HANDBOOK ON THE ECONOMIC COMPLEXITY OF TECHNOLOGICAL CHANGE

T0342072

Handbook on the Economic Complexity of Technological Change

Edited by

Cristiano Antonelli

Department of Economics, University of Turin and Collegio Carlo Alberto, Italy

Edward Elgar

Cheltenham, UK • Northampton, MA, USA

© Cristiano Antonelli 2011

All rights reserved. No part of this publication may be reproduced, stored in a retrieval system or transmitted in any form or by any means, electronic, mechanical or photocopying, recording, or otherwise without the prior permission of the publisher.

Published by
Edward Elgar Publishing Limited
The Lypiatts
15 Lansdown Road
Cheltenham
Glos GL50 2JA
UK

Edward Elgar Publishing, Inc.
William Pratt House
9 Dewey Court
Northampton
Massachusetts 01060
USA

A catalogue record for this book
is available from the British Library

Library of Congress Control Number: 2010934011

ISBN 978 1 84844 256 6 (cased)

Typeset by Servis Filmsetting Ltd, Stockport, Cheshire
Printed and bound by MPG Books Group, UK

Contents

Contributors

Cristiano Antonelli, Department of Economics 'Salvatore Cognetti de Martiis', University of Turin and Collegio Carlo Alberto, Italy

Harry Bloch, School of Economics and Finance, Curtin University of Technology, Australia

Isabel Maria Bodas Freitas, Politecnico di Torino, Italy and Grenoble Ecole de Management, France

Andrea Bonaccorsi, Department of Energy and Systems Engineering, University of Pisa, Italy

Ron Boschma, Department of Economic Geography at the University of Utrecht, The Netherlands

Uwe Cantner, Department of Economics, Friedrich Schiller University Jena, Germany and Department of Marketing and Management, I2M Group, University of Southern Denmark, Odense, Denmark

Alessandra Colombelli, CRENoS, Università di Cagliari, Italy and BRICK (Bureau of Research in Innovation Complexity and Knowledge), Collegio Carlo Alberto, Italy

Davide Consoli, Manchester Business School, UK and INGENIO (CSIC-UPV), Spain

Kurt Dopfer, Institute of Economics, St Gallen University, Switzerland

Gabriela Dutrénit, Universidad Autónoma Metropolitana, Campus Xochimilco, Mexico

Dieter Ernst, East-West Center, Honolulu, Hawaii, USA

Jan Fagerberg, Center for Technology, Innovation and Culture (TIK), University of Oslo, Norway, CIRCLE, University of Lund, Sweden and ICER, Turin, Italy

Martin Fransman, School of Economics and Institute for Japanese-European Technology Studies, University of Edinburgh, UK

Koen Frenken, Eindhoven University of Technology, The Netherlands

Aldo Geuna, Department of Economics 'Salvatore Cognetti de Martiis', University of Turin, Collegio Carlo Alberto, Italy and Grenoble Ecole de Management, France

Holger Graf, Department of Economics, Friedrich Schiller University Jena, Germany

Jarle Hildrum, Center for Technology, Innovation and Culture (TIK), University of Oslo, Norway

Jackie Krafft, University of Nice Sophia Antipolis, CNRS-GREDEG, France

David A. Lane, University of Modena and Reggio Emilia, Italy

William Latham, Center for Applied Business and Economic Research and Department of Economics, the School of Urban Affairs and Public Policy, University of Delaware, USA

Christian Le Bas, University Lyon 2, France

Albert N. Link, University of North Carolina at Greensboro, USA

Jamie R. Link, Science and Technology Policy Institute, STPI, USA

Stan Metcalfe, University of Manchester, Visiting Fellow, Cambridge University, UK, the University of Queensland and Curtin Business School, Curtin University of Technology, Australia

Paul Ormerod, Volterra Partners LLP, London and Department of Anthropology, University of Durham, UK

Pier Paolo Patrucco, Department of Economics 'Salvatore Cognetti de Martiis', University of Turin and BRICK, Collegio Carlo Alberto, Italy

Francesco Quatraro, University of Nice Sophia Antipolis, CNRS-GREDEG, France and ICER, Turin, Italy

Verónica Robert, Universidad Nacional de General Sarmiento, Argentina

Bridget Rosewell, Volterra Partners LLP, London and Greater London Authority

Federica Rossi, University of Modena and Reggio Emilia, Italy

Pier Paolo Saviotti, Laboratoire d'Économie Appliquée de Grenoble (GAEL), Institut National de la Recherche Agronomique (INRA), France

Paula E. Stephan, Andrew Young School of Policy Studies, Georgia State University and National Bureau of Economic Research, USA

Morris Teubal, The Hebrew University, Jerusalem, Israel

Nick von Tunzelmann, SPRU (Science Policy Research Unit), University of Sussex, UK

Greg Wiltshire, Volterra Consulting, London

Gabriel Yoguel, Universidad Nacional de General Sarmiento, Argentina

PART I

INTRODUCTION

1 The economic complexity of technological change: knowledge interaction and path dependence*
Cristiano Antonelli

1. INTRODUCTION

Complexity is emerging as a new unifying theory to understand endogenous change and transformation across a variety of disciplines, ranging from mathematics and physics to biology. Complexity thinking is primarily a systemic and dynamic approach according to which the outcome of the behavior of each agent and of the system into which each agent is embedded, is intrinsically dynamic and can only be understood as the result of multiple interactions among heterogeneous agents embedded in evolving structures and between the micro and macro levels.

Different attempts have been made to apply complexity to economics, ranging from computational complexity to econophysics, connectivity complexity and bounded rationality complexity. Too often these attempts have missed the basic feature of economics that consists in the analysis of the role of the intentional, rent-seeking conduct in the interpretation of the behavior of agents. Agents are portrayed as automata that are not able to implement the intentional pursuit of their interest (Rosser, 1999, 2004).

This *Handbook* presents a systematic attempt to show how, building upon the achievements of complexity theory, a substantial contribution to the economics of innovation can be implemented. At the same time it shows that an economic approach to complexity can be elaborated and fruitfully implemented. This introductory chapter articulates the view that innovation is the emergent property of a system characterized by organized complexity. It implements an approach that enables the provision of basic and simple economic foundations at the same time to analysing the outcome of the intentional economic action of agents endowed with some levels of creativity, at both micro and macro level, and to the notion of organized complexity.

According to the theory of complexity, emergence is a phenomenon whereby aggregate behaviors that arise from the organized interactions of localized individual behaviors, provide both the system and the agents with new capabilities and functionalities. Innovation and organized complexity can be seen as emerging properties of a system stemming from the combined result of the action of individual and heterogeneous agents with the structural characteristics of an organized system that is able to qualify and amplify the results of their action. The analysis of innovation as an emergent property of a system enables us to combine the individualistic analysis of innovation as the result of intentional decision making of agents with the holistic understanding of the properties of the system into which such innovative action takes place and which actually makes it possible. By the same token, the analysis of an organized complexity as an emerging property enables us to appreciate how the structural and architectural characteristics of a system are themselves the product of the interactions within the system and provide the context into which the individual reaction of agents can yield the introduction of innovations.

Here complexity theory enables a major progress in the economic analysis of innovation, especially if the latter is defined as a productivity-enhancing event. It is difficult, in fact, to understand how and why economic agents would not push innovative activities to the point where their marginal costs match their marginal revenue. The appreciation of the special features of the system into which the individual action takes place and of the specific processes by means of which the features of the system lead to the emergence of innovations, marks an important analytical progress.

Economic of innovation may help the theory of complexity, and especially its applications to economic analysis, in two ways. First, complexity theory often misses an economic analysis of the incentives and motivations of individual action. Economic agents are and remain rent-seeking individuals and it is necessary to understand why they may want to change and move in the multidimensional spaces that characterize economic systems. Here the economics of innovation may contribute to the analysis with the understanding of the out-of-equilibrium determinants of the attempt of agents to try and introduce innovations.

Second, in the complexity theory a major distinction is made between disorganized and organized complexity. In the former 'the interactions of the local entities tend to smooth each other out' (Miller and Page, 2007: 48). In the latter 'interactions are not independent, feedback can enter the system. Feedback fundamentally alters the dynamics of a system. In a system with negative feedback, changes get quickly absorbed and the system gains stability. With positive feedback, changes get amplified leading to instability' (Miller and Page, 2007: 50). Yet the theory of complexity does not provide an analysis of the endogenous determinants of the features of the system. A basic question remains unresolved in much complexity thinking: how, when and why is a system characterized by organized or disorganized complexity? The basic distinction elaborated by Hayek between cosmos and taxis, that is, spontaneous and designed order, provides basic guidance (Hayek, 1945, 1973).

The notion of organized complexity as an emerging property of an economic system enables us to grasp the endogenous dynamics of the system. The reaction of firms that happens to be creative because of the feedbacks available, affects the structure of the system and can either implement its organization or open a degenerative process. Clearly the characteristics that qualify the levels of organization of the systems complexity are endogenous to the system itself.

It seems clear that all the effort made in the identification of innovation as an emergent property of a system as a means to try and articulate its endogeneity would be spoiled if it eventually leads to the view that the organized complexity of a system is an exogenous and unpredictable characterization. Here the economics of innovation can provide important elements with its analysis of the endogenous formation of economic structures as the result of the recursive process of path dependent change.

Our attempt to implement the merging of the theory of complexity with the economics of innovation provides a complementary path to recent attempts to apply the methodologies elaborated by complexity into economics, such as complex networks (see Cowan et al., 2006, 2007), percolation (see Antonelli, 1997b; Silverberg and Verspagen, 2005), and NK-modeling (see Frenken and Nuvolari, 2004; Frenken, 2006a,

2006b), for it focuses attention upon the scope of application of the basic tools of the economics of innovation to embrace the full range of analytical perspectives brought by the analysis of innovation as an emerging property stemming from the endogenous result of both the intentional, rent-seeking conduct of individual and heterogeneous agents and the endogenous characteristics of economic systems qualified by organized complexity.

This introductory chapter articulates an approach where agents are myopic: their rationality is bounded, as opposed to Olympian, because of the wide array of unexpected events, surprises and mistakes that characterize their decision making and the conduct of their business in an ever changing environment. Our agents retain the typical characteristics of economic actors, including intentional choice and strategic conduct, augmented by the attribution of potential creativity. In our approach, however, economic agents may change both their production and their utility functions. Our agents, in fact, are endowed with an extended procedural rationality that includes the capability to learn and try to react to the changing conditions of their economic environment by means of the generation of new tastes as well as new technological knowledge and its exploitation by means of the introduction of technological innovations. In this approach agents do more than adjusting prices to quantities and vice versa: they can try and change their technologies and their preferences. Agents are intrinsically heterogeneous. Their basic characteristics differ in terms of original endowments such as learning capabilities, size, and location. Their variety is also endogenous as it keeps changing as a result of the dynamics of endogenous technological change (Albin, 1998).

The determinants and the effects of this potential creativity and the context into which it can be implemented, however, require careful investigation. The actual creativity of agents is not obvious, nor spontaneous, but induced and systemic.

To investigate the determinants of the actual creativity of agents three steps are necessary. First, the incentives to change must be identified and qualified. Agents are reluctant to change their production and utility functions and a specific motivation is necessary to induce them to try and change their routines. Second, the localized context of action and the web of knowledge interactions and externalities into which each agent is embedded are crucial to make their reaction actually creative, as opposed to adaptive, so as to shape the actual effects of their endogenous efforts to change their technologies and their preferences. Third, the sequential process of feedbacks that make the creative reaction a sustained process must be identified. The creative reaction of each agent in fact is not a punctual event that takes place isolated in time and space, but rather a historic process where the sequence of feedbacks plays a key role (Arthur, 1990).

The analysis of the effects must include, next to the introduction of innovations that increase the efficiency of the production process, the structural consequences upon the context of action. The successful introduction of new localized technologies, in fact, changes the structure of the system and hence the flows of knowledge externalities and interactions. This dynamic loop exhibits the characters of a recursive, non-ergodic and path dependent historic process. This approach enables moving away from the static, low-level complexity of general equilibrium that applies when both technologies and preferences are static, or the smooth and ubiquitous growth based upon learning processes and spontaneous spillover of the new growth theory. It also makes possible significant progress with respect to evolutionary thinking where the causal analysis of the determinants of the generation of innovations is reduced to the random walks of spontaneous variations.

This approach provides the tools to grasp the dynamics of technological change as an endogenous and recurrent process that combines rent-seeking intentionality at the agent level with the appreciation of the knowledge externalities and interactions that stem from the structural character of the system.

2. THE ECONOMICS OF INNOVATION AS AN EMERGING PROPERTY OF AN ORGANIZED COMPLEXITY

A Definition

Economics of innovation studies the determinants and the effects of the generation of new technological and organizational knowledge, the introduction of innovations in product, process, organization, mix of inputs and markets, their selection and eventual diffusion. Innovation takes place when it consists in actions that are able to engender an increase in the value of the output, adjusted for its qualitative content, that exceed their costs (Griliches, 1961).

Technological and organizational changes are defined as innovations only if and when the two overlapping features of novelty and increased efficiency coincide. Changes are innovations if they consist at the same time in the introduction of a novelty that is also able to yield an increase in the relationship between outputs and inputs. Total factor productivity can be considered a reliable indicator of the relationship between outputs and inputs of the production processes: novelties that are actually able to increase the ratio of the output to the production inputs are true innovations. Either characteristic is necessary to identify an innovation. Only if we retain such a strict definition of innovation, as a productivity-enhancing novelty, can we grasp its out-of-equilibrium characteristics.

It is clear in fact, on the one hand, that indeed total factor productivity may increase for a variety of other factors, especially if and when markets are not in equilibrium. On the other hand, however, it is also clear that often novelties do not last and are selected out in the market selection process with no actual economic effect. On a similar ground we see that minor changes in products may feed monopolistic competition and do not increase the efficiency of the production process at large. It is not surprising that much theorizing upon the new theories of growth never tackles the issue and prefers a more comfortable definition of innovation as a form of increase in the variety of products.

Innovation is the result of a variety of activities. Learning processes of various kinds play a major role in the accumulation of the competence that is necessary to generate new technological knowledge and eventually to introduce innovations. The access to external knowledge is a crucial factor in the generation of new technological knowledge. The adoption of new capital and intermediary goods incorporating technological innovations is an essential component of the innovation process. Research and development indicators are able to grasp only a fraction of such activities. Much R&D on the other hand is funded and performed to generate novelties that are not able to increase the efficiency of the production process. As is well known, only a fraction of the technological innovations being introduced is represented by patent statistics. Neither R&D nor patent statistics account for innovations in organization, input mix and markets. Innovation counts suffer the subjective character of the claims upon which they are based. Product innovations introduced by upstream producers are often considered process innovations by downstream users (Kleinknecht et al., 2002). The distinction between innovation, adoption and diffusion is more and more blurred by the increasing awareness of the amount of creative effort that is necessary to adopt and imitate an innovation. Moreover, and most importantly, the economic analysis of innovation should take into account the time distribution of adoptions, rather than their punctual introduction. Total factor productivity indicators instead can grasp the full bundle of the economic effects of the introduction and diffusion of an innovation. Hence total factor productivity indicators are likely to provide an accurate measure of the actual amount and extent of the innovations being introduced (Crépon et al., 1998).

In sum, new products, new processes, new organization methods, new inputs and new markets can be defined as innovations only if they yield an increase in total factor productivity. Hence the marginal product of innovation efforts exceeds its marginal costs. This is at the origin of a serious problem for textbook economics.

Departing from Dead-ends

This new approach overcomes the limitations of two contending approaches: general equilibrium analysis and Darwinistic evolutionary population thinking.

The merging of the theory of complexity and the economics of innovation provides a new way to integrate economic and complexity thinking and contributes to the building of an economic theory of complexity that puts the endogenous and systemic emergence of innovation at the core of the analysis. The continual introduction of new technologies and their selection is seen as the emerging and systemic property of an out-of-equilibrium dynamics characterized by path dependent non-ergodicity and interactions both among agents and between micro and macro levels. The organized complexity of the system that enables the emergence of innovations is itself the product of the recurrent and path dependent interaction of rent-seeking agents (Arthur, 1994, 1999).

Organization thinking, as distinct from population thinking, plays a crucial role in grasping the causes and the consequences of the changing structure, composition and organization of the system (Lane, 1993a, 1993b; Lane et al., 2009).

Technological and structural change are the result of a sequential process of systemic change where agents are never able to anticipate *ex ante* the outcome of their reactions to emerging surprises. The changing characters of their localized context of action in fact engender out-of-equilibrium conditions to which they react. When knowledge externalities and interactions engender positive feedbacks their reaction is creative. Firms are able to change both their technologies and the structure of the system: a recursive, historic and path-dependent process of change takes place. When the context of action does not provide knowledge externalities and interactions sufficient to engender positive feedbacks, the reaction of firms is adaptive and a single static attractor consolidates: general equilibrium analysis applies.

In general equilibrium economics, the preferences and the technologies of the representative agent and hence her production and utility functions, are allowed to change only as the result of exogenous shocks. As soon as the notion of endogenous change is introduced and heterogeneous agents are credited with the capability to change their production and utility functions in response to economic stimulations, the general equilibrium analysis appears a simplistic approach. The assumption of the necessary gravitation and convergence towards a single equilibrium point cannot be retained because of the changing centers of attraction. As soon as we acknowledge that both preferences and technologies are the result of the intentional decision making of heterogeneous actors that are part of a system of interdependencies, the foundations of general equilibrium economics collapse, yet its powerful systemic approach should be retained and implemented.

Kenneth Arrow has provided key contributions to reconcile the evidence about growth with general equilibrium analysis both with the articulated notion of learning by doing, eventually implemented with learning by using, and with the path breaking analysis of the limitation of knowledge as an economic good (Arrow, 1962a, 1962b, 1969, 1974). Building upon his legacy, the new growth theory shares the view that knowledge is characterized by an array of idiosyncratic features such as non-appropriability, non-divisibility, non-excludability, non-exhaustibility that are the cause of knowledge externalities and contribute to the continual and homogeneous introduction of innovations. The new growth theory however has not been able to appreciate the endogenous, idiosyncratic and dynamic character of knowledge spillovers. Assuming that knowledge spillovers are given and evenly distributed in time and space, the new growth theory claims that technological change takes place evenly through time and space without discontinuities and leads to smooth dynamic processes (Romer, 1994).

The main limitation of new growth theory is the underlying assumption of an automatic, spontaneous and ubiquitous trickle down of the new technological knowledge inputs into every other kind of activity in the economic system. In Aghion and Howitt's model, downstream sectors make no particular efforts to identify, understand or use the new knowledge embodied in new intermediary inputs. Technology adoption and transfer take place in the absence of effort, interaction or dedicated activity. Although perhaps not like manna from heaven, new technological knowledge rains from upstream and wets whatever is below – be it sectors or regions (Aghion and Howitt, 1992; Aghion and Tirole, 1994).

These assumptions contrast sharply with the rich evidence about the punctuated and discontinuous rates and directions of technological change and are not able to explain the wide variety across countries, regions, industries and firms in terms of rates of introduction and diffusion of innovations (Mokyr, 1990a, 1990b, 2002).

The second attempt to elaborate an evolutionary economics based upon Darwinistic population thinking, implemented by Nelson and Winter (1982) since the late 1970s, has contributed much to place innovation at the center stage of economic analysis. Evolutionary economics has built an outstanding corpus of knowledge about the characteristics of innovation and of technological knowledge with the identification of important taxonomies and significant sequences. The grafting of biological metaphors has focused on population thinking, as distinct from organization thinking, stressing the role of the natality, mortality, entry, exit and mobility of agents, while little attention has been paid to the causes and effects of the organization of economic systems. Agents are not credited with the intentional capability to change their technologies and their preferences.

Consistently with the general evolutionary frame of analysis, innovation is regarded as the product of random variations and accidental mutations, rather than the result of the intentional action of agents. The radical criticism raised by Edith Penrose against the first wave of attempts to integrate Social Darwinism into mainstream economics, based upon the well-known article by Armen Alchian (Alchian, 1950), applies very much to the second wave as well: 'to abandon [the] development [of firms] to the laws of nature diverts attention from the importance of human decisions and motives, and from problems of ethics and public policy, and surrounds the whole question of the growth of the firm of with an aura of "naturalness" and even inevitability' (Penrose, 1952: 809, 1953).

Evolutionary economics has focused much more on the analysis of the selective diffusion of new technologies rather than the analysis of the actual determinants of the generation of new technological knowledge and the introduction of innovations (Metcalfe, 1994).

The causal analysis of the determinants of technological change, however, has been left at the margin of the exploration. This seems quite paradoxical. Evolutionary economics is not able to explain the determinants of what is assumed to be the central mechanism of economic change (Hodgson and Knudsen, 2006).

Standing on Giants' Shoulders: Marshall and Schumpeter

In our approach, innovation is not only the result of the intentional action of each individual agent, but it is the endogenous product of dynamics of the system. The individual action and the system conditions are crucial and complementary ingredients to explain the emergence of innovations (see Table 1.1).

Innovation cannot be considered but the intentional result of the economic action of agents: it does not fall from heaven. Neither is it the result of random variations. Dedicated resources to knowledge governance are necessary to implement the competence accumulated by means of learning and to manage its exploitation. Agents succeed in their creative reactions when a number of contingent external conditions apply at the system level. Innovation is made possible by key systemic conditions:

> innovation is a path dependent, collective process that takes place in a localized context, if, when and where a sufficient number of creative reactions are made in a coherent, complementary and consistent way. As such innovation is one of the key emergent properties of an economic system viewed as a dynamic complex system. (Antonelli, 2008a: I)

An innovation economics approach to complexity thinking makes it possible to overcome the limitations of both general equilibrium economics and evolutionary analysis into a complex dynamics approach. It builds upon the integration of Schumpeterian analysis of innovation as a form of reaction, to the changing conditions of product and factor markets, with the Marshallian partial equilibrium approach to localized increasing returns based upon circumscribed externalities. This approach contrasts the general equilibrium analysis where economic agents are indeed embedded in a systemic analysis but are not supposed to be able to change purposely their technologies and their preferences. This effort can contribute a complex dynamics where technological change is the central engine of the evolving dynamics viewed and it is the result of the creative response of intentional agents, embedded in the organized complexity of a system populated by interacting and reactive agents (Antonelli, 2007, 2008a, 2009a).

Table 1.1   Dead ends and new prospects for the analysis of systems where innovation is an endogenous, TFP-enhancing emergent property

	Micro	Meso	Macro
General equilibrium	The representative agent can adapt but cannot innovate	Market transactions	Low-level static complexity
Marshallian partial equilibrium	Intrinsic heterogeneity and variety of agents and locations	Localized increasing returns based upon externalities	Uneven growth
Arrovian legacy	Learning; knowledge as an imperfect economic good	Knowledge spillover	Spontaneous, even and steady dynamic equilibrium
Darwinian evolutionism	Random variations and occasional mutations	Selection based upon replicator dynamics; emergence of dominant designs	Growth and change based upon selective diffusion of innovations
Complexity cum innovation	Innovation as an emergent property when individual reactions based on generative relations match organized complexity	Knowledge governance; non-ergodic changes in the organization of structures and networks	Growth and path dependent change based upon innovation within organized complexity

The Marshallian approach provides the basic frame for a systemic understanding of the behavior of heterogeneous agents that are interdependent within a dynamic context characterized by localized increasing returns and increasing levels of division of labor engendered by specialization. The Marshallian partial equilibrium analysis provides a rich analytical apparatus that emphasizes the idiosyncratic variety of agents and markets that interact in a systemic context characterized by endogenous structural change. The Marshallian partial equilibrium enables the use of the foundations of microeconomics as they provide the analytical context into which the maximizing conduct of individual agents can be interpreted and yet makes room for understanding the interactive process of structural and technological change. The integration of partial equilibria, however, does not lead to general equilibrium. As Young (1928) has shown, each change in a component of the system modifies its structural composition and organization and feeds in turn new ripples of technological change via new flows of externalities. Technological change and structural change are intertwined and necessary components of an aggregate and systemic dynamics (Foster, 2005; Metcalfe et al., 2006).

For these reasons the Marshallian approach can be retained and integrated with the Schumpeterian and classical approaches that stress the role of the creative reaction of firms caught in out-of-equilibrium conditions into an economics of complexity that emphasizes the endogenous emergence of technological change and the continual transformation of the structure of the system (Schumpeter, 1941; Downie, 1958).

The aggregate dynamics of the system, in fact, is far from the assumptions of an even, smooth and homogenous pace. It is instead characterized by strong elements of contingent discontinuity as well as historic hysteresis (Anderson et al., 1988). The understanding of the dynamics of the system requires the grasping of the causes and determinants of both individual action and the changing centers of gravitation of the system (Blume and Durlauf, 2005).

The appreciation of the systemic conditions that shape and make innovations possible, together with their individual causes lead to the identification of innovation as an emergent property of a system. This approach provides a solution to the conundrum of an intentional economic action whose rewards are larger than its costs, only if the organized complexity that enables the emergence of innovations is explained as an endogenous and dynamic process engendered by the interactions of rent-seeking agents.

The reappraisal of a somewhat forgotten contribution by Joseph Schumpeter (1947b) provides basic support in this endeavor. The direct quote of a key portion of this text seems most appropriate here:

> What has not been adequately appreciated among theorists is the distinction between different kinds of reaction to changes in 'condition'. Whenever an economy or a sector of an economy adapts itself to a change in its data in the way that traditional theory describes, whenever, that is, an economy reacts to an increase in population by simply adding the new brains and hands to the working force in the existing employment, or an industry reacts to a protective duty by the expansion within its existing practice, we may speak of the development as an adaptive response. And whenever the economy or an industry or some firms in an industry do something else, something that is outside of the range of existing practice, we may speak of creative response.

Creative response has at least three essential characteristics.

> First, from the standpoint of the observer who is in full possession of all relevant facts, it can always be understood *ex post*; but it can practically never be understood *ex ante*; that is to say, it cannot be predicted by applying the ordinary rules of inference from the pre-existing facts.

This is why the 'how' in what has been called the 'mechanisms' must be investigated in each case.

> Secondly, creative response shapes the whole course of subsequent events and their 'long-run' outcome. It is not true that both types of responses dominate only what the economist loves to call 'transitions', leaving the ultimate outcome to be determined by the initial data. Creative response changes social and economic situations for good, or, to put it differently, it creates situations from which there is no bridge to those situations that might have emerged in its absence. This is why creative response is an essential element in the historical process; no deterministic credo avails against this. Thirdly, creative response – the frequency of its occurrence in a group, its intensity and success or failure – has obviously something, be that much or little, to do (a) with quality of the personnel available in a society, (b) with relative quality of personnel, that is, with quality available to a particular field of activity relative to the quality available, at the same time, to others, and (c) with individual decisions, actions, and patterns of behavior. (Schumpeter, 1947b: 149–50)

Innovation and Organized Complexity as Emergent Properties of an Economic System

In our approach, innovation is an emergent property that takes place when complexity is organized, that is, when a number of complementary conditions enable the creative reaction of agents and make it possible to introduce innovations that actually increase their efficiency. The dynamics of complex systems is based upon the combination of the reactivity of agents, caught in out-of-equilibrium conditions, with the features of the system into which each agent is embedded in terms of externalities, interactions, positive feedbacks that enable the generation of localized technological knowledge and the introduction of localized technological change, and lead to endogenous structural change. The process is characterized by path dependent non-ergodicity.

This approach builds upon five basic points:

i.   The distinction between *ex ante* and *ex post* is crucial. Bounded rationality limits the foresight of agents. Economic agents however are credited with the basic capability to react to unexpected changes in their economic environment by changing their technology. Agents try to change their technology when their performances are both below and above their expectations.

ii.   The reaction of firms can be either adaptive or creative. Occasionally, when the context is favorable, their reaction becomes creative and they can innovate. The organization and composition of the economic structure and the quality of the external conditions add to the characteristics of the individual firms to explain whether, when, how and why their reaction can be either adaptive or creative. The levels of knowledge externalities and the quality of the generative relations that take place in the context into which firms are localized, determine the actual chances that the reaction of firms leads to the actual introduction of innovations.

iii. Their reaction is localized by the irreversibility of their tangible and intangible inputs as well as by their competence based upon learning processes and rests upon the recombinant generation of knowledge that is both internal and external. Innovation emerges as the result of the fertile interaction between the knowledge characteristics of the context and the competence of the individuals.

iv.   The introduction of innovations changes the structure of the economic system into which firms are embedded, including the availability of knowledge externalities and the quality of generative relations. These in turn affect the direction and the rate of the economic dynamics. Occasionally, loops of systemic positive feedbacks between structural and technological change lead to the emergence of organized complexity that feeds innovation cascades and Schumpeterian gales of innovations.

v.   The interaction between technological and structural change engenders dynamic processes that are non-ergodic because history exerts a strong effect in shaping their dynamics. History matters in influencing the dynamics of economic processes but innovations, introduced along the path, can alter it. History matters, yet small events can change it.

In this approach, innovation is an emergent property of the system that, when framed as an organized complexity, qualifies and makes possible the creative response of agents.

Let us now turn our attention to analyse the building blocks of our approach. The following chapters show how the integration of complexity thinking with the basic tools of the Schumpeterian economics of innovation can implement a rigorous representation of the systemic dynamics of technological change.

3.   THE DETERMINANTS OF THE CREATIVE REACTION

Consistently with the dominant view that technological change is exogenous or, at best, the automatic product of either spontaneous learning procedures within firms or uncontrolled leakage of knowledge externalities among firms, very little attention has been paid to the analysis of the determinants of innovation. This contrasts with the size and the wealth of the large literature that has explored the effects of innovation on the increase of total factor productivity and hence on growth, profitability, performance, economic and industrial structures.

Even evolutionary economics assumes that innovation is the spontaneous outcome of random mutations: agents introduce innovations occasionally without any specific motivation. In evolutionary economics there is no attempt to identify the historic, regional and institutional determinants of the decisions that lead to the generation of innovations. Much effort is made, instead, to explore the features of the selection, adoption and diffusion mechanisms of the 'spontaneous' flow of innovations. Much evolutionary economics, so far, elaborates a theory of selective diffusion of innovations, rather than a theory of innovation.

As a result, the analysis of the determinants of the introduction of innovation, considered as the result of intentional decision making, remains substantially under-investigated. This is not surprising as it is indeed difficult to provide a consistent and coherent explanation of decision-making procedures that lead to an increase of output that exceeds the increase of inputs and hence cannot be justified according to marginalistic procedures. Rational innovators in fact should stretch their innovative activities to the point where marginal costs match marginal revenues: no room for residuals should be left.

In the classical economics of technological change three different frames have been identified to try and explain the endogenous introduction of innovations: (a) the inducement approach elaborated along the lines of the early contributions of Karl Marx, (b) the demand pull approach elaborated by the Post-Keynesian school; (c) the Schumpeterian legacies.

Our approach impinges upon the late contribution of Joseph Schumpeter and focuses on the role of the relations between profitability and innovation. The analysis of the causal relations between levels of profitability, as distinct from competition, enables the elaboration of a consistent and coherent frame of analysis and integration of these different and yet complementary strands of literature that share the view that technological change is endogenous and that the decision to innovate is an intentional and relevant component of economic decision making.

The contribution of the behavioral theories of the firm provides substantial help in this effort. The decision to innovate, in fact, cannot be treated with the standard maximization procedures. The outcomes of innovations are hard to predict, and the actual chances of introduction of successful innovations are subject to radical uncertainty. The introduction of innovations is the result of a complex sequence of intentional decision making that takes place when firms are found in out-of-equilibrium conditions. According to James March (March and Simon, 1958; Cyert and March, 1963), firms are not profit maximizers. Firms are able to rely upon procedural, as opposed to substantive, rationality: firms use satisfying procedures and identify satisfactory levels of performances. Firms are risk adverse and hence reluctant to change their routines, their production processes, their networks of suppliers, their products and their marketing activities. Firms can overcome their intrinsic inertia and resistance to change only when unexpected changes in their environment push them to take the risks associated with innovation (March and Shapira, 1987).

Nelson and Winter (1982) make an important contribution along these lines:

> In the orthodox formulation, the decision rules are assumed to be profit-maximizing, over a sharply defined opportunity set that is taken as a datum, the firms in the industry and the industry as a whole are assumed to be at equilibrium size, and innovation (if it is treated at all) is absorbed into the traditional framework rather mechanically. In evolutionary theory, decision rules are viewed as a legacy from the past and hence appropriate, at best, to the range of circumstances in which the firm customarily finds itself, and are viewed as unresponsive, or inappropriate, to novel situations or situations encountered irregularly. Firms are regarded as expanding or contracting in response to disequilibria, with no presumption that the industry is 'near' equilibrium. Innovation is treated as stochastic and as variable across firms. (Nelson and Winter, 1982: 165–6)

The integration of these elements, into the single frame of the localized technological change approach, can overcome the limitations of the stochastic approach of evolutionary approaches and elaborate the hypothesis that firms try to innovate when they are found in out-of-equilibrium conditions, and more specifically when profits are either below or above the norm. When equilibrium conditions prevail and there are no extra profits, firms are not induced to try to change their technologies, nor their organizations, markets and input mixes. According to this approach a non-linear relationship between profits and innovation is at work.

Let us first review the main hypothesis elaborated about the relations between out-of-equilibrium conditions and the inducement to innovate.

The Marxian Legacies

Marx contributed the first elements of the theory of induced technological change. The introduction of new capital-intensive technologies is the result of the intentional process of augmented labor substitution. When wages increase, capitalists are induced to introduce new technologies that are embodied in capital goods. Hence technological change is introduced with the twin aim of substituting capital to labor so as to reduce the pressure of unions and increasing the total efficiency of the production process (Marx, 1867).

John Hicks (1932) and Fellner (1961) extracted from the analysis of Karl Marx the basic elements of the theory of the induced technological change: firms are induced to change their technology when wages increase. Technological change is considered an augmented form of substitution: technological change complements technical change. Binswanger and Ruttan (1978) eventually articulated a more general theory of induced technological change: firms introduce new technologies in order to save on the production factors that are relatively more expensive. Such production factors can be labor-saving, as much as energy- or even capital-saving in specific circumstances. The induced technological change approach has been criticized by Salter (1960) according to whom firms should be equally eager to introduce any kind of technological change, either labor- or capital-intensive, provided it enables the reduction of production costs and the increase of efficiency.

An important facet of the Marxian analysis is missing in the induced technological change approach. The analysis of the Marxian contribution by Rosenberg (1976) highlights the limitations of the induced technological change approach and helps to explain the key role of profitability. Firms try to reverse the decline in their profitability, stemming from the increase in wages, with the introduction of technological innovations. Starting from a common reference to Marx, Hicks paved the way to a tradition of analysis that focuses on the role of the changes in the prices of production factors in inducing technological innovations. Rosenberg, instead, stresses the role of the decline in profitability as the focusing mechanism that pushes firms to undertake innovative activities. According to Rosenberg, firms innovate in order to restore the levels of profitability (that have been undermined by the rise in wages). According to Hicks firms react to the increase in wages (and the related decline in profitability). As Nathan Rosenberg (1969) argues Marx provides elements to build a much broader inducement hypothesis, one where the levels of profitability are a cause of endogenous technological change. This line of analysis has received much less attention in the economics of innovation, and yet it provides a clear reply to Salter's arguments.

The Role of Profitability in the Demand-Pull Hypothesis

The post-Keynesian approach elaborated by Kaldor (1972, 1981) stressed the key role of demand in the explanation of the endogenous origin of technological change. To do so Kaldor revisited the dynamic engine put in place by Adam Smith. According to Adam Smith the division of labor is determined by the extent of the market and is the cause of the increase of specialization. This leads to the accumulation of new technological knowledge, and eventually to the introduction of technological innovations. Technological innovations in turn lead to an increase in productivity. The increase in productivity leads to an increase in the demand and hence of the extent of the market. According to Adam Smith the relationship between division of labor, specialization, increase of competence, introduction of technological innovations, productivity growth, increase in demand and new division of labor consists in a recursive loop. Building on this interpretation Kaldor argued that an increase in the levels of the aggregate demand would engender an increase in the division of labor, hence of specialization, and eventually of the rate of introduction of technological innovations. The so-called 'demand-pull' hypothesis was borne. Schmookler (1966) provided empirical support to the hypothesis that demand growth pulls the increase of technological knowledge, hence of inventions and eventually technological innovations. Mowery and Rosenberg (1979) provide an outstanding account of the pervasive role of the demand-pull hypothesis within the post-Keynesian approach.

Less attention has been paid to a previous contribution by Schmookler (1954) according to which the increase in demand leads to the generation of additional technological knowledge and the eventual introduction of technological innovations via the increase in the profitability of both inventors and innovators. Firms are pulled to generate new technological knowledge and to introduce technological innovations by the high levels of prices for the products that are the object of an increasing demand and by the high levels of rewards that are attached. Young scholars specialize in the fields where wages increase because of the demand for their competence. New firms enter with innovative ideas in the industries where profits are growing because of the increase of the demand.

Incumbent firms are induced to innovate by the growth in the demand and the extra profits that are attached.

Following this line of analysis we can claim that excess demand engenders out-of-equilibrium conditions that lead to an increase in prices and in profitability. Out-of-equilibrium conditions here are determined by the unexpected increase in the demand: had the firm anticipated the high levels of the demand, current supply would have already accommodated it with no increase in prices and hence in profits. When the demand fetches unexpected levels, instead, prices increase and consequently profits. Then firms are pulled to accommodate the increased levels of the demand with an increase in supply. The increase in supply however can be obtained both via investments with a given technology and an increase in productivity of the given resources, via the introduction of technological innovations. The accumulation of competence and expertise based upon learning processes enables the generation of new technological knowledge. Extra profits provide the opportunity to fund the generation of new technological knowledge and the introduction of technological innovations. Hence the increase in demand feeds the introduction of innovations by means of an increase of profits above the norm. In other words we can easily reconcile the demand-pull hypothesis with the argument that extra profits favor the introduction of additional innovations.

The chain-loop elaborated by Kaldor after Smith can be integrated with an additional ring: increase in demand, extra profits, new division of labor, specialization, increase of competence, introduction of technological innovations, productivity growth (Scherer, 1982).

The increase in demand engenders an increase in profits that in turn provides both the incentives and the opportunities for the introduction of innovations. The incentives are determined by the perspective to take advantage of the excess demand via the increase in supply by means of new productivity-enhancing technologies. The opportunities stem from the resources made available by extra profits.

The Schumpeterian Legacies

The third basic starting point to elaborate a theory of the endogenous decision making of innovation is provided by the Neo-Schumpeterian literature that has debated and implemented the so-called Schumpeterian Hypothesis on the relations between forms of competition and incentives to innovate. The consensus was reached about the argument that the rate of innovation is higher when forms of oligopolistic rivalry characterize the market structure. When perfect competition prevails, firms cannot bear the burden of research activities. When the number of competitors is too small, close to monopolistic conditions, incentives to innovate are missing. Cut-throat competition may reduce the incentives to introduce technologies because of the intrinsic non-appropriability of knowledge and the high risks of imitation and entry of new competitors that can take advantage of opportunistic behavior. Some intermediary levels of workable competition, between the extremes of monopoly and perfect competition, among large firms might favor the rate of introduction of innovations. Oligopolistic market structures and the large size of firms are viewed as positive factors able to sustain the rates of introduction of innovations (Scherer, 1967, 1970; Dasgupta and Stiglitz, 1980; Link, 1980).

The Neo-Schumpeterian school has been very selective in implementing the

Schumpeterian legacy and has neglected two crucial contributions of the late Schumpeter. As a matter of fact the scope of the analysis elaborated by Schumpeter in 1947 with two path-breaking and yet almost forgotten articles published by the *Journal of Economic History* provides ammunition to elaborate a much more radical departure from equilibrium analysis.

With the analysis of the role of creative reaction, Schumpeter (1947b) fully elaborates the view that firms and agents at large are not passive adapters but can react to the changing conditions of both product and factor markets in a creative way, with the introduction of innovations, both in technologies and organizations and by changing their products and processes. If firms are credited with the capability to innovate as a part of their business conduct, the notion of creative reaction becomes relevant. The conditions that qualify it warrant systematic investigation.

Schumpeter makes a sharp distinction between adaptive and creative responses. Adaptive responses consist in standard price/quantity adjustments that are comprised within the range of existing practices. Creative responses are triggered by strategic interactions. The rivalry among firms able to introduce – purposely – new technologies is a major factor in fostering the rate of technological change (Scherer, 1967). Here, interactions take place in the market: the extent to which firms innovate is stirred by the change in behavior of other competing agents, namely the introduction of innovations, by neighbors in the product and output markets.

Creative responses consist in innovative changes that can rarely be understood *ex ante*, but shape the whole course of subsequent events and their 'long-run' outcome: their frequency, intensity and success is influenced by a variety of conditional factors that are both internal to each firm and external. For a given shock, firms can switch from an adaptive response to a creative response according to the quality of their internal learning processes, and the context into which they are embedded. Learning in fact is a necessary but not sufficient condition for the generation of new knowledge. The notion of creative response elaborated by Schumpeter can be considered the synthesis of a long process of elaboration.

One extreme can be identified in *Business Cycles* (1939). Here the appreciation of the role of creative reaction in economic history is fully consistent with the Rosenberg–Marx line of analysis. Here Schumpeter suggests that the gales of innovations peak in the periods of decline of the rates of profitability and growth. After a sustained phase of expansion, the decline in the opportunities for further growth of output and profits induces firms to innovate. Hence the business cycle and the innovation cycle are specular. In periods of expansion the rates of introduction of innovations decline. When profitability and growth are high, firms exploit and refine the technological innovations introduced in the periods of crisis. Technological change is characterized by the introduction of minor and incremental innovations. In contrast, major breakthroughs take place when the search for new technologies acquires a strong collective character. When the rates of growth are lower, and the profitability declines, in fact, many firms try to react by means of the systematic search for new ideas.

Following Schumpeter, Nelson and Winter elaborate the hypothesis of a relationship between negative profitability and innovation performances, and implement formally the analysis of the relationship with a simulation model. According to Nelson and Winter when the profitability levels fall below average levels and enter into negative figures, firms realize that business as usual is no longer viable, take into account the need for a change in routines, and start the search for new technologies:

> . . . we assume that if firms are sufficiently profitable they do no 'searching' at all. They simply attempt to preserve their existing routines, and are driven to consider alternatives only under the pressure of adversity . . . In the simulations run here, only those firms that make a gross return on their capital less than the target level of 16 per cent engage in search. (Nelson and Winter, 1982: 211)

The formalization of the relationship between negative profitability and innovation articulated by Schumpeter in *Business Cycles*, establishes the notion of failure-induced innovation, well rooted in the Schumpeterian tradition (Antonelli, 1989).

In *Business Cycles* Schumpeter implements also the basic notion of the complementarity between innovators in the introduction of the new gales of innovations. The new gales of innovation are in fact but the result of the convergent and complementary search activity of a variety of agents who search for new technologies that enable them to reverse the decline in profitability. The new gales can emerge only when a myriad agents characterized by the variety of competences and localized knowledge is able to engage in a myriad complementary actions of exploration and search.

The generalized decline in profitability and the complementarity among individual search activities stemming from the intrinsic indivisibility of knowledge favors the emergence of collective knowledge pools and hence the chances of introduction of radical innovations. The causal relationship between profitability and innovation acquires in *Business Cycles* an aggregate dimension.

In *Capitalism, Socialism and Democracy* (1942), Schumpeter identifies the large corporation as the driving institution for the introduction of innovations. The corporation is itself an institutional innovation that favors the introduction of technological innovations for many reasons. As a large literature has stressed, the corporation can use the barriers to entry as a barrier to imitation. The risks of uncontrolled leakage of proprietary knowledge in fact are reduced when the innovator enjoys the benefits of economies of scale and absolute cost advantages so that new competitors might imitate but cannot actually enter the market place.

Schumpeter is very clear in stressing the role of the corporation as a superior allocation and selection mechanism that reduces the inefficiency of financial markets in the provision of funds to innovative undertakings and increases the matching between competence and resources available to develop new technologies. Schumpeter regards the corporation as a hierarchical system that makes possible the coordinated working of internal markets where financial resources matched with competence can be fueled towards risky but innovative undertakings.

Within the corporation the resources extracted by the extra profits match the competences of skilled managers and the vision of potential entrepreneurs. The Schumpeterian corporation can reduce the intrinsic failure of competitive markets in the allocation of resources to research, in the identification of the proper level of rewards and hence incentives for the introduction of innovations. The corporation is an effective institution able to substitute the financial markets in the provision and allocation of funds to innovative activities because it combines financial resources and learning with entrepreneurial vision within competent hierarchies, provided that extra profits can be earned

Table 1.2   Profitability and innovation: an integrative framework

	Profitability below the average	Profitability above the average
Classical inducement	The increase in factor costs engenders the fall in profitability that induces the introduction of innovations	
Demand pull		The increase in demand engenders the increase in profitability that pulls the introduction of innovations
Schumpeter: *Business Cycles*	Recession engenders the generalized fall of profitability that induces the collective search for new technologies	
Schumpeter: *Capitalism Socialism and Democracy*		Barriers to entry and to imitation favor the duration of extra profits and provide large corporations with the opportunity to fund R&D activities

and a consistent share is directed towards the generation and introduction of innovations (Penrose, 1959).

It seems clear that the careful reading of the full range of contributions by Schumpeter suggests that the two articles published in 1947 synthesize and frame the results of the long-term evolution of his thinking from the onset elaborated in *The Theory of Economic Development* (1934). Building upon this Schumpeterian legacy we can try to articulate the hypothesis that firms seek to innovate both when their profits fall below satisfying levels and when profitability provides the resources to use innovation systematically as a competitive tool. Here it is clear that the higher are the profits, the larger are the opportunities to use a share to fund research activities and hence to increase the rates of introduction of new technologies.

The appreciation of the Schumpeterian notion of creative response and the identification of out-of-equilibrium conditions in: (a) the reappraisal of the Marxian analysis of the role of the decline in profitability in pushing firms to innovate as a key component of the augmented induced technological change approach, (b) the failure-induced approach elaborated by Schumpeter in *Business Cycles*, (c) the reconsideration of the Schumpeterian analysis of the extra profits associated with the corporation as an institutional engine for continual introduction of innovations, (d) the appreciation of the role of extra profits in providing incentives and opportunities to firms to innovate in the demand-pull hypothesis, give the basic tools to articulate the hypothesis of a causal relationship between profits above and below the norm, interpreted as indicators of out-of-equilibrium conditions, and innovation.

The focus on the relationship between profitability and innovation provides key elements to integrate into a single frame the different hypotheses articulated in the literature about the endogenous determinants of innovations. Table 1.2 summarizes the main results and shows that the hypothesis of a non-linear relationship can be considered the integrative device.

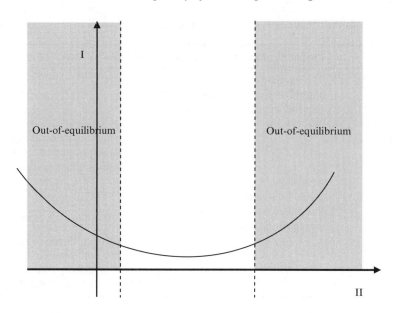

Figure 1.1   The quadratic relationship between profits and innovation

Assuming that workable competition characterizes the market place, and no monopo-listic conditions can be identified, the causal relationship between profitability and innovation can be specified by a quadratic function: with low profits, below the average, including losses, firms have a strong incentive to innovate; with high profits above the norm, firms have important opportunities to fund research activities and hence innovate; firms with normal profits miss both incentives and opportunities. The basic argument is that a combination of incentives and opportunities provides the basic mix of deter-minants to innovate. In the first case a failure inducement mechanism is at work: firms are induced to try and change their technologies and their organization when profits fall below a minimum threshold and their survival is put at risk. In the second case, incen-tives are lower but the opportunities for firms that enjoy extra profits are strong. Firms can fund risky activities with a share of extra profits and hence overcome the severe rationing of financial markets in the provision of resources for undertaking innovative activities. Firms with extra profits moreover can guide internal markets by means of competent hierarchies so as to match financial resources, competence and innovative ideas. Firms with normal profits have lesser incentives and opportunities to innovate.

The relationship between profit and innovation is shaped in Figure 1.1 where on the vertical axis I indicates the levels of innovation activity and on the horizontal axis II stands for the levels of profitability. Figure 1.1 represents the basic argument accord-ing to which the rates of innovation are likely to be higher the further away are the profitability levels of firms from equilibrium conditions. The shaded regions identify the conditions of out-of-equilibrium, as measured by the levels of profitability with respect to average values, where profitability is below and above the average.

With low profitability levels, fetching negative values, firms have a strong failure-induced incentive to innovate. Their survival is at risk. All the resources need to be mobilized in order to change the current state of activities, stop losses and introduce technological and organizational innovations that make it possible to increase their total factor productivity and hence to restore their competitiveness.

Firms with profitability in the average have no incentives and no opportunities to innovate. Rational decision making inhibits the assumption of actions in domains that are characterized by radical uncertainty such as innovative undertakings, for the well-known problems of unpredictability both in their generation and exploitation.

Finally, when firms enjoy extra profits, at levels that are above the normal profitability, managers have the opportunity to fund research and innovative activities with their own internal funds. After payments of hefty dividends, managers can retain sufficient funds to undertake innovative projects designed to stretch the duration of market power. Extra profits provide the opportunity to fund innovative activities and signal the existence of barriers to entry that increase de facto the chances of appropriability of the stream of benefits stemming from the introduction of successful innovations.

In out-of-equilibrium the rent-seeking intentionality of agents overcomes their inertia and reluctance to try to innovate. Clearly our hypothesis is complementary to the so-called Schumpeterian Hypothesis about the relations between competition and innovation. It is clear in fact that when high profitability is associated with monopolistic conditions, firms have no incentives to try to innovate; when low profits are associated with cut-throat competition firms do not have the possibility to try to innovate.[1] At the same time, however, our argument actually extends and qualifies the Schumpeterian Hypothesis because oligopolistic rivalry and workable competition are indeed likely to stir the creative response of firms, and hence to push firms to try to innovate, but only when profits are either below or above the norm.

Antonelli and Scellato (2011) have tested the hypothesis of a U-relationship between levels of profitability and innovative activity, as measured by the rates of increase of total factor productivity, on the evidence of a large sample of 7000 Italian firms in the years 1996–2005. The results are robust to different approaches to evaluate productivity growth rates and confirm that a strong causal relation holds between the quadratic specification of profitability and the growth rates of total factor productivity.

Firms can introduce productivity enhancing innovations, however, only if they can rely upon the web of knowledge interactions and externalities that qualify their localized space to activate the recombinant generation of new technological knowledge: much of their actual innovative capability is shaped by their context of action. The quality of the context plays a key role in assessing the actual possibility that the reaction of firms is creative, rather than adaptive.

4. FROM KNOWLEDGE SPILLOVERS AND INTERACTIONS TO KNOWLEDGE EXTERNALITIES

The knowledge external to the firm, at each point in time, is a necessary and relevant complement to knowledge internal to the firm, in order to generate new knowledge. The access conditions to external knowledge are a key conditional factor in assessing the chances of generation of new knowledge. The generation of new knowledge is the specific outcome of an intentional conduct and requires four distinct and specific activities:

internal learning, formal research and development activities, and the acquisition of external tacit and codified knowledge. Each of them is indispensable. Firms that have no access to external knowledge and cannot take advantage of essential complementary knowledge inputs can generate very little, if no new knowledge at all, even if internal learning, combined with research and development activities, provides major contributions. Also the opposite is true. Firms that do not perform any knowledge generating activity but have access to rich knowledge commons can generate no new knowledge.

The context in which firms try to innovate plays a key role to make the actual introduction of productivity enhancing innovations possible. Without an appropriate context that enables the access to external knowledge, the reaction of firms fails to be creative and remains merely adaptive (Antonelli, 2007).

The appreciation of the key role of the context in which firms try to innovate is the result of an articulated process initiated with the identification of knowledge spillovers, eventually implemented by the notion of knowledge interactions and finally articulated in the notion of knowledge externalities. Let us consider them in turn.

Knowledge Spillovers

The notion of knowledge spillovers has been introduced by Zvi Griliches (1979, 1992) to provide an analytical context into which the wide gap between the private and social returns of R&D expenditures could be explained. Because of low appropriability of knowledge, firms fund R&D activities but can appropriate only a fraction of the total benefits. Other firms however can take advantage of the knowledge spilling into the atmosphere. Griliches was able to appreciate the reverse side of the non-appropriability coin and to highlight its positive effects.

As a matter of fact knowledge spillovers are a direct application of the notion of technological externalities to the economics of knowledge and enable us to grasp the effects of the spontaneous availability of production factors at no costs within a given production function (Meade, 1952). Knowledge spillovers do not require any transaction between the producers and the recipients of the external effects: they can be considered a characteristic of the 'atmosphere' of the districts in which firms are based. Knowledge spillovers affect the knowledge generation function as they can account for an unpaid production factor consisting in the availability of external knowledge (Antonelli, 1999).

It seems more and more evident that the new growth theory impinges upon and elaborates the notion of knowledge spillovers initiated by Griliches. The new growth theory in fact has enriched and articulated the hypothesis that knowledge is a production factor spilling in the atmosphere of industrial districts. In this perspective the distinction between specific and generic knowledge is crucial. While specific knowledge is embedded in organizations and can be successfully appropriated by 'inventors', generic knowledge is expected to spill freely into the atmosphere, with no costs for prospective users either to acquire or to use it. Generic knowledge spills into the atmosphere like manna: it can be accessed with no search, transaction, interaction or communication costs (Romer, 1994).

Substantial empirical investigations of knowledge spillovers have made it possible to appreciate important qualifications about the characteristics of the localized context in which spillovers are found.

The application of the distinction between inter-industrial and intra-industrial externalities has been most useful. Intra-industrial spillovers, derived from MAR externalities, stress the horizontal complementarity of firms active within the same industry. When knowledge complementarity matters, firms participate in implementing a common knowledge base and each can profit from the advances of the other members of the same industry. Jacobs's spillovers (Jacobs, 1969) identify the complementarity of firms across industries. Inter-industrial flows of knowledge are most relevant when vertical flows of knowledge across many industrial filieres are relevant for the knowledge generation in a single downstream industry. The reverse also applies and takes place when the knowledge spillovers of a single industry upstream have a wide scope of application across a wide variety of industrial activities such as in the case of general purpose technologies. It is clear that the industrial structure of an economic system here plays a key role in assessing the actual flows of knowledge spillovers: holes and weaknesses in the vertical and horizontal mix of industries can play a critical role in the provision of knowledge spillovers (Audretsch and Feldman, 1996).

Spillovers are mainly local because their effects are circumscribed within a limited area of action: proximity matters. Proximity however has several dimensions. Indeed proximity in geographical space favors the dissemination of knowledge spillovers. Proximity in knowledge space however also matters as it favors the sharing of knowledge codes. In general distance in multidimensional space has strong negative effects upon the density, reliability, symmetry, recurrence and quality of knowledge spillovers (Feldman, 1999).

The rich empirical evidence gathered, however, has progressively made clear that knowledge spillovers do not take place freely in the atmosphere: interactions are necessary and crucial for the dissemination of knowledge to take place (Cohen and Levinthal, 1990).

From Social Interaction to Knowledge Interactions

The study of interactions is a growing field of economics and more specifically of the economics of complexity. The relations among agents in the economic system do not take place only in the markets and do not coincide only with market transactions. Transactions occur in the market place and are impersonal, punctual as opposed to recurrent, and individual. The notion of transaction does not apply within organizations where relations are recurrent and personal and take place in an organized context characterized by hierarchical relations. When interactions matter, prices are no longer the single vectors of all the relevant information for decision makers. The notion of transaction is not sufficient to exhaust the variety of relations that take place within markets including organized transactions, that is, transactions that are made possible by complementary interactions and the exchanges of goods are mediated by personal and recurrent contacts and contracts.

When agents are credited with no capability to change endogenously their production and utility functions, transactions are the most important, if not the single form of interaction that economics studies. When instead agents are credited with the capability to learn and to innovate, and hence to change their production and utility functions, other forms of relations, beyond transactions, become relevant.

Interactions have important effects on the behavior of agents, especially when we assume that the structure of the preferences of agents on the demand side and the structure of technological knowledge of producers is endogenous and exposed to mutual influence. Interactions are a specific form of interdependence whereby the changes in the behavior of other agents directly and explicitly affect the structure of the utility functions for households and of the production functions for producers (Durlauf, 2005). As Glaeser and Scheinkman state: 'Each person's actions change not only because of the direct change in fundamentals, but also because of the change in behavior of their neighbors' (Glaeser and Scheinkman, 2000: 1).

Interactions are a fundamental ingredient of complex dynamics. According to David Lane, complex economic dynamics takes place when the propensity to undertake specific actions of a set of heterogeneous agents changes because of their interactions with one another within structured networks.

Models of interactions have been used to analyse a variety of empirical contexts ranging from unemployment, from stock market crashes to crime, from the endogenous change of preferences to the generation of new technological knowledge. The correlated actions among interacting agents induce amplified responses to shocks. Interaction multipliers are the result of positive feedbacks (Arthur, 1990).

As a matter of fact social interaction had been widely used in the economics of innovation. The epidemic tradition of analysis of the diffusion of innovations, initiated by Zvi Griliches (1957) is based upon the notion of social interactions defined as contagion. In the epidemic tradition contagion takes place by means of interactions and it is considered as a mechanism of dissemination of information. Potential users become aware of new goods and of their superior characteristics, with respect to existing goods, by means of social interactions. Social interactions spread information about the new goods and convince reluctant adopters about the advantages. The reputation of lead users may add to the informational effects and provide incremental incentives to potential users to actually adopt the new goods. Late adopters can be considered as rational users that save on information and search costs (Lane and Arthur, 1993; Lane and Vescovini, 1996).

Recent advances in the analysis of diffusion processes have stressed the role of the structure of interactions. When the probability of interaction in the population of potential users, one of the key parameters of the logistic equation that is at the heart of the epidemic approach, is assumed to have a Pareto distribution, as opposed to a normal one, it is sufficient that a few lead adopters have a large number of social interactions to spread the epidemic contagion to a large number of potential users so as to accelerate the speed of the process that is no longer bound to follow an S-shaped process. The analysis of the working of Internet networks has in fact provided copious evidence about the key role of hubs within scale-free networks that support a very large number of connections and enable information to reach a wide range of connected users instantaneously. The analysis of scale-free networks shows how important is the structure of social interaction to grasp their role in the dissemination of information (Barabàsi and Albert, 1999).

The application of interaction models seems most appropriate to explore the role of external tacit knowledge in the generation of new knowledge. Tacit knowledge in fact can be accessed only by means of personal communications and direct interactions that cannot be analysed with the exclusive notion of transaction.[2]

The results of the empirical analyses of Lundvall (1985) and von Hippel (1976, 1998) on the key role of user-producers interactions as basic engines for the generation of new technological knowledge and the eventual introduction of new technologies confirm the relevance of the vertical interactions, both upstream with providers and downstream with customers, that complement market transactions among heterogeneous agents in the generation of knowledge.

The literature on interactions suffers from two limitations: (a) it does not consider the active and selective role of interacting agents; (b) it does not consider the effects on costs and revenues of interactions.

As a matter of fact interactions, in general, and specifically knowledge interactions, are not free and do not fall like manna from heaven. Prospective users of knowledge interactions are not just passive recipients. Prospective recipients must act in order to benefit from knowledge interactions. The pursuit of knowledge interactions may be at the origin of mobility in space or of the creation of communication channels.

A cost of knowledge interactions should be identified. It consists of the networking efforts and resources that are necessary to activate and profit from them. Knowledge interaction costs are clearly influenced by the location of firms with respect to each other. Knowledge interactions provide firms with an essential and indispensable input into the generation of new technological knowledge, at costs that are influenced by the network structure of relations among firms. The structure of interactions plays a key role in assessing their effects upon the system. Hence the analysis of knowledge interactions should consider both their costs and their actual effects, as shaped by their structure. Once again the issue of intentionality matters: agents that decide to interact are aware of the outcomes in terms of opportunity costs and possible revenues: interactions are an economic matter. Interactions are discretionary and selective: agents select those with whom they enjoy interacting and those with whom they prefer not to interact.

An important step forward can be made when we appreciate the complementarity between knowledge interactions and knowledge transactions. Knowledge transactions are possible only because of the fabric of knowledge interactions that reduce the intrinsic information asymmetry that characterizes agents with respect to the generation and exploitation of knowledge. As a matter of fact interactions make transactions possible. With no interactions, knowledge transactions are quite difficult and actually impossible: markets for knowledge require interactions to become possible.

When attention is focused upon the knowledge generation process and the role of knowledge externalities in the provision of knowledge is appreciated as a key factor combined with the intentional participation of the recipients, the notion of pecuniary knowledge externalities overlaps significantly with the notion of knowledge interaction. Pecuniary knowledge externalities provide an effective tool to analyse the costs and the effects of interactions.

Pecuniary Knowledge Externalities

The analysis of knowledge as both an input and an output and the appreciation of the costs and benefits of knowledge interactions draw attention to the notion of pecuniary knowledge externalities (Antonelli, 2008a).

In the Marshallian tradition the notion of externalities has been rooted on the supply side for quite a long time and provides an interesting device to accommodate the evidence of increasing returns without destroying the basic foundations of standard microeconomics at the firm level. Since the early Marshallian identification, externalities have received considerable attention. As a consequence many different kinds of externalities have been identified according to the specific characteristics of the external effects and the processes by means of which they take place.

Externalities owe their name to the Marshallian analysis of the causal role of factors external – as opposite to internal factors – to the firm, in the explanation of increasing returns. Externalities indeed account for factors that are external to each firm, but by no means external to the system. On the contrary they are the result of the emergence and possibly decline of the idiosyncratic characteristics of the system into which firms are embedded and that the action of firms consisting both in market strategies and in the introduction of innovations has generated. The analysis of knowledge externalities provides a clue to grasping their endogenous and dynamic character (David et al., 1995).

Recently, fresh attention has been paid, in the economics of knowledge, to the distinction introduced by Meade (1952) and Scitovsky (1954) between two quite different types of 'Marshallian externalities': (a) technological externalities and (b) pecuniary externalities. Technological externalities consist of direct interdependences among producers. Pecuniary externalities qualify the effects of external conditions upon the full range of prices of both inputs and outputs. According to Scitovsky, pecuniary externalities consist of the indirect interdependences among actors that take place via the price system. Pecuniary externalities apply when firms acquire inputs (and sell output) at costs (prices) that are lower (higher) than equilibrium levels because of specific structural factors (Antonelli, 2008a, 2008b).

Pecuniary externalities consist of indirect interdependence, mediated by the market mechanisms, via the effects on the price system. Pecuniary externalities exert an effect on both the cost of production factors and the price of products. Positive pecuniary externalities are found when the latter are below the equilibrium levels. More precisely, while technological externalities take place when unpaid production factors enter the production function of users, pecuniary externalities apply when the cost and prices of both products and factors differ from equilibrium levels and reflect the effects of external forces. Pecuniary externalities affect the knowledge generation function as well as the knowledge cost and the revenue functions and consequently have a clear effect on knowledge profit functions.

Pecuniary knowledge externalities enable analysis of the dynamics of external knowledge in its acquisition, use for the generation of new knowledge and exploitation. Let us analyse these aspects in turn.

The acquisition of external knowledge is the result of a long exploration process that includes such activities as search, screening and identification of other knowledge items. External knowledge can be accessed and eventually used in the generation of new knowledge only after dedicated resources have been invested in such activities. Knowledge interactions are not free. On the other hand, although external knowledge can be purchased, the acquisition of external knowledge cannot take place without the building of dedicated knowledge governance mechanisms, whereby transactions are possible only if implemented and complemented by significant interactions.

As far as knowledge generation is concerned we see that the analysis of knowledge externalities enables the appreciation of the effects of the external context on the actual costs of external knowledge including interaction, transaction and purchasing costs and on the intentional decision making of firms in the combination of internal and external knowledge inputs in the production of new knowledge. When knowledge externalities are important firms have a clear incentive to rely more on external rather than internal knowledge inputs in the generation of new knowledge.

Finally knowledge exploitation is affected by external effects insofar as the price of knowledge as an output is considered, as well as the opportunities for exclusive exploitation in the downstream application of new technological knowledge to introduce technological innovations.

Pecuniary knowledge externalities make it possible to appreciate the effects of transactions-cum-interactions that characterize the full range of aspects that qualify external knowledge including leakage, access, use and exploitation. Neither aspect involves either pure transactions or pure interactions. Hence neither analysis based upon sheer knowledge transactions, nor analyses based upon sheer knowledge interactions are sufficient to grasp the complex dynamics of intentional actions that characterize the use of knowledge as an external and yet indispensable input in the production of new knowledge.

Pecuniary knowledge externalities can grasp the combined effect, upon the intentional decision making of creative agents, of the full range of differences between actual and equilibrium levels both in the access, use and purchasing costs and selling prices and actual exploitation conditions of the different forms of knowledge respectively as inputs and outputs.

Firms located within a geographical and knowledge region where a concentration of knowledge intensive activities is found, benefit from the reduction in the cost of exploration of external knowledge. Proximity favors the creation of communication channels and networks where knowledge interactions are easier. Pecuniary knowledge externalities account for the reduction in the actual cost for external knowledge: proximity, in both regional and knowledge space, improves the working of organized markets for knowledge and reduces transaction costs. As far as knowledge exploitation is concerned, we see that pecuniary knowledge externalities make it possible to grasp the effects of the external context on the prices of knowledge outputs. These effects may be negative when knowledge appropriability is considered. Agglomeration and proximity may reduce knowledge appropriability and exclusive exploitation. Such circumstances vary across the specific context of action of firms and do not hold everywhere and at all times, but only in highly idiosyncratic conditions (Antonelli, 2005).

A knowledge profit function with knowledge externalities makes it possible to grasp not only the full range of factors affecting the access to external knowledge, but also both positive and negative effects of the external context in which such activities take place. Pecuniary knowledge externalities make it possible to appreciate both the positive and negative effects of the external context and their interplay as they apply not only to knowledge generation but also to knowledge exploitation and hence to knowledge generation functions as well as to knowledge cost and revenue functions. Hence a knowledge profit function that integrates the working of pecuniary knowledge externalities, provides the tools to consider both the positive effects of knowledge externalities in terms of lower interaction, access, transaction and purchasing costs of some knowledge inputs and their negative effects in terms of reduced appropriability of knowledge as an output and exclusive exploitation hence reduction of the prices for the downstream products that embody new proprietary knowledge (Antonelli, 2010c).

The new appreciation of the dynamic effects of knowledge externalities, in terms of determinants of the actual capability to introduce new technologies, has more recently pushed much effort to understanding their structural determinants, such as the size distribution of the agents, the size of the agglomeration, the network structure of the relations, the distribution of the agents in space, that qualify the context in which the external effects take place. The notion of threshold becomes central: below (above) some thresholds external effects may be positive (negative). Minimum and maximum levels can be identified with important consequences for understanding how the changing structure of innovation systems has a direct bearing on the rate and direction of technological change (Antonelli et al., 2008, 2011).

The analysis of the role of the non-divisibility of knowledge in its generation has made it possible to identify three distinct characteristics of knowledge: knowledge cumulability, knowledge compositeness and knowledge fungibility. Knowledge cumulability takes place when new knowledge is the result of the diachronic complementarity of different vintages of knowledge. When knowledge is composite, new knowledge is generated by the recombination of bits of knowledge that belong to a variety of different fields. Finally, fungibility defines the downstream complementarity of any bit of knowledge. The same core of technological knowledge and competence can be applied to the production of a wide range of new fields.

This variety of knowledge generation processes has important implications for the analysis of knowledge externalities: each of them in fact highlights and stresses a facet of the complex architecture of relations, ranging from transactions to interactions, that matters. The study of externalities and specifically of knowledge externalities enables us to grasp the relevance of the structural architecture of the system.

Knowledge externalities are essential to identify the conditions of organized complexity for which the system can attain dynamic efficiency. Knowledge externalities in fact define the context in which effective generative relations can take place so that the reaction of firms can become creative.

In this context, the notion of the generative relationship introduced by David Lane and Robert Maxfield (1997) is crucial. Generative relationships are constructive positive feedbacks that lead to the introduction of innovations, and innovations feed structural change in agent/artifact space. The process takes place through a 'bootstrap' dynamics where new generative relationships induce attributional shifts that lead to actions that in turn generate possibilities for new generative relationships. The structural characteristics of the system in terms of the distribution of agents in multidimensional spaces, of their networks of communication, relationship and interactions qualified by aligned directedness, heterogeneity, mutual directedness, permissions and action opportunities, are key elements for the sustainability of the process.

The actual conditions of knowledge externalities define the context into which complex economic dynamics takes place. Only when knowledge externalities are available, in fact, can the propensity of a set of heterogeneous agents to undertake specific actions, as a form of reaction to unexpected events, lead to the actual introduction of innovations, because of their interactions with one another within structured networks.

5. LOCALIZED TECHNOLOGICAL KNOWLEDGE AND THE EMERGENCE OF INNOVATION AS A SYSTEM PROPERTY

The appreciation of the role of intentional decision making in the generation of new knowledge and of the central role of learning processes and external knowledge qualifies the localized approach. Firms induced to innovate by irreversibility and disequilibrium in both product and factor markets search locally for new technologies. Procedural rationality, as opposed to Olympian rationality, and localized competence based upon learning processes, limit the global search of firms and constrain their search for new technologies in the proximity of the techniques already in use, upon which learning by doing and learning by using have increased the stock of competence and tacit knowledge. Both the rate and the direction of technological change are influenced by the search for new technologies that are complementary to existing ones. The quality of the context plays a key role in assessing the actual possibility that the reaction of firms is creative, rather than adaptive. In this approach the introduction of innovations and new technologies is the result of a local search, constrained by the limitations of firms to explore a wider range of technological options. This dynamics leads firms to remain in a region of techniques that are close to the original one and to continue to improve the technology in use.

The generation of new technological knowledge is the result of an intentional activity based upon four distinct and complementary inputs, namely: learning, research and development, access to tacit external knowledge and access to external codified knowledge. Each of them can be substituted only to a limited extent. In order to generate new technological knowledge firms must rely upon each of them and act as a system integrator (Antonelli, 1995, 1999).

In the localized technological knowledge framework of analysis, learning is the primary and indispensable source of competence and tacit knowledge. As a consequence firms are rooted in a limited portion of the knowledge space defined by the context in which their learning processes have been taking place, in doing, in using and in interacting. Consequently no firm can command the full range of knowledge items that are necessary to generate new knowledge, and so no firm can innovate in isolation (Antonelli, 2001).

External knowledge is an essential input into the generation of new knowledge. External knowledge can be substituted by internal sources of knowledge only to a limited extent: full-fledged substitutability between internal and external knowledge cannot apply. With proper access to external knowledge firms can complement their localized, internal competence and actually introduce new technologies. Only when a complementary set of knowledge fragments is brought together within a context of consistent interactions, can successful innovations be introduced and adopted: technological knowledge is the product of a collective activity. The access conditions to external knowledge are a key conditional factor in assessing the actual chances of generation of new knowledge. Firms that have no access to external knowledge and cannot take advantage of essential complementary knowledge inputs can generate very little, if any new knowledge at all, even if internal learning and research activities provide major contributions (Antonelli, 2003).

The reaction of firms localized in a poor context, unable to provide appropriate flows of pecuniary knowledge externalities will not be able to generate new productivity enhancing technologies and will just be adaptive: firms will move in the existing map of isoquants or introduce small changes that enable the introduction of technical change based upon substitution. Innovation will emerge as a system property when the reaction of firms, supported by the access to collective knowledge, will become actually creative and consist of the introduction of productivity enhancing technological changes that reshape the map of isoquants when their internal knowledge matches the availability of appropriate sources of external knowledge and is the result of a process of knowledge recombination.

The Recombinant Generation of Technological Knowledge

Technological knowledge internal to each firm is localized in a limited portion of the knowledge space by the learning processes that are at the origin of its accumulation: the key role of learning and tacit knowledge roots and limits the span of command of the firm in the knowledge space. In order to generate new knowledge the firm must identify other bits of complementary knowledge and recombine them with the internal one. The notion of recombinant knowledge qualifies the nature of the knowledge production activity (Antonelli, 2008a; Antonelli et al., 2010c).

The recombinant knowledge approach complements and integrates the analysis of external knowledge and localized technological knowledge. As Weitzman (1996: 209) recalls: 'when research is applied, new ideas arise out of existing ideas in some kind of cumulative interactive process that intuitively has a different feel from prospecting for petroleum.' As Arthur (2009: 21) notes: 'novel technologies arise by combination of existing technologies and . . . therefore existing technologies beget further technologies . . .' This insight leads to the recombinant growth approach which views new ideas as being generated through the recombination of existing ideas, under the constraint of diminishing returns to scale in the performance of the research and development (R&D) activities necessary to apply new ideas to economic activities (Weitzman, 1998).

A large literature on biological grafting has applied the so-called NK model in the economics of knowledge. According to Kauffman (1993) the success of a search process depends on the topography of a given knowledge landscape shaped by the complementary relations (K) among the different elements (N) of a given unit of knowledge. In the NK model, the features of the topological space within which the economic action that leads to the generation of new technological knowledge takes place, are not characterized from an economic viewpoint. Rather, the number of complementary relations and their distribution are given, as are the number of elements belonging to each unit of knowledge. As frequently occurs when biological metaphors are grafted onto economics, this is compounded by the fact that the number of components and their relations are exogenous and there is little economic analysis of their associated costs and revenues.

This approach can be implemented as soon as the characteristics of the knowledge space into which eventual recombination may take place are appreciated: some regions of the knowledge space are more fertile than others. Recombinations are seen as the products of a combinatorial engine where the location in knowledge space of each agent possessing the bits of complementary knowledge plays a key role in shaping the recombinatory process. In this view, recombination does not take place as if it were the product of a random process. On the contrary, recombination is guided by the intentional action of prospective agents seeking to solve the specific problem they are facing and is shaped by their distribution in knowledge space. Proximity in knowledge space matters as much as the actual intentionality of agents to try and change their own technologies and to participate in the recombination. Passive agents are not likely to join the recombinatory process. New technologies are the result of a recursive process of recombination of the bits of knowledge possessed by intentional agents distributed in a map that evolves together with the technology itself.

The new economics of knowledge suggests that the knowledge is a system that can be represented by means of a map where a variety of interrelated components or modules are connected by links of varying strength according to their cognitive distance. The map of the knowledge system shows that the knowledge space is rugged and is characterized by different levels of complementarity and interdependence among a variety of components. The relations among such components may be qualified in terms of fungibility, cumulability and compositeness according to the contribution that each body of knowledge is able to make in the recombinant generation of new technological knowledge. Radical technological change takes place when a variety of complementary bodies of knowledge come together to form a hub that provides knowledge externalities to the 'peripheries', which in their turn provide new inputs and help the pursuit of further recombination stretching its core (Antonelli, 1999, 2008a).

The generation of new knowledge by means of the recombination of pre-existing knowledge items does not yield the same results in all possible directions. Some recombination processes are likely to be more fertile than others. Some knowledge items happen to be central in the generation of new knowledge (Olsson, 2000; Olsson and Frey, 2002).

The empirical evidence provided by the new economics of knowledge suggests that the knowledge space is rugged and is characterized by a variety of landscapes. In some regions knowledge cores emerge and contribute to form a hub that provides knowledge externalities to the 'peripheries', which in their turn are reliant on this knowledge from the core. In other regions however such dynamics does not take place. Some regions are potentially fertile and others are not able to support the reaction of firms. The generation of new technological knowledge and the eventual introduction of productivity enhancing new technologies depend upon the quality of the context in which firms are localized, as well as on their capability to accumulate competence and implement appropriate recombination processes: organized complexity matters in the recombinant generation of knowledge.

New technological knowledge can be generated whenever, wherever and if previous and parallel knowledge is available and accessible. Moreover, at each point in time, no agent possesses all the knowledge inputs required. External knowledge is an essential input into the recombinant generation of new knowledge. Knowledge communication, both internal and external to firms, among learning agents plays a central role in the generation of new knowledge. Agents search in the knowledge space for other knowledge items, create communication channels and activate knowledge flows. Moreover firms can move within the knowledge space and select their location so as to access the new knowledge that will be most usefully recombined with their existing competences. Agents identify other agents with whom cognitive interactions and transactions are most likely to yield positive outcomes so as to benefit from localized pecuniary knowledge externalities.

In this context knowledge, external to firms, is an essential input into the generation of new knowledge. Access to external knowledge generally requires investment to enable search, screening, interaction and understanding, all of which are necessary before the external units of knowledge can be recombined with firms' internal knowledge. In certain areas of the knowledge space, fertile knowledge is available and can be accessed at a cost. Recombination will occur only if it is expected to yield net revenues in terms of the flows of knowledge outputs that it will generate.

Knowledge recombination is the process by means of which new technological systems based upon webs of complementary technologies emerge. The process is characterized by clear sequences based on highly selective exploration. The emergence of a core of complementary technologies is the first aggregating step. This initial core of technologies is very productive and is characterized by low recombination costs and high revenues from the additional knowledge generated. This engenders a process of technological convergence. The emergence of new knowledge cores pushes firms already active in existing knowledge space to explore seemingly less complementary knowledge regions in an effort to take advantage of new, marginal opportunities for knowledge recombination. Eventually, the increasing variety of these recombinations will prove less and less effective and the diminishing returns to recombination will become apparent.

In sum, according to our analysis, the generation of technological knowledge and the introduction of technological change are characterized by four assumptions: (a) firms are rooted in a limited portion of the space of technology, knowledge and geography both by the irreversibility of their stock of tangible and intangible inputs and by the competence based upon learning processes; (b) firms are characterized by bounded rationality, but their procedural rationality includes the possibility of reacting to unexpected events, generate intentionally new technological knowledge and introduce new technologies because external knowledge is an indispensable input into the generation of new knowledge and no firm or agent can command all available knowledge; (c) the quality of the reaction of each firm, whether reactive or adaptive, which depends upon (d) the amount of knowledge available in the proximity within the technological and regional space into which each agent is embedded and the viability of the knowledge governance mechanisms at work in that context.

Knowledge Positive Feedbacks and the Emergence of Innovation

Our analysis puts into context the notion of knowledge positive feedback. Knowledge positive feedbacks take place in well specified circumstances when and where the interplay between the recombinant generation of technological knowledge and the changing characteristics of the knowledge and regional space feed each other so as to support the reaction of firms and make it creative.

The notion of positive knowledge feedback has two important implications. First, recombinant knowledge and localized technological change do not provide unlimited opportunities, which are fertile at any time, and in any place. Knowledge recombination may occasionally yield positive returns in well-defined and circumscribed circumstances that take place in historic time, regional space and knowledge space, when a number of key conditions apply.

In some cases, however, the returns from recombination may be less productive.

When the structure of the system is such that knowledge externalities are not available and the access to external knowledge is burdened by heavy transaction, search and communication costs, high levels of congestion and strong appropriability, and the architecture of interactions limits knowledge interactions, single innovations may occasionally take place, but remain isolated acts of a minority of individual firms with little systemic effect. When the competitive threat to established market position is weak and hence creative social reactions are not solicited, inferior technologies are likely to be resilient. Adaptive responses, as opposed to creative ex-adaptive ones, are likely to occur when firms do not have access to knowledge social interactions and the generation of knowledge must rely only upon internal sources. Firms are not able to introduce new localized, productivity enhancing technologies and may prefer to switch, that is, just to change their techniques within the existing maps of isoquants. When the access of firms to external knowledge is costly if not inhibited, and adaptive responses, as opposed to creative ones, prevail, no technological change takes place and hence the structures of the system do not change.

The conditions for the emergence of innovations are set when the mismatch between expectation and real market conditions stirs the reaction of myopic but reactive agents and the flows of pecuniary knowledge externalities are large and consistent with their knowledge base. When both conditions apply, agents discover that their reaction is actually creative and activates a process of centred recombination that may occasionally generate new radical technologies. The actual emergence of innovations in fact takes place when active users of pre-existing technologies access the knowledge spilling over from the innovative activities of other actors co-localized in the knowledge space and combine it with their core knowledge. The larger the number of reactive agents, able to mobilize their competence and tacit knowledge and intentionally searching for new technologies, the larger is the chance that a chain reaction leading to the generation of new technological knowledge and the eventual introduction of new technologies is set forth.

When positive feedbacks qualify the individual reaction of a firm into a creative process, innovations emerge from a collective process of generation of new technological knowledge and can lead to actual innovation cascades. It is clear in fact that the larger is the number of innovations and the larger the mismatch between the plans of individual myopic firms and the actual conditions of product and factor markets, hence the number of firms that are induced to react creatively, then the larger is the amount of technological knowledge that is generated in the system. In such conditions not only are more firms induced to try and change their technology, but also a larger amount of knowledge is being generated. The chances in turn increase that the reaction of firms becomes creative and can actually lead to the introduction of successful technological innovations that increase the levels of total factor productivity (Antonelli, 2007, 2008a).

The organization, composition and distribution of the knowledge base, that is, the complementarity between the competence of reacting firms, the variety and coherence of their individual research efforts, play a key role in supporting the reaction of firms and helping the emergence of innovation (Antonelli et al., 2010c).

In special circumstances the dynamics of positive feedbacks can activate self sustained chain-reactions that lead to broader innovation cascades or Schumpeterian gales of creative destruction. New technological systems emerge and articulate around core technologies that act as general purpose technologies, that is, hubs in the collective process of knowledge generation in which all the parties involved act intentionally, within a well-identified rent-seeking perspective. Such exceptional outcomes of individual interactions are clearly influenced both by the population dynamics of the entries of more or less compatible agents with whom recombination can be practised, and the organization and composition of the knowledge base. New gales emerge from a sequential process of selective aggregation in the knowledge space of heterogeneous agents yet encompassing specific knowledge components with high levels of potential complementarity and coherence.

Schumpeterian gales of innovation can be better understood as a historical process of emergence of new technological systems based upon a selective and sequential overlapping among complementary technologies that takes place in well defined circumstances (Antonelli, 2001).

Much progress can be made by merging the literature on localized technological change and recombinant knowledge with the General Purpose Technology (GPT) literature. The notion of GPT implements and elaborates the Schumpeterian notion of the gales of technological innovations. According to Schumpeter the gales of technological innovations occur when a radically new technology with a wide scope of applicability is introduced into the system. There is today a large body of empirical and theoretical work investigating the hypothesis that when the core body of new, radical knowledge with a wide scope of application emerges out of a generalized and collective process of search and exploration, it may promote a wave of ripple effects that invest all the system (Bresnahan and Trajtenberg, 1995; Lypsey et al., 1998, 2005).

It becomes clear now that externalities are indeed endogenous. As is well known, the notion of externalities was first introduced by Alfred Marshall to identify the external causes of increasing returns at the firm level. Its meaning has been stretched so as to consider more generally the effects that an array of factors, including knowledge spillovers, external to each firm, but internal to a regional system, have on their performances. The notion of externalities has progressively acquired dynamic implications so as to include the consequences on the individuals of the changing features of the system with the notion of localized increasing returns. At the same time, however, confusion has grown about the origins of externalities.

At the system level externalities are not exogenous but rather endogenous. Externalities and specifically knowledge externalities are a specific and yet dynamic and changing attribute of the system that is produced by the interaction of the individual agents that belong to the system. This seems especially true of the generation and exploitation of knowledge: new knowledge is in fact, at the same time, an output and an input and its generation requires the participation of a variety of agents because of its intrinsic character of partial appropriability, non-exhaustibility and non-divisibility.

As soon as it is clear that externalities stem from the collective results of the behavior of individuals, however, it also becomes clear that they cannot be exogenous, but rather are endogenous to the system in which each firm is embedded. A recursive process takes place where structural change at the system level and technological change at the individual level are the two sides of the same coin. The performances of the firms and their interactions affect the structural character of the system and this in turn affects the context of action of each individual firm with external effects.

Now it becomes fully clear how, why, when and where the generation of localized technological knowledge is made possible by the positive feedback of endogenous pecuniary knowledge externalities stemming from knowledge interactions within the organized complexity provided by good knowledge governance mechanisms. The generation of localized technological knowledge enables the implementation of creative responses and the actual introduction of new productivity-enhancing technologies. Consequently it also becomes clear how and why the increase of total factor productivity is made possible by the access to external knowledge made available at costs far below equilibrium levels. Total factor productivity is explained by the role of pecuniary knowledge externalities that affect the cost equation that parallels the knowledge generation function, rather than the production function of the goods that use knowledge as an input. As such it reflects systemic conditions that are highly localized, in time and space, specific and idiosyncratic to the characteristics of the system at each point in time. This approach explains and accommodates the high levels of variance in the levels and rates of increase of total factor productivity well documented by the empirical evidence. The appreciation of innovation as the emerging property of the organized complexity of an economic system, when, where and if it is able to qualify a context of knowledge interactions that can implement and qualify the intentional action of reactive and potentially creative agents, provides a consistent explanation for total factor productivity: the basic conundrum of the economics of innovation.[3]

6. THE EMERGENCE OF THE ORGANIZED COMPLEXITY OF INNOVATION SYSTEMS: THE RECURSIVE DYNAMICS OF STRUCTURAL AND TECHNOLOGICAL CHANGE

The recursive and systemic dynamics of technological change can now be explored in more detail. The actual capability of firms to react creatively to out-of-equilibrium conditions, and to change their own technologies depends upon the proper combination of internal knowledge and competence and the localized availability of knowledge externalities and interactions. At each point in time in fact the reaction of firms is qualified and constrained by their location and the consequent conditions of access to external knowledge. When external knowledge cannot be accessed properly, the reaction of firms is adaptive and consists in standard switching upon the existing maps of isoquants.

Their reaction can become creative as opposed to adaptive and engender the actual introduction of successful, productivity enhancing innovations, when and if the interactions and feedbacks shaped by the structure of the system provide the access to external knowledge and external learning conditions. The intensity and the effects of interactions are shaped by the structure of the system and specifically by the network topology of agents distributed in the multidimensional space, at each point in time: hence innovation as an emerging property of the system into which the dynamics takes place.

The creative reaction of firms however consists both in their innovative capability and in their strategic mobility in multidimensional space. Firms can change their location, enter and exit product and factor markets, create new links and communication channels, change their position in vertical inter-industrial linkages and in regional districts and thus change their knowledge base, and hence their complementarities with respect to other firms. Firms can introduce institutional innovations that help the emergence of new markets and new forms of organization of the system at large, such as in the case of venture capitalism. The distribution of agents in the multidimensional space is itself the endogenous result of the locational strategies of agents carried out in the past. Clearly knowledge externalities are internal to the system: they depend upon the specific combination of activities and channels of communication in place among them. Knowledge externalities depend upon the structure of the system. The organization and composition of the structure of the system in which firms are localized exerts a key role in shaping the dynamics at both the aggregate and the individual level. Hence the organization of the systemic complexity is itself an emerging property.

Here it is clear how important are the contributions of both organization and population thinking. The former shows the extent to which the introduction of innovation depends upon the organization of the system, while the latter shows how population dynamics, in terms of entry and exit, reshapes the organization of the system. The analysis of the structural composition of the system, its effects on the conduct of firms and its evolution initiated by Simon Kuznets (1930, 1955, 1966, 1971, 1973) can be retrieved and enriched by the appreciation of other structural characteristics.

The systems of innovation approach has captured some aspects of the interplay between the structural characteristics of the system at each point in time and the actual capability of firms to react creatively and introduce productivity enhancing innovations (Nelson, 1993).

These structural characteristics of the system are the features of a rugged and evolving landscape which firms are at the same time rooted in and yet able to change as a result of their strategic conduct. The organization and composition of the structure of the system are neither static nor exogenous: they change through time, albeit at a slow rate, as a result of the dynamics of agents and of the aggregate. The meso-economic dynamics of the system act as a filter between the dynamics at the individual and the aggregate levels (Burt, 1992; Dopfer, 2005).

Several structural dimensions matter: institutional structures, economic structures, industrial structures, regional structures and knowledge structures, all contribute to shaping and framing the actual and effective access of firms to external knowledge and hence their chances to introduce productivity enhancing innovations.

The institutional organization of an economic system plays a crucial role in many aspects. Intellectual property right regimes qualify the exclusivity of proprietary knowledge and hence define the conditions for the use of external knowledge as an input into the generation of new knowledge. At the same time however they define the appropriability of the new knowledge generated. The interactions among users and producers of knowledge as well as the viability of the markets for knowledge are much influenced by the intellectual property right regimes. The institutional conditions for the interaction between firms and the academic and public research sector, whether based upon personal contacts or more organized transactions, are most relevant in favoring the bidirectional flows of knowledge so as to increase both the dissemination of existing knowledge and the active participation of the scientific undertaking in directions that are directly useful for the business community (Antonelli and Ferraris, 2011; Antonelli et al., 2010d).

The analysis of the structure of the endowments is crucial to grasp the incentive structures for the direction of technological change. It is clear in fact that firms have a strong incentive to introduce technological innovations that make a more intensive usage of locally abundant inputs (Kennedy, 1964; Samuelson, 1965; Binswanger and Ruttan, 1978).

The distribution and organization of markets, both intermediary and final, is far from obvious and spontaneous. The quality of markets varies across economic systems and affects their performances. The quality of the markets in terms of density of players on both the demand and the supply side, and thickness, recurrence, and distribution of transactions is a crucial structural attribute of an economic system and has powerful effects on its dynamics (Burt, 1992; Antonelli and Teubal, 2011).

The composition of the economic system in terms of primary, manufacturing and tertiary sectors and specifically the active role of knowledge intensive business service industries has a pivotal role in framing the access of firms to external knowledge. The analysis of the vertical structure of industrial and economic systems has highlighted the role of intersectoral linkages as vectors of input flows and identified the central role of key sectors in the dissemination, appropriation and exploitation of knowledge as both an input and output (Pavitt, 1984; Fransman, 2007).

The spatial distribution of the industry plays a key role. Economic geography has explored successfully the central role of regional districts and clusters as forms of governance of economic activity, analysed the effects of the spatial composition of industries and economic activities in supporting the introduction of innovations and assessed the role of spatial proximity in the dissemination of technological knowledge (Breschi and Lissoni, 2003; Boschma, 2005).

The analysis of the composition of the knowledge base of an economic system is a recent important area of fruitful investigation. Technological knowledge is far from being a homogeneous aggregate of knowledge items. Knowledge is itself a complex system of highly differentiated elements related by intricate webs of complementarity and interdependence. At the aggregate level it is more and more clear that the composition and the organization of the knowledge base in terms of variety, whether related or unrelated, coherence, specialization and concentration in specific knowledge fields has important implications for the recombinant generation of new knowledge fields (Saviotti, 1996; Frenken, 2006a, 2006b; Frenken et al., 2007). At the meso level, the structure of knowledge networks and their governance are determinant to channel knowledge externalities (Nesta and Saviotti, 2005, 2006).

According to Paul Krugman (1994) such rugged landscapes in geographical, technological, knowledge, market and product space are at the same time the consequence and the determinants of complex dynamics. The structure of the system acts as a vector of catalyzers of a self-sustained positive feedback in supporting the creative reaction of firms. Yet it is the result of their action. This approach makes it possible to pay attention to the evolution of the organization and composition of the structural characteristics of the system in terms of the distribution of agents in the different space dimensions, and to appreciate the changing architecture of the relations of communication, interaction and competition that take place among agents in assessing the rate and direction of technological change.

The structure of interactions and the flows of knowledge externalities depend upon the organization of the system in terms of the architecture of sectors and markets, the forms of competition that prevail in each of them and among them, the geographical distribution of firms, their density in regional and technological clusters, the forms of organization within and among firms, the shape and structure of knowledge networks, the vertical organization of industrial filieres, the governance mechanisms, the institutional context. All these structural elements are the meso-economic carriers of history and, as such, embody the memory of the system and, occasionally, at the same time the product of the creative reaction of firms.

It is clear that positive feedbacks take place only in specific circumstances: some structures are more conducive than others. In some circumstances structural change leads to forms of organized complexity where the reaction of firms becomes actually creative and leads to the introduction of innovations. These in turn however affect the organization, composition and architecture of the structure of the system. The organization of the structure has led to the introduction of technological changes that in turn affect the organization of the system: the dynamics loop between structural and technological change is set.

In special circumstances structural change leads to the emergence of strong innovation systems empowered by highly performing network structures that are the result of the collective dynamics of a myriad agents in search of potential, vertical and horizontal, complementarities. The emergence of highly performing innovation systems leads to Schumpeterian gales of innovations. The successful accumulation and generation of new technological knowledge, the eventual introduction of new and more productive technologies and their fast diffusion are likely to take place in a self-propelling and spiralling process and at a faster pace within economic systems characterized by fast rates of growth where interaction, feedbacks and communication are swifter. In such special circumstances, the system can undergo a phase transition leading to the introduction of a new radical technological system.

The changing structure of the system is endogenous to the system itself: the architecture of knowledge networks, as well as the industrial, sectoral, regional, knowledge and economic composition is heavily influenced by the strategies of firms seeking to improve their multidimensional location within systems of interactions.

The national system of innovations approach framed by Nelson (1993) and widely used and implemented, contributed to appreciation of the key role of the structural characteristics of economic systems in shaping their innovative capability, but clearly suffers from the basic assumption that the structure of the system is either given or exogenous. In this line of enquiry there is no effort to grasp the endogenous determinants of structural change (Patel and Pavitt, 1994).

Our approach makes it possible to focus the attention on the intertwined dynamics of knowledge externalities and interactions, localized technological changes and structural change. Our approach makes it possible to grasp that both the occurrence of creative reactions and the introduction of an innovation as well as its organized complexity are key emerging properties of an economic system.

Knowledge interactions and externalities, and hence positive feedbacks, are not exogenous, the amount of knowledge externalities and interactions depends upon the structure of the system. The structure of the system is determined by the conduct of firms including both market strategies, the introduction of innovations and new communication

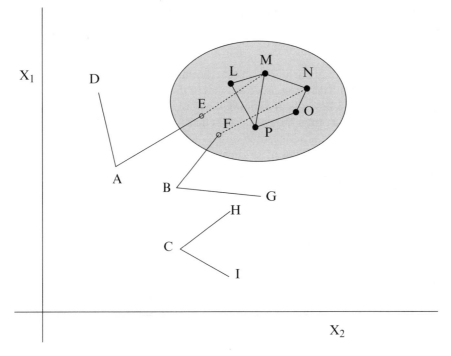

Figure 1.2   The direction of technological knowledge

and interaction networks. The activation of knowledge interactions is the result itself of intentional action.

At each point in time, in fact, agents can change both their production and utility functions and their location. Agents are mobile, albeit in a limited range constrained by relevant switching costs, and they can change their production and utility functions, building upon their experience and competence based upon learning processes, hence in a limited span of techniques and preferences practiced in their past. Firms select their interacting partners, build communication channels, elaborate governance mechanisms: all actions that favor knowledge interactions. At each point in time the map of multidimensional space into which each firm is embedded is exposed to the changes brought by the changing location of firms. Firms are both creative with respect to their technologies, and mobile, with respect to their location in the space of knowledge, technologies, and reputation, hence they can change the structure of the system. The introduction of institutional changes adds on to the endogenous evolution of economic structures.

Innovation systems consolidate through time when the structural emergent properties leading to an organized complexity feed the introduction of innovations as emergent properties that in turn are able to feed further qualifications and improvements of the organized complexity of the system.

As Figure 1.2 shows, each firm directs the generation of technological knowledge in a simple Lancastrian knowledge space with two characteristics (X_1 and X_2) depending on the opportunities to benefit from the locally available pecuniary knowledge externalities (Lancaster, 1971). At time 1 each firm moving respectively from point A, B, C, directs its technological strategy towards either D or E, F or G, H or I depending on the conditions of the external context. In turn, once rooted in either point, new possible directions can be chosen, within corridors defined by the firm's internal characteristics that include the preceding path.

The technological path of each firm reflects the characteristics of both its own internal quasi-irreversibilities and learning processes and of the structure of the local context. The initial conditions play a key role in defining the context of action. The external context, however, at each point in time, has powerful effects on the dynamics. According to the quality of knowledge interactions, some directions are favored and others impeded. In Figure 1.2 the firm in A is induced to direct its innovation process towards E rather than D by the organized complexity of the system LMNOP. The firm in B would move towards F rather than G. If other firms act as firms A and B the structure of the existing network LMNOP will change. A new architecture of the network emerges. Its governance will change according to the ability of each new and old member respectively to enter and to participate in the new communication flows within the new architecture of the network.

The new structure of the network is by no means bound to be superior to the previous one. If the structural change increases the actual amount of knowledge externalities and interactions, a self-propelling process takes place. As long as additional changes reinforce this dynamics and consolidate the network the process gains momentum.

Positive feedback is likely to reinforce the process as the effort to increase the complementarity of each firm's research activity reinforces the local pools of knowledge, which, in turn, increases the possibility to access external knowledge. At the same time increasing awareness of the opportunities for better knowledge exploitation provided by the intensive use of locally abundant and idiosyncratic production factors increases the intentional convergence of knowledge generation strategies towards a common direction shaped by the collective identification of the local idiosyncratic inputs. At the population level, the effects of individual convergence are reinforced by selection mechanisms. The success of the localized knowledge exploitation strategies acts as a powerful focusing mechanism that, through selection processes, favors the survival and growth of firms that have selected convergent paths of knowledge generation and exploitation (Antonelli, 2008b).

Each firm engaged in generating new knowledge and appropriating its benefits in terms of extra profits, discovers that the convergent alignment of its internal research activities with the complementary research activities of other firms, co-localized in both geographical and knowledge space, is a powerful factor of competitive strength. It is immediately clear in fact that the lower the unit costs of external knowledge are, the larger is the amount of knowledge that the firm is able to generate and the stronger is its localization in a specific context. A firm that is located in a conducive knowledge environment, and is able to identify and access the local pools of knowledge at low cost, is induced to take advantage of it and hence to base the generation of its new knowledge in the characteristics of its environment. This in turn is likely to affect the architecture of the local pools of knowledge and their governance.

Firms are able to try and change their environment and to influence its evolution by an array of actions ranging from intentional mobility across regional and knowledge space, the creation of new communication links with other firms and institutions active in the generation of knowledge, the organization of networks and clubs, and the introduction of better knowledge governance mechanisms. Here the notion of *coalition for innovation*, a term borrowed from political science, plays a key role. Firms and economic agents, at large, try to organize coalitions that are effective when they succeed in improving knowledge governance mechanisms by aligning and converging incentives and interactions based on their complementary competences. The *aligned* and *mutual* directedness of their interactions emerges, as the product of collective actions, aimed at increasing the quality of knowledge governance, enhancing the cohesion of the group and organizing the inherent complexity of the system around shared objectives (Antonelli, 1997b; David and Keely, 2003; Lane et al., 2009).

The dynamic coordination of creative agents emerges as a key issue. At the system level the creation of platforms that implement the dynamic complementarities of firms helps the emergence of clusters and favors the intensification of knowledge interactions and hence the rates of introduction of localized technological changes. At the firm level the counterpart consists in the design and implementation of dedicated governance mechanisms to implement knowledge interactions such alliances, technology clubs, and long-term contracts (Consoli and Patrucco, 2008).

Innovation systems emerge, through historic time, articulated in horizontal and vertical blocks of industrial sectors and filieres, technological districts, clusters, and networks when the generation of new technological knowledge is reinforced by the emerging structure of complementarities based on communication channels provided by the intentional research strategies of firms that discover new sources of complementarities and move within the knowledge space. The active role of the lead users and their fruitful interactions with their customers are encapsulated in these structures of the systems. The institutional features of the system complement the geographical and industrial ones and qualify the characterization of the mesoeconomic structure of the economic system.

The changing organization and architecture of the structure of networks within and among sectors, clusters and filieres is the result of a collective process. Each firm is able to move in such a knowledge space and generate new knowledge taking advantage of increased proximity and reinforced communication and interaction channels with other firms within knowledge coalitions clustering in nodes (the shaded region of Figure 1.2) where potential knowledge complementarities can be better understood. As a result, new systems of innovation, based upon coalitions and nodes of coherent knowledge complementarity, emerge (and others decay) while the direction of technological knowledge is shaped by the alignment towards a collective convergence of the research strategy of each firm. The levels of organization of the complexity of an economic system are endogenous and are themselves an emerging property (Antonelli, 1997b, 2010a).

Among the possible consequences, however, it is clear that, at the system level, the mix of activities that engender knowledge externalities and interactions may deteriorate over time: the entry of new members in the network as well the changes in the governance of the networks may cause congestion so as to lead to the actual decline of the amount of knowledge externalities and interactions available within the local system.

Each agent is both myopic and localized in a limited region of the space, hence it is not able to make a global choice. Exit from an old location, be it a product market, a network, an industrial sector, or a region, and entry in a new one may improve its own individual chances to access external knowledge and yet it can engender a decline in the overall viability of the innovation system.

The mobility of agents in multidimensional space affects the organization of the system. The latter in turn affects their chances to be creative and hence to introduce technological changes. Technological and structural changes are knitted in a close and dynamic interdependence. It becomes clearer how population dynamics affects the organization of the system and vice versa. Hence the need to rely upon both organization and population thinking (Lane et al., 2009).

The changes in the organization and architecture of the structure of the system have a direct bearing upon the amount and the quality of externalities interactions, and specifically upon the flows of knowledge externalities and knowledge interactions that make available, to each agent, external knowledge. The endogenous and dynamic character of externalities is set. New structures emerge and with them new architectures of externalities, communication and interactions. These in turn affect the dynamics of feedbacks and ultimately convert the chances that the creative reaction of firms leads to the actual introduction of productivity-enhancing innovations (Consoli and Mina, 2009).

Within local and sectoral systems of innovation the organization and architecture of the communication channels that link each agent to others, the distribution of nodes can be seen as the result of an endogenous process of emergence that shares the complex dynamics of Internet network creation. The evolution of these networks, however, can exhibit both positive and negative features. Scale free networks, as opposed to random networks, based upon 'preferential attachments' may emerge and favor the access to external knowledge for a variety of actors. Some firms can emerge as the stars of the system as they are able to act as general switchboards of the communication flows (Barabàsi and Albert, 1999; Barabàsi et al., 2002; D'Ignazio and Giovannetti, 2006; Pastor-Satorras and Vespignani, 2004).

The industrial structure of the system is changed by the emergence of new industries both upstream and downstream with important effects for the system at large. New markets become effective with new opportunities for supply and demand to interact and new possibilities for division of labor and specialization. New flows of intra-industrial externalities may be caused, while others may be hampered by the structural changes.

The introduction of directed technological changes biased towards the intensive use of locally abundant production factors affects their prices and hence changes the structure of relative endowments. Antonelli (2008b) has shown that when firms are able to align their research strategies so as to take advantage of locally abundant knowledge, the amount of knowledge generated is larger. The amount of external knowledge that has been used in the knowledge generation process has a direct bearing not only upon the amount of knowledge being generated and hence on the efficiency shift engendered in the production process, but also on its characteristics. Firms that rely more upon external knowledge are more likely to produce complementary knowledge (Antonelli, 2010c).

Antonelli and Teubal (2008, 2010) have shown how venture capitalism has changed the structure of interactions and transactions in financial markets with important effects upon the capability to fund, select and exploit new technological knowledge. Venture capitalism itself is a major institutional and organizational innovation that has activated a new mechanism for the governance of technological knowledge. Venture capitalism, as well, is the result of a systemic dynamics where a variety of complementary and localized innovations introduced by heterogeneous agents aligned and converged towards a collective platform. The new mechanism favors the creation of new science-based start-up and has led to the creation of new, dedicated financial markets. These new financial markets, specialized in the transactions of knowledge intensive property rights, combine the advantages of polyarchic decision making in screening and sorting radical innovations with the direct participation in the profits of new outperforming science-based start-ups typical of the corporate model.

Agglomeration within clusters in the long run may engender negative effects. Knowledge governance costs may increase along with the number of firms accessing the same knowledge pools because of congestion effects in coordination. Eventually density may have negative effects in terms of reduced knowledge appropriability: the case of excess clustering can occur when proximity favors the uncontrolled leakage of proprietary knowledge within the local system (Antonelli et al., 2008, 2011).

The convergence of the direction of technological change and the emergence of innovation systems in geographical and technological space occurs as long as the positive effects of knowledge interactions are larger than their negative effects. In specific contexts the interplay can lead to logistic processes of emergence with S-shaped dynamic processes that identify critical masses.

At each point in time the emergence of new innovation systems may be blocked by a number of countervailing forces. The process is far from being past dependent: it is shaped, at each point in time, by the ability of the actors to contrast the dissipation of pecuniary externalities. At both the firm and the regional level these processes are likely to occur with a strong non-ergodic and sequential stratification (David, 1994). The path dependent dynamics stems from the interplay between past dependence and intentional action. The internal stock of knowledge acquired through learning by each firm together with the features of the local pools of knowledge and of the economic structure is the past dependent components as at each point in time they are the result of historic accumulation. The amount of knowledge being generated, the direction of technological change being introduced, the levels of knowledge governance costs and the price of locally idiosyncratic production factors are, at each point in time, the result of the intentional action of agents. Hence they provide the opportunities for intentional action to change the original path. At each point in time the intentional action of the embedded agents adds a new layer to the original structure: the original shape exerts an effect that the new layers can modify, depending on their thickness and density. Each firm in fact is able to interact with the system and to change it. This occurs at different levels: by introducing changes to the structural conditions and the topology of the system's communication channels, with the introduction of organizational innovations in knowledge governance mechanisms, and by changes in the factor markets due to innovations that change the supply of the idiosyncratic production factors. The emergence and decline of innovation systems is the result of continual feedback between the structure of the system and the innovative action of its agents (see Figure 1.3).

When the negative effects of agglomeration exceed the positive effects, the mobility of firms in geographical and knowledge space is centrifugal and leads to divergent paths of exploration. Firms leave existing pools of knowledge and search for

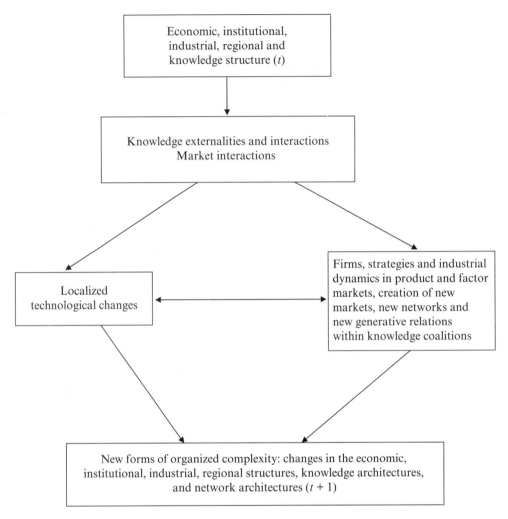

Figure 1.3   The evolving interaction between technological and structural change

new possible agglomerations around new platforms and other sources of knowledge complementarity.

Externalities are endogenous and dynamic. Their dynamics are characterized by non-ergodicity. The past has a consequence on the future. Such non-ergodicity however cannot be characterized as purely past-dependent.

Structural and technological changes interact and shape at each point in time the new architecture of the structure in which firms are localized. The new structural conditions shape the creative reaction of firms as well as their strategies. These in turn change the structure of the system. The key determinants and characteristics of the systemic dynamics of technological change are set. Technological change and structural change are intertwined and mutually interdependent. The introduction of innovations is part of a more general and dynamic process of self-organization of the structure of the system.

The actual introduction of technological and organizational innovations by each agent at each point in time is the result of a long-term process of feedbacks that make possible their creative reaction at the system level via the continual changes in product and factor markets and the related strategic reactions of firms including research and development expenditures and the mobilization of internal tacit knowledge and competence, on the one hand, and the changes in the structure of knowledge interactions and externalities that provide and implement the access to external knowledge, on the other. Hence the conversion of adaptive responses into creative reactions is not a punctual and individual event that takes place isolated in time and space, but rather a collective process that finds its sustainability at the system level. Consistently the innovative capability of a system is an emergent property of the system, a fragile process that takes place when a number of complementary conditions and circumstances are set and their coherence is the result of constant implementation and maintenance over time. The dynamic coordination of structural and technological change appears necessary and yet extremely difficult because each element in the system is changing. Here the notion of path dependence plays a key role for grasping the dynamics of innovative systems.

7. PERSISTENCE, PAST DEPENDENCE AND PATH DEPENDENCE

Historic analysis provides the key information for understanding the determinants of the long-term dynamics of economic processes. This is true at the microeconomic, mesoeconomic and macroeconomic level. Historic analysis reveals the features of the quasi-irreversibilities that shape much of the tangible and intangible assets of firms. Historic analysis provides key information for grasping the mesoeconomic features of the systems in terms of the economic, industrial and regional structures, the composition of preferences and tastes of consumers, the architecture of the networks within and among sectors, clusters and filieres into which firms are embedded and the amount of knowledge externalities and interactions that are available to each of them. Finally, historic analysis provides the key elements to understand the processes that shape the reactions of agents and make them creative, as opposed to adaptive, and hence make the actual introduction of innovations possible (Antonelli, 1997a).

At each point in time the historic processes that have defined the present conditions of each agent characterize their conduct including their capability to innovate. Hence, at each point in time, firms and agents can change their location in space, their competence, their access to external knowledge, and their systems of interactions. In so doing agents can change the structural conditions of the systems (Antonelli, 2007).

The introduction of innovation and the related generation of new knowledge is shaped by cumulative forces, substantial irreversibility and positive feedbacks and takes place only when a set of qualified circumstances applies. Hence innovation is expected to be a persistent process that is reinforced by external feedbacks and contingent factors only when the interplay between technological and structural change sustains the capability of firms to introduce innovations. The dynamics of positive feedback in fact is far from linearity with respect to an array of factors such the density of agents, the architecture of their relations, the quality of communication channels and the conditions at which the communication hubs work. Beyond some – changing – levels, congestion, exclusion and saturation may take place and negative externalities become larger than positive externalities.

Both centripetal and centrifugal effects characterize these dynamic processes with major effects in terms of discontinuity. Centripetal effects are found when the convergence towards local attractors is stronger than divergence. Technological districts, knowledge platforms and networks, new vertical filieres emerge and favor the persistence of the rates of introduction of innovations. When centripetal effects prevail the rates of introduction of innovations are stronger. At the system level growth rates increase together with the variance of the performances of firms. Eventually the diffusion of technological and organizational innovations exerts a strong effect in terms of reduction of the spatial and economic dispersion of firms. Centripetal forces prevail when congestion and knowledge dissipation cause negative net externalities that prevent the creative reaction of firms. Adaptive responses prevail and firms prefer to switch upon the existing maps of isoquants and are no longer able to change them. The rates of growth of the system decline, as well as the variance in the performances and in the characteristics of the firms. The distribution of firms in regional and knowledge spaces tends towards higher levels of homogeneity.

The persistence of the innovative activity takes place when (a) the competitive pressure pushes firms to react by means of more than traditional price–quantities adjustments but to try and change their technologies. Firms can actually react creatively to face unexpected events by means of the introduction of new technologies and new organizational methods and introduce successful innovations when two conditions are fulfilled: (b) they are actually able to learn to learn and (c) the external context qualifies the intentional action of firms and provides the access to complementary and indispensable inputs in terms of external knowledge. In such cases the dynamic process is likely to be characterized by significant hysteretic, non-ergodic features (Antonelli et al., 2010a, 2010b).

This dynamics in fact is characterized by recursive feedbacks. The introduction of new technologies and new organizational methods affects the systems on two counts as it engenders further waves of unexpected events and Schumpeterian rivalry, and, at the same time, makes available new external knowledge. Hence the introduction of innovations can be considered as the persistent and emerging property of an economic system where the interdependence between the dynamics of learning, internal to firms, and the evolving structure of interactions among firms that determines the actual amount of external knowledge available within the system, exert path dependent, rather than past dependent, effects. Non-ergodic dynamics in fact can be either past dependent or path dependent: in the latter case the effects of hysteresis are qualified and shaped by the localized context of action. In the former the process is shaped by the initial conditions only (Antonelli, 2008a).

When a process is non-ergodic, initial conditions exert their effects without alteration upon the full sequence of developmental steps and hence on the final outcome. Past dependence, or 'strong historicity', is an extreme form of non-ergodicity. Historic, as well as social and technological, determinism fully belongs to past dependence. Here, the characteristics of the processes that are analysed and their results are fully determined and contained in their initial condition.

In our approach, instead, it is clear that small and contingent events may change the fragile set of conditions that favor the persistence of innovation because of structural changes that undermine the prevalence of positive knowledge externalities and with them the chances that firms are actually capable of creative, as opposed to adaptive, reactions. This process is characterized by 'weak historicity'; as such, in fact, it may exhibit strong discontinuities. The direction of the process, moreover, may be influenced by the sequential emergence of contingent factors that can modify the path shaped by quasi-irreversible factors. Both the rate and the direction of technological change are affected by the combination of hysteresis and flexibility. The process is indeed path-dependent rather than past-dependent.

Path dependence is the specific form of complex dynamics applied to evolving economic systems. Path dependence provides a unique and fertile analytical framework which is able to explain and assess the ever-changing outcomes of the combination of and interplay between factors of continuity and discontinuity, growth and development, hysteresis and creativity, routines and 'free will', internal and external factors, all of which characterize economic action in a dynamic perspective that is also able to appreciate the role of historic time.

According to Paul David, path dependence is an attribute of a special class of dynamic processes. A process is path dependent when it is non-ergodic and subject to multiple attractors: 'Systems possessing this property cannot shake off the effects of past events, and do not have a limiting, invariant probability distribution that is continuous over the entire state space' (David, 1988, 1992: 1, 1994, 2007).

Indeed, historic analysis and much empirical evidence in economic growth and specifically in the economics of innovation and new technologies confirm that these characteristics apply and are most relevant to understanding the laws of change and growth of complex systems. Path dependence is the specific aspect of complex dynamics most apt to understand the process and the outcomes of the interactions among myopic agents embedded in their own context and constrained by their past decision, yet endowed with creativity and able to generate new knowledge by means of both learning and intentional innovative strategies as well as through structural changes. Path dependence differs sharply from past dependence.

In the theoretical economics of innovation, past dependence has often been assumed: the epidemic models of the diffusion of innovations and the notion of innovations 'locked in' a technological trajectory are typical examples of the deterministic representation of essentially stochastic technological and social phenomena. The notion of technological trajectory is another example of extreme past dependence. The development and implementation of a new technology would follow a well defined and pre-determined sequence of steps that are all defined by the initial characteristics. The notion of technological trajectory is a typical example of the so-called technological determinism according to which technology changes according to its internal rules and, while it is able to have important effects on the economic system, there is no possibility for the on-going changes in the economic system to affect the sequence of innovations that characterize its evolution.

As such, these non-ergodic models are empirically informative but analytically uninteresting. The process takes place within a single corridor, defined at the outset, and external attractors cannot divert its route, nor can the dynamics of the process be altered by transient random disturbances in its internal operations.

Path dependence differs from deterministic past dependence in that irreversibility arises from events along the path, and it is not only the initial conditions that play a role in selecting from among the multiplicity of possible outcomes. The analysis of a path-dependent stochastic system is based on the concepts of transient or 'permanent micro-level' irreversibilities, creativity and positive feedback. The latter self-reinforcing processes work both through the price system and by means of knowledge pecuniary externalities including the effects of social, strategic and generative interactions. The conceptualization of stochastic path dependence can be considered to occupy the border region between a view of the world in which history is relevant only to establish the initial conditions, but has no bearing on the developments of the process and another where the dynamics unfold along the process (Antonelli, 2006).

Path dependence takes place when events that occur along the process can have long lasting consequences and divert both its rate and its direction. A path-dependent process is a non-ergodic process that is not fully determined by its initial conditions: it allows for the contingent effects of localized events that may change the rate, the direction and the sequence of events.

Path dependence is the conceptualization of historical dynamics in which one 'accident' follows another relentlessly and unpredictably and yet the past narrows the scope of possible outcomes, shaping the corridor into which the dynamics takes place. Path dependence gives economists the scope to include historical forces without succumbing to naive historical determinism because it makes it possible to identify the reduced portions of the relevant spaces into which the system is likely to move at each point in time. The understanding of the historic forces that constrain the dynamics of both individual agents and aggregate system, in fact, provides a clue to foresee, with some degree of indeterminacy, the regions into which the future developments of a dynamic process are likely to take place. In so doing path dependences make it possible to substitute the deterministic fallacy of general equilibrium analysis with the stochastic understanding of long-term dynamic processes.

The analysis of the structural determinants of the rate and the direction of technological change enables the identification of the path-dependent interplay between structural and technological change. Technological change can alter the characteristics of the system and yet it is itself the product of the characteristics of the system at each point in time. A strong common thread links the analyses developed with the notion of life cycle and technological trajectory and the notion of path dependence. Only the latter, however, provides a theory to understand why and how technological change takes place sequentially along axes defined in terms of complementarity and cumulability, both internal and external to each firm. From this viewpoint the technological path represents significant progress with respect to both the technological trajectory and the life cycle.

Path dependence applies both to each agent and at the system level: hence we can identify and articulate an individual and a systemic path dependence. Individual path dependence provides the tools to understand the combination of hysteretic, past-dependent factors such as the quasi-irreversibility of tangible and intangible production factors, stock of knowledge and competence, and localized learning, with the generative relationships and creative reactions that make possible, at each point in time, a change in the direction of the action of each agent, including the introduction of innovations. At the firm level the generation of knowledge shares the typical characteristics of a path-dependent process where the effects of the past, in terms of accumulation of competence, mainly based on processes of learning in a localized context of interaction with a given structure of agents, exert an influence and yet are balanced by the specific creativity that is induced by the changing conditions of the system. Systemic path dependence defines the elements of non-ergodicity that characterize the changes in the industrial, regional and economic structure of the system including the architecture of the networks of social, knowledge and strategic interactions.

The notion of path dependence provides one of the most articulated and comprehensive frameworks from which to move towards an analysis of the conditions that make it possible to conceive the working of an economic system where agents are able to generate new technological knowledge, introduce new technological innovations and exploit endogenous growth. The notion of path dependence can be considered the analytical form of complexity most apt to explain the dynamics of economic systems where heterogeneous agents are characterized by some level of past dependence, as well as by local creativity, interdependence and limited mobility in a structured space that affects their behavior but is not the single determinant.

Path dependence is an essential conceptual framework that goes beyond analysis of static efficiency and enters the analysis of the conditions for dynamic efficiency. It applies to each agent, in terms of the quasi-irreversibility of their own endowment of tangible and intangible assets, networks of relations in both product and factor markets, stock of knowledge and competence, and to the system level in terms of general endowments of production factors, industrial and economic structure, and the architecture of the networks in place.

The identification and articulation of individual and system path dependence makes it possible to catch the basic laws of the continual interaction between the hysteretic effects of past dependence, both at the agent and at the system level, and the feedback dynamics that allows the intentional conduct of the creative agent to change both the course of their actions and the characteristics of the structured space. In so doing, path dependence retains the positive contributions of complexity, and at the same time has the capability to overcome the intrinsic limitations stemming from its origins built on natural sciences where human decision making is not considered. Indeed, the notion of path dependence is one of the main forays in the challenging attempt to apply the emerging theory of complexity to economics.

8. CONCLUSION

Standard economics assumes that utility and production functions are exogenous or, at best, change smoothly and evenly, following the rates of learning processes and ubiquitous positive externalities. In evolutionary economics the introduction of innovation is assimilated to the result of random mutations, and as such its causes and determinants are not investigated. No clues are provided to understand the historic, regional and institutional determinants of the generation of innovations. By contrast the selective diffusion of innovations is analysed as the result of a systemic process.

Complex dynamics elaborates the view that change and dynamics are intrinsic to systems characterized by the variety and creativity of their components. Complex systems are characterized by the heterogeneity of agents with different functions, different endowments, different learning capabilities and different perspectives, and most important, different locations in the multidimensional spaces of geography, knowledge, technology and reputation. These heterogeneous agents are complementary components of the system and their action can affect the dynamics of the system. The working of each of them as well as the working of the system can be understood only if the web of interactions and interdependencies is identified and qualified in terms of organized complexity.

The merging of the theory of complexity with the Schumpeterian and Marshallian legacies in economics provides a frame of analysis into which the systemic dynamics of technological change can be better understood, but only if the microeconomics of innovation is fully elaborated and integrated and the relations between individual and systemic change respectively at the micro and macro level are clearly articulated. Our approach makes it possible to appreciate the intertwined dynamics between the introduction of innovations and structural changes that implement the levels of organization of the complexity of the system.

The integration of the Marshallian partial equilibrium approach and Schumpeterian economics of innovation with the theory of complexity enables us to consider economic systems as complex dynamic mechanisms where innovation and organization are the key emerging properties of the system.

The actual rates and direction of change are determined by the matching between the response of creative agents anchored in a well identified portion of space by the quasi-irreversibility of their tangible and intangible inputs, and exposed to systemic and endogenous events that alter the expected conditions of product and factor markets, and the structure and quality of knowledge externalities and interactions that make external knowledge accessible within the system, according to its structure. The quality of the localized context of action is crucial to enable the creative and hence ex-adaptive, as opposed to adaptive, reaction of firms.

Organized complexity is crucial to make innovation possible. Yet the organization and composition of the structure of economic systems are themselves the endogenous result of technological change and population dynamics in terms of introduction of innovations and differential rates of natality, entry, mobility, exit and mortality. A recursive loop takes place between structural and technological change.

Summarizing the building blocks of our analysis, we have shown that out-of-equilibrium conditions push agents to react (Section 3). Their reaction builds upon localized learning processes. It can lead to the actual introduction of productivity enhancing innovation if and when the local context is structured as an organized complexity where knowledge feedback, interactions and externalities support the recombinant generation of new knowledge and hence innovative effort of firms (Section 4). The introduction of innovations is an emergent property of an organized complexity that brings together the individual efforts and the quality of the contextual feedbacks (Section 5). The introduction of innovations in turn affects the structure and architecture of the local innovation systems (Section 6). New innovation systems emerge and others decline. Resilience and persistence at both the system and the firm level shape the change of the structure of the system and lead to path-dependent dynamics. The organized complexity of the system is the complementary emerging property of an economic system able to grow (Section 7).

Some mesoeconomic architectures are clearly more conducive than others. Some knowledge structures enable the dynamics of positive feedbacks and the successful recombinant generation of new knowledge. With other structures knowledge dissipation may prevail. The architectures of the structural characters of the system may exhibit high levels of resilience, yet they are not given, nor are they exogenous. They are themselves the path-dependent products of the intentional choices of location and mobility of agents as well as of their collective interaction. Each agent is localized in a limited region as major switching costs limit mobility. Hence he cannot be fully aware of the effects of relocation in such a multidimensional space on the viability of the knowledge externalities and interactions. The topology of the network structure of interactions is also likely to be changed. New communication channels are built and the search for external knowledge is intensified. The amount of knowledge externalities and interactions is likely to increase. The amount of knowledge that each firm can now generate with a given amount of resources also increases because of the higher levels of external knowledge available and the lower costs of communication and networking.

The introduction of innovations may engender a chain reaction that leads to innovation cascades consisting in the generalized introduction of new systemic gales of innovations. In other circumstances, however, momentum can decline and adaptive reactions prevail. Contingent factors may affect the interplay between structural and technological change and tilt the dynamics of positive feedback: growth and change are characterized by discontinuity.

The relationship between the structure of the system and the actual emergence of innovation in fact is clearly recursive. The chances of introduction of innovations are indeed influenced by the structure of the system as it stands at time t. The structure of the system shapes the amount of knowledge externalities and interactions that engender positive feedbacks and hence the introduction of localized and productivity-enhancing innovations. The localized structure of interactions plays a key role in qualifying and augmenting the creative reaction of firms caught in out-of-equilibrium conditions so as to enable them to actually generate productivity-enhancing innovations. Innovations, together with other conduct, moreover engender structural change and hence influence the characteristics of the structure at time $t + 1$. A new structure is determined with effects both on the flows of knowledge externalities and interactions and on the conditions of product and factor markets. The changes in the markets cannot be fully anticipated by firms. In order to cope with them, firms elaborate new strategies that include the introduction of further innovations.

The understanding of this recursive relationship paves the way to grasping the basic elements of the continual and dynamic system of feedback between the conduct and performance of firms, and the rate and direction of technological and structural change, with a growing awareness of its evolving and historic characteristics.

A recursive loop takes place between: (a) the structural conditions of the system, (b) the ensuing amount of knowledge externalities and interactions, (c) their crucial role in enabling myopic but creative agents, caught in out-of-equilibrium conditions, to generate new technological knowledge and to introduce new localized, productivity enhancing technologies and (d) the consequent changes in the structure of the system. When such a recursive loop takes place and exhibits some level of historic sustainability, the notion of path-dependent complexity becomes relevant. The special case of the general equilibrium fades as a multiplicity of changing attractors emerges. The dynamics of markets, knowledge and social interactions feed each other and engender a dynamic process. In a system with no strategic interactions, agents are not induced to try and change their technologies. On the other hand it is clear that a system with low-level knowledge interactions is not able to convert the inducement exerted by strategic interactions into the actual introduction of technological innovations. Social interactions on the other hand have a powerful effect in terms of introducing the endogenous dynamics on the demand side.

Innovation is the emergent property of a system where there is a conducive mix of strategic interactions, able to stir the creative response of firms, and knowledge interactions, able to implement them with the supply of external knowledge. Innovation is both the result and cause of out-of-equilibrium conditions.

Complex dynamics, based upon systemic and creative reactions, substitutes adaptive convergence towards a single attractor. Complex dynamics provides an analytical framework into which much economics of innovation can be usefully encapsulated. On the other hand complex dynamics makes possible an important step forward with respect to evolutionary economics as it suggests a way to overcome the embarrassing role of random variation as a source of innovations. Innovations are the deliberate outcome of the intentional and creative action of firms localized in a well-defined context that characterizes both their competencies and their position in a web of social, strategic and knowledge interactions.

The integration of the economics of innovation and specifically of the economics of localized technological change into the frame of the economics of complexity has two important advantages. On the one hand it shows that innovations are the collective and systemic result of the intentional action of a variety of heterogeneous and interacting firms when embedded in proper innovation systems that favor their creative reaction when facing out-of-equilibrium conditions. On the other it provides the economics of complexity with an articulated analysis of the dynamic interactions between intentional decision making at the agent level and the changing characteristics of the system into which economic action takes place.

NOTES

*   I acknowledge the funding of the European Union D.G. Research with the grant number 266959 to the research project 'Policy Incentives for the Creation of Knowledge: Methods and Evidence' (PICK-ME), within the context of the Cooperation Program/Theme 8/Socio-economic Sciences and Humanities (SSH), in progress at the Collegio Carlo Alberto.
1.   The so-called Schumpeterian hypothesis recently received new attention in the context of the new growth theory. This new literature has investigated the relationship between competition and innovation with contrasting results. Aghion and Howitt (1992) at first confirmed the Schumpeterian hypothesis according to which there is a negative correlation between competition and innovation, as measured by the intensity of R&D efforts. Subsequently Aghion and Howitt (1999), however, changed their mind and elaborated the view that competition should push firms to innovate. Finally Aghion et al. (2004) elaborated a compromise, suggesting that an inverted U-shaped relation between competition and R&D expenditures might apply. The original findings of Scherer (1967) and Dasgupta and Stiglitz (1980) were confirmed after a long debate.
2.   Systematic empirical investigations have explored the role of social interactions in the generation of technological knowledge (Griffith et al., 2003; Lokshin et al., 2008). Antonelli and Scellato (2008) have applied the methodology of social interaction to test the role of knowledge spillovers at the territorial level and show how external knowledge made available by intra-industrial and inter-industrial interactions have a direct effect on total factor productivity levels of firms. They present an empirical analysis of firm level total factor productivity (TFP) for a sample of 7020 Italian manufacturing companies observed during years 1996–2005 and show that changes in firm level TFP are significantly affected by localized knowledge

interactions. Such evidence is robust to the introduction of appropriate regional and sectoral controls, as well as to econometric specifications accounting for potential endogeneity problems. Moreover, they find strong empirical evidence suggesting that changes in competitive pressure, namely the creative reaction channel, significantly affect firm level TFP with an additive effect with respect to localized social interactions deriving from knowledge spillovers.

3. See Antonelli (2011) for detailed exposition of the analytical framework, and Antonelli and Barbiellini Amidei (2011) for an empirical study of the relationship between pecuniary knowledge externalities, innovation and total factor productivity growth. The Italian evidence in the period 1950–90 shows that the continual increase of total factor productivity was a consequence of the out-of-equilibrium conditions in the knowledge cost equation rather than in increasing returns of the production function.

BIBLIOGRAPHY

Aghion, P., Bloom, N., Griffith, R. and Howitt, P. (2002), 'Competition and innovation: an inverted U relationship', NBER, WP 9269.

Aghion, P., Blundell, R., Griffith, R., Howitt, P. and Prantl, S. (2004), 'Entry and productivity growth: evidence from microlevel panel data', *Journal of the European Economic Association*, **2**, 265–76.

Aghion, P., David, P.A. and Foray, D. (2009), 'Science, technology and innovation for economic growth: linking policy research and practice in "STIG Systems"', *Research Policy*, **38**, 681–93.

Aghion, P. and Howitt, P. (1992), 'A model of growth through creative destruction', *Econometrica*, **60**, 323–51.

Aghion, P. and Howitt, P. (1999), *Endogenous Growth Theory*, Cambridge: MIT Press.

Aghion, P. and Tirole, J. (1994), 'The management of innovation', *Quarterly Journal of Economics*, **CIX**, 1185–209.

Albin, P.S. (1998), *Barriers and Bounds to Rationality. Essays on Economic Complexity and Dynamics in Interactive Systems*, Princeton: Princeton University Press.

Alchian A. (1950), 'Uncertainty, evolution and economic theory', *Journal of Political Economy*, **58**, 211–21.

Anderson, P.W., Arrow, K.J. and Pines, D. (eds) (1988), *The Economy as an Evolving Complex System*, Redwood: Addison Wesley.

Antonelli, C. (1989), 'A failure-inducement model of research and development expenditures: Italian evidence from the early 1980s', *Journal of Economic Behavior and Organization*, **12**, 159–80.

Antonelli, C. (1990), 'Induced adoption and externalities in the regional diffusion of new information technology', *Regional Studies*, **24**, 31–40.

Antonelli, C. (1997a), 'The economics of path-dependence in industrial organization', *International Journal of Industrial Organization*, **15**, 643–75.

Antonelli, C. (1997b), 'Technological externalities percolation processes and the evolution of technological clubs', *Empirica*, **24**, 137–56.

Antonelli, C. (1999), *The Microdynamics of Technological Change*, London: Routledge.

Antonelli, C. (2001), *The Microeconomics of Technological Systems*, Oxford: Oxford University Press.

Antonelli, C. (2003), *The Economics of Innovation, New Technologies and Structural Change*, London: Routledge.

Antonelli, C. (2005), 'Models of knowledge and systems of governance', *Journal of Institutional Economics*, **1**, 51–73.

Antonelli, C. (2006), 'Path dependence, localized technological change and the quest for dynamic efficiency', in Antonelli, C., Foray, D., Hall, B. and Steinmueller, E. (eds), *Frontiers in the Economics of Innovation. Essays in Honor of Paul David*, Cheltenham, UK and Northampton, MA, USA: Edward Elgar, pp. 51–69.

Antonelli, C. (2007), 'The system dynamics of collective knowledge: from gradualism and saltationism to punctuated change', *Journal of Economic Behavior and Organization*, **62**, 215–36.

Antonelli, C. (2008a), *Localized Technological Change: Towards the Economics of Complexity*, London: Routledge.

Antonelli, C. (2008b), 'Pecuniary knowledge externalities: the convergence of directed technological change and the emergence of innovation systems', *Industrial and Corporate Change*, **17**, 1049–70.

Antonelli, C. (2009a), 'The economics of innovation: from the classical legacies to the economics of complexity', *Economics of Innovation and New Technology*, **18**, 611–46.

Antonelli, C. (2009b), 'Localized appropriability: pecuniary externalities in knowledge exploitation', *Technology Analysis and Strategic Management*, **21**, 727–42.

Antonelli, C. (2010a), 'From population thinking to organization thinking: coalitions for innovation', *Regional Studies*, **44**, 513–18.

Antonelli, C. (2010b), 'The economic complexity of technology and technological innovation', *Regional Studies*, **44** (6), 801–6.

Antonelli, C. (2010c), 'Pecuniary externalities and the localized generation of technological knowledge', in Martin, R. and Boschma, R. (eds), *Handbook of Evolutionary Economic Geography*, Cheltenham, UK and Northampton, MA, USA: Edward Elgar, pp. 162–81.

Antonelli, C. (2011), 'Knowledge governance, pecuniary knowledge externalities and total factor productivity growth', WP Laboratorio di Economia dell'Innovazione Franco Momigliano, Dipartimento di Economia S. Cognetti de Martiis, Università di Torino and BRICK Working Papers, Collegio Carlo Alberto.

Antonelli, C. and Barbiellini Amidei, F. (2011), *The Dynamics of Knowledge Externalities: Localized Technological Change in Italy*, Cheltenham, UK and Northampton, MA, USA: Edward Elgar.

Antonelli, C., Crespi, F. and Scellato, G. (2010a), 'Inside innovation persistence: new evidence from Italian micro-data', WP Laboratorio di Economia dell'Innovazione Franco Memigliano, Dipartimento di Economia S. Cognetti de Martiis, Università di Torino and BRICK, Collegio Carlo Alberto.

Antonelli, C., Crespi, F. and Scellato, G. (2010b), 'Patterns of persistence in productivity growth. The Italian evidence', WP Laboratorio di Economia dell'Innovazione Franco Momigliano, Dipartimento di Economia S. Cognetti de Martiis, Università di Torino and BRICK, Collegio Carlo Alberto.

Antonelli, C. and Ferraris, L. (2011), 'Innovation as an emerging system property: an agent based model', *Journal of Artificial Societies and Social Stimulation*, **14**.

Antonelli, C., Krafft, J. and Quatraro, F. (2010c), 'Recombinant knowledge and growth: the case of ICTs', *Structural Change and Economic Dynamics*, **21**, 50–69.

Antonelli, C., Patrucco, P.P. and Quatraro, F. (2008), 'The governance of localized knowledge externalities', *International Review of Applied Economics*, **22**, 479–98.

Antonelli, C., Patrucco, P.P. and Quatraro, F. (2011), 'Productivity growth and pecuniary knowledge externalities: an empirical analysis of agglomeration economies in European regions', *Economic Geography*, **87** (1), 23–50.

Antonelli, C., Patrucco, P.P. and Rossi, F. (2010d), 'The economics of knowledge interaction and the changing role of universities', in Gallouji, F. and Djellai, F. (eds), *Innovation in Services*, Cheltenham, UK and Northampton, MA, USA: Edward Elgar, pp. 153–77.

Antonelli, C. and Scellato, G. (2008), 'Complexity and innovation: social interactions and firm level productivity growth', WP Laboratorio di Economia dell'Innovazione Franco Momigliano, Dipartimento di Economia S. Cognetti de Martiis, Università di Torino and BRICK, Collegio Carlo Alberto.

Antonelli, C. and Scellato, G. (2011), 'Out of equilibrium, profits and innovation', *Economics of Innovation and New Technology*, forthcoming.

Antonelli, C. and Teubal, M. (2008), 'Knowledge intensive property rights and the evolution of venture capitalism', *Journal of Institutional Economics*, **4**, 163–82.

Antonelli, C. and Teubal, M. (2010), 'Venture capital as a mechanism for knowledge governance', in Viale, R. and Etzkowitz, H. (eds), *The Capitalization of Knowledge*, Cheltenham, UK and Northampton, MA, USA: Edward Elgar, pp. 98–120.

Antonelli, C. and Teubal, M. (2011), 'From the corporation to venture capitalism: new surrogate markets for knowledge and innovation-led economic growth', in Dietrich, M. and Krafft J. (eds), *Handbook on the Economics and Theory of the Firm*, Cheltenham, UK and Northampton, MA, USA: Edward Elgar, forthcoming.

Arrow, K.J. (1962a), 'Economic welfare and the allocation of resources for invention', in Nelson, R.R. (ed.) *The Rate and Direction of Inventive Activity: Economic and Social Factors*, Princeton: Princeton University Press for NBER, pp. 609–25.

Arrow, K.J. (1962b), 'The economic implications of learning by doing', *Review of Economic Studies*, **29**, 155–73.

Arrow, K.J. (1969), 'Classificatory notes on the production and transmission of technical knowledge', *American Economic Review*, **59**, 29–35.

Arrow, K.J. (1974), *The Limits of Organization*, New York: W.W. Norton.

Arrow, K.J. (2000), 'Increasing returns: historiographic issues and path dependence', *European Journal of History of Economic Thought*, **7**, 171–80.

Arrow, K.J. (2004), 'Path dependence and competitive equilibrium', in Guinnane, T.W., Sundstrom, W.A. and Whatley, W. (eds), *History Matters*, Stanford: Stanford University Press, pp. 23–35.

Arthur, B. (1989), 'Competing technologies, increasing returns and lock-in by small historical events', *Economic Journal*, **99**, 116–31.

Arthur, B. (1994), *Increasing Returns and Path Dependence in the Economy*, Ann Arbor: Michigan University Press.

Arthur, B. (1999), 'Complexity and the economy', *Science*, **284**, 107–9.

Arthur, W.B. (1990), 'Positive feedbacks in the economy', *Scientific American*, **262**, 92.

Arthur, W.B. (2009), *The Nature of Technology*, New York: Free Press.

Arthur, W.B., Durlauf, S.N. and Lane, D.A. (1997a), 'Introduction', in Arthur, W.B., Durlauf, S.N. and Lane, D.A. (eds), *The Economy as an Evolving Complex System, II*, Reading: Addison-Wesley, pp. 1–14.

Arthur, W.B., Durlauf, S.N. and Lane, D.A. (eds) (1997b), *The Economy as an Evolving Complex System II*, Redwood City, CA: Addison-Wesley.

Atkinson, A.B. and Stiglitz, J.E. (1969), 'A new view of technological change', *Economic Journal*, **79**, 573–8.

Audretsch, D.B. and Feldman, M. (1996), 'Spillovers and the geography of innovation and production', *American Economic Review*, **86**, 630–40.

Barabàsi, A.L. and Albert, R. (1999), 'Emergence of scaling in random networks', *Science*, **286**, 509.

Barabàsi, A.L., Jeong, H., Neda, Z., Ravasz, E., Schubert, A. and Vicsek, T. (2002), 'Evolution of the social network of scientific collaborations', *Physica A*, **311**, 590–614.

Binswanger, H.P. and Ruttan, V.W. (eds) (1978), *Induced Innovation: Technology Institutions and Development*, Baltimore: Johns Hopkins University Press, pp. 13–43.

Blume, L.E. and Durlauf, S.N. (eds) (2001), *Social Dynamics*, Cambridge: MIT Press.

Blume, L.E. and Durlauf, S.N. (eds) (2005), *The Economy as an Evolving Complex System III*, Oxford: Oxford University Press.

Boschma, R.A. (2005), 'Proximity and innovation: a critical assessment', *Regional Studies*, **39**, 61–74.

Breschi, S. and Lissoni, F. (2003), 'Knowledge spillovers and local innovation systems: a critical survey', *Industrial and Corporate Change*, **10**, 975–1005.

Bresnahan, T.F. and Trajtenberg, M. (1995), 'General purpose technologies: "engines of growth"?', *Journal of Econometrics*, **65**, 83–108.

Burt, R.S. (1992), *Structural Holes: The Social Structure of Competition*, Cambridge: Harvard University Press.

Cohen, W.M. and Levinthal, D.A. (1990), 'Absorptive capacity: a new perspective on learning and innovation', *Administrative Science Quarterly*, **35**, 128–52.

Consoli, D. and Mina, A. (2009), 'An evolutionary perspective on health innovation systems', *Journal of Evolutionary Economics*, **19**, 297–319.

Consoli, D. and Patrucco, P.P. (2008), 'Innovation platforms and the governance of knowledge: evidence from Italy and the UK', *Economics of Innovation and New Technology*, **17**, 699–716.

Cowan, R., Jonard, N. and Zimmermann, J.B. (2006), 'Evolving networks of inventors', *Journal of Evolutionary Economics*, **16**, 155–74.

Cowan, R., Jonard, N. and Zimmermann, J.B. (2007), 'Bilateral collaboration and the emergence of networks', *Management Science*, **53**, 1051–67.

Crépon, B., Duguet, E. and Mairesse, J. (1998), 'Research and development, innovation and productivity: an econometric analysis at the firm level', *Economics of Innovation and New Technology*, **7**, 115–58.

Cyert, R.M. and March, J.C. (1963), *A Behavioral Theory of the Firm*, New Jersey: Prentice-Hall.

D'Ignazio, A. and Giovannetti, E. (2006), 'From exogenous to endogenous economic networks: internet applications', *Journal of Economic Survey*, **20**, 757–96.

Dasgupta, P. and Stiglitz, J.E. (1980), 'Industrial structure and the nature of innovative activity', *Economic Journal*, **90**, 266–93.

David, P.A. (1975), *Technical Choice Innovation and Economic Growth*, Cambridge: Cambridge University Press.

David, P.A. (1985), 'Clio and the economics of QWERTY', *American Economic Review*, **75**, 332–37.

David P.A. (1988), 'Path-dependence: putting the past into the future of economics', mimeo, Department of Economics, Stanford University.

David, P.A. (1992), 'Heroes, herds and hysteresis in technological history', *Industrial and Corporate Change*, **1**, 129–79.

David, P.A. (1994), 'Positive feedbacks and research productivity in science: reopening another black box', in Granstrand, O. (ed.), *Economics and Technology*, Amsterdam: Elsevier North Holland, pp. 65–85.

David, P.A. (2007), 'Path dependence: a foundational concept for historical social science', *Cliometrica: Journal of Historical Economics and Econometric History*, **1**, 91–114.

David, P.A., Foray, D. and Dalle, J.M. (1995), 'Marshallian externalities and the emergence and spatial stability of technological enclaves', *Economics of Innovation and New Technology*, **6**, 147–82.

David, P.A. and Keely, L. (2003), 'The endogenous formation of scientific research coalitions', *Economics of Innovation and New Technology*, **12**, 93–116.

Dopfer, K. (ed.) (2005), *The Evolutionary Foundations of Economics*, Cambridge: Cambridge University Press.

Downie, J. (1958), *The Competitive Process*, Duckworth: London.

Durlauf, S.N. (1993), 'Non-ergodic economic growth', *Review of Economic Studies*, **60**, 349–66.

Durlauf, S.N. (2005), 'Complexity and empirical economics', *Economic Journal*, **115**, 225–43.

Feldman, M.A. (1999), 'The new economics of innovation, spillovers and agglomeration: a review of empirical studies', *Economics of Innovation and New Technology*, **8**, 5–25.

Fellner, W. (1961), 'Two propositions in the theory of induced innovation', *Economic Journal*, **71**, 305–8.

Fleming, L. and Sorenson, O. (2001), 'Technology as a complex adaptive system: evidence from patent data', *Research Policy*, **30**, 1019–39.

Foster, J., (2005), 'From simplistic to complex systems in economics', *Cambridge Journal of Economics*, **29**, 873–92.

Fransman, M. (2007), *The New ICT Ecosystem and the Way Forward for Europe*, Edinburgh: Kokoro.

Frenken, K. (2006a), 'A fitness landscape approach to technological complexity, modularity, and vertical disintegration', *Structural Change and Economic Dynamics*, **17**, 288–305.

Frenken, K. (2006b), 'Technological innovation and complexity theory', *Economics of Innovation and New Technology*, **15**, 137–55.

Frenken, K. and Nuvolari, A. (2004), 'The early development of the steam engine: an evolutionary interpretation using complexity theory', *Industrial and Corporate Change*, **13**, 419–50.

Frenken, K., van Oort F.G. and Verburg, T. (2007), 'Related variety, unrelated variety and regional economic growth', *Regional Studies*, **41**, 685–97.

Glaeser, E., Sacerdote, B. and Scheinkman, J.A. (1996), 'Crime and social interactions', *Quarterly Journal of Economics*, **109**, 507–48.

Glaeser, E. and Scheinkman, J.A. (2000), 'Non-market interactions', NBER Working Paper Series 8053.

Griffith, R., Redding, S. and van Reenen, J. (2003), 'R&D and absorptive capacity: theory and empirical evidence', *Scandinavian Journal of Economics*, **105**, 99–118.

Griliches, Z. (1957), 'Hybrid corn: an exploration in the economics of technological change', *Econometrica*, **25**, 501–22.

Griliches, Z. (1961), 'Hedonic price indexes for automobiles: an econometric analysis of quality change', in NBER (eds), *The Price Statistics of the Federal Government*, New York: NBER, pp. 173–96.

Griliches, Z. (1979), 'Issues in assessing the contribution of research and development to productivity growth', *Bell Journal of Economics*, **10**, 92–116.

Griliches, Z. (1990), 'Patent statistics as economic indicators: a survey', *Journal of Economic Literature*, **28**, 1661–707.

Griliches, Z. (1992), 'The search for R&D spillovers', *Scandinavian Journal of Economics*, **94**, 29–47.

Hanusch, H. and Pyka, A. (2007), 'Principles of neo-Schumpeterian economics', *Cambridge Journal of Economics*, **31**, 275–89.

Hayek, F.A. (1945), 'The use of knowledge in society', *American Economic Review*, **35**, 519–30.

Hayek, F.A. (1973), *Law Legislation and Liberty: Volume 1, Rules and Order*, Chicago: University of Chicago Press.

Hicks, J.R. (1932), *The Theory of Wages*, London: Macmillan.

Hodgson G.M. and Knudsen T. (2006), 'Why we need a generalized Darwinism, and why generalized Darwinism is not enough', *Journal of Economic Behavior & Organization*, **61**, 1–19.

Jacobs, J. (1969), *The Economy of Cities*, New York: Random House.

Kaldor, N. (1972), 'The irrelevance of equilibrium economics', *Economic Journal*, **82**, 1237–55.

Kaldor, N. (1981), 'The role of increasing returns, technical progress and cumulative causation', *Economie Appliquee*, **34**, 593–617.

Kauffman, S. (1993), *Origins of Order: Self-Organization and Selection in Evolution*, Oxford: Oxford University Press.

Kennedy, C. (1964), 'Induced bias and the theory of distribution', *Economic Journal*, **74**, 541–47.

Kleinknecht, A.H., van Montfort, K. and Brouwer, E. (2002), 'The non-trivial choice between innovation indicators', *Economics of Innovation and New Technology*, **11**, 109–21.

Krugman, P. (1994), 'Complex landscapes in economic geography', *American Economic Review*, **84**, 412–17.

Kuznets, S. (1930), *Secular Movements in Production and Prices: Their Nature and Their Bearing upon Cyclical Fluctuations*, Boston, MA and New York: Houghton Mifflin.

Kuznets, S. (1955), 'Toward a theory of economic growth', in Lekachman, R. (ed.), *National Policy for Economic Welfare at Home and Abroad*, Garden City, NY: Doubleday, pp. 12–85.

Kuznets, S. (1966), *Modern Economic Growth*, New Haven, CT: Yale University Press.

Kuznets, S. (1971), *Economic Growth of Nations: Total Output and Production Structure*, Cambridge, MA: Harvard University Press.

Kuznets, S. (1973), 'Modern economic growth: findings and reflections', *American Economic Review*, **63**, 247–58.

Lancaster, K. (1971), *Consumer Demand: A New Approach*, New York: Columbia University Press.

Lane, D.A. (1993a), 'Artificial worlds and economics, Part I', *Journal of Evolutionary Economics*, **3**, 89–107.

Lane, D.A. (1993b), 'Artificial worlds and economics, Part II', *Journal of Evolutionary Economics*, **3**, 177–97.

Lane, D.A. (2002), 'Complexity and local interactions: towards a theory of industrial districts', in Quadrio Curzio, A. and Fortis, M. (eds), *Complexity and Industrial Clusters: Dynamics and Models in Theory and Practice*, Heidelberg and New York: Physica-Verlag, pp. 65–82.

Lane, D.A. and Arthur, W.B. (1993), Information contagion, *Structural Change and Economic Dynamics*, **4**, 81–104.

Lane, D., Malerba, F., Maxfield, R. and Orsenigo, L. (1996), 'Choice and action', *Journal of Evolutionary Economics*, **6**, 43–76.

Lane, D.A. and Maxfield, R. (1997), 'Foresight complexity and strategy', in Arthur, W.B., Durlauf, S.N. and Lane, D.A. (eds), *The Economy as an Evolving Complex System II*, Santa Fe: Westview Press, pp. 169–98.

Lane, D.A., Van Der Leeuw, S.E., Pumain, D. and West, G. (eds) (2009), *Complexity Perspectives in Innovation and Social Change*, Berlin: Springer.

Lane, D.A. and Vescovini, R. (1996), 'Decision rules and market share: aggregation in an information contagion model', *Industrial and Corporate Change*, **5**, 127–46.

Latham, W.R. and Le Bas, C. (eds) (2006), *The Economics of Persistent Innovation: An Evolutionary View*, Berlin: Springer.

Link, A.N. (1980), 'Firm size and efficient entrepreneurial activity: a reformulation of the Schumpeter hypothesis', *Journal of Political Economy*, **88**, 771–82.

Lokshin, B., Belderbos, R. and Carree, M. (2008), 'The productivity effects of internal and external R&D: evidence from dynamic panel data model', *Oxford Bulletin of Economics and Statistics*, **70**, 399–413.

Lundvall B.Å. (1985), *Product Innovation and User–Producer Interaction*, Aalborg: Aalborg University Press.

Lundvall B.Å. (1988), 'Innovation as an interactive process: from user-producer interaction to the national system of innovation', in Dosi, G., Freeman, C., Nelson, R., Silverberg, G. and Soete, L. (eds), *Technical Change and Economic Theory*, London: Frances Pinter, pp. 349–69.

Lypsey, R., Bekar, C. and Carlaw, K. (1998), 'General purpose technologies: what requires explanation', in Helpman, E. (ed.) *General Purpose Technologies and Economic Growth*, Cambridge, MA: MIT Press, pp. 193–218.

Lypsey, R., Bekar, C. and Carlaw, K. (2005), *Economic Transformations*, Oxford: Oxford University Press.

March, J.G. (1988), 'Bounded rationality, ambiguity and the engineering of choice', in Bell, D.E., Raiffa, H. and Tversky, A. (eds), *Decision Making: Descriptive Normative, and Prescriptive*, Cambridge: Cambridge University Press, pp. 33–57.

March, J.G. (1991), 'Exploration and exploitation in organizing learning', *Organization Science*, **2**, 71–87.

March, J.G. and Shapira, Z. (1987), 'Managerial perspectives on risk and risk-taking', *Management Science*, **33**, 1404–18.

March, J.G. and Simon, H. (1958), *Organizations*, New York: John Wiley and Sons.

Marshall, A. (1890), *Principles of Economics*, 8th edn (1920), London: Macmillan.

Marx, K. ([1867] 1976), *Capital: A Critique of Political Economy*, Harmondsworth: Penguin Books.

Meade, J.E. (1952), 'External economies and diseconomies in a competitive situation', *Economic Journal*, **62**, 54–67.

Metcalfe, J.S. (1994), 'Competition, Fisher's principle and increasing returns in the selection process', *Journal of Evolutionary Economics*, **4**, 327–46.

Metcalfe, J.S., Foster, J. and Ramlogan, R. (2006), 'Adaptive economic growth', *Cambridge Journal of Economics*, **30**, 7–32.

Miller, J.H. and Page, S.E. (2007), *Complex Adaptive Systems*, Princeton: Princeton University Press.

Mokyr, J. (1990a), 'Punctuated equilibria and technological progress', *American Economic Review*, Papers and Proceedings, **80** (2), 350–54.

Mokyr, J. (1990b), *The Lever of Riches. Technological Creativity and Economic Progress*, Oxford: Oxford University Press.

Mokyr, J. (2002), *The Gifts of Athena: Historical Origins of the Knowledge Economy*, Princeton: Princeton University Press.

Mowery, D. and Rosenberg, N. (1979), 'The influence of market demand upon innovation: a critical review of some recent empirical studies', *Research Policy*, **8**, 102–50.

Nelson, R.R. (1982), 'The role of knowledge in R&D efficiency', *Quarterly Journal of Economics*, **97**, 453–70.

Nelson, R.R. (ed.) (1993), *National Systems of Innovation*, Oxford: Oxford University Press.

Nelson, R.R. (2005), *Technology Institutions and Economic Growth*, Cambridge: Harvard University Press.

Nelson, R.R. and Winter, S.G. (1982), *An Evolutionary Theory of Economic Change*, Cambridge: Belknap Press of Harvard University Press.

Nesta, L. (2008), 'Knowledge and productivity in the world's largest manufacturing corporations', *Journal of Economic Behavior and Organization*, **67**, 886–902.

Nesta, L. and Saviotti, P. (2005), 'Coherence of the knowledge base and the firm's innovative performance: evidence from the US pharmaceutical industry', *Journal of Industrial Economics*, **53**, 123–42.

Nesta, L. and Saviotti, P. (2006), 'Firm knowledge and market value in biotechnology', *Industrial and Corporate Change*, **15**, 625–52.

North, D.C. (1997), 'Some fundamental puzzles in economic history', in Arthur, W.B., Durlauf, S.N. and Lane, D. (eds) (1997), *The Economy as an Evolving Complex System II*, Santa Fe: Westview Press, pp. 223–38.

Olsson, O. (2000), 'Knowledge as a set in idea space: an epistemological view on growth', *Journal of Economic Growth*, **5**, 253–76.

Olsson, O. and Frey, B.S. (2002), 'Entrepreneurship as recombinant growth', *Small Business Economics*, **19**, 69–80.
Pastor-Satorras, R. and Vespignani, A. (2004), *Evolution and Structure of the Internet*, Cambridge: Cambridge University Press.
Patel, P. and Pavitt, K. (1994), 'National innovation systems: why they are important and how they might be measured and compared', *Economics of Innovation and New Technology*, **3**, 77–95.
Pavitt, K. (1984), 'Sectoral patterns of technical change: towards a taxonomy and a theory', *Research Policy*, **13**, 343–73.
Penrose E. (1952), 'Biological analogies in the theory of the firm', *American Economic Review*, **42**, 804–19.
Penrose E. (1953), 'Biological analogies in the theory of the firm: rejoinder', *American Economic Review*, **43**, 603–9.
Penrose, E.T. (1959), *The Theory of the Growth of the Firm*, 3rd edn (1995), Oxford: Oxford University Press.
Pisano, G.P. (1990), 'The R&D boundaries of the firm: an empirical analysis', *Administrative Science Quarterly*, **35**, 153–76.
Romer, P.M. (1994), 'The origins of endogenous growth', *Journal of Economic Perspectives*, **8**, 3–22.
Rosenberg, N. (1969), 'The direction of technological change: inducement mechanisms and focusing devices', *Economic Development and Cultural Change*, **18**, 1–24.
Rosenberg, N. (1976), 'Marx as a student of technology', *Monthly Review*, **28**, 56–77.
Rosenberg, N. (1994), *Exploring the Black Box*, Cambridge: Cambridge University Press, pp. 47–61.
Rosser, J.B. (1999), 'On the complexities of complex economic dynamics', *Journal of Economic Perspectives*, **13**, 169–92.
Rosser, J.B. (ed.) (2004), *Complexity in Economics. Methodology Interacting Agents and Microeconomic Models*, Cheltenham, UK and Northampton, MA, USA: Edward Elgar.
Ruttan, V.W. (1997), 'Induced innovation evolutionary theory and path dependence: sources of technical change', *Economic Journal*, **107**, 1520–29.
Ruttan, V.W. (2001), *Technology Growth and Development. An Induced Innovation Perspective*, Oxford: Oxford University Press.
Salter, W.E.G. (1960), *Productivity and Technical Change*, Cambridge: Cambridge University Press.
Samuelson, P. (1965), 'A theory of induced innovation along Kennedy, Weiszacker lines', *Review of Economics and Statistics*, **47**, 343–56.
Saviotti, P.P. (1996), *Technology Evolution, Variety and the Economy*, Cheltenham, UK and Brookfield, VT, USA: Edward Elgar.
Scherer, F.M. (1967), 'Research and development resource allocation under rivalry', *Quarterly Journal of Economics*, **81**, 385–89.
Scherer F.M. (1970), *Industrial Market Structure and Economic Perfirmance*, Chicago: Rand McNally.
Scherer F.M. (1982), 'Demand-pull and technological invention: Schmookler revisited', *Journal of Industrial Economics*, **30**, 225–37.
Schmookler, J. (1954), 'The level of inventive activity', *Review of Economics and Statistics*, **36**, 183–90.
Schmookler, J. (1966), *Invention and Economic Growth*, Cambridge, MA: Harvard University Press.
Schumpeter, J. (1934), *The Theory of Economic Development*, Cambridge. MA: Harvard University Press. (1st German edition 1911).
Schumpeter, J.A. (1939), *Business Cycles: A Theoretical, Historical and Statistical Analysis of the Capitalist Process*, New York: McGraw-Hill.
Schumpeter, J.A. (1941), 'Alfred Marshall's *Principles*: a semi-centennial appraisal', *American Economic Review*, **51**, 85–98.
Schumpeter, J.A. (1942), *Capitalism, Socialism and Democracy*, New York: Harper and Brothers.
Schumpeter, J.A. (1947a), 'Theoretical problems of economic growth', *Journal of Economic History*, **7**, 1–9.
Schumpeter, J.A. (1947b), 'The creative response in economic history', *Journal of Economic History*, **7**, 149–59.
Scitovsky, T. (1954), 'Two concepts of external economies', *Journal of Political Economy*, **62**, 143–51.
Silverberg, G. and Verspagen, B. (2005), 'A percolation model of innovation in complex technology space', *Journal of Economic Dynamics and Control*, **29**, 225–44.
Stiglitz, J.E. (1987), 'Learning to learn, localized learning and technological progress', in Dasgupta, P. and Stoneman, P. (eds), *Economic Policy and Technological Performance*, Cambridge: Cambridge University Press, pp. 125–53.
Stoneman, P. (ed.) (1995), *Handbook of the Economics of Innovation and Technological Change*, Oxford: Blackwell.
von Hippel, E. (1976), 'The dominant role of users in the scientific instrument innovation process', *Research Policy*, **5**, 212–39.

von Hippel, E. (1998), 'Economies of product development by users: the impact of "sticky" local information', *Management Science*, **44**, 629–44.
Weitzman, M.L. (1996), 'Hybridizing growth theory', *American Economic Review*, **86**, 207–12.
Weitzman, M.L. (1998), 'Recombinant growth', *Quarterly Journal of Economics*, **113**, 331–60.
Young, A.A. (1928), 'Increasing returns and economic progress', *Economic Journal*, **38**, 527–42.

PART II

THE ECONOMIC COMPLEXITY OF INNOVATION

2 Complexity and innovation dynamics
David A. Lane

1. ARTIFACTS AND ORGANIZATIONS

Human life is impossible to conceive without two fundamental ingredients: artifacts and organizations. Just about everything we do involves interactions with artifacts, from the clothes we wear and the buildings we inhabit, to the devices through which we communicate with one another and the tools and technologies we use to make ever more artifacts. And almost all of our interactions depend for their setting, purpose and rules on organizations, whether they be churches, businesses, government agencies, political parties, law courts, police forces, armies, social clubs – or even friendship networks on the Internet.

We human beings didn't invent either artifacts or organizations: biological evolution did. Both fashioning artifacts and deploying collective action are evolutionary strategies that have been around a long time. Artifacts allow the biological individuals and species that make and use them to wrest more usable matter and energy from their environments, allow more of them to live in a given environment, and sometimes allow them to live longer and dedicate more of their time and energy to reproduction. Some biological engineers construct exquisite and complex artifacts, from the fungal agriculture of leaf-cutter ants, through the durable nests of weaverbirds and the beaver's temperature-controlled aquatic dwellings. In addition, many of these artifacts transform the environments of other biological entities as well as those that construct them, in ways that may be positive or negative for these entities' biological functionality of survival and reproduction.

Examples of collective activity among biological conspecifics range from the production of stalks and fruiting bodies by aggregations of single-celled slime molds, through ant and termite colonies, to prairie dog communities, wolf packs and primate bands. These societies, like human organizations, are characterized by differentiation of function among component individuals, not all of which necessarily benefit (or benefit equally) from the collective activity, and by control mechanisms that ensure some level of coordination among component individuals and processes.

But even if we didn't invent them, nothing in biology remotely compares with the use that we human beings have made of these two strategies. The number and complexity of the artifacts we have developed over the millennia, and in particular over the past few centuries, and the variety of activities we have organized around these artifacts, have no counterpart in the pre-human world. If three million years ago, our ancestors had essentially one kind of artifact, and fifty thousand years ago, maybe several hundred, today's inhabitant of New York City can choose among 10^{10} different bar-coded items (Beinhocker, 2006: 9), not to mention a host of other material, informational or performative artifacts currently produced by human beings for the use of human beings! Even more unprecedented are the diversity of forms and the scale of the organizations we have created, through which we collectively carry out political, economic, social and cultural functions that seem far removed from the overriding biological functional imperatives of survival and reproduction.

Since the mid-1990s, my colleagues and I have been working out a complexity-based theory of innovation that is intended to explain how human beings have managed to generate this explosion of artifacts and organizations – and the new functionalities they make possible. The theory starts from the premise that all artifacts have a history, as does the organization of the interaction modalities among people in which these artifacts figure. The aim of the theory is to describe and analyse the processes through which artifact and organizational histories are realized and interconnected. In particular, the theory addresses the following questions:

- How do new artifact types come into being?
- How do their tokens proliferate and become incorporated into patterns of human interaction?
- How do these interaction patterns give rise to new forms of organization, and how do the resulting organizations support and structure interactions among humans, artifacts and organizations?
- And how are new patterns of interaction generated?

In this chapter, I will sketch some of our answers to these questions, emphasizing two key theoretical concepts: exaptive bootstrapping, a positive feedback innovation dynamic (Section 4), and generative relationships, the locus at which new attributions of functionalities arise (Section 5). First, though, I explain what we mean by 'a complexity-based theory of innovation': what we mean by complexity (Section 2) and what this implies for what we mean by a theory – and in particular, a theory of innovation (Section 3).

2.   COMPLEXITY

The term 'complexity' is entering more and more frequently into scientific discourse, both academic and popular. Not surprisingly, in this swirl of activity, the meaning of complexity has not yet settled down, and different authors use the term in very different ways:

- For some, it refers primarily to a developing toolkit of inferential and modeling techniques, most of which depend on substantial computation.
- To others, complexity is an intrinsic and (at least in principle) measurable attribute of certain classes of mathematical or computational systems.
- Still others use the term more loosely to apply to broad classes of physical, biological or social phenomena, which are described by means of such concepts as emergence, self-organization, robustness and, more recently, networks.

In this chapter, I rely upon a particular variant of the third of these interpretations of complexity. When I say that the theory of innovation explored in this chapter is 'complexity-based', I mean that it builds upon a perspective characterized by dynamic interactionism and organization thinking. Let me now explain what I mean by these two terms.

A world is a set of phenomena that a scientist seeks to study. Worlds are unlabeled places, a flux of matter, energy and information. Scientists try to make sense out of the worlds they study by attending to certain kinds of patterns in this flux. When the scientist decides which kinds of patterns he will attend to, for the world he seeks to understand, he is making an ontological commitment: this world is made up of these kinds of things, and not others.[1] His ontological commitments determine what the scientist can talk about, and they have very important implications for what count for him as problems – and what count as solutions.

Dynamic interactionism describes a class of ontological commitments. Let's refer to a generic member of this class as DIOC. For DIOC, the world is composed of entities, which have certain properties. Entities interact with other entities, and as a result of these interactions entity properties can change. A particular kind of entity property is its interaction modalities, which specify with which other entities the entity in question can interact, and which properties of which entities change, and how, as a result of such an interaction. The patterns that matter for DIOC are functions of histories of entity interactions. In particular, DIOC is constructive: new kinds of entities, entity properties and interaction modalities can emerge in the course of interaction histories.

Virtually all scientists who identify with the streams of research that constitute complexity theory base their work on ontological commitments consistent with dynamic interactionism. This is not true, however, of the styles of theorizing that characterize many disciplines. Take economics as an example, and consider these leading styles of economic theorizing, on which various attempts to develop theories of innovation have relied:

- The ground floor of the ontology of standard econometric modeling is occupied by variables, not interacting entities.
- General equilibrium theory does commit to entities (or agents – firms and households – and markets), but does not provide an explicit representation of entity interaction, nor does it describe patterns in terms of histories of entity interactions or allow for the emergence of new kinds of entities.
- Game theory represents interactions explicitly and can describe patterns of interaction histories, but it too fails to provide an ontology that can serve as the basis for an endogenous account of the emergence of new entities, properties or interaction modalities.[2]

Thus, a commitment to dynamic interactionism requires a different approach to the problems and solutions of innovation theory than these standard styles of economic theorizing can offer.

Many of the key concepts of current complexity research gravitate around the idea of organization: emergence, self-organization, hierarchy, networks, modularity, robustness, scaling. One of the great unfinished projects of complexity research, first enunciated by Herbert Simon a half-century ago in his seminal papers entitled 'The organization of complex systems' (1973) and 'The architecture of complexity' (1962), is to construct a theory of organization for complex systems, which can provide a unified context for thinking about the concepts mentioned in the previous sentence.[3]

- What do we mean by organization? Organizations are particular kinds of interacting entities, which can be characterized by three fundamental aspects: structure, function, and process.
- Structure is recursive: it has parts, which are themselves organizations. To describe an organization's structure, one must identify its parts, the interaction modalities among its parts, and the modalities through which the organization interacts with other organizations. Hierarchy and networks are key concepts in describing organizational structure: the former, because of recursivity; the latter, because organizations engage in recurring patterns of interaction, which constitute networks – with organizations as nodes and recurring interactions as links.
- The processes associated with an organization describe the transformations (in the organization of its world) in which the organization may participate. Processes are supported by structure. To enact any of its processes, some of an organization's parts must engage in interaction events, each of which requires some particular interaction modality. Instantiating the structural support for a given process may require the activation of other processes, which we can refer to as management processes. There are three principal kinds of management processes:
  - recruitment, which induces (even constructs) parts to participate in the process;
  - differentiation or specialization, which provides these parts with the requisite interaction modalities; and
  - coordination, through which the requisite interactions are arranged and enacted in a spatiotemporal order that achieves the appropriate transformation.
- The functions of an organization provide directedness to its actions, through their role in determining which processes the organization enacts, when the organization is in a context in which more than one process could be enacted.[4]

An organization's structure, its processes and even its functions can change over time. Indeed, many human organizations can enact processes through which they themselves transform some or all of these.

For a scientist who commits to organization thinking, the important entities in the world under study (generally including the world itself) are organizations. The scientist's job is to investigate all the relationships among structure, function and process in the organizations that comprise this world: in particular, how structure supports processes, how processes build and maintain structure, how structure is shaped by function and function is enabled by structure, and how function triggers the enactment of processes and the enactment of processes effectuates function. Of particular interest are those relationships implicated in the constructive processes through which new organization emerges, and existing organizations are transformed, over time.[5]

3.   WHAT IS A 'THEORY OF INNOVATION'?

From one point of view, a 'theory of innovation' is an oxymoron. If, as many scientists believe, a theory is supposed to lead to verifiable predictions of the phenomenon under study, then a theory of innovation should predict innovations – which would mean the process leading to innovations the theory was meant to explicate is just an historical dead-end that could be replaced as innovation-generator by the theory itself! Of course, this is silly: the theory could illuminate aspects of the process without 'predicting' the new artifacts that were the process outcomes of primary economic and social interest.

But which aspects? This issue is anything but trivial: one of the first concepts my collaborators and I had to come to grips with in our theorizing was the nature of the uncertainty that surrounds innovation, and what limitations on predictability this uncertainty implies. Thinking about this problem led to the formulation of the concept of ontological uncertainty, which is explored in Lane and Maxfield (2005). Unlike truth uncertainty, in the face of which agents can formulate a logically complete set of consequences of the effects of the action possibilities they are deciding among, even if they do not know with certainty which of these consequences will actually occur, agents facing ontological uncertainty do not even know the identity of the other agents that will mediate the effects of their actions, nor do they know with which criteria they will evaluate these effects: these agents and criteria are under construction, in the course of the very processes in which our agent must act. Thus, agents facing ontological uncertainty cannot even formulate propositions that describe the possible consequences of their action, much less predict which consequences will actually occur. The more we thought about ontological uncertainty and its implications, the less attractive we found the very idea of prediction – predicting any quantitative variable – as the goal of a theory of innovation.

We ended up by adopting the following idea about what a theory of innovation ought to be – and what it ought to do. The theory itself should provide a minimal ontology for recounting historical episodes of innovation in a causally convincing way. By ontology, we mean

- kinds of entities and their properties;
- interaction modalities (which entities interact with which, under what conditions, and how entity properties change as the result of interactions); and
- a dynamic, which specifies the order in which entity interactions take place.

The ontology is minimal if each specified entity and property type and interaction modality is causally efficacious – and, of course, no other causally efficacious entity slips into the stories as they are recounted.[6] Our ontology for innovation includes such entities as agent-artifact space, market systems, competence networks, scaffolding structures, and generative relationships. I will say something about some of these later in the chapter; for an introduction to all of them, see Lane and Maxfield (2005).

Building a theory of innovation and telling stories about innovation episodes is a kind of dialogue, in which the theory informs the construction of the narrative, and the resulting narrative tests the adequacy of the theory to generate deep insights into the episode and its attendant phenomena – and when it reveals gaps and imprecision in the theory, prompts the theorist to revise it.[7]

There is another kind of dialogue that can be useful: the dialogue between theory and mathematical models. While a theory specifies the dynamics of organizational emergence and transformation qualitatively, it is difficult to rely on our own experience and research into concrete episodes to gain a deep understanding of the dynamics of complex systems. In any given story, much more is going on than what our theory picks out as important:

how can we know that particular kinds of emergent properties really depend just on the entities and interaction modalities the theory postulates? Here, mathematical models that provide abstract representations of subsets of the theory's ontology can be very useful, since if such models exhibit analogous emergent properties, they must perforce depend just on the elements and relations incorporated in the model – and nothing else. Thus, assuming that the analogy between the theory ontology as instantiated in the narrative and in the model is sufficiently convincing, the mathematical demonstration of emergent dynamics in the model enhances the causal convincingness of the analogous emergent dynamics in the narrative. In the course of developing and deepening our theory of innovation, we have constructed agent-based models that provide insight into the dynamics associated with generative relationships and exaptive bootstrapping, two theoretical concepts discussed in the following sections.[8]

4.   EXAPTIVE BOOTSTRAPPING AND INNOVATION CASCADES

One new thing leads to another: innovations occur in cascades, and involve transformations not only in artifact types, but in organizational forms and attributions as well. In this section, I sketch the theory of exaptive bootstrapping, which explains how such cascades happen. The theory, based on organization thinking, provides a qualitative description of a positive feedback dynamic in agent-artifact space, which accounts for the explosive growth that characterizes human sociocultural change, particularly over the past several centuries.

I begin by distinguishing between two different kinds of invention activities: those that are intended to deliver an existing functionality 'better-faster-cheaper' than the artifacts that currently deliver it, and those that are designed to deliver new kinds of functionality. An innovation cascade can be initiated by either type of invention, and in any cascade both types are present.

For example, the invention of printing by movable type was a 'better-faster-cheaper' innovation: Gutenberg's workshop figured out how to produce multiple copies of a manuscript more quickly and cheaply than could be done by hand-copying. But almost immediately, the first printing enterprise, headed by Gutenberg's ex-partner Fust and ex-assistant Schoeffer, had to solve a series of organizational and business problems that required new attributions of functionality: for agents, who had to pay up front for the paper for over a hundred copies (soon hundreds to several thousands) of a text, before selling any of them, and needed to work out new techniques for financing, selecting, marketing and selling their products; and for artifacts – what kinds of texts to print, and how to present them, in order to attract new customers who could not afford hand-copied manuscripts, but could pay enough for the right kind of printed book. And the solutions that the early book producers developed to these problems established new kinds of texts (and hence 'reading functionalities') that in turn induced the development of better-faster-cheaper improvements and novelties in both the physical and informational forms of books.

Though typically innovation cascades contain both types of innovation, we claim that the positive feedback dynamic depends on the existence of the second kind – in particular, on the role of new attributions of functionality in bringing these about. The theory of exaptive bootstrapping posits the following stages for the positive feedback dynamic:

1. New artifact types are designed to achieve some particular attribution of functionality.
2. Organizational transformations are constructed to proliferate the use of tokens of the new type.
3. Novel patterns of human interaction emerge around these artifacts in use.
4. New attributions of functionality are generated – by participants or observers – to describe what the participants in these interactions are obtaining or might obtain from them.
5. New artifacts are conceived and designed to instantiate the new attributed functionality.

Since the fifth stage concludes where the first begins, we have a bootstrapping dynamic that can produce cascades of changes in agent-artifact space. These cascades inextricably link innovations in artifacts, in organizational structure, and in attributions about artifact and organizational functionality.

Exaptation is the taking on of new functionality by existing structure.[9] It happens between the third and the fourth stage in this process, whereby new attributions of functionality arise from observing patterns of interaction among agents and already existing artifacts. The idea here is that artifacts gain their meaning through use, and not all the possible meanings that can arise when agents begin to incorporate new artifacts in patterns of use could have been anticipated by the designers and producers of those artifacts: the combinatory possibilities are simply too vast when a variety of different agents intent on carrying out a variety of different tasks have available a variety of different artifacts to use together with the new ones – not to mention that the designers and producers do not share the experiential base and the attribution space of all the agents that will use the artifact, in ways that depend on their own experience and attributions, not those of the artifact's designers and producers! Meaning in use is one thing – the recognition that that meaning might represent a functional novelty is another. For this to happen, some participants in (or observers of) these patterns of interaction must come to understand that something more is being delivered – or could be delivered, with suitable modifications – to some class of agents (perhaps, but not necessarily, including themselves) other than what the participants were thinking to obtain through the interactions in which they were engaging – and that these agents might come to value this new functionality. Thus, the generation of new attributions of functionality is grounded in an exaptation: from the interactions between existing structures (agents and artifacts), new functionality emerges. It may then become recognized by appropriately situated and motivated agents, and (re)cognized as a new attribution of artifact functionality.

To illustrate the stages described, consider the following example. In this example, stage 1 corresponds to the printed book, and stage 5 to the printed advertisement. The linking stages can be summarized as follows. Before printing, almost all manuscripts were produced in response to orders from a commissioning agent. Not surprisingly, this was initially the case also for the first printing firm, established in Mainz using the printing technology developed by Gutenberg and his co-workers, which was headed by the financier Johann Fust and the printer Peter Schoeffer.[10] Fust and Schoeffer had one important client, the archdiocese of Mainz, which commissioned many books from them including religious and liturgical works, references in canon law, and texts for the new humanistic school curriculum in which their clerical workers were trained. Fust and Schoeffer realized early on that they could probably find purchasers for additional copies of these books. They faced the problem of how to reach these potential purchasers and convince them to buy the printed books. One organizational solution to this problem that the firm explored was to hire traveling representatives, which constituted stage 2 of the exaptive bootstrapping cycle. These representatives of course visited fairs and festivals, but they also stopped at towns along their route. When they did so, they would have to make known to potential purchasers their whereabouts and their wares – stage 3. One approach that the firm took to this problem was exapted from their primary ongoing activity, in stage 4: they conceived the idea of using printing, the same technology they employed to produce their wares, to enhance distribution. The new artifact type they developed (stage 5) was the printed advertisement. Their earliest surviving printed advertisement dates from 1469. It is a one page broadside, which begins as follows: 'Those who wish to purchase for themselves the books listed herafter, which have been edited with the greatest care and which are set in the same Mainz printing type as this announcement . . . are invited to come to the dwelling place written in below' (quoted in Lehmann-Haupt, 1950: 86). Thus, the advertisement attests not only to the nature of the wares (the list of books that it provided), but also to their quality (the 'same Mainz printing type as this announcement'). Note that the name of the inn where the representative could be found had to be hand-written, as it changed with time and town. The printed advertisement instantiates the new attribution of functionality: the possibility of mass-circulating information about a product to recruit potential purchasers. Other instantiations of this attribution, for other classes of products, followed, and the circulation of printed catalogues soon became an important means of disseminating product information and organizing exchange activities.

Innovation cascades involve many cycles of the exaptive bootstrapping process. In addition, these cascades typically also include processes that are purely adaptive: given an attribution of functionality and an artifact that realizes it, apply a known technology to improve the artifact or its method of production to render it better (according to the values associated with the given attribution of functionality), faster or cheaper. Such processes do not require the generation of new attributions of functionality. Note, though, that better-faster-cheaper invention is not necessarily purely adaptive: when observed close up, it may require new attributions of functionality as well. For example, Gutenberg had to exapt a variety of techniques he had learned as a jeweler in quite different contexts, even with different materials, for the new functionality of typecasting. In such cases, not only the exaptation of new attributions of functionality, but also organizational transformations like those in stage 2 are required, for example in assembling a team of agents that collectively embodies the different competences necessary to achieve a complex better-faster-cheaper invention – and in developing the procedures whereby this team can sufficiently align their directedness and then attributions about each other and the artifacts with which and towards which they work to accomplish what they have come to intend to do together.

5. GENERATIVE RELATIONSHIPS: THE LOCUS OF NEW ATTRIBUTIONS

According to the previous section, the most important cognitive process in innovation is the generation of new attributions. Similarly, the most important communication processes involve the aligning of attributions among agents, otherwise the processes of recruitment, differentiation and coordination that underlie the collective action necessary to transform new attributions into new artifacts into new patterns of interaction cannot take place. As we saw, innovation often begins with a new attribution of functionality – an idea for a kind of activity in which people may wish to engage that can be realized by means of an artifact. Moreover, virtually all constructive innovation processes require new attributions of identity for the new entities in agent-artifact space that these processes generate. Since identity is relational, the construction of new entities that become incorporated in patterns of activity with previously existing entities generally requires modifications in the attributions of identity for these entities as well.

These new attributions arise in the context of a particular kind of relationship among agents, which we call generative. While the kind of ontological uncertainty that typically shrouds innovation processes makes it impossible to predict in detail what sorts of new attributions a relationship may generate, it still may be possible for agents to assess the generative potential of a relationship. This potential depends on five characteristics of the agents in the relationship and their modes of interaction with one another, and agents may not only infer the degree of these characteristics through their interactions, but may also act in such a way to increase the relationship's generative potential. These characteristics are: aligned directedness, heterogeneity, mutual directedness, appropriate permissions, and action opportunities (Lane and Maxfield, 1997, 2005).

In zones of agent-artifact space that are undergoing rapid change, identities change, and agents need to track these changes carefully in their attributions of identity of the significant agents and artifacts in their world. The process of monitoring and interpreting identities requires discourse with others, since any agent has only a partial and restricted view of what others do – never mind how they interpret what they are doing. This discourse is channeled through the agents' informational and interpretative social networks. Generative relationships emerge from these networks. These relationships may link actors who work for the same firm, groups of actors from more than one organization engaged in joint projects, or agents working together under the auspices of a market system scaffolding structure. The important point is that in generative relationships, agents have aligned directedness – that is, their interactions are focused around achieving similar transformations in the same zone of agent-artifact space – and they are characterized by significant heterogeneity. Unlike social actors who may prefer the company of like-minded others, innovative agents have to seek out and build strong relationships with others that differ substantially from them in some important respects – even if they hope to construct eventually a set of attributions about artifact meaning and agent roles sufficiently aligned to support a stable market system around the artifact family they are trying to bring into being.

Whatever the kind of heterogeneity that attracts the agents into working together – differences in competence, in position within social or economic networks, in access to particular resources – these agents are bound to have different attributions about important artifacts and agents in their common world, differences that reflect the heterogeneity of their past experiences. Attributions are not directly observable – even less so than the other sources of heterogeneity mentioned above. As agents begin to interact to establish patterns of joint action, attributional differences among them may surface – typically, in the form of utterances or actions that cannot be coherently interpreted from the point of view of the attributions the listener has assigned to the agents or artifacts to which the utterance refers or the action is targeted.

Agents may respond in several different ways to their discovery of attributional difference. They might confuse their own attributions with 'reality' and decide that the other is either ignorant or less intelligent – a reaction that can be encouraged by attributions about social or intellectual differences between discourse participants. This mode of reacting to differences undermines mutual directedness, the 'attraction' towards one another that induces partners to enter into and continue joint interactions, another of the determining characteristics of generative potential – and thus typically prevents the relationship from further development, never mind generating anything. A second reaction mode is to step carefully around any attributional differences that may surface. This reaction is more politic and may permit the relationship to continue, and it may even enhance the generative potential of the relationship if a particular attributional difference is so tied to the identity of one or the other agent that its exploration could only lead to the termination of the relationship. However, if all differences are handled in this way, the participants in the relationship do not have the appropriate permissions (what they can say to whom, about what, in which illocutionary mode) to provide generative potential to the relationship. Some permissions are explicit, others implicit; some derive through organizational hierarchies, from agents who have permissions that allow them to grant permissions (and deny them) to other agents, while others emerge from the social interactions in which agents are embedded; some are arrogated by agents for themselves, but then may become the object of contestation and negotiation among agents – negotiations channeled by other sets of permissions that characterize organizations in which the negotiations are carried out, from courtrooms to legislative bodies to trade associations to standards bodies. Analysing permissions structures is an essential element of organizational thinking – and determining which permissions are available to interacting agents is essential for establishing the generative potential of the relationship among these agents (Lane and Maxfield, 2005, 2009).

If the relationship really has generative potential, then participants can respond to attributional differences when they surface by exploring them, through extended discourse. As discourse expands around the discovered difference, semantic uncertainty (that is, uncertainty about what particular propositions mean) typically initially increases for all participants, as more and more of their attributions are linked to those for which the differences were first discovered – and differences among these too become revealed. What such a process may lead to is cascades of change in each participant's attribution set – that is, their representations of the structure of agent-artifact space. It is this process that leads to new attributions. Opening up attributions for discussion generally is not resolved through anything as simple as replacement (that is, accepting another's attribution in place of one's own) or combination (that is, merging through Boolean operations that put together one's own attributions with those of another). Rather, from what others reveal about their attributions, one may realize new dimensions for evaluating

aspects of identity – and these new dimensions may lead to new possibilities for relations among different attributions, which imply shifts in the attributions themselves. But
given the differences in starting points, and the difference in interpretations of the added
dimensions, there is no reason to think that attributions of different agents need come
'closer together' through this process, never mind come into alignment. Of course, talk
is not enough: the participants in a generative relationship must also have appropriate
action opportunities: the possibility to engage with one another in interactions that result
in transformations not just in their own attributions, but in the structure of agent-artifact
space.

To illustrate the concept of generative relationships, we return to the early days of
printing. The career of the great Venetian printer Aldo Manuzio is marked by his capacity to enter into and sustain generative relationships.[11] Manuzio was an enthusiastic
humanist knowledgeable in Latin, Greek and Hebrew, employed as a private tutor in
the household of the Pio family, lords of Carpi, who were cousins of one of the greatest (and highest-born) humanist scholars, Pico della Mirandola. Around 1490, when he
was already 40 years old, Manuzio conceived a project: to exploit the new technology of
print to increase the diffusion and appreciation of Manuzio's beloved Greek philosophy
and science. By 1490, printing had expanded well beyond its Rhineland birthplace, and
an international market system in printed books was rapidly taking shape, with production centered in Venice (where one in seven of all fifteenth-century European editions
were published) and the principal scaffolding structure (then as now, at least in Europe)
the annual Frankfurt book fair. Most texts were in Latin, with an increasing number in
local vernaculars; Italian printers had published a few Greek works, mostly grammars
and other instructional material. Medieval copyists in Western Europe produced manuscripts of Greek writers only in Latin translations (in general, from Arabic translations
of the original Greek works). Particularly after the fall of Constantinople to the Turks
in 1453, many Greek scholars fled to the West, bringing manuscripts with them. Some
of these scholars set up schools to teach their language and literature to students already
primed to learn them from their exposure to the work of the first several generations
of humanists. For Manuzio, there was already a substantial cultured public ready and
eager to benefit from the wisdom of the Greeks, and he wanted to provide this public
with philologically correct and readily available texts. Print was the ideal medium for
accomplishing this project, and the distribution channels associated with the emerging
market system in printed books provided the possibility of reaching potential readers
throughout Western Europe.

So, supported morally and financially by his devoted Pio students, Manuzio moved
to Venice and began to figure out what he needed to know to carry out his project. Four
years later, he had succeeded in putting together a partnership and a network of collaborators. One of Manuzio's partners was Andrea Torresani, one of the first Italians to enter
the print trade. Torresani was not a cultured man, and certainly knew no Greek, but he
had considerable practical experience in printing and bookselling. In the company, he
primarily concerned himself with the latter activity – Manuzio himself, after he learned
the trade from Torresani, ran the print shop, in addition to what we would now call his
work as publisher: that is, deciding what texts to print, dealing with authors or editors
and illustrators, determining the form of the book and so forth. By the 1490s, shrewd
printers like Torresani realized that the constant reprinting of a rather small number of

texts, which characterized the first several decades of the emerging industry, could not continue if particular firms and the industry as a whole were to continue to grow. He probably was convinced by Manuzio's argument that a sufficient number of the readers of the classical and humanist Latin texts currently in publication (by many different printing houses) had enough Greek to welcome the kind of text Manuzio had in mind to publish – works in philosophy and science most of which had not yet appeared even in Latin translation.

The group's other partner was a Venetian nobleman, Pierfrancesco Barberigo, son of a doge and nephew of the current doge. Undoubtedly the Pio connection was crucial to Manuzio's success in recruiting such a well-positioned member of Venetian society into his enterprise. While Barberigo was mainly an investor, he also played an important role in helping the Aldine press deal with political issues, like securing various patents and copyrights from the Venetian government, and financial ties with banks.

The partnership functioned very well, surviving several crises in the Aldine press' own affairs, the printing business in general, and Venetian politics. In 1505, Manuzio married Torresani's daughter, and the families set up a joint household, over the printing shop. The Barberigo family continued to participate in the press and draw their share of the profits after Pierfrancesco's death.

Even this brief description suffices to illustrate both the heterogeneity and the aligned directedness of this partnership, which became a generative relationship: note that the alignment is towards what we might call the development of a particular zone in agent-artifact space, but undoubtedly did not extend to a shared vision of the importance of publishing Greek works to deepen the understanding of the world on the part of a cultural elite. (In fact, as we will see, the practical bookseller Torresani and the profit-seeking Barberigo family pushed Manuzio to change direction, as the Greek books they produced sold considerably more slowly than they had initially hoped.)

Initially, the network of collaborators of the Aldine press consisted of eminent Greek scholars, who edited the works that Manuzio published; collectors of manuscripts, like the nobleman Bernardo Bembo, who provided the texts with which Manuzio and his editors worked; and a group of avid Venetian students of Greek, who helped provide Manuzio with a sounding-board for ideas on which texts to publish. The latter group organized itself in 1500, under Manuzio's leadership, as the 'New Academy', whose members agreed to speak Greek at their meetings, where they were to discuss themes of common interest.

In 1495, the Aldine press began publishing, with a grammar by the most eminent Greek immigrant currently teaching in Italy, Constantine Lascaris, and the first volume of its most important and ambitious Greek language project, the collected works of Aristotle. Manuzio obtained the Lascaris' text in manuscript from Pietro Bembo, the young son of Bernardo, who had just returned from two years of study under Lascaris' direction in Messina.[12] For centuries, male members of the Venetian patriciate chose one (or sometimes more) of three possible careers: public service in the Venetian administration (or navy), commerce, or the church, a choice usually possible only for younger sons. Pietro Bembo's father had been one of the first generation of Venetian patricians to embrace humanism while studying at the University of Padua, and throughout his long and distinguished career as a diplomat and administrator[13] he collected manuscripts and developed friendships with leading scholars. Growing up in this cultivated household, young Pietro early developed strong scholarly and literary inclinations. When he returned from Messina, he wrote a short work in elegant Latin, *De Aetna*, recounting some of his experiences to his father, which was published, probably as a return favor for the Lascaris manuscript and Bernardo's cooperation, by Manuzio in 1495.[14] By the time he finished his studies at Padua, he was not attracted by either public service or commerce. He spent several years at the court of the Este family in Ferrara, consorting with such literary luminaries there as Ariosto, and he began himself to compose works in the vernacular (including the beginning of a dialogue on romantic love, Gli Asolani, eventually published by Manuzio in 1505). More and more, he dedicated himself to literature, and so he increasingly departed from the life-ways his society considered appropriate for a Venetian patrician. Both Manuzio and Bembo, starting from very different positions in Quattrocento Italy, were constructing new kinds of identities as the new Cinquecento dawned.

By 1500, it was becoming clear to the partners in the Aldine press that the magnificent Greek folio volumes they were producing were selling too slowly to justify the investments they required. Until then, Manuzio had yet to enter the overcrowded but high-volume market of Latin classics. As he considered alternative new publication projects, he began to reflect on a new way to present these books. In general, the classics had been published as weighty tomes, usually folios or quartos, smothered in commentary to help the reader understand the text. Manuzio, though, envisioned a particular kind of reader: active and cultivated men, like Bernardo Bembo, who might enjoy reading for their pleasure and edification whenever they had a spare moment from their labors, and who didn't need to be led by the hand by an intrusive editor's selected commentaries, but would prefer direct, 'personal' interaction with the ancient authors. Such men would demand a high level of rigorous philology in the preparation of the text, with perhaps an introduction explaining issues encountered in choosing between variant manuscripts, but no commentaries. Without commentaries, the texts would be considerably shorter, and it might be feasible to bring out smaller books that readers could carry with them on their travels, in their saddlebags or even in their pockets. So Manuzio had the idea of publishing a series of Latin books in ottavo, designed for easy readability, printed in a new kind of font, in italics, which he thought was both more pleasing to the eye and more intimate than the standard fonts used heretofore.

Manuzio discussed this idea with his circle of friends and collaborators, among whom was Pietro Bembo. Bembo was attracted to Manuzio's project, so compatible with his own view of the meaning and value of literature, but he urged Manuzio to go a step further, by including 'classics' in the vernacular in the new series: to Bembo, Manuzio's idea represented a great opportunity to boost the status of vernacular literature, by associating it with the aura of cultivation and gentlemanly entertainment that Manuzio's format was designed to confer. Manuzio himself had little interest in vernacular literature: before 1500, he had published only two – one a religious work of Saint Catherine of Siena, and the other the bizarre *Hypnerotomachia Polifili*, neither then nor ever considered a 'classic' (although the Aldine edition is regarded as one of the most beautifully illustrated books ever published).[15] However, Manuzio accepted Bembo's advice, and Bembo himself edited the first of these (and the third overall in the series, after a volume of Virgil and one of Horace): Petrarch's *Cose Volgari* of 1501. Bembo's role as editor was not explicitly acknowledged in the book, since he was not yet ready to embrace fully

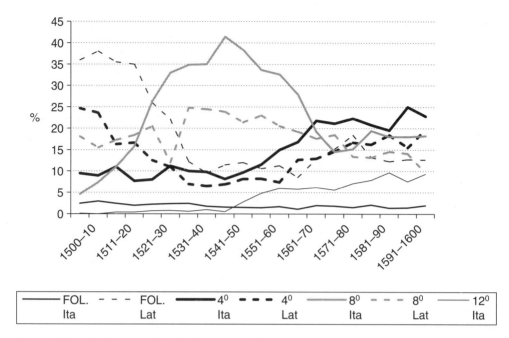

Figure 2.1   The Venetian book: format and language

a role absolutely extraneous to the Venetian patrician way of life: a professional man of letters, whatever that might mean in 1500.

As editor of the Petrarch text, Bembo introduced a number of important innovations, beyond the ottavo form and the italic font. To implement Manuzio's vision of easy read-ability, the book introduced several novel punctuation marks, including the apostrophe to indicate contractions, and the comma. In addition, Bembo applied philological princi-ples in an attempt to reconstruct Petrarch's original text (his principal manuscript source was in Petrarch's own hand, from Bernardo's collection); before this, editors felt free to change words to conform to current usage or different vernacular dialects – or even to 'clarify' the meaning of difficult passages. Finally, and most importantly for the future, Bembo's introduction defended his editorial practice, by developing an evolutionary theory of language, according to which languages 'mature' to a certain point of perfec-tion and then begin to decline – and he argued that the Tuscan dialect reached its apex in the age of Petrarch (for poetry; he later added Boccaccio for prose), which was the lan-guage he sought to uncover and which he proposed as a model for all future literature in vernacular. In a sense, this introduction is the first formal proposal of the vernacular as a literary language, with its own rules and literary history – an argument to which Bembo returned in 1525, with the publication of *Prosa della volgar lingua*, which many consider the formative work for the construction of an Italian language.

In their work in conceiving and producing the new series, Bembo and Manuzio formed a generative relationship,[16] and the attributions and artifacts to which this relationship gave rise have an importance that is difficult to overestimate. Their Petrarch volume was the first ottavo in vernacular published in Venice – but not the last, as Figure 2.1 shows.

Bembo's introduction sparked an intense debate about the vernacular as a literary language, to which such luminaries as Machiavelli and Castiglione contributed with alternative proposals, but by the 1530s Bembo's ideas had swept the field. Indeed, all vernacular writers understood that 'good literature' requires a language with an established lexicon and structured syntactical rules, which provide the background constraints on which their own particular usage patterns can generate an emergent 'style'. That Bembo's vision of what that lexicon and syntax should be would become the canonical one was by no means a foregone conclusion, but the immense success of the Petrarch volume was an important step along that path. Moreover, Bembo's punctuation aids, along with his 'de-latinized' vocabulary and spelling, also triumphed. More important, the new form and format of the Aldine series, especially in its vernacular volumes, helped generate a larger reading public, who began to read in new ways appropriate to reading as entertainment and pastime, rather than reading as serious study in a contemplative space.

This enlargement of the reading public was very much helped along by an exaptation from the Aldine innovation in form and font. The first volumes of the series, released in 1501, were a big success, and some Lyonnais printers quickly provided another interpretation of ottavo in italics: the italic font allowed more characters per line than a standard font with the same legibility, and the smaller ottavo format permitted more characters per area of paper used. So the new format could be exploited to produce cheaper books – an idea quite foreign to Manuzio's way of thinking about books! They immediately copied Manuzio's work, squeezing more lines per page than his aesthetics permitted, using inferior paper, inks and italic characters – but producing books with record low cost, making them accessible to a larger potential public. A new innovation cascade was underway, with new kinds of texts produced and published to satisfy the emerging tastes of an expanding reading public. By 1540, a new role had come into being: the professional author, who earned his (usually precarious) living by providing these texts,[17] working closely with increasingly entrepreneurial publishers (another new role!) who were particularly apt in anticipating the kinds of texts that would both satisfy some existing set of readers and recruit new ones. It was these new kinds of texts and new readers that account for the explosion of vernacular ottavos between 1500 and 1545 portrayed in Figure 2.1:[18] the tradesmen who pored over vernacular ottavo 'how-to' books, the professional people who read the letter collections[19] that they adopted as models for their own correspondence, not to mention all those who were entranced by the first 'puzzle books', or were entertained and informed by expositions of the wonders of nature, including guides to self-medication for all sorts of common afflictions. Because the new ottavos in vernacular were highly portable, increasingly cheap, with contents appealing to an ever more popular reading public, new distribution channels were initiated to carry them to parts of the public off the beaten track: in particular, the male populations of whole mountain villages began to be recruited by publishers to carry their wares into smaller remote population centers, and the book peddler began to become a familiar figure throughout the Western European countryside. And because the volumes these peddlers sold were so small, when necessary they could also be carried surreptitiously, hidden in clothing or concealed under other kinds of goods: ideal for some of these peddlers to smuggle Protestant texts from Germany and Switzerland into French and Italian territories, whose rulers were intent on stamping out the new heresies in their lands.

Note how different is this sort of innovation cascade from another concept in the innovation literature that links different inventions together, the technological trajectory. The latter is characterized by predictability: the inventions all do the same kind of thing, pushing further along a well-demarcated and collectively recognized trajectory in artifact space. Of course, agents are necessary to work out the technological details that join one point in the trajectory to another, but the trajectory itself appears as some sort of natural kind. The trajectory of changes in the innovation cascade that follow from Manuzio and Bembo's new attributions and the artifact they constructed to instantiate it is anything but linear and predictable. It passes through changes in artifact type, attributions, agent organization, impinges on technology, aesthetics, social organization, politics – each change contributing as a precondition but hardly determining those that follow, each of which is constructed through the interactions of many different kinds of agents, with different intentions, creating through their interactions new emergent patterns and structures that no-one could have foreseen, but which retrospectively had to be incorporated into new attributions of agents seeking to make sense of their world in order to act to change it. The trajectory of an innovation cascade is an historical process, no natural kind, and can be understood only from an historical perspective, based on some set of ontological commitments about the kinds of interacting entities, interaction modalities and ensuing dynamics that provide the framework in which the trajectory's emergence can be narrated.

NOTES

1. The fact that most scientists inherit their ontological commitments from the disciplines in which they work, and as a result don't think they are actually making ontological commitments but rather studying the world as it is – is completely irrelevant to the point I am making here. Nor am I saying that quarks and spin, genes and heritability, or markets and democracy are mere inventions of the scientists who first used these terms to describe patterns they were interested in understanding. Some ontological commitments give a lot more purchase on the flux of matter, energy and information that underlie the phenomena we observe and try to study than others.
2. The theory of repeated games does allow for the emergence of strategies but not new rules for the game.
3. Simon's theory, based on the idea of nearly decomposable hierarchies, is full of suggestive ideas, but it does not do the job. In particular, of the three aspects of organization discussed below, it is long on structure, weak on function, and almost totally ignores process. See Lane (2006) for an extended critique, along with a discussion of some other important contributions to a complexity theory of organization by Phil Anderson and John Holland.
4. Obviously, the concept of function is irrelevant for organizations that are never in such contexts – or if, when they are, chance rather than the organization determines which process is enacted. This is the case for physical systems. Function begins with biology.
5. See Lane et al. (2009a), Read et al. (2009), and van der Leeuw et al. (2009) for a detailed discussion of organization thinking and its implications for understanding innovation and social change.
6. I have used the term causally (efficacious or convincing) rather cavalierly: efficacious or convincing for whom? We have come to believe that there is no dodging the fact that for any theory this question has to be raised – and answered, by specifying a particular community that uses the theory in question to tell stories among themselves about the phenomena in which they are interested. There are lots of different ways to tell stories about particular episodes in the history of innovation. Each of them will be based, implicitly or explicitly, on some ontology; a sufficiently abstract form of ontology that allows one to tell lots of stories about other episodes of artifact innovation would count as a theory, perhaps alternative to the one we have developed. The power of these theories can be assessed by how deeply (in any given episode), widely (over a set of episodes that share the phenomenon of theoretical interest, in this case artifact innovation as we have defined it, but differ with respect to other characteristics, like time, space, artifact type) and convincingly (within the community of reference) are the stories constructed with their ontologies. Related ideas about what constitutes a theory for understanding social phenomena are developed in much more depth and philosophical precision in Hacking (2002) and Davidson (2001).

7. Examples of dialogues between historical narratives and various aspects of our theory include Lane and Maxfield (1997, 2005, 2009), Russo (2000), Bonifati (2008), Rossi et al. (2009).
8. See Lane et al. (2004), Villani et al. (2007), Serra et al. (2009) and Villani et al. (2009) for details.
9. For introductions to and references about exaptation, see Gould (2002, Chapter 11), in the biological context, and Villani et al. (2007, plus discussion), in the sociocultural context.
10. Gutenberg himself was an early example of an inventor who failed to make the transition to innovating entrepreneur. See Lehmann-Haupt (1950) for an account of the history of the interactions among Gutenberg, Fust and Schoeffer.
11. For Manuzio, see for example Lowry (1979), Marcon and Zorzi (1994), Richardson (1994) Dionisotti (1995), and Zeidberg (1998).
12. For Bembo, see Richardson (1994), Dionisotti (2002), Kidwell (2004).
13. While serving as Venetian *rettore* in Ravenna, he commissioned the beautiful monument that marks the tomb of Dante in that city.
14. The press's first publication in Latin.
15. It remains a mystery why Manuzio published this work, so different from anything else released from his press. There are indications that he wished to dissociate himself from the book, despite its beauty.
16. I leave it as an exercise to the reader to verify the generative potential conditions.
17. See Grendler (1969), Larivaille (1997) and Richardson (1999).
18. Which may resemble the sort of S-shaped curves that innovation 'diffusion' theorists love to model – but which is due to a constructive dynamics, featuring cascades of innovations in artifact types, agent roles, attributions and the organization of the market system around books, as far from a passive 'diffusion' dynamics as one could well imagine!
19. Pioneered by Aretino, who had them published mainly to blackmail leading political figures to induce him to sing their praises instead of making them the targets of his withering sarcasm; while his clever publisher Marcolini brought out volumes of Aretino's letters in ottavo because he had intuited just how big a market there might be for gossip about the doings of the rich and the famous.

REFERENCES

Beinhocker, E. (2006), *The Origin of Wealth: Evolution, Complexity, and the Radical Remaking of Economics*, Boston: Harvard Business School Press.
Bonifati, G. (2008), *Dal Libro Manoscritto al Libro Stampato: Sistemi di Mercato a Bologna e a Firenze agli Albori del Capitalismo*, Turin: Rosenberg & Sellier.
Davidson, A. (2001), *The Emergence of Sexuality: Historical Epistemology and the Formation of Concepts*, Cambridge, MA: Harvard University Press.
Dionisotti, C. (1995), *Aldo Manuzio Umanista e Editore*, Milano: Edizioni il Polifilo.
Dionisotti, C. (2002), *Scritti sul Bembo* (ed. Claudio Vela), Turin: Einaudi.
Gould, S. (2002), *The Structure of Evolutionary Theory*, Cambridge, MA: Harvard University Press.
Grendler, P. (1969), *Critics of the Italian World (1530–1560): Anton Francesco Doni, Nicolo Franco and Ortensio Lando*, Madison, WI: University of Wisconsin Press.
Hacking, I. (2002), *Historical Ontology*, Cambridge, MA: Harvard University Press.
Kidwell, C. (2004), Pietro Bembo: Lover, Linguist, Cardinal, Montreal: McGill-Queens University Press.
Lane, D. (2006), 'Hierarchy, complexity, society', in Pumain, D. (ed.), *Hierarchy in Natural and Social Sciences*, Berlin: Springer-Verlag, pp. 81–119
Lane, D. and Maxfield, R. (1997), 'Complexity, foresight and strategy', in Arthur, W., Durlauf, S. and Lane, D. (eds), *The Economy as a Complex Evolving System II*, Redwood City CA: Addison-Wesley, pp. 169–98.
Lane, D. and Maxfield, R. (2005), 'Ontological uncertainty and innovation', *Journal of Evolutionary Economics*, 5, 3–50.
Lane, D. and Maxfield, R. (2009), 'Building a new market system: effective action, redirection and generative relationships', in Lane, D., Pumain, D., van der Leeuw, S. and West, G. (eds), (2009), *Complexity Perspectives on Innovation and Social Change*, pp. 263–88.
Lane, D., Maxfield, R., Read, D. and van der Leeuw, S. (2009a), 'From population to organization thinking', in Lane, D., Pumain, D., van der Leeuw, S. and West, G. (eds), (2009a), *Complexity Perspectives on Innovation and Social Change*, pp. 11–42.
Lane, D., Pumain, D., van der Leeuw, S. and West, G. (eds), (2009b), *Complexity Perspectives on Innovation and Social Change*, Berlin: Springer-Verlag.
Lane, D., Serra, R., Villani, M. and Ansaloni, L. (2004), 'A theory-based dynamical model for innovation processes', *Complexus*, **2**, 177–94.

Larivaille, P. (1997), *Pietro Aretino*, Rome: Salerno Editrice.
Lehmann-Haupt, H. (1950), *Peter Schoeffer of Gersheim and Mainz*, Rochester, NY: Leo Hart.
Lowry, M. (1979), *The World of Aldus Manutius*, Oxford: Blackwell.
Marcon, S. and M. Zorzi (1994), *Aldo Manuzio e l'ambiente veneziano 1494–1515*, Venice: Il Cardo.
Read, D., Lane, D. and van der Leeuw, S. (2009), 'The innovation innovation', in Lane, D., Pumain, D., van der Leeuw, S. and West, G. (eds), *Complexity Perspectives on Innovation and Social Change*, pp. 43–84.
Richardson, B. (1994), *Print Culture in Renaissance Italy: The Editor and the Vernacular Text, 1470–1600*, Cambridge: Cambridge University Press.
Richardson, B. (1999), *Printing, Writers and Readers in Renaissance Italy*, Cambridge: Cambridge University Press.
Rossi, F., Bertossi, P., Gurisatti, P. and Sovieni, L. (2009), 'Incorporating a new technology into agent-artifact space: the case of control system automation in Europe', in Lane, D., Pumain, D., van der Leeuw, S. and West, G. (eds), *Complexity Perspectives on Innovation and Social Change*, pp. 289–310.
Russo, M. (2000), 'Complementary innovations and generative relationships: an enthnographic study', *Economics of Innovation and New Technology*, **9**, 517–57.
Serra, R., Villani, M. and Lane, D. (2009), 'Modeling innovation', in Lane, D., Pumain, D., van der Leeuw, S. and West, G. (eds), *Complexity Perspectives on Innovation and Social Change*, pp. 361–88.
Simon, H. (1962), 'The architecture of complexity: hierarchic systems', *Proceedings of the American Philosophical Society*, **106**, pp. 467–82.
Simon, H. (1973), 'The organization of complex systems', in Pattee, H. (ed.), *Hierarchy Theory: The Challenge of Complex Systems*, New York: George Braziller, pp. 3–27.
Van der Leeuw, S., Lane, D. and Read, D. (2009), 'The long-term evolution of social organization', Lane, D., Pumain, D., van der Leeuw, S. and West, G. (eds), *Complexity Perspectives on Innovation and Social Change*, pp. 85–116.
Villani, M., Bonancini, S., Ferrari, D. and Serra, R. (2009), 'Exaptive processes: an agent-based model', in Lane, D., Pumain, D., van der Leeuw, S. and West, G. (eds), *Complexity Perspectives on Innovation and Social Change*, pp. 413–32.
Villani, M., S. Bonacini, D. Ferrari, R. Serra and D. Lane (2007), 'An agent-based model of exaptive processes', European Management Review, **4**, 141–51.
Zeidberg, D. (ed.) (1998), *Aldus Manutius and Renaissance Culture: Essays in Memory of Franklin D. Murphy*, Florence: Leo Olschki.

3 Complexity in the theory of the developing firm
Harry Bloch and Stan Metcalfe

INTRODUCTION

We begin this chapter with a straightforward question. What kind of theory of the firm is appropriate to the study of an evolving, complex, developing economy? A suitable answer clearly depends on what are considered to be the salient properties of an evolving, developing economy. To facilitate the following discussion we list them seriatim without further comment.

- An economy is a highly ordered system based on the division of labour within and between firms and industries. The division of labour is rendered productive and viable by the self organizing properties of the system, properties that make purposeful connections between the elements of the economic system.
- Modern economies are open systems, characterized by far from equilibrium, ordered states; they are necessarily self transforming as well as self organizing although the pattern of transformation is very uneven.
- The manner of self transformation is premised on the manner of self organization with the remarkable implication that the rules which facilitate the generation of order and stability are the same rules that render possible transformation of order and thus instability.
- The principal source of instability arises through innovation, the invasion of the prevailing system by novelties of which those in relation to technology and organization have proved particularly powerful, the theme encapsulated in Schumpeter's notion of creative destruction.
- The firm is a principal locus of innovation but to innovate it must have adaptive capacity, while the wider consequences of that innovation depend on the market system having adaptive capacity so that the impact of novelty may be widely diffused.
- The context for future oriented decision making is uncertainty and, to use Shackle's terminology 'unknowledge', the inescapable requirement to base decisions on imagination and conjecture premised on an imperfect command of the facts relevant to the outcome of a decision. Consequently, investment and other future oriented decisions frequently turn out, *ex post*, to have been based on a false conjecture. Yet 'disaster' can be as instructive as 'triumph' in the growth of economically useful knowledge.[1]

These are the complexity-based themes that link the development of an economy as a whole to the development of its constituent firms and vice versa. A satisfactory answer to our opening question must offer a concept of the firm that is consistent with a broader view of the economy as a complex system. It must allow for the firm to have emergent properties, for the firm to develop internally as well as adapt to changes in its external environment. The most appropriate way to do this is to explore the idea of the firm as a particular kind of knowledge-based system, operating within the wider knowledge based system that is the market process and its yet wider frame of instituting rules and norms. The fundamental difference between the firm and market as systems is that one is a designed order while the other is a spontaneous order, to borrow Hayek's distinction, although as we shall see the boundary between the two kinds of order is not always clear.

To explore this perspective we need a particular approach to the idea of the evolving and developing firm and we shall trace this to the ideas expressed in Marshall and Penrose, with other supporting contributions from Richardson, Coase, Boulding and Arrow, and more recently by Nelson and Winter.[2] This view of the firm does not stand in isolation but sits within a parallel view of the evolving and developing market process, a view that we trace to Smith and Hayek. Our central theme now becomes clear, firms and markets are distributed knowledge systems that, on the one hand, serve to accommodate behaviour to limitations on individual human knowing, while, on the other hand, they serve to recreate those same limitations on human knowing.

This is why there is an ever present sense in modern capitalism of an inbuilt red-queen effect, a sense that the search for new knowledge to generate market advantage serves to stimulate rivals in the same countervailing endeavour. That is to say, the instituted process of competition in the market is both a device for establishing order, purposeful patterns of human interaction, and a device for transforming that order. The market process like the firm turns out to be a system based on distributed intelligence, an intelligence that depends on each individual knowing a great deal about very little. It is the systemic properties of the economic system that transform the very uneven distribution of individual knowledge into a collective but distributed intelligence within firms and markets.

This was Adam Smith's great insight, that a division of labour is a division of knowing that must be organized through connecting processes if it is realize its full effects. That is the deep purpose of organization, and firms and markets are different forms of organization to promote joint action. Indeed, our standard of living depends crucially on this ability to make use of the limitations on personal knowing; modern societies are collectively 'smart' while the individuals within them are comparatively 'ignorant'. Indeed, we consider it to be one of the great strengths of the adaptive complexity approach that it privileges the importance of the highly uneven distribution of human knowing and the consequential highly uneven distribution of human creativity.

Moreover, as with all evolutionary theory of the variation cum selection kind, it is the generation of variation that drives change in organizations and in markets. To paraphrase Ross Ashby, 'variety destroys variety', but the sources of variety creation are also unevenly distributed. That is the significance of innovation: it points to the crucial role of the firm as an agent of organization and as an agent of transformation. It also points to the limitations of Olympian rationality as a basis for economic theory: it may be far better to start from the assumption of human ignorance rather than perfect knowing if we are to grasp the nature of our ever evolving economic world.

The remainder of this chapter is organized as follows. We begin with a discussion of the evolution of knowledge as a problem solving process and proceed to link this to the ideas of complexity and emergence. From there we review the development of ideas in relation to the evolving and developing firm drawing principally on the ideas contained in Marshall and elaborated by Penrose and Richardson and later scholars.

KNOWLEDGE AND INFORMATION

The idea of the firm and the economy as distributed knowledge systems owes a great deal to Adam Smith and his principle of the division of labour. For the device of linking superior productivity to the specialization of task is in fact a device for pointing to the importance of the specialized and distributed nature of human knowing. The employees in the pin factory have detailed knowledge of only part of the process, the makers of machines have detailed knowledge that is different from the users of machines and the philosophers and men of speculation are each expert in their own particular sub branch of knowledge. Highly localized knowing of course generates a problem, the problem of how the actions of different individuals are to be connected and coordinated so that joint action is possible. This is the problem of organization and from this perspective firms and the markets within which they function are different forms of organization. In each case, the role of organization is in part to transmit flows of information between its different participating actors. This is not to agree that firms and markets are substitutable forms of organization, quite the opposite, they are complementary and firms do what markets cannot do and vice versa. We are already beginning to outline the three elements of any organization as a system, be it firm or market, that it is defined within boundaries, that it is composed of component parts (actors) and that these component parts are connected in specific spatiotemporal contexts. This epistemic view leads to several interwoven ideas that will be important in our discussion of complexity and the firm.

The most important idea is that only individuals can be said to know; knowledge is a state of mind and necessarily idiosyncratic. The flows of information that are essential for coordinating human action are not flows of knowledge but rather representations of individual knowings, the effect of which is to induce shared states of understanding, so that the same question or instruction elicits the same answer or response across the appropriate group of individuals. The possibility of sustaining these shared states of understanding depends not only on traditional modes of cultural transmission but on the ability to represent human knowing in a great range of durable and communicable forms of information, from Gutenberg to Gates as it were. It is the complex of innovations in information technology that have rendered possible the modern form of a knowledge-based society. The pervasive communication of information to enable the formation of shared states of understanding at the many different levels that underpin coordinated actions creates a need for correlating processes, of which those carried out by organizations are one major form. The degree to which there is a requisite need for the correlation of understanding varies greatly with the context. In some cases the understandings need to be society wide (the rules of the road, the understanding of time zones, the law on property transfer, for example) in other cases they are localized and specific, as they typically are within a firm and even more within its sub departments.

The net effect is that each individual is dependent in their daily action on the knowledge of others and on the organized forms of information flow that allow mutually beneficial action in common. In the case of a firm its central activity is the organization of the production and marketing process, the elements of which are Smith's discrete sequence of specialized activities that have to be operated in a particular pattern if the purpose of the firm is to be met. Each individual production or marketing stage may be operated by a team in which case there must also be local rules for connecting their different roles to achieve the desired outcome. If that outcome is realized, then coordination, the correlation of efforts, has been achieved. The greater part of managerial effort is focused on these coordination tasks, and the preparation, transmission and interpretation of the information necessary for this.

The distinction between knowledge and information, between private knowing and shared understanding is important not only in relation to the process of organization in firms and markets but for what it implies about the process of changing knowledge. Organization is premised on a desire for order, for connections that achieve desired effects, yet the same processes give rise to reasons to transform those orders. For what information communicates is a representation of some pre-existing knowing with the intention of correlating understanding and thus behaviour. Yet continued progress depends on decorrelating prevailing states of understanding: only in the stationary state is human knowing fully correlated and at rest. Abandon the stationary state and the processes for decorrelating understanding are essential to the possibility of changes in the pattern of human knowing. These are truly processes of creative destruction in the epistemic realm. Because information is not knowledge its transmission gives rise to the potential that what is 'transmitted' is not always what is 'received', and it is this disjuncture that we usually associate with the entrepreneur or the paradigm-breaking scientist both of whom work within organized information systems and share in many elements of a common information flow, and yet come to understand that their respective worlds can be organized differently. The implication is that much that is conjecture in science as in enterprise turns out to be misguided. Imagination implies unpredictability of outcome and this 'experimental' dimension of modern economic systems is crucial to their ongoing development. Here lies one of the great fault lines in our understanding of the firm. On one side lies the need for its members to have the processes and understanding to maintain coherence and order, for predictability and the justification of results, the strand that appeals to rational behaviour. On the other side lies the need to incorporate processes that disrupt order, that bring the disruptive influence of innovation and novelty, that accept the importance of the unexpected and the irrational imagined. The fault line separates different modes of management and the balancing of the two is perhaps the greatest of managerial challenges. Without coherence immediate viability is threatened, without innovation longer term viability is undermined. That is the dilemma.

The restless nature of human knowing is at the core of a process of knowledge accumulation in which new understandings become emergent phenomena premised on the interacting creativity of specific individual minds.[3] If new knowledge is an emergent property of individual minds, correlated understanding is an emergent property of organized social systems, an emergent property contingent upon the correlating effects of organization and its instituted frames. Consequently, a distributed knowledge system is generative of order, the particular patterns of correlated understanding that underpin current action, and of the transformation of that order, the creation of new patterns of correlated understanding that underpin new patterns of action. This is the great importance of the line of reasoning that flows from specialization and the division of labour, the line that suggests that firms and markets are not only self organizing forms of organization but self transforming forms of organization. It is why we can speak, like Schumpeter, of the idea of *development from within*, perhaps the most important of the threads in the evolutionary economic tradition.

In relation to the firm in particular, this should cause one to pause carefully before representing the firm as a globally rational agency that is always in equilibrium with its environment. The equilibrium theory of the firm has a long tradition in neoclassical economic theory, where it is designed as one part of the theory of a stationary economy. Because of the static nature of the analysis it is of no intellectual cost to treat all the firms in an industry as identical, the uniform firm that is summarized by its (unexplained) cost curves. But the firm cannot be in equilibrium since there is no sense to be made of the idea of human knowing being in equilibrium, and so no sense to be made of knowledge-based organizations being in equilibrium. There are always pressing reasons to seek changes in knowledge even if the capacity to do so is very unevenly distributed. However, the resulting systems are not randomly ordered – their order reflects the structuring role of institutions and norms. It is this epistemic frame that leads us directly to the developing, evolving firm, but before exploring this idea in more detail it will help to locate our discussion within the broader idea of complexity.

COMPLEXITY

Many phenomena can be called complicated in terms of the difficulty the human mind has in describing and comprehending them in detail and scope, but this is not all that we have in mind when the idea of complexity is discussed. The idea of an economy as an interplay of countless consuming and producing activities, as portrayed by a general equilibrium system, or a more practical instantiation of an input output table is, of course, explicit recognition that an economy is a complicated system of parts and connections. Economics as a discipline has reflected the systemic complications of the real world for a long time, but addressing complication and addressing complexity are not the same thing. Rather, complexity is a dimension of systems that arises not only from the difficulty of enumerating the number of components and kinds of connection within the system, but from the difficulty in comprehending the significance of the connections. The creation of novelties in connections and parts is both the meaning of economic development and the essence of complexity; they are always historically embedded phenomena (Foster, 2011). Thus complexity means more than a difficulty in understanding a particular system; it is rather a unique property of a form of system dynamics, the property of generating emergent phenomena. Innovations and changes in knowledge are emergent phenomena, they are novelties, the occurrence and nature of which cannot be explained entirely by reference to particular causes, so emergence is necessarily connected to indeterminacy and uncertainty, to surprise, ignorance and wonder, to the language of history. Expressed so, emergence leads to the openness of systems, that there are emergents that did not exist in the past, which from the perspective of the past could not have been predicted.[4] The systems dimension makes the connection between development and emergent novelty, novelty that is not imposed from outside the operation of the system but arises from its internal operation. That is to say, complexity arises because economic systems are self-transforming as well as self-ordering, and the manner of their transformation is a consequence of the nature of their ordering processes. Order and transformation are rule based. The rules establishing locally reliable patterns of order impose a particular process of development, and if these rules are changed then so is the future evolution of the system.

The most important reason for subscribing to this view is that adduced above, namely that all forms of organization are knowledge-based systems dependent on intensive flows of specialized information between the many actors, and that the very operation of the system gives rise to new understandings, new beliefs and thus new possibilities for economic activity. The testing of these conjectured beliefs may lead to new, reliable economic knowledge but in so doing serves only to stimulate fresh conjectures as to how the economic world can be differently arranged. Such changes in human knowing arise from within the system; they depend on the distribution of experience and thus on the patterns of connection that coordinate different activities, and there is no obvious reason for them ever to cease.

If economies are problem-solving systems, the central problem being the scarcity of means relative to the attainment of the desired objectives of countless individuals, then we might say that the solution of problems serves only to define new problems, *ad infinitum*. Just as no one should plausibly expect any basis for the stagnation of scientific knowledge so no one should expect an end to the development of the many other forms of knowledge that shape economic activity. By this process the prevailing order is always open to unpredictable change such that the nature and composition of economic activity ten, twenty, a hundred years hence is simply beyond present understanding.

Complexity is a property of systems; and it places systems thinking within boundaries set by methodological individualism and holism. Individuals matter greatly in economic systems but so do the connections between them, and connections cannot be a property of any one individual. They must define a 'whole', with parts constituted by several individuals. It is fundamental to what follows that we understand that economic systems are based on relations between components. Thus the firm as an organized system is not an agglomeration of individuals arranged at random, rather it is purposefully structured to combine, that is, relate those individuals to achieve the desired effect as defined by its theory of action. We do not have to choose between holism and individualism, as Bunge (2003) has noted – systems thinking is an autonomous middle ground that can draw on both, indeed must draw on both. However, the pattern of connections is rarely complete in the sense that every element connects directly to every other element within the system, and this incompleteness is essential to understanding how systems differ. The sources of difference are threefold: differences in the elements within the system's boundary, differences in the pattern of connection, and differences in the meaning of connection.[5] Firm A differs from firm B, for example, precisely because they are combinations of different individuals and because they connect these individuals differently to generate different internal understandings of their functioning. Change the elements or the pattern of connections and we not only have a different firm, we have a firm that is on a different development trajectory. This is why stepping inside the black box matters, if we are to understand the reasons why firms evolve and develop differently. Indeed, much organizational change can be interpreted in terms of a reshaping of the connections between its operating units, changes that are designed to alter the future development path of the firm.

A taxonomy of systems is immediately in view, encompassing the enumeration of elements and the enumeration of connections and relations. Hayek (1967), for example, has defined complexity in terms of 'the minimum number of elements (components and connections) of which an instance of the pattern must consist in order to exhibit the entire range of characteristic attributes of the class of patterns in question.' In Hayek's understanding, complexity arises from incomprehension of whole patterns of interlinked behaviour, not individual events. The great difficulty lies in ascertaining all of the relevant data required to predict a particular instantiation of the whole patterns that a system can generate. Point prediction becomes impossible, and, instead, we are interested in the *ex post* relations between particular whole patterns and defined circumstances. These relations are a product of the particular rules that govern the formation of order within a system, as in the general theory of evolution which describes a process which is independent of the particular circumstances in which it takes place. In an evolutionary context, different circumstances would produce quite different outcomes within an invariant set of rules. At the base of Hayek's view is one brute fact, the ultimate unpredictability of human behaviour. No external observer can list all of the events that shaped a mind or spontaneous change of mind: hence, the ineluctable connection between complexity and the distributed nature of human ignorance. Distributed systems of knowing and not knowing are perhaps the most significant examples we have of complexity at work.

This line of reasoning ties complexity to the idea of complication beyond reason but this is only part of the meaning of complexity. The missing dimension is the link between complexity and the process of change that is a characteristic feature of complex systems. The fundamental point is that complex systems are evolving systems. Here it is useful to draw attention to a paper by John Foster (2005) on the epistemic base of economic systems. Foster spells out the fundamental issues with particular clarity by focusing on the architecture of complex systems expressed in terms of a fourfold schema, in which increases in complexity are linked to higher degrees of epistemic development. The simplest forms of system do not have the capacity to transform their internal structure; they are purely reactive automata whose survival prospects are not in their own command.[6] Hard wired systems of this kind are common in the worlds of nature and technological artifice, they can be complicated but they are not characteristic of human systems and social arrangements. These have the capacity to draw on the information flow emanating from their environment to generate new understandings of internal connections, or new components or changes in the characteristics of existing components. In turn, this epistemic capability generates a higher order of emergent complexity when we add the capacity to imagine new mental models, that is to say new theories of action that are products of experience. When the different mental models within a system interact with each other and are revised in relation to their performance we have reached Foster's fourth order complexity in which new ideas stimulate new ideas. It is a very accurate description of a modern, entrepreneurial economy, in which the capacity to imagine alternative economic worlds lies at the core of economic development but only because different imaginings are connected systemically. One might put it rather succinctly as enterprise stimulates enterprise, emergent novelty calls forth emergent novelty.[7] The importance of Foster's paper is to connect complexity with the epistemic realm of the human mind and its connections to other minds within a context of ignorance, partial knowing, indeterminacy and non computability.[8] Economic systems are complex because the knowledge systems on which they are unavoidably based are complex systems, systems that jointly evolve by changing boundaries, making and breaking connections and adding new components or subtracting preexisting components.

The discussion so far points to two puzzles connecting our interest in complexity to our interest in the developing firm. The first is the problem of stability and instability, the second is that of rationality. For a system to function at all there must be a minimal stability in its component parts and their interconnections, otherwise it ceases to be a coherent system. Order is needed to enable purpose (that of the functioning of the organization) and this is as true of an individual firm as it is of an industry or entire economy. Yet the development of a system depends on a capacity to add novel elements and make novel connections, and in this regard the system must be unstable enough to be open to invasion by innovations. Perhaps one of the most remarkable features of the instituted rules of modern capitalism is that stability in the large is consistent with innovation-based instability in the small.

There is an important connection here too with the limitations of Olympian rationality in any complexity-based analysis, although this is quite consistent with limited, local rationality in the sense of actors seeking to do the best they can when tying goals to immediate circumstances. The important point is not that action is rational in general but that it is locally and circumstantially rational and therefore different between individuals even when they act in similar circumstances. Such a pragmatic sense of rationality dispenses with invariant means ends relationships, and allows individuals to experiment and conjecture alternative possibilities, an evolutionary process of selection that is open ended and admits no steady states.

What is decisive in relation to the development of complex systems is selection between rival claims for the verisimilitude of conjectures, not optimization. Moreover, selection is only possible if we have variety creating processes generating novelties to be tested against the prevailing environment. As Hayek and Shackle have pointed out, this indeterminacy imposes a cost on human affairs, in that the future of knowledge-based systems is fundamentally uncertain. We cannot by the meaning of the words prefigure human knowing so we cannot predict who will innovate, or when or to what degree. We are simply ignorant of these novelty generating events. What we can form reasonable understandings about, are the processes involved in novelty creation and the processes of subsequent adaptation of the system to the imminent possibilities that are latent in emergent novelty. These are the processes that reflect most directly the instituted rules of each particular economic system, some of which are locally designed, others of which frame the whole spontaneous order of human interaction.

Whether we are speaking of a designed order as with a firm, or a spontaneous order as with a market process, we have to recognize that the boundaries between the two organizational forms are necessarily blurred. Yet the distinction is none the less pointing to a vitally important contrast between different ways in which the inconsistent plans of different individuals are reconciled. Moreover, a crucial feature of such spontaneous orders is their systemic breadth which takes them beyond the comprehension of any individual mind or group of minds, and the corollary that their development is entirely open and unpredictable in terms of specific details, even when the general order forming rules are unchanged. Firms, like markets, are capable of spontaneous orderings, and the central reason for this is that both forms of order are premised on the existence of networks of human relations, networks of connections that promote the flow of information and invite changes in human knowing. So the idea of a firm as a structured but incomplete network is paralleled by the notion of a market as a structured but incomplete network and in each case the structure shapes the pattern of information flow and thus the adaptive properties of the two kinds of network (Potts, 2000).[9]

THE DEVELOPMENT OF THE THEORY OF THE DEVELOPING FIRM

With these remarks in mind we can now begin to trace the evolution of the theory of the firm in economic theory from Marshall onwards. The start is promising: Marshall works with the developing, innovating firm reaping its quota of internal and external economies of expansion. That is to say, the firms that reshape the economic landscape are dynamic, expanding organizations. However, in the hands of Marshall's followers this developmental perspective is quickly tamed and we are left with the equilibrium firm, an automaton response mechanism, passively adjusting to factor and product prices over which signals it has no control. This is Foster's lowest order of organization. The reason for this change in the nature of the theory of the firm is very clear: Marshall's followers changed the economic question, substituting the analysis of the stationary state for the analysis of economic evolution and development which was Marshall's aim. To be clear, in the context of stationary analysis, the treatment of each firm in terms of an identical cost function along the lines subsequently specified by Pigou and Viner is not at all out of place. Once we turn to the questions of evolution and development, however, it becomes entirely inadequate. This is not because pricing and cost behaviour become irrelevant, far from it, but rather because the firm has to be understood in terms of many more dimensions than that.

All of Marshall's insistent emphasis on differences between firms even in the same line of competition, and these differences are his chief source of (evolutionary) progress, is rendered obsolete in a non evolving industry and economy.[10] In a stationary state there is no evolution and so by construction all firms in an industry have to be the same, know the same facts and operate with the same theories of action. This is not Marshall's world.

Several features of Marshall's approach need to be highlighted. The first is the central place that he gives to knowledge aided by organization as the principal sources of economic progress. Organization, in turn, is a matter of managing the division of labour within and between firms and, crucially, the tasks of management are also subjected to the growth of specialized knowledge and a division of labour (Loasby, 1989, 2006; Metcalfe, 2006, 2007; Nelson, 1991). The growth of specialized functions is a consequence of the increasing complexity of large scale business affairs, the development that makes 'handicraft' managerial methods quite inappropriate to the task of modern business management. This requires a new division of administrative labour, premised on organizational innovation, with specialized business leaders who collectively undertake risks, bring together capital and labour, engineer the general plan and superintend the details of the business. The distinguishing feature of these tasks is the distinctive knowledge and specialized mental effort that they entail. Management in its new forms is a matter for the intellect and involves much more than the superintendence of labour.

Managerial services fall within two broad categories of action: first, the ability to appoint and lead a team of subordinates and to make the most of their abilities while preserving order and unity in the plan of the business; and, secondly, to 'know the trade'. By this short phrase, Marshall means activities that are closely tied to enterprise and innovation, and included in this category are the ability to forecast demand (expectations, as always, play an important role in Marshall's assessment of how people act and different individuals hold substantively different expectations[11]), the facility to judge risks boldly but with care, and, finally, the capacity to innovate through the perception of opportunities to supply new commodities or improve methods of production. Thus Marshall's organic view of the managerial team, consisting of grades of different ability carrying out interlinked, networked tasks, organized on different lines, whether partnerships or private companies, but always held together by business leadership.

In *Industry and Trade*, (1919), the list of attributes of business leaders and their chief subordinates is spelled out even more clearly, as follows: the personal qualities of judgement and enterprise, prudence and fortitude in risk making; an alertness to adopting new techniques and initiating them; a high power of organization; the ability to read and handle character in subordinates; and, finally, the skill to allocate employees to tasks to which they are most suited. All of these are needed even in a business of moderate size and a fortiori in the larger business they are required by the senior management team and its head in particular.[12] It cannot be said that Marshall did not have innovation and enterprise very firmly in his grasp when he wrote about the distinctive contribution of management to economic organization.

In passing we should also note a significant addition to Marshall's treatment of management that appears in *Industry and Trade*, namely his treatment of the growth of the scientific management movement and its implications for work and the organization of the firm. The central theme is a familiar one, namely the organization and management of the flow of information required to coordinate the division of labour in a firm, but Marshall goes to great lengths to explain how greater information and its organization through new principles of work allocation and evaluation allows further rationalization of the division of labour. Cost accounting is one example but the chief exhibit is the work of F.W. Taylor, for it leads to a possibility not previously considered, namely, a deeper division of labour between the physical work, 'the doing' and the mental work, 'the planning', the former distributed but the latter centralized.[13]

The distinctive role of planning and the conception of alternative futures for a firm is now identified as a task of the senior management team, and it is clear that Marshall considers the rise of professional management to give further advantages to the large scale organization, where the head can be devoted to 'the broadest and most fundamental problems of his trade' neither troubled with details nor with routine work but 'keeping his mind fresh and clear *for thinking out* [our emphasis] the most difficult and vital problems of his business' (*Principles*, IV, 11, p. 284). While the smaller business may have some advantages of direction and close control of fine detail, its most fundamental disadvantage is in making experiments (innovating) so that the small business must generally follow rather than lead. Here we see the logical division between the control of an existing business and the ability to change the business in technique, organization or market. It constitutes today a central managerial dichotomy. As always, Marshall's non essentialist approach leads to important qualifications. The small business, exceptionally, may become large by overcoming formidable barriers. To do so, the business leader must adapt to the larger sphere, must retain his 'originality and versatility, his perseverance, his tact and his good luck for very many years together' (*Principles*, IV, 9, p. 285) so that a larger market can be secured, credit established, and subordinates attracted of more than ordinary zeal and ability. Bad luck may thwart such efforts and the ultimate barrier to growth may be decay if not of the faculties then of the willingness to work hard. In Marshall, great stress is placed on the elemental fact that time is the ultimate scarce resource at the disposal of the individual.

There is a further factor in favour of the exceptional small business – its access to external knowledge in the form of scientific, technical and trade literature that may substitute for the internal allocation of resources to innovation. This raises the important Marshallian idea of the external connectedness of the firm not only to its product and factor markets but more broadly to the relevant innovation systems. External economies, however, do not come for free. The firm must organize itself to gather the advantages that are available and we are left in no doubt that different firms differ in their ability to form and to capitalize on these external network relationships. That is to say, the differential reaping of external economies is a reflection of differential managerial ability. Two forms of external relationship are given particular emphasis by Marshall and both are premised on networked relationships, namely the industrial district and the innovation system.[14] In relation to the latter Marshall is very explicit about the different kinds of actors in innovation systems, universities and other research intermediaries as well as firms with technical laboratories, and the importance of how the different actors interconnect in the solution of innovation problems. Thus external economies in Marshall are not an answer to a problem of how competitive conditions can be rendered safe from the depredations of increasing returns but an answer to a quite different set of questions about the development path of a firm and the growth of its knowledge.

There is a final dimension to Marshall's theory that it is important to recognize: not only do firms vary in multiple dimensions, but the scope and dimensionality of these variations varies over time. This is the famous imagery of the trees in the forest, the perception that firms are developing differentially, the hint that ambition and adaptive ability are not timeless attributes of a management team. No subsequent orthodox economist of note accepted this imagery because their purpose was not Marshall's purpose, they had lost the evolutionary, adaptive perspective with differentiated, developing firms, and at great cost. It has taken many years for Marshall's threads to be picked up again.

One of the first so to do was Kenneth Boulding (1951) who, drawing on the emerging self organization and cybernetics literature of the time, picks up on Marshall's themes of the role of organization, management and the growth of knowledge. Boulding (1951) starts from the premise of the impossible information requirements implicit in profit maximizing behaviour, and the need for a research agenda that connects with how firms operate in reality. How they operate is intimately connected to what they can be said to know and thus becomes a question of the relation between organization, flows of information and the growth of understanding within the firm.

Boulding's firm is part of a more general theory of organization premised on the idea of self-ordering behaviour such as is provided by a theory of homeostasis, which entails the negative feedback control of decision variables within upper and lower bounds. In this sense, it is a forerunner of Simon's satisfycing theory of decision making. Stabilization requires a control mechanism, and the theory of control points to several key elements, namely, sensors and information receptors, communication channels, decision makers and nodes, and effectors who take instructions from the decision makers.

From this perspective Boulding's firm is a connected structure for generating and processing information. The points of decision are the effective components of the firm and the channels through which information flows constitute the pattern of connectivity, the twin elements of organizational structure in terms of who is informed of what, within an authority structure indicating who each individual responds too. Here Boulding is making an important distinction between the gathering of information in the course of a firm's day to day activities and the pattern of communication of that information, which is a matter of deliberate decision. Thus the central implication of this systemic view of the firm, that it can only react to and change decisions on the basis of the information it has chosen to gather and communicate is a natural reflection of its theory of action and its current state of knowing.

There are two qualifications to this model that need to be highlighted. Some information is generated externally to the firm, yet it can be of significance for decisions and actions. As in Marshall, the firm needs its external organization of sensors and communication channels, as provided by sales staff who interact with customers, or service staff who correct faults for customers, and these must be integrated into the internal control structure. Secondly, it is insufficient to argue that a change of information alone is the *sine qua non* of a change in decision, as probability-based decision theory articulates. Beliefs can also change independently of the flow of information, once we allow decision makers to have mental frames that develop as a result of introspection and those internal processes of the mind that are the essence of much that we call the exercise of imagination. New information is neither necessary nor sufficient for a development in understanding and we must not assume that the failure to receive new information is the sole reason for inaction. Thus the importance of the theories that decision makers hold in determining what is deemed to be relevant information. Change in the operating business theory at different levels of the firm becomes the basis for innovation in method or organization or market focus.

A further development, very much in line with the Boulding approach, is contained in Arrow (1974). Arrow starts from the same position as Marshall and Boulding: coordinated action in common requires understanding in common and this requires the exchange and interpretation of information. The most important aspect of Arrow's argument is the idea that the organization of the firm, Boulding's control structure, does not come for free – it is a matter of investment and of the design of communication channels and decision nodes. Since information is scarce, it requires costly activities to gather, process, and communicate, and these costs have the characteristic of fixed costs in relation to the degree to which information is used in the firm's activities. Three aspects of these costs are singled out as being of particular importance: the limited capacity of individuals to gather and interpret information; the capital costs of establishing communication codes to interpret and transmit information; and the costs of establishing the firm's own specialized language and interpretive conventions. Information costs are not equal in all directions. The fact that firms differ in their internal communication codes and structures is not unrelated to the fact that the founders of the firm start from distinctive knowledge and expectation of what the firm will be. The irreversibility of the investment is productive of inertia so that we can interpret these possibilities of sunk costs and path dependence as a further part of the story of inter-firm differentiation. That different firms have different codes also reflects the combinatorial richness in the possible set of codes and the scope for effectively unlimited variation of practice.

RONALD COASE AND THE BOUNDARIES QUESTION

By drawing attention to communication structures and information flows Boulding and Arrow are implicitly focusing on the network of connections within an organizational system. But as with any network, there is always a question of those connections that are internal to the firm and those that connect it to its external environment, the old Marshallian issue of how a firm is to gain access to external economies. It is standard practice in economics to argue that firms and markets are a different form of instituted human organization: in the one, concentrated administrative authority controls the disposition of resources; while in the other, that function is taken over by the distributed price mechanism. What determines the boundary between the two forms of organization? Why, instead of being under the control of one large integrated unit of managerial control, might activities be divided between many independent firms who make their transactions through markets? This is the famous question addressed by Ronald Coase (1937) and it has a considerable bearing on the operation of complex systems precisely because it impinges on the drawing of boundaries.

Let us note first that Coase is not asking why there are firms. Firms, like households, are specialized organizations, designed to do what markets cannot do, that is, they conduct transformational activities of their choosing. Thus the answer to the question 'Why do firms exist?' is no more complicated than the claim that they are organizations to facilitate production. This is understood most transparently in a hypothetical, minimalist circular flow economy where single proprietor, single employee firms produce final goods and utilize markets to sell them to households and to buy the factor inputs that households supply (Knight, 1951). This is the economics of the division of labour, not in Smith's sense of the internal operation of the firm but in terms of the operation of an economic system as a whole in which each household is far less specialized in its consumption than is each firm in its production. Households and firms are the transforming organizations, markets for goods and productive factors are the transacting organizations. They are simply not of the same kind.[15] As McNulty (1968) astutely observes, it is firms who ultimately decide not only how to produce but what to produce and in this role they have no peer. We might equally say of households that they decide what to use and how to use it to satisfy their needs. The firms and households could be one and the same in the sense that every proprietor/employee is also a member of some household but no one, we imagine, has argued that the boundaries between firms and households are a problem worthy of investigation.

But this is not the issue that concerns Coase; he is far more attentive to the significance of the roundabout division of labour in a modern production system in which many firms produce means of production (steel billets, basic chemicals, accounting services and machine tools) that are sold not to households but to other firms. Coase's question is, when do firms bring these intermediate production stages in house and when do they rely on a supply chain market mediated or filiere arrangement? That is to say, how do they choose to balance internal and external relationships? His answer is a powerful evocation of the marginal principle and is in two parts. First, just as the internal articulation of transformation activities generates coordination as well as production costs for the firm, so the transactional activities that must be performed to operate a market generate coordination and production costs in relation to transactions services. These so-called transaction costs are charges over and above the supply price posted by an external supplier and include the costs of acquiring price information, the costs of writing and enforcing contracts and any taxes or other imposts on market transactions. Secondly, the boundary of the firm is determined by a marginal comparison of these alternative costs of organization, leading to the general principle that the range of the firm's activities are extended up to the point where the internal costs of performing the marginal activity are equal to the costs of acquiring the particular good or service in a market transaction. This means of course that a firm only sources externally from a supplier who can conduct the activity more cheaply, the difference in production costs being necessary to defray the costs of transacting. The corollary is clear: if all firms were equally efficient in all their activities, all the activities would be conducted in house with no resort to the market. It is the fact that the clock maker is not as efficient at rolling brass sheet as the brass founder that makes the symbiosis of firm and market so relevant. It is a natural consequence of the division of knowing. Notice also that this is a claim in relation to the size of the firm, measured not in terms of its scale of final output but rather in terms of the number of activities that lie within its managerial boundary.

Within Coase's framework, a firm with a given rate of output may be large or small according to the net advantages of internal versus external sourcing of a range of complementary activities that contribute to its chosen stage of production. In its essentials, this is an argument about the scope for vertical integration in the complementary activities that turn resources into goods and goods into consumer satisfactions. Moreover, the make or buy decision is only one way of altering the boundary of the firm. The market for corporate control provides another very important route to change the composition of a firm's activities, by buying and selling the relevant business units – a procedure that is very relevant to the innovation process. To the extent that changing the boundary of a firm requires it to invest in or divest activities, that firm depends upon the working of the capital market and Coase is implicitly considering a case in which finance is not a constraint on the broader operation of his marginal principle. However, if funds are limited, the choice becomes dependent not simply on the net gains from integration but on these relative to the net gains from that alternative project which is squeezed out by the Coaseian boundary changing project. Different firms may legitimately be differentially placed to make these decisions, thus adding a further source of variety to the organization of economic activity.

From our perspective it is very important to recognize Coase's claims that his is a dynamic principle of shifting boundaries between hierarchy and market. Changes in technology, particularly changes in information technology, transport technology and the technology of managerial control may radically shift the balance of net advantages between internal activation and external sourcing. So, as Stigler (1951) subsequently pointed out, the principles underlying the division of labour and the distribution of increasing returns to particular sub activities play a major role in shaping the boundaries of a firm. In particular, an activity that is subject to increasing returns is a likely candidate for outsourcing by the majority of firms, while one that is subject to diminishing returns is likely to be operated internally by a majority of firms. In this way the balance of relative advantages changes with the growth of the economy as a whole, and with the differential growth of the broad branches within it. This echo of Allyn Young's (1928) famous argument is an important aspect of any systems dynamics perspective on economic development. There is yet a further way in which Coase's argument is dynamic, in that bringing activities within the boundary of managerial control leads to new experiences in operating activity and thus to the potential growth of new knowledge, with further implications for the cost structure and boundaries of the firm. From this angle the firm is to be construed as a centre for learning and knowledge acquisition, and where this knowledge is deemed to be part of its proprietary advantage there will be powerful reasons not to outsource it to another supplier.

Coase's justly celebrated account of the economics of organization in the broadest sense provides ample material for understanding why firms may be differentiated in terms of the activities they undertake, and how the balance of internal versus external sourcing may be reflected in the differential costs of production or the quality of final output. The link between the firm's boundaries and the growth of its knowledge also provides a powerful continuing source of differentiation: if firms organize differently, they must be expected to learn and accumulate knowledge differently. Indeed if we lose sight of this connection between the growth of knowledge and the structure of economic organization we risk nullifying the importance of the dynamics of the division of labour as a method of distributing the accumulation of experience and thus understanding. It is to Edith Penrose that we turn to bring this line of reasoning to fruition.

THE REVIVAL OF COMPLEXITY: EDITH PENROSE AND THE RESTLESS FIRM

It is Edith Penrose in her *Theory of the Growth of the Firm* (1959) who returns us to the Marshallian tradition in which the firm derives its importance within a long period perspective linking profits, investment behaviour and innovation. Penrose's firm is not in equilibrium, there are always endogenously generated possibilities for its further development. Such opportunities are necessarily generated differently in different firms and acted upon differentially by them according to the distribution of entrepreneurial vigour and managerial capability. The essential point is that the firm develops because its managerial team is always gaining experience, experience which develops their capabilities and opens up opportunities for expansion. This is the epistemic dynamic of a distributed knowledge system outlined above. Thus the fundamental reason why the Penroseian firm is not an equilibrium firm is that no meaning is to be attached to the idea that knowledge can be in equilibrium. Penrose's managers are living individuals operating in a world of continual information flux, not uniform automata.

The Penroseian firm is defined by the boundaries of its administrative organization, as in Coase, within which it controls the disposition of bundles of resources that it either owns or rents from the market. The physical resources are not the inputs into the productive process, rather they are funds from which heterogeneous services are drawn, and the services that are so drawn from any one resource depend on the complementary services that are available to the firm. Thus the services derived from any given manager in a given time interval, for instance, are not simply an invariant property of that manager but rather they are a potential that is to be realized, a potential which depends on the surrounding managerial team and organizational context and which in its realization changes the ability of that manager. In short, they depend on who that manager is connected to. This is the nub of her link between the development of the firm and the development of its managerial team. As in Marshall, management is the basis of performance, and management is an integrated team activity dependent on the practice of working together. This is not incompatible with the idea that the firm is a bundle of contracts but it is essential to the argument that the contracts as to what services come from what resources cannot be perfectly specified, and they cannot be perfectly specified because the conduct of the activity in the business changes the entities in the contractual relationship. Thus it is more accurate to say that Penrose's firm is a bundle of relationships jointly partaking in decision making rather than a bundle of contracts. It is a view that gravitates naturally to the emphasis given by Nelson and Winter (1982) to firms as bundles of interdependent routines.

The logic of firm differentiation and development follows immediately once we recognize the epistemic element in Penrose's theory. In order to operate effectively, the management team must develop a coherent sense of common understanding as to their respective duties and how these are to be coordinated in the organization. Correlation of understanding, as we explained above, is essential for the performance of any activity. But performance changes individual knowing and gives rise to new understandings in the form of unexploited, latent managerial services for the firm to act upon. Thus, Penrose's firm is neither an equilibrium firm nor a uniform firm and it is this fact which makes managerial strategy meaningful. Enterprise in this scheme involves the decorrelation of understanding, the conception of alternative ways of conducting the activities of a firm and of putting the new perspectives into effect. Enterprise, like management, is multi dimensional and a given team may vary in its entrepreneurial versatility, fund raising ingenuity, ambition, and judgement in assessing and taking risks, all dimensions that impinge heavily on the development of the firm. If enterprise and innovation are at the core of what we mean by economic development then a theory of development needs a Penrose style theory of the firm.

The development of the firm will usually involve growth of scale and with it the discovery of new opportunities for specialization and co-ordination within and between activities. Here there is a degree of interdependence between those external factors creating opportunities for growth and the internal factors that are at the core of her discussion. The net outcome is the creation of growth and development opportunities that depend on how other firms are simultaneously creating their own developmental possibilities and how these differences are resolved in the market process. How one manager develops relatively to another manager is mirrored in the question of how one firm develops relatively to another. The firm is an unfolding entity and its unfolding depends on its internal organizational form and on the competitive interaction with its rivals. Complexity means that markets and firms cannot be separated from a developmental viewpoint.

The importance of Penrose's contribution lies not only in bringing management back into an understanding of why firms differ but in making the link between the Marshallian competitive process tradition and the more recent development of a strategic view of the firm expressed in terms of the articulation and development of capabilities.

G.B. RICHARDSON: CAPABILITIES AND THE DEVELOPING FIRM

A particularly rich and persuasive enunciation of this theme is due to G.B. Richardson (1972). Richardson begins with the Coase question, 'Why is the internal/external boundary of the firm drawn in a particular way?' but articulates the answer so as to privilege the many different ways in which the components of an economic system can be connected. At one extreme lies the spontaneous order of spot market transactions, those transactions that imply no obligations as to the future conduct of the contracting parties. But these are not exhaustive of the possible external connections: there are many other intermediate forms of cooperative arrangement, that are found in practice and range from sub contracting to formal arrangements to cooperate in the conduct of some activity such as the development of a particular technology, or to supply a very specific quality of a productive input. The chief characteristic of these intermediate forms is that they entail investment by both parties in the sense of current outlay made in anticipation of returns in a more distant future.

Here we might add to Richardson's argument. If the system of spot markets were complemented by a system of futures markets then many of these intermediate forms of cooperation would be rendered unnecessary but this is not the case. The set of futures markets is virtually empty and it is so precisely because of uncertainty and ignorance about the future which prevents the specification of the terms of a future contract. How can you place an order today for a specified quantity of an unspecified commodity, one that has yet to be invented? The solution is the formation of cooperative connections to substitute for the absence of futures markets, connections that are particularly important when coordination of the qualitative characteristics of a good as well as its quantitative characteristics is important. Such forms of connectivity provide the assurance that would otherwise be given by a futures contract but they do so by generating mutual obligations as to what is appropriate conduct of the parties. This is the dimension in which they differ from spot contracts; they are instituted connecting devices to give a degree of confidence and certainty by generating information and correlating understanding to a degree that would otherwise not be available.[16]

The second strand of Richardson's argument relates more to the internal connections of the firm for it explains why different firms have comparative advantages in the performance of different activities, and therefore tend to specialize in those activities. The clue is to be found in the idea of capabilities, broadly defined, as in Marshall, in terms of 'the roles of organization, knowledge, experience and skills' (Richardson, 1972: 888) that define the activities a firm can articulate and turn to profit. Activities that depend on the same capabilities are called similar activities even if they may be productive of dissimilar products serving dissimilar market demands. As in Penrose, particular bundles of capabilities define an expansion path for a business which, if followed, is productive of new experiences, new understandings and knowledge and thus new patterns of connection within the firm. Specialization invokes a dynamic process, not a state of unchanging affairs. The fact that different firms tend to be specialized around similar activities then creates the problem of how complementary activities that depend on different capabilities are to be coordinated and so brings us back to Richardson's, and indeed Adam Smith's, initial question.

There is space to mention here only one of many developments in the capabilities perspective on the firm. Nelson and Winter have produced a very influential account of the firm interpreted as a bundle of interacting routines (rules for action), predicated on the capabilities as Richardson has defined them. Within their evolutionary framework, the articulation of different routine bundles gives each firm a different economic signature. Each routine relates to some task, cognitive or physical, within a specific activity, and provides the instructions for action according to the circumstances prevailing (Nelson and Winter, 1982; Dosi and Marengo, 1994). But routines do not operate in isolation and the important point is that the firm's behaviour depends upon the interaction and connectivity between its bundles of routines; capability is something which relates to the integration and joint operation of routines. Hence it is not always possible to link specific behaviours to single routines for the reasons that Arrow drew attention to. For one thing routines vary considerably in the specificity of the action they stimulate and in the nature of the information by which they are triggered. Certain routines may brook no deviation from a performance template and be entirely automatic in operation, being invoked purely by habit. Other routines may admit a great deal of interpretative flexibility so that the outcome varies with the individual or team performing the routine, and the other teams with which they interact. This is particularly likely with respect to the sets of higher level routines, such as those which guide innovative activities, since their purpose is to encourage and accommodate creativity.

WIDER SYSTEM BOUNDARIES

As a way to understanding the processes of firm differentiation through innovation, the capabilities literature has proved to be remarkably fruitful, but a careful consideration of Penrose's and Marshall's analysis of the self transformation of the firm demonstrates that these internal processes have to fit with an analysis of the external environment. As with our discussion of Coase and Richardson we have to cross the boundary and acknowledge the wider system in which any firm is embedded. This is particularly important in assessing how firms experience differential success in accessing resources and customers, and indeed in their attempts to shape market institutions to their advantage. Here, we can draw a connection with the analysis of Schumpeter (1934 and 1942) where he focuses on the difficulties faced by the enterprising firm in finding room for itself in an existing order. The difficulties are twofold: to raise the capital to exploit the innovation and to convince sceptical consumers to change their expenditure pattern in favour of the innovator. Neither difficulty is straightforward to address, the order maintaining properties of a prevailing system create barriers to protect it from invasion by novelties, and this is why Schumpeter puts so much emphasis on the exceptional qualities of the entrepreneur in overcoming hostility to that which is new. Entrepreneurs need not only to imagine differently, they need to have the differential leadership capacity to bring their plans to fruition (Witt, 1998). Thus, for example, in the case of a firm's financing requirements, it is because the entrepreneur's knowledge is distinctive and novel that it can be only imperfectly understood by external parties. There is an inherent barrier to the willingness to provide finance to the entrepreneur so that they can wrest control of productive resources from other firms, and the entrepreneur may require exceptional powers of persuasion to overcome this differential understanding.[17]

Steindl (1945) goes further and argues that the access of entrepreneurs to finance is also limited by their own private wealth. The skewed distribution of private wealth then restricts the ability of most entrepreneurs to take advantage of economies of scale through the division of labour within the firm. Successful entrepreneurs earn profits that allow their firms to grow through reinvesting the profits in expanding productive capacity (internal accumulation). However, this is a slow process and, as a result, many firms fail to fully exploit economies of scale, and firms that do achieve large size are able to earn above average profits for extended periods of time.

Entrepreneurs also face resistance from buyers for innovative products, when products are sold into new markets and even when established products are sold for new purposes. This is clearly a problem of divergent knowledge sets that limits the rate at which a firm can connect to new customers. To overcome resistance, entrepreneurs provide free information for the buyers or provide inducements to the buyers (for example, free samples or advertisements attached to free entertainment), hence the role of modern marketing. A special case of overcoming the resistance of buyers occurs where innovation takes the form of reducing production costs. Even when products are relatively homogenous, the innovator needs to win over the custom from other suppliers. This generally requires price reductions or costly inducements (for example, free delivery or better payment terms). Yet, the innovator can accept the lower prices or higher distribution costs due to its advantage in production costs, something the rivals can't afford to match. Where there are unexploited internal economies of scale, the innovator's advantage increases over time as higher sales volume begets even lower production cost. Both Marshall and Schumpeter recognized and were troubled by the growth potential of large firms, especially as research and development activities become dominated by the laboratories of large firms in at least some industries. The ability to generate new products in the laboratories together with the deployment of managerial capabilities to related lines of business, as suggested by Penrose, mean that the innovating and enterprising firm can overcome the external limits associated with the size of individual product markets, which implies a theory of the firm in which growth and dominance are irresistible outcomes of the self transformation of innovating and enterprising firms.

These are not peripheral concerns. The ability of some firms to acquire capabilities that transcend managerial limits on size destroys the possibility of perfect competition and all the implications this has for economic theory. Evolutionary economics has no problems with increasing returns but recognizes an important question. What is it about the environment, if anything, that can create external limits to growth to balance alongside the familiar Penrosian internal limits? Bloch and Finch (2010) point to the unresolved tension in Marshall regarding the limits to the firm's size and growth. In the *Principles of Economics*, Marshall (1920, p.287) suggests a natural limit is imposed by the decay of entrepreneurial faculties over generations, where the third generation of managers lack the personal motivation, commitment and vigour of the founders. While this sociological approach perhaps has merit for family firms, in *Industry and Trade*, Marshall

(1919) recognizes the influence of scientific management and joint stock companies as factors negating the influence of the individual on the fate of firms. Whether there are other factors that limit the growth of joint stock companies is not clarified. In effect, the distributed nature of knowledge justifies Marshall's ambiguity. Firms are irreducibly heterogeneous in multiple dimensions as noted above: they make different investment choices; they make different choices as to the markets they compete in; different choices over where to locate their plants; and, perhaps most crucially of all, they innovate differently. Thus some firms will excel in marketing, others in technology development, still others in supply chain management. It is these sources of differentiation that generate the variety which renders competition an evolutionary process rather than a state of equilibrium affairs. Moreover, because different firms act differently, they experience economic activity differently and they generate new knowledge differently, in the style emphasized by Marshall, Schumpeter and Penrose.

The interaction of the forces destroying and creating order is reflected in the statistics of the size distribution of firms in any industry. The implication of a theory of uniform firms is that the variance of firm size is zero, but this could not be further from the facts of the matter. The contrast to firm size distributions exhibiting substantial variance when knowledge is distributed unevenly across firms is a direct implication of Schumpeter's concept of creative destruction. Creative destruction is the process by which innovating firms displace established producers in the market order and impose patterns of growth and decline both absolute and relative across the population of rival producers, so creating a variance in firm size. Steindl (1976) also analyses the effect of differential production costs on increasing concentration, with firms moderating their investment to expand productive capacity as industry concentration grows. He associates the moderation of investment with a process he terms 'industry maturity'. This captures in a prosaic way the notion that learning can occur at a level beyond the individual firm, as might be expected in a complex system undergoing continual development.

The fundamental empirical fact about the size distribution of firms is that they are highly skewed and this skewness is a product of the wide variety in the growth paths realized by different firms. It is vital to grasp that growth opportunities are very unevenly distributed and that only a very few firms out of the many grow to any significant relative size in an industry or indeed its separate market segments. But it is the outlying members of the 'fat tails' that provide the overwhelming evolutionary impulses for economic change and development. Exceptional firms, like Schumpeter's exceptional entrepreneurs, are precisely that: exceptional and thus relatively rare. Evolution is driven by the few not the many, but no one can accurately predict which of a given cohort of firms will have greatness thrust upon them. That is the view that we are inevitably drawn to when we combine evolutionary and systems thinking.

CONCLUDING REMARKS

We began this chapter with a series of claims about the nature of a complex evolving economy. In the light of these claims, we have sought to demonstrate that the developing firm is a system within systems of higher orders of complexity. Complexity has two characteristics, the property of complication, which is a consequence of the multiple differentiated components at each system level, and the combinatorial ways that they can be imperfectly connected (Potts, 2000). The consequence of imperfect connectivity is the vast number of different ways that disturbances within a system are transmitted to its different elements; unpredictability in this sense is the consequence of not knowing the whole system. But complication is not enough, the characteristic of complex economic and social systems is that they are self transforming and they are self transforming because they are epistemic systems with multiple parts and combinatorially incomplete connections. Emergent knowledge for the individual, and emergent correlated understanding for the group, are the deep consequences of this systemic view. Such systems can never be in equilibrium because their movement through time serves only to generate different patterns of knowing and understanding. Firm and economy are restless because human knowing is restless. The nature of emergence is that neither the list of system components, nor their individual characteristics nor their pattern of interconnectivity are ever stationary. The theories of the firm promulgated by Marshall, Penrose and the others discussed here are systemic theories that comprehended the complex, epistemic nature of the firm from the outset. The fundamental difference they highlighted is that between the passive and the active firm. The difference as Schumpeter expressed it is between creative action or response, and adaptive action or response contingent on whether or not we are considering 'the doing of new things or the doing of things that are already being done in a new way' (Schumpeter, 1947: 151). Passive adaptation is not absent from the conventional theory of the firm, indeed it is essential to it, but it is treated as an automatic response when, in fact, adaptation is neither automatic nor certain. As we have already pointed out, passive adaptation is the lowest rung on the ladder of responsive behaviour.

If we are to understand the rate and direction of economic development, we need a higher level of intelligence from the firm. Such an understanding must also comprehend the reasons not to adapt and create, the reasons why the need to maintain the existing activity and organization sets limits on what can be changed within any time interval. Adaptation and innovation are certainly not to be presumed, and as we have pointed out above, the capacity to achieve them is very unevenly distributed across the firms in an economy. This is the force of the claim that each firm is a unique individual but that its individuality changes with the passage of time and is dependent at each point in time on its internal organization of a particular set of individuals, their knowledge and skills.

Much of what we have highlighted is an elementary consequence of the division of labour and its necessary coordination through processes of connection. This suggests an important feature, namely, that the economic system contains more adaptive capability than its individual firm components precisely and only because those firms are different and because their heterogeneity extends in many dimensions. It is central to the case made for the benefits of a market economy that there are multiple and autonomous sources of adaptability and innovation, giving to the system more enduring survival and developmental prospects than its component parts. It suggests a remarkable feature of any economic system, capitalism in particular, that the rules that provide it with a capacity to self-organize the division of labour are the same rules that create the incentives to transform that division of labour. There cannot usefully be a separate theory of statics and a separate theory of dynamics for we are always dealing with inseparable phenomena: economic order and transformation have to be understood as the direct consequences of one another not as separate, non-communicating economic phenomena. That is the most important lesson to be drawn from the economic systems perspective.

NOTES

1. A theme that Mokyr (1990, 2002) has developed with great effect.
2. The literature on the strategic theory of the firm is vast and ever growing. We can deal neither with it nor with the complementary reasoning of Herbert Simon and the Carnegie School in this chapter, though we hope the connections will be clear to a management scholar.
3. See Bunge (2003) for an extended discussion of emergence and its twin strands, qualitative novelty and unpredictability of the relation between lower and higher levels in a system.
4. See Lovejoy (1927) for a thorough discussion of the concept of emergence. Shackle (1966) also makes the connection between the possibility of emergence, interpreted as non-deterministic history, and the non-illusory nature of human decision making, 'a history that is to say, in which we need not regard every situation or event as the inevitable, sole and necessary consequence of antecedent situations or events' (p. 107). As he goes on to say, emergence is not chaos but rather a consequence of the particular form of order that is an economy. This is very much the theme of this chapter, that prevailing and emergent structures are squabbling twins. See also Shackle (1961) Part 1. For an illuminating discussion of Shackle's thought in relation to his theory of the firm, consult Loasby (2010).
5. Jason Potts (2000) has explored the significance of incomplete connectivity, contrasting it with the complete connectivity of general equilibrium theory. Paradoxically, as he points out, the complete connectivity of large economic systems in which each agent is a price taker allows the analyst to ignore connectivity completely. See Chapter 3, in particular, for a detailed elaboration of this contrast between fully connected and imperfectly connected systems.
6. Hayek (1973) uses the example of a crystal to illustrate the occurrence of complexity in nature.
7. Recent developments in computational science have made clear the superior problem solving capabilities of networks of computers but this is a latter day elaboration of the old principle of the benefits to be found in the division of labour, or rather the interconnection of local pools of differentiated knowledge and capability. On the connection with the development of evolutionary computing systems (super Turing computational systems), consult Wiedermann and van Leeuwen (2002).
8. On complexity as non computability, as distinct from greater computing effort, see Boschetti and Gray (2007).
9. As Potts points out, the functioning of a complex system is a reflection of the imperfect connectivity of agents who are largely ignorant of the wider context in which they operate – that they know the few relevant things, not everything. There are connections here with Smith's division of labour, with Simon's idea of decomposable systems and Kauffman's idea of a system boundary between order and disorder. See p. 97 *et seq.* for further discussion.
10. The reader might here recall Chamberlin's struggles to free the firm from the straitjacket of uniformity (Chamberlin, 1933). His firms are meant to be differentiated by the product produced but when it comes to his group analysis they produce the same products with identical production methods. This left his analysis wide open to the Chicago critique that it added nothing to that which was already known from the extremes of monopoly and perfect competition. More precisely it adds nothing to an equilibrium scheme of competition and the firm. See the excellent discussion in Triffin (1941) and Robinson (1971).
11. See Loasby (1990) for further elaboration. We note in passing that a business does not expect to make profits, or losses for that matter, by having the same expectations as rivals. At a minimum, rational expectations in relation to business prospects must mean variform expectations.
12. *Industry and Trade*, II, 10: 355.
13. See Whitaker (1999) for extended discussion of Marshall's attitude to the Taylorism movement.
14. Marshall's writing on industrial districts is rather more familiar than his writing on innovation systems. For an introduction to a large literature on the former see Becattini (2006).
15. It is for this reason that we have little sympathy with the Arrow (1974) inspired view that firms are a response to market failures or with its surely implicit corollary that markets are a response to firm failures. Neither firms nor markets are perfect answers to the questions they are designed to address and if asymmetric understandings cause problems for market efficiency they also, as Hayek well knew, create opportunities for market creativity. In short, the failure language is not helpful. See also Roberts (2004), Chapter 3, for a very good account of the failure-based perspective.
16. Because they tend to be temporary bilateral arrangements a potential market in any one type of highly

specific arrangement is necessarily thin, and because there are costs of forming markets this weighs heavily in preventing the organization of a market for so few transactions.

17. This provides a different way of viewing the reluctance of external parties to provide finance than that put forward under the concept of moral hazard. Even without fraud or deceit, there is difficulty due to the different knowledge of the entrepreneur and the financier. Contractual instruments can't overcome this difference in knowledge, so that at least some elements of the barriers to securing finance are irreducible.

REFERENCES

Arrow, K. (1974), *The Limits of Organization*, New York: Norton.
Becattini, G. (2006), 'The industrial district and development economics', in Rafaelli, T., Becattini, G. and M. Dardi (eds), *The Elgar Companion to Alfred Marshall*, Cheltenham, UK and Northampton, MA, USA: Edward Elgar, pp. 664–710.
Bloch, H. and Finch, J. (2010), 'Firms and industries in evolutionary economics: lessons from Marshall, Young, Steindl and Penrose', *Journal of Evolutionary Economics*, **20**, 139–62.
Boschetti, F. and Gray, R. (2007), 'Emergence and computability', *E-CO*, **9** (1–2), 120–30.
Boulding, K. (1951), 'Implications for general economics of more realistic theories of the firm', *American Economic Review*, **42** (May), 35–44.
Bunge, M. (2003), *Emergence and Convergence: Qualitative Novelty and the Unity of Knowledge*, Toronto: University of Toronto Press.
Chamberlin, E.H. (1933), *The Theory of Monopolistic Competition*, Cambridge, MA: Harvard University Press.
Coase, R.A. (1937), 'The nature of the firm', *Economica*, **4** (16), 386–405.
Dosi, G. and Marengo, L. (1994), 'Some elements of an evolutionary theory of organizational concepts', in England, R.W. (ed.), *Evolutionary Concepts in Contemporary Economics*, Michigan: Michigan University Press, pp.157–78.
Foster, J. (2005), 'From simplistic to complex systems in economics', *Cambridge Journal of Economics*, **29**, 873–92.
Foster, J. (2011), 'Complex economic systems', in Hooker, C. (ed.) *Philosophy of Complex Systems: Handbook of Philosophical Science*, Amsterdam: Elsevier.
Hayek, F. (1967), 'The theory of complex phenomena', *Studies in Philosophy, Politics and Economics*, London: Routledge & Kegan Paul, pp. 22–42.
Hayek, F.A. (1973), *Law, Legislation and Liberty*, Volume 1, Chicago: Chicago University Press.
Knight, F. (1951), *The Economic Organisation*, New York: Augustus M. Kelley.
Loasby, B. (1989), 'Knowledge and organization: Marshall's theory of economic progress and coordination', *The Mind and Method of the Economist*, Aldershot, UK and Brookfield, VT, USA: Edward Elgar.
Loasby, B. (1990), 'Firms, markets and the principle of continuity', in Whitaker, J.K. (ed.), *Centenary Essays on Alfred Marshall*, Cambridge: Cambridge University Press, pp. 108–27.
Loasby, B. (2006), 'Industrial organization', in Raffaelli, T., Becattini, G. and Dardi, M. (eds), *The Elgar Companion to Alfred Marshall*, Cheltenham, UK and Northampton, MA, USA: Edward Elgar, 371–8.
Loasby, B. (2010), 'Uncertainty and imagination, illusion and order, Shackleian connections', G.L.S. Shackle Memorial Lecture, St Edmund's College Cambridge.
Lovejoy, A.O. (1927), 'The meaning of "Emergence" and its modes', *Journal of Philosophical Studies*, **2** (6), 167–81.
Marshall, A. (1919), *Industry and Trade*, London: Macmillan.
Marshall, A. (1920), *Principles of Economics*, 8th edn, London: Macmillan.
McNulty, P.J. (1968), 'Economic theory and the meaning of competition', *Quarterly Journal of Economics*, **82**, 639–56.
Metcalfe, J.S. (2006), 'Evolutionary economics' in Raffaelli, T., Becattini, G. and Dardi, M. (eds), *The Elgar Companion to Alfred Marshall*, Cheltenham, UK and Northampton, MA, USA: Edward Elgar.
Metcalfe, J.S. (2007), 'Alfred Marshall and the general theory of evolutionary economics', *History of Economic Ideas*, **15** (1), 81–110.
Mokyr, J. (1990), *The Lever of Riches*, Oxford: Oxford University Press.
Mokyr, J. (2002), *The Gifts of Athena*, Princeton: Princeton University Press.
Nelson, R.R. (1991), 'Why do firms differ; and how does it matter', *Strategic Journal of Management*, **12**, 61–74.
Nelson, R.R. and Winter, S.G. (1982), *An Evolutionary Theory of Economic Change*, Cambridge, MA: Harvard University Press.

Penrose, E.T. (1959), *The Theory of the Growth of the Firm*, Oxford: Basil Blackwell.
Potts, J. (2000), *The New Evolutionary Microeconomics: Complexity, Competence and Adaptive Behaviour*, Cheltenham, UK and Northampton, MA, USA: Edward Elgar.
Richardson, G.B. (1972), 'The organisation of industry', *Economic Journal*, **82**, 883–96.
Roberts, J. (2004), *The Modern Firm*, Oxford: Oxford University Press.
Robinson, R. (1971), *Edward H. Chamberlin: Columbia Essays on Great Economists*, New York: Columbia University Press.
Schumpeter, J.A (1934), *The Theory of Economic Development*, Oxford: Galaxy Books.
Schumpeter, J.A. (1942), *Capitalism, Socialism and Democracy*, New York: Harper.
Schumpeter, J.A. (1947), 'The creative response in economic history', *Journal of Economic History*, **7** (2), 149–59.
Shackle, G.L.S. (1961), *Decision Order and Time in Human Affairs*, Cambridge: Cambridge University Press.
Shackle, G.L.S. (1966), 'The dilemma of history', in *The Nature of Economic Thought; Selected Papers, 1955–1964*, Cambridge: Cambridge University Press.
Steindl, J. (1945), *Small and Big Business: Economic Problems of the Size of Firms*, Oxford: Blackwell.
Steindl, J. (1976), *Maturity and Stagnation in American Capitalism*, New York: Monthly Review Press.
Stigler, G. (1951), 'The division of labour is limited by the extent of the market', *Journal of Political Economy*, **59** (3), 185–96.
Triffin, R. (1941), *Monopolistic Competition and General Equilibrium Theory*, Cambridge, MA: Harvard University Press.
Whitaker, J.K. (1999), 'Alfred Marshall and scientific management', in Dow, S.C. and Earl, P.E. (eds), *Economic Organisation and Economic Knowledge: Essays in Honour of Brian J. Loasby Volume 1*, Cheltenham, UK and Northampton, MA, USA: Edward Elgar.
Wiedermann, J. and van Leeuwen, J. (2002), 'The evolving computational potential of evolving artificial life systems', *AI Communications*, **15**, 205–15.
Witt, U. (1998), 'Imagination and leadership – the neglected dimension of an evolutionary theory of the firm', *Journal of Economic Behaviour and Organization*, **35**, 161–77.
Young, A.A. (1928), 'Increasing returns and economic progress', *Economic Journal*, **38**, 527–42.

4 The persistence of innovation and path dependence
Alessandra Colombelli and Nick von Tunzelmann

1. INTRODUCTION

The persistence of innovation has been the subject of a recent body of literature. Most of the contributions consist of empirical analyses carried out with time series tools or transition matrixes. The theoretical underpinnings of this approach lie in the concepts of cumulativeness and technological learning. However this literature fails to grasp the systemic character of persistent processes.

In this chapter we develop an integrated framework able to graft the persistence of innovation within a complex dynamic framework. We therefore try to establish a link between persistence and path dependence by putting particular emphasis on the dynamics of local attractors. In particular we focus on innovation considered as a dynamic process characterized by persistence and path dependence. More precisely, we develop the kinds of local attractors that distinctively create persistent and path dependent processes of technological change. The rationale behind our study is the understanding of innovation processes, organizational change, growth, and systemic dynamics.

In our approach, the generation of new knowledge and the introduction of innovation are the results of cumulative patterns and learning dynamics. This pattern of technological accumulation is at the base of the persistence of innovation. This means that current innovation is explained by past innovation and, thus, innovation has enduring effects as a result of knowledge cumulability and learning processes.

We also retain that innovation persistence is path dependent as opposed to past dependent. While past dependent processes are fully determined by the initial conditions, path dependent processes are affected by contingent factors that intervene in modifying the rate and the direction of technological change. As such, path dependent processes are shaped by the localized context of action.

Hence in our view, innovation is a collective process that takes place when systemic conditions are at work. Thus, following Antonelli (2008), 'innovation is one of the key emergent properties of an economic system viewed as a dynamic complex system'.

Under the assumptions that the introduction of innovation is persistent, path dependent and has a systemic character, in this chapter we investigate the role and the different kinds of local attractors that may influence the dynamics of technological change. In our view, local attractors may foster technological accumulation and learning dynamics and, as a consequence, the persistence of innovation. They are the driving forces that influence the rate, the sequence and the direction of the path and, thus, introduce discontinuity in the process making it a path dependent process. Hence, local attractors engender the systemic conditions at the base of knowledge and social interactions and, thus, give rise to the introduction of technological innovations. In the very long term, the technologies and their local attractors develop reverse links, promoting complex dynamics. In our view, attractors result from localized increasing returns or at least through offsets to diminishing returns, particularly through the generation of what we refer to as 'dynamic and interactive economies of scale and scope'. Some examples of contexts where such kinds of gains are significant and hence local attractors play a major role are technological districts, regional innovation systems and innovative milieux, but also knowledge platforms and networks.

Our work can contribute to the literature under three perspectives. First, we try to enclose the concepts of persistence and path dependence in a common framework. Second, we draw attention to the local attractors that may influence the dynamics of technological change. Finally, we analyse the dynamics at the base of local attractors' generation not only in the geographical space but also in the knowledge space.

The chapter is organized as follows. The second section discusses the literature on the persistence of innovation. The third section provides an overview of the local attractor concept and develops an interpretative framework that links it to the notion of path dependence and persistence. Following our interpretative framework, Section 4 critically reviews the theoretical and empirical literature on technological change in order to capture the role of local attractors under different perspectives. In Section 5 we outline our conclusions.

2.   THE PERSISTENCE OF INNOVATION

The persistence of innovation activities has been largely analysed from a theoretical viewpoint and empirically confirmed only to a limited extent. According to neo-Schumpeterians, knowledge accumulation and technological learning account for the main forces leading to innovation persistence. Schumpeter himself distinguished between two different patterns of innovations. In *The Theory of Economic Development* (1912), the 'creative destruction' process is conceptualized. In this model, knowledge is conceived as a free good and, thus, all the firms can fish in the same pool of accessible technologies. As a consequence, new innovators introduce new technology while old innovators stay stuck in old innovation. On the contrary, in *Capitalism, Socialism and Democracy* (1942) Schumpeter emphasizes the cumulative nature of technological change. In this view, the innovation process is described as a process of 'creative accumulation'. Knowledge is created and accumulated within firms. This builds high barriers to entry and, as a consequence, established large firms become key actors in the process of technological change. Within this framework success breeds success, current innovation is explained by past innovation and, thus, innovation is persistent (Alfranca et al., 2002).

In evolutionary theory, the persistence of innovation activities stems from competition and selection mechanisms. In this view, the accumulation of knowledge and learning dynamics lead to the formation of firm-specific routines that may generate a stable pattern of economic activities. Yet, the inertia stemming from routines can be counteracted by dynamic forces like technological competition and innovation that push the economic system towards evolution (Nelson and Winter, 1982). As a consequence, firms that survive to the market competition are those that persistently implement new techniques and introduce new ideas, which, in turn, increase their profitability and market share. Thus, the selection mechanism that pushes firms to persistently rely on innovation is a function of their internal competencies, technological capability and profitability.

A recent strand of literature has tried to empirically analyse the persistence of innovation. It is possible to distinguish two main lines of research in this area. A first set of studies aims at analysing the persistence in the introduction of innovation, trying to understand whether innovators have a stronger probability than non-innovators to keep innovating. In particular, these empirical works focus on the determinants and the features of the persistency by observing firms' patenting activity over time (Geroski et al., 1997; Malerba et al., 1997; Cefis and Orsenigo, 2001; Alfranca et al., 2002; Cefis, 2003) or the introduction of product and process innovation as revealed by innovation surveys repeated along time (Raymond et al., 2006; Roper and Hewitt-Dundas, 2008; Peters, 2009). These works, explicitly or implicitly, are based on the dynamic capabilities theory (Teece and Pisano, 1994) and refer to the idea that technical change builds upon accumulated competencies and that new knowledge is generated by what has been learned in the past. A second set of studies examines persistency in the effects of innovation rather than the persistence of innovation per se (Cefis and Ciccarelli, 2005; Latham and Le Bas, 2006). These works build upon the idea that the stream of profits generated by past innovation gives firms the opportunity to keep on innovating and confirm that the impact of innovation on performance is cumulative and long lasting (Antonelli et al., 2010a, 2010b).

While the importance of internal technological capabilities and financial resources has been widely analysed by both the theoretical and empirical literature on the persistence of innovation, less attention has been paid to the environment in which firms operate. However, the role of the external context should not be neglected as technological change is the joint outcome of innovation and learning activities within organizations and interaction between these and their environments (Fagerberg, 1994). The external context is a fundamental condition to the introduction of innovation as it provides firms with access to complementary and indispensable inputs in terms of external knowledge. Without an appropriate context that enables the access to external knowledge, the reaction of firms fails to be creative and, hence, the generation of new knowledge cannot persist over time.

The literature on knowledge spillovers and knowledge externalities allows for appreciating the key role of the context into which firms innovate (see Antonelli, Chapter 1 in this volume). Yet, this strand of the literature fails to account for the fundamental role of interactions among agents within the system in the process of technological change. Interactions are instead a fundamental ingredient of complex economic dynamics. For this reason we develop an integrated framework able to graft the persistence of innovation within a complex dynamic framework by putting particular emphasis on the dynamics of local attractors. In our view, the concept of local attractor accounts for interdependences and networks among agents in the system that engender positive feedbacks leading to the introduction of innovations. Local attractors promote knowledge externalities and interactions and, in turn, favor the persistence of the rates of introduction of innovations. Hence, firms are able to change both their technologies and the structure of the system following a recursive, historic and path-dependent process of change. In this view the introduction of innovation is the result of a persistent process endogenous to both the firm and the system.

3.   THE ROLE OF LOCAL ATTRACTORS IN COMPLEXITY

Local Attractors

The attractor concept was first developed by Lorenz (1963) in a model of atmospheric convection and has remained a cornerstone in chaos theory (Prigogine and Stengers, 1984), first, and complexity theory (Kauffman, 1993, 1995) later on. In chaos theory the local attractor concept has been used for stressing the sensitivity to initial conditions in the evolution of a system. Following the Lorenz work on atmospheric forecasting, the attractor concept has also been explained by means of the well known 'butterfly effect' metaphor. It suggests that small events, like the flap of a butterfly's wings, can engender large effects in the trajectory of the system, like a hurricane in another continent. It is worth stressing that the local attractor, as it is conceptualized in chaos theory, describes deterministic processes which lead to unpredictable results. In other words, initial conditions are important and their effects can be magnified during the process, thus leading to unpredictable outcomes.

The literature on non-linear and complex systems offers a different perspective for understanding the local attractors concept. Here the term 'attractor' indicates a limitation in possibilities. Stuart Kauffman asserts that 'attractors "box" the behaviour of a system into small parts of its state space, or space of possibilities' (1993: 174). Every dynamical system has attractors that limit the possible states a system can reach.

Following the mathematical formalization, an attractor can be defined as a set of values in the phase space to which a system migrates over time. The phase space is an abstract space used to represent the behavior of a system which has as many dimensions as the variables of the system. Thus a point in the phase space defines a potential state of the system.

Each attractor has a basin of attraction, a region in the phase space which represents the set of all (initial) points that go to that attractor. In this way the literature on non-linear and complex systems introduces the idea of patterning. The emergence of patterning within a given system results from 'attractors'. As a consequence of local attractors a dynamic system does not move over time through all possible parts of a phase space but instead occupies a restricted part of it. Local attractors represent a set of possible states or phase space which a time series generated by a dynamical system tend to take over time. They represent the outcome that a dynamic system eventually can reach.

In this line of thought, the process is no more deterministic as it is influenced not only by initial condition but also by its iterative function. Hence, in complex theory the sensitivity to both initial condition and chance events make the dynamic process a stochastic process as opposed to a deterministic one. In this line of thoughts, Prigogine (1997) underlines how complexity theory allows mediating

> between two alienating representations: that of a deterministic world and that of an arbitrary world subject to pure chance. Systems are thus seen as being 'on the edge of chaos'. Order and chaos are in a kind of balance where the components are neither fully locked into place but yet do not fully dissolve into anarchy. Time flows with minor changes in the past being able to produce potentially massive effects in the present or future. Such small events are not 'forgotten'.

Multiple Attractors and Path Dependence

How does an outcome (attractor) come to be selected over time when there are several possible long-run outcomes?

History may decide the outcome. When many outcomes are possible, chance events become magnified by positive feedbacks and drive the system towards the actual outcome to be selected. Positive feedbacks magnify the effects of small shifts in the system. There is thus a self-reinforcing mechanism that makes the system move towards a new configuration. Small or chance events (à la David), perturbations or historical accidents (à la Arthur) at critical times influence which outcome is selected and the chosen outcome may have higher energy than other possible end states. Early perturbations become important in the selection of the structure.

Positive feedback is an essential concept in order to capture the role of local attractors in complexity. The trajectory of dynamical systems is attracted towards an attractor through positive feedback occurring over time. Positive feedbacks exacerbate initial stresses in the system, so rendering it unable to absorb shocks and re-establishing the original equilibrium. Very strong interactions occur between the parts of a system and there is an absence of a central hierarchical structure able to 'govern' outcomes. Positive feedbacks occur when a change tendency is reinforced rather than dampened down as occurs with the negative feedback and hence engender out of equilibrium conditions.

In economics, positive feedbacks engender increasing returns and are strictly related with the path dependence concept (Arthur, 1994). Increasing returns make for many possible outcomes. When the process leading to the selected outcome is a function of history, it is said to be a path dependent process. In order to define it, Paul David (2001) first draws on a negative definition opposing path dependent to path independent dynamic processes. Path independent processes possess the property of convergence to a unique, globally stable equilibrium configuration (single attractor) and, hence, history does not matter, meaning that it cannot affect the processes' asymptotic distribution among the states. These processes are said to be ergodic as they are not influenced by their past states. On the contrary, 'processes that are non-ergodic, and thus unable to shake free of their history, are said to yield path dependent outcomes' (David, 2001). Converting this last definition in a positive perspective, 'a path dependent stochastic process is one whose asymptotic distribution evolves as a consequence (function of) the process's own history' (David, 2001). In path dependent processes the system does not converge to a single attractor. The evolution of the system may have multiple steady states. 'Once there are multiple stationary points of a dynamic process, path dependence follows automatically, since each stable stationary point has a basic of attraction' (Arrow, 2000: 178). Then the outcome to which the system eventually converges depends on its path. The selected steady state is determined not only by arbitrary initial conditions but also by chance events which occur during the process. These events that arise along the path are non-reversible. Path dependent processes are thus characterized by local irreversibilities.

Multiple Attractors and Persistence

How long does the dynamic system occupy the same region in the phase space?

Once the outcome has been selected, a new structure of the system emerges. As the new structure is subject to long-term self-reinforcement mechanisms, it is difficult to change it. Each attractor has a basin of attraction which represents a region in phase space composed by the set of all points that pull the system towards the attractor. When the system enters into the orbit of one attractor the system may eventually lock into its new configuration.

Yet, the dynamic system's new configuration may be ever changing when the impulse to change comes from within the system and as such the process of change is endogenous. The system can adapt and evolve but only within a limited set of possibilities. As it moves around the attractor, the dynamic system may evolve toward a new configuration which is roughly the same but not exactly the same as the previous one.

In economics, this means that increasing returns are localized. The dynamic system can adapt and evolve following self-organizing and self-reinforcing mechanisms. If one product, a firm or even a nation in a competitive marketplace gets ahead in the development process by chance it tends to stay ahead and even increase its lead (Arthur, 1994). Localized increasing returns thus allow for persistence in the process of change.

Movements Toward a New Attractor

When does the complex dynamic system move from one attractor to another?

When discontinuities and radical perturbations arise the actual configuration becomes unattractive. The system moves unpredictably and irreversibly away from the old local attractor when its development is constrained within a progressively narrower range of possibilities that lead to decline. In other words, when localized features built over time shift from being advantageous to become barriers to future development and change of a system, the latter is pushed away from the old attractor towards a new one.

It is worth stressing an important distinction between social and natural sciences on this point. What distinguishes social from natural phenomena is that change arises from intentional choices by agents. As a consequence, while in natural sciences radical perturbations occur exogenously, we maintain that when considering social phenomena the perturbations are endogenous.

4. THE KINDS OF LOCAL ATTRACTORS IN THE COMPLEX DYNAMICS OF TECHNOLOGICAL CHANGE

We now mean to analyse technological change within a complex dynamic framework paying particular attention to the role and kinds of local attractors. Our unit of analysis is the economic system which is defined as follows:

- Our economic agents are heterogeneous agents that are interconnected and networked with other agents in the system in order to exploit complementarities and interdependence.
- The heterogeneous agents are firms and also public and private institutions and organizations.
- The introduction of innovation stems from intentional choices by economic agents.
- The structure of the system changes endogenously.

Following the complexity theory the interactions between economic agents are as fundamental as the behavior of economic agents themselves. The system's properties emerge from the interactions between heterogeneous agents and are, thus, generated by system dynamics. These collective emergent properties are different from those of the agents composing the system. In this line of reasoning, innovation emerges from the systemic interactions among firms and the other agents and is different from each other alternative innovation which would arise from the individual agent alone. In complex theory, this concept is commonly explained by saying that 'the sum is greater than the size of its parts'. This suggests that the innovation process is not only differentiated but is also magnified by systemic dynamics.

The intentional interactions among agents engender the generation of unexpected events and, as a consequence, new configurations of the system structure endogenously emerge. This generates path dependence and the persistence of innovation.

In order to discuss our approach, we analyse technological change in two phase spaces: geographical and knowledge space. Their structure matters in that they provide the context for actions of innovating agents. In each space attractors can have as many dimensions as the number of variables that influence its system.

As far as geographical space is concerned, the literature on agglomeration and dynamic processes leading to innovation is fertile (Boschma and Lambooy, 1999; Boschma and Frenken, 2006; Martin and Sunley, 2006; Martin, 2010). There are also some interesting applications of the complexity approach in urban and regional economics (Allen, 1997; Garnsey, 1998; Garnsey and McGlade, 2006). Yet, there is still space for exploring this stream of the literature.

In contrast, the application of complexity theory to the knowledge space is less diffused. Moreover, in this literature the unit of analysis is knowledge itself and the complex system is composed by networked pieces of knowledge that recombine in complex ways. In our framework, knowledge space represents a context of action for heterogeneous agents. In our view, knowledge space gives a new perspective for understanding the role of local attractors in making technological change a persistent and path dependent process. We think this is a new avenue to be exploited by the literature.

Movement in Geographical Space

What makes a possible outcome a base of attraction in geographical space?

The literature on agglomerations is an important reference on this point. This literature emphasizes that firms locating first in a place create an attraction for new firms to move there, and these in turn make an even stronger attraction for more firms to move there (Arthur, 1994). Initial conditions, historical accidents and self-reinforcing mechanisms play a crucial role in the process. In our view, this means that the process of agglomeration is a path dependent and persistent one.

A number of emergent properties or conditions of the local system can make a place in geographical space more attractive than others. This attractiveness in turn influences the process of technological change as spatial proximity supports the introduction of innovations and the dissemination of technological knowledge (Breschi and Lissoni, 2003; Boschma, 2005). Different mechanisms of attraction and agglomeration in a bounded geographical space have been highlighted by the literature, such as the access to a market for specialized labor (Marshall, 1890; Krugman, 1991), access to localized and dynamic capabilities (Maskell and Malmberg, 1999; von Tunzelmann and Wang, 2003), the reduced costs for shared infrastructures and other collective resources, and the reduced transaction costs for co-located trading partners (Arthur, 1994). Knowledge spillovers, knowledge and pecuniary externalities are other mechanisms behind the agglomeration of firms in geographical space. These mechanisms give firms access to external knowledge at costs that are lower than equilibrium levels. This in turn affects firms' knowledge production function (Antonelli, 1999, 2008). The institutional endowment also has an impact on the emergence of local attractors. As the movement in the geographical space is governed by institutional rules, routines and practices (Nelson and Winter, 1982; Lundvall, 1992; Arthur, 1994) the institutional set-up (North, 1990) or institutional thickness (Amin and Thrift, 1994) can favor agglomeration phenomena. Finally, proximity to scientific institutions and universities and an attractive social environment (Aydalot, 1986; Camagni, 1991; Maillat, 1995; Etzkowitz and Leydesdorff, 1997, 2000; Cassia et al., 2009) engender collective learning processes which in turn foster the agglomeration of firms (see Frenken and Boschma, Chapter 14 in this volume).

It is now clear how the structure of the system and the mechanisms operating within it can act as an attractor. The interaction and networks of local actors that allow for the exploitation of complementarities and interdependences, reinforced by the technological and industrial specialization of the area, the institutional endowment and by a common local culture of trust, based on shared practices and rules, are centripetal forces that make a base of attraction of the local system.

However, it is not only the local attributes or conditions but rather the sequence of cumulative interactions between them and positive feedbacks that give rise to a local complex system. Both geographic attractiveness and accidental historical order of choice generate agglomerations (Arthur, 1989, 1994).

Thus the agglomeration process is a path dependent process. This means that the rate, the direction and the sequence of the economic agent actions can be intentionally changed. Path dependence is thus opposed to past dependence. The latter gives a deterministic interpretation to the patterns followed by economic agents. On the contrary, the path dependence concept allows taking history into account. This means that the technological process is influenced by arbitrary initial decisions taken by the economic agent under uncertain conditions but it is also determined by chance events arising during the process and by the local context of action. In this sense the past narrows but not univocally determines the final outcome and the space of action of economic agents. The creative response of heterogeneous agents to changes in the local context of action can modify unpredictably the rate and the direction of the innovation process.

If we apply our interpretative framework to the literature in the area of economic geography, evolutionary and institutional economics, it is possible to identify some concepts that fit with the local attractor one. These are the following:

- agglomeration and cluster (Porter, 1990; Arthur, 1994)
- innovation systems (Freeman, 1987; Lundvall, 1992)
- innovative milieu (Aydalot, 1986; Maillat, 1995).

Once the local attractor has emerged following a path dependent process, heterogeneous agents within it are subject to self-reinforcing mechanisms of the innovation process. The process of increasing returns is self-reinforcing since the benefits of remaining in the current path are higher than the cost of switching to an alternative path. Localized increasing returns operate as a selection mechanism and favor the survival and growth of firms that are well established in the local system and take part in the local dynamics of technological change. Thus, if one firm gets ahead by chance in the innovation process it tends to stay ahead and even increases its lead (Arthur, 1994). Innovation has enduring effects and the introduction of innovation is thus a persistent process.

As discussed in Section 2 on the persistence of innovation, the successful introduction of innovation takes place when the internal capabilities accumulated by means of learning processes lead to the generation and exploitation of new knowledge. Another fundamental condition to the introduction of innovation is when the external context provides the access to complementary and indispensable inputs in terms of external knowledge. The generation of new knowledge requires both internal learning and the acquisition of external tacit and codified knowledge. Hence, knowledge accumulation and technological learning account for the main forces leading to innovation persistence. In this view, the introduction of innovation is a process of 'creative accumulation'. Knowledge is created and accumulated within firms and, thus, established firms become key actors in the process of technological change.

Similar arguments have been applied at the macro level in the works trying to answer the question why growth differs across countries (see Fagerberg, 1994). Starting with the neoclassical growth model proposed by Solow (1956, 1957), technological progress was included as an additional – exogenous – variable to account for long-run growth in GDP per capita. In this interpretation, technology is accessible for everybody free of charge. On this assumption the neoclassical model of economic growth predicts that, in the long run, GDP per capita in all countries will grow at the same, exogenously determined rate of technological progress. Subsequent contributions belonging to the technology-gap approach to economic growth and to the 'new growth theories' conceive technology in a different way. While in works based on traditional neoclassical theory of economic growth technology is assumed to be a public good and, as such, cannot be the source of cross-country differences in GDP per capita, in the technology-gap approach technological differences are the prime cause for differences in GDP per capita across countries (Ames and Rosenberg, 1963). This stream of the literature recognizes the tacit nature of knowledge. As a result technological knowledge is difficult and costly to transfer. Knowledge is generated and exploited mainly within organizations and is at the base of internal capabilities formation. The process of technological change is the outcome of knowledge accumulation and learning activities and is influenced by country-specific factors (Nelson and Wright, 1992). In this line of reasoning, the country leading in technology can be overtaken only if the 'national system of innovation' of some country, through the creation of a new 'national technology' succeeds in embarking on a new, superior path of technological change. New growth theories lead to similar conclusions. According to this stream of the literature, technological progress is not exogenous but it is the result of intentional activities by firms. Cross-country differences affect differences in cross-country rates of growth. Lock-in situations may occur and, thus, rich countries stay rich and poor countries stay poor.

Comparing the two debates in the literature, the first on innovation persistence and the second on the growth theory, it is possible to notice many similarities. As a result of knowledge cumulability and learning processes, innovation has enduring effects. Thus, new innovators are old innovators and the leader firm or country remains at the technology frontier. Increasing returns thus lead to the localized, persistent and path dependent process of technological change.

Why and How Do Local Attractors Become Unattractive?

When the leadership of the innovating firm is set, adaptive behaviors can emerge and consequently a lock-in situation arises. The dynamic system moves around the attractor and evolves toward a new configuration which is roughly the same as the previous one. Congestion, over-specialization and limited appropriability within the local attractor lead firms to exploit incremental innovation and rely mainly on internal knowledge and capabilities. As a consequence, localized capabilities deteriorate, routines become obsolete and the region loses market share and innovation capacity.

In this case the negative effects of agglomerations are higher than the positive ones. As shown in Antonelli et al. (2011), there is an inverted U-shaped relationship between the agglomeration of innovation activities and regional productivity growth. Authors refer to the concept of pecuniary knowledge externalities for appreciating both positive and negative effects of agglomeration. The gains of regional concentration of knowledge generating activities are related with the reduction in the prices of knowledge as an input while the losses are related to the reduction in the prices of knowledge as an output. As a consequence agglomerations yield positive net knowledge externalities only until a given threshold. The main argument is that the advantages in terms of knowledge externalities are dissipated by the losses engendered by reduced appropriability.

Firms within the local attractor understand that the benefits of remaining in the current technological path, that in turn has engendered the current local attractor, are lower than the cost of shifting to an alternative path and, thus, to an alternative attractor. Firms are induced to react creatively to changing local conditions. The collective process of search for new technology may finally engender radical changes in the technological paradigm and lead to Schumpeterian gales of creative destruction. Only the creation of a new and radical knowledge with a wide scope of application allows the disruption of the established innovators' leadership and lets new innovators to be new leaders in the technological frontier.

The emerged radical innovation generates a perturbation in the system. The creation of a new technology and radical changes in the technological paradigm make the system move unpredictably and irreversibly away from the old local attractor. Positive feedbacks and network externalities sustain this process of technological change and define the basin of attraction of the new attractor.

It is worth noting that in this interpretative framework the process of technological change is endogenous. Previous contributions in economic geography and evolutionary economics on path dependence assert that once the system has been locked into one attractor, the break of the current path and the switch to another attractor can be caused only by external shocks (Nelson, 1993; David, 2005). In this line of reasoning, the process of technological change is exogenous. On the contrary, in our interpretative framework we claim that the process is endogenous. Firms within the old attractor are induced by negative feedbacks to react creatively to changing conditions. Their intentional search for a new path-breaking technology promotes the process of technological change and leads to innovation cascades. A new structure of the system emerges and, as a consequence, firms can move in geographical space towards the new base of attraction.

Movement in the Knowledge Space

What makes a possible outcome a base of attraction in the knowledge space?

The economics of knowledge literature offers the main concepts for explaining the behavior of firms moving in the knowledge space. In particular, our framework on complex dynamics refers to both the localized technological knowledge and the recombinant knowledge approaches. The former assert that the stock of knowledge and competence internal to a firm are localized and constrained in a limited area in the knowledge space. In the latter the generation of new knowledge stems from the recombination of a variety of knowledge bits. Following a cumulative and interacting process, existing ideas are recombined in order to generate new ideas (Weitzman, 1996).

Different mechanisms make a restricted area in the knowledge space a base of attraction. First, the stock of knowledge and competence of firms is the result of a process of learning by doing, using and interacting. In this way firms accumulate knowledge that constrains their ray of action in the knowledge space and limits their possibilities to exploit alternative and unrelated knowledge. Secondly, the search for complementarities as conceived in the recombinant approach attracts firms toward a bounded area in the knowledge space. In order to complement their internal knowledge and generate new technology, firms can move in the knowledge space and search for external knowledge. As a consequence firms are attracted towards a restricted area in the knowledge space which is composed by knowledge complementary to the internal knowledge. The search for external knowledge is thus local.

A number of emergent properties or conditions of the local system can make a place in knowledge space more attractive than others. In our view, the properties defining the structure of the knowledge space are knowledge proximity, knowledge coherence and knowledge variety, related or unrelated (Saviotti, 1996, 2004, 2007; Nesta and Saviotti, 2005; Frenken et al., 2007). Local attractors are thus areas characterized by high levels of knowledge proximity, knowledge coherence and knowledge related variety that allows the generation and exploitation of new technological knowledge. As suggested by Antonelli et al. (2010c) in a study on the emergence of the new technological system based upon information and communication technologies, the recombination process has been more effective in areas characterized by higher levels of coherence and specialization of their knowledge space.

It is now clear that local attractors are areas in the knowledge space where fertile knowledge is accessible and makes possible the generation of new knowledge through learning, accumulation and recombinant processes. Yet, at a given time, firms can select among multiple outcomes. Their location choice can be directed towards different places and is influenced by both their internal characteristics, which include the preceding path, and external characteristics, which depend on the location strategies of other agents carried out in the past. Hence the concentration of innovating firms in the knowledge space and the consequent introduction of innovation stemming from the knowledge base available in the local attractor is a path dependence process.

With reference to the economics of knowledge literature, the kinds of knowledge attractors we identify are:

- Dominant design (Utterback and Abernathy, 1975)
- Core technologies
- Knowledge platforms (see Consoli and Patrucco, Chapter 8 in this volume).

Firms are attracted towards the knowledge attractor until the profits stemming from their innovation activities are above the equilibrium one. The selection mechanism depends on the profits realized by each firm. Extra profits and increasing returns of the innovation activities engender positive feedbacks and self-reinforcing mechanisms that sustain firms' creative behaviors and the persistence of innovation activities. The attractiveness of a place persists as long as the returns of knowledge recombination processes are positive.

Once an innovating agent has approached a local attractor in the knowledge space it is likely to introduce new technologies with a high degree of relativeness, similarity and coherence with the technologies already in place. As a consequence, the features of new technology change slowly and profits reach the equilibrium level. In this case, adaptive responses are likely to occur while knowledge externalities and interactions decrease. Inertial forces keep the economic system in equilibrium conditions and hence firms are not induced to change their technologies and innovate.

As soon as the level of profits falls below the equilibrium level, negative feedbacks arise and the local attractor becomes unattractive. The mismatch between expected and real returns on knowledge production activities pushes firms to react creatively to out of equilibrium conditions. Firms try to innovate and search for complementary knowledge to recombine with their internal one. New core technologies and drastic innovation emerge from a collective process of knowledge recombination. General purpose technologies represent an example of such a drastic innovation. According to Helpman (1998: 13), 'a drastic innovation qualifies as a "general purpose technology" if it has the potential for pervasive use in a wide range of sectors in ways that drastically change their modes of operation', and thus can provoke a perturbation in the system. The addition of a radically new technology decreases coherence and proximity in the local attractor and increases unrelated variety. These dynamics will disadvantage the firms within the local attractor where knowledge externalities and interactions are deteriorated. As a consequence the creation of such new drastic innovations makes the system move unpredictably and irreversibly away from the old local attractor in search of a new one. A new structure of the system emerges endogenously from the new architecture of externalities, interactions and networks set by innovating firms.

5. DISCUSSION

In this chapter we developed an interpretative framework able to link the persistence and path dependence concepts and to graft them within a complex dynamic framework by putting particular emphasis on the dynamics of local attractors.

Complex theory allows for the appreciation of system dynamics of technological change as it investigates emergent, dynamic and self-organizing systems that evolve and adapt in ways that deeply influence the probabilities of later events (Prigogine, 1997; Urry, 2006). This means that the dynamics of systems arise endogenously through a persistent and path dependent process.

We can highlight the theoretical foundations of our approach as follows. Economic agents are heterogeneous individuals. The introduction of innovation stems from intentional choices that are shaped by learning dynamics and the cumulativeness of knowledge. In this line of reasoning, innovation has enduring effects and the introduction of innovation is thus a persistent process.

The rate, direction and sequence of technological change can be intentionally changed by the heterogeneous agents that are able to select among multiple outcomes. This makes the introduction of innovation a path dependent process.

Positive feedbacks arising by knowledge externalities and interactions in the system influence the innovation process that consequently is a persistent, path dependent and systemic process.

As the system evolves and self-organizes through time following the reactions of heterogeneous agents to changing conditions, the introduction of innovation is an endogenous process.

Local attractors fuel the mechanism at the base of these dynamics. A number of emergent properties of the local system, positive feedbacks and the interactions and networks of local actors that allow for the exploitation of complementarities and interdependences are centripetal forces that make a place in both the geographical and knowledge space more attractive than others.

Attractors stem from localized increasing returns and maintain their basis of attraction as long as positive feedbacks and self-reinforcing mechanisms sustain firms' creative behaviors and the returns of the innovation process are positive.

BIBLIOGRAPHY

Alfranca, O., Rama, R. and von Tunzelmann, N. (2002), 'A patent analysis of global food and beverage firms: the persistence of innovation', *Agribusiness*, **18**, 349–68.
Allen, P.M. (1997), *Cities and Regions as Self-Organizing Systems: Models of Complexity*, Amsterdam: Gordon and Breach Science Publishers.
Ames, E. and Rosenberg, N. (1963), 'Changing technological leadership and industrial growth', *Economic Journal*, **73**, 13–31.
Amin, A. and Thrift, N. (1994), *Globalization, Institutions, and Regional Development in Europe*, Oxford: Oxford University Press.
Antonelli, C. (1999), *The Microdynamics of Technological Change*, London: Routledge.
Antonelli, C. (2008), *Localized Technological Change: Towards the Economics of Complexity*, London: Routledge.
Antonelli, C., Crespi, F. and Scellato, G. (2010a), 'Inside innovation persistence: new evidence from Italian micro-data', WP Laboratorio di Economia dell'Innovazione Franco Momigliano, Dipartimento di Economia S. Cognetti de Martiis, Università di Torino and BRICK, Collegio Carlo Alberto.
Antonelli, C., Crespi, F. and Scellato, G. (2010b), 'Patterns of persistence in productivity growth. The Italian evidence', WP Laboratorio di Economia dell'Innovazione Franco Momigliano, Dipartimento di Economia S. Cognetti de Martiis, Università di Torino and BRICK, Collegio Carlo Alberto.
Antonelli, C., Krafft, J. and Quatraro, F. (2010c), 'Recombinant knowledge and growth: the case of ICTs', *Structural Change and Economic Dynamics*, **21**, 50–69.

Antonelli C., Patrucco, P.P. and Quatraro, F. (2011), 'Productivity growth and pecuniary knowledge externalities: an empirical analysis of agglomeration economies in European regions', *Economic Geography*, **87** (1), 23–50.

Arrow, K.J. (2000), 'Increasing returns: historiographic issues and path dependence', *European Journal of History of Economic Thought*, **7**, 171–80.

Arthur, W.B. (1989), 'Competing technologies, increasing returns, and lock-in by historical small events', *Economic Journal*, **99**, 116–31.

Arthur, W.B. (1994), *Increasing Returns and Path Dependence in the Economy*, Ann Arbor: University of Michigan Press.

Aydalot, P. (1986), *Milieux innovateurs en Europe*, Paris: GREMI.

Boschma, R.A. (2005), 'Proximity and innovation: a critical assessment', *Regional Studies*, **39**, 61–74.

Boschma, R.A. and Frenken, K. (2006), 'Why is economic geography not an evolutionary science? Towards an evolutionary economic geography', *Journal of Economic Geography*, **6**, 273–302.

Boschma, R.A. and Lambooy, J.G. (1999), 'Evolutionary economics and economic geography', *Journal of Evolutionary Economics*, **9**, 411–29.

Breschi, S. and Lissoni, F. (2003), 'Knowledge spillovers and local innovation systems: a critical survey', *Industrial and Corporate Change*, **10**, 975–1005.

Camagni, R. (1991), *Innovation Networks: Spatial Perspectives*, London: Belhaven Press.

Cassia, L., Colombelli, A. and Paleari, S. (2009), 'Firms' growth: does the innovation system matter?', *Structural Change and Economic Dynamics*, **20**, 211–20.

Cefis, E. (2003), 'Is there persistence in innovative activities?', *International Journal of Industrial Organization*, **21**, 489–515.

Cefis, E. and Ciccarelli, M. (2005), 'Profit differentials and innovation', *Economics of Innovation and New Technology*, **14**, 43–61.

Cefis, E. and Orsenigo, L. (2001), 'The persistence of innovative activities. A cross-countries and cross-sectors comparative analysis', *Research Policy*, **30**, 1139–58.

David, P.A. (2001), 'Path dependence, its critics, and the quest for "historical economics"', in Garrouste, P. and Ioannidis, S. (eds), *Evolution and Path Dependence in Economic Ideas: Past and Present*, Cheltenham, UK and Northampton, MA, USA: Edward Elgar pp. 15–40.

David, P.A. (2005), 'Path dependence in economic processes: implications for policy analysis in dynamical systems contexts', in Dopfer, K. (ed.), *The Evolutionary Foundations of Economics*, Cambridge: Cambridge University Press, pp. 151–94.

Etzkowitz, H. and Leydesdorff, L. (1997), *Universities in the Global Economy: A Triple Helix of University-Industry-Government Relations*, London: Cassell Academic.

Etzkowitz H. and Leydesdorff L. (2000), 'The dynamics of innovation: from 'National Systems' and 'Mode 2' to a triple helix of university-industry-government relations', *Research Policy*, **29**, 109–23.

Fagerberg, J. (1994), 'Technology and international differences in growth rates', *Journal of Economic Literature*, **32**, 1147–75.

Freeman, C. (1987), *Technology, Policy, and Economic Performance – Lessons from Japan*, London: Pinter Publishers.

Frenken, K., van Oort, F.G. and Verburg, T. (2007), 'Related variety, unrelated variety and regional economic growth', *Regional Studies*, **41**, 685–97.

Garnsey, E. (1998), 'The genesis of the high technology milieu: a study in complexity', *International Journal of Urban and Regional Research*, **22**, 361–77.

Garnsey, E. and McGlade, J. (2006), *Complexity and Co-evolution: Continuity and Change in Socio-economic Systems*, Cheltenham, UK and Northampton, MA, USA: Edward Elgar.

Geroski, P., Van Reenen, J. and Walters, C. (1997), 'How persistently do firms innovate?', *Research Policy*, **26**, 33–48.

Helpman, E. (1998), *General Purpose Technologies and Economic Growth*, Cambridge, MA: MIT Press.

Kauffman, S. (1993), *Origins of Order: Self-Organization and Selection in Evolution*, Oxford: Oxford University Press.

Kauffman, S. (1995), *At Home in the Universe: The Search for Laws of Complexity*, Oxford: Oxford University Press.

Krugman, P. (1991), *Geography and Trade*, Leuven and Cambridge, MA: Leuven University Press and MIT Press.

Latham, W.R. and Le Bas, C. (2006), *The Economics of Persistent Innovation: An Evolutionary View*, Berlin: Springer.

Lorenz, E.N. (1963), 'Deterministic nonperiodic flow', *Journal of the Atmospheric Sciences*, **20**, 130–41.

Lundvall, B.-Å. (1992), *National Systems of Innovation – Toward a Theory of Innovation and Interactive Learning*, London: Pinter Publishers.

Maillat, D. (1995), 'Territorial dynamic, innovative milieu and regional policy', *Entrepreneurship & Regional Development*, **7**, 157–65.

Malerba, F., Orsenigo, L. and Petretto, P. (1997), 'Persistence of innovative activities, sectoral patterns of innovation and international technological specialization', *International Journal of Industrial Organization*, **15**, 801–26.

Marshall, A. (1890), *Principles of Economics* (8th edition, 1920), London: Macmillan.

Martin, R.L. (2010), 'Rethinking regional path dependence: beyond lock-in to evolution', Roepke Lecture in Economic Geography, *Economic Geography*, **86**, 1–27.

Martin, R.L. and Sunley, P.J. (2006), 'Path dependence and regional economic evolution', *Journal of Economic Geography*, **6**, 395–438.

Maskell, P. and Malmberg, A. (1999), 'Localized learning and industrial competitiveness', *Cambridge Journal of Economics*, **23**, 167–85.

Nelson, R.R. (1993), *National Systems of Innovation*, Oxford: Oxford University Press.

Nelson, R. and Winter, S. (1982), *An Evolutionary Theory of Economic Change*, Cambridge, MA: Harvard University Press.

Nelson, R. and Wright, G. (1992), 'The rise and fall of American technological leadership: the postwar era in historical perspective', *Journal of Economic Literature*, **30**, 1931–64.

Nesta, L. and Saviotti, P. (2005), 'Coherence of the knowledge base and the firm's innovative performance: evidence from the US pharmaceutical industry', *Journal of Industrial Economics*, **53**, 123–42.

North, D.C. (1990), *Institutions, Institutional Change and Economic Performance*, New York: Cambridge University Press.

Peters, B. (2009), 'Persistence of innovation: stylized facts and panel data evidence', *Journal of Technology Transfer*, **34**, 226–43.

Porter, M.E. (1990), *The Competitive Advantage of Nations*, New York: The Free Press.

Prigogine, I. (1997), *The End of Certainty*, New York: The Free Press.

Prigogine, I. and Stengers, I. (1984), *Order Out of Chaos: Man's New Dialogue with Nature*, Boulder, CO: New Science Library.

Raymond, W., Mohnen, P., Palm, F.C. and Schim Van Der Loeff, S. (2006), 'Persistence of innovation in Dutch manufacturing: is it spurious?', CESifo Working Paper Series No. 1681.

Roper, S. and Hewitt-Dundas, N. (2008), 'Innovation persistence: survey and case-study evidence', *Research Policy*, **37**, 149–62.

Saviotti, P.P. (1996), *Technology Evolution, Variety and the Economy*, Cheltenham, UK and Brookfield, VT, USA: Edward Elgar.

Saviotti, P.P. (2004), 'Considerations about the production and utilization of knowledge', *Journal of Institutional and Theoretical Economics*, **160**, 100–21.

Saviotti, P.P. (2007), 'On the dynamics of generation and utilisation of knowledge: the local character of knowledge', *Structural Change and Economic Dynamics*, **18**, 387–408.

Schumpeter, J.A. (1912), *The Theory of Economic Development*, Cambridge: Harvard Economic Studies.

Schumpeter, J.A. (1939), *Business Cycles*, New York: McGraw-Hill.

Schumpeter, J.A. (1942), *Capitalism, Socialism and Democracy*, New York: Harper and Brothers.

Solow, R.M. (1956), 'A contribution to the theory of economic growth', *Quarterly Journal of Economics*, **70**, 65–94.

Solow, R.M. (1957), 'Technical change and the aggregate production function', *Review of Economics and Statistics*, **39**, 312–20.

Solow, R.M. (1970), *Growth Theory: An Exposition*, Oxford: Clarendon Press.

Teece, D. and Pisano, G. (1994), 'The dynamic capabilities of firms: an introduction', *Industrial and Corporate Change*, **3**, 537–55.

Urry, J. (2006), 'Complexity', *Theory Culture & Society*, **23**, 111–17.

Utterback J.M. and Abernathy, W.J. (1975), 'A dynamic model of process and product innovation', *Omega*, **3**, 639–56.

von Tunzelmann, G., Malerba, F., Nightingale, P. and Metcalfe, S. (2008), 'Technological paradigms: past, present and future', *Industrial and Corporate Change*, **17**, 467–84.

von Tunzelmann, G. and Wang Q. (2003), 'An evolutionary view of dynamic capabilities', *Economie Appliquée*, **16**, 33–64.

Weitzman, M.L. (1996), 'Hybridizing growth theory', *American Economic Review*, **86**, 207–12.

Winter, S.G. (2003), 'Understanding dynamic capabilities', *Strategic Management Journal*, **24**, 991–95.

5   The symbiotic theory of innovation: knowledge creation and the evolution of the capitalist system
Martin Fransman

INTRODUCTION

Remarkably, economics has very little to say about the process of knowledge creation in capitalist economies.[1] This is remarkable because economists acknowledge the crucial role that increasing knowledge plays in the process of economic change. Edith Penrose's comment in this regard is just as true now as it was when she wrote it: 'Economists have, of course, always recognized the dominant role that increasing knowledge plays in economic processes but have, for the most part, found the whole subject of knowledge too slippery to handle . . .' (Penrose, 1959: 77).

The human complex system (of which the economy is a part) is in one respect fundamentally different from biological and physical complex systems. It is based on the creation of knowledge by human beings. It is this knowledge that injects *novelty* into the system, causing a rupture with the past and driving its dynamics.[2] In order to understand the workings of this system, therefore, it is necessary to understand how knowledge is created in it.

In recent years some economists have acknowledged the importance of paying more attention to the creation of knowledge. Cristiano Antonelli (2008), for example, has emphasized the centrality of what he calls 'knowledge interactions' in economic complex systems, also referred to as 'generative relationships' by Lane and Maxfield (1997). Ulrich Witt (2002) has argued that although Schumpeter's entrepreneur has been credited with the creation of what in this chapter will be referred to as innovation knowledge (that is, knowledge embodied in new products, processes and technologies, new forms of organization and markets), Schumpeter himself did not deal adequately with the process of knowledge-creation.[3]

In this chapter a framework will be proposed for analysing how innovation knowledge is created in capitalist systems.

KNOWLEDGE CREATION AND THE CAPITALIST SYSTEM

The Importance of Changing Knowledge

Knowledge is central to all economic and social decision-making. The reason, simply, is that we think and act on the basis of what we know (or, more accurately, what we believe we know).

Changing knowledge is the most important driver of the dynamics of the capitalist system. The reason is that a change in the knowledge of players in the system may lead to a change in their actions. In turn other players may change in reaction. In short, changing knowledge challenges the status quo and unleashes movement in the system.

Changing knowledge is the result of processes in the human mind and interactions with other human minds. All change in knowledge is social change. The ability of humans to think and as a result change their knowledge has no direct counterpart in the natural (physical and biological) worlds. This makes human systems fundamentally different from natural systems with different dynamics.

Theoretically, the most important challenge facing analysts of the capitalist system is to understand how knowledge changes and how this impacts the dynamics of the system. The magnitude of this challenge is enormous because of the complexity of the determinants of change in knowledge. Complexity makes it dangerous to tackle the problem of changing knowledge head-on by attempting to explain how and why knowledge changes. Not only is the analytical journey that would be required tortuous, there is little likelihood that a researcher's choice of route and the destination arrived at would be widely acceptable. The analytical problem, therefore, is one of rendering the process of knowledge change tractable, both theoretically and empirically.

It is worth noting that orthodox economics, as noted above by Penrose, sidesteps the challenge of changing knowledge. It does so by assuming, implicitly or explicitly, that knowledge is complete, knowable (though not necessarily known by all), and given. Furthermore, knowledge does not change. The economic problem is then to analyse how players will act and interact so as to optimize their actions and the consequences of their actions on the basis of the *given* knowledge. Above all, players do not create new knowledge. Orthodox economics, therefore, is static in the specific sense that knowledge is given and does not change.[4]

It is not surprising that orthodox economics takes this evasive response. To do otherwise, to attempt to incorporate the process of changing knowledge into economic thinking, would necessitate the admission of unpredictability and indeterminacy into economics. The reason is that the process of knowledge change and the resulting knowledge are irreducibly unpredictable and indeterminate. And orthodox economics has always pretended to be an 'exact science' which is uncomfortable with unpredictability and indeterminacy. The cost of this response, however, is to fail to come fully to grips with the dynamics of the capitalist system. In turn this limits understanding of this system.

Innovation Knowledge

The approach taken in this chapter is to restrict attention to a single category of knowledge, referred to here as innovation knowledge. Innovation knowledge is knowledge embodied in new products, processes and technologies, forms of organization, and markets. In short, innovation knowledge is what Joseph Schumpeter referred to as new combinations. He argued that this category of knowledge plays a particularly important role in the dynamics of the capitalist system since it is responsible for the system's 'incessant change' and restlessness.

The question that will be explored in this chapter is, how is innovation knowledge created?

HOW INNOVATION KNOWLEDGE IS CREATED – 1: THE PRIMARY SYMBIOTIC RELATIONSHIPS

Innovation knowledge (of the kind embodied in new products, processes and technologies, forms of organization, and new markets) is created primarily in firms, although other influences (such as universities, government research institutes, intellectual property law, and standards) also shape the process of knowledge creation and its content.

But what is a 'firm'? The answer is contingent on the questions that are being asked about firms. Different questions yield different answers. For present purposes the firm is an entity that transforms inputs into outputs that are to be sold for gain. The transformation process requires knowledge regarding how inputs should be turned into sellable outputs. Technology refers to the use of existing knowledge in turning inputs into outputs. Innovation refers to new ways of transforming inputs into outputs for gain.

In creating value, firms participate in a dense web of relationships with other firms and other organizations and ultimately the knowledge that they create, which they embody in their offerings, is a product of their own knowledge and these interactions. In order to examine these interactions in more detail it is necessary to distinguish a firm's primary relationships (that is, relationships that a firm has with other firms) from the wider context which shapes these relationships.

The primary relationships are shown in Figure 5.1.

In Figure 5.1 a firm's four primary relationships are shown. These are relationships with a firm's customers, suppliers, partners, and competitors.

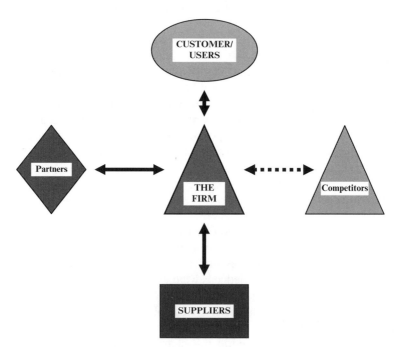

Figure 5.1   *The primary knowledge-creating symbiotic relationships: the firm as part of a web of symbiotic knowledge interactions*

These relationships may be analysed in two different ways. The first is static where it is assumed, first, that the firm already has the knowledge it needs to create value with its customers, suppliers, partners, and competitors and, second, that this knowledge is held constant over time. The second is dynamic, that is, the knowledge of the four groups of players changes over time as they interact with each other.

The Static Approach to the Primary Relationships

The static approach is familiar from standard microeconomics. The relationship between firms and their suppliers is dealt with through an analysis of input markets. By aggregating the input demand of firms in the market, input demand curves are derived. By aggregating the supply of inputs by input suppliers supply curves are derived. The demand and supply curves determine the set of input prices. The same is done for output markets (which deal with the relationship between firms and their customers), providing output prices. Output prices minus input prices determine firms' profits, which in turn determine how firms grow.

With knowledge held constant, the relationship with competitors (unless, of course, there is monopoly) is essentially determined by how many competitors there are. The more competitors and the less differentiated the products, the greater the constraint on the firm's ability to set its prices. Standard microeconomics distinguishes in this way between different market structures, ranging from perfect competition at the one extreme to monopoly at the other.

The Dynamic Approach to the Primary Relationships

Less familiar, however, is what will happen, and how to analyse, when knowledge changes. Rather than seeing firms and customer-users as the suppliers and demanders of given inputs and outputs embodying given knowledge, we can now see them also as the creators and users of knowledge. This approach is evident in a dynamic analysis of a firm's[5] relationship with its customers.

A firm's dynamic relationship with its customer-users

Firms supply their knowledge (in the form of products and services) to their customer-users. But this is only the starting point in their relationship with their customer-users. In purchasing the product and using it the customer acquires a particular kind of knowledge, namely knowledge of the product-in-use. In short, the customer becomes a specialist in the use of the product and acquires knowledge gained through use, knowledge relating to the strengths and weaknesses of the product when used for the customer's purposes.[6] This specialist user-knowledge may be fed back in various ways to the supplying firms. (The different ways in which user-knowledge may be fed back and the effectiveness of these ways constitutes a significant field of research in its own right.[7]) In turn, the supplying firms may use this knowledge as an input in the creation of further knowledge that will be passed back to the customer-user in a second round of mutual knowledge creation.[8]

Through their interactions, therefore, firms and customer-users create and use knowledge in an ongoing symbiotic process. This process never ends as users acquire knowledge

---

BOX 5.1   IMPACT OF THE INTERNET ON THE ROLE OF CONSUMER-USERS IN KNOWLEDGE CREATION

The Internet radically changes:

- the quantity of information available to buyers and sellers;
- the cost of information, including search costs;
- the ability to interact of buyers and sellers;
- the ability to aggregate users and create long-tail effects;
- the ability to visualize, vision being one of the most important ways of providing information and communicating.

---

of the products-in-use and this knowledge is fed back to the creators who over time use it to create further knowledge for consumer-users. Sometimes, however, it is the users themselves, using the knowledge they have accumulated, who make improvements.

But the relationship between the creators and users of knowledge will often involve more than the products that they are exchanging. Through their relationships with their customer-users firms will also acquire information about customers' broader needs, capabilities and contexts. This information may be used by firms to take a more proactive role in anticipating future desirable products and services, even before a demand for them has been articulated by consumer-users. Here an opportunity is created for future innovations.[9]

As this discussion, schematic as it is, makes clear there is far more that goes on in market processes of buying, using and selling than appears in the orthodox economics narrative. By explicitly or implicitly assuming given products embodying given knowledge, orthodox economics ignores the process of innovation knowledge creation that occurs as the creators and users of knowledge symbiotically interact, the users also becoming creators and the creators too becoming users.

The evolving role of consumer-users

Consumer-users have always played an important role in the creation of innovation knowledge although it is only relatively recently that their contribution has been the subject of academic study.[10] More recently, however, structural changes have occurred in the economic system that have radically transformed the role of the customer-user in the knowledge-creation process.

The structural changes referred to have been brought about by the global diffusion of the Internet from around 1995. Widespread use of the Internet has brought about a number of important transformations shown in Box 5.1. These transformations have changed radically the role of consumer-users in the innovation knowledge-creation process.

These systemic changes have altered the symbiotic relationships just as have earlier changes such as electricity and radical transport innovations (like the railways and internal combustion engine). In the case of innovation knowledge creation the changes shown in Box 5.1 have allowed consumers to be far more proactive, expanding their contribution to the knowledge-creation process and having a much greater impact. In some cases they have even allowed consumers to break the link with the original creators of the knowledge and to take control of the subsequent knowledge-creation process.

These radical changes blur further the very distinction between the creators and users of knowledge since users may become creators and vice versa. These systemic changes make it imperative to amend the standard Schumpeterian account of the innovation process, reconstructing the role played by consumer-users and the demand side more generally.

Suppliers and partners

The second and third primary relationships (shown in Figure 5.1) are with suppliers and partners. Here too there has been significant change although the underlying processes have been present as long as has capitalism.

Marshall discussed these processes in proposing a 'general rule' which he thought expressed the 'fundamental unity of action' between the laws of the physical and human worlds:

> This central unity is set forth in the general rule, to which there are not very many exceptions, that the development of the organism, whether social or physical, involves an increasing subdivision of functions between its separate parts on the one hand, and on the other a more intimate connection between them. (Marshall, 1890: 200–201)

Marshall continues,

> Each part gets to be less and less self-sufficient, to depend for its well-being more and more on other parts, so that any disorder in any part of a highly-developed organism will affect other parts also. This increased subdivision of functions, or 'differentiation', as it is called, manifests itself with regard to industry in such forms as the division of labour, and the development of specialized skill, knowledge and machinery: which 'integration', that is, a growing intimacy and firmness of the connections between the separate parts of the industrial organism, shows itself in such forms as the increase of security of commercial credit, and of the means and habits of communication by sea and road, by railway and telegraph, by post and printing-press. (ibid.)

One important consequence of the joint process of differentiation and integration – with significant implications for the creation of innovation knowledge – is that, *increasingly, knowledge of relevance to the firm is located outside the firm*. This necessarily implies that firms often have no option but to go outside their gates in order to access the complementary knowledge that they need to create their own knowledge. This requires the *external organization of the firm*, complementing its internal organization. From the point of view of the knowledge-creation process this shifts the boundary of the firm (even if from a legal or ownership perspective the boundary remains the same). In creating knowledge the firm becomes part of a wider web of symbiotic knowledge-creating relationships.

Competition in the dynamic approach

In the static approach competitors, by definition, are not creators and providers of knowledge. They exert their disciplining effect by supplying their given, substitutable products. However, in the dynamic approach competing firms become part of the knowledge-creation dynamic.

Regarding the creation of knowledge there are two aspects to inter-firm competitive rivalry. The first is responsive, responding to knowledge-based advantages that a competitor enjoys in the selection process in the market. This response aids the process of diffusion of knowledge. The second aspect is anticipatory, searching for and attempting to create new knowledge that will in the future give the firm a selection advantage. This involves imagining the future, creating hypotheses about the future that will then be tested in the market. These hypotheses (as with Popper's conjectures) are also part of the process of knowledge creation.

The responsive aspect involves learning from one's competitors, for example by imitating or improving on their offerings, and is an important source of knowledge for most firms. In making improvements, however, a response can also become anticipatory, bringing the two aspects together.

Creating knowledge for users under competitive conditions is very different from creating it when there are no competitors. Under competition it is necessary, not only to take account of the user's present and future requirements, but also to allow for the initiatives and responses of competitors.

SYMBIOTIC OPEN INNOVATION AND THE CREATION OF INNOVATION KNOWLEDGE

Symbiosis comes from the Greek meaning living together. Frequently symbiotic relationships are mutually beneficial. (However, this is not always the case, as, for instance, in a parasitic symbiotic relationship.)

A firm, as our discussion of the four primary relationships makes clear, is never an independent, isolated entity. Rather it is always part of a web of symbiotic relationships as the firm lives with, and interacts with, its customers, suppliers, partners and competitors. In playing their role in this web of interdependent actors firms accumulate innovation knowledge. From a knowledge point of view, therefore, the firm can never be an isolated unit of analysis (even though from a legal, financial and decision-making perspective it may be). Just as individuals in isolation can never create knowledge[11] so firms alone are severely constrained in their ability to create innovation knowledge.

The key point is that living together over time (that is, in human systems) *always* implies changing knowledge. The reason is that human minds in interaction are constantly involved in thinking, making new connections, experimenting, questioning, learning, and creating. Through a firm's symbiotic interactions with its customers, suppliers, partners and competitors – which simultaneously influence interactions within the firm – the knowledge of the firm itself as an individual player in the web, and the knowledge of the web as a whole, is *constantly* in a process of change. To assume that knowledge is given is to freeze the human players, to assume they are dead.

EX ANTE UNCERTAINTY AND UNPREDICTABILITY

One important logical consequence of the present analysis is unavoidable *ex ante* uncertainty and unpredictability in the knowledge-creating process. Although knowledge is in a constant process of becoming, it is not possible to predict the form that this knowledge in the future will take. This, in turn, implies that over time surprise and error are the rule rather than the exception. The human actors in this complex system have no option in this context but to create their own expectations of what might happen. However, a further feature of the human ability to imagine and create is that in the same situation different people will come up with different expectations. While this does lead to inconsistency, it also generates the variety that together with selection drives the evolutionary processes that change the system.

These 'givens' of human complex systems, as already noted, present difficulties for formal analyses seeking to calculate determinate outcomes. While these analyses may aid logical understanding, they may not help, or may even hinder (as a result of the explicit and implicit assumptions that they make) an understanding of how the system works and the implications for the system's actors. Formal analysis, therefore, should be treated as an aid to understanding rather than as being sufficient for understanding.

HOW INNOVATION KNOWLEDGE IS CREATED – 2: CONTEXTUAL DETERMINANTS

Some of the contextual determinants that influence the creation of innovation knowledge are shown in Figure 5.2.

The way in which competition affects the four primary knowledge-creating symbiotic relationships has already been discussed. Of the contextual determinants depicted in

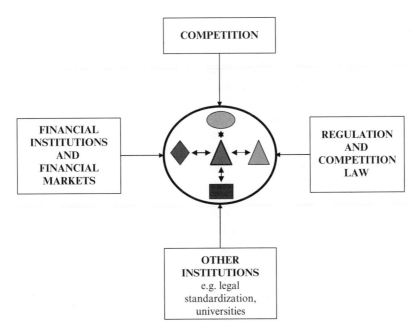

Figure 5.2   Contextual determinants of the creation of innovation knowledge

Figure 5.2 will be briefly examined here. These are financial institutions and financial markets; universities; and regulation.

Financial institutions and financial markets

Financial institutions will influence the primary relationships in a number of ways. One advantage of a severe financial crisis (if it can be seen as an advantage) is that it lays bare the implications of the functioning (and malfunctioning) of financial institutions.

Credit allows a firm to buy before it sells; to buy inputs before having to sell the output. As Schumpeter stressed, credit is necessary so that entrepreneurs can pull resources away from the old activities and direct them to the new. Credit gives entrepreneurs time to develop their innovative new products and services so that they can be sold. Conversely, the breakdown of the credit supplying mechanism inhibits the process of innovation knowledge creation.

However, the market for the funding of innovation is tricky, even if financial institutions are able to provide a sufficient supply of credit. The first reason for the difficulty is uncertainty. *Ex ante* there is no guarantee that intended innovation activity will result in desired innovation. The would-be creator of new knowledge does not know whether the knowledge will ultimately succeed in being created. If he or she did know, the knowledge would be old knowledge already established. Under these conditions it is impossible for the supplier of funds for innovation to be sure about the returns that the funds will generate.

But there is also another possible problem: asymmetric information. Usually, the demander of funds, the innovator, will have more information than the supplier regarding the uses to which the funds will be put and the returns that might be (even with uncertainty) expected. Even if the demander does not act opportunistically (defined by Williamson (1975) as self-seeking with guile) – although this may in some cases happen – it is possible that the demander will be unduly exuberant about the prospects for the innovation. If the supplier were uncritically to act on the demander's information, unrealistic expectations might be formed leading later to frustration.

However, forms of funding have evolved in order to deal with these problems. In the earliest stage, when the difficulties of uncertainty and asymmetric information are at their greatest, the entrepreneur has little option but to self-finance activity. But in the next stage, when things become a little clearer, there may be angel investors who are willing to step in. Not only do angel investors have available funding, they have also 'been there and done it themselves' with the result that the degree of asymmetry of information may be reduced.

In the following stage (often when a prototype has been produced, reducing uncertainty somewhat) venture capital funding might be available from specialists in particular areas. Much later, when the firm has a financial and profit track record it will be easier for the suppliers of funding to form a judgment regarding the firm's prospects (although a degree of uncertainty will still persist). Here financial institutions such as commercial and investment banks and corporate investors may be willing to provide funding, and capital markets may fund IPOs. In this way financial specialization has evolved in order to deal with the problems of uncertainty and asymmetric information in the financing and creating of innovation knowledge (although there is no guarantee that the solutions are perfect).

But what is the causal connection between the funding of innovation and innovation itself? For example, does the availability of venture capital increase innovation or is it innovation that elicits a supply of venture capital? One recent study suggests that it is the latter that usually applies (Vass, 2008), although there is also evidence that firms receiving more venture capital are more likely to patent (Kortum and Lerner, 2000).

Universities

In some sectors (particularly science-based sectors) firms depend on knowledge created in universities. However, the symbiotic relationship between firms and universities is significantly different from that between firms. The reason is the different motivations and incentives of firms and universities and of their knowledge-creators.

The main objective of firms is to make profit. Universities traditionally have had two objectives: research and teaching. More recently, a third objective has been added: the commercialization of research. Knowledge-creators in firms may have a variety of personal motivations.[12] However, generally firms will try (with greater or lesser success) to ensure that their knowledge-creators contribute to the shorter or longer run profitability of the firm.

The situation in universities is more complicated as a result of their objectives. To begin with, there is the possibility of conflicts between their three objectives, leading to trade-offs. For example, leading-edge research (measured and motivated by peer-reviewed publications in leading journals) may conflict with commercialization objectives. The focus on research may be at the expense of teaching quality, and vice versa. Furthermore, the performance incentives created by universities in pursuance of research objectives (such as their promotion criteria) may be inconsistent with commercial objectives. For instance, publication in leading journals (often a necessary condition for promotion) may not contribute to, and indeed may frustrate, the furtherance of commercialization. On the other hand, the time spent by university researchers working for firms may conflict with their role as academic researchers and teachers.

In addition, there is the question of the motivations of researchers. Where there is a significant difference in the remuneration of researchers in given areas in the private and university sectors it may be the case that there are also different motivations. It may be the case, for example, that university researchers are more motivated by status and the freedom to pursue their own intellectual interests and less motivated by monetary gain than their private sector counterparts. Different motivations may influence the symbiotic creation of knowledge although they may result in both advantages and disadvantages.

These problems may make it difficult for firms seeking to access the knowledge potentially available in universities. This is not to say that the problems, trade-offs and differing motivations cannot be resolved, even if imperfectly. The point remains, however, that the symbiotic relationships between firms and universities will often be complicated, making the process of joint knowledge creation potentially difficult.

Regulation

Regulation is an example of an institution that, in Douglass North's (1990) definition, determines the rules of the game. However, standard regulation theory and practice has tended to follow the static approach referred to earlier, not taking into account the process of innovation knowledge creation.

To simplify (but not to unduly distort), standard regulation theory and practice are informed by the static economic theory of perfect competition. This theory teaches that social welfare (specifically, the welfare of consumers and producers) will be maximized when the conditions of perfect competition are fulfilled. In regulation theory and practice perfect competition is treated as an ideal benchmark, acknowledging that real-world circumstances are likely to diverge from this ideal but assuming that the closer that it is possible to get to perfect competition the more favourable the outcome.

However, there are two sets of problems that follow from this approach. First, it is questionable whether perfect competition provides a meaningful benchmark. The reason is that the assumptions of perfect competition in both the short and the long run (such as homogeneous products, perfect information on the part of producers and consumers, and equilibrium) exclude the possibility of innovation and the creation of new knowledge.

The second is the assumption that is implicitly made in regulation practice that competitive conditions are both necessary and sufficient for the realization of internationally competitive innovation knowledge creation. (This assumption does not follow from regulatory theory since, as already noted, standard regulatory theory does not incorporate the knowledge-creation process.) If this assumption were true, regulators would only have one problem to solve, namely the creation of competitive markets. The achievement of internationally competitive innovation knowledge creation would follow automatically from competitive markets. However, as has been made explicitly and implicitly clear in the discussion of the creation of innovation knowledge in this chapter, competitive markets may be neither necessary[13] nor sufficient for the attainment of internationally competitive innovation.

How should regulation be rethought if innovation knowledge creation is to be adequately taken into account? Several points may be made in answer to this question.

To begin with, it is indeed necessary to rethink regulation. As has been seen, regulation is largely about the establishment of competitive markets. However, competition is not an end in itself but a means to the achievement of other ends. The ends include increasing efficiency (defined dynamically), productivity, economic growth, equity, and sectoral objectives (such as health aims). As we have argued, competition is neither necessary nor sufficient for the achievement of these ends, although competition may help. Innovative knowledge creation is probably both necessary and sufficient for attaining increasing productivity and economic growth and it may help for some sectoral objectives. Ideally, therefore, an appropriate approach to regulation (and government policy) ought to take both competition and innovation knowledge-creation into account.

It would be convenient if it were possible to establish all the conditions that are both necessary and sufficient for the achievement of internationally competitive innovation knowledge creation and to determine whether or not in a real situation these conditions exist. The remaining problem would then be to determine what needs to be done to create the conditions where they do not exist. But unfortunately, the human complex system does not allow this to be done. In part this is due to complexity itself, the complex interactions between the many factors that determine such knowledge-creation. But it is also due to the uncertainty and unpredictability that, as has been shown, is an inherent part of the process of the creating of knowledge.

So how should we proceed in rethinking regulation? This is a matter for further analysis and debate. But it is possible to suggest one way of proceeding.

The first step is to try and understand how the relevant innovation knowledge creation process is working, including its strengths and weaknesses. This may be at a national level, a sectoral level, a regional level, or in particular firms and non-firm bodies. In order to undertake this investigation it will be helpful to have an appreciation of the innovation process itself. In addition, it will be useful to have indicators of performance.

With this appreciation and performance indicators it may be possible to establish whether the absence of competition is constraining performance. If it is, and if something can be done about it, there will be reason to use regulatory solutions designed to increase competition or to ameliorate its absence. These solutions will have to be dynamically conceived, taking account of the process of knowledge-creation. (Of course, there may be other reasons quite apart from innovation considerations for going down this regulatory road, such as negative effects on consumers.)

But is this approach practically achievable? Do not complexity, uncertainty and unpredictability stand in the way of useful, practical regulation? In short, to return to Penrose, is not the problem of knowledge still too slippery to handle?

Two answers may be given to these questions. The first is that yes, there are significant analytical and practical problems in pursuing this path. However, not to pursue it is to continue to ignore the process of innovation knowledge creation which is the key driver of the dynamics of human complex systems. (The story of the drunk searching under the street-light because this is where he can see is well known.)

The second answer is that some comfort can be derived from the current financial crisis. The workings of global financial markets are also complex, uncertain and unpredictable. But the threat of their failure has made it imperative to go beyond the 'street light', to try and understand what the problems are and attempt to devise appropriate solutions. The relatively easy world of static economics (although it too has its own difficulties), where the slipperiness of knowledge is avoided, may be a more comfortable habitat. But its ability to help deal with dynamic problems associated with the creation of innovative knowledge is limited. As in the case of the financial crisis, therefore, we have little alternative but to press on and deal with the creation of knowledge.

THE EVOLUTION OF INNOVATION KNOWLEDGE

Innovation knowledge evolves. It evolves, as do all evolutionary processes, as a result of the interaction between the generation of variety and selection from this variety.

In the capitalist system variety in innovation knowledge is generated as people create different kinds of knowledge. Of particular concern in this chapter is innovation knowledge, that is, knowledge embodied in new products, processes and technologies, forms of organization, and markets. New innovation knowledge leads to variety in these areas.

It is firms that specialize in the creation of innovation knowledge, although they may be helped (or hindered) by other bodies (for example, universities or government research institutes) and institutions (such as intellectual property rights or regulation). A firm's innovation knowledge is embodied in its output (products and services). This output must be sold if the firm is to generate the revenue to renew its operations.

It is in the process of selling and buying that market selection enters the picture. Buyers, on the demand side of the market, choose from the products that are available. This selection process winnows the variety through the selection of the products of some firms and the rejection of others. In this way the market process acts as a selection mechanism.[14]

The successful sale of the innovation knowledge embodied in the products that have met the selection processes' criteria will contribute to the reproduction of the firm. It will do this by adding to the firm's revenue and perhaps profits. Over time more profitable firms will expand relative to less profitable ones. As the former expand and increase the output of their successful products so the use of the innovation knowledge embodied in these products will grow. Conversely, the use of the innovation knowledge in the de-selected products will decrease. In this way the content of the stock of innovation knowledge will evolve over time.[15]

SECTORAL ECOSYSTEMS AND THE CREATION OF INNOVATION KNOWLEDGE

It has been shown in this chapter that symbiotic open innovation relationships are essentially interactions between the creators and users of innovation knowledge. It has also been emphasized that in the process of innovation knowledge creation the distinction between creators and users becomes blurred, with users frequently also being the creators of knowledge and vice versa.

Until this point the discussion of the relationship between creators and users has been primarily at the micro level, that is, at the level of individual firms (including their suppliers, partners, and competitors) and their customers. However, symbiotic open innovation relationships also exist between groups of firms, and groups of customer-users, who perform the function of creating and using innovation knowledge.

These group relationships are best analysed at the level of the sector. Indeed, the sectoral level, rather than that of the aggregate macro-economy, becomes an important unit of analysis precisely because of the distinctive knowledge-creating and using relationships in each sector. Furthermore – going beyond the groups of firms – there are other determinants that exist at the level of the sector that also influence the symbiotic relationship between creators and users in the process of innovation knowledge creation. For example, universities play a key role in innovation in the biomedical sector, a role that is very different from that performed by universities in, say, the motor car or heavy engineering sectors.

But how might the symbiotic relationship between the groups of firms that create and use knowledge be analysed at the sectoral level? This question will be pursued by taking the ICT sector as an example.

The Example of the ICT Ecosystem[16]

An ecosystem consists of groups of organisms (or species) that interact with one another and with their environment. This biological metaphor is useful in analysing socio-economic systems precisely because, as Alfred Marshall put it more than a century ago, at its heart is 'living force and movement'.[17] In strong contrast, the standard metaphor in orthodox economics is one of optimization and equilibrium where the actors involved have reached their optimal positions and are in a state of rest. Knowledge remains constant in this state. Were it to change, and were different actors able to create different knowledge which would not instantaneously be shared by all, equilibrium would be impossible. On the other hand, in biological ecosystems all species, and possibly their environment, are in a constant process of change.

Ecosystems exist at both the micro and sectoral levels of the socio-economic system. For example, the primary symbiotic relationships of a firm situated within a broader context of institutions and other influences, discussed earlier in this chapter, may be thought of as a micro-ecosystem. The ecosystem conceptualization is also useful at the sectoral level as will be shown now in connection with the ICT ecosystem.

The four main groups of players in the ICT ecosystem

Who are the main groups of players – groups that through their symbiotic relationships create and use innovation knowledge – in the ICT sector? Four groups may be distinguished: ICT equipment providers; network operators (including telecoms, cable, and satellite operators, as well as broadcasters); platform, content and applications providers; and final consumer-users. (The first three groups are intermediate consumer-users, each buying and using the output of the other two groups as well, perhaps, as some of their own output.)

These four groups of players are organized into a layered, hierarchically structured, architecture. Each layer defines a set of functions that are necessary for the layer above to perform its role in the ICT ecosystem. A diagrammatic depiction of the ICT ecosystem is shown in Figure 5.3.

In Layer 1, ICT equipment makers (including both hardware and software) provide the elements that go into information and communications networks (such as phones, computers, servers, routers and transmissions equipment). The network operators in Layer 2 purchase network elements which are strung together in the form of networks. In turn, these networks and their elements provide platforms on which content and applications providers, located in Layer 3, create offerings for their customers (final customers in Layer 4 as well as intermediate customers in the other three layers).

The players in this ecosystem, it should be noted, may be involved in more than one layer. Furthermore, over time the boundaries between layers tend to shift (as indicated by the dotted boundary lines).

What drives evolutionary change in the ICT ecosystem, making it the restless system that it is? The answer is changing innovation knowledge, that is, new products and services, new processes and technologies, new forms of organization, and new markets. But how do these innovations happen? The answer to this question is that innovation emerges largely from the symbiotic open innovation relationships between the four groups of players.

Symbiotic open innovation in the ICT ecosystem

In the ICT ecosystem each of the four groups of players interacts with all the others, making a total of six open symbiotic relationships. It is out of these relationships that most innovation emerges. The six relationships are shown in Figure 5.4.

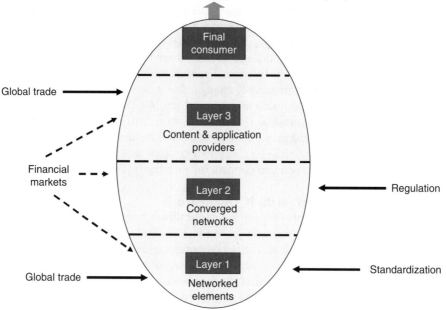

Source: Fransmann (2010).

Figure 5.3   A simplified model of the new ICT ecosystem

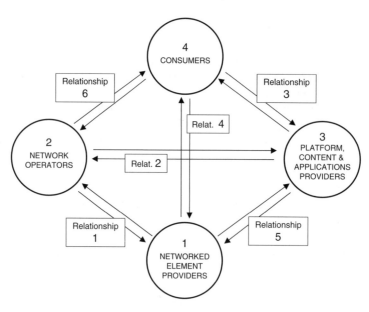

Source: Fransmann (2010).

Figure 5.4   Relationships in the ICT ecosystem

However, these six symbiotic open innovation relationships are not the end of the story. The reason, simply, is that the relationships themselves are shaped by a set of other factors that must therefore be included in the analysis. These factors include institutions which Noble Laureate Douglass North defines as the rules of the game that include, for instance, regulation and competition law. Universities and standardization are other institutions which, although not defining formal rules, will influence the symbiotic relationships. Other determinants such as the financial ecosystem will also influence the relationships (as the current global financial crisis is teaching us).

Examples of knowledge creation in these six symbiotic open innovation relationships are to be found in Fransman (2010).

CONCLUSION

Knowledge may, as Edith Penrose suggests (see first paragraph of this chapter), be slippery and difficult to handle. However, it is essential for economists to bite the bullet and attempt to deal adequately with it. To refuse to do so is, in effect, to fail to understand the dynamics of the uniquely human complex system that is the socio-economy.

In this chapter one way forward has been proposed. This has involved the analysis of changing innovation knowledge (that is, knowledge embodied in new products, processes and technologies, forms of organization, and markets) through an examination of the symbiotic open innovation relationships between firms and their customer-users, suppliers, partners and competitors co-evolving within a broader institutional context.

NOTES

1. The emphasis here is on the way in which knowledge is created as opposed to the incentives to create knowledge and the institutions that facilitate knowledge creation. The latter issues have received widespread treatment in economics.
2. As Darwin (1859) said, *natura non facit saltum* (nature does not make a jump). But the human mind does as knowledge is created. In the capitalist human system, as Schumpeter stressed, the rupture is incessantly produced from within; it is the 'fundamental impulse that sets and keeps the capitalist engine in motion'. Rupture occurs continuously as a result of innovation knowledge creation.
3. 'An explanation of how new knowledge is created, and what the feedback relationships between search, discovery, experimentation, and adoption of new possibilities look like, and the respective motivations – all this would be necessary in order to really be able to treat economic change as being endogenously caused. With [Schumpeter's] focus on entrepreneurial skills in *promoting* innovations, rather than conceiving them, attention is diverted from general human creativity and inventiveness and the motivations underlying it as crucial elements of evolutionary change' (Witt, 2002: 15).
4. In some economic models some 'knowledge' does change. One example is models dealing with so-called learning-by-doing. But in these models the 'knowledge' that is assumed to change and the new knowledge that replaces it are highly constrained. The process of knowledge change, therefore, is crude, simplistic, and mechanistic and falls far short of the process of knowledge creation in the world that we know.
5. It should be noted that reference here is to *a* firm, rather than *the* firm (the latter designating a representative firm, a term frequently used in orthodox economics). The reason for reference to an individual firm is simply that firms differ. Accordingly, different firms will have different relationships with their customers, suppliers, partners, and competitors and these different symbiotic relationships will be accompanied by the creation of different innovation knowledge.
6. Different customers will have different purposes and therefore will acquire different sets of knowledge as they put the product to use to serve their varying purposes within varying contexts.

7. The work of Eric von Hippel and Bengt-Åke Lundvall on user-producer interactions has been an important stimulus in this field.
8. As Nathan Rosenberg (1976) has pointed out in his study of capital good providers, in some cases firms may also be users of their own products (for example machine tools). This internalizes within the firm the user-feedback process allowing the firm to act on the basis of its own information in order to make improvements.
9. One example that I have studied in detail is the relationship between telecoms network operators and their specialist equipment providers. This relationship took significantly different forms in the US, Japan and Europe and as telecoms services markets were liberalized from the mid-1980s the knowledge-creation process changed as more of the R&D-intensive activities passed to the equipment providers. See Fransman (1995) and (2004).
10. A landmark study is Eric von Hippel's book, *The Sources of Innovation* (von Hippel, 1988).
11. The psychoanalyst, Wilfred Bion, examines the growth of knowledge in the newly born infant, locating this process in the relationship between the infant and its mother. Later in life the growth of individual knowledge remains a social process. See, for example, W.R. Bion (1984).
12. For example, there are well-known cases of firm-based researchers continuing 'underground' with their research even though their managers have decided that the research should be terminated. One instance is Theodore Maiman, who produced the first working laser on 16 May 1960 in Hughes Research Laboratory in California, persisting with his ground-breaking research in defiance of instructions to stop.
13. One example of successful innovation occurring under monopolistic product market conditions is the telecoms services market in the main industrialized countries until the mid-1980s when these markets were liberalized. Indeed, during the monopoly era some of the most important innovations were made in the R&D laboratories of the main telecoms operators (such as AT&T's Bell Laboratories, France Telecom's CNET Laboratories, and BT's Martelesham Laboratories). These included, for example, the transistor, the laser, cellular communications, the C software language, and so on. The 'children' of these innovations are still amongst the most important drivers of today's ICT sector.
14. Apart from market selection there are other forms of selection in capitalist economies that also influence the evolution of innovation knowledge. However, these are not discussed here.
15. The material in this section is a brief summary of a complex process about which there is a large literature in evolutionary economics. Just a few points will be made here. In their seminal contribution Nelson and Winter (1982) propose that firms should be conceived of as repositories of knowledge. Firms differ in terms of their knowledge. Their knowledge is contained in their routines, which include routines used in searching for new knowledge. The routines of the firm are analogous to the genes of a biological organism (although firms may be able to change their routines in a way that biological organisms cannot change their genes). However, selection works on the phenotype, that is, the characteristics of the organism that determine its fitness in the selection environment. For the firm involved in market selection the phenotype refers to those product characteristics about which consumers express their preferences in deciding whether or not to buy the product. Just as genotype and phenotype interact in biological organisms so routines interact with product characteristics. But there is a further point that needs to be made in connection with firms. Firms are usually multi-product entities. But the profits that determine firms' evolutionary success are a magnitude aggregated over all the firm's products. Accordingly, some of a firm's products that have not fared well in the selection process may nevertheless be reproduced together with the innovation knowledge they embody. Where this happens the effect of market selection on the evolution of innovation knowledge will be weakened.
16. This section draws on the present author's book, *The New ICT Ecosystem – Implications for Policy and Regulation* (Fransman, 2010).
17. See the preface to Fransman (2010).

BIBLIOGRAPHY

Antonelli, C. (2008), 'The system dynamics of technical change', draft, pp. 8–10.
Antonelli, C. (2009), 'The economics of innovation: from the classical legacies to the economics of complexity', *Economics of Innovation and New Technology*, **18**, 611–46.
Bion, W.R. (1984), *Second Thoughts. Selected Papers on Psycho-Analysis*, London: H. Karnac.
Darwin, C. (1859), *On The Origin Of Species By Means Of Natural Selection, Or The Preservation Of Favoured Races In The Struggle For Life*, London: John Murray.
Fransman, M. (1995), *Japan's Computer and Communications Industry: The Evolution of Industrial Giants and Global Competitiveness*, Oxford: Oxford University Press.

Fransman, M. (2004), 'The telecoms boom and bust 1996–2003 and the role of financial markets', *Journal of Evolutionary Economics*, **14** (4), 369–406.

Fransman, M. (2010), *The New ICT Ecosystem – Implications for Policy and Regulation*, Cambridge: Cambridge University Press.

Hippel, E. von (1988), *The Sources of Innovation*, New York: Oxford University Press.

Kortum, S. and Lerner, J. (2000), 'Assessing the contribution of venture capital to innovation', *Rand Journal of Economics*, **31** (4), 674–92.

Lane, D.A. and Maxfield, R. (1997), 'Foresight complexity and strategy', in Arthur, W.B., Durlauf, S.N. and Lane, D.A. (eds), *The Economy as an Evolving Complex System II*, Reading, MA: Addison-Wesley, pp. 169–98.

Lundvall, B.Å. (1988), 'Innovation as an interactive process: from user-producer interaction to the national system of innovation', in Dosi, G., Freeman, C., Nelson, R. and Soetc, L. (eds), *Technical Change and Economic Theory*, pp. 349–69, London: Pinter.

Marshall, A. (1890), *Principles of Economics*, London: Macmillan.

Nelson, R.R. and Winter, S.G. (1982), *An Evolutionary Theory of Economic Change*, Cambridge: The Belknap Press of Harvard University Press.

North, D.C. (1990), *Institutions, Institutional Change and Economic Performance*, Cambridge: Cambridge University Press.

Penrose, E.T. (1959), *The Theory of the Growth of the Firm*, 3rd edn (1995), Oxford: Oxford University Press.

Rosenberg, N. (1976), *Perspectives on Technology*, Cambridge: Cambridge University Press.

Schumpeter, J.A. (1934), *The Theory of Economic Development*, New York: Oxford University Press.

Schumpeter, J.A. (1939), *Business Cycles*, New York: McGraw-Hill.

Schumpeter, J.A. (1942), *Capitalism, Socialism and Democracy*, New York: Harper and Brothers.

Vass, Thomas E. (2008), 'Will more venture capital spur regional innovation?', Private Capital Market Working Paper No. 2008-08-04 (available at SSRN: http://ssrn.com/abstract=1269405).

Williamson, O. (1975), *Markets and Hierarchies*, New York: The Free Press.

Witt, U. (2002), 'How evolutionary is Schumpeter's theory of economic development?', *Industry and Innovation*, **9** (1/2), 7–22.

PART III

THE ECONOMIC COMPLEXITY OF KNOWLEDGE

6. Knowledge, complexity and networks*

Pier Paolo Saviotti

1. INTRODUCTION

Knowledge is becoming the most important factor determining the competitiveness of firms and the growth of countries. However, do we know what knowledge is? Can we represent it in such a way that it can be measured and modelled as a component of economic processes? The limited understanding that economists have so far acquired of knowledge comes mostly from studies of innovation, that is, of processes which in order to give rise to new artefacts use and create knowledge. The tools which economists of innovation have developed rely on indicators of innovation, most of which are also indicators of knowledge. Publications and patents are traces of knowledge which have been left by processes of knowledge creation and utilization. However, while both publications and patents are related to knowledge we do not know exactly how. In order to make progress in the construction of an economics of knowledge we need to find an adequate, sufficiently general and operationally useful, definition of knowledge. Such a definition should allow us to detect units of knowledge which can be observed and used to measure and model processes of knowledge creation and utilization. In what follows a definition of knowledge which is both general and operationally useful will be given and a representation of the knowledge base of firms will be derived from it. Furthermore, the dynamics of knowledge will be interpreted using a number of complexity based concepts. In what follows we outline a number of such concepts and discuss the meaning they can acquire in the context of the representation of knowledge. Amongst the most general of these concepts is that of networks which in, this chapter will be applied both to the representation of the knowledge base of firms and to that of networks constructed by knowledge producing or using organizations.

2. COMPLEXITY AND KNOWLEDGE

2.1 Emergence

Emergence can be defined as the arising of novel and coherent structures, patterns and properties during a process of self-organization in complex systems (Goldstein, cited in Corning, 2002). The common characteristics of emergence are: (1) radical novelty (features not previously observed in systems); (2) coherence or co-relation meaning integrated wholes that maintain themselves over some period of time; (3) a global or macro 'level', that is, there is some property of 'wholeness'; (4) it is the product of a dynamical process (it evolves); (5) it is ostensive (it can be perceived) .

Emergence can be weak or strong. Weak emergence occurs when properties arise in a system as a result of the interactions at an elemental level. However, some systems can have properties not directly traceable to the system's components. In this case the emergent properties are irreducible to the system's component parts (Laughlin, 2005). Then the whole is not only greater than the sum of its parts but irreducible to them. In this case we speak of strong emergence.

The concept of emergence, and particularly that of strong emergence, is closely related to a number of concepts used in the economics of innovation and increasing in the economics of knowledge. Amongst those concepts are:

(i)   Qualitative change
(ii)   Discontinuity
(iii)   Paradigms (scientific, technological)
(iv)   Natural, technological trajectories
(v)   Radical, incremental innovations

To say that economic development is characterized by qualitative change means that some entities emerge in the process which are not comparable to (Saviotti, 2007), and thus not explicable by, or not reducible to, the properties of pre-existing entities. When these new entities arise they lead to a discontinuity. It is precisely this type of discontinuity which is captured by concepts such as scientific paradigms (Kuhn, 1962), technological paradigms (Dosi, 1982), natural (Nelson and Winter, 1977) or technological (Dosi, 1982) trajectories, competence disrupting or competence enhancing technological change (Tushman and Anderson, 1986), exploration or exploitation (March, 1991). In scientific or technological paradigms the revolutionary phase of the initial emergence is followed by a more incremental phase, called normal science, during which the leading principles of the new paradigm are applied to a growing range of situations. In the same way as Copernican astronomy is not reducible to Ptolemaic astronomy (Kuhn, 1962) molecular biology is not reducible to the concepts of traditional biology. It must be pointed out that the emergence of a new discipline in science following the onset of a new paradigm can give rise (even if with a delay) to a new technological paradigm once some of the potential industrial applications of the new scientific knowledge begin to be exploited.

The emergence of discontinuities and of qualitative change is closely related to a number of concepts such as creativity, creative reaction (Antonelli, 2008), to the debate between gradualism and saltationism (here see the comparison of Marshall and Schumpeter in Antonelli, 2008), to punctuated equilibrium, and to micro-diversity (Allen et al., 2006).

2.2   System Structure and Dynamics

Another very important concept in the analysis of complex systems is that of structure. The structure of a complex system is constituted by its components and by their interactions. Of course, the representation of the system's structure varies depending on the level of aggregation since each component has an internal structure with its own components and interactions. Such structure is created by particular phenomena which make the system *irreducible* to the previous state of the separated components. In a dynamical sense the important questions to ask about structure are: (i) why and how does this structure emerge? And (ii) why and how does a given structure disappear to be substituted by one or more different and non comparable structures? Question (i) leads us back to the concept of order which Hayek (1978) judges more relevant than that of equilibrium. The emergence of an initial structure and transitions towards qualitatively different systems are examples of strong emergence in the previous sense. A theory of long run economic development must be able to explain why and how transitions towards qualitatively different states occur. For example, an important question could arise about the nature of the Industrial Revolution. Was it indeed a revolution involving the emergence of new components or simply the accumulation of components which had been present in the economic system but the interactions of which changed? Of course, this question can be reduced to the relationship between gradualism and saltationism already referred to in the previous section. In terms of innovation the previous question could be formulated as: did the Industrial Revolution arise from a number of important and radical innovations which collectively induced the emergence of a new industrial system, or was that emergence due to the changing interactions of previously existing components? We could talk of strong emergence in the former case and of weak emergence in the latter. The same question could be asked about processes of knowledge creation. For example, is molecular biology the result of radically new concepts or is it the result of assembling differently concepts which had been present before? It must be pointed out that the so called *recombinant theories* of knowledge (Fleming, 2001; Sorenson et al., 2006) attribute the creation of innovations and of new knowledge to the recombination of previously existing ideas. This point will be discussed in greater detail later but we can already see that both radical novelty and the recombination of pre-existing ideas can give rise to emergence.

Knowledge can then be considered a complex system the structure of which changes at particular times in ways which we need to understand. Our task is to find out the components of the knowledge system, why and how they come about and how they change in the course of time. For what concerns social systems we can find that important changes occur both in the elemental components, for example in the competencies of individuals, and in the interactions giving rise to different levels of aggregation such as meso or macro. At a very general level of analysis the elementary interactions occurring in a social system can be analysed by means of two amongst the oldest and more fundamental concepts in economics: division of labour and coordination. Thus, the new competencies to which either radical innovations or the finer subdivision of existing processes give rise are new forms of division of labour, as well as the new scientific disciplines which are increasingly underlying the emergence of innovations and of new industrial sectors. The division of labour is useless by itself without the forms of coordination by means of which partial outcomes are transformed into final outputs which are sellable, or socially useful. In fact, one could argue that one of the main objectives of the structure of modern organizations is to provide the required coordination of all the steps in the division of labour that they contain. As far as knowledge is concerned, one of the fundamental questions arising is: 'why and how do new forms of knowledge (disciplines) emerge, how are they interacting amongst themselves and with pre-existing types of knowledge, and how do they contribute to the emergence of new technologies?'

2.3 Diversity, Variety and System Evolution

During economic development new industrial processes and new organizational forms arose. Such changes required the emergence of new competencies and of new forms of knowledge. Sometimes the new competencies and forms of knowledge replace pre-existing ones, sometimes they are added to them. This process of pronounced structural change corresponds to Schumpeter's creative destruction (Schumpeter, 1934), although whether the amount of creation and that of destruction are identical is an open research question. The variety of a system is determined by the number of its distinguishable components. The emergence of new types of competencies, of new organizational forms and of new types of output can change the variety of an economic system. Thus, variety is a sensitive indicator of structural change, although when the extent of destruction is equal to the extent of creation no net change in variety will result. In this case new economic species emerge and the same number of existing ones becomes extinct. However, if variety were to rise or fall persistently in the course of economic development then an arrow of time would be present. Not only would there be structural change but it would move predominantly in one direction. There is increasing, although not definitive, evidence that output and export variety rise in the course of economic development (Frenken et al., 2007; Saviotti and Frenken, 2008; Saviotti et al., 2008; Saviotti and Nesta, 2009; Funke and Ruwhedel, 2001a, 2001b). Even in the case of knowledge there is structural change determined by the emergence of new knowledge types (for example, paradigms) and by the extinction of older ones. Even for knowledge, variety is a sensitive indicator of structural change and it is particularly useful when variety grows or falls persistently in the course of time. Knowledge variety would clearly be affected by the specialization or by the broadening of given research fields. Similarly to what occurs for industrial processes, variety can be measured at different levels of aggregation.

2.4 Networks as the Structure of Systems

Recently networks have been one of the most lively research fields within complexity. Their importance lies in the fact that they can be considered a good representation of complex systems and of socio-economic systems in particular. Network nodes are the components of socio-economic systems and their links are the interactions. The usefulness of networks lies in the fact that some of their properties depend exclusively on network geometry irrespective of the nature of their components or nodes. For example, a class of networks which has been recently discovered and which is called 'scale free' (Barabasi et al., 1999; Barabasi and Reka, 1999; Reka et al., 2000; Barabasi, 2002; Reka and Barabasi, 2002; Barabasi and Bonabeau, 2003) has a highly asymmetric distribution of links around nodes: few nodes have many links and many nodes have few links. This distribution is very different from that predicted for previously studied networks, called exponential networks, which had a much more egalitarian distribution of links around nodes. Scale free networks have a power law distribution while exponential networks have a Poisson distribution of links around nodes. As a consequence, scale free networks have the interesting property of being very resistant to random attack: almost 80 per cent of the links can be cut before a scale free network is destroyed while the corresponding percentage for an exponential network is less than 20 per cent. However, a targeted attack selectively cutting links around the most central nodes (hubs) destroys the network by cutting less than 20 per cent of the links. Two conditions are required in order for scale free networks to exist: (i) growth – the number of nodes must grow; (ii) preferential attachment – new links tend to be formed more easily with already linked nodes. These conditions are often present in socio-economic networks. In general the observed growth in variety of a number of economic species (technologies, and so on) can be expected to lead to a growing number of nodes. Thus, growing variety could supply one of the two conditions required for the existence of scale free networks. In socio-economic networks the second condition – preferential attachment – depends on sources of increasing returns to adoption. Examples of these sources are reputational structure and various types of resources. Let us take the example of an alliance between an incumbent large diversified firm (LDF) and a start up. In its choice of partner the start up is likely to favour the LDF with the best reputation. If the alliance leads to a further enhancement of the LDF's reputation, other start ups will continue to favour it with respect to other LDFs. Moreover, if a growing number of alliances raises the resource base of incumbent LDFs, those already having a greater number of alliances will be better able to form further ones than other LDFs. Thus, conditions (i) and (ii) can often be found in socio-economic networks. The presence of these two conditions leads to a higher probability of creation of scale free networks than to other types of networks, or to a higher relative rate of *variation* for this type of network. This condition is at best necessary, but not sufficient, to justify a high concentration of scale free networks. However, one of the most important findings about this type of network its resistance to attack. If we interpret attack as selection, scale free networks are likely to have a high rate of variation and a low rate of selection whenever conditions (i) and (ii) are satisfied. On the other hand, since conditions (i) and (ii) are often present in socio-economic networks, we can expect the scale free geometry to be quite common in this type of network.

These network properties are obviously interesting and highly relevant for socio-economic networks. However, although research in scale free networks has concentrated on the distribution of links around nodes, other related network properties are of great importance. For example, the existence of scale free networks implies an uneven distribution of the degree of centrality of nodes. Few nodes are highly central while others have a low centrality. Furthermore, the distribution of centrality is likely to change dynamically, for example with the distribution becoming at times more skewed or more even, as the relative centrality of some nodes falls and that of others rises. Another property whose role has already been discussed is connectivity. We have already seen how we can expect connectivity to rise or to fall during the evolution of networks. The meaning of this property will be discussed in greater detail in the next section.

The previous considerations focus predominantly on the static structure of networks. However, for us it is equally important to understand how network numbers and structures change in the course of time. Prigogine (see for example, Nicolis and Prigogine, 1989) supplied us with ideas which are very useful in this context. For example, an important distinction needs to be introduced between closed and open systems. The former are closed because they do not exchange anything (such as matter and energy) with their environment. Only closed systems can achieve an equilibrium, which corresponds to the maximum possible disorder or randomness of the components of the system, that is, to the contrary of the order we observe in economic development. Open systems exchange matter, energy, information and so on with their environment. The rates of flow through the boundaries of the system measure the distance of such system from equilibrium: the more intense such flows, the more the system moves away from equilibrium. The interesting behaviour of these systems only emerges when they are far enough away from equilibrium. In these conditions structure may emerge first and transitions between different types of structure can occur subsequently. Transitions occur when the system, as a consequence of its previous development, becomes unstable and undergoes a transition to a different configuration. According to Prigogine, instability arises in the form of *fluctuations* in some system variables. When fluctuations become sufficiently intense they induce *bifurcations*, or transitions to different configurations of the system, which are not only different from pre-transition ones but can be present in higher numbers. As a consequence of bifurcations the number of possible states of the system can increase, thus providing an in-principle justification for the growing variety of the economic system.

Thus, Prigogine's theory gives a potential explanation to (i) the emergence of structure, (ii) the presence of transitions between distinguishable states of the system, and (iii) the growth in the number of possible system states after the transition. Prigogine's theory provides a potential explanation for the stylized facts listed above. Incidentally, let us note that some very similar stylized facts apply to biological development. Prigogine's ideas provide an underlying theoretical framework for both biological and economic development. Of course, the existence of this underlying theoretical framework does not mean that exactly the same type of explanation will apply to biological and economic phenomena. Complexity theory is expected to be applicable to many different types of systems at a high level of generality. The complete analysis of each system involves both such a general level and a more specific one requiring the use of concepts and variables specific to the system itself. Thus, the actual dynamics of biological and of economic systems cannot be expected to be identical even if at a high level of generality they share the non-equilibrium nature of evolution and the possibility of bifurcations.

In this context fluctuations take an interesting meaning. Instability within an existing structure/network is likely to arise as a consequence of the instability of some existing links. This instability can be interpreted as a departure from dominant rules, which in turn can allow the exploration of new subsets of ExtEnv and the creation of innovations. (For brevity in what follows we will refer to the external environment as ExtEnv.) This would be compatible with observations which imply that historically innovations have tended to arise more frequently in societies which were freer and less bound by tradition (see for example Landes, 1999).

In terms of networks an increase in the variety of the economic system during the process of economic development could imply that the number of networks within the system increases. Another important feature of network dynamics is the evolution of their connectivity. In fact the variety of an economic system at best measures the number of its nodes but does not say anything about its links, which are an important part of its structure. Therefore, connectivity is an important part of network dynamics. We can expect innovations to be introduced by entrepreneurs in a rule poor environment, which provides the required freedom and the scope for fluctuations. Not all fluctuations are successful. At any time most of them are likely to be selected out. Precisely for this reason, a society which is able to create more fluctuations will have a greater chance of having successful ones. However, if the innovation is successful we can expect it to be widely imitated and to diffuse gradually in society. In order to acquire its 'economic weight' an innovation also requires the co-evolution of appropriate institutions (Nelson, 1994). The creation of complementary technologies and of appropriate institutions enhances the potential market size of the new technology. In presence of such institutions the output corresponding to the new technology increases, thus inducing further growth in the institutions. This form of positive feedback, which enhances the output of new technology producing firms and can raise their number and size, is equivalent to *autocatalysis*, a phenomenon which, according to Nicolis and Prigogine (1989), is responsible for the emergence of dissipative systems. Furthermore, the co-evolution of technologies and of appropriate institutions can lead to the formation of new links, thus raising the connectivity of the system. For example, the creation of a regulatory institution can be expected to lead to interactions with the firms and the other organizations responsible for the production and use of the new technology. These interactions may be impersonal and simply provide constraint, as would happen in the case of standard creating institutions, or be more localized and directed, as in the case of a firm producing complementary inputs to the innovation and technology concerned. Examples of these situations for the automobile could be (i) the ministries responsible for issuing driving permits or driving rules, or (ii) the firms producing and distributing tyres or petrol (Saviotti, 2005). In all these cases the general meaning of links is that they reduce the number of degrees of freedom of each node and provide constraint. The behaviour of the nodes then becomes more highly co-related. This progressive increase in connectivity, as an innovation and the relative technology mature on the one hand, increases the potential market size of the new technology by improving the technology with respect to its initial form but, on the other hand, makes the new technology progressively more rigid, even if more coherent. In this way an increasing connectivity allows a technology to acquire its full 'economic weight' but contributes to the process whereby diminishing returns gradually take over and slow down the rate of improvement of maturing technologies.

Network dynamics at the industry/technology level can be expected to be characterized by low connectivity during the emergence phase and by growing connectivity as the sector matures. At the aggregate level of the whole economic system increasing diversity/ variety means an increasing number of nodes. However, this increase is likely to be unevenly distributed in time and space. The creation of new nodes cannot be expected to be followed immediately by the creation of new links. The emergence of important innovations can be expected to lower connectivity while the subsequent process of diffusion can be expected to raise connectivity. Thus, aggregate connectivity cannot be expected to grow at all times, but it could easily oscillate around a given value.

We can then expect some relationships to exist between the evolution of variety and that of networks. Variety grows by the creation of new economic species (new products, services and so on).

- First, we can expect the creation of new economic species to lead to a growing number of distinguishable networks.
- Second, we can expect the phase of emergence of new economic species to occur in an institutionally poor environment characterized by a low connectivity, but we

can also expect the subsequent phases of diffusion and of maturation of new technologies to lead to a growing connectivity.

3.   TOWARDS A GENERAL REPRESENTATION OF KNOWLEDGE

In what follows two properties of knowledge that are considered to be very general and applicable to any type of knowledge, from scientific to more empirical and craft based, are described. These two properties do not constitute a complete description of knowledge, but, as will be seen, they provide a surprisingly powerful basis to analyse processes of knowledge creation and utilization. The two properties are:

(P1)   Knowledge is a co-relational structure.
(P2)   Knowledge is a retrieval or interpretative structure.

3.1   Knowledge as a Co-relational Structure

Human beings interact with this external environment by means of their sense organs and by means of a series of enhanced sense organs and tools. Initially human beings had to rely only on their sense organs for any observations on the external environment. In the course of human evolution they developed enhanced sense organs (for example, telescopes, measuring devices, scanners, and so on) that allowed them to access parts of the external environment not directly accessible through their primary sense organs. Furthermore, they developed a series of tools (for example, axes, hammers and so on) that allowed them to modify purposefully their external environment, tools that Georgescu-Roegen (1971) called exosomatic organs. We find here already the basic distinction between two distinguishable but intimately interconnected activities. On the one hand there is a need to observe and to know, on the other hand there is a need to modify the external environment. The activities corresponding to the two needs are clearly separable, at least conceptually, but closely related because it is easier to modify the external environment if we know its structure and properties. In fact, these two needs and the related activities correspond to what we currently call science and technology. Science is the activity that understands and knows our external environment and technology is the activity that modifies the same environment. Examples of the relatedness of these two activities can be found from very ancient times, for example in the field of navigation. However, until the second half of the nineteenth century such relationships were more occasional than systematic. The situation is very different today in the societies characterized by a high intensity of R&D.

The distinction between science and technology corresponds roughly to that between *to know what* and *to know how* (Loasby, 1999). To know how allows us to modify our external environment. To know how can be made easier by knowing what happens in the particular subset of the external environment that we intend to modify. However, the knowledge of *what* of the particular subset is not always available, thus sometimes knowledge of *how* has to be developed without the knowledge of *what* of the subset considered. This does not imply that know-how is not knowledge, but that it is knowledge of a different type with respect know-what. These differences are by no means easy to understand and to explain and we will come back to them later. Johnson et al. (2000) use a more sophisticated classification of knowledge types, including know-why and know-who. In this chapter the distinction between know-what and know-how is considered more fundamental than the other two. Know-why and know-who are two categories which, while very useful, are in principle derivable from know-what and know-how. This close connection between science and technology is considerably enhanced by the truth criterion we normally use. A theory is considered to be 'temporarily' correct if its predictions correspond to empirical observations of the ExtEnv. This close connection between the nature of theories and the structure of ExtEnv lies at the roots of our ability to use theoretical knowledge to modify our ExtEnv.

For the time being, let us proceed to explain what is meant by co-relational structure. We can identify in our external environment a number of observables, that is, of entities that can be responsible for observed phenomena. To each observable we can associate one or more variables that represent and measure different aspects of the observable. In this chapter no particular assumption is made about the truthfulness of the observables and of the variables representing them. In other words, we are not assuming the observables to be real entities that can be observed in an unbiased way by human observers. Observables and variables are mental representations (Loasby, 1999; Saviotti, 2004, 2007) that allow us to explore the external environment and to establish in it a series of constituting entities and structures. All theories are conceived in the space of mental representations. Of course, we have to assume that our mental representations and the theories that are based on them are potentially isomorphic with respect to the ExtEnv. We have to bear in mind that mental representations can be generated at will but that not all of them will pass the required tests. The test that is commonly used is that of correspondence between the predictions of a theory and empirical observations. In other words, the variety of mental representations that can be constructed is much greater than that of the mental representations surviving empirical tests. The ExtEnv constitutes a set of constraints that cannot be easily overcome, either to know or to modify it. What needs to be retained of this section is that observables and variables are mental representations and that they are parts of a theoretical construction that has to be largely isomorphic with external reality.

If we then start from the possibility to detect observables and to create variables representing them, we can immediately see that at least some theories are co-relational structures. Let us briefly say that knowledge can be subdivided into disciplines or fields, each discipline or field attempting to explore and explain a subset of the ExtEnv. Within this subset the discipline/field identifies observables and variables and establishes the extent of co-relation between different variables. Important and frequently used examples of co-relations between different variables are given by the law of ideal gases (Equation 6.1), Newton's laws of dynamics (Equation 6.2), and Fisher's fundamental theorem (Equation 6.3).

$$PV = nRT \tag{6.1}$$

$$F = ma \tag{6.2}$$

$$dr(t)/dt = \sigma_r^2(t) \tag{6.3}$$

where P is the pressure of a gas, V its volume, n the number of moles of the gas and T its temperature, with R a general constant. F is the force exerted on a particular body, m is its mass and a the acceleration the body acquires. Fisher's theorem (6.3) (Roughgarden, 1996: 54–55) is used in biology, although with possible implications for the social sciences (see Nelson and Winter, 1982; Andersen, 1994). The theorem states that the rate of growth of a population ($r(t)$) depends on the variance of the fitness of the same population ($\sigma_r^2(t)$). These equations tell us that all these variables are co-related in such a way that, for example, if we raise the temperature, the volume and the pressure of the gas have to increase in order for Equation (6.1) to keep being satisfied. In other words, Equation (6.1) represents the co-relation of the behaviour of a number of variables of the gas. All equations of this type are part of theoretical models, which in turn are components of broader theories. This is the most extreme example of a theory as a co-relational structure. In this case the co-relation takes on a very accurate and quantitative character. As we will see later, this is not always the case. In many cases the co-relation provided by a theory can be more qualitative and loose while still being a co-relation.

Examples of accurate and quantitative co-relations are found mainly in the physical sciences, although they can be found also in the biological and social sciences, even if with a lower frequency. In spite of the great number of these laws and equations that can be found, they do not represent the majority of our knowledge, except for a few fields. A large number of theories of the ExtEnv have to be content with much looser and less accurate co-relations. However, they end up with some kind of co-relation. For example, the so called Engel's law (Hirshleifer, 1988: 98–100) states that the share of income spent on basic commodities, such as food, housing and so on, falls as the average income per head increases. Here the co-relation between income per head and expenditures in particular categories of commodities can be detected empirically and measured, but there is no complete theory of Engel's law. A complete theory would show the relationships of the variables involved in Engel's law (income per head and expenditures on commodities) with all other possible variables in the economic domain. Such a complete theory does not exist for any economic law, and it would in fact be incompatible with the local character of knowledge. However, well established generalizations in any field are linked by a dense network of connecting relationships to other variables in the same field, and in particular to variables which are considered fundamental. We can derive Engel's curves from an income consumption curve and use it to classify goods as superior or inferior. However, we cannot predict how the purchasing behaviour of consumers for particular types of goods and services will depend on changes in income per head. The only possible generalization in this direction is that the expenditure on basic necessities, of which food is the most often quoted example, is likely to fall as income per head grows. This seems to imply a hierarchical theory of consumption, but such a theory has never been adequately developed. Thus, in spite of its great usefulness and of its strong empirical corroboration, Engel's law remains an empirically based observation relatively poorly connected to the rest of economic theory.

An even looser, even if very interesting, type of co-relation, can be found in Max Weber's theory linking the protestant ethic and the spirit of capitalism (Weber, 1968). The co-relation can be stated in the following form: countries/societies/groups adhering to a protestant religion have a higher probability of giving rise to a capitalist economic system than non protestant ones. It is of no consequence for the objective of this chapter that today many scholars criticize this theory of Max Weber's. The point to be made here is not the truthfulness of the theory, but the form in which it is created, and this form is that of a co-relation. The theory co-relates in a loose and non quantitative way religious or cultural beliefs and economic performance.

A particular place in this context must be reserved for econometric analysis. Econometric equations provide an example of very accurate co-relations, but they are co-relations of a different type with respect to those of so called analytical models. Analytical models are created by assuming that a reduced number of simple entities are the fundamental determinants of a large range of phenomena, and by working out how the relationships and interactions of the basic entities (co-relations) lead to the observed phenomena. In econometric models, on the other hand, we know that some variables are co-related, but we do not attempt to determine the precise nature of the interaction of the basic variables. By fitting the equation to a set of data we optimize the co-relation *at a given form* of co-relation. Thus econometric analysis establishes the *presence* of a co-relation, rather than its precise form as could be done in an analytical model. In summary, the property of being a co-relational structure can be considered a general property of knowledge. This has both limits and many interesting implications.

3.2 Knowledge as a Network

According to the previous considerations knowledge establishes co-relations, or connections, between different concepts and variables. It is therefore possible to represent knowledge as a *network* the nodes of which are concepts or variables and the links of which are given by the joint utilization of the concepts or variables. In this representation we would attain a complete knowledge of our ExtEnv if we had all the nodes corresponding to all the concepts and/or variables of our ExtEnv and if the corresponding network was fully connected. However, if we examine the way knowledge develops we can realize that we are very far from complete knowledge. As the exploration of our ExtEnv proceeds we detect new observables and create appropriate variables. This is typically done by casual observations or in order to find a solution for a practical problem (see also Popper, 1972). The subsequent evolution of different fields of knowledge gives rise to disconnected networks. Let us take an example.

In the past astronomy and medicine developed in completely separate ways. There was no awareness that the entities to which the problems could be reduced in the two fields had anything in common. Thus, astronomy proceeded by identifying observables (the sun, the earth, planets, stars and so on) and constructed models of the movements of these entities. Medicine on the other hand proceeded by identifying organs and by trying to explain the behaviour of the whole body by means of its organs. The awareness that organs were constituted by cells, cells by molecules and molecules by protons, electrons and neutrons took centuries to come. In other words, the networks of knowledge of astronomy and medicine were for a very long time separate and it was not realized that they could in principle be connected. The awareness of the potential connectedness of these two and of other networks of knowledge only came during the nineteenth century and gave rise to the so called Laplacian dream (Mirowski, 1989). One could say that the research program of molecular biology aims at connecting the networks of biology and of physics. However, and in spite of the considerable successes achieved in this direction in the last thirty years, we are still very far from having identified all the possible nodes and links. Thus, we can conclude that, although the final objective of knowledge is to construct a complete network, containing all the possible variables of our ExtEnv and all the possible connections linking these variables, the present state of our knowledge is very far from that.

Some observations can help in understanding the present state of our knowledge network. First, new observables are continuously discovered, although at a different speed in different disciplines. Some disciplines (for example, chemistry) are closer to maturity and generate few new observables, others (for example, biology) keep generating new observables and variables. Second, the rate of creation of new nodes by the discovery of new observables and variables precedes in general the creation of links between the corresponding variables. In many cases we can expect the construction of links to be a much slower process than the creation of new nodes. When, as a result of new discoveries, new nodes are introduced in our network of knowledge we can expect connectivity to fall. As links are established with the newly created nodes, the connectivity of the system can start rising again. We can reinforce here some trends we had already seen at a more general level:

(i)   The emergence of novelty tends to create new but poorly connected nodes, thus temporarily reducing the connectivity of the system.
(ii)   The subsequent diffusion of the innovations establishes new links and raises again the connectivity of the system.
(iii)   As a result of (i) and (ii) the connectivity of the system is likely to fluctuate around a given value.

It is important to realize here the role that connectivity can play in the dynamics of socio-economic networks. Connectivity is generally measured by the density of links per node in a network. Since in knowledge networks links represent the existence of co-relations between nodes/variables, in a high connectivity knowledge network variables are highly co-related. In turn, the existence of co-relations leads to a high probability of predicting the values of some variables from those of other co-related variables. On the whole a high connectivity knowledge network leads to a high probability of predicting the behaviour of some parts of the network starting from the knowledge of other parts. When our knowledge network is used to modify a subset S of ExtEnv, a higher probability of predicting some parts of the knowledge network leads to lower costs of modifying a subset S (ExtEnv) (Saviotti, 2004). Thus, connectivity is a relevant property of a knowledge network, both in a cognitive and in a technological sense.

The dynamic representation of knowledge used in this chapter (but see Saviotti, 2004, 2007 for greater details) is compatible with Kuhn's (1962) analysis of the evolution of science. New observables and variables are likely to be created when new paradigms emerge. In this early phase we can expect new variables to be poorly connected to those existing in the previous network of knowledge. Thus, the emergence, or revolutionary, phase of a new paradigm is likely to be accompanied by a falling connectivity of the network of knowledge. On the other hand, we can expect the subsequent phase of normal science to be characterized by a growing number of links and thus by a growing network connectivity.

In a broader sense the representation of knowledge as a co-relational and as retrieval/interpretative structure is compatible with the idea of knowledge as an organized structure, to which both Kuhn's and Lakatos' theories belong (Chalmers, 1980). In particular, the representation of knowledge described in this chapter is compatible with some structuralist theories of science (Balzer et al., 1987; Franck, 1999) according to which the collection of all empirical science forms a theoretical *holon*, composed of constellations of elementary theories, theories that would be *connected* by inter-theoretical links of different types, such as equivalence, specialization, connection and so on. Furthermore, the representation of knowledge as a network encompasses both the emergence of radical novelty and the recombination of existing ideas (Nightingale, 1998; Fleming, 2001; Katila and Ahuja, 2002; Sorenson et al., 2006). The former case corresponds to the detection of completely new observables or to the definition of new variables related to these observables. The latter case involves the formation of new links between pre-existing variables.

3.3 Knowledge as a Retrieval or Interpretative Structure

At any time individuals and organizations have some type of knowledge which we will call *internal*. In a dynamic economic system individuals and organizations need to learn knowledge new to them (external) and to use existing information. Their existing internal knowledge determines their ability to learn external knowledge and to use existing information.

One of the properties commonly attributed to knowledge is its cumulative character. We can describe any type of knowledge by its location in knowledge space and by its distance with respect to the scientific or technological frontier of the time. Learning any new type of knowledge can only occur by proceeding from the most basic to the most advanced parts of discipline. We can expect an economic agent to learn more easily types of knowledge similar to the one(s) in his/her internal knowledge than very different ones.

Thus, knowledge is a retrieval/interpretative structure both for other more advanced pieces of knowledge within the same discipline and for knowledge belonging to different disciplines. It can be noticed here that the concept of knowledge as a retrieval/interpretative structure bears a considerable resemblance to that of absorptive capacity (Cohen and Levinthal, 1989, 1990) although the latter was formulated with reference to R&D. R&D is not only useful to create new knowledge but it can also help a firm to learn (absorb) external knowledge created by another firm or research institution, or simply stored in the scientific and technical literature. The probability that a firm, having performed a given type of R&D, can absorb some external knowledge depends on the *similarity* of the internal R&D and the external knowledge.

According to information theory (Shannon and Weaver, 1949), information does not have meaning, it is purely factual. In this sense information is different from knowledge. Based on the previous characterization we could say that knowledge provides co-relations between different variables while information is constituted by the numerical values of the variables. However, while information does not in itself carry any meaning, its use requires knowledge of the context in which information was created (see also Cowan et al., 2000). Thus, data sets on atomic transition frequencies or on the distribution of some biological populations would not be interpretable by an observer who does not know the relevant theoretical framework. Thus, information is not generally interpretable by a non knowledgeable agent/actor, but any information set requires the knowledge of one or more subsets of ExtEnv. In this sense knowledge can be considered a retrieval/interpretative structure.

The representation of knowledge described so far does not constitute a complete theory of knowledge. However, it is compatible with widely accepted epistemological theories. First, the creation of new observables and variables constitutes conjectures, to be tested by their correspondence to empirical observations. As Popper (1934) demonstrated, existing observables, variables and connections can never be proved to be true or correct. Their validity can only be corroborated by new experiments, but it is limited to the set of experiments carried out up to that point. Even in this limited sense knowledge can be very useful to modify our ExtEnv in the subsets of ExtEnv where the theory has been adequately tested.

The property of knowledge as a co-relational structure allows us to represent knowledge as a network in which variables constitute nodes and co-relations/connections constitute links. We can expect that observables will be discovered and relevant variables will be defined by a gradual process. We can expect that once new variables have been defined they will not immediately be co-related to all the pre-existing variables. Using a network analogy we can expect that the process of creation of new nodes/variables will be faster than the process of establishing links/co-relations between existing nodes/variables. Thus, in periods in which many new variables are introduced we can expect the average density of linkages in the network of knowledge to fall. Conversely, when no new variables are introduced we can expect the density of linkages/co-relations in the network of knowledge to increase (Saviotti, 2005).

Finally, the representation of knowledge as a co-relational and as a retrieval/interpretative structure can be used for both true and false theories. Different networks of knowledge, consisting of different variables and connections, will exist at different times. The evolution of knowledge will be represented by the transition between these different networks. The nodes and links of a theory which is proposed at a given time and at later times turns out to be false or incorrect will be replaced by new nodes and links.

3.4   The Local Character of Knowledge

Based on the considerations of the previous section we can never expect the knowledge network to be fully connected. This occurs for a number of reasons:

(1)   The process of creation of nodes can be expected to be faster than the creation of links within the new nodes and between the new and the old ones.
(2)   Co-relations can be established over a limited number of variables.
(3)   Co-relations can be established over a limited range of values of the variables.

(1) Has been analysed in the previous section.

(2) Analytical equations can contain a very limited number of variables. It is possible to write equations containing a large number of variables but it becomes increasingly difficult to solve them. Furthermore, even if it were possible to solve equations with a very large number of variables, it would become increasingly difficult to interpret the results.

Thus the number of variables involved in each co-relation is limited. Finally, even the mathematical co-relations used in the most advanced theories are approximations valid only for limited ranges of values of the variables included. For example, the relationship of pressure, volume, temperature and the number of moles of an ideal gas (6.1) is valid only for low pressures and high temperatures and it needs to be modified for different conditions. This property is not specific to the model considered. Any model is then always a simplified analogue of reality, containing a lower number of variables and of interactions with respect to the subset S_i(ExtEnv) that it intends to represent. The model is then going to be a good representation of reality to the extent that the neglected variables and interactions contribute weakly to the behaviour of the system. Such weak contribution is in general unlikely to persist over the complete range of possible values of all the variables and interactions or with respect to all the properties of the system. Thus, we can expect that the validity of most models will be limited to some ranges of the values of the variables and interactions of the subset S_i(ExtEnv). Moreover, even within the range of validity, the ability to co-relate variables varies, and precisely it falls gradually as we move away from the ideal conditions of the model.

There is even a further way in which knowledge can be considered local. According to the second property of knowledge mentioned above, that of being a retrieval or interpretative structure, any further or more advanced piece of knowledge within a given discipline can only be learned by human actors who already know the fundamental parts of the same discipline. If we now consider that the whole external environment can be subdivided into different subsets, each studied by a discipline, we can realize that different disciplines may have very different or very closely related observation spaces. For example, physics and chemistry have very similar and partly overlapping observation spaces, while physics and anthropology have very different observation spaces. As a consequence we can imagine ranking disciplines in terms of the similarity of their observable spaces in such a way that neighbouring disciplines are very similar, and disciplines that are far apart are very different. This point will be developed in greater detail later. Here let us note that the learning ability conferred upon people/agents/ actors already holding given pieces of knowledge is not only limited within a discipline. Knowledge of a given discipline A increases the probability of learning a similar discipline B more than that of learning a very different discipline C. If we consider that disciplines are themselves heterogeneous and that they tend to become increasingly heterogeneous in the course of time, we can give the previous considerations a more general form as follows. Assume that the ExtEnv can be represented by a very large number of observables and of related variables, and that such observables and variables can be ordered along a mono-dimensional space. The total observation space corresponding to ExtEnv (O(ExtEnv)) can be partitioned into subsets that may cover part or all of O(ExtEnv). In O(ExtEnv) we can imagine being able to measure the distances between any two pieces of knowledge, located either within the same discipline or in two different disciplines. The local character of knowledge can then be represented in the following way:

The probability that a human actor/agent holding at time t a given type of knowledge (actor's internal knowledge) can learn another piece of knowledge (external) increases in a way inversely proportional to the distance between the internal and the external knowledge.

This statement can be expressed concisely by means of the following formula:

$$P_{Ki \to (Ki+Ke)} \propto 1/D_0(K_i, K_e) \qquad (6.4)$$

where $P_{Ki \to (Ki+Ke)}$ is the probability that a given actor having internal knowledge K_i at time t can learn external knowledge K_e, and $D_0(K_i, K_e)$ is the distance of the internal and external pieces of knowledge in O(ExtEnv).

The considerations presented so far were developed based on evidence from the history of science, that is, on the outcome of cognitive processes. It is interesting that the concept of the local character of knowledge finds confirmation in the work of cognitive psychologists. For example, it seems that we remember better items that are related to what we actually do than items completely new to us (Buenstorff, 2001: 3). To the extent that memory influences our selection of problems and interpretation of phenomena it can be one of the causes of the local character of knowledge. More generally, both the interpretation of new stimuli and the formation of expectations are performed in accordance with existing schemata and categories which tend to be resistant to change. Thus, the features of cognitive processes that lead to a local character of knowledge also tend, if left undisturbed, to make our individual mental representations increasingly rigid over time (ibid).

The two meanings previously described of the local character of knowledge refer to different levels of aggregation. The second meaning of the local character of knowledge is related to the limitation of our individual knowledge. The range of knowledge possessed by any individual is very limited but it can be partly overcome by division of labour and coordination (Saviotti, 2004). The first meaning described above refers to a limitation of human knowledge as collectively achieved. Although our collectively created knowledge is much wider and more advanced than any individual knowledge, even the latter is still limited and local. Even the most advanced theories and models created by the work of many scientists are local. Of course, this local character can be partly overcome in the course of time as scientists find new relations, or connections, between previously discovered variables. In principle if no new variables were to be discovered it would be possible to raise continuously the connectivity of the network of knowledge, although not necessarily to its maximum value. However, such an outcome is unlikely since the progress of science keeps creating new observables and variables. We can then expect that even the network of knowledge collectively created will never be completely connected.

Let us observe here that the local character of knowledge has some explicit and implicit precedents, although they are far less general than the version of the concept presented here. Atkinson and Stiglitz (1969) introduced a production function in which only a limited number of techniques is actually feasible. Improvements in technology do not concern the whole production function, but affect only one or few techniques. Innovations are concentrated in the technology that is currently in use, while other technologies remain largely unaffected. Thus only a limited number of choices is available to a firm at a moment in time. Nelson and Winter (1982) talked about the local character of search in a similar sense. In their model each firm at a given time can be represented in input factor coefficient space by a point, corresponding to the technique used by the firm (pp. 180–83). According to their model the probability that as a result of an innovative process a firm ends up with a different ratio of input factor coefficients is inversely proportional to the difference between the initial and the final ratios, or equivalently, to their distance in input factor space. This of course implies that local search involves incremental modifications of existing techniques and that ratios near the initial one are the most probable. A concept perhaps more closely related to the local character of knowledge as expressed in this chapter is that of absorptive capacity (Cohen and Levinthal, 1989, 1990). A firm can only absorb some external knowledge *similar* to that it already holds. According to Cohen and Levinthal firms do R&D not only to create novelty but also to understand what other firms are doing. In this sense the knowledge acquired by firms doing R&D enables them to retrieve/interpret other firms' knowledge to the extent that their own R&D has been carried out in similar fields. For example, a firm doing R&D on RNA silencing will not acquire an absorptive capacity in low temperature physics or in electronics. Thus, the concept of absorptive capacity on the one hand confirms the property of knowledge as retrieval/interpretative structure and, on the other hand the local character of knowledge. Antonelli (2008) gives a central role to local technological change and focuses both on the limitations of individual agents because they are located in a limited space in the wide cognitive map (p. 49), but takes into account also that a new technology to diffuse needs to be superior only locally and that it can be inferior in other ranges of technology space (p. 53).

Summarizing, we can say that knowledge has a local character because:

(a) The creation of new nodes can be expected to precede the creation of links within the new nodes and between the new and the old ones.
(b) Knowledge can provide co-relations only over a small number of variables at a time.
(c) It can provide co-relations only over a limited range of values of the variables considered.
(d) The probability that a human actor holding a given internal knowledge K_i learns some piece of external knowledge K_e is inversely proportional to the distance between K_i and K_e in the observable space O(ExtEnv).

3.5 Measurable Properties of Knowledge

In the following sections some applications of the previous representation of knowledge will be described. These applications are based on complexity concepts. Central amongst them will be that of networks, but other measurable properties will be described. One of the most fundamental features of complex systems is that of emergence. In its strong sense emergence implies qualitative change and discontinuities.

Cognitive distances and indices of similarity Although to measure qualitative change is intrinsically impossible a number approximations can be derived in the form of *distances* in particular types of spaces. In the case of knowledge we can measure *cognitive distances*, which are the inverse of indices of *similarity*. Such distances, often developed by ecologists to calculate the number of species in a biological habitat (for example, Pielou, 1984), can be interpreted as measures of the extent of discontinuity in the emergence of new types of knowledge. Cognitive distances and indices of similarity can be used to detect both weak and strong emergence and can be calculated at different levels of aggregation. For example, we can calculate cognitive distances and indices of similarity for the same firm at different times, for different firms at the same, for knowledge fields or industrial sectors, for different countries and so on. A cognitive distance is not a measure of the proximity of a firm or country to the existing frontier of knowledge but it defines the location of any particular agent or organization in a knowledge space defined by the existing subdivisions of knowledge (disciplines, specialties and so on). We expect cognitive distance to have the highest values in the initial phase of a new paradigm and to fall gradually as the paradigm matures.

Indicators of differentiation or specialization   The extent of specialization, or of its inverse, differentiation, is one of the main characteristics of the knowledge base of firms or organizations. Differentiation can be measured in a number of ways. The one which will be used here is based on variety, which will be calculated by means of the informational entropy function. Knowledge variety can be measured at different levels of aggregation, for example at a low level of aggregation within a small group or at the highest possible level of aggregation. The former will be called related variety and the latter unrelated variety. We expect unrelated variety to rise rapidly in the initial phases of a new paradigm but possibly to be overtaken by related as the paradigm matures.

Coherence   As was previously pointed out, the production of knowledge is carried out by means of division of labour and coordination. The division of labour determines the tasks which each worker will carry out. In the case of knowledge this amounts to the classification of knowledge into divisions at different levels of aggregation (disciplines, specialties and so on). For the production of both more aggregate forms of knowledge and for that of technological artefacts many pieces of knowledge need to be combined or coordinated. Coherence measures the ability of firms or organizations to combine, or coordinate, different pieces of knowledge. The ability to do this varies amongst firms and in the course of time. Particularly interesting is the variation which occurs during the lifecycle of a type of knowledge within a scientific or technological paradigm. The onset of a new paradigm is likely to cause pronounced structural change in knowledge by quickly introducing new variables and new subsets of knowledge and by eliminating older ones. We can expect the initial phases of a new paradigm to be characterized by a loss of coherence since the new variables introduced are likely to be poorly connected to the pre-existing ones. As the paradigm matures or moves towards normal science we can expect firms to improve their ability to connect different, older and newer, pieces of knowledge. Thus, we expect coherence to fall in the initial phase of a new paradigm (for example a scientific revolution) and to rise subsequently as the paradigm matures or moves towards normal science.

4.   EXAMPLES OF KNOWLEDGE NETWORKS

4.1   The Knowledge Base of Firms and Organizations

We can define the knowledge base (KB) of a firm or organization as the collective knowledge that can be used to achieve the firm's productive objectives. The term collective is due to the fact that the process of knowledge creation in the firm is based on division of labour and on coordination. Many individuals, departments, subsidiaries and so on of the firm contribute to the creation of new knowledge, each carrying out a small subset of the whole process. The production of the resultant knowledge necessarily involves the coordination of all these activities. Clearly the organizational structure of a firm can be expected to have an impact on the process of knowledge creation. The knowledge base is itself a structure, the components of which are the types of knowledge used by the firm or organization and the interactions of which are determined by their joint utilization. Furthermore, the above defined coherence gives us an indication of the ability of firms or industrial sectors to combine different types of knowledge arising from different sources. Thus, coherence represents an important property of the knowledge base of such firms or sectors.

The study of firms' (and organizations') KBs is a very important component of the creation of an economics of knowledge. In this section two different methods to map the KB and to measure its properties will be described. In both cases we start by identifying some basic units of knowledge. In principle we could refer to the considerations of Section 2.1 and attempt to find all the variables corresponding to a given piece of knowledge. This is generally impossible and we use instead more aggregate units of knowledge, such as the technological classes contained in patents or the themes contained in patents or publications. The representation of the KB that we obtain by examining, for example, the patents of a firm is a network in which the nodes are constituted by our units of knowledge and the links by the interactions of the units of knowledge. In the work described here the interactions are measured by the co-occurrence of the units of knowledge in the patents or in the other sources of information that we are using.

The two methods we use to study firms' KBs are different in that they refer to different levels of aggregation. The first method, lexicographic analysis (LA), detects the units of knowledge in the texts that we use as sources of information. LA can detect in the text of patents short phrases corresponding to technological themes, or alternatively the technological classes contained in the patent. The links of these units are determined by their frequency of co-occurrence in the patents used. This provides us with a graphic representation of the network of knowledge constituting the KB at a given time. Repeating the study at different times we can map the evolution of the KB and relate it to changes in firm strategy, firm organization, and so on. (see Saviotti et al., 2003, 2005). In other words, LA allows us to represent the 'brain' of the firm.

The second method we use starts by constructing a matrix of co-occurrences of technological classes and provides us with a more aggregate representation of the KB. In particular, it allows us to measure some of the properties of the KB, such as its coherence, specialization, differentiation, and similarity. On the basis of these measures it is possible to show that the KB of a firm is a determinant of the firm's performance (Nesta and Saviotti, 2005, 2006). These two methods are complementary. LA provides us with a more disaggregate representation, by means of which we can enter the firm's KB, while the method based on co-occurrence matrices gives us measures of the resultant properties of each KB. The graphic representation we show here (Figures 6.1 to 6.5) was obtained by means of LA.

Figures 6.1 and 6.2 represent the KB of Hoechst for the periods 1993–95 and 1996–98.

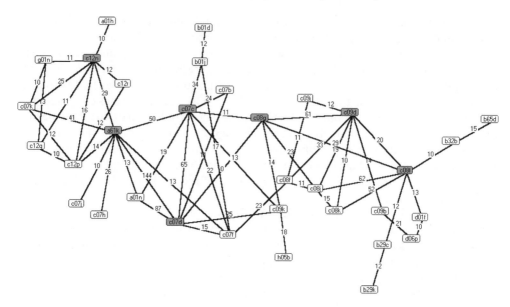

Note: The most central classes are represented in dark grey.

Source: Saviotti et al. (2003).

Figure 6.1   *The KB of Hoechst for period 1 (1993–95) of the co-occurrences between the main International Patent Classes (IPC) of its patents*

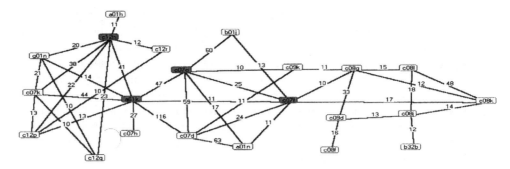

Note: The most central classes are represented in dark grey.

Source: Saviotti et al. (2005).

Figure 6.2   *The KB of Hoechst for period 2 (1996–98) as represented by the co-occurrences between the main International Patent Classes (IPC) of its patents*

Figures 6.3 and 6.4 represent the KB of Rhône-Poulenc for the periods 1993–95 and 1996–98. Figure 6.5 represents the KB of Aventis, the firm created by the merger of Hoechst and Rhône-Poulenc. We can immediately notice some properties of this KB network:

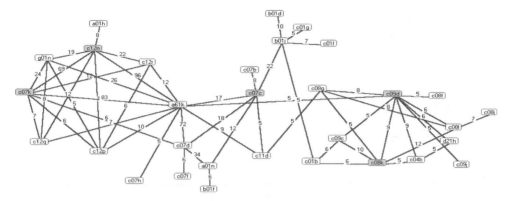

Note: The most central classes are represented in dark grey.

Source: Saviotti et al. (2003).

Figure 6.3 *The KB of Rhône-Poulenc for period 1 (1993–95) as represented by the co-occurrences between the main International Patent Classes (IPC) of its patents*

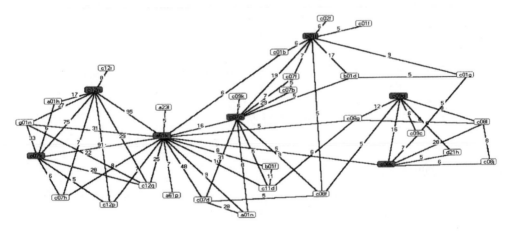

Source: Saviotti et al. (2005).

Figure 6.4 *The KB of Rhône-Poulenc for period 2 (1996–98) as represented by the co-occurrences between the main IPC classes of its patents*

- The distribution of the frequencies and intensities/strengths of links around nodes is highly heterogeneous. Few nodes have many links and other nodes have very few links. Also, some nodes have very strong links while others have very weak ones.
- In the KBs of both Hoechst and Rhône-Poulenc we can see two parts which have a high internal density of links while being very lightly connected to each other. Each of the two separate subsets of the KB of Hoechst and Rhône-Poulenc corresponds

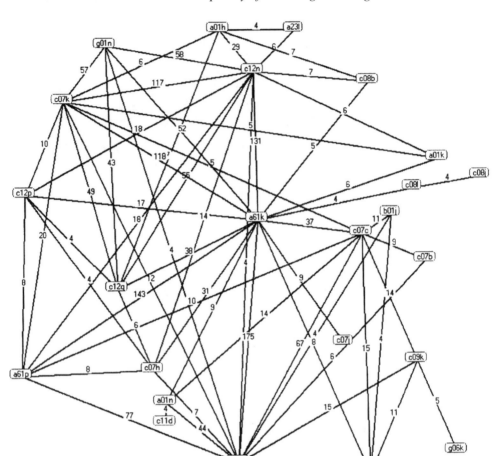

Source: Saviotti et al. (2005).

Figure 6.5   *The KB of Aventis after the merger, as represented by the co-occurrences of the technological classes in the patents of Aventis*

to a different type of knowledge, chemistry and biology respectively. Taking into account that during the period studied the two firms were attempting to move away from chemistry and towards the life sciences, the two subsets correspond to the past and to the intended future of the firm respectively. In other words, Figures 6.1 to 6.4 represent the changes in the KB of both firms following from their strategic reorientation.

• Figure 6.5, representing the KB of Aventis after the merger, no longer shows the separation into two distinguishable subsets, corresponding to chemistry and to the life sciences. The whole KB seems to be better connected, realizing a more complete integration of old and new knowledge. This better integration is confirmed by a measure of the number of links per node, which can be considered an approximate measure of network density, and which is considerably higher for Aventis after the

Table 6.1   Number of nodes, links and links per node in the KB* of Hoechst, Rhône-Poulenc and Aventis

	Hoechst		Rhône-Poulenc		Aventis
	P1 (1993–95)	P2 (1996–98)	P1 (1993–95)	P2 (1996–98)	2002
Nodes (N)	33	22	31	32	24
Links (L)	55	36	46	54	73
L/N	1.67	1.64	1.48	1.69	3.04

Note: * As shown in Figures 6.1–6.5.

merger with respect to both Hoechst and Rhône-Poulenc before the merger (Table 6.1). Furthermore, the distribution of links around nodes is highly asymmetrical.

4.2   Innovation Networks

Another type of knowledge related network is that of innovation networks, also called technological alliances. The ones described here occur in biotechnology but similar networks exist in other fields, such as electronics or telecommunications. In biotechnology they are constituted by small dedicated biotechnology firms (DBFs), large diversified firms (LDFs), mostly pharmaceutical but sometimes belonging to other sectors, and by public research institutes (PRIs). These three types of actors interact by forming alliances, one of the main objectives of which is the creation of new knowledge. These networks were studied during the period 1973–99 using data from the RECAP database. Innovation networks (INs) are part of a class of inter-firm alliances which emerged in the early 1980s. At that time INs were considered by many economists to be a temporary form of industrial organization. Existing economic theories predicted that only markets and hierarchical organizations could be stable. Inter-firm alliances were considered a temporary response to shocks, a response which would have disappeared once the shocks had been absorbed by the economic system. Yet twenty five years later the number of INs keeps increasing (Saviotti and Catherine, 2008). INs seem to have become a new and stable form of industrial organization. However, the full answer is more subtle than that.

If we break down the whole period 1973–99 into two sub periods distinguished by the main technologies used in each one, the picture becomes considerably different. If we consider that modern biotechnology was created by the potential industrial applications of molecular biology, we can distinguish in its subsequent evolution two generations of biotech, linked to recombinant DNA and monoclonal antibodies and to genomics respectively. The former begins in the mid 1970s and the latter in the late 1980s. By classifying all the technological alliances in the data set as belonging either to the first or to the second generation, we can plot separately curves describing their numbers, represent separately their networks and measure properties of these networks, such as density, centrality, and so on (Figures 6.14 and 6.15 and Tables 6.2 and 6.3). A number of interesting results emerge.

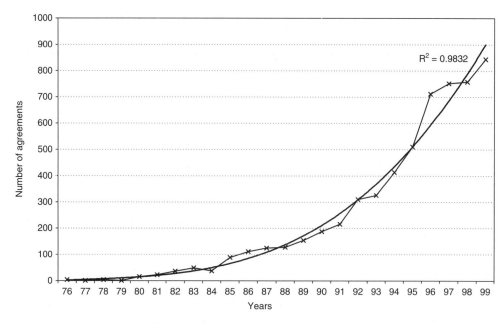

Figure 6.6   Total number of agreements in biotechnology, 1973–99

- First, the total number of INs in biotechnology keeps increasing (Figure 6.6).
- Second, the number of INs corresponding to the first generation reaches a maximum in 1996 and then starts declining (Figure 6.7).
- Third, if in each generation we separate the alliances linked to R&D from those linked to marketing we see that they have different dynamics. In particular, alliances related to R&D dominate in the early phases but peak out and decline later, while marketing alliances emerge later but dominate the late phases of the life cycle of the biotech generation we are considering (Figures 6.8 and 6.9).

One of the most interesting results of this study is that INs in each generation of biotechnology follow a life cycle, in which the number of INs rises at first, reaches a maximum and then declines. In the meantime the type of agreement changes from R&D to marketing, passing from the early to the late phases of the life cycle.

Other interesting results emerge when we represent graphically the INs corresponding to the two generations (Figures 6.10 to 6.13). Here we can see that for each generation both the number of nodes and the number of links rises during the life cycle. However, the density of links seems to be falling throughout the life cycle, with the possible exception of the very late phases of the first generation (Figures 6.14 to 6.16).

Finally, the centrality of the different actors changes during the evolution of the life cycle (Tables 6.2 and 6.3). The Ndegree centrality of DBFs is high initially and tends to fall as the life cycle tends towards maturity; that of LDFs falls slightly while remaining rather high; that of PRIs is initially high but falls to the lowest values of the three actors. The first and second generation show qualitatively the same type of evolution but differ for the relative extent of decline as the life cycle moves towards maturity: in the case of

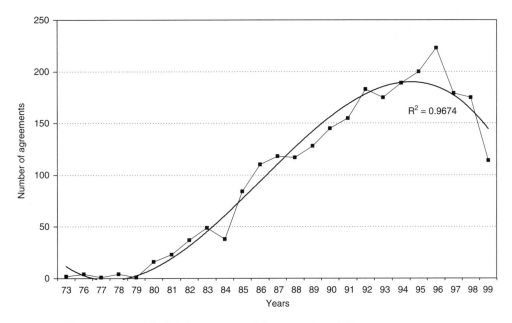

Figure 6.7 Number of agreements in the first generation of biotechnology

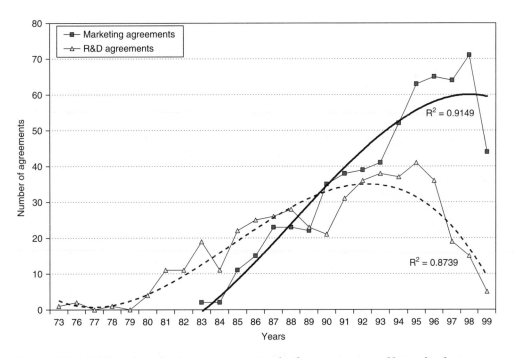

Figure 6.8 R&D and marketing agreements in the first generation of biotechnology

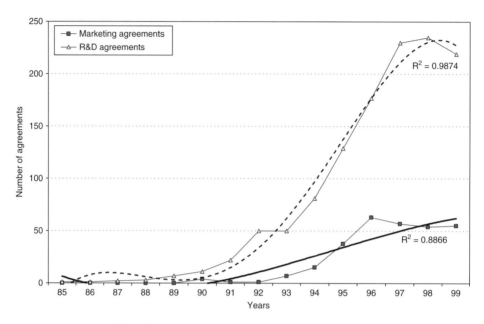

Figure 6.9   R&D and marketing agreements in the second generation of biotechnology

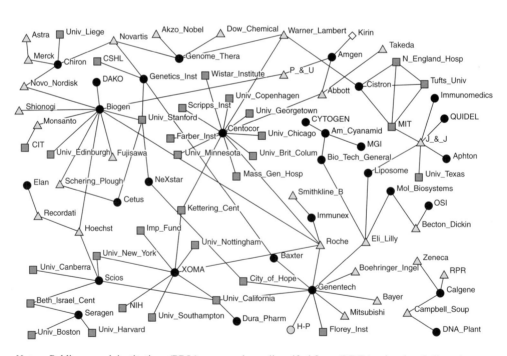

Note: Public research institutions (PRIs): squares; large diversified firms (LDFs): triangles; dedicated biotechnology firms (DBFs): circles.

Figure 6.10   Innovation networks, first generation, 1973–84

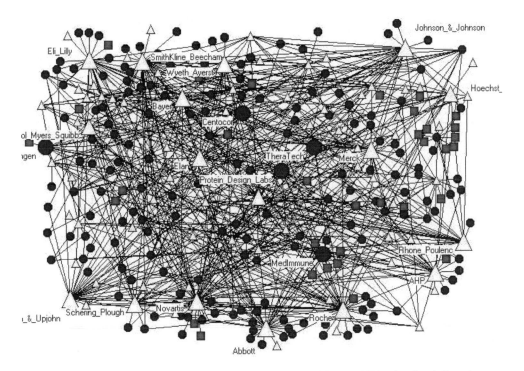

Note: Public research institutions (PRIs): squares; large diversified firms (LDFs): triangles; dedicated biotechnology firms (DBFs): circles.

Figure 6.11   Innovation networks, first generation, 1993–99

genomics the Ndegree centrality shows a more moderate fall, perhaps due to the shorter duration of the period studied.

Summarizing the results of this section we could say that:

- Innovation networks in biotechnology seem to undergo a life cycle in which the number of alliances rises at first, reaches a maximum and then declines. During the same life cycle the character of alliances changes from mostly R&D based in the early phases towards mostly marketing based in the late phases.
- This cyclical behaviour can be observed only at the level of aggregation of the generation of biotechnology (first generation: recombinant DNA + monoclonal antibodies; second generation: genomics). The overall time profile of the number of alliances shows a continuous growth.
- The networks of both generations of biotechnology show an asymmetrical distribution around nodes. The distribution has not yet been measured.
- During the life cycle observed so far the number of nodes grows and the number of links grows but network density seems to fall.
- The Ndegree centrality of the different actors involved in the networks (DBFs, LDFs, PRIs) tends to fall at different rates, that of LDFs remaining the highest in the long run.

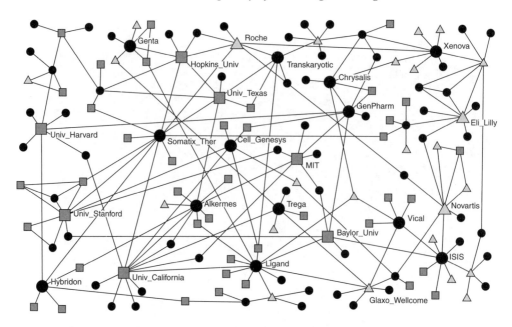

Note: Public research institutions (PRIs): squares; large diversified firms (LDFs): triangles; dedicated biotechnology firms (DBFs): circles.

Figure 6.12   Innovation networks, second generation, 1985–92

A short comment is required here to interpret the meaning of network density in this case. The creation of new nodes is here due to the creation of new firms. At the beginning we can expect these firms to be relatively poorly connected to the existent economic system. Their early emergence can be expected to be accompanied by a low density of their networks, thus reducing the overall density of the networks in which they can be embedded. However, in order to grow the new firms have to establish interactions with dealers, regulators, customers, suppliers and so on, thus leading to a growing density of their networks. The same situation is likely to apply to all firms in new, emerging sectors. Thus, we can expect new sectors to start with low density networks and to undergo a growth of network density as they mature. In this sense we can expect new sectors to benefit from the growth in network density occurring during their maturation, although this greater density will also imply a greater difficulty of introducing into the sector further innovations, especially if they are challenging the existence of the links already formed in the network. Of course, the same reasoning can be expected to apply to the technologies which give rise to the creation of new sectors or sub-sectors, as in this case. In fact, one of the main reasons for which network density can be expected to behave in the way described above is the role played by knowledge in the creation and in the dynamics of industrial sectors.

4.3   The Dynamics of Knowledge Intensive Sectors

In this section a brief description of a study of knowledge intensive sectors (KIS) will be given. The objective of this study was to map the dynamics of knowledge in three KIS,

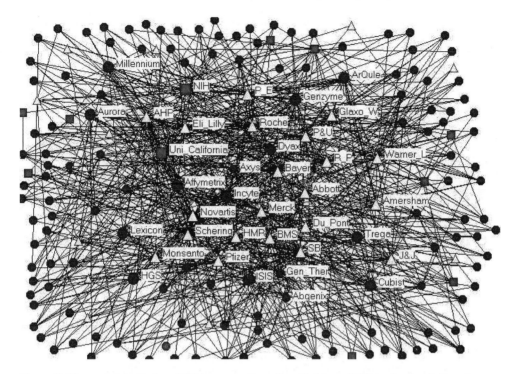

Note: Public research institutions (PRIs): squares; large diversified firms (LDFs): triangles; dedicated biotechnology firms (DBFs): circles.

Figure 6.13   Innovation networks, second generation, 1993–99

biotechnology, telecommunications and electronics, in order to test the idea that recent changes in industrial organization, such as the emergence of innovation networks, were at least partly determined by the dynamics of knowledge.[1] The main objective of this section is to show the intellectual continuity of the topics described in this chapter and their relationship to the same intellectual framework.

Biotechnology, telecommunications and electronics were chosen for the ANR study because they have a higher than average knowledge intensity. They were studied for the period 1981–2003 using the EPO patent database. In the initial phase of the project the knowledge base of the three sectors was studied by measuring some of its properties, namely related and unrelated variety, coherence and cognitive distance. Furthermore, the networks representing the knowledge base of biotechnology at different times have been plotted. In other words, the same two complementary techniques consisting of (i) plotting the knowledge base as a network, and (ii) measuring the properties of the knowledge base, which were already used to study the knowledge base of firms, have been applied here.

These three sectors are not only knowledge intensive but have been affected by an important discontinuity in their knowledge base. For example, modern or third generation biotechnology, which emerged due to advances in molecular biology, changed radically the knowledge base of firms in the pharmaceutical and in the agrochemical industries by replacing organic chemistry as their main source of knowledge. Likewise,

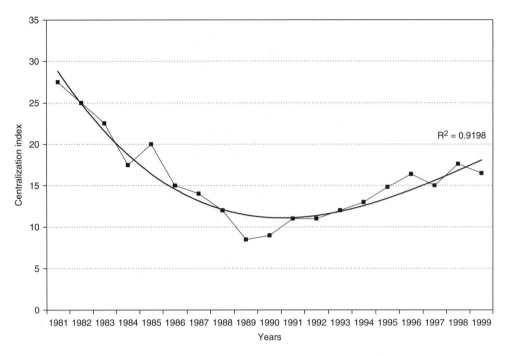

Figure 6.14   Evolution of network density for first generation biotechnology

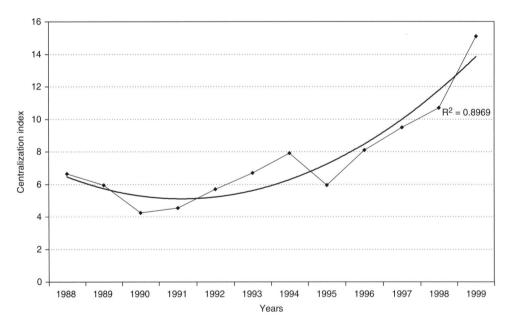

Figure 6.15   Evolution of network density for second generation biotechnology

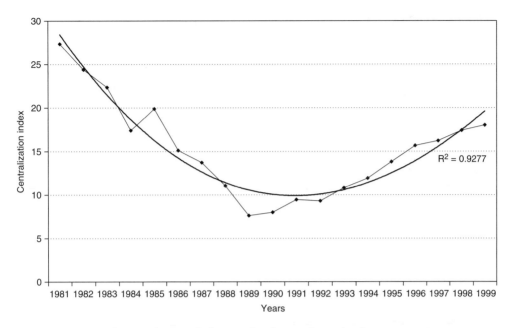

Figure 6.16   Evolution of network density for the two biotechnology generations combined

Table 6.2   Centrality of the different actors (DBFs = dedicated biotechnology firms, LDFs = large diversified groups and PRIs = public research institutions) involved in the first generation of biotechnology alliances

1st generation biotechnology	Period 1976–84			Period 1985–92			Period 1993–99		
Actor's type	DBF	LDF	PRI	DBF	LDF	PRI	DBF	LDF	PRI
Average number of agreements	5.67	3.20	2.63	6.20	10.79	2.61	6.12	15.50	2.05
Average Ndegree centrality	5.84	3.30	2.71	1.71	2.97	0.72	1.41	3.58	0.47
Median Ndegree centrality	3.09	2.06	2.06	1.10	1.38	0.55	0.92	1.73	0.23
Average betweenness centrality	4.95	2.82	0.85	0.71	1.38	0.20	0.40	1.40	0.10
Median betweenness centrality	1.17	0	0	0.20	0.53	0	0.07	0.18	0

telecommunications and electronics were deeply affected by the emergence of the transistor. In the rest of this chapter the focus will be mainly on the methodology used. Thus, only the results obtained for biotechnology will be discussed.

4.3.1   Properties of the knowledge base

Figures 6.17, 6.18 and 6.19 show that for biotechnology the variety of the knowledge base increased, the coherence increased and the cognitive distance fell during the period 1981–2002. Furthermore, unrelated variety was dominant until 1983 while related variety became dominant in the following period. As previously pointed out, the low initial value of coherence fits very well with the recent emergence of a knowledge discontinuity.

Table 6.3   Centrality of the different actors (DBFs = dedicated biotechnology firms,
LDFs = large diversified groups and PRIs = public research institutions)
involved in the second generation of biotechnology alliances

2nd generation biotechnology	Period 1985–92			Period 1993–99		
Actor's type	DBF	LDF	PRI	DBF	LDF	PRI
Average number of agreements	5.98	5.90	5.48	12.50	25.13	9.27
Average Ndegree centrality	2.48	2.45	2.27	1.68	3.38	1.25
Median Ndegree centrality	2.08	1.66	1.66	1.21	1.55	0.81
Average betweenness centrality	2.70	2.21	2.69	0.41	0.97	0.13
Median betweenness centrality	1.91	1.36	2.14	0.18	0.15	0.07

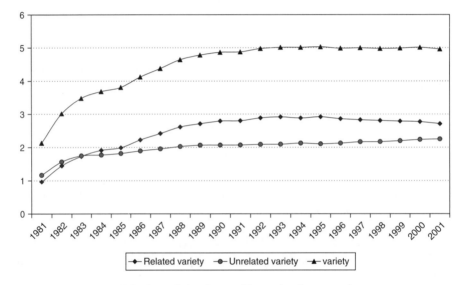

Figure 6.17   Variety of the knowledge base of biotechnology

The rise in variety, both related and unrelated, means that after its emergence the new knowledge base of the pharmaceutical and agrochemical industries started diversifying by identifying new extensions and applications. The shift away from unrelated to related variety means that the process of diversification of the knowledge base started by exploring parts of the knowledge space but, after a number of promising applications were identified, continued by differentiating 'around' these applications. This transition, which in previous papers (Grebel et al., 2006) had been identified as moving from *random* to *organized search*, is likely to occur systematically when a knowledge discontinuity emerges. The fall in cognitive distance confirms the previous interpretation. We can expect that when firms start using a radically new type of knowledge the cognitive distance between their present and past knowledge base is suddenly going to increase. After the principles of the new knowledge have been absorbed, as the new paradigm moves to maturity, we can expect cognitive distance to fall even in the presence of a continued

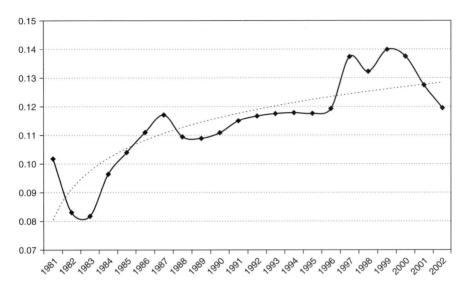

Figure 6.18   Coherence of the knowledge base of biotechnology

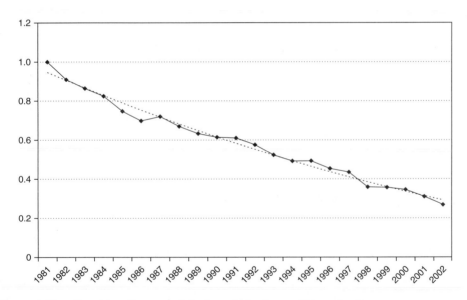

Figure 6.19   Cognitive distance of the knowledge base of biotechnology

differentiation of the knowledge base. As the search moves away from unrelated to related variety further progress occurs by means of the same set of concepts.

4.3.2   Knowledge networks

Figures 6.20a–6.20d show the changes which have taken place in the network of knowledge of biotechnology in the period 1981–2000 (Krafft et al., 2009b). We can see that

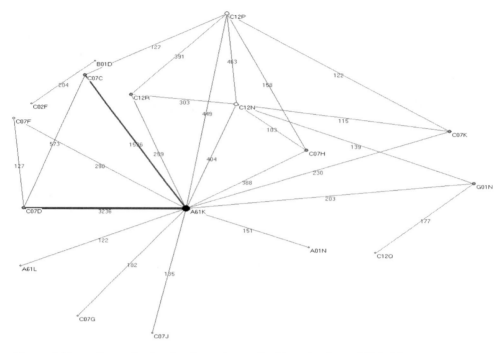

Figure 6.20a   Network of technology classes for biotechnology, 1981–85

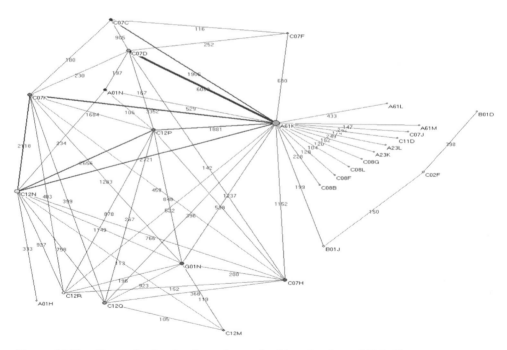

Figure 6.20b   Network of technology classes for biotechnology, 1986–90

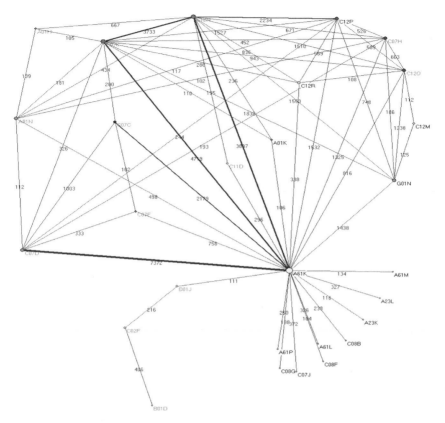

Figure 6.20c   Network of technology classes for biotechnology, 1991–95

all these networks have a small number of very important nodes and that the important nodes change in the course of time. Furthermore, the strength of the links between the nodes varies considerably at a given time and in the course of time. The importance of each node and of the corresponding IPC class depends on the number of occurrences of the class and on the number and strength of its links. The technological class A61K is always the most important node. This is not surprising since most of the patents are aimed at the pharmaceutical industry of which A61K is one of the main technological classes. In fact, A61K corresponds to a large number of market oriented applications of the pharmaceutical industry. Two other classes, C07C and C07D, are chemical classes which are still used in the pharmaceutical industry but the importance of which has been declining. A number of new classes corresponding to biology enter the knowledge networks and acquire a greater importance. Examples of these rising classes are C12N, C12P, C12Q. A physical class, G01N, emerges relatively late but acquires a considerable importance. The strength of the links of these emerging classes with A61K increases gradually in the course of time, while that of 'older' links between A61K and the surviving chemical classes C07C declines. The later rise in importance of G01N is likely to be due to the emergence of the second generation of modern biotechnology described in the section about innovation networks. G01N is likely to capture the applications of

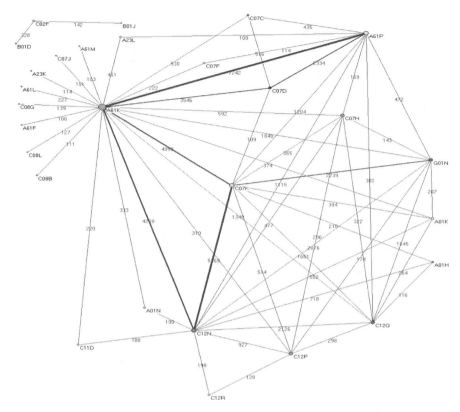

Figure 6.20d   Network of technology classes for biotechnology, 1996–2000

bioinformatics to the sequencing of DNA, which allowed the completion of the human genome project in the second generation of modern biotechnology. In other words, the evolution of these networks of knowledge shows a pronounced structural change occurring by means of (i) the emergence of new technological classes linked to biology and partly to physics, (ii) the disappearance or gradual loss of importance of classes linked to the previous knowledge base, organic chemistry, (iii) the gradual rise in strength of the links between A61K and the emerging classes and the gradual fall in strength of the links between A61K and the older classes, (iv) a growth in the number of important nodes and of important links, corresponding to an overall process of diversification of the knowledge networks, and (v) the persistence of A61K, showing that the new knowledge is used to attain market objectives similar to the past ones in the pharmaceutical industry.

These findings complement nicely those based on the properties of the knowledge base and allow us to provide a meaningful representation of what occurs when firms are faced with a discontinuity in their knowledge base. In biotechnology the discontinuity was constituted by the replacement of organic chemistry by the modern biotechnology which arose from the progress of molecular biology. The discontinuity gave rise to a structural change in knowledge in which new classes emerged, older ones disappeared or declined, and the pattern of links was largely reorganized. As a consequence of these underlying changes at the emergence of a discontinuity cognitive distance rapidly increases and then starts falling, coherence falls rapidly and then starts rising, variety grows with the emphasis gradually shifting away from unrelated to related variety.

5. SUMMARY AND CONCLUSIONS

In this chapter a general representation of knowledge which could be used to map, measure and model processes of knowledge generation and utilization was presented. This representation is based on two general properties of knowledge, that of being a co-relational structure and that of being a retrieval/interpretative structure. From these two properties it can be inferred that (i) knowledge is a network and that (ii) knowledge is local. The dynamics of knowledge generation and utilization is interpreted on the basis of a number of complexity concepts such as emergence, discontinuity, system structure, fluctuations and bifurcations, networks, and so on. For example, cognitive distance can be considered a measure of the extent of discontinuity occurring when a new type of knowledge is developed or starts to be used by a firm or organization. Cognitive distance is an indicator of emergence as discussed in this chapter. Furthermore, knowledge in general and knowledge bases in particular are structures with components given by different types of knowledge and interactions determined by the joint utilization of these types of knowledge. Structural change occurs in knowledge bases when firms or sectors adopt new types of knowledge. Diversification occurs during the evolution of a scientific or technological paradigm as new types of knowledge are added to the initial ones constituting the foundations of the paradigm. However, such differentiation can occur by adding to the knowledge bases of firms or organizations completely new or closely related pieces of knowledge, the former case corresponding to a radical innovation and the latter to a more incremental innovation. The representation of the knowledge base as a network allows us to exploit the usual network properties (density, centrality, and so on) in the study of the evolution of knowledge.

The representation of the KB of the firm is carried out by means of two complementary techniques, one which allows us to map the network connecting the components of the KB of a firm at different times and the other measuring some properties of the KB of the firm. The former shows the changes which occur in the KB as a consequence of a change in strategy while the latter shows that the properties of the KB are determinants of the performance of the firm. The same two approaches are used to study the dynamics of knowledge in biotechnology considered as a sector. The combination of the variety, coherence and cognitive distance allows us to map the life cycle of biotechnology beginning with the discontinuity represented by molecular biology and proceeding with the gradual absorption of the new knowledge by pharmaceutical or agrochemical firms. The evolution of the network of knowledge of biotechnology shows a high degree of structural change in which new technological classes corresponding to biotechnology emerge and older technological classes corresponding to chemistry disappear. In this chapter the network approach is used not only for knowledge but also for knowledge producing or using organizations. In particular it is applied to innovation networks in biotechnology. The dynamics of these networks is studied by measuring their density and the centrality of different actors. The methods of measurement and of mapping described in this chapter can be very useful in the construction of an economics of knowledge by allowing us to understand mechanisms of knowledge generation and utilization and their impact on industrial performance in a way which is both coherent with a general representation of knowledge and with a number of complexity based concepts.

NOTES

*   Part of the material described in this chapter is based on joint work with Jackie Krafft and Francesco Quatraro carried out within the ANR (Agence Nationale de la Recherche) funded project, contract number: ANR JCJC06_141306, 'Knowledge Intensive Sectors: Models and Evidence'.
1. This project, funded by the ANR (Agence Nationale de la Recherche), which is being carried out in collaboration with Jackie Krafft and Francesco Quatraro, is not yet complete (see Krafft et al., 2009a, 2009b).

REFERENCES

Allen, P., Strathern, M. and Baldwin, J. (2006), 'Evolution, diversity and organization', in Garsey E. and McGlade J. (eds), *Complexity and Co-Evolution*, Cheltenham, UK and Northampton, MA, USA: Edward Elgar.
Andersen, E.S. (1994), *Evolutionary Economics, Post-Schumpeterian Contributions*, London: Pinter.
Antonelli, C. (2008), *Localised Technological Change: Towards the Economics of Complexity*, London: Routledge.
Atkinson, A.B. and Stiglitz, J.E. (1969), 'A new view of technological change', *The Economic Journal*, **99**, 573–78.
Balzer, W., Moulines, U. and Sneed, J. (1987), *An Architectonic for Science: The Structuralist Program*, Dordrecht: D. Reidel Publishing Co.
Barabasi, A. (2002), *Linked: The New Science of Networks*, Cambridge, MA: Perseus Publishing.
Barabasi, A. and Bonabeau, E. (2003), 'Scale-free networks', *Scientific American*, **5**, May, 52–9.
Barabasi, A. and Reka, A. (1999), 'Emergence of scaling in random networks', *Science*, **286**, 509–12.
Barabasi, A., Reka A. and Jeong H. (1999), 'Mean field theory for scale free random networks', *Physica*, A 272, 173–87.
Buenstorff, G. (2001), *Dynamics of Knowledge Sharing: From Cognitive Psychology to Economics*, Jena: Evolutionary Economics Unit, Max Planck Institute for Research into Economic Systems.
Chalmers, A.F. (1980), *What Is This Thing Called Science?*, Milton Keynes: Open University Press.
Cohen, M. and Levinthal, D. (1989), 'Innovation and learning: the two faces of R&D', *Economic Journal*, **99**, 569–96.
Cohen, M. and Levinthal, D. (1990), 'Absorptive capacity: a new perspective on learning and innovation', *Administrative Science Quarterly*, **35**, 128–52.
Corning, P.A. (2002), 'The re-emergence of emergence: a venerable concept in search of a theory', *Complexity*, **7** (6), 18–30.
Cowan, R., David, P. and Foray, D. (2000), 'The explicit economics of knowledge codification and tacitness', *Industrial and Corporate Change*, **9**, 211–54.
Dosi, G. (1982), 'Technological paradigms and technological trajectories: a suggested interpretation of the determinants and directions of technical change', *Research Policy*, **11**, 147–62.
Fleming, L. (2001), 'Recombinant uncertainty in technological search', *Management Science*, 117–32.
Franck, R. (1999), 'La pluralité des disciplines, l'unité du savoir et les connaissances ordinaires', *Sociologie et Société*, **XXXI**, 129–42.
Frenken, K., van Oort, F.G. and Verburg, T. (2007), 'Related variety, unrelated variety and regional economic growth', *Regional Studies*, **41**, 685–97.
Funke, M. and Ruhwedel, R. (2001a), 'Product variety and economic growth: empirical evidence for the OECD countries', *IMF Staff Papers*, **48** (2), 225–42.
Funke, M. and Ruhwedel, R. (2001b), 'Export variety and export performance: empirical evidence from East Asia', *Journal of Asian Economics*, 12, 493–505.
Georgescu-Roegen, N. (1971), *The Entropy Law and the Economic Process*, Cambridge, MA: Harvard University Press.

Grebel, T., Krafft, J. and Saviotti, P.P. (2006), 'On the life cycle of knowledge intensive sectors', *Revue de l'OFCE*, June, 63–85.

Hayek, N. (1978), *New Studies in Philosophy, Politics, Economics and the History of Ideas*, London: Routledge, p. 184.

Hirshleifer, J. (1988), *Price Theory and Applications*, Englewood Cliffs, NJ: Prentice Hall.

Johnson, B., Lorenz, E. and Lundvall, B.-Å. (2000), 'Why all this fuss about codified and tacit knowledge?', *Industrial and Corporate Change*, **11** (2), 245–62.

Katila, R. and Ahiya, G. (2002), 'Something old, something new: longitudinal study of search behavior and new product introduction', *Academy of Management Journal*, **45** (6), 1183–94.

Krafft, J., Quatraro, F. and Saviotti, P.P. (2009a), 'Evolution of the knowledge base in knowledge intensive sectors', LEI-BRICK working paper no 06/2009.

Krafft, J., Quatraro, F. and Saviotti, P.P. (2009b), 'The evolution of knowledge base in knowledge-intensive sectors: social network analysis of biotechnology', presented at the dime workshop 'The structure and dynamics of knowledge networks', Eindhoven, 12–14 May.

Kuhn, T.S. (1962), *The Structure of Scientific Revolutions*, Chicago: The University of Chicago Press.

Landes, D. (1999), *The Wealth and Poverty of Nations*, New York: WW Norton & Company.

Laughlin, R. (2005), *A Different Universe: Reinventing Physics from the Bottom Down*, New York: Basic Books.

Loasby, B.J. (1999), *Knowledge, Institutions and Evolutionary Economics*, London: Routledge.

Losee, J. (1977), *A Historical Introduction to the Philosophy of Science*, Oxford: Oxford University Press.

March, J. (1991), 'Exploration and exploitation in organizational learning', *Organization Science*, **2** (1), 71–87.

Mirowski, P. (1989), *More Heat than Light*, Cambridge: Cambridge University Press.

Nelson, R.R. (1994), 'The co-evolution of technology, industrial structure, and supporting institutions', *Industrial and Corporate Change*, **3** (1), 47–63.

Nelson, R. and Winter S. (1977), 'In search of useful theory of innovation', *Research Policy*, **6**, 36–76.

Nelson, R. and Winter, S. (1982), *An Evolutionary Theory of Economic Change*, Cambridge, MA: Harvard University Press.

Nesta, L. and Saviotti, P.P. (2005), 'Coherence of the knowledge base and the firm's innovative performance: evidence from the U.S. pharmaceutical industry', Journal of Industrial Economics, **53** (1), 123–42.

Nesta, L. and Saviotti, P.P. (2006), 'Firm knowledge and market value in biotechnology', *Industrial and Corporate Change*, **15** (4), 625–52.

Nicolis G. and Prigogine, I. (1989), *Exploring Complexity*, New York: Freeman.

Nightingale, P. (1998), 'A cognitive model of innovation', *Research Policy*, **27**, 689–709.

Pielou E.C. (1984), *The Interpretation of Ecological Data*, New York: Wiley.

Popper, K.R. (1934), *The Logic of Scientific Discovery*, London: Hutchinson, 1968.

Popper, K.R. (1972), *Objective Knowledge, An Evolutionary Approach*, Oxford: Oxford University Press.

Reka, A. and Barabasi, A. (2002), 'Statistical mechanics of complex networks', *Reviews of Modern Physics*, **74**, 47–97.

Reka, A., Jeong, H. and Barabasi, A. (2000), 'Error and attack tolerance of complex networks', *Nature*, **406**, 378–82.

Roughgarden, J. (1996), *Theory of Population Genetics and Evolutionary Ecology, An Introduction*, Upper Saddle River NJ: Prentice Hall.

Saviotti, P. (2004), 'Considerations about knowledge production and strategies', *Journal of Institutional and Theoretical Economics*, **160**, 100–121.

Saviotti, P.P. (2005), 'On the co-evolution of technologies and institutions', in Weber, M. and Hemmelskamp, J. (eds), *Towards Environmental Innovation Systems*, Berlin, Heidelberg, New York: Springer.

Saviotti, P.P. (2007), 'Qualitative change and economic development', in Hanusch. H. and Pyka, A. (eds), *The Elgar Companion to Neo-Schumpeterian Economics*, Cheltenham, UK and Northampton, MA, USA: Edward Elgar, pp. 820–39.

Saviotti, P.P. and Catherine, D. (2008), 'Innovation networks in biotechnology', in Patzelt, Holger and Brenner, Thomas (eds), *Handbook of Bioentrepreneurship*, New York: Springer.

Saviotti, P.P., de Looze, M.A. and Maupertuis, M.A. (2005), 'Knowledge dynamics and the mergers of firms in the biotechnology based sectors', *Economics of Innovation and New Technology*, **14** (1–2), 103–24.

Saviotti, P.P., de Looze, M.A., Maupertuis, M.A. and Nesta, L. (2003), 'Knowledge dynamics and the mergers of firms in the biotechnology based sectors', *International Journal of Biotechnology*, **5**, 371–401.

Saviotti, P.P. and Frenken, K. (2008), 'Export variety and the economic performance of countries', *Journal of Evolutionary Economics*, **18**, 201–18.

Saviotti, P.P. and Nesta, L. (2009), 'Trajectories, convergence and divergence in economic development', Paper presented at the 7th Globelics Conference, 'Inclusive growth, innovation and technological change: education, social capital and sustainable development', held in Dakar, Senegal on 6–8 October.

Saviotti, P.P., Nesta, L. and Javaid, M.N. (2008), 'Is there a direction in economic development? And, if so, what does it imply for emerging countries?', Presented at the 6th International GLOBELICS Conference

'New insights for understanding innovation and competence building for sustainable development and social justice' held in Mexico City on 22–24 September.

Schumpeter, J. (1934), *The Theory of Economic Development*, Cambridge, MA: Harvard University Press, original edition 1912.

Shannon, C.E. and Weaver, W. (1949), *The Mathematical Theory of Communication*, Urbana, IL: University of Illinois Press.

Smith, A. (1776), *The Wealth of Nations*, Penguin English Library, 1972 and following reprints.

Sorenson, O., Rivkin, J.V. and Fleming, L. (2006), 'Complexity, networks and knowledge flow', *Research Policy*, **35** (7), September, 994–1017.

Tushman, M.L. and Anderson, P. (1986), 'Technological discontinuities and organizational environments', *Administrative Science Quarterly*, **31**, 439–65.

Weber, M. (1968), *The Protestant Ethic and the Spirit of Capitalism*, London: Unwin University Books (First British edition, 1930).

7 The dynamics of technological knowledge: from linearity to recombination
Jackie Krafft and Francesco Quatraro

1. INTRODUCTION

Innovation and technological knowledge have long attracted the interest of scholars in economics. Most of the attention has been paid by the pioneers in the economics of innovation to the economic effects of the introduction of new technological knowledge as well as to the structural conditions better triggering innovative performances. This has paved the way to an empirically grounded research tradition which has initially considered knowledge as a homogeneous stock, as if it were the outcome of a quite uniform and fluid process of accumulation made possible by R&D investments, the same way as capital stock. This made it possible to include knowledge capital stock within an extended production function framework, as an additional input to labour and fixed capital (Griliches, 1979; Mansfield, 1980).

The focus therein was on the empirical assessment of the impact of technological knowledge on economic performances. Yet, very little was known about how new knowledge is brought about and, consequently, about how to provide a representation of knowledge that could be meaningful also from the epistemological viewpoint. Technology was mostly a black box, which began to be explored in depth with a significant lapse of time. The idea progressively arose that knowledge was something more than the mere outcome of a linear accumulation process. Indeed such an idea was grounded on theoretical reflections on the nature of knowledge creation processes, with a particular emphasis on the concept of search and on the institutions involved in the production of new technologies (Nelson, 1982, 1986; Nelson and Winter, 1982; Rosenberg, 1982).

Drawing on insightful intuitions of Schumpeter (1912, 1942) and Usher (1954), an increasing share of scholars in the economics of innovation has more recently elaborated theoretical approaches wherein the process of knowledge production is viewed as the outcome of a recombination process, according to which innovations stem either from the combination of brand new components or from the combination of existing components in new ways (Kauffman, 1993; Weitzmann, 1998). These theoretical efforts are in turn complemented by a well-defined cognitive approach to innovation as well as by the increasing availability of historical accounts and sectoral studies on the dynamics of technological knowledge (Vincenti, 1990; Nightingale, 1998; Fleming, 2001; Katila and Ahuja, 2002; van der Bergh, 2008).

Such a framework has been largely used to build empirical studies aimed at investigating the dynamics of knowledge from the viewpoint of the complex systems approach. Knowledge was indeed seen as a set of elements connected by a network of relationships, the architecture of which affects its performances. However, despite the emergence of these new lines of inquiry in the economics of knowledge, only a few efforts can be found in the literature attempting to analyse their empirical consequences, with respect to (i) the identification of the relevant properties that better proximate the concept of recombinant knowledge, and hence provide a more sensible representation of knowledge on the one hand; (ii) the operational translation of such properties, as well as the identification of the most appropriate analytical tools on the other hand. Moreover, such approaches are also characterized by an important theoretical limit, according to which the architecture of knowledge structure is stable over time, that is, complexity is exogenous rather than endogenous.

This chapter aims at providing an original review of the main theoretical approaches to technological knowledge, both implicit and explicit, and of their empirical counterparts in the field of economics of innovation. While there are in the literature interesting contributions aiming at assessing the relative goodness of the different proxies used in empirical analysis of innovation (see for example Kleinknecht et al., 2002), there is a lack of effort explicitly directed towards synthesis of theoretical and empirical issues in a historical perspective.

In this direction, we will go through the most recent debates on the dynamics of knowledge by proposing new methodologies for identifying relevant properties of knowledge that are consistent with the recombinant knowledge concept and allow for its grafting in the complex system dynamics approach, in a different way from the extant literature.

In particular, such methodologies are well suited to reconcile two different aspects of the analysis of the complex dynamics of technology, that is, the view of technology as an artefact and as an act (Arthur, 2009; Lane et al., 2009). Indeed, by proposing that knowledge is the outcome of a collective process of recombination, we may argue that technological knowledge itself is characterized by an internal structure emerging out of a complex dynamics that is strictly connected to the dynamics affecting the formation and evolution of technology coalitions (David and Keely, 2003).

The chapter is organized as follows. Section 2 provides an overview of the main different approaches to technological knowledge, in both empirical and theoretical terms. Section 3 lays down the basic ingredients of complex system dynamics and establishes the linkages with knowledge dynamics. In Section 4 we discuss the operational implications of knowledge understood as a complex system, by proposing a set of indicators that may fit this framework. Section 5 provides the conclusion and establishes an agenda for future research.

2.   TECHNOLOGICAL KNOWLEDGE: FROM KNOWLEDGE CAPITAL STOCK TO COMPLEX KNOWLEDGE

2.1   Knowledge Capital Stock and the Linear Model

The importance of creativity for the production of goods and wealth is not a recent discovery within economics. The earlier treatment can indeed be found already in Adam Smith's first four books of the *Wealth of Nations*. After more than a century, Alfred Marshall elaborated upon Adam Smith's contribution, by proposing a systemic account of the role of knowledge in the production process. In particular, Marshall made it very clear both in *Industry and Trade* (1919) and in the *Principles of Economics* (1920) that knowledge is a key input in the production process and the main engine of economic growth.

Despite the venerable origins of the interest in technological knowledge within the field of economics, attempts to provide empirical accounts of the dynamics and the effects of innovation appeared only in the late 1950s. The studies by Griliches (1957) and Mansfield (1961) on the diffusion of innovation can be viewed as the earliest empirical efforts in this sense. However, very little was known at that time about knowledge and in particular about its production and exploitation. The earliest empirical works in which the word 'knowledge' appeared to refer to a factor affecting the production of firms can be dated back to the late 1970s. Zvi Griliches turned out to be a pioneer in the field again. In his 1979 paper indeed he proposed the famous extended production function, which paved the way to a wide body of empirical investigations. In the paper the traditional production function was extended so as to include an additional explanatory variable, as follows:

$$Y_i = C_i^\alpha L_i^\beta K_i^\gamma \tag{7.1}$$

Where C is the fixed capital stock, L stands for labour services and K is the knowledge capital used by firm i. Strangely enough, the empirical literature has generated a great deal of confusion on this contribution, as it is usually taken as a key reference in papers using the so-called 'knowledge production function' approach. We believe this is due to a basic misunderstanding. Indeed, Professor Griliches in his article made some steps towards giving an empirical meaning to the K term. To this purpose he proposed the following relationship:

$$K = G[W(B)R, \upsilon] \tag{7.2}$$

where R is R&D expenditures and υ is a set of unobserved disturbances. The term $W(B)$ is instead a lag polynomial describing the relative contribution of past and present R&D expenditures to the accumulated level of knowledge. Clearly, this representation is one more application of the distributed lag literature, which influenced Griliches to a great extent. Far from proposing a knowledge production function, this relationship simply was the formalization of the concept of knowledge capital stock, which the author subsequently used in his 1980 paper on the US productivity slowdown (Griliches, 1980). In a nutshell, the 1979 paper offered the formal basis to the application of the permanent inventory method to calculate the knowledge stock starting from R&D expenditures, which are then considered as a flow measure.

The specification of knowledge capital also called for a proper account of the effects of knowledge spillovers, that is, knowledge borrowed or stolen from other firms or industries that can equally affect productivity of the observed firm or industry. Knowledge spillovers have been accommodated in an extended production function at the firm level by including a proxy for the aggregate stock of knowledge available within the industry firm i to which the firm belongs:

$$Y_i = C_i^\alpha L_i^\beta K_i^\gamma K_a^\mu \tag{7.3}$$

This equation enables us to distinguish between the total effect of aggregate private knowledge and the total spillover effect. Since all private knowledge is supposed to spill over to some extent, the total effect of all private knowledge at the aggregate level is given by $\gamma + \mu$ (Griliches, 1979, 1992).

On the basis of the argument elaborated so far, we may provide some insights about the possible theoretical underpinnings to the concept of knowledge capital stock. Indeed, we lack an explicit theoretical reasoning on technological knowledge leading to its operationalization in terms of knowledge capital stock. A quote from Griliches (1967) may be of some help here:

> For example, let investments affect the level of patenting with a lag whose generating function is given by $W_1(z)$, let these new inventions be embodied in new investment with a lag $W_2(z)$ and let new investment affect total factor productivity with a lag $W_3(z)$; then the total lag distribution of productivity behind investment is given by $W(T) = W_1(z) W_2(z) W_3(z)$. (Griliches, 1967: 20)

It is clear that the application of lag generating functions to investments measures so as to get a stock implies an underlying sequential process that starts with R&D investments to yield a proxy of cumulated knowledge that in turn is supposed to show some effects on economic performances. In this direction, we believe it would not be inappropriate to say that knowledge capital stock implies a vision of knowledge accumulation as an outcome of a linear process such as this: science precedes technology development, which then comes to be adopted by firms, and finally affects production efficiency.

After all, Vannevar Bush's report to the US president had long been the main reference text to students of science and technology. Therefore it's likely that the articulation of the linear model he proposed has influenced the way scholars from other fields looked at technological knowledge as well. Moreover, Kline and Rosenberg's critique came only in the 1980s, and so did many of the works that opened up a new view on knowledge and innovation providing the basis to the knowledge production function approach (Bush, 1945; Kline and Rosenberg, 1986; Balconi et al., 2009).[1]

2.2   Knowledge Production Function

The inclusion of knowledge capital stock within an extended production function approach allows economists to preserve the basic microeconomic assumptions about production sets out of which firms take their profit-maximizing choice. However, such an approach assumes the existence of a separate R&D sector that is partly responsible for the change in the production technology, and hence for the shift of the production function (Nelson, 1980).

Because of this limitation, such a representation began to be challenged mainly by evolutionary economists, who proposed to expand the view upon technological knowledge so as to account for its inherent compositeness. At the same time, scholars of science and technology started criticizing the linear model, by proposing an alternative view basically drawing upon systemic models of innovation based upon the interaction among different and yet complementary institutions involved in the complex business of knowledge production (Kline and Rosenberg, 1986; Gibbons and Murphy, 1992).

A couple of Dick Nelson's contributions in the early 1980s provided a clear statement of the problems with the concept of knowledge capital stock, along with the theorization of a more articulated concept of knowledge, understood as a set of capabilities guiding the search processes undertaken by organizations performing R&D. Such capabilities may be themselves the outcome of R&D activities, and are likely to improve over time due to dynamic increasing returns stemming from learning by doing dynamics (Nelson, 1980, 1982).

In this sense, such contributions may be viewed as pioneering in the attempt to open the black box of technological knowledge so as to explicitly improve upon Griliches' and Mansfield's former operationalizations. Moreover, they also proposed a more realistic view in which science and technology are far from being sharply differentiated. There are a number of institutions producing knowledge, some of them public and some private, and it is not possible to identify a one-to-one mapping from science to public institutions or from applied technology to private business firms. Scholars must acknowledge that different kinds of organizations take part in the process of knowledge production, such as firms, research labs and universities (Nelson, 1982, 1986).

This set of arguments has been well received mostly in the literature dealing with knowledge production at the aggregate level. In particular the literature on regional systems of innovation provided a fertile ground to develop the implications of this new view (Cooke, 1996; Cooke et al., 1997). Regional economists translated the idea that knowledge is the result of the interaction of a number of complementary inputs provided by different research institutions, into the concept of knowledge production function. The differences with the concept of knowledge capital stock are clear. Knowledge is no longer the mere result of cumulated R&D spending subject to decreasing returns. The knowledge production function provides a mapping from knowledge inputs to knowledge outputs that appears as follows:

$$\log(K_t) = \alpha + \beta\log(R_t) + \gamma\log(U_t) + \delta\log(Z_t) + \varepsilon \qquad (7.4)$$

where K stands for a measure of knowledge output, say patents, R stands for the industry R&D and U represents the university research, while Z includes a proxy for the concentration of a given type of activity (Acs et al., 2002; Fritsch, 2002). Equation (7.4) represents a production function, the arguments of which enter a multiplicative relationship, and hence are seen as complementary rather than substitute. The coefficients are in turn the elasticities of knowledge output to knowledge inputs.

On a fairly similar ground, the localized technological change approach has stressed that the dynamics of knowledge production are characterized by the joint utilization of internal and external knowledge, both tacit and codified. Mechanisms of learning, socialization and recombination are considered as crucial in a context characterized by the production of knowledge by means of knowledge itself (Antonelli, 1999).

The knowledge production function approach represents an improvement both from the theoretical and the empirical viewpoint, with respect to the concept of knowledge capital stock. It allows a better understanding of the interactive dynamics leading to the production of technological knowledge, by accounting for possible dynamic increasing returns stemming from learning dynamics as well as knowledge externalities. However, knowledge on the left hand side of the equation is still conceived as an homogeneous stock, and little is said about the intrinsic heterogeneity of the knowledge base. In other words such a representation still lacks proper cognitive models of knowledge production.

2.3   Complex Knowledge and NK Models

The development of the knowledge production approach inevitably leaves a basic question as to what are the micro-founded mechanisms underlying knowledge production. In this respect, the interest in the cognitive mechanisms leading to production of new technological knowledge has recently emerged in the field of economics of innovation. This strand of analysis has moved from key concepts brought forward by Schumpeter (1912, 1942) and Usher (1954), and then elaborated upon the models proposed within evolutionary economics (Nelson and Winter, 1982).

In his seminal works, Schumpeter proposed a view of innovation as the outcome of a recombination process. Most innovations brought about in the economic system stem from the combinations of existing elements in new and previously untried ways. Such innovations appear to be mainly incremental. Radical innovations stem instead from the combination of existing components with brand new ones.

The contributions by Weitzman (1996, 1998) represent the first, and very impressive, attempt to draw upon such assumptions. His recombinant growth approach provides a sophisticated analytical framework grafting a micro-founded theory of knowledge production within an endogenous growth model. The production of knowledge is seen as the outcome of an intentional effort aimed at reconfiguring existing within a genuine cumulative perspective. However, there is no particular focus on the constraints that the combination of different ideas may represent, especially when these ideas are technologically distant. The only limiting factor seems to be the bounded processing capacity of economic agents.

The recombinant knowledge approach is based on the following assumptions. The creation of new knowledge is represented as a search process across a set of alternative components that can be combined. However, within this framework a crucial role is played by the cognitive mechanisms underlying the search process aimed at exploring the knowledge space so as to identify the pieces that might possibly be combined together. The set of potentially combinable pieces turns out to be a subset of the whole knowledge space. Search is supposed to be local rather than global, while the degree of localness appears to be the outcome of cognitive, social and technological influences. The ability to engage in a search process within spaces that are distant from the original starting point is likely to generate breakthroughs stemming from the combination of brand new components (Nightingale, 1998; Fleming, 2001).

Incidentally, such an approach also helps to better qualify the distinction between exploration and exploitation articulated by March (1991). Most of the research in organization studies has seen search processes as ranging between two poles of a one-dimensional continuum, that is, exploration and exploitation. The view of knowledge as an outcome of a recombination activity allows the introduction of two nested dimensions, defined according to the degree to which agents decide to rely on exploration or on exploitation, or on a combination of both. To this purpose concepts like search depth and search scope have been introduced. The former refers to degree to which agents intend to draw upon their prior knowledge, while the latter refers to the degree to which agents intend to rely on the exploration of new areas in the knowledge space (Katila and Ahuja, 2002).

Recombination occurs only after agents have put much effort into searching within the knowledge space. This strand of literature posits that knowledge so obtained is complex, meaning that it comprises many elements that interact richly (Simon, 1966; Kauffman, 1993). This has paved the way to an increasing number of empirical works based on the NK model proposed by Kauffman, according to which the search process is conducted across a rugged landscape, where pieces of knowledge are located and which provides the context within which technologies interact.

The bulk of the focus is on the concept of interdependence among the pieces that are combined together, while complexity is defined as the relationship between the number of components and the degree of interdependence (Fleming and Sorenson, 2001; Sorenson et al., 2006). Following the intuition on the importance of patent citations contained in the seminal paper by Manuel Trajtenberg (1990), the empirical implementation of the interdependence concept is based on the deployment of the information contained in patent documents, that is, technological classes and citations to other patents. In particular, interdependence is considered as a powerful explanatory variable building upon the technological classes the patent is assigned to. The interdependence of a patent l is obtained in two steps. First of all one has to calculate the ease of recombination for each subclass i (E_i), defined as the count of subclasses $j \neq i$ previously combined with class i weighted by total number of patents assigned to class i:

$$E_i = \frac{\sum j \neq i}{\sum l_i} \tag{7.5}$$

Then one can calculate the degree of interdependence of patent l (K_l) by inverting its average ease of recombination:

$$K_l = \frac{\sum i \in l}{\sum_{i \in l} E_i} \tag{7.6}$$

This empirical approach allows for evaluating the relative probability of recombination of each technological class observed in the patent sample, and then to assign an average recombination score to a patent. The basic idea is that the more combinable are the classes contained within a patent, the lower the degree of interdependence, as the technology is susceptible to be developed in a larger number of directions. On the contrary, should the classes be less combinable, then a relatively low number of possible combinations is possible, for which the technology turns out to show a high degree of interdependence. Such a measure of interdependence is in turn expected to explain differentials in usefulness of inventions as proxied by the flow of citations received by patents over time.

This framework clearly has the merit to push the economic discussion about technological knowledge beyond the conventional vision considering it as a sort of black box. It sheds light on the possibility to further qualify knowledge as proxied by patents, by better exploiting the information contained in patent documents. Moreover, it provides an innovative link between knowledge and complexity.

However, the notion of complexity used therein seems to be constrained to a generic definition of an object, the elements of which are characterized by a high degree of interaction. As an implication the empirical effort does not go beyond the count of classes and of patents assigned to classes. The NK models fail to identify knowledge as an emergent property of an adaptive complex system, characterized by an architecture that can influence the actions at the micro and meso levels as well as be influenced as a result of what happens at lower layers. This requires first an explicit concept of knowledge structure and then an exploration of the different tools made available by different methodological approaches.

Summing up, the grafting of complexity theory into economic sciences has proved to be particularly fertile, especially for what concerns the economics of knowledge and innovation. The explicit reference to the NK model by the recombinant knowledge literature provides a clear example in this respect.

Most NK models are however affected by a severe limit, which constrains their usefulness. The complex system is characterized by a set of elements and the connections amongst them. The configuration of the linkages connecting the elements of the system is likely to affect agents' performances. The main problem here is that the architecture of the system is often considered as stable over time rather than evolving (Frenken, 2006). This amounts to considering the degree of complexity of the system as exogenous, defined *ex ante*. The contribution by Fleming and Sorenson discussed above presents exactly this limitation, which makes it unsuitable for the analysis of the evolutionary and path dependent dynamics of technological change.

3.   ENDOGENOUS COMPLEXITY AND TECHNOLOGICAL KNOWLEDGE

The main issue to be considered now is that the architecture of a complex system may well change over time, and so may the structure of epistatic relationships. This may occur either due to a change in the relative weight of some elements in the system, these elements switching from a non-influential to an influential position, or by means of introduction of new elements within the system. This is in turn likely to alter the existing structure of relationships. Within this context, the pleiotropy represents the number of elements in the system that are affected by the appearance of new elements. It is clear that the higher the pleiotropy, the greater the change in the architecture of the system that the inclusion of new elements may engender.

The model of constructional selection by Altenberg (1994, 1995) represents one of the few attempts to cope with the issue of changing architectures of complex systems. As noted by Frenken (2005, 2006), this class of models is well suited to investigate the evolution of technologies considered as artefacts made of interdependent elements (Lane and Maxfield, 2005).

The viewpoint of endogenous complexity makes the analysis of knowledge dynamics particularly appealing and challenging. Knowledge can indeed be represented as an emergent property stemming from multi-layered complex dynamics (see Figure 7.1). Knowledge is indeed the result of a collective effort of individuals who interact with one another, sharing their bits of knowledge by means of intentional acts of communication (Saviotti, 2007; Antonelli, 2008). In other words, the adoption of an endogenous complexity made possible by the recombination approach allows for the combination of the view on technology as an artefact with the view of technology as an act, that is, as

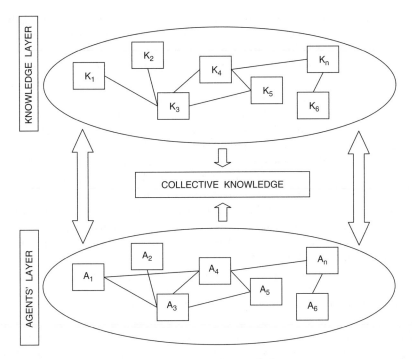

Figure 7.1   Multi-layered complex dynamics of knowledge

the product of collective actions involving agents with converging incentives and aligned interests (Arthur, 2009; Lane et al., 2009).

The structure of the network of relationships amongst innovating agents represents therefore a crucial factor able to shape the ultimate outcome of knowledge production processes. Constructional selection matters, in that new institutions entering the network need first of all to choose which incumbents they want to be linked with. The concept of preferential attachment applies to this situation. In a wide number of contexts, the new nodes in a network generally end up linking with those 'old' nodes already characterized by a large number of connections (Barabasi and Albert, 1999). As a consequence, the entrance of new actors in the network is likely to reshape the relative weight of nodes, and hence modify the structure and the balance of relationships.

Collective knowledge so produced stems from the combination of bits of knowledge dispersed among innovating agents. Creativity refers to the ability of agents to combine together these small bits of knowledge so as to produce an original piece of technological knowledge. This in turn may be thought about as a collection of bits of knowledge linked with one another. The knowledge base of a firm can be therefore imagined as a network in which the nodes are the small bits of knowledge and the links represent their actual combination in specific tokens. Knowledge in this sense turns out to be an emergent property of complex dynamics featuring the interdependent elements of the system, that is, the bits of knowledge.

This is a quite unexplored consequence of the collective character of knowledge production, which provides further richness to its dynamics. Such a complex system may be represented as a network, the nodes of which are the smaller units of knowledge while the edges stand for their actual combination. Hence the knowledge base is characterized by a structure with its own architecture. This in turn may evolve over time, as an effect of the introduction of new small bits of knowledge and the consequent change in the relative weight of the nodes within the network. Indeed, as in the networks of innovators, new nodes will be attached to some existing nodes, the centrality of which will be altered. Learning dynamics and absorptive capacity represent a channel through which the topology of knowledge structure affects search behaviour at the level of agents' networks. Indeed, agents move across the technology landscape in regions that are quite close to the area of their actual competences. Technological change is localized as an effect of the interactions between the complex dynamics at the knowledge and the agents' level. However the topology of knowledge structure is in turn shaped by the choices made by innovating agents as to which bits of knowledge combine together. A self-sustained process is likely to emerge, according to which the knowledge creation process tends more and more towards a local attractor in which they are locked (see Colombelli and von Tunzelmann, Chapter 4 in this volume).

This dynamics indeed makes preferential attachment work also at the knowledge level. Agents' search behaviour is indeed constrained by the topology of the knowledge structure. In this direction, those small bits of knowledge which have grown in importance are likely to exert a much stronger influence. This process is rooted in historical time, according to which the gradual sorting out of knowledge bits which have proved to be not so fertile, leaves the floor to fewer, more fertile bits. New bits of knowledge entering the knowledge base later on are likely to be linked to these few pillars.

Preferential attachment introduces a great deal of path dependence in system dynamics of technological knowledge. It articulates the concept of persistence beyond the rate of introduction of innovations, so as to apply it to the centrality of the specific smaller bits of knowledge which make the structure of the knowledge base.

Still, while this self-enforcing process is likely to trap the search process within a bounded area, the dynamics of technological communication at the agents' level as well as the capabilities to cope with search in areas that are far away from the competences of innovating agents are likely to introduce discontinuities in the evolutionary pattern. This introduces a wide variety of new bits of knowledge which are loosely related with those already existing in the knowledge base, so as to give rise to radically new combinations. The process of evolution, fed by learning dynamics and cumulativeness, leads to the gradual selection of the best combinations, which grow in centrality and hence begin to constrain agents' search behaviour.

Knowledge sharing and technological communication ensure therefore the emergence of new variety, which is more likely to occur in transition phases. At this stage a wide range of alternatives are viable, and multiple local attractors are likely to emerge from mutual influences between complex dynamics at the knowledge and the agents' layers.

4.   SOME OPERATIONAL METHODOLOGIES

The outcome of considering endogenous complexity in technological knowledge is that the layout of knowledge structure appears to be both an outcome and a determinant of agents' search. This deserves further careful attention and more in depth analysis. In what follows we propose two alternatives methodologies which have been relatively recently introduced, and are equally suitable to improve our empirical ability to measure the various facets of the evolution of the knowledge base, including the occurrence of path dependency and persistence phases as well as the emergence of variety and discontinuity phases.

4.1   Measures based on Co-occurrence Matrixes

The purpose of this first methodology consists in the exploration of the evolution of the properties of the knowledge base, with particular emphasis on the issues of variety, similarity and complementarity.

1. Variety can be measured by using the information entropy index. Entropy measures the degree of disorder or randomness of the system, so that systems characterized by high entropy will also be characterized by a high degree of uncertainty (Saviotti, 1988).

   The information entropy has some interesting properties, and especially a property of multidimensional extension (Frenken and Nuvolari, 2004). Consider a pair of events (X_1, Y_j), and the probability of co-occurrence of both of them p_{lj}. A two dimensional total variety (TV) measure can be expressed as follows:

   $$TV \equiv H(X,Y) = \sum_l \sum_j p_{lj} \log_2\left(\frac{1}{p_{lj}}\right) \qquad (7.7)$$

   If one considers p_{lj} to be the probability that two technological classes l and j co-occur within the same patent, then the measure of multidimensional entropy focuses on the variety of co-occurrences of technological classes within regional patents applications.

   Moreover, the total index can be decomposed in a 'within' and a 'between' part any time the events to be investigated can be aggregated in a smaller numbers of subsets. Within-entropy measures the average degree of disorder or variety within the subsets, while between-entropy focuses on the subsets measuring the variety across them. Frenken et al. (2007) refer to between- and within-group entropy respectively as unrelated and related variety.

   It can be easily shown that the decomposition theorem holds also for the multidimensional case. Hence if one allows $l \in S_g$ and $j \in S_z$ ($g = 1, \ldots, G; z = 1, \ldots, Z$), we can rewrite $H(X, Y)$ as follows:

   $$TV = H_Q + \sum_{g=1}^{G} \sum_{z=1}^{Z} P_{gz} H_{gz} \qquad (7.8)$$

   where the first term of the right-hand side is the between-entropy and the second term is the (weighted) within-entropy. In particular:

$$UTV \equiv H_Q = \sum_{g=1}^{G} \sum_{z=1}^{Z} P_{gz} \log_2 \frac{1}{P_{gz}} \qquad (7.9)$$

$$RTV \equiv \sum_{g=1}^{G} \sum_{z=1}^{Z} P_{gz} H_{gz} \qquad (7.10)$$

$$P_{gz} = \sum_{l \in S_g} \sum_{j \in S_z} p_{lj}$$

$$H_{gz} = \sum_{l \in S_g} \sum_{j \in S_z} \frac{p_{lj}}{P_{gz}} \log_2 \left(\frac{1}{p_{lj}/P_{gz}} \right)$$

We can therefore refer to between- and within-entropy respectively as unrelated technological variety (UTV) and related technological variety (RTV), while total information entropy is referred to as general technological variety.

2.   The similarity amongst different types of knowledge can be captured by a measure of cognitive distance. A useful index of distance can be derived from the measure of technological proximity originally proposed by Jaffe (1986, 1989), who investigated the proximity of firms' technological portfolios. Subsequently Breschi et al. (2003) adapted the index in order to measure the proximity, or relatedness, between two technologies. The idea is that each firm is characterized by a vector V of the k technologies that occur in its patents. Knowledge similarity can first be calculated for a pair of technologies l and j as the angular separation or un-centered correlation of the vectors V_{lk} and V_{jk}. The similarity of technologies l and j can then be defined as follows:

$$S_{lj} = \frac{\sum_{k=1}^{n} V_{lk} V_{jk}}{\sqrt{\sum_{k=1}^{n} V_{lk}^2} \sqrt{\sum_{k=1}^{n} V_{jk}^2}} \qquad (7.11)$$

The idea underlying the calculation of this index is that two technologies j and l are similar to the extent that they co-occur with a third technology k. The cognitive distance between j and l is the complement of their index of the similarity:

$$d_{lj} = 1 - S_{lj} \qquad (7.12)$$

Once the index is calculated for all possible pairs, it needs to be aggregated at the industry level to obtain a synthetic index of technological distance. This can be done in two steps. First of all one can compute the weighted average distance of technology l, that is, the average distance of l from all other technologies.

$$WAD_{lt} = \frac{\sum_{j \neq l} d_{lj} P_{jit}}{\sum_{j \neq l} P_{jit}} \qquad (7.13)$$

where P_j is the number of patents in which the technology j is observed. Now the average cognitive distance at time t is obtained as follows:

$$CD_t = \sum_l WAD_{lit} \times \frac{P_{lit}}{\sum_l P_{lit}} \qquad (7.14)$$

Complementarity: typically a firm needs to combine, or integrate, many different pieces of knowledge to produce a marketable output. In order to be competitive a firm not only needs to learn new 'external' knowledge. It also needs to learn how to combine it with other, new and old, pieces of knowledge. We can say that a knowledge base, in which different pieces of knowledge are well combined, or integrated, is a coherent knowledge base. Such technologies are by definition complementary in that they are jointly required to obtain a given outcome. We can now turn to calculate the coherence (R) of the knowledge base, defined as the average relatedness of any technology randomly chosen within the sector with respect to any other technology (Nesta and Saviotti, 2005, 2006; Nesta, 2008). To yield the knowledge coherence index, a number of steps are required however. In what follows we describe how to obtain the index at the sector level. First of all, one should calculate the weighted average relatedness WAR_l of technology l with respect to all other technologies present within the sector. Such a measure builds upon the measure of technological relatedness t_{lj} (see Nesta and Saviotti, 2005). Following Teece et al. (1994), WAR_l is defined as the degree to which technology l is related to all other technologies $j \in l$ in the sector, weighted by patent count P_{jt}:

$$WAR_{lt} = \frac{\sum_{j \neq l} \tau_{lj} P_{jt}}{\sum_{j \neq l} P_{jt}} \qquad (7.15)$$

Finally the coherence of knowledge base within the sector is defined as weighted average of the WAR_{lt} measure:

$$R_t = \sum_{l \neq j} WAR_{lt} \times \frac{P_{lt}}{\sum_l P_{lt}} \qquad (7.16)$$

It is worth stressing that this index, implemented by analysing co-occurrences of technological classes within patent applications, measures the degree to which the services rendered by the co-occurring technologies are complementary with one another. The relatedness measure τ_{lj} indicates indeed that the utilization of technology l implies that of technology j in order to perform specific functions that are not reducible to their independent use.

4.2 Measures based on Social Network Analysis

The starting point of this second methodology is to consider that a network may be defined as a graph made of nodes that are tied to each other by one or more types of interdependency. Relationships among nodes are expressed by arcs, which in turn may be directed or undirected. Two nodes that are connected by a line are said to be adjacent to one another. Adjacency is therefore the graphical expression of the fact that two nodes are directly related or connected to one another. The points to which a particular point is adjacent are termed its neighbourhood. Points may be directly connected by a line, or they may be indirectly connected through a sequence of lines. It may be thought of as a 'walk' in which each point and each line are distinct. This is called a path. The length of path is measured by the number of lines that constitute it. The distance between two points is the shortest path (the geodesic) that connects them.

One of the most widely used measures to describe a network is the density. It describes the general level of linkage among the points in a graph. The density of a network is therefore defined as the total number of actual lines, expressed as a proportion of the maximum possible number of lines:

$$\Delta = \frac{l}{n(n-1)/2} \tag{7.17}$$

A network is complete when all the nodes are adjacent, and the measure of density attempts to summarize the overall distribution of lines in order to assess how far the network is from completion. Density depends upon two other important parameters of the network, that is, the inclusiveness and the sum of the degree of its points. Inclusiveness can be defined as the share of network nodes that are not isolated, that is, the share of nodes that are connected to at least one other node. For example, in a network of 20 nodes with 5 isolated nodes the inclusiveness is 0.75. The more inclusive the graph, the more dense the network will be.

However some nodes will be more connected than others. The degree of a node is an important measure of centrality that refers to the total number of other points in its neighbourhood. Formally one can represent the degree by the following equation:

$$D(v) = \sum_{s \in V \neq v} x_{vs} \tag{7.18}$$

This measure is obviously biased by the network size. Therefore it is useful to use a standardized measure, which consists in dividing the degree measure by its maximum value as follows:

$$ND(v) = \frac{D(v)}{n-1} \tag{7.19}$$

The higher the degree of the connected points in the network, the higher will be the density. For this reason the calculation of density needs to take into account both measures. It should compare the actual number of lines present in the graph with the total number of lines that the graph would show if it were complete.

While the density describes the network as a whole, the measures of centrality refer to the relevance of the nodes belonging to the network. A point is locally central if it has a large number of connections with other points in its immediate environment, that is, other points in its neighbourhood. Global centrality refers instead to the prominence of the node with respect to the overall structure of the network. Measures of global and of local centrality have a different meaning.

Measures of global centrality are expressed in terms of the distance among various points. Two of these measures, that is, closeness and betweenness, are particularly important. The simplest notion of closeness is that calculated from the 'sum distance', the sum of geodesic distances to all other points in the graph (Sabidussi, 1966). After having calculated the matrix of distances among the nodes of the network, the sum distance is the row of column marginal value. A point with a low sum distance is close to a large number of other points, and so closeness can be seen as the reciprocal of the sum distance. Formally it can be expressed as follows:

$$C(v) = \frac{1}{\sum_{t \in V \neq v} d_G(v, t)} \tag{7.20}$$

where the denominator represents the sum of the geodesic distance of the vertex v to all other points.

The betweenness measures the extent to which a particular point lies 'between' the other points in the graph: a point with a relatively low degree may play an important intermediary role and so be very central to the network (Freeman, 1979). The betweenness of a node measures how much it can play the part of a broker or gatekeeper in the network. Freeman's approach is built upon the concept of local dependency. A point is dependent upon another if the paths which connect it to the other points pass through this point. Formally, let G be a graph with n vertices, then the betweenness is calculated as follows:

$$B(v) = \sum_{\substack{s \neq v \neq t \in V \\ s \neq t}} \frac{\sigma_{st}(v)}{\sigma_{st}} \tag{7.21}$$

where σ_{st} is the number of shortest geodesic paths from s to t, and $\sigma_{st}(v)$ is the number of shortest geodesic paths from s to t passing through a vertex v.

The centrality measures discussed above, allow us to characterize each single network node. However, it is also possible to calculate the sector averages for all of the three indexes. In this direction, one must consider that each node corresponds to a technological class observed with a specific relative frequency, which must be taken into account when averaging out the centrality measures. We can then propose weighted average centrality measures as follows. Let $Z(v)$ be one of the three centrality measures referred to the generic node v, the weighted average centrality at time t is:

$$\overline{Z(v)} = Z(v) \times \frac{P_v}{\sum_v P_v} \tag{7.22}$$

where P_v is the number of patents in which the technology v is observed.

5. CONCLUSION: AVENUES FOR FUTURE RESEARCH

The chapter was intended to provide an original and creative review of the literature on the dynamics of technological knowledge. Table 7.1 provides a synthesis and a taxonomy of the different approaches to technological knowledge, as well as of their theoretical underpinnings and empirical consequences.

Table 7.1   Taxonomy of the different approaches to technological knowledge

Early 1980s	Extended production function	Knowledge capital stock as explanatory variable	Homogeneous good	Linear model	Linear mode and top down process R&D and specialized institutions of knowledge Large, vertically related companies Internal financial markets
Late 1980s Early 1990s	Knowledge production function	Knowledge capital stock as dependent variable	Homogeneous good	Systemic interactions	Learning effects and bottom up process Markets for knowledge and strong IPR regimes Small, specialized firms Venture capital and IPOs
Late 1990s Early 2000s	Exogeneous complexity	Citations and ease of recombination	Heterogeneous good	Emergent property of a given architecture	Search conducted across a rugged landscape Explain differentials in usefulness of inventions
Early 2000s	Endogeneous complexity	Technological classes and knowledge structure	Heterogeneous good	Emergent property of a changing architecture	Knowledge discontinuities and search strategies Stable innovation networks with large and small firms retain and reinvest, long term investors' strategies

We argue that among the new developments on the theme, the investigation on endogenous complexity in technological knowledge is certainly the most promising. First it provides an accurate representation of how knowledge is created and diffused at the analytical level, and second it also has empirical value since it can be expressed by a wide range of indicators and measures. In particular, we claimed that such a framework has great potential in that it provides both the theoretical and empirical grounds to carry out an interdependent analysis of technology as an act and as an artefact. In this direction, the structure of technological knowledge is represented as a network, the architecture of which is in turn influenced by the architecture of the network of innovation, and vice versa. It follows a never ending process of mutual influences that keeps the system constantly out of equilibrium (see Antonelli, Chapter 1 in this volume).

The notion of coalitions for innovation gains momentum in this context (David and Keely, 2002). They can be regarded as the product of spontaneous order, yet their emergence can be guided and designed by means of the intentional intervention of policy makers as well as corporate strategies. The successful introduction of an innovation may be regarded as the result of a hegemonic coalition, that is, a coalition that has been able to design a group of complementary agents, coordinate their incentives and integrate their competences so as to achieve hegemony in a given technological space. The design of coalitions for innovation is therefore likely to exert a great deal of influence on the direction of technology evolution, and hence on future developments of the knowledge space. Within non-ergodic systems, this is likely to favour the lock-in engendered by path dependent dynamics, unless the structures of the two nested networks change so much that a new hegemonic coalition emerges, able to introduce a discontinuity in the technology space.

The implications of this approach are far reaching. One of the major domains of application so far has been the analysis of the technological basis of knowledge of firms, characterized by patent portfolios (see Nesta, 2008). Further applications have been proposed in empirical studies dealing with the evolutionary patterns of development of knowledge intensive sectors, especially focused on the identification of the introduction of discontinuities and the periodicity of random screening and organized search stages (Krafft et al., 2009, 2011; Antonelli et al., 2010).

A non exhaustive list of potential applications can be elaborated, and each element in this list can be considered as a major avenue of research to be explored in the future:

Industrial dynamics and evolution   The fact that, in an industry, knowledge can either come from a recombination of existing knowledge or from the creation of new knowledge has an impact on industrial evolution. Incumbents may play the role of efficient recombination of existing knowledge, but very often may also rely on new entrant firms for the creation of new knowledge. Depending on the share of combination of existing knowledge versus creation of entirely new knowledge, incumbents or new entrants may act as leaders in the industry.

Networks   In most industries, networks occur among firms, and appear more and more as a stable form of industrial organization. Endogenous complex knowledge allows an accurate mapping of the formation of networks, and their transformation over time. Moreover depending on preferential attachment characteristics of the agents within the network, it is possible to identify the centrality of some actors in the network at some point in time, and to predict how it may change over time with the entrance of new actors.

Geographical issues   The recent debates on knowledge cities, or the more traditional ones on learning regions, gain new resonance from the use of the analysis of complex knowledge. On this theme, the approach can provide new quantitative results on the importance of geography in the creation and recombination of knowledge. In particular, it is possible to assess quantitatively how new actors bringing new pieces of knowledge may aggregate with other actors already installed, or not, and eventually how these new actors may over time gain some weight (or centrality) over older ones, thus shaping the technological characteristics of a region.

NOTE

1. We do not intend to go into the debate on the virtues and drawbacks of the linear model. The work by Balconi et al. (2009) provides an excellent synthesis in this direction.

REFERENCES

Acs, Z.J., Anselin, L. and Varga, A. (2002), 'Patents and innovation counts as measures of regional production of new knowledge', *Research Policy*, **31**, 1069–85.

Altenberg, L. (1994), 'Evolving better representations through selective genome growth', in Schaffer, J.D., Schwefel, H.P. and Kitano, H. (eds) *Proceedings of the IEEE World Congress on Computational Intelligence*, Piscataway, NJ: IEEE, pp. 182–87.

Altenberg, L. (1995), 'Genome growth and the evolution of the genotype–phenotype map', in Banzhaf, W. and Eckman, F.H. (eds), *Evolution and Biocomputation*, Berlin and Heidelberg: Springer-Verlag, pp. 205–59.

Antonelli, C. (1999), *The Microdynamics of Technological Change*, London: Routledge.

Antonelli, C. (2008), *Localized Technological Change: Towards the Economics of Complexity*, London: Routledge.

Antonelli, C., Krafft, J. and Quatraro, F. (2010), 'Recombinant knowledge and growth: the case of ICTs', *Structural Change and Economic Dynamics*, **21**, 50–69.

Arthur, W.B. (2009), 'Complexity and the economy', in Rosser Jr, J.B. (ed.), *Handbook of Research on Complexity*, Cheltenham, UK and Northampton, MA, USA: Edward Elgar, pp. 12–21.

Balconi, M., Brusoni, S. and Orsenigo, L. (2010), 'In defence of the linear model: an essay', *Research Policy*, **39** (1), 1–13.

Barabasi, A.L. and Albert, R. (1999), 'Emergence of scaling in random networks', *Science*, **286**, 509–12.

Breschi, S., Lissoni, F. and Malerba, F. (2003), 'Knowledge relatedness in firm technological diversification', *Research Policy*, **32**, 69–97.

Bush, V. (1945), *Science the Endless Frontier. Report to the President*, Washington DC: United States Government Printing Office.

Cooke, P. (1996), 'The new wave of regional innovation networks: analysis, characteristics and strategy', *Small Business Economics*, **8**, 1–13.

Cooke, P., Uranga, M. and Etxebarria, G. (1997), 'Regional innovation systems: institutional and organisational dimensions', *Research Policy*, **26**, 475–91.

David, P.A. and Keely, L.C. (2002), 'The economics of scientific research coalitions: collaborative network formation in the presence of multiple funding agencies', Wisconsin-Madison – Social Systems, Working Papers, no. 11.

David, P.A. and Keely, L. (2003), 'The endogenous formation of scientific research coalitions', *Economics of Innovation and New Technology*, **12**, 93–116.

Fleming, L. (2001), 'Recombinant uncertainty in technological search', *Management Science*, **47**, 117–32.

Fleming, L. and Sorenson, O. (2001), 'Technology as a complex adaptive system: evidence from patent data', *Research Policy*, **30**, 1019–39.

Freeman, L.C. (1979), 'Centrality in social networks: conceptual clarification', *Social Networks*, **1** (3), 215–39.

Frenken, K. (2005), *Innovation, Evolution and Complexity Theory*, Cheltenham, UK and Northampton, MA, USA: Edward Elgar.

Frenken, K. (2006), 'Technological innovation and complexity theory', *Economics of Innovation and New Technology*, **15**, 137–55.

Frenken, K. and Nuvolari, A. (2004), 'Entropy statistics as a framework to analyse technological evolution', in

Foster, J. and Hölzl, W. (eds), *Applied Evolutionary Economics and Complex Systems*, Cheltenham, UK and Northampton, MA, USA: Edward Elgar, pp. 95–132.

Frenken, K., von Oort, F. and Verburg, T. (2007), 'Related variety, unrelated variety and regional economic growth', *Regional Studies*, **41** (5), 685–97.

Fritsch, M. (2002), 'Measuring the quality of regional innovation systems: a knowledge production function approach', *International Review of Regional Science*, **25**, 86–101.

Gibbons, R. and Murphy, K.J. (1992), 'Optimal incentive contracts in the presence of career concerns: theory and evidence', *Journal of Political Economy*, **100** (3), 468–505.

Gibbons, M., Limoges, C., Nowtny, H., Schwartzman, S., Scott, P. and Trow, M. (1984), *The New Production of Knowledge: The Dynamics of Science and Research in Contemporary Societies*, London: Sage.

Griliches, Z. (1957), 'Hybrid corn: an exploration in the economics of technological change', *Econometrica*, **25** (4), 501–22, reprinted in Fox, K.A. and Johnson, D.G. (eds) (1969), *AEA Readings in Agricultural Economics*, London: Allen & Unwin.

Griliches, Z. (1967), 'Distributed lags: a survey', *Econometrica*, **35**, 16–49.

Griliches, Z. (1979), 'Issues in assessing the contribution of research and development to productivity growth', *Bell Journal of Economics*, **10** (1), 92–116.

Griliches, Z. (1980), 'R&D and the productivity slowdown', *American Economic Review*, **70**, 343–48.

Griliches, Z. (1992), 'The search for R&D spillovers', *Scandinavian Journal of Economics*, **94** (Supplement).

Jaffe, A. (1986), 'Technological opportunity and spillovers of R&D: evidence from firms' patents, profits, and market value', *American Economic Review*, **76** (5), 984–1001.

Jaffe, A. (1989), 'Real effects of academic research', *American Economic Review*, **79** (5), 957–70.

Katila, R. and Ahuja, G. (2002), 'Something old, something new: a longitudinal study of search behaviour and new product introduction', *Academy of Management Journal*, **45**, 1183–94.

Kauffmann, S. (1993), *Origins of Order: Self-Organization and Selection in Evolution*, Oxford: Oxford University Press.

Kleinknecht, A.H., van Montfort, K. and Brouwer, E. (2002), 'The non-trivial choice between innovation indicators', *Economics of Innovation and New Technology*, **11**, 109–21.

Kline, S.J. and Rosenberg, N. (1986), 'An overview on innovation', in Landau, R. and Rosenberg, N. (eds), *The Positive Sum Strategy*, Washington DC: National Academy Press, pp. 275–306.

Krafft, J., Quatraro, F. and Saviotti, P.P. (2009), 'Evolution of the knowledge base in knowledge intensive sectors', LEI and BRICK Working Paper, No. 06/2009.

Krafft, J., Quatraro, F. and Saviotti, P.P. (2011), 'The evolution of knowledge base in knowledge-intensive sectors: social network analysis of biotechnology', *Economics of Innovation and New Technology*, forthcoming, **20** (5), 1–31.

Lane, D. and Maxfield, R. (2005), 'Ontological uncertainty and innovation', *Journal of Evolutionary Economics*, **15** (1), 3–50.

Lane, D., Pumain, D., van der Leeuw, S.E. and West, G. (eds) (2009), *Complexity Perspectives in Innovation and Social Change*, Methodos Series, vol. 7, New York: Springer.

Mansfield, E. (1961), 'Technical change and the rate of imitation', *Econometrica*, **29** (4), 741–66.

Mansfield, E. (1980), 'Basic research and productivity increase in manufacturing', *American Economic Review*, **70**, 863–73.

March, J. (1991), 'Exploration and exploitation in organizational learning', *Organization Science*, **2** (1), 71–87.

Nelson, R.R. (1980), 'Production sets, technological knowledge, and R&D: fragile and overworked constructs for the analysis of productivity growth', *American Economic Review*, **70**, 62–67.

Nelson, R.R. (1982), 'The role of knowledge in R&D efficiency', *Quarterly Journal of Economics*, **97**, 453–70.

Nelson, R.R. (1986), 'Institutions supporting technical advance in industry', *American Economic Review*, **76**, 186–89.

Nelson, R.R. and Winter, S. (1982), *An Evolutionary Theory of Economic Change*, Cambridge: Harvard University Press.

Nesta, L. (2008), 'Knowledge and productivity in the world's largest manufacturing corporations', *Journal of Economic Behavior and Organization*, **67**, 886–902.

Nesta, L. and Saviotti, P.P. (2005), 'Coherence of the knowledge base and the firm's innovative performance: evidence from the US pharmaceutical industry', *Journal of Industrial Economics*, **53** (1), 123–42.

Nesta, L. and Saviotti, P.P. (2006), 'Firm knowledge and market value in biotechnology', *Industrial and Corporate Change*, **15** (4), 625–52.

Nightingale, P. (1998), 'A cognitive model of innovation', *Research Policy*, **27**, 689–709.

Rosenberg, N. (1982), *Inside the Black Box: Technology and Economics*, Cambridge: Cambridge University Press.

Sabidussi, G. (1966), 'The centrality index of a graph', *Psychometrika*, **31** (4), 581–603.

Saviotti, P.P. (1988), 'Information, variety and entropy in technoeconomic development', *Research Policy*, **17** (2), 89–103.

Saviotti, P.P. (2007), 'On the dynamics of generation and utilisation of knowledge: the local character of knowledge', *Structural Change and Economic Dynamics*, **18**, 387–408.

Schumpeter, J. (1912), *The Theory of Economic Development*, Cambridge: Harvard University Press.

Schumpeter, J. (1942), *Capitalism, Socialism and Democracy*, New York: Harper and Row.

Simon, H. (1966), *The Sciences of the Artificial*, Cambridge, MA: MIT Press.

Sorenson, O., Rivkin, J.W. and Fleming, L. (2006), 'Complexity, network and knowledge flows', *Research Policy*, **35**, 994–1017.

Teece, D., Rumelt, R. Dosi, G. and Winter, S. (1994), 'Understanding corporate coherence: theory and evidence', *Journal of Economic Behavior and Organization*, **23** (1), 1–30.

Trajtenberg, M. (1990), 'A penny for your quotes: patent citations and the value of innovations', *Rand Journal of Economics*, **21**, 172–87.

Usher, A. (1954), *History of Mechanical Inventions*, Cambridge: Harvard University Press.

van der Bergh, J.C.J.M. (2008), 'Optimal diversity: increasing returns versus recombinant innovation', *Journal of Economic Behaviour and Organization*, **68**, 565–80.

Vincenti, W. (1990), *What Engineers Know and How They Know It*, Baltimore and London: Johns Hopkins University Press.

Weitzman, M.L. (1996), 'Hybridizing growth theory', *American Economic Review*, **86**, 207–12.

Weitzman, M.L. (1998), 'Recombinant growth', *Quarterly Journal of Economics*, **113**, 331–60.

8. Complexity and the coordination of technological knowledge: the case of innovation platforms*

Davide Consoli and Pier Paolo Patrucco

1. INTRODUCTION

The chapter integrates insights from complexity theory into the economics of technological knowledge in order to reflect systematically on the variety of forms and processes that underpin knowledge production, dissemination and coordination. In so doing the chapter brings together two complementary bodies of scholarly research: the analysis of multiple interactions occurring within network-type structures which is typical of the literature on complex dynamic systems; on the other hand the study of learning processes as intentional, mindful and purposive behaviors set in motion by myopic agents, which is at the heart of the economics of innovation. For what concerns the formalization of structured interactions and the emergence of networks we draw from complexity theory and emphasize the intentional nature of those interactions aimed at sourcing external knowledge and competences, and integrating them in the extant repertoires. In this view actors possess limited resources and knowledge, and their ability to innovate is contingent to the implementation of selective interactions by means of research, development and learning processes.

Complexity theories emerge in economics as a response to the need of understanding systematically the dynamics of innovation and technological knowledge taking place in increasingly dispersed contexts (see Antonelli, Chapter 1 in this volume). This approach facilitates the appreciation of both structural and dynamic properties of evolving economic systems; the changing forms of interaction across actors are crucial for the evolution of the system at the aggregate level as much as the changing characteristics of individual actors at micro level. The network of interactions between agents is central to accessing and creating new knowledge, and in particular exploiting complementarities with other organizations embedded in the network. Innovative firms are therefore able to select and manage efficiently external linkages while implementing learning processes enabled by both external linkages and strategic investments in technological communication with other organizations.

These complex nets of interactions and the transformation that their structures undergo call for purposeful coordination in order to reap the potential of knowledge creation and dissemination that is typical of diverse environments. The chapter focuses on innovation platforms, that is, systemic infrastructures for the organization and coordination of distributed innovation processes. Their recent emergence responds to the rationale of maximizing variety in the ecology of knowledge types while maintaining coherence by means of some degree of hierarchy. In platform-type structures, key nodes are crucial in determining at once the relative contribution of peripheral units as well as the performance of the whole system. There is growing evidence on the significance of innovation platforms in different sectoral contexts where innovation and the successful exploitation of new technological knowledge require integrating a variety of complementary competences.

To analyse this phenomenon the chapter taps into two complementary bodies of scholarly research: the analysis of multiple interactions occurring within collective structures, which is typical of the literature on complex dynamic systems, and the study of learning processes as purposive behaviors set in motion by myopic agents, which stands at the heart of the economics of innovation. More to the point, our study builds on the appreciation of three distinctive dynamic structural properties of innovation platforms: hierarchical causation; coordinated variety; and selective openness. The juxtaposition of these three, it is argued, shapes the structure of non-redundant connections that make up innovation platforms. The chapter is structured as follows. Section 1 introduces the basic conceptual framework; Section 2 overviews the literature on complexity and its connection with innovation and technological change with various articulations in relation to intertwined organizational and cognitive dynamics. Section 3 introduces the concept of innovation platform and the underpinning component processes. The last section concludes and summarizes.

2.   BACKGROUND

Let us begin with a concise appreciation of the fact that the nature of the innovation process has changed over the last two decades.[1] Three of those changes deserve closer attention. The first is that products, services and processes have progressively drawn on wider ranges of constituent parts and, a fortiori, of knowledge bases. This phenomenon is ascribed to the search for both cost reductions and differentiation as well as to increased availability of specialized components. The second type of change is the growing tendency of products, services and processes to be used in symbiotic fashion. The resulting trajectory is one in which products that were originally conceived as meeting different needs co-exist in a systemic context of use. Yet one more important change concerns the type of knowledge that best enables and facilitates innovation in such a fast-changing scenario. It is clear that combined together the first two points entail for individual firms the challenge to enlarge the range of capabilities while at the same time preserving internal coherence.

Summing up, as the technological complexity embedded in products and services increases and the contexts of use grow diverse while remaining symbiotic, other things being equal, the reliance of a firm on its own resources does necessarily diminish. These phenomena are widely discussed in the scholarly debate, especially in two areas of research. The first is the theory of complex systems, whose convergence towards social sciences began in the 1990s under the pressure of economists who sought to understand the dynamics of collective processes. These approaches adopt as a unit of analysis the interactions across the components rather than the individual parts; such interactions, in turn, define the criteria of access to as well as the rules that govern cooperation within collective environments. In the evolution of complex systems the aggregate and the individual dimensions are intertwined (Arthur et al., 1997; Foster, 2005). The corollary is that the architecture of such systems is not a datum but rather a dynamic, emergent property stemming from the coordination of a myriad individual characteristics and behaviors.

The economics of innovation is the second body of work that is most directly relevant to the phenomena discussed before. In a nutshell this area of scholarly research aims at understanding how wealth is created from human knowledge. The starting point is that economic agents are boundedly rational, and deal with innate uncertainty by building on experience and learning to develop skills and decision rules (Simon, 1962; Nelson and Winter, 1982; Loasby, 1998; Antonelli, 2008). Strong emphasis is placed in this context on the sources of human knowledge, on the procedures by which this is applied to solve specific problems, and on the effects that the latter bears on the context of application. A crucial point, different from other approaches to economic agency, is that these interactions are explicitly embedded in a context, that is to say, a time and a place. Accordingly the relevant metric for these processes is historical – as opposed to spatial (see O'Driscoll and Rizzo, 1985) – time: the gist of economic actions is the development of cognitive processes and of associated choices along an irreversible time arrow.

This frame entails a view of human agency that is of development and not of mere allocation, and elucidates on the *trait d'union* between the two approaches. To bring the argument home, a staple of the economics of innovation is that as individual actors possess limited resources and knowledge, they necessarily need to search, develop and establish interactions in evolving environments. Moreover like complex systems theory, the economics of technological change focuses on non-deterministic, multi-level relationships which are a necessary but not sufficient condition to organize successfully for innovation.

From the foregoing discussion it is clear that in dynamic environments characterized by recurrent changes in product characteristics and production technologies, the internal capabilities of individual firms hardly suffice. It is also clear that strategies for the governance of knowledge are critical for survival (Pavitt, 2002; Antonelli, 2008). To this end firms deepen specialization and establish connections to access and contribute to collective knowledge. New knowledge is facilitated by complementarities, rather than substitutability, between internal and external knowledge: the greater the scale of networking, the more intense the internal know-how needed to understand, command and recombine external capabilities (Patrucco, 2008). On the basis of prospective costs associated to changes in their knowledge base, firms position themselves along a strategic spectrum whose extremes are either vertical integration or the market.

Notwithstanding the widespread significance of vertical disintegration, some forms of production and provision cannot be served efficiently by market mechanisms and managed through vertical disintegration and total outsourcing only. Hybrid solutions, like networks, are more appropriate when the design of inter-organizational relationships seeks to minimize costs due to external coordination, and to maximize the creative contribution of individual firms (Langlois, 1992). In turn, complex dynamic systems feature simultaneous availability of the outlined options and cyclical adaptation of strategic designs (Ethiraj and Levinthal, 2004). Put another way, decision-making in such contexts is driven by 'dynamic' coordination, that is, by generative interactions that facilitate changes in production, technologies, networks of suppliers, and in the modules of relevant knowledge (Lane and Maxfield, 1997; Loasby, 2002; Potts, 2001).

The paper illustrates the case of innovation platforms, an emerging form of knowledge governance which has captured the attention of scholars and policy-makers alike in recent years.

2.1   Complex Systems and the Dynamics of Knowledge

The theory of complexity is progressively emerging in the evolutionary economics of innovation as a new paradigm able to explain the structural and dynamic properties of knowledge generation and diffusion as well as the related emergence of innovation. Complexity theory is intrinsically both systemic and dynamic, and may be most useful in the understanding of the characteristics and processes of knowledge creation, diffusion and exploitation, as well as the emergence and transformation of architectures for the coordination of knowledge through time (Antonelli, 2008).

In broad terms, complex economic systems can be defined as a set of heterogeneous actors that interact in order to create new knowledge as well as to organize and change their activities through time. However, a closer look at the properties of complex systems highlights a variety of intertwining elements within complex systems. First, actors within complex systems are heterogeneous in terms of the competencies and knowledge they possess; second and consequently, actors have access only to portions of knowledge that are feasible through the cognitive map underpinning their search heuristics. In this sense they use limited cognitive resources and create new knowledge through trial and error and continuous revision of their behaviors. Third, interaction between heterogeneous actors is central to the effect of both creating and enabling access to knowledge. Moreover, these interactions occur in a local space defined by shared economic, social, technological, cognitive and geographical settings. Because of this, the behaviors of actors will likely feature some degree of inflexibility and stickiness in adapting and reacting to changes in the environment. In particular, the structure of the environment bounds such adaptation and reaction and in turn the conduct of actors is limited by irreversibility (Arthur et al., 1997; Rosser, 1999).

Recent advances in the evolutionary school provide major contributions to integrate and improve such understanding. Evolutionary economists built upon Nelson and Winter's (1982) analysis by developing the idea that the features of economic change are biased by the behavior of actors with idiosyncratic competencies, especially with regard to innovative capabilities and technological skills. Each firm is distinct and unique with respect to the technological knowledge and the ability to introduce innovation. Therefore there is very limited interchangeability and substitutability, high complementarity and strong specialization and differentiation in the space of technological competencies.

Along this line, the integration of the analysis of the characteristics of knowledge and of the process of knowledge creation is a major step forward in the understanding of the dynamic properties of complex economic systems. When looked at through the lenses of the complexity perspective the infrastructures aimed at the creation and use of technological knowledge are characterized by (1) intrinsic and radical uncertainty, that is, the mismatch between firms' expectations, planned strategies and actual results (for instance because of failures in facing changes in consumers' needs through new products), and (2) non-decomposability, that is, complex systems are irreducible systems, where the behavior and performance of a single actor may affect the behavior and performance of the entire system. Although agents are myopic and characterized by irreversibility in their choices and behaviors, they are also creative and can react to unplanned and unexpected interdependencies typical of complex environments. Imagination and creativity are required in order to introduce changes in the environment as well as for the environment itself to evolve. In turn, the changes and the evolution of both the system and the behaviors of agents can be understood only in historical time: complex systems are intrinsically dynamic. In a dynamic perspective, therefore, in such systems the behaviors of individual agents and the evolution of the environment shape each other because of the interaction between individual creativity and structural irreversibility. The dynamics of complex systems depends upon the interaction both between micro and macro elements, and between individual actors themselves (Foster, 1993, 2005; Loasby, 2002; Lane and Maxfield, 2005; Antonelli, 2007; Arthur, 2007; Hanusch and Pyka, 2007).

Complex economic systems are characterized by non-ergodicity, social interactions, phase transition and emergent properties. Non-ergodic path dependency applies when a little shock at one point in time, and not necessarily at the onset of the process, affects the long run dynamics of a system. Phase transitions consist in qualitative changes that can be determined by small changes in the parameters of the system. Emergent properties are properties of a system that apply at a specific level of aggregation of a system. In the theory of complexity, feedback and interactions play a key role in assessing the conduct of agents and specifically the chances of changing their behavior[2] (Durlauf, 2005).

Most importantly, complex dynamic systems are distinguished by processes of true transformation (rather than mere transition), where the changes in the system affect both the properties of the architecture of the system and the properties of its entities, namely firms and organizations. The dynamics of complex systems are based on evolutionary processes that are not driven by variety and selection (as traditionally in evolutionary thinking) but by differentiation of the activities of actors and the changes in the institutions that coordinate the division of labor among those actors. In other words, two kinds of differentiation are at work here: (1) differentiation in the functional and technological specialization of firms; (2) differentiation in the architecture of the system. These transform the relationships between actors, in turn transforming the architecture of the system, that is, the structure of interactions between actors. The two processes clearly co-evolve by means of the feedbacks between the behaviors of actors and the architecture of the system in which firms are embedded. Such a co-evolution qualifies the openness of the system and the coordinating architecture (Lane et al., 2009; Metcalfe, 2007).

The structural and dynamic characteristics of complex systems involve the integration of different and complementary elements and components, which in turn reflect different and complementary spaces of technological competencies. Individual actors put in place connections in order to access and generate new knowledge, and thus to react to cognitive and structural boundaries and the changes that have occurred in the environment. Learning takes place in myopic (that is, characterized by limited and specific knowledge), but creative firms and this learning underpins the generation of new knowledge. The process of creation of new knowledge relies upon the complementarity between internal and external portions of knowledge (Patrucco, 2009). The larger the adoption of networking as a means to access and use external knowledge modules, the larger the complementary internal know-how required by the firm to be able to understand, command and recombine these modules of external knowledge. Increasing returns in the generation of new knowledge build upon the exploitation of complementarities between internal and external knowledge and the implementation of a collective pool of knowledge and competencies through interactions (Patrucco, 2008). In turn, creative firms benefiting from complementary modules of knowledge are able not only to introduce new knowledge but also to change the structure of their connections and the architecture of the network in which they are embedded, eventually modifying the processes and mechanisms of coordination.

In this respect, interactive learning from external sources provides new ideas able either to improve existing technologies or to be the basis for the development of brand new ones. Knowledge creation is not only a collective process, that is, depending upon the contribution of different and complementary actors, but also a recombinant, cumulative and path-dependent one (Weitzman, 1996, 1998). The creation of new knowledge is seen as building upon itself through the new recombination of existing ideas. Such recombination is clearly affected by both the structural characteristics of the network in which it takes place and the historical sequence of previous combinations of ideas.

Focusing on the organization of knowledge interactions, rather than merely on the structure of their net is a crucial analytical shift in order to grasp the causes and the consequences of the changing structure, composition and coordination of the system in which actors interplay (see Antonelli, Chapter 1 in this volume). The network of interactions between agents is the central mechanism through which they can access and create new knowledge, exploiting complementarities. Changes in the organization and structure of this network, introduced by myopic but creative agents as a response to modification in their environment, induce changes in the institutions of coordination of complementary activities and competencies. The feedbacks between micro behaviors and the structural boundaries of the system in turn shape the evolution of the system itself (Arthur, 2009).

Economic complexity is an emerging phenomenon that is the outcome of a continuously transforming process of interaction between firms, each of which is characterized by different capabilities and placed in a different technological domain. The notion of the coordination of knowledge is central in this context, in order to understand in which way complex systems evolve and the dynamics of knowledge creation and change take place. Knowledge coordination occurs through the generative structure of interactions between actors and the changes in such networks operated by bounded but creative actors (Lane and Maxfield, 1997).

The notion of coalitions for innovation has been recently outlined (Antonelli, 2010) precisely to shift attention to the role that the coordination of inter-organizational linkages has on the implementation of effective innovation as well as the generation of new productive and technological knowledge. When innovation and knowledge are collective features of the interactions between different actors, effective coalitions for innovation align the heterogeneous capabilities of the partners embedded in the network and achieve the mutual directedness of their strategic interactions in order to guarantee the cohesion and the coordination of the complex net of interactions that characterizes the innovation process, as well as to cope with the structural uncertainty of the innovation process through some degree of hierarchical authority and power centrality in the network.

The next sub-section frames the analysis of the different modes through which economic actors can organize and govern technological knowledge. This paves the way for introducing and articulating the concept of 'innovation platforms' in Section 3.

2.2 Governing Technological Knowledge: Integration, Modularity and Networking

The analysis of the organization of innovative activities and the management of knowledge generation and diffusion in complex systems has been at the centre of an intense and rich debate between scholars about how technological knowledge can be successfully coordinated and which is the more effective organizational form through which firms can acquire and manage their innovative and productive capabilities in particular. As is well known, three types of organization received attention in the literature: the vertically integrated firm, the market-based and modular organization, and the hybrids such as networks and collaborative ventures.

The role of managerial authority, command and hierarchy has been central through almost the entire twentieth century and different authors have argued that the vertically integrated firm is a superior solution, either because of scale, scope and learning economies in R&D (Penrose, 1959; Chandler, 1990) or because, as David Teece (1984) argued, it is more efficient in managing radical (or 'systemic', to use his words) innovation. According to the definition introduced by Teece (1984), a new product or technology that requires changes in different and connected elements of the system in which it will be placed, can be defined as a systemic innovation – in contrast to 'autonomous' innovations that easily fit into the system already existing without calling for consequent, diffused and simultaneous changes elsewhere in the system. Following this work, in the literature about the organization and management of innovation, it has been often presumed that the more radical or 'systemic' the innovation, the more appropriate and efficient is vertical integration and the coordination of the change within a single organization.

However, more recently innovation scholars rediscovered the seminal work of Herbert Simon (Simon, 1962, 2002) on modularity, and shifted their attention to the wide range of decentralized and 'market-based' or 'virtual' (for example, Chesbrough and Teece, 1996) organizations opened up by the vanishing out of large firms (Langlois, 2002, 2003). Herbert Simon, through his frequently cited example of Tempus and Hora (Simon, 1962: 470) defined the notion of near-decomposability and claimed that a complex system is composed by different modules – or sub-systems – in such a way that interactions between sub-systems are much weaker than interactions within sub-systems (that is, between elements of the same sub-systems). Modules are almost independent of one another and changes occurring in one element of the system do not affect either the other elements or the overall structure of the system.[3]

Elaborating upon Simon's perspective, in recent years the economics and managerial literature on modularity distilled and addressed the benefits that make modular organizational structures and contracts-based relations between buyer and suppliers more suitable than vertical integration (for example, Sanchez and Mahoney, 1996; Arora et al., and Rullani, 1998; Ethiraj and Levinthal, 2004; Langlois and Garzarelli, 2008). In particular, Baldwin and Clark (1997) and Langlois (2002) view the organization of production and innovation through modular strategies as the more efficient way to manage extremely complex and otherwise troublesome organizations and technologies.

When systems grow extensively and the interconnections between the different elements and sub-systems become so numerous, their coordination under an integrated structure is almost unfeasible. In such circumstances, firms can switch from integrated to modular strategies for acquiring and coordinating their productive and innovative capabilities, in relation to the changing characteristics of the technologies and the competencies they build upon in order to introduce novelty (for example, Chesbrough and Teece, 1996). The more interconnected and articulated are the knowledge bases and technologies necessary to innovate – that is, according to the view of Herbert Simon, the more complex is the system – the more advantageous is the adoption of a modular organization and the use of formal contracts and market transactions.

However, various contributions highlighted that the literature on modular and contract-based organizations underestimates the important effects that interdependencies between firms (for example, Kogut and Zander, 1996; Stacey, 1995), as well as inertia (Brusoni and Prencipe, 2001) and high switching costs (Gilson et al., 2009) have on the coordination of knowledge.

In this respect, innovation scholars are reaching increasing consensus about the fact that inter-firm ties exploit resource heterogeneity and reduce the disadvantages of accessing dispersed and diverse sources of knowledge, enabling therefore new knowledge creation, by combining the flexibility of markets with the visible hand of organization (Powell, 1990; Kogut and Zander, 1992; Powell et al., 1996; Uzzi, 1997; Ahuja, 2000; Burt, 2000; Kogut, 2000).

Contributions have paid attention to the qualitative structure of the network and the role played by individual actors, thus identifying different network structures and their relative advantages. In particular, two configurations have been contrasted in the literature: networks characterized by what Coleman (1990) described as structures with strong and redundant ties have been opposed to Burt's (1992) 'structural holes' and structures characterized by weak and non-redundant ties.[4]

Brusoni and Prencipe (2001) elaborated upon the contrasting evidence about which kind of network is better equipped to organize the accumulation and acquisition of knowledge, and with a special emphasis on complex environments, revisited the notion of loosely coupled networks (Orton and Weick, 1990).

Orton and Weick (1990) describe the structure of inter-firm networks according to the degree of responsiveness and distinctiveness networks show. They define distinctiveness as the ability to command and produce a range of complementary technological competences in order to introduce novelty, while responsiveness is the active and intentional management of inter-firm relations to provide the network with cohesion, and to coordinate different sources of learning.

> If there is neither responsiveness nor distinctiveness, the system is not really a system and it can be defined as a non-coupled system. If there is responsiveness without distinctiveness, the system is tightly coupled. If there is distinctiveness without responsiveness, the system is decoupled. If there is both distinctiveness and responsiveness, the system is loosely coupled. (Orton and Weick, 1990: 205, quoted in Brusoni and Prencipe, 2001: 1026)

We argue that innovation platforms share some of the properties of loosely coupled networks in that they combine elements of both modular and integrated systems, as well as of sparse and dense networks. Innovation platforms are characterized by structural holes, arbitrating through a hierarchy the interactions between organizations that are not directly connected. In this regard, for example, system integrators firms (Sturgeon, 2002; Prencipe et al., 2003), that are well known in a number of sectors, such as the automobile, software and PC, microelectronics, and aviation industries, are a defined specific type of structural holes at the center of the recombinatorial flows of different bodies of technological knowledge in complex innovations. However, the increasing division of labor brought about by complexity in both products and knowledge engenders an increase in the number of specific components and bodies of knowledge that need to be recombined in the final product. Redundant connections are often necessary in order to complement different specialized skills and directly share the relevant knowledge among different firms in the systems. Direct collaboration, that is, not mediated by a structural hole, between for instance two specialized suppliers, can be necessary to co-define and co-implement a new component or a sub-system of a complex product. In this case the network has some features of the dense and flat structure described by Coleman and Uzzi. Here, specialization requires the broadening of the knowledge base of system integrators as coordinating organizations in order both to understand innovations and knowledge sourced externally and to manage the network of outsourced components and sub-systems of technologies and knowledge. The competence of a system integrator in this case involves the ability to govern the networked process by which innovations are collectively produced and shared (Kogut, 2000). In this regard, networks where system integrators play as central brokers do not suffer the weaknesses of pure modular strategies, where the system is conceived as easily decoupled in interdependent chunks.

The remainder of the chapter illustrates the case of innovation platforms as organizational forms aimed at the coordination of collective and distributed innovation activities. Because of the coordinating role played by central nodes, innovation platforms combine elements of hierarchical coordination and elements of decentralization of innovative and productive capabilities, based either on modular outsourcing and market transactions, or on collaborations. Let us focus now on their characteristics.

3. INNOVATION PLATFORMS: THE BUILDING BLOCKS

Innovation platforms are systemic infrastructures for the organization and coordination of distributed innovation processes that feature high degrees of complexity. The creation of innovation platforms consists in the design and establishment of architectures for inter-organizational coordination (Sah and Stiglitz, 1986, 1988): these define the levels of engagement of each peripheral unit, the characteristics of the flows (that is, unidirectional or bidirectional) of information and knowledge, and the extent of exchange across organizations.[5] The design of a platform determines *ex ante* but evaluates (and eventually adapts) *ex post* the creation and the use of knowledge (Garicano, 2000). Wheelwright and Clark (1992) first talked of platform products whose core design seeks to appeal to a large customer base while its openness to marginal modifications attempts to captivate peripheral users with more specific needs. A few years later Kim and Kogut (1996) talked about platform technologies referring to models for the coordination of complementary components such as computers. Rochet and Tirole (2003) first ventured beyond the physical features of artifacts thinking of platforms as a design concept and giving them operational functioning with a clear articulation of how products and services stand in functional relation to a collective endeavor, and of the mediating role of leader organizations within such constructs.

The phenomenon of collective structures striving for the participation of multiple business entities is not new, and platforms are certainly not the first instantiation. Modeling of networks has probably been the archetypal point of reference for this class of phenomena. Network economics approaches propose that increasing returns to scale are at the core of strategic coordination across competing firms (Pennings and Harianto, 1992; Economides, 1996). Networks have higher capacity to manage large-volume trans-actions compared to closed proprietary circuits, and given a large enough customer base the expected profitability of joining is high and the benefits outweigh the costs (Saloner and Shepard, 1995; Shy, 2001). A critical assumption underpinning this theory is that technologies, like the component organizations, are given and constant. This static view leaves out important features for the observed growth of variety in both the network participants as well as the kinds of interrelations across them (Consoli, 2008).

Innovation platforms differ in some crucial aspects from the above characterization. In these structures a variety of agents participates in the production and supply of products and services; each unit exists independently according to its own goals and capacity but, at the same time, responds to a collective goal through shared communication rules. The point, though, is that such differences across agents matter to a great degree. In turn, the architectures in which they operate are flexible and can be configured in different ways for different uses, very much akin to computer platforms. A central component for the rationale underpinning platforms is maximizing the variety of contributions stemming from a variegated knowledge base while maintaining coherence though a minimum level of hierarchy. As will be discussed further, innovation platforms are purposefully open to entry of new actors and, thereby, of new competences: the extent of contribution by each additional unit depends endogenously on the relative value of internal competences measured against the collective goal. At the core of the logic of a platform stand three powerful sources of increasing returns: economies of scale due to increased volumes of throughput; economies of scope due to lower costs of producing variations around the core product and services of the platform; and economies of system, that is, the creation of dedicated control procedures to improve utilization of the installed capacity. Another crucial characteristic of platforms is the functional relation in which services and manu-facturing activities stand to one another (Suarez and Cusumano, 2009). The provision of some services, in fact, enables closer customer-producer interaction and opens up impor-tant feedback mechanisms that contribute to adapting the organization of the platform, or some of its components, towards emerging features such as unmet customer needs, skill gaps, and future product developments.

Relevant dynamics within platforms span technological and organizational levels, and bear upon both the static and the dynamic coordination of knowledge. From a static viewpoint, platforms connect and integrate activities and capabilities of relevant agents within an industry, thus supporting specialization and favoring the accumulation of specific knowledge. From a dynamic viewpoint, platforms stimulate changes in both the structure of the network and the mechanisms for the governance of technological knowledge.

The phenomenon of innovation platforms stirs an intense debate across disciplines. Management scholars connect them to the challenges and the strategic implications associated to the emergence of open systems for production, exchange and governance competencies (Gerstein, 1992; Ciborra, 1996; Garud and Kumaraswamy, 1996; Ethiraj

and Levinthal, 2004, Jacobides and Billinger, 2006). In the policy realm innovation platforms are looked at as a key reference model for the creation and management of mixed
(that is, public and private) coalitions (European Commission, 2004). In the context of
innovation studies Antonelli (2006) argues that platforms are especially appropriate
when technological knowledge exhibits levels of compositeness and cumulability that
imply too high coordination costs for a single firm. Recent contributions by Baumol
(2002) and von Hippel (2005) further stress the incentives of knowledge-sharing for firms
within a platform. Efficiency in knowledge creation, they observe, stems from both internal investments and external learning and is higher than if it relied exclusively on either
internal creation (that is, vertical integration of R&D) or external acquisition (that is,
outsourcing of R&D and design).

Innovation platforms underpin the development of physical technologies too. These
integrate a variety of inputs from a range of industries and firms and include innovations such as Internet services, enhanced broadband fibre optics, Asynchronous Digital
Subscriber Lines, and Universal Mobile Telecommunications System. As each allows
the integration of a variety of content, services, technologies and applications, platform-
based technologies are both composite and fungible (Fransman, 2002; Antonelli, 2006).

Let us now draw attention to some of the dynamic properties that characterize innovation platforms, namely: hierarchical causation; coordinated variety; and selective openness. The juxtaposition of these three, it will be further argued, gives way to the texture
of connections that make up innovation platforms.

3.1   Hierarchical Causation

What stimulates the emergence of collective structures such as innovation platforms? Let
us, in answering this question, adopt a functional approach and argue that platforms are
purposive responses to specific problems that no individual firm can solve in isolation. The
general phenomenon is very common across most modern industries. Each firm possesses
a knowledge base which is usually accumulated by blending information inputs, know-
how and capabilities while searching for and developing innovative solutions (Nelson
and Winter, 1982; Teece, 1986; Cohen and Levinthal, 1989). Industries with a complex
knowledge base accelerate the obsolescence of firm-specific knowledge assets thus forcing
them to either invest in human capital or sourcing knowledge externally. Each of these
solutions however carries its own risk. On the one hand the adaptation of channels for
the supply of up-to-date training depends on adjustments within and between complementary institutional domains (Vona and Consoli, 2009). In practice, highly specialized
knowledge is sticky and therefore unlikely to become available through training programs
quickly enough, especially knowledge that is close to the frontier. On the other hand
significant communication costs stand in the way of latent knowledge spillovers among
firms. Such costs are affected by specific characteristics of the competitive environment in
which firms operate (Patrucco, 2008). Either way, a firm under pressure needs to adopt
effective governance mechanisms to overcome the barriers to creative reaction.

For example, in the auto industry in the Turin area, Fiat experienced strong competitive pressure and risked failure. As a reaction, Fiat adopted governance mechanisms to
reconfigure the organization of internal as well as external competencies. In this new
system, Fiat retained hierarchical control over the net of suppliers and partners.

The notion of hierarchical causation refers to the fact that the search for knowledge and the associated reorganization of activities are essentially problem-based processes. This carries important consequences. First, newly emerged problems reverberate from past decisions, not necessarily because of a mistake but simply because modified conditions make the current set of activities no longer adequate. In this fundamental sense firms' knowledge accumulation and learning are path dependent, that is, they are at once directed but also limited by the current knowledge base. Secondly, and related to the former, knowledge growth is an essentially uncertain process. As a result the ability to calculate the outcomes of each individual's decisions as well as the strategies available to others is rather limited. Clearly the sources of complexity and the associated coordination challenges increase when individual actions are drawn together in collective structures like a platform. As Burt (2008) remarks, learning is not an optional attribute of collective structures: in dynamic environments where the scope of collaboration and the operative rules are liable to change, inclusion depends on the ability to remain relevant. That is to say, participation is contingent to learning and adaptation.

3.2   Coordinated Variety

Innovation scholars advocate that the growth of knowledge is rarely, if ever, the outcome of isolated action, but rather of collective learning and cumulative interactions. On the one hand, the development of tacit knowledge moulds individuals' responses and is a source for new ideas and solutions; on the other, codified and practical knowledge are crucial to facilitate exchange and interactions across individuals. Contrary to the common view that these dimensions are dichotomic, we stress their complementary aspects: new knowledge grows as a result of coordination across individual experiences and the development of shared understanding. At the same time, variety and heterogeneity are not sufficient to replenish the knowledge base and individual specialization is most effective when coordinated through formal and informal standards (Prahalad and Hamel, 1990; Langlois, 2002; Antonelli, 2008). The collective character of knowledge, in turn, elucidates the importance of establishing sound governance mechanisms (Antonelli, 2008). Previous literature sidestepped these points by assuming implicitly that agents learn and adapt swiftly to collective environments. If instead we focus on the juxtaposition of complementary dimensions such as individuals' knowledge bases, routines of communication across them and the criteria that define their collective scope, a great deal of effort is necessary to make these diverse pieces fit together. For, as Nelson (2003) remarks, all such dimensions evolve in a symbiotic, yet uneven, fashion.

The paradigm of the system of Electronic Funds Transfer at the Point of Sale (EFTPOS) in the UK banking industry is a good case in point. After the 1970s the basic rationale of innovation in banking was the replacement of the paper-based regime with automated transactions along the trajectory inspired by the Automated Cash Machines (Consoli, 2005). The EFTPOS concept embodied the grand ambition of implementing a unique system of peripherals which connected directly the point of sale, that is, the retailer, with the terminals of the bank. This major step change in the management of retail payments was happening at a time when the largest clearing banks had already developed their own proprietary systems for the provision of other automated services. The philosophy underpinning EFTPOS was therefore twofold: increasing the current scale of the network for payments, and expanding the number of services available to customers. Such a purpose required a physical infrastructure of access points, nodes and terminals for the management of the information flow as well as the harmonization of diffuse interests across diverse parties such as financial institutions and retailers. The first step in this direction was the creation of an umbrella organization, EFTPOS Development, under which the major financial institutions were committed to collaborate for the definition of blueprints of the collective network. The initiative however stumbled upon lack of cooperation from its inception as the clearing banks, especially the largest, pursued the expansion of their proprietary schemes. This in turn led to a patchwork of processing systems, front-end terminals and card schemes which was inefficient for both customers and the banking firms. More cogently, individual proprietary schemes discouraged service diversification (Howells and Hine, 1993; Consoli, 2008).

Later in the decade, under the pressure to reduce wasteful dual standards British banks resorted to the collaborative plan in a different fashion, by handing the task of designing a common blueprint over to external organizations like LINK and BACS.[6] These two organizations brought coherence by establishing a semi-hierarchical structure in which proprietary infrastructures and end terminals adapt to a central scheme. Banking firms and retailers are therefore the peripherals of a standardized system whose goal is no longer maximizing traffic (for example economies of scale) but rather rationalizing it. In this new framework horizontal entry entails the involvement of previously unrelated organizations, for example supermarkets or specialized intermediaries like Paypal, which in turn stimulate the diversification of retail payment services. Similarly, information processing in the upstream market has evolved into a self-standing business through increasing recourse to outsourcing.

This example illustrates the trade-offs involved in the pursuit of specialization when a large knowledge base is available (Kogut, 2000; Crémer et al., 2007). In fact, such a trade-off defines the scope, the boundaries and the forms of inter-organizational relations within a platform. On the one hand specialization favors efficient communication within a narrow set of partners but limits both the scope for coordination and accessibility to innovative opportunities. On the other hand the coordination of a bundle of interfirms and inter-organization linkages opens up new opportunities but lowers the scope for specialization and the benefits of communication (see Kogut and Zander, 1992). The implementation of innovation platforms contributes to reduce the inefficiencies associated to these trade-offs.

3.3 Selective Openness

The problem based perspective outlined so far bears another important consequence for the phenomenon of innovation platforms. Inclusion in collective structures for knowledge sharing does not diminish the uncertainty associated with competition in fast-changing contexts but rather changes the nature of such uncertainty. To be viable, infrastructures such as innovation platforms require on the one hand a degree of stability that confers coherence to a shared goal and, on the other hand, room for further novelty. From this it follows that a necessary condition for the emergence of novelty is that a system maintains a degree of openness to be able to adapt to modified circumstances.

The key point is that the implementation of major technical changes generates new opportunities for learning but in so doing also leads to skill gaps or shortages. Empirical works such as those by Brynjolfsson and Hitt (2000) and Bresnahan et al. (2002) demonstrate that the large scale diffusion of Information and Communication Technologies (ICTs), often the backbone of innovation platforms, stimulates the emergence of new tasks and of wholly new occupations (Vona and Consoli, 2009). In turn, where matching skills come from and how long it takes to correct for the imbalances depends on the degree of openness of the platform. The case of UK banking is again suggestive in this sense. The growing role of informational and strategic systems entailed an unexpected demand for middle- and back-office technical skills as well as new high-level managerial skills, crucial for business development. In part this skill imbalance has been met by outsourcing of business processing. Such changes need not apply exclusively to physical technologies. The ability of the British National Health Service (NHS) to support the development of innovative practices stemming from the front line of health care delivery has been a matter of debate for some time. The main culprit, it has been observed, was the lack of appropriate innovation management skills that would facilitate the translation of feedback from patient care into systematic (and systemic) innovation (Cooksey, 2006). The recent creation of the Institute for Innovation and Improvement aims at supporting the connection between basic research and clinical practice (UK Evaluation Forum, 2006), as well as supporting the diffusion of improvements in routine patient care beyond the source unit (Department of Health, 2003). The new organizational platform operates across nine geographical jurisdictions within the UK through local hubs which offer a broad variety of services such as training, technology audits and IP management, to name but a few (Consoli and Patrucco, 2008). By and large the activity of the hubs generates benefits that stretch beyond the life cycle of individual solutions, be they medical products or clinical services. In so doing they ensure a degree of openness towards the screening and the absorption of new skills and forms of knowledge.

As anticipated by Richardson (1972) and reiterated by many others, when coordination between closely complementary activities and competencies is essential for the success of innovation firms rely upon a variety of inter-organizational arrangements – such as joint ventures, equity agreement, R&D partnerships, coalitions and consortia – to blend market- and contract-based and integral solutions, strong and weak relations, in order to acquire and coordinate the necessary productive and innovative knowledge. Complex and articulated governance forms emerge when the task is the coordination of knowledge sourced both internally and externally, and multisided learning.

Notions of 'architectural knowledge' (Henderson and Clark, 1990), or 'architectural capability' (Jacobides, 2006) have been put forward precisely to characterize the key ability possessed by networks' leaders, to coordinate and direct the working of increasingly complex organizations, and more precisely to combine and adapt elements of integration, such as authority, with elements of modularity, such as openness, in order to choose which elements and competencies are required to be included in the network.

In the car industry, for instance, this seems precisely to be the case of the design and development of Electric Vehicles (EVs), where large partnerships, often embedding public actors and newcomers, have been implemented, with the scope of learning and acquiring selective technological and market competencies developed outside the car industry strictly considered, as the illustrative evidence of the cooperation between Betterplace and Renault clearly suggests (Aggeri et al., 2009; Beaume and Midler, 2009).

The introduction of electric vehicles (EVs) can be depicted as a collective innovation wherein different actors such as traditional original equipment manufacturers (OEMs), automobile batteries producers, utilities and system integrators contribute with complementary resources as well as technologies, and converge towards common goals and incentives. Evidence from Israeli and Danish experiences in the introduction of electric vehicles largely supports this view (see Beaume and Midler, 2009).

At the same time, some elements of managerial authority are still likely to characterize such models in that directedness is required in order to guarantee both cohesion within the network and the convergence of the complex system of goals, incentives and interactions that characterizes such an articulated innovation process (Enrietti and Patrucco, 2010). The entry of newcomers like Betterplace in the car industry as well as of car battery producers from the electronic sector that parallel the role of traditional carmakers, and emerge as new platforms' leaders, points in this direction: preliminary evidence on the implementation of EVs indicates that integration, coordination and direction of the different strategies and goals of various organizations that take part in the platform should be a central issue not only for the platform management (Gawer, 2009) but also for the design of innovation and industrial policies that support the formation of broad coalition for innovation in the car industry.

4. CONCLUDING REMARKS AND PROSPECTIVE RESEARCH

This chapter proposed an integration between elements of the economics of innovation and of complexity theory. This exercise, it has been argued, opens up interesting new avenues for research on the organization of innovative and productive knowledge. In constructing this point we illustrated the empirical case of innovation platforms as an emerging form of organization featuring common elements between the two research strands indicated above.

Building upon the pioneering analysis of Nelson and Winter (1982) scholars of innovation made much headway in elaborating a framework based on the analysis of purposeful yet limitedly rational agents; to overcome their intrinsic limitations these engage in learning activities and in so doing develop idiosyncratic capabilities and moving goals. Each agent is distinct and unique in relation to the way in which technological knowledge is created and used and, a fortiori, in the ability to succeed. Consistent with the basic tenet of complexity theory, interchangeability and substitutability is limited and the emergent patterns of specialization are likely to display significant variety. In such a framework the dynamic acquisition and coordination of new knowledge is the central issue (Teece et al., 1997; Winter, 2002).

The concept of coalitions for innovation (Antonelli, 2010) displays its interpretative power precisely in this context and in our opinion deserves to be further developed and understood in the future as a general form of hierarchical networks, among which innovation platforms are a specific manifestation. Coalitions emerge when the diverse incentives and capabilities of a variety of heterogeneous actors are organized so as to display a character of alignment and convergence. In fact, 'only the convergence of a plurality of complementary actions aligned though sequential chains of user-producer relations can shape the actual direction and speed of the process. The architecture of coalitions plays a key role here' (Antonelli, 2010: 515). The inclusion and exclusion of specific actors, characterized by idiosyncratic productive and innovative capabilities, as well as incentives, change the strategic behavior of the coalition, its objectives and the likely actions through which these can be achieved. The need for dynamic coordination, that is, coordination at each point in time of the heterogeneous actors embedded in the network is clear, if the goal is to be the successful realization of a common innovation. In such a systemic context, dynamic coordination requires some forms of hierarchical organization and yet, for the complexity involved in the system, no single firm commands both the technological and managerial resources necessary to make such coordination effective technologically and efficiently in terms of the coordination costs. Some intermediate forms of organization are required and it is likely that the implementation of coalitions centered on key firms and their strategic action emerges as more appropriate than extreme solutions such as market exchange and vertical integration. Coalitions for innovation as hybrid organizational forms emerge precisely as the appropriate strategy in order to make possible bureaucratic organizations reacting to improvements in products or services by acquiring externally the know-how necessary to innovate.

In a context of distributed capabilities and knowledge often sourced externally, the challenge for individual firms is to enlarge the range of external capabilities that can be accessed and integrated with internal ones, while guaranteeing efficiency and cohesion in access and integration of external knowledge as well as the distinctiveness of capabilities. In this chapter, also through illustrative examples derived from a variety of technologies and industries, we pay attention to the implementation of hierarchical networks that integrate the characteristics of distributed markets and directed organizations and qualify the innovation platform as a specific form of hierarchical network appropriate to govern knowledge interactions and to face that challenge.

NOTES

*   The order in which the authors are listed is alphabetical and does not imply differential contribution. The authors would like to thank the participants to the BRICK workshop on 'The System Dynamics of Technological Change' held at the Collegio Carlo Alberto in Moncalieri, 4–5 December 2009, and the editor of this book, Cristiano Antonelli, for their stimulating feedbacks and suggestions.
1.   Of course to scholars of innovation and technological change such a statement is almost tautological since for years they insisted that innovation is an essentially dynamic phenomenon.
2.   Complex systems are characterized by phase transition precisely because, in a non-decomposable system, a shock occurring to a single actor, for instance a firm unable to face the structural uncertainty of changing market conditions, has effects that dramatically impinge on the behavior of the interdependent actors. The innovation we eventually observe is exactly an emergent property of the creative reaction of the system of interactive firms to the shock and the changes in the performance of the system itself.
3.   This is what Herbert Simon defined as a loosely coupled structure.
4.   The purpose of the paper is not to describe and compare the advantages and disadvantages of the different structure. However, for the sake of clarity, Burt (1992) argues that networks with weak links and structural holes – that is, brokers that arbitrate and flow of knowledge between firms and groups of firms that are not tied to each other – are more efficient organizational forms and benefit from a kind of hierarchical structure. On the contrary, Coleman (1990) and Uzzi (1997, 1999), suggest that dense and redundant networks have a clear advantage when firms need to exchange and communicate complex knowledge because they promote trust-based relations and support more effectively cooperative behaviors, since they support repeated exchanges and a balanced distribution of power in the network.
5.   The notion of innovation platforms elaborated here differs from that of technological platform. The latter accounts for ICT-based innovations like virtual networks, and the associated infrastructures, and

interfaces and standards (Gawer and Cusumano, 2002). Technology platforms facilitate interoperability and coordination between different firms and technologies in the context of high-tech industries (see for example Consoli, 2005) as well as scientific clusters (Robinson et al., 2007). Innovation platforms are strategic organizational vehicles for coordinating specialized agents. ICTs and virtual networks are thus instrumental and yet subsidiary elements. Common to both technology and innovation platforms is the notion of directed and coordinated organization as opposed to 'spontaneous' organization typical of market processes.

6. Bankers Automated Clearing Services Limited (BACS) manages electronic transfer of funds between banks. Since 2003 BACS has become the platform for processing telephone and Internet banking payments in the UK. LINK is the network that connects 90 per cent of ATMs in the UK's banking system.

BIBLIOGRAPHY

Aggeri, F., Elmquist, M. and Pohl, H. (2009), 'Managing learning in the automotive industry: the innovation race for electric vehicles', *International Journal of Automotive Technology and Management*, **9** (2), 123–47.

Ahuja, G. (2000), 'Collaboration networks, structural holes and innovation: a longitudinal study', *Administratively Science Quarterly*, **45** (3), 317–43.

Antonelli, C. (2006), 'The business governance of localized knowledge: an information economics approach for the economics of knowledge', *Industry and Innovation*, **13** (3), 227–61.

Antonelli, C. (2007), 'The system dynamics of collective knowledge: from gradualism and saltationism to punctuated change', *Journal of Economic Behavior and Organization*, **62** (2), 215–36.

Antonelli, C. (2008), *Localized Technological Change: Towards the Economics of Complexity*, London: Routledge.

Antonelli, C. (2010), 'From population thinking to organization thinking: coalitions for innovation', *Regional Studies*, **44** (4), 513–18.

Arora, A., Gambardella, A. and Rullani, E. (1998), 'Division of labour and the locus of inventive activity', *Journal of Management and Governance*, **1** (1), 123–40.

Arthur, W.B. (2007), 'The structure of invention', *Research Policy*, **36** (2), 274–87.

Arthur, W.B. (2009), *The Nature of Technology: What It Is and How It Evolves*, New York: The Free Press.

Arthur, W.B., Durlauf, S.N. and Lane, D.A. (eds) (1997), *The Economy as an Evolving Complex System II*, Reading, MA: Addison-Wesley.

Baldwin, C.Y. and Clark, K.B. (1997), 'Managing in the age of modularity', *Harvard Business Review*, **5** (75), 84–93.

Baumol, W.J. (2002), *The Free-Market Innovation Machine: Analyzing the Growth Miracle of Capitalism*, Princeton: Princeton University Press.

Beaume, R. and Midler, C. (2009), 'From technology competition to reinventing individual ecomobility: new design strategies for electric vehicles', *International Journal of Automotive Technology and Management*, **9** (2), 174–90.

Bresnahan, T.F., Brynjolfsson, E. and Hitt, L.M. (2002), 'Information technology, workplace organization, and the demand for skilled labor: firm-level evidence', *Quarterly Journal of Economics*, **117** (1), 339–76.

Brusoni, S. and Prencipe, S. (2001), 'Managing knowledge in loosely coupled networks: exploring the links between product and knowledge dynamics', *Journal of Management Studies*, **38** (7), 1019–35.

Brynjolfsson, E. and Hitt, L.M. (2000), 'Beyond computation: information technology, organizational transformation and business performance', *Journal of Economic Perspectives*, **14** (4), 23–48.

Burt, R.S. (1992), *Structural Holes: The Social Structure of Competition*, Cambridge, MA: Harvard University Press.

Burt, R.S. (2000), 'The network structure of social capital', in Sutton, S.I. and Staw, B.M. (eds), *Research in Organizational Behaviour*, vol. 22, Greenwich, CT: JAI Press, pp. 345–423.

Burt, R.S. (2008), 'Information and structural holes: comment on Reagans and Zuckerman', *Industrial and Corporate Change*, **17** (5), 953–69.

Chandler, A.D. (1990), *Scale and Scope: The Dynamics of Industrial Capitalism*, Cambridge, MA: Belknap Press.

Chesbrough, H. and Teece, D. (1996), 'When is virtual virtuous: organizing for innovation', *Harvard Business Review*, **74** (1), 65–74.

Ciborra, C. (1996), 'The platform organization: recombining strategies, structures and surprises', *Organizational Science*, **7** (2), 103–18.

Cohen, W.M. and Levinthal, D.A. (1989), 'Innovation and learning: the two faces of R&D', *Economic Journal*, **99** (397), 569–96.

Cohen, W.M. and Levinthal, D.A. (1990), 'Absorptive capacity: a new perspective on learning and innovation', *Administrative Science Quarterly*, **35** (1), 128–52.

Coleman, J. (1990), *The Foundations of Social Theory*, Cambridge, MA: Harvard University Press.

Consoli, D. (2005), 'The dynamics of technological change in UK retail banking services: an evolutionary perspective', *Research Policy*, **34** (4), 461–80.

Consoli, D. (2008), 'Systems of innovation and industry evolution: the case of retail banking in the UK', *Industry & Innovation*, **15** (6), 579–600.

Consoli, D. and Patrucco, P.P. (2008), 'Innovation platforms and the governance of knowledge: evidence from Italy and the UK', *Economics of Innovation and New Technology*, **17** (7), 701–18.

Cooksey, D. (2006), 'A review of UK health research funding', Report to HM Treasury.

Crémer, J., Garicano, L. and Prat, A. (2007), 'Language and the theory of the firm', *Quarterly Journal of Economics*, **122** (1), 373–407.

Department of Health (2003), 'The NHS as an innovative organisation: a framework and guidance on the management of intellectual property in the NHS'.

Durlauf, S. (2005), 'Complexity and empirical economics', *Economic Journal*, **115** (504), 225–43.

Economides, N. (1996), 'The economics of networks', *International Journal of Industrial Organization*, **14** (6), 673–99.

Enrietti, A. and Patrucco, P.P. (2010), 'Open innovation and systemic reconfiguration in the car industry: the case of electric vehicles', LEI and BRICK – Laboratorio di economia dell'innovazione 'Franco Momigliano' Bureau of Research in Innovation, Complexity and Knowledge, Collegio Carlo Alberto, Working Paper No. 08/2010.

Ethiraj, S.K. and Levinthal, D. (2004), 'Modularity and innovation in complex systems', *Management Science*, **50** (2), 159–73.

European Commission (2004), 'Technology platforms: from definition to implementation of a common research agenda', 21 September, EUR 21265, Directorate-General for Research, Luxembourg: Office for Official Publications of the European Communities.

Foster, J. (1993), 'Economics and the self-organisation approach: Alfred Marshall revisited?', *Economic Journal*, **103** (419), 975–91.

Foster, J. (2005), 'From simplistic to complex systems in economics', *Cambridge Journal of Economics*, **29** (6), 873–92.

Fransman, M. (2002), *Telecoms in the Internet Age: From Boom to Bust to . . .?* Oxford: Oxford University Press.

Garicano, L. (2000), 'Hierarchies and the organization of knowledge in production', *Journal of Political Economy*, **108** (5), 874–904.

Garud, R. and Kumaraswamy, A. (1996), 'Technological designs for retention and reuse', *International Journal of Technology Management*, **11** (7/8), 883–91.

Gawer, A. (ed.) (2009), *Platforms, Markets and Innovation*, Cheltenham, UK and Northampton, MA, USA: Edward Elgar.

Gawer, A. and Cusumano, M.A. (2002), *Platform Leadership: How Intel, Microsoft, and Cisco Drive Industry Innovation*, Cambridge, MA: Harvard Business School Press.

Gerstein, S. (1992), 'From machine bureaucracies to networked organizations: an architectural journey', in Nadler, D.A., Gerstein, M.A. and Shaw, R.B. (eds), *Organizational Architecture: Designs for Changing Organizations*, San Francisco: Jossey-Bass, pp. 11–38.

Gilson R.J., Sabel, C. and Scott, R. (2009), 'Contracting for innovation: vertical disintegration and interfirm collaboration', *Columbia Law Review*, **109**, 431–502.

Hanusch, H. and Pyka, A. (2007), 'Principles of Neo-Schumpeterian economics', *Cambridge Journal of Economics*, **31** (2), 275–89.

Helper, S., MacDuffie, J.P. and Sabel, C. (2000), 'Pragmatic collaborations: advancing knowledge while controlling opportunism', *Industrial and Corporate Change*, **9** (3), 443–88.

Henderson, R.M. and Clark, K.B. (1990), 'Architectural innovation: the reconfiguration of existing product technologies and the failure of established firms', *Administrative Science Quarterly*, **35**, 9–30.

Hippel, E. von (2005), *Democratizing Innovation*, Cambridge, MA: MIT Press.

Howells, J. and Hine, J. (1993), *Innovative Banking: Competition and the Management of a New Networks Technology*, London: Routledge.

Jacobides, M.G. (2006), 'The architecture and design of organizational capabilities', *Industrial and Corporate Change*, **15** (1), 151–71.

Jacobides, M.G. and Billinger, S. (2006), 'Designing the boundaries of the firm: from "make, buy, or ally" to the dynamic benefits of vertical architecture', *Organization Science*, **17** (2), 249–61.

Kim, D. and Kogut, B. (1996), 'Technological platforms and diversification', *Organization Science*, **7** (2), 283–301.

Kogut, B. (2000), 'The network as knowledge: generative rules and the emergence of structure', *Strategic Management Journal*, **21** (3), 405–25.

Kogut, B. and Zander, U. (1992), 'Knowledge of the firm, combinative capabilities, and the replication of technology', *Organization Science*, **3** (3), 383–97.
Kogut, B. and Zander, U. (1996), 'Knowledge of the firm, combinative capabilities, and the replication of technology', *Organization Science*, **3** (3), 383–97.
Lane D.A. and Maxfield R. (1997), 'Strategy under complexity: fostering generative relationships', in Arthur, B., Durlauf, S. and Lane D. (eds), *The Economy as an Evolving Complex System II*, Reading, MA: Addison-Wesley, pp. 169–98.
Lane, D.A. and Maxfield, R.R. (2005), 'Ontological uncertainty and innovation', *Journal of Evolutionary Economics*, **15** (1), 3–50.
Lane, D., Pumain, D., van der Leew, S. and West, G. (eds) (2009), *Complexity Perspectives on Innovation and Social Change*, Berlin: Springer.
Langlois, R.N. (1992), 'Transaction-cost economics in real time', *Industrial and Corporate Change*, **1** (1), 99–127.
Langlois, R.N. (2002), 'Modularity in technology and organization', *Journal of Economic Behavior & Organization*, **49** (1), 19–37.
Langlois, R.N. (2003), 'The vanishing hand: the changing dynamics of industrial capitalism', *Industrial and Corporate Change*, **12** (2), 351–85.
Langlois, R.N. (2004), 'Chandler in a larger frame: markets, transaction costs, and organizational form in history', *Enterprise & Society*, **5** (3), 355–75.
Langlois R.N. and Garzarelli, G. (2008), 'Of hackers and hairdressers: modularity and the organizational economics of open-source collaboration', *Industry & Innovation*, **15** (2), 125–43.
Loasby, B.J. (1998), 'The organisation of capabilities', *Journal of Economic Behavior & Organization*, **35** (2), 139–60.
Loasby, B.J. (2002), 'The division and coordination of knowledge', in Dow, S. and Hillard, J. (eds), *Post Keynesian Econometrics, Microeconomics and the Theory of the Firm, Vol. 1*, Cheltenham, UK and Northampton, MA, USA: Edward Elgar, pp. 6–14.
Metcalfe, J.S. (2007), 'The broken thread: Marshall, Schumpeter and Hayek on the evolution of capitalism', presented at the Brisbane Club Meeting on Innovation and Complexity, Pollenzo (Italy), 1–3 June.
Nelson, R.R. (2003), 'On the uneven evolution of human know-how', *Research Policy*, **32** (6), 909–22.
Nelson, R.R. and Winter, S. (1982), *An Evolutionary Theory of Economic Change*, New York: Belknap Press.
O'Driscoll, G.P. Jr and Rizzo, M.J. (1985), *The Economics of Time and Ignorance*, New York: Basil Blackwell.
Orton, J.D. and Weick, K.E. (1990), 'Loosely coupled systems: a reconceptualization', *Academy of Management Review*, **15** (2), 203–23.
Patrucco, P.P. (2008), 'The economics of collective knowledge and technological communication', *Journal of Technology Transfer*, **33** (6), 579–99.
Patrucco, P.P. (2009), 'Collective knowledge production costs and the dynamics of technological systems', *Economics of Innovation and New Technology*, **18** (3), 295–310.
Pavitt, K. (2002), 'Innovating routines in the business firm: what corporate task should they be accomplishing?', *Industrial and Corporate Change*, **11** (1), 117–33.
Pennings J.M. and Harianto, F. (1992), 'Technological networking and innovation implementation', *Organization Science*, **3** (3), 356–82.
Penrose, E.T. (1959), *The Theory of the Growth of the Firm*, Oxford: Oxford University Press.
Potts, J. (2001), 'Knowledge and markets', *Journal of Evolutionary Economics*, **11** (4), 413–31.
Powell, W. (1990), 'Neither market nor hierarchy: network forms of organization', *Research in Organizational Behaviour*, **12**, 295–336.
Powell, W., Koput, K.W. and Smith-Doerr, L. (1996), 'Interorganizational collaboration and the locus of innovation: networks of learning in biotechnology', *Administrative Science Quarterly*, **41** (1), 116–45.
Prahalad, C.K. and Hamel, G. (1990), 'The core competence of the corporation', *Harvard Business Review*, **68** (3), 79–91.
Prencipe, A., Davies, A. and Hobday, M. (eds) (2003), *The Business of System Integration*, Oxford: Oxford University Press.
Richardson, G.B. (1972), 'The Organisation of Industry', *Economic Journal*, **82**, 883–96.
Robinson, D.K.R., Rip, A. and Mangematin, V. (2007), 'Technological agglomeration and the emergence of clusters and networks in nanotechnology', *Research Policy*, **36** (6), 871–79.
Rochet, J.C. and Tirole, J. (2003), 'Platform competition in two-sided markets', *Journal of the European Economic Association*, **1** (4), 990–1029.
Rosser Jr, B.J. (1999), 'On the complexities of complex economic systems', *Journal of Economic Perspectives*, **13** (4), 169–92.
Sah, R.K. and Stiglitz, J.E. (1986), 'The architecture of economic systems: hierarchies and polyarchies', *American Economic Review*, **76** (4), 716–27.
Sah, R.K. and Stiglitz, J.E. (1988), 'Committees, hierarchies and polyarchies', *Economic Journal*, **98** (391), 451–70.

Saloner, G. and Shepard, A. (1995), 'Adoption of technologies with network externalities: an empirical examination of the adoption of automated teller machines', *Rand Journal of Economics*, **26**, 479–501.
Sanchez, R. and Mahoney, T.T. (1996), 'Modularity flexibility, and knowledge management in product and organization design', *Strategic Management Journal*, **17**, 63–76.
Shy, O. (2001), *The Economics of Network Industries*, Cambridge: Cambridge University Press.
Simon, H.A. (1962), 'The architecture of complexity', *Proceedings of the American Philosophical Society*, **106** (6), 467–82.
Simon, H.A. (2002), 'Near decomposability and the speed of evolution', *Industrial and Corporate Change*, **11** (3), 587–99.
Stacey, R.D. (1995), 'The science of complexity: an alternative perspective for strategic change processes', *Strategic Management Journal*, **16** (6), 477–95.
Sturgeon, T.J. (2002), 'Modular production networks: a new American model of industrial organization', *Industrial and Corporate Change*, **11** (3), 451–96.
Suarez, F.F. and Cusumano, M.A. (2009), 'The role of services in platform markets', in Gawer, A. (ed.), *Platforms, Markets and Innovation*, Cheltenham, UK and Northampton, MA, USA: Edward Elgar, pp. 77–98.
Teece, D.J. (1984), 'Economic analysis and strategic management', *California Management Review*, **26** (3), 87–110.
Teece, D.J. (1986), 'Profiting from technological innovation: implications for integration, collaboration, licensing and public policy', *Research Policy*, **15** (6), 285–305.
Teece, D., Pisano, G. and Shuen, A. (1997), 'Dynamic capabilities and strategic management', *Strategic Management Journal*, **18** (7), 509–33.
UK Evaluation Forum (2006), 'Medical research: assessing the benefits to society', Report by Academy of Medical Sciences, Medical Research Council and Wellcome Trust.
Uzzi, B. (1997), 'Social structure and competition in interfirm networks: the paradox of embeddedness', *Administrative Science Quarterly*, **42** (1), 35–67.
Uzzi, B. (1999), 'Embeddedness in the making of financial capital: how social relations and networks benefit firms seeking financing', *American Sociological Review*, **64** (4), 481–505.
Vona, F. and Consoli, D. (2009), 'Innovation, human capital and earning distribution: towards a dynamic life-cycle approach', SENTE Working Paper, Tampere University (FI).
Weitzman, M.L. (1996), 'Hybridizing growth theory', *American Economic Review*, **86** (2), 207–12.
Weitzman, M.L. (1998), 'Recombinant growth', *Quarterly Journal of Economics*, **113** (2), 331–60.
Wheelwright, S.C. and Clark, K.B. (1992), 'Creating project plans to focus product development', *Harvard Business Review*, **70** (2), 70–82.
Winter, S.G. (2002), 'Understanding dynamic capabilities', *Strategic Management Journal*, **24** (19), 991–95.

9 Causes, consequences and dynamics of 'complex' distributions of technological activities: the case of prolific inventors
William Latham and Christian Le Bas[1]

1. INTRODUCTION

In this chapter individuals constitute the unit of analysis. Individuals must be considered because innovation is not simply a product of firms and organizations, it requires individual creativity. A century ago Schumpeter clearly identified the individual entrepreneur as essential to technological development. We follow this Schumpeterian notion that innovation, a form of creativity very much like entrepreneurial activity, is fundamentally individual in its genesis. Firms and organizations can create conditions that enhance or detract from the innovative activity of individuals, but it is the individuals who innovate. Yet we also know that *not all individuals innovate (or invent) equally*. Among individuals, even among individual entrepreneurs or firm innovators, innovation is not uniformly distributed. This heterogeneity among individuals is, of course, not unrelated to the existence of technological gaps across firms and organizations as far as innovation activities are concerned. Variation across firms is especially important in evolutionary economics and was recognized explicitly by Alfred Marshall. It is a natural outcome in a world marked by competition where organizations have heterogeneous bases of competences, different sets of strategies and, as a consequence, perform differently (see Metcalfe, 1995). In other words, we are in Antonelli's world of 'organized complexity' as he describes it in the introduction to this book.

Figure 9.1 illustrates heterogeneity among inventors using the distribution of US patents for the most productive French inventors (those with 15 or more inventions) over the period from 1975 to 2002. The distribution is characterized by heterogeneity and skewness.[2] The distributions for the other countries that we have examined, as expected, appear to be quite similar The most noticeable and significant characteristic of these 'long-tailed' distributions is that high-frequency or high-amplitude populations are followed by low-frequency or low-amplitude populations whose frequencies or amplitudes 'tail off' asymptotically to zero.

This chapter provides an understanding of the causes and the consequences of the particular shapes of the distributions of individual inventors' productivities that have been observed. It has long been acknowledged that technological activities are characterized by asymmetrical distributions. The basic question underlying this chapter is this: what can we learn about individual innovation from the analysis of similar phenomena observed in scientific productivity? In Section 2 we review a literature that begins with Lotka's (1926) 'law' regarding his observations about the persistence of diversity in scientific productivity at any point in time and also over time. We note that Lotka's model has been extended to technological activities and has proved useful for describing and

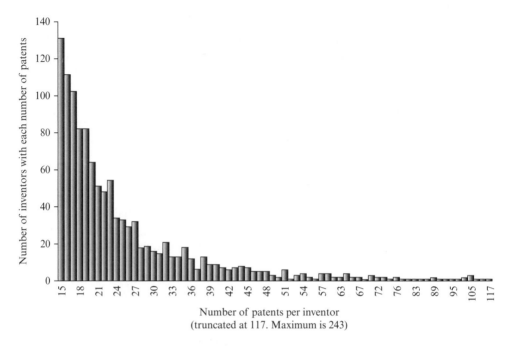

Figure 9.1   Number of French inventors with each number of US patents >14

understanding inventor productivity distributions. In Section 3 we survey empirical work regarding the utility of the 'power law' and the Pareto distribution to describe and explain empirically observed distributions. Section 4 is devoted to the economics of 'prolificness'. Here we are especially interested in the highly productive, or more 'prolific', inventors from the upper parts of the frequency distributions for inventors. While the identifying characteristic of prolific inventors is that they individually contribute to the production of more than the average number of patents (which can be termed 'quantity' productivity), we hypothesize that prolific inventors also contribute to the production of patents having greater than the average values (which can be termed 'value' productivity). Our focus on 'prolificness' allows us to explore the processes underlying knowledge accumulation at the individual level including its features, characteristics, and structural trends. We show that 'prolificness' is a dual process. First, we show, as has been shown in numerous empirical studies, that some inventors are able to reach the upper end of the 'quantity' productivity distribution by accumulating much larger than the average numbers of patents. Second we explore the specific processes by which these individuals create, maintain, and increase knowledge accumulation as their careers evolve.

2.   'LOTKA' WORLD: A COMPLEX SYSTEM OF CREATIVITY

The Lotka world simply generalizes to more activities the highly skewed distribution of productivity among scientists first identified by Lotka (1926). The first work to extend the 'Lotka model' to the productivity of inventors was Narin and Breitzman's (1995) paper on prolific inventors. They found a 'Lotka-like distribution' in the semi-conductor sector, and suggested that the same type of 'law' governs the productivity distribution for the creation of new ideas in science and in technology.[3]

2.1 Empirical Issues Related to the Lotka Model

2.1.1 Introduction to the issues

Among the well-known examples of skewed distributions of human creative activity that we will describe are the following: (1) the small proportion of individuals who ever patent an invention, (2) the extremely highly concentrated nature of eminence in science as described by Derek Solla Price (1965), (3) the fact that only a small fraction of patents receives most citations while most patents receive few citations, (4) the same citations pattern is observed for academic publications as for patent citations. All of these frequency distributions – of patents per inventor, publications per academic, citations per patent, and citations per academic publication, as well as many others – are not symmetric but highly skewed. We refer to them as 'complex' distributions because the observed varieties in individual creative capacity are the product of complex forces involving individuals, firms, organizations, and external effects across space and time. We contrast these skewed distributions with the assumption of normal (Gauss-Laplace) distributions for the characteristics and behaviours of the agents implicit in much of standard neo-classical economics. In the latter framework, the law of large numbers applies, and thus the mean is often a suitable representation for an entire distribution. By contrast, in complex technological-economic systems we show that understanding the nature of long-tail distributions, those that are highly right-skewed (such as the Pareto, log-normal, and others) is crucial. The 'long-tailed' distributions describe a kind of diversity in their asymmetric shapes: a high-frequency population is followed by a low-frequency population which 'tails off' asymptotically to zero.

Since Lotka's seminal work on the subject many additional works in different disciplines and over varied time periods have confirmed this long-tailed form for the distribution of creativity. It has been shown that the distribution is even more skewed when the scientific productivity is measured by patent citations. For us the significant feature of the Lotka world is simply the highly skewed distribution of productivity among scientists and inventors.

2.1.2 Detailed explanation of the Lotka law

Lotka's law of scientific productivity states that the number of scientists y_x each having produced x number of papers, is inversely proportional to x, which is the output of each individual author. The relation may be expressed as:

$$x^n y_x = C \qquad\qquad 9.1$$

where n and C are two constants that can be estimated with data on the numbers of scientific publications by author. Lotka's own calculations gave values to C of 0.61 and 0.57 for $n = 2$ and $n = 1.888$, respectively. Thus in Lotka's distribution 6 per cent of scientist publishers produce half of the papers (Stephan, 1996). Some authors claim that a generalized form of Lotka's law is the 'inverse power law' discussed in the next section below (Bookstein, 1976). Since the publication of Lotka's paper many studies have tested the existence of Lotka's law on particular samples. There have been too many studies for us to report on the results of each one in this chapter. For our purposes it is sufficient to note that some of these works have shown that Lotka's law does not apply to specific data sets. Nevertheless the nature of the distributions found remain the same: all are very skewed to the right with a long tail.

We note that the research program on Lotka's distribution is not really complete. We find in the recent literature a large number of papers that continue to deal with it.[4] Efforts to explain why Lotka's law 'works' to the extent that it does constitute another branch of research relative to the law. For instance Huber (2002) develops a new model for a process that generates Lotka's law. He shows that four relatively mild assumptions create a process that fits five different 'informetric' distributions: rate of production, career duration, randomness, and Poisson distribution over time, as well as Lotka's law. By simulation, he obtains good fits to three empirical samples that exhibit the extreme ranges of the observed parameters. The overall error is 7 per cent or less. An advantage of this model is that the parameters can be linked to observable human factors. The model is not merely descriptive, but also provides insights into the causes of differences between samples. Furthermore, the differences can be tested with powerful statistical tools.[5]

2.1.3   Explanatory frameworks

We contrast two older proposed explanations or 'frames of thinking about' the observed asymmetric distributions of innovative productivity: (1) the 'sacred star' and (2) the 'cumulative advantage' hypotheses of Allison and Stewart (1974). These two remain the most acknowledged explanatory frames. We discuss the supporting evidence for each hypothesis including empirical findings.

The first, the 'sacred star', refers to the hypothesis that differences in creative productivities of scientists are largely determined before their careers even begin. For instance the productive capacity might be linked to the formation of the scientist, to his/her motivation and to general ability. Many academics are reluctant to consider this hypothesis because, in general, measures of intellectual ability have low correlations with creative productivity. David (1994) has identified another limit of this first approach: if a predetermined distribution of abilities can perhaps explain the static cross-sectional distribution of productivity, it does not explain why the dispersion of productivity appears to increase over the life of cohorts of scientists.

The second explanation for asymmetry, 'cumulative advantage', is much better known. It has been proposed as an explanation by Allison and Stewart:

> First, scientists who have been recognized as having significant advances will be motivated by additional publications, and will be influenced by their colleagues' expectations that they repeat or exceed those achievements. Second beyond these direct effects, recognition usually implies increased access to resources which facilitates research. . . . (Allison and Stewart, 1974: 597)

So they conclude that cumulative advantage is the relevant explanation for the increase in productivity inequality. Cole and Cole (1973) have assembled some positive evidence in favour of this approach. Moreover they note that the cumulative advantages thesis is strongest where individuals are rewarded according to their merits (in this case, the

'Matthew effect' (the phenomenon whereby 'the rich get richer and the poor get poorer') is particularly important).[6] One point remains obscure and consequently would deserve more attention: is this cumulative advantage approach compatible with the pre-existing differences approach (which is the foundation of the 'sacred star' hypothesis)? Surely, 'yes' in theory, but perhaps it is less so in practice. All these issues are discussed in detail by Allison and Stewart (1974) and Cole and Cole (1973). Turner (2003) explicitly considers three laws of scientist productivity: (1) uneven distribution of productivity, (2) persistence of the hierarchy, and (3) reinforcement of the productivity gap (Turner, 2003).[7]

Strangely, there are only a few studies that provide empirical support for either of the two theses.[8] On the one hand Allison and Stewart (1974) confirmed the relevance of 'cumulative advantages'. They show, with cross-sectional data for chemists, physicists and mathematicians, that the distribution of productivity becomes increasingly unequal as a cohort ages. Resources and esteem increase too as career age increases. Levin and Stephan (1991) analysed scientist productivity in terms of career life-cycle (see also Stephan, 1996). After controlling for motivation and ability, they show that, in general, life-cycle has effects on productivity. As a consequence, this approach confirms and expands Allison and Stewart (1974). But, by contrast and much more recently, empirical work by Mairesse and Turner (2002) gives different results. They have a data set on physicists from the French CNRS. They do not confirm that the thesis of 'cumulative advantage' applies.

Six issues need to be considered in discussing the two approaches:

(1) The 'cumulative advantage' hypothesis is sometimes considered as a generalization of the Matthew effect, built on two feedback loops through recognition and resources. Although a variety of factors are at work in the process, the 'winner takes all' manifestation in the reward structure in science translates small differences in human capital endowments into large differences in the economic reward (Stephan, 1996).

(2) An important contribution is the idea that the two theses ('sacred star' and 'cumulative advantage') might be two special cases of a more general approach based on heterogeneity and stochastic reinforcement models (mathematical formulations of which were proposed by Simon, 1957). By contrast David (1994) has shown how Polya Urn schemes (processes first identified by Polya in probability theory in which a winning draw is reinforced) can be used for analysis of the cumulative advantage process, an idea first suggested by Price (1965).

(3) Interestingly, with both these approaches we are entering into the working of complex systems. The heterogeneity hypothesis tells us that individuals perform tasks differently (for instance inventive productivities differ). The reinforcing process delineates how the propensity to perform changes over time and, especially how, according to the 'cumulative advantage' thesis, small differences may become large.

(4) It may be that the studies reviewed here do not sufficiently account for the characteristics of the modern process of invention in science and in technology: the production of new ideas is done by teams. Some studies have tested Lotka's law with institutional productivity data, where the institutions are viewed as teams. In general negative binomial distributions fit these data better than Lotka's

distribution.[9] Of course this type of research opens the way to bibliometric studies and the ranking of institutions. These works are different from Shockley (1957) who analysed the distribution of publications among scientists in a particular institution and found them to be distributed in a lognormal way. From this point of view the work by Mairesse and Turner (2002) fills a gap. They include in their models variables measuring the influence of research teams. The size of the team, its productivity and the quality of publications of the team are found to be positively related (although the size of the team only has a weak impact on the other variables). We note that team interactions takes place within 'local or global networks', in small worlds, where scientists are mobile and collaboration between individuals is common (Fleming and Marx, 2006). This last behaviour, collaboration, is more prevalent for inventors than for scientists.

(5)   Often the productivity of scientists is defined equivalently by either the quantity of publications or by their quality (as measured by the number of citations they receive). We believe it is necessary to distinguish explicitly between the quantity of publications and their quality as researchers do with patented inventions.[10]

(6)   An intriguing question is posed by the empirical literature: does the same law that describes scientists' productivity also apply to inventors 'in technology' as well. In others words are scientists and inventors in the same Lotka world? After Lotka himself the works by Shockley (1957), Price (1976) and Seglen (1992) tend to confirm the main findings of the seminal Lotka study. But all these studies have been confined to the creative productivity of scientists. To our knowledge the first work that tries to extend the 'Lotka world' to the productivity of inventors is Narin and Breitzman (1995) who focused on prolific inventors. They found in the semiconductor sector a 'Lotka-like distribution' of the number of patents per inventor: a relatively small number of highly productive inventors and a large number of inventors having only one patent. In brief they suggest that the same type of 'law' governs the productivity distribution in the activity of creation of new ideas in science and in technology.[11]

2.2   A Competitive Explanation of the Distribution of Creativity: An Evolutionary Model of Breakthrough Inventions

Fleming and Szigety (2006) provided a fascinating model that enables us to understand the creation process at the core of Lotka's law but which is general enough to be applied to contexts other than scientific discovery.

They start their study with a psychological model first elaborated by Simonton (1999). Inventors generate new ideas through combinatorial thought trials subject to psychological and social selection processes (see also Fleming, 2007). They note that individuals who simultaneously juxtapose, combine, and evaluate a stream of uncombined inputs will be more creative. The generative creativity is an assemblage or rearrangement of new combinations. The more the inventor tries recombinant actions, the more he/she increases the likelihood of a productive hit. As a consequence we hypothesize a correlation between an inventor's total output and the likelihood that he/she finds inventions with high impact ('a one-hit wonder is very unlikely', Fleming and Szigety, 2006: 340). 'The most prolific inventor is the one most likely to invent a breakthrough' (ibid.).[12] A scientist who has produced very highly cited publications has probably also published a lot of papers that are poorly cited, as Simonton (1999) noted. If we rank scientists (inventors) according to their productivity in terms of total number of papers (patents) we will find the 'genius creators' with the most influential ideas are in the extreme right tail of the distribution of productivity.

Simonton (1999) has framed creativity as an investigation of the distributional moments of inventive output. He noted that the ratio of the number of major works to the number of minor works remained constant over a productive career. Fleming and Szigety (2006) make an inventory of the factors (technological and social-psychological variables) that have an influence on 'the second moment of the creative outcome distribution' and consequently also affect the propensity to create breakthroughs. For example, among the important variables that have an expected positive impact on the variance of the distribution are: diversity of collaborators, dissolution of collaborative relationship, and changes of creative fields: as has been noted by many researchers an inventor cannot invent alone, he/she invents collectively and within an 'ecological context'.[13] As a consequence there are organizational influences on the evolution of the distribution of inventive behaviour as well. In another paper Fleming (2007) finds empirical results in favour of his thesis. However, Mairesse and Turner (2002) find evidence contesting the trend for scientists (they investigate French physicists). They find that at some point in time there seems to be a substitution between the quantity of publications and their quality. That is not in accordance with the law pictured by Fleming and Szigety (2006).[14]

We have reviewed theoretical and empirical analyses reported in the literature relating to scientists' productivity distributions. These analyses led us into the workings of complex systems. The heterogeneity hypothesis tells us that individuals perform tasks differently; for example, inventive productivities differ. The reinforcing processes hypothesis provides the dynamics in the system, delineating how the propensity to perform changes over time and how, according to the 'cumulative advantage' hypothesis, small differences may become larger.

3. THE 'LONG TAIL' STORY: THE POWER LAW AND THE PARETO DISTRIBUTION IN TECHNO-ECONOMIC SYSTEMS

The 'long tail' is the name for a long-known feature of some statistical highly right-skewed distributions. The feature is also known as 'heavy tails', 'power-law tails', or 'Pareto tails'. The main characteristic of 'long-tailed' distributions is that a high-frequency or high-amplitude population is followed by a low-frequency or low-amplitude population which gradually 'tails off' asymptotically. Some authors have also noted that this long tail is also bigger (higher). The events at the far right end of the tail have extremely low probabilities of occurrence but these probabilities are nonzero, as emphasized by Taleb (2007). This type of distribution often follows a power law qualitatively quite different from the 'normal' or 'Gaussian' type distributions (which are narrower, symmetric and peaked) used to describe phenomena such as histograms of people's heights. A vast range of natural and social phenomena follow such distributions.[15]

For a distribution having the power law general form, the power law can be expressed as

$$p(x) = C. x^{\alpha}, \tag{9.2}$$

where α is the exponent and the constant $C = e^c$. In the case of a cumulative distribution, the exponent of the power law will be $(1 - \alpha)$.

To check if an empirical distribution fits a power law, we can simply plot the data on a log-log scale. A power law distribution appears as a straight line (because $\log_e [p(x)] = c + \alpha * \log_e (x)$ is a straight line). Equivalently we can plot the *cumulative distribution* and it will give a straight line as well. We will utilize these characteristics of power laws to represent the distribution of numbers of patents by inventors.

3.1   Variety in Highly Right-skewed Distributions: Some Definitions

Newman (2006) uses the distribution of the population of all US cities to illustrate the power law. The right-skewed form of the distribution indicates that most US cities have small populations while there are a small number of very large cities. Price (1965) finds that the numbers of citations received by scientific papers can be described as a power law distribution.

Many skewed distributions are well known. They include power law cumulative distributions that are sometimes called 'Pareto distributions', a type of continuous power law distribution first identified by Pareto (also known as the '80–20' distribution because 80 per cent of the total density is accounted for by 20 per cent of the range of values). Pareto observed that 80 per cent of Italy's wealth was owned by 20 per cent of the population. He then carried out surveys on a variety of other countries and found that a similar distribution applied. The 80–20 Pareto principle states that, for many events, 80 per cent of the effects come from 20 per cent of the causes. It has many applications beyond the world of economics, especially in engineering and business management. An advantage of the Pareto power law is that the exponent α offers a measure of the concentration. There is a direct (and clear) relationship between it and the Lorenz concentration index (Bouget and Viénot, 1995).

It is important not to confuse the general phenomenon of the long tail, the power law that provides the general mathematical structure for the long tail, and the Pareto distribution as a particular (and popular) type of power law distribution.

Zipf's law leads to one of a family of related discrete power-law probability distributions first proposed by Zipf (1935, 1949). If we rank a collection of individuals each having the rank r, by the size of the individual z_r, the following relationship defines Zipf's law:

$$r^{\beta}. z_r = \text{a constant}, C,$$

where β is Zipf's parameter.

For the distribution of people by their wealth, we can rank the people beginning with the wealthiest person (rank = 1). The individual with the wealth, w_r, has the rank r. In this context the function shows how w_r is a power-law function of r (see, for example,

Klass et al., 2007).[16] Such power-law cumulative distributions are also called rank/ frequency distribution (see Newman, 2006). For relevant applications in the field of economic phenomena see Axtell (2001) and Naldi (2003).

Note that, for small values of the variable being measured (that is, for values of $x <$ x_m), a distribution often may not follow a power law.[17] Consequently estimating the value of the coefficient α only for the values of $x > x_m$ requires making a judgment about the value of x_m.

Also note that a large number of highly right-skewed distributions do not follow power laws (Newman, 2006). There are other types of laws that can generate highly skewed distributions. Surprisingly, the second most popular distribution after Pareto's law is not a general power-law distribution but is the so-called 'Gibrat law', the log-normal law,[18] that describes the distribution of firms by size in particular industries. However, recent studies have shown that the parameters for Gibrat's law in this situation are not stable (Sutton, 1997).[19] In addition, its value as a descriptive device has been challenged by other laws.[20] Pareto's distribution and the log-normal law yield very similar distributions. In some cases it is impossible to choose between the two (Petruszewycz, 1972). It is acknowledged that the foundations in terms of probability are clear concerning the log-normal law and somewhat fuzzy for Pareto's distribution (Bouget and Viénot, 1995).

3.2 The Distribution of Prolific Inventors According to their Patents

We propose to illustrate these different types of distributions using data collected by Le Bas et al. (2010) and Latham et al. (2009) on the distribution of inventor productivity in terms of inventions patented.

For defining who is a prolific inventor we decided to use the threshold of 15 US patents granted over the time period under observation (1975–2002). We have examined the distributions for alternative numbers of patents. There is no large gap between the numbers of inventors having 13 or 14 patents and the (prolific) inventors having 15 or 16 patents. In other words, if we had fixed the threshold at 13 or 14 patents, the number of prolific inventors would have been larger, but this increase would not have been dramatic. We justify choosing 15 patents as our threshold for identifying prolific inventors as follows: Trajtenberg (2004), in his report on inventors in the US patenting system, notes that in the period 1975–99 the average number of patents per inventor was 2.74 (for all countries). Our period of observation is longer, extending through 2002. We know that patenting strongly increased toward the end of the period under consideration. Thus we might expect that the average number of patents per inventor would have risen to about 3.0. It seems to us that a *prolific* inventor would be an individual with productivity (in terms of patents) at least five times higher than the average.[21] We use data for US patents issued to more than 55 000 individual prolific inventors from five countries in our analysis. The countries are those with the largest numbers of patents in the US patent system: the US, Japan, Germany, France and the UK.

We have calculated the distribution of this population of prolific inventors according to their individual levels of patenting. Figure 9.2 displays the relationship between the log of the number of patents per inventor (recall that the patenting begins at 15) and the log of cumulative decreasing frequency of individuals with the number of patents for France. For a large section of the observed distribution of points, a linear relationship fits well.

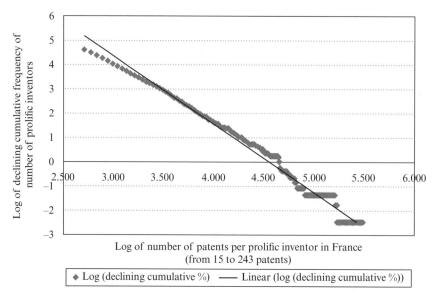

Figure 9.2   Application of power law to patenting by prolific French inventors

As noted by many authors the right hand end of the distribution is noisy because of the sample size. So we are in the frame of a power law distribution. We could have used simple OLS regressions to calculate slope parameters for the linear functions for each of the five countries. However, Newman (2006) showed that this method of estimation is biased. Fortunately he derived an alternative way of estimating these slope coefficients. Using Newman's method, we estimate the slopes as follows: Japan 1.5, Germany 1.4, US 1.34, France 1.52, and UK 1.74.[22] The larger is the value of the coefficient, the steeper is the slope and the smaller the skewness. The US has the distribution that is the most skewed, and the UK's is the least skewed. Surprisingly the US has a much larger number of prolific inventors than the UK. It may be that the size of the sample (which is much larger for the US) influences the results but more studies will be necessary to get the right explanation. Note that we could also perform this same analysis using the number of patents by technological fields or we could do it after pooling the data across all five countries.

3.3   The Quest for Explanation: The Frameworks[23]

We hypothesize that an empirical distribution fitting a power law is stable (that the exponent α is constant when we calculate it for different time periods or different economic entities). This stability means mechanisms exist working for maintaining the stability of distributions.

Many theoretical frameworks have been proposed to explain why stable power-law distributions arise in the natural and social worlds. From the point of view of mathematical structures, a combination of exponentials can be sufficient for producing power-law distributions. Regarding the basic mechanisms, some researchers have turned to the tools of 'complex systems' such as 'self-organized criticality' or 'highly-optimized tolerance'.

Other researchers hypothesize that the well-known Yule process[24] can be applied to economic phenomena such as the growth of cities, the distribution of wealth, the number of citations to a paper, and so on. In these applications the probability of gaining a new member, or of increasing revenues, or of receiving a new citation is proportional to the number the object already has. The dynamic process is reinforcing.[25] According to various researchers we have phenomena such as the Matthew effect and the cumulative advantage process, both of which we have discussed in previous sections.

4. ANALYSING THE UPPER END OF THE PERFORMANCE DISTRIBUTION: THE ECONOMICS OF 'PROLIFICNESS'

Previous studies on prolific (or key) inventors have focused on firms or industries. For example Narin and Breitzman (1995) use four firms in one sector in their seminal work. Pilkington et al. (2008) use two industries. We have another perspective: we have adopted the individual inventor as the unit of analysis. We choose to focus our analysis around comparisons of individual inventors across countries, across technological fields, and across individuals. We use the empirical results and analysis summarized in the following four papers: Gay et al. (2008), Le Bas et al. (2010), Laredo et al. (2009) and Latham et al. (2009). As previously indicated we use a large database on US patenting from 1975 to 2002, for the five largest countries in terms of scale of technological activities: France, Germany, the UK, the US and Japan. It contains more than 55 000 prolific inventors. This database provides systematic empirical evidence on the main trends concerning prolific inventors. First we summarize some salient stylized facts drawn from our previous studies. Then we will provide more details on the explanatory framework we propose for 'prolificness'.

4.1 Some Stylized Facts on 'Prolificness'

(1) Macro patterns
(a) The size of the relative population of prolific inventors as a proportion of the total number of inventors, a first index of prolificness, and the number of their patents as the proportion of total patenting, a second index of prolificness, differ across countries (see Table 9.1). Note that there is a strong asymmetry between the proportion of prolific inventors and the proportion of their patenting. In fact, this asymmetry defines what we term 'prolificness'.
(b) The country ranking in terms of 'prolificness' according to the first index is: Japan, Germany, US, France, and the UK (the US and France change places with the second index). The country ranking that we found is coherent (correlated) with what we know about the primary national technological indicators such as R&D expenditures funded by enterprises, triadic patents,[26] and private industrial R&D.
(c) We observe that prolific inventor patenting is distributed unevenly across technological fields in all countries. We also observe a close relationship between the degree of a country's technological specialization and the importance of its prolific inventors (measured by their patents as a proportion of all of a country's patents).
(d) The significance of the correlation between technological specialization and

Table 9.1   Prolific inventors: number, indexes of prolificness, and average productivity by country

	GB	France	US	Germany	Japan
Total number of prolific inventors	813	1157	26279	5270	19418
Index of prolificness (1)					
Number of prolific inventors / total number of inventors	1.32	1.75	2.66	3.77	7.31
Index of prolificness (2):					
Number of prolific inventors' patents / total number of patents	20.27	34.62	33.72	40.02	66.61
Average number of patents per inventor for all inventors	2.34	2.38	2.80	3.49	4.94
Average number of patents per inventor for prolific inventors	24.63	26.34	25.77	30.05	31.14

Source: Le Bas et al. (2010).

prolificness is confirmed by a strong correlation between the Revealed Technological Advantages (RTA) Index and the proportion of prolific inventors at technological subcategory level for 37 subcategories of technology.[27] When we regress the RTA and the proportion of prolific inventors at the technological field level, we obtain an R^2 of 47.7 per cent. In an expanded model dummy variables to control for country fixed effects are not significant and broad technological class fixed effects for six categories are significant only for Chemicals. This model has an R^2 of 53.3 per cent (Adjusted R^2 = 50.6 per cent). The slope coefficient for the proportion of prolific inventors is significant at the 1 per cent level.

(e)   From this last evidence it is possible to provide a tentative explanation. The evidence raises the following question: what is the relationship between country technological specialization and the technological importance of prolific inventors (measured here by their relative number)? It may be that the relationship is simultaneous. On the one hand as more R&D investments are made in the fields in which a country is specialized, there will be more inventions and consequently the more prolific inventors (indirect effects). On the other hand, the strengths of each country are reflected in the presence of large nationally based firms (Patel and Pavitt, 1995) which are able to maintain their specialization persistently in the context of competitive pressures if they hire the best technological knowledge workers available (prolific inventors). Supporting this interpretation, Pilkington et al. (2008) have shown that key inventors are primarily located within a limited number of key firms that show real technological leadership (Pilkington et al., 2008). If this view is correct, we would have a 'virtuous circle' linking national technological specialization (countries), technological leadership (firms) and highly productive human capital (inventors). Positive feedbacks stand at the core of the process and self-reinforcing processes are at work. We find here many of the processes depicted by Antonelli in the introduction to this book, especially irreversibility due to path dependence or deterministic past dependence.

(2) Micro patterns

(a)   Almost 30 per cent of our population of prolific inventors got their first patent at the outset of the period of time under observation (1975). In the US a high proportion of prolific inventors (20 per cent) have their first patent after 1990. The variable patent duration (a proxy for the length of an inventor's career) differs greatly across inventors (and countries). Some inventors are active over only 5 years, others are active for more than 35 years. Japanese inventors have shorter periods of activity, Germans have longer periods. This variable should be used for building a taxonomy of inventors: inventors who patent persistently become prolific over time, others are prolific quickly (the study should control for inter-industrial differences).

(b)   Inventor productivity. Negative binomial regressions explaining the inventor productivity (number of patents) show that interfirm and international mobility and technological variety (at the inventor level) positively affect inventor productivity after controlling for patent duration and time concentration. The overall results suggest that the same factors positively impact productivity across countries with few exceptions (Le Bas et al., 2010).

(c)   Mobility.[28] The 'dominant design' as far as the effects of inventor mobility are concerned is based on knowledge spillovers. In standard microeconomics it is acknowledged that individual mobility is an important source of knowledge externalities (Griliches, 1992; Moen, 2005). Mobility is mainly a local phenomenon; in general knowledge flows between economic units are localized to the extent labour mobility also is (Breschi and Lissoni, 2003). We present evidence for national inter-firm mobility: around 20 per cent of the prolific inventors do not move during the period under observation and international mobility of prolific inventors is very weak (all results shown by Le Bas et al., 2010). The mobility equations for the five countries (France, Japan, Germany, UK, USA) show that productivity is positively associated with mobility. The more prolific an inventor is, the more mobile he/she is (in accordance with what the recent literature tells us).

(d)   Patent value. Following Fleming and Szigety (2006) who described an evolutionary model of breakthrough invention directly linked to prolificness, we thought a priori that the more productive a prolific inventor is, the more valuable his/her inventions would be. This follows directly from the idea that the most prolific inventor is the one most likely to invent a breakthrough. In fact, our findings do not confirm this implication of creativity. The regressions carried out by Latham et al. (2009) for three countries (France, Germany, and the UK) show a consistent negative and significant relationship between value and inter-firm mobility. These results are surprising. A priori we expected that value would be enhanced by mobility. Instead we are left to conclude that while mobility may increase patenting, there is more value produced when inventors remain where they begin. The negative relationship with productivity lends credence to the idea of a trade-off for prolific inventors between value and productivity. At this stage of the research we have to remain cautious for two reasons: (a) we measure value of patent by citations and numerous authors have emphasized that this measure may be misleading in particular for patents receiving high numbers of citations; and (b) so far we have studied the relationship between productivity and value only for the population of prolific inventors. When we conduct a comparison between prolific and non-prolific inventors, as we did in a previous study, the evidence showed clearly that having prolific inventors in the team of inventors is a factor increasing the number of citations (Gay et al., 2008).

(3) Micro-micro patterns

(a)   Gay et al. (2008) show that prolific inventors work with larger teams than others and produce inventions having more value after controlling for technological field effects.[29] These results suggest that a prolific inventor can act as a 'knowledge system integrator'. The 'knowledge system integrator' (the prolific inventor) coordinates the competence and capabilities of the members of the team in order to increase the firms' technological performance and its economic competitiveness. This view tends to confirm that human resources are the most important factor for R&D performance (and maybe for scientific research as well), not only because of the individual talents and qualifications of scientists, but also because of their capacity to create and develop ties with other scientists, the scientific 'communities' and networks (Laredo et al., 2009).

(b)   Econometric analysis suggests that the presence of a foreign inventor (who may or may not be prolific) on the inventive team has a positive effect on the value of invention. This witnesses the actual importance of the international networks within which large, often multinational, corporations operate (Cantwell and Iammarino, 2003). Firms extend their knowledge activity abroad in order to extract local knowledge for their global production of new ideas.

4.2   Introductory General Remarks on an Explanatory Framework for 'Prolificness'

Our empirical findings to date have enabled us to propose a tentative explanatory framework. Our feeling is that there are two fundamental processes that explain the prolificness of inventors. First, prolificness is linked to the role of these inventors as gatekeepers for 'science in the making' (in particular in science-based industries). Second, prolificness is linked to the capacity of inventors to aggregate resources, mainly human resources, for deploying their inventions to the extent that they can be patented (see Laredo et al., 2009), not only because of their individual talents and competence, but also because of their capacity to create and develop ties with other scientists, the scientific 'communities' and networks. Their creativity tends to define, to some extent, a form of localized technological change (Antonelli, 2008) to the smallest level of analysis: an individual.

These general remarks do not even begin to adequately explain the mechanisms that determine the precise levels of inventor productivity. Our basic hypothesis is that the models laid out in the previous section enable us to account for much of the upper end of the tail of the productivity distribution. But they can help us only to a limited extent. Both of the two main hypotheses regarding the productivity of prolific inventors, the 'sacred star' and the 'cumulative advantage' hypotheses, seem to be at work. We observe in some cases an inventor is immediately prolific. His/her level of patenting is high. In general he/she is productive over a short period of time. For example, the 'star scientists', when they patent, enter this category. We can think they have high capabilities in their academic and technological fields and stay strongly motivated. By contrast, some achieve a few patents per year but persistently over a long time period. They accumulate knowledge step by step. The 'cumulative advantage' hypothesis fits well their career or professional trajectory. But at this point of our own research we are not sure that a pattern of 'increases in productivity inequality' really works. It sets out the limits of the comparison between inventors and scientists. A Matthew effect is not observed here, or if it is, only with special insights. Surely an inventor must receive financial incentives for researching, inventing, and accumulating knowledge, but the incentives are not the same kind as the rules governing the awards system in science. It may be that the Matthew effect works since a good productive inventor will receive more money from the firm for developing his/her research program. Basically industrial firms are in a competitive environment: they have to survive and they search for new technological knowledge, not for the sake of increasing the current stock of knowledge but for innovating in a business environment (the users' part of the knowledge economy). The recognition of the inventor is linked to a great extent to his/her capacity to produce new knowledge that is economically useful (innovation). The awards come from the market, not from the 'community of inventors'. Of course, in science, the opinion of peers is of paramount importance.

5.   CONCLUSION

The preceding discussion has placed the analysis of prolific inventors at the heart of understanding the dynamic complexity of innovation and technological change. Our analysis has been based on only preliminary analyses, ours and those of others that have been completed to date. We hope that those analyses and our discussion of them will provide guidance in the continuing development of empirical research programs on innovative productivity. We hope to contribute to the emergence of both a useful inventor productivity taxonomy and a coherent explanatory framework for the observed patterns of innovative behaviour.

   We believe that the preliminary work suggests some implications for policy and management. Regarding the relations between mobility and productivity, the policy implications of our findings are clear but puzzling: more total value will be created in R&D if incentives are used to keep inventors where they are. It seems that the externality spillover losses from mobility in the firms from which inventors move are not offset by the gains in productivity in the firms to which inventors move. This is a classic example of private markets not being able to adequately balance private individual gains with global losses.

   Prolific inventors make up a very special variety of human resources that require particular management. First, policies and incentives are needed in order to both motivate these productive people to share their knowledge and know-how and simultaneously discourage movements that are not likely to be productive or, at least, to discourage them from moving too quickly.[30] Leonard and Swap (2005) have described some criteria for the management of 'deep smarts', the people who have a high level of expertise in all the areas of industrial life. It may be useful to apply their analysis to prolific inventors.

NOTES

1.   The authors thank L'Agence nationale de la recherche, Paris for funding our research on prolific inventors regarding the characteristics, the productivity distributions, and the time paths of the careers of

prolific inventors in the five largest countries in terms of overall technological activity (see Le Bas et al., 2010; Latham et al., 2009). Christian Le Bas acknowledges the funding and support of the International Center for Economic Research, Torino where he was a Fellow in 2008 and 2009. We also thank Riad Bouklia Hassan, Naciba Haniba and Dmitry Volodin for their valuable research assistance.

2. The distribution shown is truncated because our data set has no information before 1975 or after 2002 and thus we do not have completed information for inventors who were at mid-career at the beginning and the end of our data. However, we have also examined the distribution for inventors whose entire careers begin and end within the data and know that the truncation does not affect the fundamental characteristics of the distribution.

3. See also Göktepe (2007).

4. Two illustrative papers showing the kind of interest in the topic that is ongoing are: Kretschmer and Kretschmer (2007) and Morris and Goldstein (2007). See Egghe (2005) as well.

5. Note that Lotka's analysis does not deal with the 'value' of publications (which has been measured by citations).

6. Cumulative advantage is a general mechanism for inequality across any temporal process in which a favourable relative position becomes a resource that produces further relative gains. DiPrete and Eirich (2006) show that the concept of cumulative advantage has developed multiple meanings in the sociological literature, in particular in the areas of education, careers, and related life course processes. It is well known in economics, explaining, for example, the productivity gap between individuals (inventors), firms, regions, and nations.

7. Recently this approach has been challenged by Harhoff and Hoisl (2006). They note that pre-existing differences and cumulative advantages affect differences in output not in quality.

8. Some of them are reviewed by David (1994).

9. Nearly identical results are obtained from the analysis of the productivity of industrial firms in terms of patents.

10. Mairesse and Turner (2002) show that the trend between the two indicators might be divergent.

11. See also Göktepe (2007).

12. This point is controversial. Recent work on the private value of patents confirms the existence of a significant relationship between inventor productivity and value of inventions. The characteristics of the inventor, in particular his or her past number of patents, is the main determinant of this value, even more important than the characteristics of the organization in which he or she is employed (Gambardella et al., 2006).

13. It appears that for Fleming and Szigety the same mechanisms of creativity apply both in science and in technology.

14. Analysis of 'star scientists' such as those in Zucker, Darby and Torero (2002) is relevant in this context. 'Star scientists' have high-quality intellectual capital (measured in terms of number of citations) and make major discoveries (Zucker and Darby, 1996, 2001). The stars are also in the extreme upper tail of the productivity distribution. The observation that, in the biotechnology sector, 'the labour of the most productive scientists is the main resource around which firms are built or transformed' can be generalized to high-tech industries (Zucker and Darby, 2006).

15. See Newman's (2006) survey.

16. Zipf's law refers to frequency distributions of 'rank data,' in which the relative frequency of the Nth-ranked item is given by the Zeta distribution that is the discrete form of the probabilistic Pareto law.

17. Reed (2001) proposes a model that predicts there is a power law fitting the lower tail as well.

18. We have already noted it is close to the Pareto distribution.

19. Simon and Bonini (1958) show under some general conditions that this distribution might be a power law.

20. See in particular Bottazzi et al. (2007).

21. Another option would have been to retain the top 1% or top 5% of patenting inventors. Trajtenberg (2004) observes that inventors present in 10 patents and more represent the top 5% of the inventor population. We thus estimate that with our threshold of 15 patents we focus on the 3% top inventors (in the US patent system) and thus our figures can be compared with those cited in debates about top or star scientists.

22. The ranking of countries as far as this estimator is concerned is virtually identical to those obtained with the OLS estimates and the actual values of the estimated slopes are also very similar.

23. In this section we follow Newman's (2006) survey.

24. In a Yule process, entities get random increments of a given property in proportion to their present value of that property.

25. See Simon (1955). Recall that the power-law distribution has a 'broad dynamic range'.

26. Triadic patents are those filed in the US, Japan and Europe.

27. We measure a country's technological specialization with an index of revealed technological advantage (RTA) as developed and used previously by many authors (see Le Bas and Sierra, 2002). Denoting P_{ij}

as the number of patents granted in technological field j to country i, the RTA index is calculated on the sample of countries used in this study as follows: $\text{RTA}ij = (P_{ij}/\sum_i P_{ij}) / (\sum_j P_{ij}/\sum_{ij}\sum P_{ij})$. When $\text{RTA}ij > 1$, technological field j is revealed to be a strength for country i.

28. We envisage here only inter-firm mobility. Latham et al. (2009) deal with geographic mobility and technological mobility (intellectual mobility).

29. This evidence is consistent with the hypothesis that firm size matters as well. Kim et al. (2004) report that inventor productivity is higher in large firms.

30. Inventor mobility must also now be understood as a component of the firm's overall competitive strategy. High tech firms seek competitive advantages by actively encouraging defections among their competitors' technological personnel (Kim et al., 2004). See also Fleming and Marx (2006).

REFERENCES

Allison, P.D. and Stewart, J.A. (1974), 'Productivity differences among scientists: evidence for cumulative advantage', *American Sociological Review*, **39**, 596–606.

Antonelli, C. (2008), *Localised Technological Change: Towards the Economics of Complexity*, London: Routledge.

Axtell, R. (2001), 'Zipf Distribution of US firm sizes', *Science*, September, **293** (5536), 1818–20.

Bookstein, A. (1976), 'The bibliometric distributions', *Library Quarterly*, **46**, 416–23.

Bottazzi, G., Cefis, E., Dosi, G. and Scecchi, A. (2007), 'Invariances and diversities in the patterns of industrial evolution: some evidence from Italian manufacturing industries', *Small Business Economics*, **29** (1–2), 137–59.

Bouget, D. and Viénot, A. (1995), *Traitement de l'information: statistiques et probabilité*, Paris: Vuibert.

Breschi, S. and Lissoni, F. (2003), 'Mobility and social networks: localized knowledge spillovers revisited', CESPRI Working Paper Series 142.

Cantwell, J. and Iammarino, S. (2003), *Multinational Corporations and European Regional Systems of Innovation*, London: Routledge.

Cole, J. and Cole, S. (1973), *Social Stratification in Science*, Chicago University of Chicago Press.

David, P.A. (1994), 'Why are institutions the "carriers of history"? Path dependence and the evolution of conventions, organizations and institutions', *Structural Change and Economic Dynamics*, **2** (5).

DiPrete, T.A. and Eirich, G.M. (2006), 'Cumulative advantage as a mechanism for inequality: a review of theoretical and empirical developments', *Annual Review of Sociology*, **32**, 271–97.

Egghe, L. (2005) *Power Laws in the Information Production Process: Lotkaian Informetrics*, Amsterdam: Elsevier Academic Press.

Fleming, L. (2007), 'Breakthroughs and the "long tail" of innovation', *MIT Sloan Management Review*, **49** (1).

Fleming, L. and Marx, M. (2006), 'Managing creativity in small worlds', California Management Review, **48** (4), 6–27.

Fleming, L. and Szigety, M. (2006), 'Exploring the tail of creativity: an evolutionary model of breakthrough invention', *Strategic Management*, **23**, 335–59.

Gambardella A., Harhoff, D. and Verspagen, B. (2006), 'The value of patents', Paper presented at an NBER Conference 'The Economics of Intellectual Property', Cambridge, MA.

Gay, C., Le Bas, C. and Latham, W. (2008), 'Collective knowledge, prolific inventors and the value of inventions: an empirical study of French, German and British owned US patents, 1975–1998', *The Economics of Innovation and New Technology*, **17**, 5–22.

Göktepe, D. (2007), 'Profiling serial innovators' creative research milieus. What Matters: nature or nurture?', mimeo, DRUID Summer Conference in Copenhagen, Denmark.

Griliches, Z. (1992), 'The search for R&D spillovers', NBER Working Papers, 3768.

Harhoff, D. and Hoisl, K. (2006), 'Institutionalized incentives for ingenuity, patent value and the German employees' inventor act', Munich School of Management, University of Munich, Discussion Paper 2006-12.

Huber, J.C. (2002), 'A new model that generates Lotka's law', *Journal of the American Society for Information Science and Technology*, **53**, 209–19.

Kim, J., Lee, S.J. and Marschke, G. (2004), 'Research scientist productivity and firm size: evidence from panel data on inventors', mimeo.

Klass, O.S., Biham, O., Levy, M., Malcai, O. and Solomon, S. (2007), 'The Forbes 400, the Pareto power-law and efficient markets', *European Physical Journal B – Condensed Matter and Complex Systems*, **55**, 143–7.

Kretschmer, H. and Kretschmer, T. (2007), 'Lotka's distribution and the distribution of co-author pairs' frequencies', *Journal of Informetrics*, **1**, 308–37.

Laredo, P., Le Bas, C. and Redor, D. (2009), 'Prolific inventors in science-based industries: profiles, interactions with their knowledge environment, and trajectories', Research Project Report.

Latham, W., Le Bas, C. and Volodin, D. (2009), 'Inventor mobility, productivity and patent value for prolific inventors in France, Germany and the UK: 1980–2002', Paper presented at the VU. University & Tinbergen Institute workshop, 'Creative, intellectual and entrepreneurial resources for regional development', Amsterdam.

Le Bas, C., Cabagnols, A. and Bouklia, R. (2010), 'Prolific inventors? Who are they and where do they locate? Evidence from a five countries US patenting data set', International Centre for Economic Research Working Paper No. 14/2010. Available at SSRN: http://ssrn.com/abstract=1625743.

Le Bas, C. and Sierra, C. (2002), 'Location versus home country advantages in R&D activities: some further results on multinationals' locational strategies', *Research Policy*, **31**, 589–609.

Leonard, D. and Swap, W. (2005), *Deep Smarts: How to Cultivate and Transfer Business Wisdom*, Boston, MA: Harvard Business School Press.

Levin, S.G. and Stephan, P.E. (1991), 'Research productivity over the life cycle: evidence for academic scientists', *American Economic Review*, **81**, 114–32.

Lotka, A.J. (1926), 'The frequency distribution of scientific productivity', *Journal of the Washington Academy of Sciences*, **16**, 317–23.

Mairesse, J. and Turner, L. (2002), 'Différences de productivités dans la recherche académique, Une étude à partir d'un échantillon de physiciens du CNRS', mimeo.

Metcalfe, J.S (1995), 'Technology systems and technology policy in an evolutionary framework', *Cambridge Journal of Economics*, **19**, 25–46.

Moen, J. (2005), 'Is mobility of technical personnel a source of R&D spillovers?', Department of Economics Discussion paper 05/01, Norwegian School of Economics and Business Administration, Oslo.

Morris, S.A. and Goldstein, M.L. (2007), 'Manifestations of research teams in journal literature: a growth model of papers, coauthorship, weak ties, authors, collaboration, and Lotka's law', *Journal of the American Society for Information Science and Technology*, **58**, 1764–82.

Naldi, M. (2003), 'Concentration indices and Zipf's law', *Economic Letters*, **78**, 329–34.

Narin, F. and Breitzman, A. (1995), 'Inventive productivity', *Research Policy*, **24**, 507–19.

Newman, M.E.J. (2006), 'Power laws, Pareto distributions and Zipf's law', *Contemporary Physics*, **46**, 323–51.

Patel, P. and Pavitt, K. (1995), 'Patterns of technological activity: their measurement and interpretation', in P. Stoneman (ed.), *Handbook of the Economics of Innovation and Technical Change*, London: Blackwell, pp. 14–51.

Petruszewycz, M. (1972), 'Loi de Pareto et loi log-normal: un choix difficile', *Mathématiques et Sciences Sociales*, **39**, 37–52.

Pilkington, A., Lee, L., Chan, C. and Ramakrishna, S. (2008), 'Defining key inventors: a comparison of fuel cell and nanotechnology industries', *Technological Forecasting and Social Change*, **76** (1), 118–27.

Price, D.J. de Solla (1965), 'Networks of scientific papers', *Science*, **149**, 510–15.

Price, D.J. de Solla (1976), 'A general theory of bibliometric and other cumulative advantage processes', *Journal of the American Society for Information Science*, **27** (5–6), 292–306.

Reed, W.J. (2001), 'The Pareto, Zipf and other power laws', *Economics Letters*, **74** (1), 15–19.

Seglen, P.O. (1992), 'The skewness of science', *Journal of the American Society for Information Science*, **43**, 628–38.

Shockley, W. (1957), 'On the statistics of individual variations of productivity in research laboratories', *Proceedings of the IRE*, **47**, 279–90.

Simon, H.A. (1955), 'On a class of skew distribution functions', *Biometrika*, **42**, 425–40.

Simon, H.A. (1957), *Models of Man*, New York: John Wiley and Sons.

Simon, H. and Bonini, C.P. (1958), 'The size distribution of business firms', *American Economic Review*, **48** (4).

Simonton, D.K. (1999), *Origins of Genius: Darwinian Perspectives on Creativity*, New York: Oxford University Press.

Stephan, P.E. (1996), 'The economics of science', *Journal of Economic Literature*, **34**, 1199–62.

Sutton, J. (1997), 'Gibrat's legacy', *Journal of Economic Literature*, **35** (1), 40–59.

Taleb, N.N. (2007) *The Black Swan: The Impact of the Highly Improbable*, New York: Random House.

Trajtenberg, M. (2004), 'The names game: using inventors' patent data in economic research', Power-point presentation http://www.tau.ac.il/~manuel/.

Turner, L. (2003), 'La recherche publique dans la production de connaissances. Contribution en Economie de la Science', thesis, Paris 1, Paris.

Zipf, G.K. (1935), *The Psychobiology of Language*, New York: Houghton-Mifflin.

Zipf, G.K. (1949), *Human Behavior and the Principle of Least-Effort*, New York: Addison-Wesley.

Zucker, L.G. and Darby, M.R. (1996), 'Star scientists and institutional transformation: patterns of invention and innovation in the biotechnologies industry', *Proceedings of the National Academy of Sciences, USA*, **93**, 12709–16.

Zucker, L.G. and Darby, M.R. (2001), 'Capturing technological opportunity via Japan's star scientists: evidence from Japanese firms' biotech patents and products', *Journal of Technology Transfer*, **26** (1–2), 37–58.

Zucker, L.G. and Darby, M.R. (2006), 'Movement of star scientists and engineers and high-tech firm entry', NBER Working Papers 12172, National Bureau of Economic Research.

Zucker, L.G., Darby, M.R. and Torero, M. (2002), 'Labor mobility from academe to commerce', *Journal of Labor Economics*, **20**, 629–60.

10 The biomedical workforce in the US: an example of positive feedbacks
Paula E. Stephan[1]

1. INTRODUCTION

The standard neoclassical model of the labor market assumes that negative feedbacks occur, causing the market to self-correct if it is out of equilibrium. Thus, for example, an oversupply of workers in a specific sector leads wages to decline relative to those in other sectors. This in turn leads to a decrease in supply, resulting in an eventual increase in wages. The contraction in supply is accomplished through the outward mobility of workers to higher wage sectors as well as the choice by potential entrants of alternative sectors in which to work.

In the 1970s radical political economists proposed that not all labor markets were characterized by negative feedback. Instead, they argued that, because of segmentation, labor markets existed in the secondary sector that were characterized by positive feedbacks. As a result, low relative wages persisted, coupled with signs of oversupply. Moreover, they argued that the welfare system was an 'integral part of this vicious circle' acting on the one hand to provide 'a payroll subsidy to secondary employers' and on the other hand, to maintain 'living levels low enough to force a steady flow of labor supply into the secondary labor market' (Vietorisz and Harrison, 1973: 366).

While dual labor market economists focused on the low-wage-low-skill sector, in recent years several scholars have suggested that positive feedback is not limited to the low-skill sector. Indeed, a market which has many positive feedback characteristics is thriving among those who have ten-plus years of post-baccalaureate training. Furthermore, the government, by providing much of the funding for the market, plays an integral part in perpetuating the positive feedback in this market. The market in question is that for biomedical workers; the government agency that plays a leading role is the National Institutes of Health (NIH).

In a 2008 article, Michael Teitelbaum, a demographer by training, characterized the disequilibria in biomedical research in the United States (discussion to follow) as caused by 'structural problems' and pointed out in an article in *Science* that research funding in the biomedical sciences is subject to 'positive-feedback loops' that 'drive the system ineluctably toward damaging instability' (p. 644). He went on to point out that while in theory the poor job market outcomes experienced by individuals in the biomedical workforce should result in negative feedback 'that would tend toward more stable equilibria', because of structural problems this has not occurred (p. 644). Seven years earlier, Richard Freeman et al. asked in another article in *Science* 'why in the face of poor career prospects has the field [of biomedical science] increased its supply of students relative to other PhD fields?' (2001: 2294)

In this chapter we extend the argument of Freeman et al. and Teitelbaum, making the case as to why the biomedical workforce is characterized by positive feedback. To do so requires background information on (1) the way in which research is structured in the biomedical sciences; (2) the reward structure among biomedical researchers; and (3) the funding enterprise for biomedical sciences. After addressing these three key components, we set out to examine what these mean in terms of the market for graduate students, postdocs and faculty. We then explore ways in which the positive feedback mechanisms could be dampened.

2. HOW RESEARCH IS STRUCTURED IN THE BIOMEDICAL SCIENCES

The majority of biomedical research in the US is performed at universities and medical schools. For example, 75.5 per cent of all papers authored by US scientists in the field of biological sciences are produced in the university sector (National Science Board, 2010, Appendix Table 5-42).[2] The vast majority of this research is conducted in a lab setting, led by a faculty member, known as the principal investigator (PI).

How labs are staffed varies across countries. For example, in Europe research labs are often staffed by permanent staff scientists, although increasingly these positions are held by temporary employees (Stephan, 2008). In the United States, while positions such as staff scientists and research associates exist, the majority of scientists working in the university lab are doctoral students and postdocs. Stephan, Grant Black and Tanwin Chang's study (2007) of 415 labs affiliated with a nanotechnology center, while not specific to the biomedical sciences, makes the point, finding that the average lab has 12 technical staff, excluding the PI. Fifty per cent of these are graduate students; 16 per cent are postdocs and 10 per cent are undergrads.[3] Some labs are quite large. A case in point is the Susan Lindquist lab at MIT which has 36 members (excluding Lindquist herself) – 20 postdocs, 7 graduate students, 1 visiting scientist, 1 staff scientist, 3 technicians, and 4 administrators.[4]

This way of staffing labs has been embraced in the US for a variety of reasons. Pedagogically, it is an efficient training model. It is also an inexpensive way to staff laboratories. Moreover, and as faculty are not abashed to note, it provides a source of 'new' ideas, especially given the relatively young age of doctoral students and postdocs. To quote Trevor Penning, while serving as the Associate Dean for Postdoctoral Research Training at the University of Pennsylvania School of Medicine, 'A faculty member is only as good as his or her best postdoc' (Penning, 1998). In addition, funding is often more readily available for predoctoral and postdoctoral students than for staff scientists. The typical NIH grant, for example, supports both types of training, as do many other forms of grants. There is also the added advantage that postdocs and graduate students, with their short tenure, provide for more flexibility in the staffing of laboratories than do permanent technicians.

Labs at US universities 'belong' to the faculty PI, at least in name if not in fact, as is readily seen by the common practice of naming the lab for the faculty member. A mere click of the mouse, for example, reveals that all of the 26 faculty at MIT in biochemistry and biophysics use their name in referring to their lab.[5] Sometimes, as in the case of the Nobel laureate Philip Sharp, lab members and former members are referred to using a play on the PI's name – in this case 'Sharpies'.[6]

Research is expensive. Personnel costs alone for a small-to-medium lab, composed of three GRAs, one postdoc, one technician and the PI are approximately $210 000 including salaries and benefits but excluding the cost of buying out the PI's time for research. Each additional graduate student adds approximately $37 000; each additional postdoc adds approximately $52 000.[7] Additional expenses include the cost of supplies and equipment. For research in the life sciences, supplies can easily average $18 000 per year per lab member, or add another $108 000 to the costs for a lab of six including the PI (Pelekanos, 2008). This excludes the cost of animals, which can be quite expensive. An off-the-shelf mouse costs between $17 and $60 (US) in 2009; mutant strains begin at around $40 and can go to more than $500. The cost to recover a mouse from a strain that is only available from cryopreserved material is $1900 (Stephan 2010). With the large number of mice in use (over 13 000 are already published), the cost of mouse upkeep becomes a significant factor in doing research. US universities, for example, charged from $.05 to $.10 per day per mouse (mouse per diem) in 2000 (Malakoff, 2000).[8] Equipping a lab adds considerably more to expenses. Pelekanos (2008) estimates that start-up equipment for a lab in the life sciences costs about $60 000. But equipment can cost much more than this. The next generation sequencing machines, such as Illumina's Genome Analyzer System, cost approximately $470 000 (Stephan, 2011).

In order to get started on an independent research career, faculty usually receive resources from the dean at the time they are hired. Included in these start-up packages are funds for equipment and stipends to hire graduate students, staff scientists and postdocs. Also, and of crucial importance in the lab sciences, they are assigned lab space. Ehrenberg et al. (2007) surveyed US universities regarding start-up packages in the early 2000s. They found that the average package for an assistant professor in biology was $403 071. At the high end it was $437 000. For senior faculty they report start-up packages of $957 143 in biology (high end is $1 575 000).

Start-up packages are exactly that. After several years, the faculty member becomes responsible for procuring the resources for the lab. Faculty do this primarily through the grants system, writing proposals and, if successful, receiving funds from Federal agencies and private foundations.[9] Faculty also receive support for their labs from industry. One exception to the rule is that faculty sometimes host postdocs who have received funding through a fellowship or graduate students supported on training grants (awarded to the department) who work (on a rotation basis) in a faculty lab.[10] Increasingly, faculty are expected not only to cover the research expenses of the lab through grants and contracts, but also to cover a portion of their own salary. Indeed, it is becoming increasingly common for faculty in tenured positions at US medical institutions to be required to procure a portion of their salary from grants.[11]

Organizationally, PI labs in the United States are structured as pyramids. At the pinnacle is the faculty principal investigator. Below the PI are the postdocs; below the postdocs are graduate students and undergraduates. Some labs also have scientists who have completed postdoctoral training in this or another lab and are hired in such non-tenure-track positions as staff scientists and research faculty. The pyramid analogy does not stop here, however. In certain ways the research enterprise itself resembles a pyramid scheme. In order to staff their labs, faculty recruit PhD students into their graduate program with funding and the promise of interesting research careers (Stephan and Levin, 2002). Upon receiving their degree it is mandatory for students who aspire to a faculty position to first take an appointment as a postdoc. Postdocs then seek to move on to tenure-track positions in academe. The Sigma Xi study of postdocs, for example, found that 72.7 per cent of the postdocs who were looking for a job were 'very interested' in a job at a research university and 23 per cent were 'somewhat interested' (Davis, 2005). In recent years, however, the transition from postdoc to tenure track has been slowed as the number of tenure-track positions has failed to keep pace with the increase in supply (discussion to follow).

Faculty actively recruit and select the students who work in their lab. Unlike admission decisions to PhD programs, however, which generally occur at the department level, decisions regarding staffing are usually made by the faculty member who, in effect, is paying for the student. Recruitment is even more direct in the case of postdocs, since the department plays no intermediate role in terms of admission. All decisions are the domain of the faculty member.

Not surprisingly, given the role faculty play in staffing decisions, networks or what may more accurately be described as 'affinity effects' appear to play a role in staffing. Tanyildiz (2008) has studied paired labs in 82 departments of engineering, chemistry, physics and biology. In each case she matches a lab directed by a 'native' PI (as established by name and undergraduate institution) to a lab directed by a foreign PI, of Chinese, Korean, Indian or Turkish background. She then studies the graduate student composition of the labs, assigning nationalities to the students based on the common-name methodology used by Kerr (2008). She finds significant differences in the role that ethnicity plays in staffing. The mean paired difference in the per cent of Chinese students in a lab directed by a Chinese PI versus a lab in the same department directed by a 'native' US faculty is 37.8 per cent; that for Koreans is 29.0 per cent; that for Indians is 27.1 per cent; that for Turkish is 36.3 per cent (very small sample). When she compares labs directed by natives to non-natives from one of these four groups the mean paired difference is 28.9 per cent. Clearly clustering by ethnicity occurs in labs. Tanyildiz also finds that affinity effects are more common in 'bottom'-ranked departments; less common in 'top' departments.[12] In related work, Gaulé and Piacentini (2010) find that around 40 per cent of the dissertation advisors of Chinese students in the US are themselves Chinese.

3.   THE INCENTIVE SYSTEM IN BIOMEDICAL SCIENCES

Scientists are motivated to do research because of their interest in solving puzzles; they also do research because of a desire to be recognized as being first, or as Robert Merton articulated, establishing priority of discovery. Moreover, they are not immune to the reward of money. Paula Stephan and Sharon Levin (1992) describe these three components as 'puzzle, ribbon and gold'.

By far the most important of these motives, at least from the point of view of this chapter, is the interest in recognition, which comes by being the first to solve a particular problem. The recognition that the scientific community bestows on priority has varied forms, depending on the importance it attaches to the discovery. Heading the list is eponymy, the practice of attaching the name of the scientist to the discovery. The hunt for the Higgs particle, for example, is in the news these days with the completion of the new accelerator at CERN (the LHC) and its associated four colliders. The particle is named for the Scottish physicist Peter Higgs, who was first to postulate a theory (in 1964) to explain why fundamental particles have mass, and predict a new particle that subsequently bore his name. Many other examples of eponymy exist: Haley's comet, Planck's constant, Hodgkin's disease, the Copernican system, Boyle's law, RSA, to name but a few.[13]

Recognition also comes in the form of prizes; sometimes for a particular discovery, in other instances in recognition of a scientist's life work. Among prizes, the Nobel is the best known, carrying the most prestige and a large – although not the largest – purse of approximately $1.3 million. But hundreds of other prizes exist, a handful of which have purses of $500 000 or more such as the Lemelson-MIT prize with an award of $500 000, the Crafoord Prize ($500 000), the Albany Medical Center Prize ($500 000), the Shaw prize ($1 million), the Spinoza Prize (1.5 million euros), the Kyoto Prize ($460 000) and the Louis-Jeantet Prize (700 000 CHF) to name but a sampling.

Other forms of recognition exist. For example, many countries have societies to which the luminaries are elected: the National Academies of Science, Engineering, and Medicine in the United States, the Royal Society in England, the Académie des Sciences in France.

The importance scientists attribute to priority and reputation can be inferred by a variety of social conventions and practices in science. It is not unknown for scientists to argue about the order in which they appear on a program. Two issues are at stake: not wanting to be scooped, and enjoying the prestige associated with being listed first. Scientists have been known to collect class notes from students in an effort to stave off the competition, or, in the case of mathematicians, to leave out a key point of a proof. Disputes regarding author order can also occur.

The research enterprise in the biomedical sciences has characteristics of what economists call a tournament model (Lazear and Rosen, 1981; Freeman et al., 2001). Such contests are characterized by offering contestants the chance to win a large prize such as becoming a principal investigator, receiving tenure, holding an endowed chair, winning a prestigious prize, being elected to the National Academy. Because small differences in productivity can be amplified into large differences in rewards, tournament models are characterized by intense competition. A researcher can be scooped by another, merely because her article arrived several days later; a principal investigator can fail to get his grant renewed, missing out by a tenth of a per cent.

The tournament nature of the research enterprise puts enormous pressure on faculty members: since 'the slightest edge can make the difference between success and failure.' (Freeman et al., 2001: 2993). Given the pressure to publish and publish quickly, PIs work long hours. Moreover, they look for ways to increase speed and output. One way to accomplish this is to increase the size of one's lab: the easiest (and cheapest way) to do so is to recruit more graduate students and postdocs. Graduate students and postdocs are, as noted above, full of fresh ideas and are relatively inexpensive. Moreover, they are dispensable if one's financial fortunes decline. The tournament nature of research also creates students and postdocs with narrow specialties. Faculty, after all, have narrow foci (essential for establishing a reputation); they recruit graduate students to work with them and they 'keep' them in their lab for four or five years.

4. THE FUNDING ENTERPRISE FOR BIOMEDICAL SCIENCES IN THE UNITED STATES

US universities in 2008 spent almost $52 billion on research (in 2008 dollars). The largest contributor to research by far was the federal government (60.2 per cent), followed by universities themselves (20.1 per cent). Considerably less came from state and local governments (6.6 per cent), industry (5.5 per cent) and other sources (7.6 per cent) such as private foundations (Britt, 2009: Table 1).

The percentage change in funding for US university research by field is given in Figure 10.1 for the entire period 1975–2006 and for the later period, 1995–2006. The decline of the physical and engineering sciences and the growth of the biomedical sciences are abundantly clear. Over the entire period, only three areas of research have experienced an increase in share: computer science, engineering, and the life sciences. The share of funds going to the physical, environmental and social sciences, psychology and math has declined. In the most recent period, the share going to the life sciences has increased at the expense of the share going to all other fields of research.

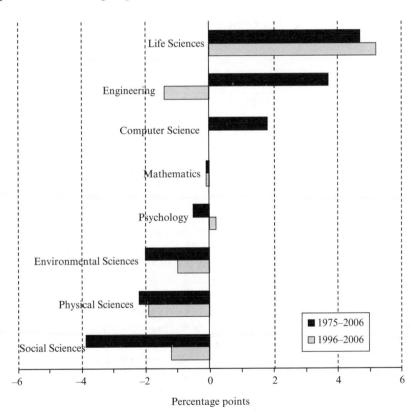

Source: National Science Board (2008), Figure 5-7.

Figure 10.1 Changes in share of academic R&D in selected S&E fields, 1975–2006 and 1996–2006

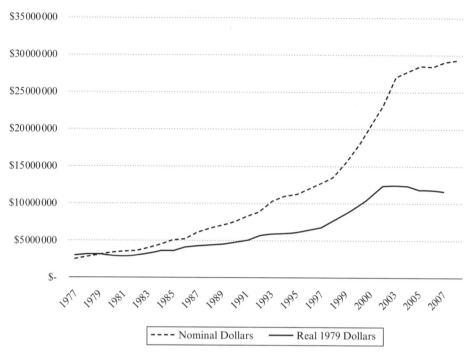

Source: National Institutes of Health (2009).

Figure 10.2   NIH budget, 1977–2008

Federal funding for biomedical research comes primarily from NIH. Figure 10.2 shows the NIH budget in current and real terms over the period 1997 to 2009. Although growth has been far from steady, especially when the budget doubled between the years 1998 and 2002, the upward trend is impressive and the envy of the physical and engineering sciences as well as of biomedical researchers in other countries.

The US love affair with funding for the life sciences, especially the biomedical sciences, is not difficult to understand. It is far easier for Congress to support research that the public sees as benefiting their well-being. Moreover, a large number of interest groups constantly remind Congress of the importance of medical research for 'their' disease. The age distribution of Congress does not hurt. The average member of the House of Representatives in 2009 was 56.0; the average senator was 61.7.[14] Both houses are considerably older than they were at their 'youngest' in 1981 when the average member of the House of Representatives was 48.4 and the average Senator was 52.5 (Congressional Quarterly 2008). Certain senators are particularly focused on biomedical research. Senator Arlen Spector (born in 1930), for example, has long been a champion of NIH funding and almost single-handedly increased the amount that NIH got out of the 2009 stimulus funds (officially referred to as the American Recovery and Reinvestment Act – or ARRA) from $3.9 billion to $10.4 billion. He is also a three-time survivor of cancer.

The ARRA package, as noted above, included a substantial amount of funds for NIH to be spent over a two-year period.[15] By the end of the first year of the stimulus awards, fully a third of these funds had been committed to administrative supplements to existing awards, provided to 'accelerate the tempo of research' by hiring more people or buying more equipment. The supplements are reviewed by NIH staff, not peer reviewed. Although it is too early to know exact numbers, many of the new hires are postdoctoral scholars and graduate students.

NIH spent an additional 33 per cent of the first year funding on projects that had been reviewed prior to the stimulus package, but had missed the payline. Many of these projects will involve graduate students and postdocs, as well. In addition, it spent approximately a quarter of the first-year funds on projects submitted in response to the stimulus announcement; some of these will also involve graduate students and postdocs.[16]

Support for research in the biomedical sciences also comes from private foundations. The most prominent among these is the Howard Hughes Medical Institute (HHMI). Established in 1953 by Howard Hughes, the Institute acquired a stronger footing when it sold the Hughes Aircraft Company to General Motors in 1985, thus establishing the Institute's endowment at $5 billion.[17] In 2008 its endowment was valued at close to $18 billion. By law HHMI is required to distribute 3.5 per cent of its assets each year. It has done so by supporting between 300 and 350 HHMI investigators at research universities, funding a number of training programs, and establishing the Janelia Farm Research Campus, in Ashburn, Virginia, which opened in 2006 with the goal of bringing 25 interdisciplinary teams together to study neural circuits and imaging (Kaiser, 2008a).

The decision as to whether or not NIH will support a particular research project is determined through a process of peer review. It begins when the Principal Investigator submits a proposal to NIH; the proposal is then assigned to a 'study section'. Study section members review proposals in advance of the meeting. When the study section meets, a process of triage occurs which results in approximately half of the proposals not being formally discussed and not scored. Investigators whose proposals are not scored receive no written comments. Proposals that survive the triage process are discussed in some detail and scored to one decimal point by members of the study section on a 1 to 5 scale, 1 representing the most favorable review and 5 representing the least favorable. An average of the reviewers' scores (rounded to two decimal points) is then computed and multiplied by 100.[18] Scores are standardized by pooling them with those given in other recent meetings. The resulting priority score and accompanying written review is forwarded to the specific institute (there are 27 institutes and centers at NIH) and reviewed by the institute's national advisory committee. Percentile cutoffs are important in determining who gets funded, although NIH does fund PIs whose proposals fall outside the cutoff. Investigators whose proposals are turned down have the right to resubmit two additional times. Most do. It is particularly challenging to resubmit if one's proposal is not scored, for then there are no written comments to address. This is a particularly serious problem for new, not established investigators.[19]

The review process puts considerable weight on past accomplishments, which are enumerated on a standardized NIH biosketch form. Results from the previous grant (if there was one) also play an important role in the evaluation. The presence of demonstrated expertise and strong preliminary data also play an especially key role in the review process. A major reason that universities provide start up funds is to permit the newly hired faculty member time to continue the process of collecting preliminary data for an

NIH proposal. Researchers must also demonstrate that they have adequate space at their university in which to conduct the research.

Historically anywhere between 10 and 40 per cent of applications have been funded. Success obviously depends on the number of applications, the cost of the proposals being considered and the availability of funding. It is also institute specific. For example, in 2008, the highest success rate was for applications reviewed by the National Eye Institute (29.5 per cent); the lowest was for proposals reviewed at National Institutes of Child Health and Human Development (16.8).[20] In 2001, during the doubling, several institutes had success rates above 35 per cent; many more had success rates above 30 per cent.[21]

The R01 grant, the 'bread and butter' for university investigators, typically lasts for three to five years. Researchers can apply to renew their grant. This is the norm, not the exception. It is greatly encouraged by the fact that renewals do much better in the review process than new proposals. It is not unknown for researchers to be supported on the same grant for 40-plus years. Or even 50-plus. Harold Scheraga (Cornell University) has had the same NIH grant to study protein folding for 52 years.[22]

The NIH grants system has not been friendly to the young. In recent years, for example, the number of new investigators funded by NIH has remained almost constant while the number of experienced investigators increased (more to follow). And success, when it comes, increasingly comes to older scientists. The average age at which one receives first independent funding increased from 37.2 to 42.4 between 1985 and 2006 (American Academy of Arts and Sciences, 2008: 11). At least three factors contribute to this outcome. First, the need for preliminary results biases funding decisions towards more established researchers and delays the submission of grants by investigators just starting out. Second, more than 70 per cent of new investigators must resubmit their proposals before receiving funding; thirty years ago over 85 per cent of all new investigators received funding on their first submission. Resubmission can easily add an additional year to the process. Third, people increasingly are older at the time that they get a tenure-track position (American Academy of Arts and Sciences, 2008: 12).

It's tempting to assume that more money will translate into higher success rates and better outcomes for the young. But this did not occur when the NIH budget doubled between 1998 and 2002. By the time the doubling was over, success rates were no higher than they had been before the doubling. By 2009, and partly because of the real decreases that NIH experienced in the intervening years, success rates were considerably lower than they had been before the doubling. Faculty were spending more time submitting and reviewing grants. The per cent of proposals funded on the first submission fell from over 60 per cent in the early 2000s to 30 per cent.[23] Over one-third of all funded R01 proposals were not approved until their last and final review. This not only took time and delayed careers; the perception was that these 'last chance' proposals were favored over others, creating a system that, according to Elias Zerhouni, the former director of NIH, awarded 'persistence over brilliance sometimes' (Kaiser, 2008c: 1169). Moreover, and jumping ahead to the discussion in Section 5, there is little evidence that the increase translated into permanent jobs for new PhDs, as had been the case in the 1950s and 1960s when government support for research expanded.

A major cause of this seeming paradox was the response of universities to the doubling. Some universities saw the doubling as an opportunity to move into a new 'league' and establish a program of 'excellence'. Others saw it as an opportunity to augment the strength they already had. For others, expansion of their existing programs was simply necessary if they were to remain competitive in biomedical research. Regardless, the end result was that the majority of research universities went on an unprecedented building binge.[24] Universities used philanthropic, local, and state resources, as well as debt, to finance the expansion. They hired additional faculty and research scientists, many in soft-money positions. Universities also encouraged faculty who had heretofore not applied for grants from NIH, to apply. They also encouraged those who had NIH grants to get additional grants: not one grant or two grants but three became the expectation at many research institutions. New buildings with larger labs required more resources to support them.

Not surprisingly, the number of applications for new and competing research projects grew. In 1998, NIH received slightly over 20 000 applications for R01 awards; by 2003 it received 24 634 and by 2008, long after the doubling had ended, it received 26 648. Success rates, which initially grew, declined from 32 per cent to 23 per cent.[25] Some of the new grants went to researchers who had heretofore not received NIH funds. But the vast majority of new grants went to established researchers: the per cent of investigators who had more than one R01 grant grew by one-third during the doubling, going from 22 per cent to 29 per cent. (Davis, 2007). The number of first time investigators grew by no more than 10 per cent.[26]

Young researchers were at a disadvantage competing against more seasoned researchers who had better preliminary data and more grantsmanship expertise; at every submission stage the success rates of new investigators was lower than for established researchers submitting a proposal for a new line of research.[27] The increased number of grants for experienced investigators and minimal growth in grants for first time investigators resulted in a dramatic change in the age distribution of PIs. In 1998 only a third of awardees were over 51: almost 25 per cent were under 40. By 2003 42.3 per cent were over 51 while less than 17 per cent were under 40. Fully a quarter were over 55 (Stephan, 2007).

5. THE MARKET FOR PHD STUDENTS, POSTDOCTORAL SCHOLARS AND FACULTY

In 1996 the National Research Council formed a committee to study trends in early careers of life scientists. The impetus for the study was that the number of PhDs in the life sciences had grown substantially in recent years but the job market opportunities for young life scientists had not kept pace. Increasingly, young life scientists had found themselves in a 'holding pattern', waiting for a permanent position (National Research Council, 1998).

There were a number of disturbing trends. Time to degree had increased, the percentage of life scientists holding postdoc positions had grown, and the duration of the postdoc position had also increased. Moreover, the likelihood that a young life scientist would hold a tenure track position, especially at a research university, had declined. Furthermore, young faculty were experiencing increasing difficulty getting their NIH grants funded and were getting funded for the first time at later and later ages.

To be a bit more specific, during the 10-year period 1985–95, the number of PhDs awarded in the biomedical sciences in the US had increased by almost 40 per cent.[28] Median time to degree, which was just over seven years in 1995, had increased to eight years. Sixty per cent of all new PhDs took a postdoc position, up from around 55 per cent a decade earlier. Over 30 per cent of PhDs who had been out of graduate school for three to four years held a postdoc position, up from 25 per cent a decade earlier. And the per cent who held a postdoc position for five to six years had grown by approximately 50 per cent.[29]

Obtaining a tenure-track position had become increasingly unlikely. In 1985 the odds were about one in three that someone who had received a PhD five to six years before (1979–80) held a tenure track position at a PhD-granting institution. By 1995 the odds were approximately one in five that a recent PhD held a tenure-track position. Not only had the odds declined; the actual number of young faculty holding tenure-track positions at PhD-granting institutions had declined. The big growth was in 'other' positions, a category that included postdocs, staff scientists and other non-tenure-track positions, as well as those who were working part-time.

After documenting and studying these trends, the committee made five recommendations: (1) restraint in the growth of the number of graduate students in the life sciences, (2) dissemination of accurate information on career prospects of young life scientists, (3) improvement of the educational experience of graduate students; (4) enhancement of opportunities for independence of postdoctoral fellows, and (5) alternative careers for individuals in the life sciences. The committee's intent regarding recommendation five was to convey the conviction that 'the PhD degree [should] remain a research-intensive degree, with the current primary purpose of training future independent scientists' (National Research Council, 1998: 8). In other words, the committee did not endorse the idea of training PhDs in the life sciences who would then pursue alternative careers.

The committee expanded on recommendation three in the text of the report, encouraging federal agencies to place greater emphasis on training grants and individual fellowships for supporting predoctoral training – as opposed to indirectly supporting training through the funding of graduate research assistantships on research projects. Their rationale was that training grants are pedagogically superior because the quality of the training is peer-reviewed, while the quality of training is not considered in the review of research projects. In addition, training grants minimize potential conflicts of interest that can arise between the trainer and trainee since the graduate student is not 'indentured' to a faculty member. Despite the advantages of training grants, the number of students supported on training grants had remained fairly constant for a number of years, while the number supported on research assistantships had grown dramatically.[30]

The life science community did not embrace the recommendations. Graduate programs continued to grow, little effort was made to disseminate information concerning career outcomes, and there was virtually no reallocation of funds between training grants and research assistantships. Indeed, while training grants used to fund two-thirds of graduate students and post docs, today they fund about 15 per cent.[31] Primarily at the initiative of the Alfred P. Sloan Foundation, a number of professional masters programs were started in the life sciences in the late 1990s. The hope was that such programs could prepare individuals for non-research positions in industry.[32]

Then, in 1998 the NIH budget began its five-year doubling. Many hoped that the doubling would be particularly beneficial to the young. This was not to be the case, although conditions initially marginally improved. The probability that a biomedical PhD aged 35 or younger held a tenure-track position, which had declined from around 10.3 per cent in 1995 to 6.9 per cent in 2001 'rebounded' to 10.4 per cent by 2003. The per cent of individuals remaining in a postdoc position for six plus years declined.[33] There was considerable growth in non-tenure track positions, especially at medical schools,[34] as well as considerable growth in non-academic jobs. But by 2005 the number of new PhD faculty hires at medical schools began to decline.[35]

In short, the pickup in academic jobs was relatively modest for the young. There were some other, disquieting trends. For example, there was an increase in the per cent of young PhDs working part time, and the age at which new faculty with PhDs were hired at medical schools increased by two years between 1992 and 2004, reaching 39.[36] Moreover, the young, as we have seen, had a hard time competing for funding. The number of awards to first-time investigators, which had initially increased, declined.[37] The 'spread' between the success rate on grant applications from established investigators and that for new investigators grew. In 1996 the difference was about 2.6 percentage points.[38] By 2003 it was over 6 percentage points. Career trajectories of young life scientists were sufficiently bleak to prompt the journal *Nature* to run an editorial entitled 'Indentured labour' which argued that 'too many graduate schools may be preparing too many students, so that too few young scientists have a real prospect of making a career in academic science'.[39]

During this entire time the number of PhDs awarded in the biosciences continued to grow. In 1980, for example, the US produced 3733 PhDs in the biosciences. By 1995, just before the NRC committee was constituted, the number had reached 5300. By 2006 it had grown to 6313 and by 2008 it exceeded 7500 (see Figure 10.3). At least three factors contributed to the increase: first, the success of early biotechnology companies as well as a number of research breakthroughs in the late 1980s and 1990s bestowed 'hot field' status on the biosciences. The field was seen as having a future. Second, the heavy emphasis in the US on Federal funding for biomedical research meant that graduate research assistantships were readily available for doctoral study. This attracted students, particularly international students, to study in the field. While only one in ten of the PhDs bestowed in the biosciences in 1980 went to someone on a temporary visa, by 2008, close to one in three went to someone on a temporary visa. Third, while the evidence suggests that US males are somewhat sensitive to market opportunities in choosing a field of study, the evidence is less clear that women make choices regarding field of study based on market signals. And this was a period when increasing numbers of US women headed to graduate school.

The number of individuals holding postdoctoral positions also grew dramatically during these years (see Figure 10.4). For example, NSF estimates that there were approximately 7000 postdocs working in academe in the biosciences – regardless of where the postdoc received their PhD – in 1980. By 1995, the number stood at 14 500 and by 2006 the number exceeded 19 000. A large percentage of these postdocs were in the US on temporary visas. Indeed, while slightly less than 30 per cent were on temporary visas in 1985, by 2006 fully 57 per cent were on temporary visas. The growth is easy to understand: first the NIH budget increase meant that ready funds were available for

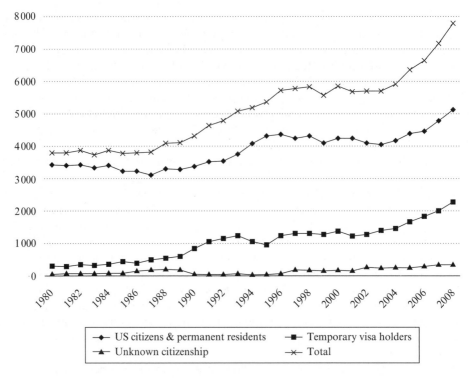

Sources: National Science Foundation (2009a), Table 11 and National Science Foundation (2009b).

Figure 10.3   Doctorates awarded in biosciences, 1980–2008

postdocs. While $37 000 – the initial salary for many postdocs – may not be a princely sum to a US citizen, it is highly attractive to an international scholar, especially scholars coming from Asia. Moreover, once the scientist enters the US, the probability increases that the scientist will eventually become a permanent resident and thus be able to stay in the US. Second, being a postdoc is a necessary milestone on the route to becoming an independent researcher at a university – a goal that the majority of doctoral scientists in the biomedical sciences hold, despite the poor job prospects.[40] Third, when jobs are tight, people remain in postdoc positions for a longer period of time, increasing the number of postdocs at any one time.

The counts of postdoctoral fellows produced by the National Science Foundation are known to be an undercount of the actual number of postdoctoral fellows. The extent of the undercount is difficult to determine, however. Problems in enumerating the total arise in part because postdocs work for individual faculty members and this makes it more difficult to collect data. It is also difficult to determine who exactly is a postdoc because it is not uncommon for individuals who are essentially postdocs to be called by another title, such as research scientist.

To summarize, the supply of life scientists being trained in the US has increased dramatically in the recent past despite considerable evidence that permanent jobs are scarce, especially permanent positions in academe. A back of the envelope estimate suggests

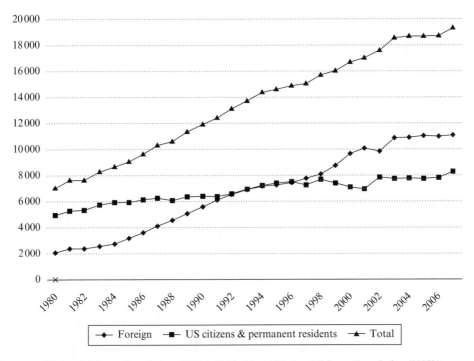

Sources: National Science Foundation (2009a), Table 37 and National Science Foundation (2009b).

Figure 10.4   Postdoctorates in biosciences, 1980–2007

that the probability of a US trained PhD being hired into a tenure track position and becoming a PI is less than 5 per cent. And for the lucky few, this only occurs when the PI is in her 40s. Moreover, conventional negative feedback models predict that such a situation cannot persist: bleak job prospects, long periods of postdocing, and the low probability of receiving funding should make the field relatively less attractive. This does not appear to be the case in the biomedical sciences. In Section 6 we examine why this has occurred.

6.   THE FAILURE OF NEGATIVE FEEDBACKS

At least two factors discourage the negative feedback process from occurring. First, and as noted above, there is a severe lack of information regarding job prospects in the biomedical sciences. Second, the supply of foreign-born wishing to study in the US, both for a PhD and for a postdoc, is quite elastic. Money speaks and the increase in the NIH budget has meant that funds are readily available for graduate and postdoctoral study. Finally, and integral to the first two points, faculty incentives are incompatible with negative feedback: graduate students and postdocs are key to faculty advancing in the tournament. And when competition is fierce, more research staff is always better. We address each of these below.

Information

The lack of accurate information concerning the placement of graduates contributes to the growth in the number of individuals going to graduate school. In the US, information, especially with regard to the job outcomes of recent graduates, has typically not been readily available from graduate programs. By way of example, in the late 1990s, and by way of an experiment, the economist Paul Romer (2000) asked a research assistant to initiate application to the top ten graduate departments of mathematics, physics, chemistry, biology, computer science and electrical engineering in the US, as measured by *US News and World Report*. For purposes of comparison, the student also began to apply to the top ten business and law schools. The student's efforts resulted in

> not one response giving information about the distribution of salaries for graduates, either in the initial information packet or in response to a follow-up inquiry from him. In contrast, he received salary information for 7 of the 10 business schools in the application packet, and in response to his second request, he was directed to a web page with salary information by one of the three non-respondents . . . Four out of the 10 law schools gave salary information in the application packet and three more of them directed him to this information in response to a second request. (Romer, 2000: 3)

The spread of information technology has not improved the amount of information that departments make available concerning the job outcomes of their graduates. An examination of the web pages of fifteen top programs in each of the fields of electrical engineering, chemistry and biomedical sciences in the winter of 2008 found that only two of the forty-five programs listed actual information on placements. Four others provided some information on placements but did not list specific information regarding the placements. By way of contrast, seven of the fifteen programs in economics provided a list of students and where they were placed, year by year (Stephan, 2009).[41]

It is easy to understand why departments are reluctant to provide placement data given that faculty are in the business of recruiting students to staff their labs. Revealing placement data could discourage potential applicants and thus place their research in jeopardy. The culture of the university also stresses careers in academe, rather than careers in industry. Most graduate students with academic ambitions, especially in the biomedical and physical sciences, take a postdoc position after receiving their PhD. In this sense, they have a job, albeit in a temporary, training position after they graduate. The ready availability of postdoc positions also conveniently lets the department 'off the hook' for helping to provide permanent placements. They have, after all, placed the student. The MIT program in biology can thus safely state on its webpage that the 'majority [of PhD recipients] . . . go on to a postdoctoral position in an academic setting'.[42]

The Presence of International Students and Scholars

The ready supply of international students, extremely responsive to the availability of financial support for graduate study, is another factor that dampens the negative feedback process. To understand just how important international students are to US science education, consider the fact that three of the top five BA-source institutions for those receiving PhDs in science and engineering in the US are located outside the US.

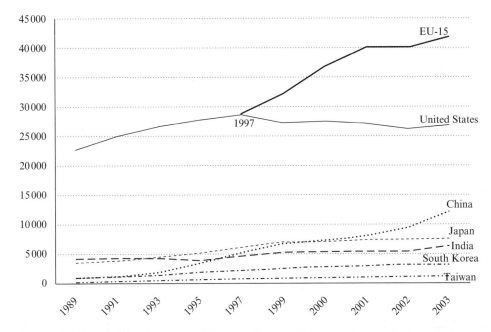

Source: National Science Foundation (2007: 5).

Figure 10.5   *Science and engineering doctorate production, selected country/economy, 1989–2003*

To be more specific, Tsinghua University heads the list, followed by its neighbor Peking University. The University of California Berkeley is third and Seoul National University takes fourth place. Cornell follows in fifth (Mervis, 2008).[43] It is not difficult to understand why students come to the US to pursue graduate study. Admission for full-time students generally comes with a research assistantship which pays between $20 000 and $30 000 as well as full tuition.

Some would argue that the supply of international graduate students is likely to diminish because of increasing competition, both outside the primary source countries of Asia as well as within these countries. And this is a factor that must be taken into consideration. As Figure 10.5 demonstrates, the US's position as the dominant trainer of PhDs in the world is being challenged by other countries and regions of the world. The EU-15 production, for example, has surpassed US production since 1997. More importantly, China, which produced less than 5 per cent of the number of PhDs produced by the US in 1989, produced approximately 50 per cent of what the US produced in 2003 (the latest date for which data are readily available).

This is only part of the story, however, given that the supply of those eligible to pursue graduate study is growing more rapidly outside the US than within. To wit, the number of Chinese students who have completed a BA in science and engineering has doubled in recent years, going from 268 400 in 1990 to 533 600 in 2002. By way of comparison, the number of BAs in science and engineering awarded in the US increased from 329 100 to 415 600 (an increase of 26 per cent) (National Science Foundation, 2007: Table 2).

Table 10.1   First-time full-time enrollment citizenship in US graduate programs in the biological sciences

Field/citizenship	2000	2001	2002	2003	2004	2005	2006	2007
US citizen/permanent resident	8355	8768	9261	9763	9808	9925	9946	10230
Temporary resident	2600	2840	2866	2956	2988	2993	3109	3255

Sources: Data for 2000–06 come from National Science Board (2008), Appendix Table 2-18. Data for 2007 come from Burns et al. (2009).

The dramatic increase in the number of PhDs bestowed outside the US also means that there is a growing supply of individuals to come to the US for postdoctoral training after receiving their PhD. And this is compatible with an incentive system which encourages faculty to substitute postdoctoral fellows for graduate students in their lab, given that graduate students, especially in private institutions, can cost the faculty more than a postdoc, since the PI is responsible not only for the stipend but also for tuition.

The stipends associated with postdoctoral positions make them particularly attractive to those on temporary visas. NIH guidelines, issued 27 March 2009, state a minimum of $37368 for those starting out; a minimum of $51552 for postdocs with seven or more years of experience. Some institutions pay more than this. Stanford University, for example, starts postdocs at $40785 and the Whitehead Institute starts postdocs at $47000. It is no wonder that the number of postdocs who are in the US on a temporary visa has grown dramatically. The advent of the 2009 stimulus package will, without a doubt, increase the number further.

Many assumed that visa restrictions associated with the US response to the events of September 11 would curtail the flow of graduate students and postdocs to the US. And it did in certain fields. But not in the biomedical sciences. Indeed, and unlike the overall trend, in no year since the data have been collected have first-time enrollments among full-time students in the biological sciences on temporary visas declined at US graduate schools. This is seen in Table 10.1.

7.   DISCUSSION

The positive feedback character of the biomedical labor market in the US is not inherent in the way in which research is conducted. Rather, it has evolved from a structure that has placed biomedical research in an institutional setting that has the license to staff labs with temporary workers. These temporary workers eventually leave with credentials that allow them to (try to) compete in the biomedical research tournament. It has been fed by a public, and a receptive Congress, eager to provide research funds to address 'popular' diseases.

There are a variety of ways to attenuate the positive-feedback mechanisms at work in this market. Three are discussed here. First, and most obvious, is a permanent and substantial cut in the research budget of US universities. Without research funds, many universities, especially those with lower-tier graduate programs, would be forced to dramatically cut or eliminate their PhD programs. Fewer students and postdocs would be trained and the pyramid nature of the research enterprise would be attenuated.

Is this likely to occur? Absolutely not. The public is too hungry for cures and Senators and Representatives are too happy to oblige, especially if it means supporting research in their state or district.[44] Moreover, pharmaceutical companies, who have benefited from much of the research performed in the university sector, represent a formidable lobby. The Congress may temporarily halt increases in funding for research, as it did in the years 2002–09, but a permanent and dramatic cut appears to be outside the political will. Furthermore, even if the Federal government were to curtail support for biomedical research, other sources of support exist. States have embraced biomedical research as a mechanism for economic growth and development; private foundations provide support; and industry also provides funds for biomedical research at universities.

A second alternative is to decouple the biomedical workforce from the training enterprise. The most straightforward way to do this is to staff university labs with permanent staff scientists, rather than with graduate students and postdocs. To some extent, this is already occurring, but not on a large enough scale to make a sizeable impact. Moreover, the staff scientist positions that have evolved often pay little more than a senior-postdoc position and offer little job security. For this alternative to have teeth, the position of staff scientist would need to be upgraded in three respects: (1) salary; (2) job security and (3) research independence. If PIs were increasingly to staff their labs with such staff scientists, research would be less coupled to training. NIH could encourage this by providing funds to support career-path staff scientist positions in the NIH budget.

University faculty, however, are likely to resist such a plan. PIs like the status quo: it provides flexibility, allowing them to downsize their labs in lean times and grow them when resources are plentiful, and graduate students and postdocs provide fresh, new ideas, which are absolutely key for faculty to do well in the biomedical tournament. Moreover, more permanent positions could provide competition for research space, always a concern at a university.

A third approach is to shift control of training funds away from PIs and towards the trainee or the department in which training occurs. The former could be done by awarding more fellowships for study directly to students. This accomplishes two things. First, it encourages selection on the basis of quality rather than on the basis of availability to staff a lab and meet a research objective of the PI. Second, it allows trainees to 'vote with their feet'. If students and postdocs are free agents they will arguably select programs that focus on addressing student needs. Moreover, they are more likely to inquire about job prospects if they are in a position to select where they train. A related way of addressing this goal is to place greater emphasis on training grants, providing resources to the department for training rather than to the PI. Such grants are peer-reviewed, while the quality of training, as we noted above, is not considered in the review of a research project. Moreover, training grants generally require students to rotate across labs, thereby decreasing the possibility that a student 'belongs' to a faculty member.

Again, this is unlikely to occur. For almost fifteen years, committees have been making such a recommendation. But the biomedical community is extremely resistant to such suggestions; the incentives are far too strong to cause them to shift course. And it is the senior investigators, not the trainees, who influence how funds are allocated.

In short, the presence of positive feedbacks in the biomedical workforce is a result of system-wide problems. Any fix requires changing incentives. This is unlikely to occur as long as the US Congress and faculty have their way.

NOTES

1. The author wishes to thank Erin Coffman for research assistance and Bill Amis for helpful suggestions on an earlier draft of this chapter. Portions of this chapter are drawn from Stephan (2011).
2. Computed on the basis of fractional counts.
3. Approximately a third of the PIs were affiliated with departments of engineering, a third with departments of chemistry and the remainder with departments of physics.
4. The Lindquist lab is large compared to the labs of her colleagues at MIT in biochemistry and biophysics, which have an average of 6.3 graduate students (median of 7) and average of 5.25 postdocs (median of 5).
5. Details regarding research and staffing are available for 17 of the 26 via lab web pages. Three other faculty have web pages for their labs that are not fully developed. For the other six one can find reference to the name of their lab when searching the Internet.
6. In a similar manner, graduate students and postdocs working in Alexander Pines' lab at Berkeley, are referred to as 'pinenuts' and alumni are referred to as 'old pinenuts' (http://waugh.cchem.berkeley.edu/people/).
7. The graduate student amount includes stipend, fringe benefits and tuition and is based on the amount allowed by NIH for the Ruth Kirstein NRSA fellowship for FY 2007. Many institutions pattern their support for other students on the Kerstein fellowship. The postdoc figure includes stipend and fringe benefits; it is the average paid under NIH guidelines for postdocs with varying experience. The fringe estimate comes from Pelekanos (2008), as does the cost estimate for the technician.
8. The cost of mouse upkeep can rapidly add up. Irving Weissman of Stanford University reports that before Stanford changed its cage rates he was paying between $800 000 and $1 million a year to keep the 10 000 to 15 000 mice in his lab. Costs for keeping immune-deficient mice are far greater (on the order of $.65 per day), given their susceptibility to disease.
9. The primary sources of federal funds are National Institutes of Health (NIH), the Department of Energy (DOE), the Department of Defense (DOD) and, to a lesser extent, the National Science Foundation (NSF).
10. MIT, for example, distinguishes between postdoctoral associates and postdoctoral fellows. The former are supported through grants that faculty have procured at MIT; the latter have received fellowships or stipends to work with a faculty member at MIT.
11. A survey of medical schools found that tenure is accompanied with no financial guarantee for 35 per cent of basic science faculty and 38 per cent of clinical faculty (Bunton and Mallon, 2007).
12. Using National Research Council rankings, she finds that the mean difference is 25.9 per cent in 'top' departments; 35.9 per cent in 'middle' departments and 53.2 per cent in 'bottom' departments. These calculations do not include mean differences between native students in native labs versus native students in non-native labs.
13. RSA, an algorithm for a public-key cryptosystem and the algorithm of choice for encrypting Internet credit-card transactions, was published in 1977 by Ron Rivest, Adi Shamir, and Leonard Adleman (hence the name RSA). Recognition is also awarded by attaching a scientist's name to a building, professorship, or lecture series, although this form of recognition usually comes after the death of the scientist while eponymy can occur during the scientist's life.
14. http://www.centeroncongress.org/learn_about/feature/qa_members.html#age.
15. At the time of this writing, it is unclear what the fate of the NIH budget will be after the stimulus funds expire. To be more precise, it is unclear whether NIH will receive funds to offset the loss of stimulus moneys.
16. NIH spent the rest of the first-year stimulus funds on competing revisions (supplements to existing awards) and on summer supplements ('Preliminary NIH ARRA FY2009 Funding', see http://report.nih.gov/PDF/Preliminary_NIH_ARRA_FY2009_Funding.pdf).
17. http://www.hhmi.org/about/growth.html.
18. http://www.niaid.nih.gov/ncn/newsletters/2008/1217.htm#n01.
19. NIH recently made major modifications in its peer review system in an effort to address various concerns. To wit, it has restricted the length of the proposal (cutting it from 25 to 12 pages beginning in January of 2010), and streamlined the quantity and format of written comments expected from reviewers. NIH also modified the scoring system, resulting in a two-digit score rather than a three-digit score, and instituted a policy to score and rank all proposals, thereby effectively abolishing triage.
20. See http://report.nih.gov/award/success/Success_ByIC.cfm. Excluded from the discussion are institutes that received fewer than 500 proposals and the NCCAM (National Center for Complementary and Alternative Medicine).
21. http://report.nih.gov/award/success/Success_ByIC.cfm.
22. Scheraga, who was born in 1921, may be the oldest NIH investigator. In March of 2009 he wound down another NIH grant for experimental work and in the process freed up lab space for a new faculty member. (see Kaiser, 2008b).

23. PowerPoint 'Update on NIH Peer Review', distributed by National Institute of General Medical Sciences Advisory Council.
24. See Heinig et al. (2007) for a discussion of the dramatic increase in building that occurred at American medical schools.
25. See Research Portfolio Online Reporting Tool RePORT, http://report.nih.gov/NIHDatabook/Charts/SlideGen.aspx?chartId=126&catId=1.
26. The number of first-time investigators who received R01 (or equivalent funds) from NIH went from 1439 in 1998 to 1559 in 2003 (NIH, Office of Extramural Research). There was a considerable increase, however, in the number of R03 and R21 awards made to new investigators. Both are small (the R03 is for $50 000 for two years; the R21 is for two years and cannot exceed $275 000 in direct costs). ⸱
27. PowerPoint 'Update on NIH Peer Review', distributed by National Institute of General Medical Sciences Advisory Council.
28. Data in the report allow one to differentiate between general life sciences and the biomedical sciences. The data provided here are for the biomedical sciences.
29. All data are taken from National Research Council, (1998).
30. Training grants were established in 1974 when Congress established the National Research Service Awards (NRSA). In the early years, the program provided over two-thirds of the support for graduate and postdoctoral training. Today it funds about 15 per cent of the total number of trainees. See Committee to Study the Changing Needs for Biomedical, Behavioral, and Clinical Research Personnel hand-out distributed at NIGMS.
31. Data come from presentation made to members of an ad hoc committee assembled to discuss workforce issues, American Association of Medical Colleges, 5 March 2008.
32. It is still too early to know the degree to which such programs have been successful.
33. This decline, of course, may be in name only since at approximately the same time many institutions, in response to the gentleman's agreement that a postdoc position not last longer than five years, began to develop new, creative titles, for senior postdocs.
34. 33 per cent of US-trained PhDs working at medical schools were in non-tenure track positions in 1993. By 2003, 45 per cent were in non-tenure track positions.
35. Biomedical Research Workforce, Background Information, 7 September 2007. Prepared by OER, NIH. Slide 29.
36. Faculty Roster Data, American Association of Medical Colleges.
37. Elias Zurhuni and the NIH leadership put special emphasis on the young; the number awarded to new investigators has grown in very recent years.
38. Data come for OER, NIH, and were prepared for GREAT. See Stephan, 2007.
39. Editorial, *Nature*, 23 August 2007, 448, pp. 839–40. The editorial was based on data released by FASEB, summarizing the career trajectories of young life scientists.
40. Davis (2005) reports that 1110 of the 2770 respondents in the survey of postdocs that he fielded indicated that they were looking for a job. Among these, 72.7 per cent were 'very interested' in a job at a research university and 23.0 per cent were 'somewhat interested'.
41. For each field, the top ten programs, as ranked by the National Research Council in 1995, were surveyed, as well as the five programs rated 21–25.
42. The web page goes on to say 'Other areas . . . include medical school, teaching, science publishing, investment banking, patent law and venture capital' but provides no specific placement information.
43. The calculations are for degrees awarded between 2004 and 2006. The University of Michigan, Ann Arbor holds sixth place. Just a few years earlier the University of California Berkeley was the number-one undergraduate institution.
44. Congressional representation affects NIH allocations and (indirectly) the distribution of grants. Powerful congressmen, for example, can provide guidance on the allocation and disbursement of appropriated funds, and can direct reallocations among various NIH institutes and support funds for specific diseases. In recent years, having an additional member on the appropriate subcommittee of the House Appropriations Committee that deals with the NIH budget increased NIH funding to public universities in the member's state by 8.8 per cent (Hedge and Mowery, 2008).

REFERENCES

American Academy of Arts and Sciences (2008), 'Investing in early-career scientists and high-risk, high-reward research: Advancing Research in Science and Engineering (ARISE) report', American Academy of Arts and Sciences, http://www.amacad.org/ariseFolder/ariseReport.pdf.

Britt, R. (2009), 'Federal government is largest source of university R&D funding in S&E: share drops in FY 2008', *InfoBrief*, Science Resources Statistics, National Science Foundation, 09-318.

Bunton, S.A. and Mallon, W.T. (2007), 'The continued evolution of faculty appointment and tenure policies at US medical schools', *Academic Medicine*, **82**, 281–89.

Burns, L., Einaudi, P. and Green, P. (2009), 'S&E graduate enrollments accelerate in 2007: enrollments of foreign students reach new highs', National Science Foundation 09-314, Division of Science Resource Statistics, National Science Foundation.

Congressional Quarterly (2008), *Guide to Congress*, 6th edition, Washington, DC: CQ Press.

Davis, G. (2007), 'NIH budget doubling: side effects and solutions', Presentation, Harvard University, 12 March.

Davis, J. (2005), 'The Sigma Xi Postdoc Survey', Sigma Xi, http://postdoc.sigmaxi.org.

Ehrenberg, R., Rizzo, M. and Jakubson, G.H. (2007), 'Who bears the growing costs of science at universities?', in Stephan, P. and Ehrenberg, R. (eds) *Science and the University*, Madison, WI: University of Wisconsin Press, pp. 19–35.

Freeman, R., Weinstein, W., Marincola, E., Rosenbaum, J. and Solomon, F. (2001), 'Competition and careers in biosciences', *Science*, **294**, 2293–4.

Gaulé, P. and Piacentini, M. (2010), 'Chinese graduate students and US scientific productivity: evidence from chemistry', http://www.ucl.be/cps/ucl/doc/econ/documents/IRS_Piacentini.pdf.

Hedge, D. and Mowery, D.C. (2008), 'Politics and funding in the US public biomedical R&D system', *Science*, **332**, 1797–98.

Heinig, S.J., Krakower, J.Y., Dickler, H.B. and Korn, D. (2007), 'Sustaining the engine of US biomedical discovery', *The New England Journal of Medicine*, **357**, 1042–47.

Kaiser, J. (2008a), 'HHMI's Cech signs off on his biggest experiment', *Science*, **320**, 164.

Kaiser, J. (2008b), 'The graying of NIH research', *Science*, **322**, 848.

Kaiser, J. (2008c), 'NIH urged to focus on new ideas, new applicants', *Science*, **319**, 1169.

Kerr, W. (2008), 'Ethnic scientific communities and international technology diffusion', *Review of Economics and Statistics*, **90**, 518–30.

Lazear, E.P. and Rosen, S. (1981), 'Rank order tournaments as optimum labor contracts', *Journal of Political Economy*, **89**, 841–64.

Malakoff, D. (2000), 'The rise of the mouse: biomedicine's model mammal', *Science*, **288**, 248–53.

Mervis, J. (2008), 'Top PhD feeder schools are now Chinese', *Science*, **321**, 185.

National Institutes of Health (2009), *NIH Almanac*, Office of Communications and Public Liaison, National Institutes of Health, Bethesda, Maryland.

National Research Council (1998), *Trends in the Early Careers of Life Scientists*, Committee on Dimensions, Causes and Implications of Recent Trends in the Careers of Life Scientists, The National Academies Press.

National Science Board (2008), *Science and Engineering Indicators 2008*, 2 vols, Arlington, Virginia: National Science Foundation.

National Science Board (2010), *Science and Engineering Indicators 2010*, 2 vols, Arlington, Virginia: National Science Foundation.

National Science Foundation (2007), *Asia's Rising Science and Technology Strength: Comparative Indicators for Asia, the European Union, and the United States*, NSF 07-319, Arlington, Virginia.

National Science Foundation (2009a), *Doctorate Recipients from US Universities: Summary Report 2007–08*, Arlington, Virginia.

National Science Foundation (2009b), WebCASPAR database, National Science Foundation, Arlington, Virginia, http://webcaspar.nsf.gov.

Pelekanos, A. (2008), 'Money management for scientists: lab budgets and funding issues for young PIs', *Science Alliance eBriefing*, New York Academy of Sciences, http://classic.nysa.org/SA/Career/Career.asp?articleID=60.

Penning, T. (1998), 'The postdoctoral experience: an associate dean's perspective', *The Scientist* **12**, 9.

Romer, P. (2000), 'Should the government subsidize supply or demand in the market for scientists and engineers?', National Bureau of Economic Research Working Paper 7723.

Stephan, P. (2007), 'Early careers for biomedical scientists: doubling (and troubling) outcomes', Presentation, Harvard University, 26 February.

Stephan, P. (2008), 'Job market effects on scientific productivity', in Albert, M., Schmidtchen, D. and Voigt, S. (eds), *Scientific Competition*, Tübingen: Mohr Siebeck.

Stephan, P. (2009), 'Tracking the placement of students as a measure of technology transfer', in Libecap, G. (ed.), *Measuring the Social Value of Innovation: A Link in the University Technology Transfer and Entrepreneurship Equation*, Bingley, UK: JAI press, pp. 113–40.

Stephan, P. (2010), 'The economics of science', in Hall, B. and Rosenberg, N. (eds), *Handbook of the Economics of Innovation*, Vol. 1, Oxford: Elsevier Press, Chapter 5.

Stephan, P. (2011), *Economics of Science*, in progress.

Stephan, P., Black, G. and Chang, T. (2007), 'The small size of the small scale market: the early-stage labor market for highly skilled nanotechnology workers', *Research Policy*, **36**, 887–92.

Stephan, P. and Levin, S. (1992), *Striking the Mother Lode in Science: The Importance of Age, Place and Time*, New York: Oxford University Press.

Stephan, P. and Levin, S. (2002), 'The importance of implicit contracts in collaborative scientific research', in Mirowski, P. and Sent, E.-M. (eds), *Science Bought and Sold: Essays in the Economics of Science*, Chicago and London: University of Chicago Press, pp. 412–30.

Tanyildiz, E. (2008), 'The effects of networks on institution selection by foreign doctoral students in the US', PhD Dissertation, Georgia State University.

Teitelbaum, M. (2008), 'Structural disequilibria in biomedical research', *Science*, **321**, 644–45.

Vietorisz, T. and Harrison, B. (1973), 'Labor market segmentation: positive feedback and divergent development', *American Economic Review*, **63**, 366–76.

11 University–industry interactions: the unresolved puzzle

Isabel Maria Bodas Freitas, Aldo Geuna and Federica Rossi

1. INTRODUCTION

Theoretical advances in the economics of knowledge and innovation since the 1980s conceptualize knowledge as partly tacit, sticky, context-dependent and idiosyncratic, and see knowledge creation as a collective, localized and path dependent process (Antonelli, 2005). Consistent with this view of knowledge is the argument that interactions among economic agents to acquire particular skills, are fundamental to the production and exchange of knowledge – particularly 'qualified' interactions that last over time and often involve the establishment of organizational frameworks to support the collaboration (as opposed to 'spot' market transactions) (Lundvall, 1985; Nooteboom, 2004).

The term 'university–industry knowledge transfer' is used to indicate a wide range of interactions at different levels, involving various activities aimed mostly at the exchange of knowledge and technology between universities and firms. These interactions on the side of universities are often described as 'third stream' or 'third mission' activities. They include, for example, collaborative research with firms, contract research and academic consulting commissioned by industry, the development and commercialization of intellectual property rights (IPRs), the creation of start-up firms to exploit university inventions, co-operation with firms on graduate training, and training and exchanges with industry researchers (Debackere, 2004; D'Este and Patel, 2007).

In most advanced economies since the 1980s, views have changed regarding the role of universities in the economic system. From being seen as 'ivory towers' where academics performed research in isolation, the contemporary university is seen as an economic organization that engages actively with external stakeholders. At the same time, the scale and scope of university–industry knowledge transfer activities have increased. These increases can be measured quantitatively in terms of university-assigned patents (Henderson et al., 1998; Geuna and Nesta, 2006), papers co-authored with industry (Hicks and Hamilton, 1999), income from royalties (Feller, 1990; Argyres and Liebeskind, 1998; AUTM, 2002), and industry funding for academic research (Slaughter and Rhoades, 1996; Geuna, 1999). The period 1980–2000 was characterized by a marked transformation in the mode of governance of university–industry interactions. The traditional models were personal contracts between academic scientists and company researchers, and intermediation through dedicated public research centres. However, new methods have been developed to achieve prompt transfer and exchange of knowledge, which is crucial for firms facing continuously increasing competition from low cost producers, and rapid obsolescence of products. Many attempts (in different countries) have been made to develop a new institutional infrastructure able to support knowledge diffusion between universities and firms (Block, 2008; Geuna and Muscio, 2009). A central tenet of these new systems is that the university must take an active part in the governance of knowledge transfer. Knowledge transfer is becoming institutionalized, and seen as a new role conferred on the university, rather than on individual university researchers or public research organizations. This qualitative change in the nature of the relationships between industry and academia has been accompanied by the emergence of visible new organizational forms such as university–industry liaison offices, technology licensing offices, technology transfer offices, industry–university research centres, research joint ventures, university spin-offs and technology consultancies (Peters and Etzkowitz, 1990; Cohen et al., 2002; Rothaermel and Thursby, 2005; Link et al., 2007). It has also entailed the development of a new set of 'rules of engagement' to coordinate the interactions between academic and company scientists.

This chapter focuses on the knowledge transfer processes involved in university–industry research collaborations based on contractual arrangements – personal and institutional – as opposed to purely commercial relationships based on the exchange of intellectual property, or student placements and staff secondments. It attempts to explain the rationales behind different forms of governance for university–industry collaboration, and the factors for success in a dynamic context. Although several studies examine the determinants of university–industry collaboration, very little work has been done on their modes of governance. Thus, we do not know what are the effects of personal contractual as opposed to institutional governance, on knowledge transfer and subsequent economic development, or what might be the best form of governance for these collaborations. The discussion is limited to universities since, in most countries, public research centres have become relatively less important since the 1990s (Senker, 1999).

This chapter is organized in three main sections. Section 2 discusses the context surrounding university–industry relationships and tries to explain why some 30 years of policy action have not yet succeeded in creating an organic infrastructure to support interactions between firms and universities. We argue that in order to understand these interactions it is necessary to understand the different governance models for university–industry collaboration (personal contractual and institutional). Failure to appreciate the specificities of these two models, their mutual feedbacks and the historical reasons for their persistence, has led to policies that overlook an important part of the knowledge transfer phenomenon and create incentives that can impede rather than support knowledge flows. We suggest that policy often emphasizes the role of institutionalized knowledge transfer channels, at the expense of less visible, but equally important personal contractual channels. We propose a framework to analyse the advantages and limitations of these governance models. Section 3 discusses the complexity of university–industry interactions. It reviews and synthesizes the large body of empirical evidence on university–firm interactions across countries, focusing on three main levels of analysis, the firm, the university and the researcher (Sections 3.1, 3.2, 3.3). We then discuss the measurement problems that affect the study of the phenomenon (Section 3.4). Section 4 describes a specific case of university–industry collaboration in the Piedmont region, in the north of Italy, and provides evidence of the coexistence and importance of personal and institutional governance structures. The data were collected via two original surveys (one addressed to a sample of regional firms and the other to a sample of industry inventors resident in the region), which provide detailed information on both types of interactions and the impact of interaction on innovation in companies. Section 5 offers some conclusions.

2.   A CRITICAL FRAMEWORK TO ANALYSE UNIVERSITY– INDUSTRY RELATIONSHIPS

There is empirical evidence of more intense university–industry collaboration since the 1980s. There are several arguments in the economics of knowledge production and use as to why interaction with universities has become more attractive for firms, and why policymakers are putting pressure on universities to engage in knowledge-based transactions with industry partners.

The economic understanding of knowledge has changed considerably since the 1950s (Dosi et al., 2006). Initially, knowledge was seen as equivalent to information – that is, the symbolic representation of the knowledge content that is tangible and transmissible. In discussing the properties of information as an economic good, Arrow (1962) highlighted appropriability issues related to information being non-rivalrous, non-excludable and asymmetric in terms of assessments of its content (which leads to the so-called 'Arrow's paradox'). These problems have resulted in the failure of decentralized markets to provide a sufficient amount of this good. Scientific knowledge in particular, was regarded as possessing many of the features typical of durable public goods: '(i) it does not lose validity due to use or the passage of time per se, (ii) it can be enjoyed jointly, and (iii) costly measures must be taken to restrict access to those who do not have a "right" to use it' (Dasgupta and David, 1994: 493). Nelson (1959) showed that private investment in basic research activities is likely to be suboptimal, because of the serendipity, large externalities and uncertainty that characterize research outcomes, and which cause their social returns to be larger than their private returns. To overcome the market inefficiencies associated with basic research, public intervention is required (Mowery, 1983): governments can engage directly in the production of knowledge, making it freely available for use, or they can provide subsidies to private knowledge producers in return for research outcomes being made public (Dasgupta and David, 1994). The latter scheme corresponds to the academic research system: businesses accept a system of taxation, which results in revenue being transferred to academia, which, in its turn, manages the open science system of knowledge production (Antonelli, 2008a).

Progressively, contributions from various sources have led to the emergence of a different view of knowledge, characterized by different and more complex economic properties than those encompassed by either fully public or fully private goods. Even before the 1970s, studies of human learning were demonstrating that individual learning always includes a tacit, non-expressible dimension and, consequently, that knowledge exchange is not instantaneous, but requires practice and the active participation of learning partners (Ryle, 1949; Polanyi, 1966). The recognition that knowledge cannot be reduced to information, undermines some of the assumptions that underpin the conventional economic interpretation of knowledge-producing activities. First, since knowledge is often specific to the context in which it was generated, it may be difficult to transfer without the assistance of its creator and, consequently, its imitation costs may be high: certain forms of knowledge have quite high levels of in-built appropriability and exclusivity (Levin et al., 1987). Second, attention to the tacit dimension of knowledge has led scholars to re-examine the nature of scientific research activity leading to agreement that scientific knowledge is to an extent tacit. It draws upon skills and techniques 'that are acquired experientially, and transferred by demonstration, by personal instruction and by the provision of expert services (advice, consultations, and so forth), rather than being reduced to conscious and codified methods and procedures' (Dasgupta and David, 1994: 494). This blurs the distinction between scientific and technological knowledge: both types of knowledge contain tacit and codified elements.[1] Third, there is increasing agreement that the production of new knowledge often requires the recombination of knowledge from several sources. Interactions among agents possessing different cognitive resources are considered crucial for the production of new knowledge (Nooteboom, 2004): the semantic ambiguity that results from these relationships is a powerful mechanism for innovation (Lane and Maxfield, 1997, 2005; Fonseca, 2002). These interactions need to be longer lasting than spot market transactions in order to reduce the cognitive distance among the agents involved, to facilitate communication. Knowledge transmission requires cognitive, geographical, cultural and social proximity among agents (Balconi et al., 2004).

The importance of these types of relationships has increased over time for several reasons. First, the production of new knowledge requires the integration and recombination of existing sources of knowledge. The complexity of the knowledge base of innovative firms increases depending on its cumulative (building on existing knowledge), complementary (requiring the integration of complementary types of knowledge), and composite (requiring the combination of different 'bits' of knowledge held by multiple agents) nature. Several studies support the claim that, as technological knowledge cumulates and expands, firms become increasingly dependent on a wider range of knowledge fields to develop innovations (Powell et al., 1996; Pavitt, 1998a; Nesta and Saviotti, 2005). Over time, the increased complexity of products and processes induces firms to seek complementary competences outside their boundaries. Second, uncertainty plays a role. In addition to uncertainty about the outcome of research activities – in terms of timing, direction, potential to open up new avenues of research – the economic context in which firms operate is another major source of uncertainty. The increasing pace of organizational and technological change generates what Lane and Maxfield (2005) define as 'ontological uncertainty' or situations that render economic agents uncertain about what processes and what other agents are likely to impinge on their actions. In these conditions, agents become not only unable to formulate a probability distribution for a set of outcomes – as in the concept of non-probabilizable risk which characterizes Knightian uncertainty – but may be unable even to conceive a tentative list of outcomes. Firms that face ontological uncertainty have a strong incentive to pursue qualified interactions with other organizations, in order to exert some influence over the many complex processes that ultimately will affect the results of their own activities. Organizations can counter uncertainty by constructing long lasting inter-organizational structures (what Lane and Maxfield (1997) call 'scaffolding structures'), which provide relatively stable contexts for shorter-term inter-organizational interactions and planning. Examples of scaffolding structures are inter-firm alliances, user organizations, forums, trade associations, fairs and exhibitions, standards setting organizations, and so on.

The increasing uncertainty of the economic environment combined with the increased complexity of technological systems, is driving innovation processes to become more open and distributed (Chesbrough, 2003; Powell and Grodal, 2005). In such conditions of high uncertainty and complexity, pursuing qualified interactions with universities can be advantageous for firms (Rossi, 2010):

- they can access wide, international networks of scientists with heterogeneous competences; this provides increasing opportunities to establish relationships with high potential to generate innovations (Lane and Maxfield, 1997; Antonelli, 2008a), especially as industrial production has a growing scientific and technological content (Geuna, 1999; Mokyr, 1990);
- they can hedge against uncertainty through the opportunity to monitor numerous innovation processes at the same time and keep up to date with scientific developments (Meyer-Krahmer and Schmoch, 1998);
- learning and research opportunities are enhanced by the possibility to access new knowledge in the form of infrastructures (laboratories, databases) and secondments of researchers and scientists to academic institutions.

Thus, university–industry interaction as a means of access to and development of knowledge cannot be one-off (Meyer-Krahmer and Schmoch, 1998; Cohen et al., 2002).

Interaction with universities can also be cost effective for firms. The economics of knowledge shows that the costs of knowledge production are lower in the academic than in the private research system because of the split structure of academic salaries (Dasgupta and David, 1994). University researchers' fixed costs are covered by the payment received for their teaching activities, so that 'the compensation schemes practiced in the academic system allow the supply side to operate on a variable cost base' (Antonelli, 2008a: 12). Also, a university affiliation signals quality and competence, based upon the institution's reputation in the open science system: the existence of an independent system that confirms the competence of academic researchers lowers firms' search costs for high quality competences and reduces the agency problems inherent in collaborations with knowledge workers whose skills are difficult to assess (Antonelli, 2008a).

At the same time, universities have become more interested in collaborating with firms. On the one hand, the historical context, such as the reduced drive to fund university research for military reasons, and the move towards reduced government intervention in the economy, have encouraged universities actively to seek commercial transactions with external stakeholders in order to reduce their dependence on public grants (Geuna and Muscio, 2009). On the other hand, many governments have introduced incentives for universities to engage in third stream activities, premised on the expectation that university–industry interactions will increase the rate of innovation in the economy (Spencer, 2001). The argument that enforcement of property rights could foster the emergence of efficient markets for knowledge, was the justification for the introduction, in the 1980s and 1990s, of policies to promote patenting by universities, while the interpretation of knowledge as partly tacit, cumulative and collective, has fostered the view that the transfer of knowledge requires purposeful interaction among economic agents, and justified the creation of incentives for universities to engage in direct interactions with industry in the context of qualified relationships. Since the 1970s, governments have supported numerous such programmes (Cohen et al., 2002). In the US, the National Science Foundation established the first set of university–industry cooperative research centres in 1975, in the first steps towards instituting direct knowledge transfer to industry as a university mission. In 1980, the Stevenson–Wyndler Act in the US, mandated that Federal Laboratories spend part of their funds on technology transfer activities, and encouraged them to engage in direct collaborations with state and local governments, universities and private firms. These measures were followed by many others aimed at strengthening the basis for collaboration between universities and firms (for example, the 1985 Federal Technology Transfer Act, the 1986 National Competitiveness Technology Transfer Act, the 1989 Small Business Research and Development Act). Similar measures were introduced in Europe. In 1983, the UK launched the Alvey Programme to support university–industry research projects in information technology. This was followed by a range of government programmes aimed at strengthening links with industry, which culminated in the launch of the Higher Education Innovation Fund in 2001. University–industry interactions were a part of the ESPRIT programme (started in 1983) and one of the building blocks of the European Commission's Framework Programmes, the first of which was launched in 1984.

Most of the policies introduced to promote university knowledge transfer activities emphasize the role and importance of institutional university–industry relationships mediated by specialized units such as knowledge transfer organizations (KTOs), or by university departments and other administrative units. Consequently, in most cases, the creation of an institutional infrastructure for knowledge exchange between universities and firms has been the outcome of policy actions oriented to the creation of structured third stream activities within the university (Macdonald, 2010). Exceptions include Stanford and Katholieke Universiteit Leuven, where the creation of such an infrastructure was based on a request for institutional support from the academics involved in these interactions and the universities' desire to regulate and benefit from industry contracts.

A problem with this approach to knowledge transfer policy is that it ignores the specificities of the socio-economic-institutional context and the fields of research. It is possible that different disciplines and research areas, and also different types of higher education institutions embedded in different local contexts, would fit with different models of knowledge transfer. There is, in fact, another important mode of governance for university–industry collaboration: formal personal contractual collaborations between university researchers and firm engineers and researchers (Geuna and Muscio, 2009). This type of governance is based on participation in the same social and professional networks (Colyvas et al., 2002), and some form of trust (sometimes a common educational background, as in the case of alumni members or of the *esprit de corps* of the French Grandes Écoles and the Italian Politecnici). However, these interactions generally are not informal: they are usually defined in binding contracts and agreements which are not mediated by university structures. Historically, personal contractual collaboration predates the institutionalization of university–industry linkages: individual collaborations between academics and industry scientists were taking place at the end of the nineteenth century in Germany, and in the early twentieth century in the US (Meyer-Thurow, 1982; Liebenau, 1985; Swann, 1989; MacGarvie and Furman, 2005). This type of governance structure tends to be dismissed as being of lesser importance, sometimes confused or mixed with personal informal relationships or subsumed under 'consulting' and assumed to be 'soft' rather than 'hard' research. However, empirical evidence confirms that these relationships involve knowledge production as well as the transfer and application of existing knowledge (see empirical analysis in Section 4).

Gibbons et al. (1994) and Etzkowitz and Leydesdorff (2000) argue that the supposedly more efficient new institutional knowledge transfer model is substituting for the older model, which as a result is disappearing. We would suggest instead that these models of governance are coexisting and have important positive and negative interdependencies that need to be understood for the development of an effective and efficient knowledge transfer infrastructure. We would argue that, although (for the reasons described above) qualified interactions mediated by university institutional structures may be more attractive when firms need to manage complex projects characterized by uncertainty and technological complexity, personal contractual interactions present advantages in terms of immediacy, flexibility and convenience. Different firms may be inclined to use different forms of collaboration depending upon the resources they can dedicate to cooperative activities and the organizational forms they rely on to innovate. In addition, use of these two models of governance of collaboration by a firm is not mutually exclusive: firms can choose between modes, depending on their needs and the types of support they need to access. Finally, and relatedly, the policy framework is important in driving firm choice: that public funds often are available only for university-mediated interactions, for example, is an important determinant of the firm's choice to set up an institutionalized form of collaboration. In countries where there are fewer public policies to support the institutional model, we would expect both models of governance of university–industry relationships to thrive in response to different knowledge exchange needs. Section 4 provides some evidence of the co-existence of these two models in Piedmont, and discusses their specificities and relative advantages for knowledge transfer.

An exclusive focus on the institutionalization of knowledge transfer has informed a large number of attempts to improve firm–university interactions, which are sometimes much less successful than expected. For example, income from technology transfer is very skewed, with very few universities making much money from patents and licences (Charles and Conway, 2001; Bulut and Moschini, 2006), the direct costs of IPR usually exceed revenues (Charles and Conway, 2001) and many university technology transfer offices struggle to be profitable (Kenney, 1986). It appears also that technology transfer offices play a very small part in establishing links with industry (Colyvas et al., 2002), most of which are based on the personal contacts of academics (Jansen and Dillon, 2000). Thus, culture, history and values affect the impact of economic incentives in the development of new institutional set ups. The analysis below of the evolving problems and failures in university–industry interactions sheds interesting light on the complexities characterizing the developing disintegrated market for knowledge and the related governance structures.

3. WHAT WE KNOW AND DON'T KNOW ABOUT UNIVERSITY–INDUSTRY RELATIONSHIPS

University–industry relationships involve collaboration between at least two types of organizations, a firm and a university – a department or a faculty, and perhaps mediation by a Knowledge Transfer Office (KTO). They are based on collaboration (or contracting) between academic researchers and firm researchers/project managers. We provide a brief review of the literature based on evidence collected in recent years on the characteristics of firms, universities and researchers. Although we can point to some stylized facts, no clear cut picture emerges. We also discuss the conceptual and measurement problems associated with lack of a clear understanding of the governance of university–industry collaboration and specifically personal contractual collaboration arrangements.

3.1 Firm Characteristics

Organizational characteristics, such as size, technological capabilities, industry and level of internationalization, affect the innovative objectives of firms and their motivations to collaborate with universities over research and development (R&D). Several studies show that firm size influences both the decision to interact with a university, and the content of the interaction. Larger firms and spin offs benefit most from public research, even after controlling for industry (Cohen et al., 2002; Belderbos et al., 2004b). For large firms, collaboration with universities may be a strategy designed to strengthen their skills and knowledge, and to gain access to non-core technologies; for small firms, university collaboration tends to focus on problem solving in core technological areas (Santoro and Chakrabarti, 2002) and gaining access to university facilities. Small firms do not seem to differ from larger ones in the use of students, publications, patents and labour mobility as channels of knowledge transfer. Small firms are less likely to engage in 'collaborative or contract research' to access university knowledge, mostly due to their limited financial and skills resources (Bekkers and Bodas Freitas, 2008). However, university spin-offs, and high-tech companies more generally (as in the case of the biotechnological industry), tend to engage in intensive interactions with universities and university researchers (Zucker et al., 2002). Evidence shows also that firms that invest heavily in R&D, especially within a diversified portfolio of innovative activities, have the absorptive capabilities to learn, and to maintain linkages with universities and public research institutes (Cohen et al., 2002; Fontana et al., 2006a; Bodas Freitas et al., 2011). Large firms that are active in R&D can derive benefits from collaboration across a wider spectrum of research/innovation activities. Collaboration with universities is more likely among firms that put greater effort into searching for external knowledge by screening publications databases, and that signal their competence by patenting (Laursen and Salter, 2004; Belderbos et al., 2004b; Fontana et al., 2006a). Collaboration with universities and government research institutes enables firms to improve their access to an even wider pool of sources (Bodas Freitas et al., 2010). Feldman and Kelley (2006) find that firms involved in collaborative research projects with universities financed by public grants develop more diverse sets of linkages to other firms and exhibit greater openness in terms of communicating their research results, than firms that do not engage in such projects.

The level of competition seems also to affect the likelihood of a firm innovating and collaborating with external actors (Laursen and Salter, 2006). Therefore, if the firm's largest market is the international market, it will be more likely to interact with public research organizations (Laursen and Salter, 2006; Bodas Freitas et al., 2011). Similarly, firms with very challenging innovation strategies are also more likely to collaborate. In particular, firms involved in radical innovation and integration of market and production objectives, generally are more likely to collaborate with public research organizations (Belderbos et al., 2004a; Bodas Freitas et al., 2011).

Finally, based on industry differences in patterns of technological change and innovation development, interaction with and access to knowledge developed at universities may be uneven across industries (Pavitt, 1984; Marsili, 2001; Salter and Martin, 2001; Grimpe and Sofka, 2009). Cohen et al. (2002) show that public research is critical for a small number of industries, and 'moderately important' in most of the manufacturing sector. Industry–university interaction is crucially important for science-based technologies when product innovation is based on a recent scientific discovery (Beise and Stahl, 1999; Koumpis and Pavitt, 1999; Schartinger et al., 2002; Monjon and Waelbroeck, 2003). Indeed, in industries where the technology develops fast, firms need to explore multiple technological trajectories, which often involves collaboration with universities (Belderbos et al., 2004a). For this reason, university collaboration is widespread in the biotechnological and pharmaceutical industries, which depend heavily on academic knowledge and very basic scientific research (McMillan et al., 2000; Cohen et al., 2002). However, science-based industrial activities may not be similar across countries. In some countries firms operating in science-based activities seem more dependent on collaboration with public research organizations; in others these firms follow a more market-oriented collaborative strategy for innovation development (Bodas Freitas et al., 2011). Also, Beise and Stahl (1999) find that the share of sales from products based on public research does not depend on whether or not the firm sector is R&D-intensive. University–industry collaboration may play different roles and be configured in different ways, in different industries. Meyer-Krahmer and Schmoch (1998) show that in science-based fields, university collaboration is focused on basic research and keeping abreast of knowledge developments, while in other fields, university collaboration focuses mainly on finding solutions to technical problems. Similarly, Bekkers and Bodas Freitas (2008) find that the differences in the use of a wide variety of channels do not depend on the industrial activities of firms, but rather on the context and the characteristics of the underlying knowledge and of the researchers involved.

3.2   University Characteristics

The propensity of universities to collaborate with firms varies and is strongly related to the disciplinary focus of the university. Other characteristics, such as research quality and technology transfer policies, may also have an effect.

Work on industrial firms shows that the more basic sciences (that is, mathematics, physics and biology, but not chemistry) tend to be seen as less important than applied science and engineering disciplines (Klevorick et al., 1995; Cohen et al., 2002). Industry is much more interested in collaborating on applied science, especially in disciplines like materials and computer science. However, as several authors note, the basic sciences are extremely important for the development of industrial innovation, although their effect is more often channelled through the applied sciences and engineering fields (Klevorick et al., 1995; Pavitt, 1998b; Cohen et al., 2002; Meyer-Krahmer and Schmoch, 1998). Based on interviews with industry and university researchers, Bekkers and Bodas Freitas (2008) find that the disciplinary origin of the knowledge affects the form of interaction used for the development and transfer of knowledge between academia and industry.

The research orientations of university departments have an impact on attitudes to knowledge transfer to industry. University departments focused on applied research and technological development tend to be more involved in the processes of knowledge transfer to industry (Lee, 1996; Bozeman, 2000; O'Shea et al., 2005). The organizational characteristics of research centres and faculties, on the other hand, seem not to affect the level and intensity of interactions with industry. For instance, Bozeman (1994) shows that there is no relationship between the effectiveness of technology transfer activities and the organization of university departments in terms of size, administrative intensity, hierarchy and number of organizational levels (that is, principal investigator, departments, projects, others).

There is empirical evidence suggesting that the university's technology transfer policy may influence the level of interaction with industry. US universities, which give higher percentages of royalty payments to their faculty members, are involved in more intense and more efficient technology transfer activities such as spin-offs and start-ups (Link and Siegel, 2005). Other studies show that the entrepreneurial activity of the research departments, measured as spin-off activity, decreases the higher is the share of the university licensing royalties allocated to inventors and their department (O'Shea et al., 2008; Markman et al., 2004).

Institutional differences in terms of amounts of industry financing received and quality of the university (obviously correlated) are good predictors of the involvement of scientists with industry (Ponomariov and Boardman, 2008). This appears to be related to the fact that top universities seem to provide easier access to the diverse set of resources required to create start-ups (Di Gregorio and Shane, 2003, O'Shea et al., 2008). Finally, D'Este and Patel (2007) show that the quality of university research does not affect the intensity of industrial interaction; in the case of UK universities, institutional characteristics are not as important as the characteristics of individual scientists, which is the subject of the next subsection.

3.3   Researcher Characteristics

The characteristics of individual researchers matter for the process of knowledge transfer. Highly productive tenured and senior academic researchers are more experienced and are more willing to participate in collaborative projects with industry (D'Este and Patel, 2007). Bozeman and Corley (2004) analyse the collaborative behaviours of scientists and find that researchers who take on mentoring roles (that is, help junior colleagues and graduate students by collaborating with them) are more enthusiastic about working with industry.

There is no strong evidence of substitution or crowding-out between patenting and publishing (Agrawal and Henderson, 2002; Jensen et al., 2003; Lee and Gaertner, 1994) and the most scientifically productive researchers are often those with the most patents, although this is likely to differ significantly across scientific fields with more basic fields showing some evidence of crowding-out (Geuna and Nesta, 2006; Stephan et al., 2007; Crespi et al., 2011). In basic science, researchers who interact with industry in a minor way (that is, the returns from this activity do not exceed 15 per cent of the researcher's budget), are more productive than those that do not collaborate with industry at all (Manjarrés-Henríquez et al., 2008). Also, researchers who interact with industry are more likely to obtain higher funding from competitive public sources than those who engage only in research (Bozeman and Gaughan, 2007; Manjarrés-Henríquez et al., 2008). However, the productivity of the highest performing scientists decreases with involvement in long-term relationships with one specific industry-related sponsor (Goldfarb,

2008). Researchers that own several patents and who are more entrepreneurial are more willing to engage in knowledge transfer to industry (Zucker et al., 2002; D'Este and Patel, 2007). Researchers who become entrepreneurs are likely to be older, to have a good scientific record and to be extroverts, and to have worked in departments that have produced prestigious scientists and have a track record for entrepreneurialism (O'Shea et al., 2008). At the same time, several studies find that academic entrepreneurship is driven mainly by the expectation of generating results that will improve the researcher's academic position, creating stimuli for further research activities, and resulting in prestige and reputation as a leading academic rather than as a business entrepreneur (Baldini et al., 2007; Fini et al., 2009; Baldini, 2008; Franzoni and Lissoni, 2009).

The importance attributed by academic and industrial researchers to university–industry interactions, the forms and channels of and barriers to these interactions, are related to the researchers' characteristics in terms of experience in patenting, in being entrepreneurial and in publishing (Bekkers and Bodas Freitas, 2008). Also, the research environments in universities and industries with a specific disciplinary emphasis and different focus on basic, applied and technological developments, create different incentives to use particular knowledge development and transfer mechanisms (Bekkers and Bodas Freitas, 2008).

3.4   A Conceptual and Measurement Puzzle

The discussion above shows how much work has been done on the characteristics of university–industry collaboration, and how little attention has been paid to the forms of governance of this relationship. There is no consensus on whether there is, or what is, the best form of governance, or on actual results in terms of level of knowledge transfer and specific contribution to economic development. Most empirical studies focus on high-tech industries, although the availability of Community Innovation Survey (CIS) type data has enabled the development of econometric analyses controlling for sector and technological differences. Discrepancies in the conclusions reached by these analyses are often associated with the methodology, with detailed interview-based case studies tending to highlight the importance of personal contacts and mobility in the transfer of knowledge, and quantitative studies underscoring the success of informal contacts and formal knowledge transfer channels managed by universities.

One reason for these inconsistent results is that most studies rely on imprecise measurements due to a lack of standardized, validated data on university–industry relationships. In addition to the common problem of data availability and comparability (most studies are based on one-off survey data or internal university information that is not standardized across universities), there are some conceptual and empirical sources of mis-measurement.

Although work on identifying communication channels has become quite sophisticated, it is limited by the implicit assumption that personal contacts are mainly informal, and thus considers more formal channels of knowledge transfer to be university-managed. Some firms and researchers may be bound by strict contracts which are managed personally without going through the university administration (personal contractual collaborations, in our framework). Many studies are based only on data made available by KTOs and, thus, capture only the set of interactions managed directly by the university (see, for example, Joly and Mangematin, 1996; Thursby et al., 2001). In the Anglo-Saxon context, where consultancy (formal personal contracts) is allowed and is formally regulated (depending on contracts and university regulations, faculty are usually permitted to spend one day a week on consulting) and reported (faculty are required to submit annual reports on outside professional activities), a few studies have considered formal academic consulting explicitly as a channel for knowledge transfer distinct from university-managed collaborations (see for example, Rebne, 1989; Cohen et al., 1998; D'Este and Perkmann, 2007; Jensen et al., 2010). These studies highlight the importance and specificity of personal arrangements.

Empirically, several studies use data collected via surveys of academics or/and firms, allowing consideration of a wider range of alternative knowledge transfer channels. However, these channels are investigated from different viewpoints and often are categorized differently. There is disagreement in the literature on their relative importance, although there is some consensus that several different channels often are used at the same time and that formal channels allowing commercialization of university knowledge (that is, spin offs, licences, patents) are among the least frequent (Schartinger et al., 2001; Cohen et al., 2002; D'Este and Patel, 2007). For example, Mowery and Sampat (2005) show that conferences and publications are more frequent channels of communication than patents and licences, and Cohen et al. (2002) confirm that formal transfers of IPR are not necessarily the most successful and common form of interaction.[2] According to Bruneel et al. (2009), for firms, conference attendance and graduate recruitment are the main types of interaction with universities, while Abreu et al. (2008) suggest that the most frequent types of interactions are within networks of collaborative research. D'Este and Perkmann (2007) analyse universities in the UK; they find that collaborative research projects, including consultancy, are a more important source of income than licensing. A study by Schartinger et al. (2001) highlights crucial inter-sectoral and inter-disciplinary differences with respect to the intensity with which the different channels are used. In categorizing knowledge transfer channels, Perkmann and Walsh (2006) propose a distinction between socialized and non-socialized collaborations, that is, between collaborations that involve the establishment of social relationships (sponsored research projects, research consortia, collaborative joint ventures, research centres) and those that are purely contractual (licensing, specific ad-hoc consultancy). However, other scholars highlight that all knowledge transfer channels, including less personalized ones, such as access to scientific publications and university patent licensing, are accompanied by the establishment of social relationships (Meyer-Krahmer and Schmoch, 1998; Bozeman et al., 1995).

The development of CIS surveys is providing researchers with comparable data to study university–industry linkages. However, the information is limited since these surveys simply ask whether firms have relationships with universities and, if so, for an indication of their importance. The CIS includes a question about the type of cooperation partner the firm found most valuable for its innovation activities. But respondents are not asked about the nature or governance of these relationships, which confuses university-mediated, institutional relationships with personal (formal or informal) collaborations. In addition, surveys are often responded to by managers who are probably more aware of commercial/business rather than science-related activities. An analysis of the responses to the CIS indicates that universities or other higher education institutions are generally considered not very important sources of information (in CIS-4 only 3 per cent of firms considered universities and other higher education institutions as highly important sources of information), and that companies collaborate with universities less frequently than with other partners. Such results are often emphasized in the policy literature, and point to a secondary role of university research as a source of knowledge for the innovation processes of companies (Paravan, 2007). However, when we consider the results of surveys, such as Yale (US), Carnagie-Mellon (US), and PACE (EU), which focus exclusively on knowledge flows and surveyed large R&D performing companies (and were addressed to R&D managers), the importance of university research increases (Cohen et al., 2002; Arundel and Geuna, 2004). The difference in part can be ascribed to the sampling procedure (CIS considers firms of all sizes) and to the fact that CIS results are not weighted by R&D spending. Arundel and Geuna (2004) show that for comparable samples, CIS results tend to be similar to PACE results showing higher importance of university research. Firm size, however, does not explain all the difference found. Indeed the focus of the survey on knowledge flows rather than on company innovation in general (such as CIS) can steer the attention of the respondents to a specific topic. Fontana et al. (2006b), using data from the KNOW survey (a survey focused on knowledge flows) of small and medium sized enterprises in Denmark, France, Germany, Greece, Italy, the Netherlands and the UK, find higher importance and higher use of university research than the CIS.

University–industry relationships have also been measured through international surveys addressed to inventors (company researchers) rather than R&D or other managers. Two recent examples are the European Community Inventor Survey – PatVal (Giuri et al., 2007) and Georgia Tech/RIETI Inventor Survey for the US and Japan (Walsh and Nagaoka, 2009). Analysis of the results of these surveys indicates high importance for university research. Although in Europe, research from universities seems to be less important than results from other sources (only public research organizations are considered less important than universities), it is considered highly important by 14 per cent of the respondents (compared to 19 per cent for suppliers) and much more important than in the case of the CIS survey. For the US (but not Japan), universities are on a par with competitors and suppliers as sources of research. Similarly, when we look at co-inventors and collaborative partners, universities are ranked just below suppliers and customers (Walsh and Nagaoka, 2009).

The evidence from survey-based measurements of university–industry collaboration indicates possible respondent and sample biases. First, comparing responses from managers, R&D managers and inventors, the importance and use of university research increases. Second, in CIS, sources of knowledge include universities, scientific publications and conferences: the focus is on knowledge channels rather than on knowledge contributions. However, this framing of alternatives does not include many of the channels of knowledge transfer from universities discussed in the literature. It also biases downwards the ranking of university knowledge, as the overall source of knowledge is the sum of the knowledge directly obtained from universities and the knowledge obtained from scientific publications and conferences that is mainly produced by academics. Policy often considers only statistics related to 'university and other higher education institutions', overlooking the fact that academic researchers are involved in the majority of scientific publications and conference presentations. Third, the aim and focus of CIS and surveys of knowledge flows are on capturing innovation (business) related activities and sources, which orients the respondents to focus upon industry, accountable, 'concrete' types of activities and sources. This usually results in comparative bias, that is, respondents are inclined to rank the most concrete sources of knowledge highest, and to understate the importance of interactions (for example personal contracts) that do not involve a clearly identified organization. It should be remembered also that sampling strategies (in relation to size and R&D) affect the way that academic knowledge is seen as contributing to firm innovation. This makes the use of aggregate statistics questionable, since smaller and less innovative firms are over represented while it is well known that radical innovation is concentrated in few large (or very small) high-tech companies and that its diffusion in the economy happens via user-producer interaction. Academic knowledge absorbed by large R&D intensive companies is subsequently transferred to the rest of the economy via commercial linkages, more efficiently than being transferred directly from universities (or university researchers). Small companies that lack the resources for interaction with universities inevitably will rank commercial sources as much more important than academic sources.

The evidence presented in this section together with the theoretical discussion in Section 2, emphasizes the complexity in the interactions between science and innovation represented by university–industry relationships. It highlights the need for a better understanding of their governance and points to the need for better conceptual and empirical measurement of the university–industry complex to inform policy action.

4.   THE CASE OF UNIVERSITY–INDUSTRY RELATIONSHIPS IN PIEDMONT

In this section, we provide some evidence on the two non-exclusive governance models of university–industry interactions presented in the previous section in the case of the Piedmont region in the North-West of Italy. We rely on two original surveys conducted in 2008–09: UIPIE (firm level) and PIEMINV (inventor level). We underline that the firms surveyed are all located in Piedmont, that is, in the same institutional, social and economic setting. This is important because it allows us to control for some of the determinants of different types of interactions.

Before discussing the governance of university–industry relationships in Piedmont we briefly examine the importance of universities as a source of information and as a innovation partners for companies and inventors on the basis of the information contained in the CIS and PatVal surveys. We use weighted data for the companies extracted from the national statistical office, ISTAT, CIS database. Universities are ranked as a highly important source by only 1.2 per cent of the respondents and 85 per cent consider this source of information as not useful.[3] When we look at co-operation partners, 5.3 per cent of companies collaborated with universities. This is similar to the rate of collaboration with competitors (5.4 per cent) and clients (5.1 per cent) and slightly lower than with suppliers (7.6 per cent) and consultants and other private research centres (7.0 per cent). Using information from the PatVal dataset for the sample of Piedmontese inventors, we find that the share of inventors reporting university laboratories and faculty as highly important sources of information is 8.2 per cent unweighted (24 per cent had used this

Table 11.1　Choice of governance mode for university–industry collaborations (firms)

	Observations	Share (%)
Sample	1 052	100
No collaboration	865	82.2
Institutional collaboration	104	9.9
Personal collaboration but no institutional collaboration	83	7.9

source), fourth after Customers (1), Competitors (2) and Suppliers (3) but higher than the score in the CIS.[4] The evidence presented confirms the discussion in Section 3 on differences in the various measurements of university–industry interaction. The importance (use) of universities for industry innovation varies depending on who responds to the survey, and on its objectives and structure.

Next we look at the co-existence of the personal and institutional modes of governance for university–industry interactions. Based on data from the UIPIE survey[5] of Piedmontese firms (Bodas Freitas et al., 2010), Table 11.1 reports the shares of: firms that engaged in institutional collaborations with universities; firms that engaged only in personal contractual collaborations with individual university researchers; and firms that did not collaborate at all.

Based on data from the PIEMINV survey of Piedmontese inventors,[6] Table 11.2 presents the shares of inventors and the channels of knowledge-transfer within different governance modes.

The results of these two surveys are consistent in showing that personal contractual collaborations are as important as institutional cooperation. Thus, a focus on the latter overlooks an important part of this phenomenon. The managers' survey (Table 11.1) shows that in 2006–08, 10 per cent of Piedmontese firms engaged in institutional collaboration and 8 per cent in personal contractual collaboration. Among the inventors surveyed (Table 11.2), at least 25 per cent reported engaging in institutional collaboration with a university and just less than 25 per cent had collaborated through personal contracts. As expected, surveying inventors rather than firms, where a manager is the respondent, increases the importance and use of university research.

Table 11.3 shows that there is positive correlation between the use of either governance form as well as some other forms: in other words, firms use the various governance forms in complementary ways. This applies particularly to different kinds of institutional collaborations where a very high share of firms collaborating with universities with the support of public funds, also engage in institutional contracts financed by the firms themselves. The correlations are positive but lower for institutional and personal contractual collaborations, and for these and informal contacts, indicating that a number of firms uses only one of these governance forms. This suggests that different types of firms may use different forms of governance for university–industry collaborations.

Bodas Freitas et al. (2010), based on UIPIE data, show that larger firms that invest internally in innovation through R&D or design are more likely to enter an institutional collaboration with a university. Firms that collaborate through personal contractual linkages tend also to be smaller than non-collaborators. These firms also invest more in acquiring knowledge through patents and know-how than firms that collaborate

Table 11.2   Governance modes in university–industry collaborations (inventors)

Types of knowledge transfer channels	In order to make your inventions, how important were the following ways of accessing university knowledge?	Used, but of little importance (%)	Used and of high importance (%)	Used (%)
University–industry research collaborations	Institutional research collaborations between your company and the university (department, faculty, university, technology transfer office), financed by the company	14.0	12.4	26.4
	Institutional research collaborations between your company and the university, financed through public funds (regional, national or international)	13.4	11.2	24.6
	Personal contracts between your company and individual university researchers	12.6	11.3	23.9
	Informal, personal contacts between your company and university researchers	16.9	8.0	24.9
	Sharing facilities (e.g. laboratories, equipment) with the university	9.8	7.3	17.1
Open science channels	Participation in conferences and workshops	28.8	18.8	47.6
	Scientific papers in journals	22.3	31.1	53.4
	Other publications, including professional publications and reports	29.0	25.7	54.7
Commercial channels	Attending university organized business training or initiatives to promote knowledge transfer	14.0	6.1	20.1
	University researchers or staff employed part-time or on a temporary basis by your company	9.4	4.2	13.6
	Reading university patents	14.9	5.3	20.2
Education and employment-based channels	Your staff employed part-time or on a temporary basis at a university	3.6	0.7	4.3
	University researchers or staff employed part-time or on a temporary basis by your company	10.6	6.4	17.0
	Collaborations based on co-supervision of Masters or PhD students	14.5	11.3	25.8
	University students working for your company as trainees	21.0	12.0	33.0
	Full time hiring of university graduates or researchers	18.8	18.6	37.4

Source: PIEMINV survey.

Table 11.3   Forms of governance for collaboration: Pearson correlation coefficients

	Institutional research collaborations financed through public funds	Personal contracts between your company and individual university researchers	Informal, personal contacts between your company and university researchers
Institutional research collaborations financed by the company	0.542***	0.421***	0.306***
Institutional research collaborations financed through public funds		0.434***	0.360***
Personal contracts between your company and individual university researchers			0.386***

Source: PIEMINV survey.

Table 11.4   Effectiveness of institutional and personal collaborations with university across innovative objectives

Objectives	Institutional collaborations more effective (%)	Personal contracts more effective (%)	Both equally effective (%)
Non-competitive (basic research) projects	**32.6**	20.8	**34.2**
Applied research projects to develop new products	14.8	**49.4**	26.0
Applied research projects for production activities	12.7	**48.4**	25.6
To identify the best students for recruitment	20.9	**41.8**	27.2
To keep up to date on new knowledge developments	28.6	17.6	**40.6**
To get ideas for new product development	15.5	**34.3**	**37.3**

Source: PIEMINV survey. Question: 'In order to reach the following objectives, which is more effective: collaborations with a university or personal contracts with individual university staff?'

institutionally, and are more likely to adopt 'open' innovation strategies based on the exchange of technological knowledge with external partners than firms that do not collaborate at all. Hence, personal contractual collaborations with individual university researchers, as opposed to institutional collaborations, may be more appropriate for small firms, because they are more flexible and easier to manage.

The choice of a governance form for collaboration may be related also to the type of knowledge being developed and shared. Table 11.4 uses information from the PIEMINV survey to show the effectiveness of institutional and personal contractual collaborations for specific industrial knowledge development goals.

Results suggest that personal contractual collaborations are particularly important for solving problems related to product development and production activities, and to identify students to recruit. In the case of non-competitive basic-research projects institutional collaboration is preferred or is at least as relevant as personal contractual arrangements. This may be related to the infrastructure, resources and international networks of contacts that may be required to accomplish basic research projects. Both personal contractual and institutional collaborations are used to update knowledge and to get new ideas for product development – with the latter showing some preference towards personal contractual.

Overall, for university–industry interactions in Piedmont, both personal contractual and institutional arrangements are important, which means that both models of governance must be taken into account when studying the impact of knowledge transfer, and when designing science and technology transfer policies. The choice of governance form for a university–industry collaboration may be related to the characteristics of firms and the type of knowledge that is being developed and shared. Our evidence shows that institutional governance may be more effective when the basic research content of the industrial innovation objective is larger, while personal contractual arrangements seem to be particularly effective when the innovation objective is mainly applied research and problem solving. Smaller firms that are more reliant on the acquisition of external knowledge and favour more open innovation strategies based on the exchange of technological knowledge with external partners, are more likely to favour personal contractual rather than institutional forms of collaborations.

5. CONCLUSIONS

Theoretical developments in economic thinking (Freeman, 1974), and primarily the economic debate on knowledge-driven economic growth (Foray, 2004) have shaped how we look at the contribution of universities (teaching and research) to society. Models of growth driven by increased human capital show that increasing the stock of knowledge embodied in skilled workers increases the productivity of the inputs and, hence, leads to higher levels of per-capita output from the economic system (Lucas, 1988). Other endogenous growth theory models emphasize the role of disembodied knowledge as a non-excludable and non-rival factor of production that generates increasing returns to scale in the production function and drives the economy towards higher rates of aggregate output growth (Romer, 1990). For these reasons, augmenting the stock of knowledge produced in the economic system is increasingly considered the key to greater innovation and productivity growth. The most important agents in this process, based on their function as producers of new knowledge (in the form of scientific publications and human capital), are universities (Aghion et al., 2008). The central economic role of universities is highlighted in the broader discourse on the features of the 'knowledge economy', which is characterized by faster rates of technological progress and by the greater economic importance of the industries that produce and trade knowledge products (Quah, 1998). While the provision of higher education is still regarded as the main function of universities, especially in light of the increased numbers of higher education students thought to be essential for the knowledge economy, the role of universities in the direct transfer of new knowledge in the form of technologies and intellectual property is also increasing.

This chapter has provided a theoretical and empirical rationale for the different forms of governance of university–industry collaboration. We examined the knowledge transfer processes that occur through university–industry research collaborations – personal contractual and institutional – compared to purely commercial relationships based on the exchange of IP or on exchanges of personnel and students.

Section 2 examined the importance of university–industry relationships for dealing with the increasingly uncertain economic environment and ever more complex technological systems, which lead to more open and distributed innovation (Chesbrough, 2003; Powell and Grodal, 2005; Rossi, 2010) The existence and the role of personal contractual and institutional governance of university–industry collaboration was discussed in the light of the literature. The complexities of university–industry interaction and the existence of more than one mode of governance, reflects the multiple, non-linear relationships between modes of interaction and the characteristics and objectives of the actors, and also the empirical and conceptual issues involved. Section 3 presented evidence on how different knowledge development processes require specific forms of organization, with the result that firms, universities and researchers with different characteristics engage in specific linkages and modes of knowledge transfer. We discussed the issues related to the conceptualization and measurement of university–industry interactions and their consequences. This chapter highlights the need for a better appreciation of their governance and points to the need for better conceptual and empirical measurement of the university–industry context to inform policy action.

The analysis in this chapter used two new original databases providing information on university–industry relationships in the Piedmont region in the North-West of Italy, on the basis of which we discussed the co-existence and importance of personal contractual and institutional governance modes of collaborations. Evidence collected from firm managers, R&D managers and inventors in Piedmont suggests that personal contractual collaborations are as important as institutional ones and that the two are complemented by informal contacts. Our evidence suggests also that the choice of governance form for collaboration depends on the characteristics of firms and the type of knowledge that is being developed and shared. Institutional collaborations appear to be slightly more effective if the industrial innovation objective involves more basic research, while personal contractual collaborations are particularly effective when the innovation objectives involve mainly applied research and problem-solving activities. Smaller firms that are more reliant on external knowledge and adopt more open innovation strategies based on the exchange of technological knowledge with external partners, are more likely to favour personal contractual rather than institutional arrangements (Bodas Freitas et al., 2010).

The results in this chapter have important implications for policymakers. Both personal contractual and institutional governance models are important for interactions and knowledge transfer between university and industry and the former seems more appropriate for small companies. These results are somewhat paradoxical as policy support for the development of institutional forms of governance of university–industry relationships is based mostly on the view that universities are self-contained and unable to respond to the applied knowledge needs of small companies. Both personal contractual and institutional collaboration need to be considered in examining the contribution of universities to economic development. Instead of focusing only on supporting institutional collaborations (perhaps cumbersome for small firms) policy should aim at stimulating personal contractual collaborations through proper regulation of part-time professorships and consulting.

NOTES

1. Studies in the history and sociology of science and technology confirm that they are mutually dependent and often difficult to distinguish (Mokyr, 1990; Nelson and Rosenberg, 1996; MacKenzie and Wajcman, 1999).
2. Data availability means that most econometric analyses use IPR-related information.
3. Analysis of CIS-4 weighted responses for Italy indicates that only 2.1 per cent rate universities as a highly important source of information (ISTAT, 2008).
4. For all Italian respondents the values were 8.8 per cent and 26.5 per cent respectively.
5. The UIPIE questionnaire was administered in autumn 2008 to a sample of representative firms in the Piedmont region. From a representative sample of 1058 firms, we obtained 1052 valid responses. The sample was developed and validated by the local Chamber of Commerce, which sent out our questionnaires with their quarterly regional economic foresight survey.
6. The PIEMINV questionnaire was sent out in autumn 2009 and spring 2010 to the population of inventors with a Piedmont address, that had applied for an EPO patent in the period 1998–2005 (about 4000 patents and 3000 inventors in Piedmont). We obtained just over 865 valid responses from 2800 questionnaires (response rate 31 per cent).

REFERENCES

Abreu, M., Grinevich, V., Hughes, A., Kitson, M. and Ternouth, P. (2008), 'Universities, business and knowledge exchange', London and Cambridge: Council for Industry and Higher Education and Centre for Business Research.

Aghion, P., Dewatripont, M. and Stein, J. (2008), 'Academic freedom, private sector focus, and the process of innovation', *Rand Journal of Economics*, **39** (3), 617–35.

Agrawal, A. and Henderson, R. (2002), 'Putting patents in context: exploring knowledge transfer from MIT', *Management Science*, **49** (1), 44–60.

Antonelli, C. (2005), 'Models of knowledge and systems of governance', *Journal of Institutional Economics*, **1** (1), 51–73.

Antonelli, C. (2008a), 'The new economics of the university: a knowledge governance approach', *Journal of Technology Transfer*, **33**, 1–22.

Antonelli, C. (2008b), 'Pecuniary externalities: the convergence of directed technological change and the emergence of innovation systems', *Industrial and Corporate Change*, **17** (5), 1049–70.

Argyres, N.S. and Liebeskind, J.P. (1998), 'Privatizing the intellectual commons: universities and the commercialization of biotechnology', *Journal of Economic Behaviour and Organization*, **35**, 427–54.

Arrow, K.J. (1962), 'Economic welfare and the allocation of resources for invention', in R.R. Nelson (ed.), *The Rate and Direction of Inventive Activity: Economic and Social Factors*, Princeton, NJ: Princeton University Press, for NBER, pp. 609–25.

Arundel, A. and Geuna, A. (2004), 'Proximity and the use of public science by innovative European firms', *Economics of Innovation and New Technology*, **13** (6), 559–80.

AUTM (2002), 'Licensing survey: FY 2000', Baltimore University, The Association of Technology Managers Inc.

Balconi, M., Breschi, S. and Lissoni, F. (2004), 'Networks of inventors and the role of academia: an exploration of Italian patent data', *Research Policy*, **33** (1), 127–45.

Baldini, N. (2008), 'Negative effects of university patenting: myths and grounded evidence', *Scientometrics*, **75** (2), 289–311.

Baldini, N., Grimaldi, R. and Sobrero, M. (2007), 'To patent or not to patent? A survey of Italian inventors on motivations, incentives, and obstacles to university patenting', *Scientometrics*, **70**, 333–54.

Beise, M. and Stahl, H. (1999), 'Public research and industrial innovations in Germany', *Research Policy*, **28**, 397–422.

Bekkers, R. and Bodas Freitas, I.M. (2008), 'Analysing preferences for knowledge transfer channels between universities and industry: to what degree do sectors also matter?', *Research Policy*, **37**, 1837–53.

Belderbos, R., Carree, M. and Lokshin, B. (2004a), 'Cooperative R&D and firm performance', *Research Policy*, **33**, 1477–92.

Belderbos, R., Carree, M., Lokshin, B. and Veugelers, R. (2004b), 'Heterogeneity in R&D cooperation strategies', *International Journal of Industrial Organization*, **22**, 1237–63.

Block, F. (2008), 'Swimming against the current: the rise of a hidden developmental state in the United States', *Politics & Society*, **36** (2), 169–206.

Bodas Freitas, I.M, Clausen, T., Fontana, R. and Verspagen, B. (2011), 'Formal and informal external linkages and firms' innovative strategy. A cross-country comparison', *Journal of Evolutionary Economics*, **21** (1), 91–119.

Bodas Freitas, I.M., Geuna, A. and Rossi, F. (2010), 'The governance of regional university–industry knowledge transfer: are different models coexisting?', LEI & BRICK Working Papers 2010, Turin: University of Turin Department of Economics.

Bozeman, B. (1994), 'Evaluating government technology transfer: early impacts of the "cooperative technology paradigm"', *Policy Studies Journal*, **22** (2), 322–37.

Bozeman, B. (2000), 'Technology transfer and public policy: a review of research and theory', *Research Policy*, **29**, 627–55.

Bozeman, B. and Corley, E. (2004), 'Scientists' collaboration strategies: implications for scientific and technical human capital', *Research Policy*, **33**, 599–616.

Bozeman, B. and Gaughan, M. (2007), 'Impacts of grants and contracts on academic researchers' interactions with industry', *Research Policy*, **36**, 694–707.

Bozeman, B., Papadakis, M. and Coker, K. (1995), 'Industry perspectives on commercial interactions with federal laboratories: does the cooperative technology paradigm really work?', Report to the National Science Foundation, Research on Science and Technology Program.

Bruneel, J., D'Este, P., Neely, A. and Salter, A. (2009), 'The search for talent and technology', AIM research paper, Imperial College London.

Bulut, H. and Moschini, G. (2006), 'US universities' net returns from patenting and licensing: a quantile regression analysis', Working Paper 06-WP432, Center for Agricultural and Rural Development, Iowa State University.

Charles, D. and Conway, C. (2001), *Higher Education – Business Interaction Survey*, London: Higher Education Funding Council for England.

Chesbrough, H.W. (2003), *Open Innovation: The New Imperative for Creating and Profiting from Technology*, Boston, MA: Harvard Business School Press.

Cohen, W.M., Florida, R., Randazzese, L. and Walsh, J. (1998), *Industry and the Academy: Uneasy Partners in the Cause of Technological Advance*, Washington, DC: The Brookings Institution.

Cohen, W.M., Nelson, R.R. and Walsh, J. (2002), 'Links and impacts: the influence of public research on industrial R&D', *Management Science*, **48** (1), 1–23.

Colyvas, J., Crow, M., Gelijns, A., Mazzoleni, R., Nelson, R., Rosenberg, N. and Sampat, B. (2002), 'How do university inventions get into practice?', *Management Science*, **48** (1), 61–72.

Crespi, G., D'Este, P., Geuna, A. and Fontana, R. (2011), 'The impact of academic patenting on university research and its transfer', *Research Policy*, **40** (1), 55–68.

D'Este, P. and Patel, P. (2007), 'University–industry linkages in the UK: what are the factors underlying the variety of interactions with industry?', *Research Policy*, **36**, 1295–313.

D'Este, P. and Perkmann, M. (2007), 'Why do academics collaborate with industry? A study of the relationship between motivations and channels of interaction', paper presented at the DRUID Summer Conference, Copenhagen, 18–20 June.

Dasgupta, P. and David, P.A. (1994), 'Toward a new economics of science', *Research Policy*, **23** (5), 487–521.

Debackere, K. (2004), 'Introduction', *R&D Management*, **34** (1), 1–2.

Di Gregorio, D. and Shane, S. (2003), 'Why do some universities generate more start-ups than others?', *Research Policy*, **32** (2), 209–28.

Dosi, G., Llerena, P. and Sylos Labini, M. (2006), 'Science–technology–industry links and the "European Paradox": some notes on the dynamics of scientific and technological research in Europe', *Research Policy*, **35** (10), 1450–64.

Etzkowitz, H. and Leydesdorff, L. (2000), 'The dynamics of innovation: from national systems and "Mode 2" to a triple helix of university–industry–government relations', *Research Policy*, **29** (2), 109–23.

Feldman M.P. and Kelley, M.R. (2006), 'The ex ante assessment of knowledge spillovers: government R&D policy, economic incentives and private firm behaviour', *Research Policy*, **35**, 1509–21.

Feller, I. (1990), 'Universities as engines of R&D based economic growth – they think they can', *Research Policy*, **19** (4), 335–48.

Fini, R., Grimaldi, R. and Sobrero, M. (2009), 'Factors fostering academics to start up new ventures: an assessment of Italian founders' incentives', *Journal of Technology Transfer*, **34**, 380–402.

Fonseca, J. (2002), *Complexity and Innovation in Organizations*, London: Routledge.

Fontana R., Geuna, A. and Matt, M. (2006a), 'Factors affecting university–industry R&D projects: the importance of searching, screening and signalling', *Research Policy*, **35**, 309–23.

Fontana R., Geuna, A. and Matt, M. (2006b), 'Firm size and openness: the driving forces of university–industry collaboration', in Caloghirou, Y., Constantelou, A. and Vonortas, N.S. (eds), *Knowledge Flows in European Industry*, London: Routledge, pp. 185–209.

Foray, D. (2004), *The Economics of Knowledge*, Cambridge, MA: MIT Press.

Franzoni, C. and Lissoni, F. (2009), 'Academic entrepreneurship: critical issues and lessons for Europe', in Varga, A. (ed.), *Academic Entrepreneurship and Regional Development*, Cheltenham, UK and Northampton, MA, USA: Edward Elgar, pp. 163–90.

Freeman, C. (1974), *The Economics of Industrial Innovation*, Harmondsworth: Penguin.

Geuna, A. (1999), *The Economics of Knowledge Production*, Cheltenham, UK and Northampton, MA, USA: Edward Elgar.

Geuna, A. and Muscio, A. (2009), 'The governance of university knowledge transfer: a critical review of the literature', *Minerva*, **47** (1), 93–114.

Geuna, A. and Nesta, L.J.J. (2006), 'University patenting and its effects on academic research: the emerging European evidence', *Research Policy*, **35** (6), 790–807.

Gibbons, M., Limoges, C., Nowotny, H., Schwarzman, S., Scott, P. and Trow, M. (1994), *The New Production of Knowledge: The Dynamics of Research in Contemporary Societies*, London: Sage Publications.

Giuri, P., Mariani M., Brusoni, S. and Verspagen, B. (2007), 'Inventors and invention processes in Europe. Results from the PatVal-EU survey', *Research Policy*, **36**, 1107–27.

Goldfarb, B. (2008), 'The effect of government contracting on academic research: does the source of funding affect scientific output?', *Research Policy*, **37**, 41–58.

Grimpe, C. and Sofka, W. (2009), 'Search patterns and absorptive capacity: low- and high-technology sectors in European countries', *Research Policy*, **38**, 495–506.

Henderson, R., Jaffe, A. and Trajtenberg, M. (1998), 'Universities as a source of commercial technology: a detailed analysis of university patenting, 1965–1988', *Review of Economics and Statistics*, **80** (1), 119–27.

Hicks, D. and Hamilton, K. (1999), 'Does university-industry collaboration adversely affect university research?', *Issues in Science and Technology*, **15** (4), 74–5.

ISTAT (2008), *Statistiche sull'innovazione nelle imprese*, Rome: ISTAT.

Jansen, C. and Dillon, H. (2000), 'Where do the leads for licences come from?', *Industry & Higher Education*, **14** (3), 150–56.

Jensen, R.A., Thursby, J.G. and Thursby, M.C. (2003), 'Disclosure and licensing of university inventions: "The best we can do with the s**t we get to work with"', *International Journal of Industrial Organization*, **21** (9), 1271–300.

Jensen, R., Thursby, J. and Thursby, M.C. (2010), 'University–industry spillovers, government funding, and industrial consulting', NBER Working Paper 15732, Cambridge, MA: National Bureau of Economic Research.

Joly, P.B. and Mangematin, V. (1996), 'Profile of public laboratories, industrial partnerships and organisation of R&D: the dynamics of industrial relationships in a large research organisation', *Research Policy*, **25**, 901–22.

Kenney, M. (1986), *Biotechnology: the University–Industry Complex*, New Haven, CT: Yale University Press.

Klevorick, A.K., Levin, R.C., Nelson, R.R. and Winter, S.G. (1995), 'On the sources and significance of inter-industry differences in technological opportunities', *Research Policy*, **24**, 185–205.

Koumpis, K. and Pavitt, K. (1999), 'Corporate activities in speech recognition and natural language: another "new science"-based technology', *International Journal of Innovation Management*, **3**, 335–66.

Lane, D.A. and Maxfield, R. (1997), 'Foresight, complexity and strategy', in Arthur, B., Durlauf, S. and Lane, D.A. (eds), *The Economy as a Complex Evolving System II*, Reading, MA: Addison-Wesley, pp. 533–65.

Lane, D.A. and Maxfield, R. (2005), 'Ontological uncertainty and innovation', *Journal of Evolutionary Economics*, **15** (1), 3–50.

Laursen, K. and Salter, A. (2004), 'Searching low and high: what types of firms use universities as a source of innovation?', *Research Policy*, **33**, 1201–15.

Laursen, K. and Salter, A. (2006), 'Open for innovation: the role of openness in explaining innovation performance among UK manufacturing firms', *Strategic Management Journal*, **27**, 131–50.

Lee, Y.S. (1996), 'Technology transfer and the research university: a search for the boundaries of university–industry collaboration', *Research Policy*, **25**, 843–63.

Lee, Y.S. and Gaertner, R. (1994), 'Technology transfer from university to industry: a large-scale experiment with technology development and commercialization', *Policy Studies Journal*, **22** (2), 384–99.

Levin, R., Klevoric, R., Nelson, R.R. and Winter, S. (1987), 'Appropriating the returns from industrial research and development', *Brookings Papers on Economic Activity*, **3** (Special Issue on Microeconomics), 783–831.

Liebenau, J.M. (1985), 'Innovation in pharmaceuticals: industrial R&D in the early twentieth century', *Research Policy*, **14**, 179–87.

Link, A.N. and Siegel, D.S. (2005), 'Generating science-based growth: an econometric analysis of the impact of organizational incentives on university–industry technology transfer', *European Journal of Finance*, **11**, 169–81.

Link, A.N., Siegel, D.S. and Bozeman, B. (2007), 'An empirical analysis of the propensity of academics to engage in informal university technology transfer', *Industrial and Corporate Change*, **16** (4), 641–55.

Lucas, R. (1988), 'On the mechanics of economic development', *Journal of Monetary Economics*, **22** (1), 3–42.

Lundvall, B.-Å. (1985), *Product Innovation and User–Producer Interaction*, Aalborg: Aalborg University Press.

Macdonald, S. (2010), 'Seducing the goose: patenting by UK universities', University of Sheffield.

MacGarvie, M. and Furman, J. (2005), 'Early academic science and the birth of industrial research laboratories in the US pharmaceutical industry', NBER Working Paper 11470, Cambridge. MA: National Bureau of Economic Research.

MacKenzie, D. and Wajcman, J. (1999), *The Social Shaping of Technology*, Milton Keynes: Open University Press.

Manjarrés-Henríquez, L., Gutiérrez-Gracia, A. and Vega-Jurado, J. (2008), 'Coexistence of university–industry relations and academic research: barrier to or incentive for scientific productivity', *Scientometrics*, **76** (3), 561–76.

Markman, G.D, Gianiodis, P.T., Phan, P.H. and Balkin, D.B. (2004), 'Entrepreneurship from the Ivory Tower: do incentive systems matter?', *Journal of Technology Transfer*, **29**, 353–64.

Marsili, O. (2001), *The Anatomy and Evolution of Industries: Technological Change and Industrial Dynamics*, Cheltenham, UK and Northampton, MA, USA: Edward Elgar.

McMillan, G.S., Narin, F. and Deeds, D.L. (2000), 'An analysis of the critical role of public science in innovation: the case of biotechnology', *Research Policy*, **29**, 1–8.

Meyer-Krahmer, F. and Schmoch, U. (1998), 'Science-based technologies: university–industry interactions in four fields', *Research Policy*, **27** (8), 835–52.

Meyer-Thurow, G. (1982), 'The industrialization of invention: a case study from the German chemical industry', *Isis*, **73** (3), 363–81.

Mokyr, J. (1990), *The Lever of Riches*, New York: Oxford University Press.

Monjon, S. and Waelbroeck, P. (2003), 'Assessing spillovers from universities to firms: evidence from French firm-level data', *International Journal of Industrial Organization*, **21**, 1255–70.

Mowery, D. (1983), 'Economic theory and government technology policy', *Policy Science*, **16** (1), 27–43.

Mowery, D. and Sampat, B. (2005), 'The Bayh–Dole Act of 1980 and university–industry technology transfer: a model for other OECD governments?', *Journal of Technology Transfer*, **30**, 115–27.

Nelson, R.R. (1959), 'The simple economics of basic scientific research', *Journal of Political Economy*, **67** (3), 297–306.

Nelson, R.R. and Rosenberg, N. (1996), 'The role of universities in the advance of industrial technology', in Rosenbloom, R.S. and Spencer, W.J. (eds), *Engines of Innovation*, Harvard: Business School Press, pp. 87–109.

Nesta, L. and Saviotti, P.P. (2005), 'Coherence of the knowledge base and the firm's innovative performance: evidence from the US pharmaceutical industry', *Journal of Industrial Economics*, **53** (1), 123–42.

Nooteboom, B. (2004), *Inter-firm Collaboration, Learning and Networks. An Integrated Approach*, London and New York: Routledge.

O'Shea, R.P., Allen, T.J., Chevalier, A. and Roche, F. (2005), 'Entrepreneurial orientation, technology transfer and spinoff performance of US universities', *Research Policy*, **34**, 994–1009.

O'Shea, R.P., Chugh, H. and Allen, T.J. (2008), 'Determinants and consequences of university spinoff activity: a conceptual framework', *Journal of Technology Transfer*, **33**, 653–66.

Paravan, S.-V. (2007), 'Weak link between innovative enterprises and public research institutes/universities', *Statistics in Focus*, **81**.

Pavitt, K. (1984), 'Sectoral patterns of technical change: towards a taxonomy and a theory', *Research Policy*, **13** (6), 343–73.

Pavitt, K. (1998a), 'Technologies, products and organization in the innovating firm: what Adam Smith tells us and Joseph Schumpeter doesn't', *Industrial and Corporate Change*, **7** (3), 433–52.

Pavitt, K. (1998b), 'The social shaping of the national science base', *Research Policy*, **27**, 793–805.

Perkmann, M. and Walsh, K. (2006), 'Relationship-based university–industry links and open innovation: towards a research agenda', AIM Working Paper Series n. 41, Imperial College London.

Peters, L. and Etzkowitz, H. (1990), 'University–industry connections and academic values', *Technology in Society*, **12** (4), 427–40.

Polanyi, M. (1966), *The Tacit Dimension*, New York: Doubleday.

Ponomariov, B. and Boardman, C. (2008), 'The effect of informal industry contacts on the time university scientists allocate to collaborative research with industry', *Journal of Technology Transfer*, **33**, 301–13.

Powell, W. and Grodal, S. (2005), 'Networks for innovators', in Fagerberg, J., Mowery, D. and Nelson, R. (eds), *The Oxford Handbook of Innovation*, Oxford: Oxford University Press, pp. 56–85.

Powell, W.W, Koput, K.W. and Smith-Doerr, L. (1996), 'Interorganizational collaboration and the locus of innovation: networks of learning in biotechnology', *Administrative Science Quarterly*, **41** (1), 116–45.

Quah, D. (1998), 'A weightless economy', *UNESCO Courier*, 18–21 December.

Rebne, D. (1989), 'Faculty consulting and scientific knowledge: a traditional university–industry linkage', *Educational Administration Quarterly*, **25**, 338–57.

Romer, P.M. (1990), 'Endogenous technological change', *Journal of Political Economy*, **98** (5), 71–102.

Rossi, F. (2010), 'The governance of university–industry knowledge transfer', *European Journal of Innovation Management*, **13** (12), 151–71.

Rothaermel, F.T. and Thursby, M.C. (2005), 'University-incubator firm knowledge flows: assessing their impact on incubator firm performance', *Research Policy*, **34** (3), 305–20.

Ryle, G. (1949), *The Concept of Mind*, London: Hutchinson.

Salter, A.J. and Martin, B.R. (2001), 'The economic benefits of publicly funded research: a critical review', *Research Policy*, **30**, 509–39.

Santoro, M.D. and Chakrabarti, A.K. (2002), 'Firm size and technology centrality in industry–university interactions', *Research Policy*, **31**, 1163–80.

Schartinger, D., Rammera, C., Fischer, M.M. and Fröhlich, J. (2002), 'Knowledge interactions between universities and industry in Austria: sectoral patterns and determinants', *Research Policy*, **31**, 303–28.

Schartinger, D., Schibany, A. and Gassler, H. (2001), 'Interactive relations between universities and firms: empirical evidence for Austria', *Journal of Technology Transfer*, **26** (3), 255–69.

Senker, J. (1999), *Changing Structure, Organisation and Nature of European PSR Systems*, Synthesis Report, Brighton: SPRU, University of Sussex.

Slaughter, S. and Rhoades, G. (1996), 'The emergence of a competitiveness research and development policy coalition and the commercialization of academic science and technology', *Science, Technology, & Human Values*, **21** (3), 303–39.

Spencer, J.W. (2001), 'How relevant is university-based scientific research to private high-technology firms? A United States–Japan comparison', *Academy of Management Journal*, **44** (2), 432–40.

Stephan, P.E., Gurmu S., Sumell, A.J. and Black, G. (2007), 'Who's patenting in the university? Evidence from a survey of doctorate recipients', *Economics of Innovation and New Technology*, **16** (2), 71–99.

Swann, P. (1989), *Academic Scientists and the Pharmaceutical Industry: Co-operative Research in Twentieth-Century America*, Baltimore, MD: Johns Hopkins University Press.

Thursby, J.G., Jensen, R. and Thursby, M.C. (2001), 'Objectives, characteristics and outcomes of university licensing: a survey of major US universities', *Journal of Technology Transfer*, **26**, 59–72.

Walsh, J.P. and Nagaoka, S. (2009), 'How "open" is innovation in the US and Japan? Evidence from the RIETI-Georgia Tech Inventor Survey', RIETI Discussion Paper Series 09-E-022, The Research Institute of Economy, Trade and Industry, Tokyo.

Zucker, L.G., Darby, M.R. and Armstrong, J.S. (2002), 'Commercializing knowledge: university science, knowledge capture, and firm performance in biotechnology', *Management Science*, **48** (1), 138–53.

12 A functional theory of technology and technological change

Andrea Bonaccorsi[1]

INTRODUCTION

The field of economics of innovation is rich in various ways to represent technology, sometimes descriptively, sometimes with models, algorithms and quantitative variables. It is our contention that existing representations do not do justice to the complexity of the nature and dynamics of technology. In particular, they almost invariably fail to recognize the *dual* nature of technology, that is, the fact that it takes place simultaneously in a space of physical embodiments (attributes, characteristics) and in a space of representations, whose main organizing principle is abstraction. And even those authors that recognize the importance of this distinction, do not capture it in modeling technology.

The goal of this chapter is to introduce in the economics of innovation a representation of technology, labeled *functional representation*, which is more articulated than the ones currently available and addresses some of the limitations in the literature. In order to develop a functional representation, we will draw on bodies of knowledge that range from formal theories of design in engineering, to artificial intelligence, to the philosophy of technology and biology. We will also make use of a recently developed functional base, containing a full scale dictionary of functional expressions, using which it is possible to draw highly informative maps of technologies or artifacts.

The chapter will try to persuade the profession that assuming such a representation is worthwhile and not cumbersome. On the contrary, it will help to address some of the main weaknesses of existing representations in the economics of innovation. Based on the representation, a theory of search can be developed, fully compatible with the notion of procedural rationality, and with a number of testable propositions. A short retrospective case study will show how a functional representation allows, with the benefit of hindsight, to reconstruct the long term technological evolution of an industry and to identify key turning points.

The economic implications of this approach will then be spelled out in some detail. They will address some of the classical topics in the economics of innovation (technological trajectories, paradigms, technological bottlenecks, reverse salience, path dependency, user initiated innovation), in industrial dynamics (persistence of innovators, radical innovation, industry life cycle, diversification), and in IPR (patentability, patent scope).

This effort is close to the one developed by Rikard Stankiewicz, with the notion of design spaces, by Stan Metcalfe and Paolo Saviotti with a model of service characteristics, and by David Lane, with a full fledged theory of generative relationships. We consider these efforts as an important attempt to free the economics of innovation from simplistic analogies with biology and from purely combinatorial representations of technology and search. However, differently from them, we make full use of a large body of literature that has developed the notion of *functions* in considerable detail, and which is largely unknown to the economics profession.

In addition, we will explicitly develop a language for representation, which can be the basis for future empirical work in the field. A constructive proof will be offered that by using functional language, a function space with the mathematical properties of a vector space can be obtained. If this is true, then a number of distance functions in topology can be used in order to address important problems in economics of innovation.

1.   DOES TECHNOLOGICAL DYNAMICS TAKE PLACE (ALMOST RANDOMLY) IN THE SPACE OF ATTRIBUTES?

1.1   A Review of Some Models of Technology and Technological Change

In this section we try to address the issue of how models represent technology and technological change when they move from appreciative theorizing to full scale models.

NK models

A well developed tradition in economic modeling makes use of Stuart Kauffman's NK approach (Kauffman, 1993). There is a complex system, made of many elements that are bound by interdependence relations, which affect the performance of the system. The interdependence is described by the notion of epistatic relation: when the state of an element changes, this affects its own functioning and the functioning of all elements to which it is epistatically related. In the NK model, N stands for the number of elements of the system, K for the number of other elements affected by each element. Note that in the original formulation K is a parameter, that is, all elements are affected by the same number of other elements.

A string is then formed of N elements, each of which is affecting K elements, to which a fitness value is associated for each state. For each state of the system there is a fitness value, computed as a mean fitness of each element. A mutation dynamics is applied to this system, whereby the state of an element is mutated randomly and the fitness value is calculated. The mutation is accepted, hence the old string is substituted by a new string, only if the new fitness value is larger than the previous one. This problem is exponential in K and is subject to many local optima, generating a rugged fitness landscape.

The parallel between this formalism and a representation of technology is evident (Frenken, 2006a): all products are composed by a number of elements, and the overall performance is usually the result of design interdependencies among them. The designer problem is to find the best performance by changing the architecture (that is, the elements in the string), mutating their state, or modifying the interdependence relations.

In NK models mutation is random. The search space for this problem grows exponentially, so that heuristic strategies based on local search are used. In addition, selection based on fitness takes place in an independent way with respect to mutation. The interest of the model is in identifying suitable search strategies given the dimensionality of the design space.

Genetic algorithms

A variation of NK models is found in genetic algorithm (GA) models. Here the idea is to introduce cross-over, similar to sexual reproduction in animals. By reproduction the genetic material of two individuals is combined. In genetic algorithm models, a point in the sequence of two parent strings is randomly identified and the resulting sub-strings are swapped between the two (Holland, 1975; Goldberg, 1989). This modeling strategy has been applied to technological evolution by Birchenhall (1995) and Windrum and Birchenhall (1998).

As Holland puts it:

> a general theory of complex adaptive systems . . . will be built, I think, on a framework that centers on three mechanisms: *parallelism, competition,* and *recombination. Parallelism* lets the system use individuals (rules, agents) as building blocks, activating sets of individuals to describe and act upon changing situations. . . . *Competition* allows the system to marshal its resources in realistic environments where torrents of mostly irrelevant information deluge the system. Procedures relying on the mechanism of competition – credit assignment and rule discovery – extract useful, repeatable events from this torrent, incorporating them as new building blocks. *Recombination* underpins the discovery process, generating plausible new rules from building blocks that form parts of tested rules. (Holland, 1992: 197; see also Holland, 1995)

By introducing recombination, or cross-over, the power of heuristic strategies increases significantly, because through recombination it is possible to discover new rules, or, in other words, to build more complexity from elementary building blocks.

Generalized NK models

A variation of NK models has been proposed by Altenberg (1994, 1995, 1997), by making K variable, that is, eliminating the parameter. A generalized NK model contains N elements (n = 1,. . .N) and F functions (f = 1, . . .F). While the Kauffman model has made the number of elements equal to the number of functions, the generalized Altenberg model allows any number of elements and functions to be treated, assuming that each element can affect any number of functions and, vice versa, that each function can be affected by any number of functions. The number of functions affected by a particular element is called *pleiotropy* of the element. The number of elements that affect a given function is called *polygeny* of the function. Thus the relation is many-to-many, a feature that indeed resembles the one in design.

In order to initialize the model

> each element is assumed to affect at least one function. If an element does not serve a function, it is redundant in the description of the system, and, each function is assumed to be affected by at least one element. When a function is not affected by any element, its fitness is zero by definition. (Frenken, 2006a: 33)

Thus by definition the set of functions must be defined *ex ante*. A constructional selection model is then built by adding new elements over time, while leaving the list of functions unchanged. When a new element is introduced, it affects a number of functions defined by its pleiotropy value, so that the overall fitness value is changed. An important result by Altenberg is that the overall fitness value of constructional selection is larger than the one found in NK models of the same size. The introduction of new elements changes the architecture of the system, allowing the identification of superior solutions.

It must be admitted that generalized NK models come close to our notion of search in the function space. However, there are still limitations. The most important limitation is that the number of functions is fixed, while the number of elements is variable. While this representation is a major step beyond simple NK models, still it does not solve the issue of where the functions come from, nor the issue of endogenous generation of functions through the technological dynamics.

It is somewhat puzzling that, while evolutionary economics has deepened the use of NK models, welcoming the generalized Altenberg version, the father of NK models has somewhat called for a departure from the original formulation, introducing the notion of non-algorithmic nature of evolution and accepting the idea of exaptation (Kauffman, 2000), as we will see below.

Problem decomposition

Developing the deep insight of Herbert Simon, that in order for complex systems to be evolutionarily stable they must exhibit quasi-decomposability, a stream of literature has examined the implications for technology search of alternative decomposition schemes (Marengo et al., 2000; Cooper, 2000; Marengo and Dosi, 2005). Typically, such schemes are also associated to organizational architectures (for example, centralized versus decentralized search). Different problem decompositions entail different patterns of division of labor, in turn generating variable results in the speed of convergence to solutions (Dosi and Grazzi, 2010).

This literature comes close to the notion that the search in the function space should be represented separately from the search in the space of structure, objects, or technologies, as we will discuss later, but does not develop it. An important reason might be that the lack of a standardized language for functions has hampered any attempt to model search separately.

Recombinant growth

In a different tradition, that is, growth theory, Martin Weitzman has developed formally the old Schumpeterian idea that 'the new combinations must draw the necessary means of production from some old combinations', that is, new ideas come out from existing ideas. He exploits the mathematical properties of combinatorial processes and shows that, if all ideas can be hybridized with all other ideas, and a certain proportion of newly generated ideas has some productive potential, then the long run growth of an economy is not limited by the supply of ideas, but only by the ability to exploit them (Weitzman, 1998). The combinatorial explosion generated by the hybridization mechanism means that technological evolution becomes less determined over time:

> At the beginning of the economy's history there are only a few ideas, like 'fire', 'clay', or 'water', whose combinations are intensively scrutinized so that, in a manner of speaking, every viable combination is fully explored, and the economy's evolution is determinate. As the economy evolves further, the opposite scenario eventually emerges. There are so many different sources of energy, or types of materials, or anything else, that the number of possible combinations becomes astronomical. The degree of 'path dependence' becomes ever greater. (Weitzman, 1998)

This idea has been further developed by Ola Olsson (2000), who introduces the possibility that the space of ideas, as proposed by Weitzman, is non-convex, so that not all combinations are admissible. This simple modification brings about a few important implications: when all convex combinations have been found, technological opportunities are exhausted, creating room for paradigm shift. In addition, the cost of combination increases with technological distance (Olsson and Frey, 2002). In this simple framework, some of the stylized facts about technology, such as trajectories, paradigms, and cycles can be generated.

Another way of expanding on the notion of recombinant growth is to admit that ideas can be combined in order to generate structures of higher level, which in turn are again combined, and that ideas must meet social needs. Brian Arthur and Wolfgang Polak (2004) have built a simple simulation setting in which

> new technologies are constructed by randomly wiring together existing ones and testing the results to see whether they satisfy any existing needs. If (a technology) proves useful – satisfies some need better than its competitors – it replaces the one that previously satisfied that need. It then adds to the active collection of technologies and becomes available as an element for the construction of still further technologies. (Arthur and Polak, 2004: 2)

They show that simple technologies can be assembled into more complex ones, and some of them prove critical in generating waves of substitution, that is, breakthroughs. That simple technologies may be assembled into more complex ones, which remain stable and are subject to further recombinations is an important idea, which Arthur labels *recursiveness* (Arthur, 2005) and which is at the basis of his ambitious general theory (Arthur, 2009).

These contributions are interesting because they explore where one can arrive by deliberately ignoring the directedness of technological change and leaving all the explanatory power to the virtues of massive computation. In fact, there are good reasons to believe that technological progress does *not* take place via a combination of all existing objects (fire, clay, water . . .) with all others, nor by randomly constructing intermediate structures.

Entropy and variety
The issue of variety has been at the core of a long term research effort by Paolo Saviotti (Saviotti, 1988, 1991; Saviotti and Trickett, 1992; Saviotti and Mani, 1995) and his coauthors, particularly Koen Frenken (Frenken, 2000, 2006b; Frenken et al., 1999, 2000). The process of economic growth in the very long term is expected to lead to an increase in the variety of products offered to consumers, and hence of underlying technological solutions needed to increase the features or attributes of products. In a Lancaster space of product attributes, this implies a positive correlation between economic growth and the rate of expansion of the space.

This idea is important to address one of the main predictions of structural models of growth, such as the one developed by Pasinetti (1963). In Pasinetti's model, in fact, consumers' needs come inevitably to satiation due to economic growth, so that industries producing goods subject to satiation do not grow any longer, leading to a halt in growth (Pasinetti, 1974, 1993). The idea of increase in product variety suggests that consumers never get satiated, because they substitute old needs with new needs, as the economy grows. In particular, products may receive new features that do not add functionalities, but symbolic value.

The degree of variety is then measured using entropy measures, particularly Theil's index from information theory. For the moment let us note that entropy measures are taken directly in physical attributes of products over time.

1.2   A Few Remarks on the Literature

In modeling the evolution of technology, it is interesting that economics of innovation made de facto a number of choices.

First, the distinction between causal and functional explanation has been downplayed. In order to escape from representations that imply human intentionality, evolutionary economics has represented technology directly in the space of physical embodiments, for example in terms of technical coefficients, or product attributes, or characteristics, that are directly observable and over which causation can be predicated. The relation between characteristics and physical structures is verified *ex post*, through the calculation of fitness, while the *ex ante* reasons are ignored. Consequently, all discursive reconstructions of technological change, by necessity, give an account of intentional activities of scientists, engineers and designers in reaching some desired state of the art, but this activity is immediately lost in formal modeling. The historical reconstructions of Walter Vincenti (1990) on aeronautical engineering, or Edward Constant (1980) on the turbojet are discursively recognized, but no serious theory of design is implemented. Nothing in combinatorial mechanisms of search resembles the way in which engineering decisions are made. As we will see, however, it is not intentionality that is the real problem. A coherent theory of technology may be built even without intentionality, or the 'design stance' (Dennett, 1987). The real difficulty is how to maintain separate, although interdependent, representations of structure and function. We suggest that in this theory-building approach an important role has been played by the need to minimize the role of human rationality in economic evolution, in order to avoid a choice-theoretic framework.

Second, evolutionary models adopt a representation of mutation that closely resembles the Darwinian notion of small, incremental, piecewise changes that take place in genetic materials. It is symptomatic that, after the publication of Nelson and Winter's book (1982), a stream of models has explicitly adopted formalisms such as genetic algorithms, classifier systems, or NK models, all of which are based on the idea of random variations of states of variables, taken one by one.

Third, the dynamics of variety generation is, roughly speaking, non-directed, or random. The overall dynamics is much more influenced by selective pressures (fitness) than by properties of the novelty generation process, which is left a black box. As Stadler et al. (2001) note, this amounts to assuming that genetic states can be accessed from everywhere, so that the space of variations is not structured or constrained, so that the bulk of the explanation lies not in the structure but in the selection process, or fitness.

As for socio-technical systems, Witt (2004) has noted that there is a fundamental distinction between assuming randomness in the variation stage and in the selection stage, or evaluation of alternatives: 'we can create as many combinatory extensions as we wish with a computer program – yet the associative act of meaning attribution at the core of the evaluation process still needs to be done by a human brain which, after all, is the bottleneck in the human creation of novelty' (p. 131). Therefore leaving the burden of the explanation of novelty just on the massive power of computation misses the point.

Fourth, it is assumed that variation is independent of selection. Variation takes place randomly (more or less) and then selection takes place in the market. Alternatively, it is somewhat assumed that selection takes place in a non-market context, for example in the R&D department of a large company following hierarchical managerial rules. But this does not change the implicit assumption that mutation is independent of selection. This strong feature makes it difficult to articulate any dialogue with those positions in sociology of technology that have underlined the fact that technological decisions are shaped by social considerations (Bijker et al., 1987; Bijker, 1995) and that often users influence deeply the way in which technological problems are framed (Oudshoorn and Pinch, 2003). If selection acts only *ex post*, then the role of social needs is only one of accepting or rejecting new solutions. In order to accommodate considerations of users and social shaping, it is essential to break with the notion of fitness and introduce exaptation as a crucial mechanism.

All these modeling assumptions have a common ground: the desire of evolutionary economics to reach, as much as possible, the scientific status of a particular kind of evolutionary theory in biology, the one associated with the works of Maynard Smith or Dawkins. In this tradition, sometimes labeled neo-Darwinism (Eldredge, 1995, 1999) the Darwinian natural selection theory is interpreted in its strictest form: mutations are small, random, blind, non-purposeful, and the evolutionary pattern can only be observed *ex post*, after selection has taken place. Transmission of heritable features can only take place through the genes and DNA, then through their molecular or chemical constitution, not outside it.

The attitude of evolutionary economics with respect to the already established evolutionary biology discipline must be justified in the light of the current scientific debate in the formation period, that is, the 1980s. However, it is time to reconsider the whole problem in the light of new conditions.

1.3   Unsolved Puzzles in Models of Technology

We suggest that models of technology developed so far in the tradition of evolutionary economics are subject to a paradox. They admit exploration and search in a space which is defined only in terms of physical elements (technical coefficients, product attributes, product characteristics); furthermore, they largely assume random search, or combinatorial search, with feedback from fitness functions. Elements subject to variations, or alleles, can be represented as long strings of binary values. Now, one can ask how large is the space of possible solutions. If agents must find and test all possible combinations by mutating alleles and, more importantly, if there is interdependency between the states of alleles, then it is possible to show that the size of the search space escalates rapidly with the number of elements and the degree of interdependence (Kauffman, 1993, 2000). Assuming that each trial requires a finite amount of resources and time, and each test requires a minimum amount of time, it is easy to conclude that, for moderately complex technological problems, the expected time to find a solution exceeds the life of humans on Earth.

It is a classical result of Kauffman's work that 'the expected time to reach an optimum is proportional to the dimensionality of the space' (Kauffman, 1993: 49). So as the number of elements N increases and the number of epistatic relations K increases, the time needed to reach an optimum grows. Now, suppose that, contrary to computer simulations, which take place almost in real time, each step in the adaptive walk in the fitness landscape takes time. Each engineering solution must be designed, prototyped, tested, then adopted or discarded. Each of these explorations is costly, placing a limit on the number of parallel paths that can be pursued by the same agent. Thus, roughly speaking, if all agents are doing the adaptive walk, the number of explorations per period equals the number of agents involved in exploration, times the number of different explorations per period, times the average number of parallel explorations afforded.

Another important result is called 'complexity catastrophe':

> As systems with many parts increase both the number of those parts and the richness of interactions among the parts, it is typical that the number of conflicting design constraints among the parts increases rapidly. Those conflicting constraints imply that optimization can attain only ever poorer compromises. No matter how strong selection may be, adaptive processes cannot climb higher peaks than afforded by the fitness landscape. That is, this limitation cannot be overcome by stronger selection. (Kauffman, 1993: 53–4)

Why, on the contrary, do we see such rapid technological progress in many fields? Furthermore, there is large evidence from the history of technology that technological progress does not follow a linear path, but shows accelerations and periods of stagnation. A quite impressive summary of this evidence is offered by Kline (1995), who normalized the growth in performance of ten technologies that enlarge human powers (such as transport, communication, or weapons) and plotted it over time. A sharp acceleration takes place circa 1840, after which date the evolution of technological performance becomes approximately linear in logarithmic scale.

As we will show below, several theories of technical progress that take into account this stylized feature have been proposed, but none of them offers an explanation of *why* we see sudden accelerations, nor *where*, or in which technologies, we see them. As remarked by Levinthal (1998), rapid technological change seems to have a 'slow pace'. And, as Nelson has noted (Nelson, 2003) the reason why we see such an uneven distribution of rates of progress is still not well understood.

Thus a related question, still unsolved, is: where do discontinuities come from?

A solution to this problem has been offered in terms of decomposition. Since the search space is extremely large and rugged, exhaustive search strategies, like hill climbing, end up in local optima, not global optima. By decomposing the search space into sub-spaces and searching for solutions that are optimal for each sub-space, overall solutions can be identified. Decomposition is clearly a powerful search heuristic, as the classical discussion by Simon demonstrated (Simon, 1962; 1969).

As Frenken (2006a) has shown, effective decomposition has been responsible for the extremely successful search strategy followed by the Wright brothers in inventing the airplane. The example is illuminating. Instead of combining piecewise many solutions to components of the airplane, as their contemporaries did, the Wright brothers addressed the three main functional problems of man-controlled flight, that is, control, lift and thrust, and addressed them separately, decomposing the overall problem of flight (Bradshaw and Lienert, 1991; but see also Copp and Zanella, 1993; Riddle and Sinnott, 2003; Johnson-Laird, 2005, for a more complete reconstruction).

While decomposition is clearly part of the solution, it is not at all sufficient. The difficult question in fact is: why the decomposition into {control, lift, thrust} was the appropriate one? How was it discovered? While it is accepted that a good decomposition makes the design problem tractable, it is also clear that there are many possible decompositions. Indeed, searching for the right decomposition may be as cognitively complex as the overall search in the space. Thus we need more than that. We definitely need to jump to a different representation.

1.4   The Changing Intellectual Landscape of Evolutionary Biology

Interestingly, we are now in a much better position than in the 1980s to build a theory that fully capitalizes on advances in the other large field of evolutionary theories – that is, biology. We do not subscribe to the notion that economics should follow biology, in any possible sense. The fact is that *both* depend critically on the particular notion of functions they adopt.

In fact, the strict neo-Darwinian representation of evolution is today challenged by other evolutionary approaches, most of them still fully compatible with Darwin's ideas. While we do not have time here to review the literature, let us briefly revisit the crucial points. First, the idea that variation is not random, but is guided or directed, is now widely accepted. In his monumental end-of-life work, Stephen Jay Gould (2002) has shown that directed variation comes from two sources:

> some adaptive features of organisms may be directly molded by, or may originate as immediate and deterministic consequences of the physical properties of matter and the dynamical nature of forces [while some] features arise nonadaptively as physically necessary consequences of other changes that may (and, in all probability, usually do) have an adaptive basis. [so called *spandrels*] (p. 1054)

Consequently,

> natural selection must therefore operate in a context of far greater constraints (in both the 'negative' sense of limits upon freedom to craft particular adaptive solutions, and in the 'positive' sense of synergism in the specification of preexisting or preferred internal channels) than the usual functionalist characterization of Darwinian theory envisages. (p. 1065)

There is no need, according to Gould, to invoke teleology to abandon a view of random variation (Eldredge, 1995; Shanahan, 2004; Pigliucci and Kaplan, 2006; see also Sterelny, 2007). A rigorous evolutionary account can include various forms of directedness.[2]

In this direction, a particularly elaborate discussion of the way in which the relations between genotype and phenotype can be modeled is offered in Stadler et al. (2001). They rightly argue that fitness landscape models are based on the wrong assumption that each point of the phenotypic and genetic states could be easily accessible from other points, using a mathematical structure of Euclidean distances. New notions of punctuated change, developmental constraints, and directionality of evolution all require a fundamentally different mathematical representation. Second, the molecular view of evolution, strictly associated to the discovery of the chemical constitution of DNA, is now complemented by systems biology, a view that admits not only bottom up causation (from elements to higher order levels) but also regulatory, or top down or downward causation, which can be hardly explained by reference to massive variation of chemical elements in the genetic material (Noble, 2006). The discovery of epigenetic mutations, or mutations that take place outside DNA, have also deeply changed the way in which evolution at molecular level is conceived. Along the same lines, the mapping of the human genome has revealed that only a tiny part of genetic material is involved in DNA replication, so that the molecular biology dogma is now largely abandoned.

Third, it is now recognized that evolution takes place at different levels of organization, not only at the level of genes. Jablonka and Lamb (2005) have suggested that it takes place at genetic, epigenetic, behavioral and symbolic levels. The latter two levels open the way for reconsidering the relation between genetic variation and cultural variation (Boyd and Richerson, 1985; Cavalli Sforza, 2001; Changeux, 2003, 2008; Richerson and Boyd, 2005), as well as for re-addressing the debated issue of the relations between genetic variation and the environment (Lewontin, 2000). All these developments are clearly relevant for evolutionary theories of artificial systems, such as technology, and call for an explicit treatment of the relation between evolution at the level of physical constituents (in our case, artifacts) and at the level of representations.

In these developments, an important role is played by the notion of *exaptation*, introduced by Stephen Gould and Richard Lewontin (1979) and further developed with Elisabeth Vrba (Gould and Vrba, 1982; Vrba and Gould, 1986). This notion will be crucial for our theory of dynamics in the function space. The idea of exaptation was introduced to react to the tendency of evolutionary biology to explain all observed features of the living world as a consequence of adaptiveness. This is not necessarily true, Gould and Lewontin suggested: sometimes a given feature is generated without any adaptive property, is retained simply because it does not harm the organism, and receives a functional role later, usually for completely different reasons (see below).

This notion is important because it permits the relation between physical constraints and adaptiveness to be articulated in a more sophisticated way. Physical constraints act on living and artificial matter and channel the direction of possible evolution. New physical configurations may have several functions and may be retained and survive thanks to just one or a subset of them. For many features, there is simply no functional explanation for their appearance, only a physical explanation related to their feasibility, or conditions for existence. But, here is the most interesting part of the theory, new functions can be discovered *ex post*. Once a feature survives because it is associated to other features that have a function, it may be discovered that it can serve a completely new function. This process is called exaptation.

This problem, although in a different form, resonates also in the most recent work of Stuart Kauffman (2000), which departs from his early works in a significant way. He reports on the pioneering work of Walter Fontana, a theoretical chemist at Santa Fe Institute who has developed a Lisp program (Alchemy) able to perform computations on expressions in such a way that these expressions can be transformed, as happens in chemical reactions, and become themselves operators for further transformations. New expressions are continuously created from these operations; new expressions which appear more frequently are retained, while the less frequent are eliminated. By keeping the total number of expressions constant (at $n = 10\,000$) it is possible to observe the creation of expressions of increasingly higher complexity, operating on other expressions of lower complexity. This work attracted enormous interest in the 1990s, because it promised to reveal principles of self-organization that could be general. What happened,

Kauffman says, was however rather disappointing. Alchemy creates expressions of type 1, similar to replicators, and expressions of type 2, close to autocatalytic chains. Less frequently, it creates expressions of type 3, similar to eukaryote cells. Nothing more. The system is unable to generate any expression of higher complexity, and no one knows exactly why.

Interestingly, Kauffman suggests an articulated functional explanation. The emergence of expressions of higher complexity requires that their collective properties are recognized and retained, avoiding disruptions. In other words, expressions of higher complexity are less probable and more unstable, so they can be disrupted more easily. What Alchemy lacks, suggests Kauffman, is a mechanism that recognizes collective properties of structures of increasing higher complexity, because these properties increase the fitness. We may translate his explanation in the following way: a world without functions is a world of limited complexity.

There must be a mechanism that drastically reduces the exploration. This is the mapping between configurations of physical (or chemical) elements in nature and possible functions, that preserve the configuration from disruption and disappearance. It is not possible to compute the space of all possible mappings, even if we knew in detail (as happens in Newtonian, quantum or relativity physics) all the possible physical configurations.

In order to explain the non-algorithmic nature of natural selection, Kauffman makes an interesting use of the notion of exaptation: it is not possible to generate the new configuration algorithmically, because its functions are discovered only after it appears, thanks to the co-evolutionary interactions of it with other elements of the biosphere. To predict the functions, one should tell the entire history of the evolution of the configuration until the final point, including all the elements that lead to the discovery of the new function – something that clearly contradicts the notion of algorithm. Thus we have to abandon the idea that evolutionary dynamics can be computed and accept that it has a history, that is, something that can be told but not algorithmically compressed. This is a remarkable departure from his previous works, in which the distinction between natural and artificial, or between the physico-chemical building blocks and the emergent order, were a matter of computation, not of logical difference.

Summing up, evolutionary economics has now a much larger menu of theories in evolutionary biology to look at, instead of just the neo-Darwinian perspective. The narrow adoption of a simple modeling approach of non-directed search can be fruitfully substituted by more promising models.

2.   NOT ONLY TACITNESS. THE SECOND HALF OF MICHAEL POLANYI

In Chapter 4 of *An Evolutionary Theory of Economic Change*, Nelson and Winter introduced to the economics profession the work of the late scientist-philosopher Michael Polanyi (Nelson and Winter, 1982). In two books published in 1958 (*Personal Knowledge. Towards a Post-critical Philosophy*) and 1967 (*The Tacit Dimension*), Polanyi developed an articulated theory of knowledge, based on the notion that 'we know more than we can tell', and that there are limits to the degree to which knowledge can be articulated and expressed in language. The notion of tacitness gained enormous success in the economics of innovation and was adopted as an essential part of explanation in several fields.

There are good reasons for this success.

First, the idea of tacit knowledge helps to explain why organizational routines tend to be sticky and idiosyncratic, so that knowledge is attached to firms and transmitted in the form of routines. If on the contrary knowledge were fully codifiable, then it would rather be a matter of rational decision (for example, a matter of cost of knowledge acquisition) which piece of knowledge to use in any given situation, as happens in mainstream economics. Therefore it was a crucial element of the claim that evolutionary mechanisms of mutation, retention and selection are at play in the economic system, because these mechanisms require that instructions, or information, are not transmitted separately from their embodiment (for example, genetic material).

Second, it helped to reframe the economics of innovation, far from the assimilation of knowledge to information (and then of economics of innovation as a sub-discipline of the economics of information). Most theorems in the informational view of innovation developed by Arrow or Hirshleifer rely crucially on the idea that knowledge can circulate freely and transmission of knowledge does not impair the content (Arrow, 1962, 1969; Hirshleifer, 1971; Lamberton, 1971). These ideas have been subsequently elaborated (Arrow, 1974, 1994, 1996; Hirshleifer and Riley, 1992), but keeping the central notion intact. One might then ask why the system does not identify these complex structures simply by following an algorithmic procedure, that is, exploring the space of states of the system. The answer is that the size of the space is of higher dimensionality than the life of the universe or the total number of particles in the universe. This argument leads Kauffman to an interesting conclusion: the number of all possible configurations of the portion of universe subject to natural selection, that is, the biosphere, is not infinite but transfinite, that is, no computational system in the universe can compute it. This means that the evolution of the biosphere cannot be conceived as an exploration, by random mutations, of all possible configurations. The dynamics is highly non-ergodic.

The idea of tacitness radically alters this view, suggesting that making knowledge articulable may be costly, even prohibitively costly:

> costs matter. Whether a particular bit of knowledge is in principle articulable or necessarily tacit is not the relevant question in most behavioral situations. Rather, the question is whether the costs associated with the obstacles to articulation are sufficiently high so that the knowledge in fact remains tacit. (Nelson and Winter, 1982: 82)

From this remark a large stream of studies originated, leading to an economics of knowledge almost entirely based on the economic analysis of codification costs (Senker, 1995; Cowan et al., 2000; Foray, 2000; see Balconi et al., 2007).

Third, the variable combinations between codified and tacit knowledge resulted in a useful foundation for a theory of industrial dynamics based on localized technological change (Antonelli, 1995), for a theory of contracts in which tacitness is a key source of transaction costs (Teece, 1986), and for theories of organizational learning based on socialization and articulation (Nonaka and Takeuchi, 1995).

In the light of this success, it is remarkable that few authors took the trouble to explore other dimensions of the theory of knowledge of Polanyi. Interestingly, it contains a full scale discussion of the nature of technology. Even more interestingly, this discussion can be linked to a large stream of literature in various fields that has addressed similar problems and can offer valuable inputs to economic thinking and modeling about complexity.

How can objects be described? Among many others, this question was clearly addressed by Polanyi in *Personal Knowledge* (Polanyi, 1958), wrongly famous only for the notion of tacitness.

In articulating this relation, Polanyi addresses a classical problem in the philosophy of scientific explanation and develops a distinction which has a more general validity. Take an object as the reference point. How many different descriptions are possible for any given object? There are many possible descriptions regarding its physical structure, depending on the scale of observation (object, parts of the object, molecules, atoms, particles), the aspects described (geometry, materials, physical properties such as mass or weight, and so on), the coarseness of description and the like. Ultimately, all descriptions of this type have the same logical nature and are mutually reducible to each other, shifting the frame of reference. Let us call them *structural descriptions*. A structural description regards an object according to its structure or form, or it contains structural properties of the object. Generally, structural properties are related to two main elements: materials and shape. Thus a structural description includes an object into one or more classes of objects that share the same properties. There are many classes to which an object may be ascribed according to its properties: the class of all objects with the same weight, with the same shape, made of the same material and so on. The number of classes is an open question, but for all practical purposes let us assume that it is a large number. As the description is based on physical properties, and as physical objects are finite by definition, this number would be probably finite, but for all practical purposes it may be considered very large.

Thus a structural description is a very rich one, since it allows many levels and permits the connection with many other structural descriptions. In general, it is possible to generate many descriptions that have the same logical nature, that is, can be transformed into each other provided a sufficiently rich vocabulary is developed. Thus a description in terms of molecular structures can be transformed into a description in terms of atomic structures provided the chemical and physical laws relating the two levels are specified, and some level of approximation is introduced for calculation (Klein and Lachièze-Rey, 1999). The question is: is this the only admissible *type* of description?

According to Polanyi there is another type of description, which is called *functional description*. In this type of description, the object is considered in relation to its behavior or effect, not structure. To describe the behavior of an object it is necessary to specify the conditions under which the behavior is observed. A behavior under a general class of conditions is called a function.

So we say that the function of a heart is to pump blood. Or the function of a hammer, under the conditions that a force is exerted on the wooden body around a fulcrum, is to push a nail in the wall. Functional descriptions apply well to biology and technology, or to living and artificial systems, although there are important differences between the two fields. Why do we use such a term in our descriptions? The answer of Polanyi is clear: structural and functional descriptions are both necessary, but they have a different logical nature. It is not possible to derive a functional description by recombining structural information – it requires information of a different kind. Technology works according to reasons and operational principles, while structural descriptions are based on causes, as highlighted by scientific knowledge. Technology must be evaluated in terms of success, not truth. The success of a machine is explained in terms of its operational principles, not the physical or chemical causes, although the former must be compatible with the latter.

The problem discussed by Polanyi refers, in a non-technical way and without many quotations to the relevant literature, to an old but still controversial ontological problem, that is, identity and diversity. In *Fedone* (58A), Plato talked about the ship used by Theseus, to save himself and seven pairs of youths. In order to thank Apollo for rescuing the youths, Athenians promised to send the very same ship of Theseus each year to Delos, and to refrain from death penalties during the whole period of the journey. To realize this promise, they had to do extensive maintenance of the ship each year and substitute damaged parts. So the problem is: was the ship the very same ship of Theseus, or rather, piece after piece, had the identity of the ship changed? What constituted the identity of the ship, the physical constitution of any single piece of wood, or some other property?

This problem has been repeatedly discussed by philosophers, such as Leibniz, Hobbes, Locke and Hume until recent times, in which the problem of identity, or persistence of objects, has been made central to modern metaphysics, philosophy of mind (Chisholm, 1976; Hirsch, 1982; van Inwagen, 1990; Merricks, 2003; Elder, 2004; Thomasson, 2007) and ontology (Casati and Varzi, 1999; Varzi, 2001, 2005; Ferraris, 2005). From more of an engineering perspective such a problem has been widely studied in seminal papers by Gero (1990), and then by Vermaas (2007) and Dorst and Vermaas (2005).

It is our contention that all this literature is highly relevant for a deep understanding of technology and of the evolution of economic systems. It sheds light on the dual logical nature of functions, and then on the need to build up a theory that appropriately represents this distinction. On one hand, the ship *must* be made of wood or other material. Without the physical embodiment of the ship, there is no entity called ship. At the same time, describing the ship only in terms of the exact physical constitution is not adequate either, because there is no way to avoid the paradoxical implication that by changing the pieces the ship is no longer the same, which is contrary to evidence. There must be, as suggested by Polanyi, another level of description, one which is compatible with the physical description but is not completely determined by it.

This argument, in our view, is logically compelling. No description in purely structural form, that is, whose arguments refer only to physical entities and causal chains operating on them, is able to represent evolutionary systems, either in biology or technology. Evolutionary economics has paid service to the need to represent functions, but then has developed all models only as a search in the space of attributes or similar. It is time to take on board the second half of Polanyi and try to develop a more comprehensive theory.

3.   FUNCTIONAL REPRESENTATIONS: A PHILOSOPHICAL INTRODUCTION

Needless to say, however, things are not stuck at the point where Polanyi left them. In the last thirty years his problem, once considered marginal in philosophy, gained momentum.

The notion of function has indeed a troubled history in logic and philosophy of science, particularly after the rejection of the notion of teleological cause introduced by Aristotle. The main reason is that the notion of functions implies a dimension of *normativity*. According to philosophers Krohs and Kroes:

> The ascription of a function to a biological trait goes beyond a mere description of what the trait does. Mammalian hearts move blood, and like most but not all other hearts, they move it through the animal's blood vessels. This biological finding is descriptive in the same way that the geological finding that magma chambers below the bases of volcanoes extrude lava out of a crater through a conduit in the volcano or the physical finding that two masses attract each other are descriptive. However, biologists ascribe to the heart not only the action but also the function of pumping blood. In contrast to the mere description, the function ascription allows one also to talk about malfunction or dysfunction, a situation in which a function is impaired or not performed at all. This contrasts sharply with the situation in physics. (Krohs and Kroes, 2009: 3; see Franssen, 2006)

Because of the difficulty of articulating normativity without making reference to teleology, the logical validity of functional description was put in doubt by such eminent philosophers as Hempel in the 1950s, and the whole issue became rapidly obsolete. Hempel (1959) tried to subsume the functional description as part of the nomological-deductive explanation, where the function is inferred from the underlying causal relations (that is, because a muscular structure shaped like a heart invariably produces pumping, we say it has the function of pumping). A functional explanation is a deductive explanation in which the condition is the effect produced by the object, and the cause (the function of the object) is inferred by necessity. If we are not wrong, however, despite his relevance to the argument, Hempel is not cited by Polanyi in his *Personal Knowledge*. It is important to recall this approach, because most economic analysis (implicitly) follows it, downplaying the distinction between causal and functional explanation.

Because functional explanations can appear to be bound up with teleology, philosophy of science prefers to deal with notions of causality and causal explanation, rather than functional explanation (McLaughlin, 2001). However, the overall question has been reopened by an article by Wright in 1973, that offered an etiological definition of functions, fully compatible with a naturalistic view: 'The function of X is Z means: (a) X is there because it does Z, and (b) Z is a consequence (or result) of X's being there' (Wright, 1973).

This reformulation of the traditional notion opened the way to several naturalistic conceptualizations, starting with Cummins's functional analysis (Cummins, 1975) and culminating in Millikan's proposal of a unified framework (Millikan, 1984, 1993). It may be interesting to the economics profession to look at the extremely rich literature that developed in philosophy in the two and half decades after Millikan's landmark book, because it is the very same foundational period of evolutionary economics.

All these contributions accept the logical distinction between physical description and functional description. The strategy of reducing functional descriptions to a nomological-deductive scheme, as suggested by Hempel, has logical flaws, as Polanyi clearly noted. *There are always many ways in which a given cause may be produced*: for example blood may be pumped by an artificial heart or by a system of valves. An inference from the effect to the presence of the cause is *not* logically binding.

At the same time, once one has started to describe an object according to its function, immediately it becomes clear that it may have many other functions, perhaps less trivial. A hammer can be used to keep a door open, or to support the body of a plant, or to weigh down a stack of paper sheets so that they do not fly away. In describing these functions it is necessary to change the conditions under which the behavior is observed. Once one has generated some examples of plausible functions for the object several questions arise, such as: how many functions are there for an object? And: what is the relation between describing an object according to its function and describing it according to its structure?

The number of functions is an open question, but there is nothing logically absurd in admitting they are potentially a large number. Of course not all changes in conditions are admissible, so not all functions are plausible for an object. Ultimately, functions must be described in terms of physical variables. 'Pushing a nail into the wall' can be translated into 'exerting a pressure of X kilograms per square millimeter following a movement with angle k on axis Y around a fulcrum at the bottom of the object' or the like. Thus we may agree on the intuition that the number of functions must be finite but very large. Then why do we identify only a few? We suggest that this question is a fundamental one to understand radical innovation.

A promising way to answer this question is to propose that functions are the result of a *selectional* process, similar to that assumed in evolutionary biology (Millikan, 1984; Neander 1991a, 1991b, 1995). In this way a function is ascribed to an object not in virtue of its actual or possible functions, but in virtue of the fact that that function must be the result of a selectional process that occurred in the past, with some ancestors. This also explains why we tend to identify a small number of functions to objects, even though there may be others. The realized mapping we observe (the fact that a hammer is normally used for pushing nails in the wall) must result from a process of selection among many possible mappings.

This points to the final question. Given that the descriptions according to functions and according to structures are different, the relation between the two cannot be logically binding. This is the fundamental contribution of the critique to Hempel's attempt to reduce functions to deductive reasoning. There is nothing logically compelling in establishing a relation between a structure and a function. There has to be a translation or *mapping* between the two.

Philosophical theories, interestingly, differentiate among themselves on the basis of the specific selectional mechanism assumed as the explanation for the emergence of functions (Perlman, 2004, 2009). Thus Cummins's theory admits only a causal mechanism operating at the same timescale as the object of which the functions are investigated (Cummins, 1975), or is present-looking. On the contrary, backward-looking theories of functions try to reconstruct the etiological, or historical sequence of causal factors that have led to the selection of a function. So called theories of the recent past justify functions on the basis of events immediately antecedent to the manifestation of the function, so assume goal-directedness (Boorse, 1976; Nagel, 1977; Godfrey-Smith, 1994), or teleological explanations. On the other hand, theories of the distant or ancient past admit that the explanation for the emergence of a function may lie well back historically in an etiological chain and try to identify the evolutionary causation (Millikan, 1984, 1993; Neander 1991a, 1991b; Griffiths, 1993). A minority position admits a forward-looking perspective, assuming that objects may have *propensities* (Bigelow and Pargetter, 1987).

Vermaas and Houkes (2003) summarize the debate pointing to three general approaches: the I(ntentionalist), C(causal-role), and E(volutionist) theories, and suggest an integrative model, called ICE (see also Vermaas and Houkes, 2006) in which intentional and structural descriptions are jointly used.

An interesting debate takes place in the philosophical literature as to whether the notion of function applies equally well to natural and to artificial systems, to evolutionary biology and to technology. There are some technical difficulties, such as the need to make intentionality in the description of technology logically redundant, or the difference in ascription of functions to wholes and parts between organisms and artifacts, or the time scale for selection.

Indeed, as the careful study of Lewens (2004) has shown, an important distinction to be drawn is between *selection*, which only applies to the level of population, and *selective forces*, which apply to individuals and whose outcomes also depend on developmental constraints. Thus the appeal to intentionality of designers in technology is not at all a solution and the appeal to a general theory of functions is promising:

> explanations in terms of intention often explain not the makeup of an artefact but the actions of the artificer; intentional actions can affect individual objects, while evolutionary functions refer to population-level phenomena; many artifacts have evolutionary functions that are not intended functions, for these artifacts have effects that augment their fitness even though these effects are unintended; many artifacts have intended functions that are not evolutionary functions, for the intention of the artificer mistakes the selection pressures at work on the items, or because the intention of the artificer in some particular token case does not reflect the general selection pressures at work on artifacts of the type. (Lewens, 2004: 166)

Even taking into account these differences, most authors claim that a general theory of functions can be built. According to Krohs and Kroes (2009) there are striking similarities between natural and artificial systems that warrant a unified theory: they have hierarchically organized systemic structures, are subject to evolution, exhibit development (in the biological sense or in technical construction), are capable of reproduction (or technical series production) and try to maintain integrity through recovery, regulation and self-repair.

Indeed, McLaughlin has suggested that the appeal to functions 'explains the existence and properties of those parts of a self-reproducing system that contribute to the self-reproduction of that system. What functions explain is systems whose identity conditions consist in the constant replacement, repair, or reproduction of their component parts' (McLaughlin, 2001: 209). The statement that functions and structures call for logically different types of descriptions is supported also by Nicholas Rescher. In his view, the information contained in a structural description does not logically imply the information in a functional description (Rescher, 1996).

These views point to an important point, that is, *that functional descriptions can be ultimately written in physical terms*. Any function can be described as a statement in physical language. In other words, functional and structural descriptions must be compatible, since ultimately the behavior of the object must be realized in the physical world. Still, the crucial point is that these representations are *logically different*.[3]

4.   FUNCTIONAL REPRESENTATION AS DISTINCTIVE HUMAN ABILITY: INSIGHTS FROM RECENT SCIENTIFIC DISCOVERIES

From the philosophical discussion above a clear insight is to be retained: functional representations, and the associated normativity, are a necessary ingredient for understanding all systems that exhibit properties of survival and evolution – namely, biological and technical systems. Is this insight just a philosophical suggestion, or do we find evidence in empirical sciences that this is, indeed, the case?

Interestingly, we have identified several fields of science in which compelling arguments have been recently developed in support of the notion of functional representation. Thus the philosophical argument has a detailed counterpart in recent advancements in human and social sciences, such as neuroscience, paleoanthropology, development psychology and history of technology.

The separate representation of functions and structures is most likely at the origin of the technical capabilities of mankind, which is highly distinctive of the species, and which has probably evolved slowly in the natural history. One of the reasons is that it requires the development of an operational memory of sufficient size (Schick and Toth, 1993; Boncinelli, 2006; de Beaune, 2009). Recent neuro-physiological research on mirror neurons suggests that humans recall the function of an action (for example, picking up a cup of coffee) even when the physical realization of the action is experimentally interrupted, that is, maintain a functional representation in the mind independent of the causal representation offered by visual clues (Rizzolatti and Sinigaglia, 2006; Iacoboni, 2008). This mechanism may be at the origin of the ability to form functional representations in the absence of sensory stimuli, and to work on them in the operational memory.

It is most likely that this capability is peculiar to humans. Animals can learn simple functional relations from repetition of causal actions, but cannot develop machines. Biologists studying the differences between men and monkeys and apes show that, although the latter are able to solve correctly elementary problems of functions (for example, filling the blank card between an apple and a cut apple with the card representing a knife), they are not able to solve problems that require maintaining a representation of the functions for a certain time interval (Tomasello, 1999; Premack and Premack, 2003).

Also, some evidence is accumulating on the peculiar development process by which human children start to acquire the ability to think functionally, as a separate ability from thinking causally (Corballis and Lea, 1999; Kelemen 1999; Kelemen and Di Yanni, 2005; Margolis and Laurence, 2007).

Finally, historians of technology emphasize that the distinctive capability of humans to manipulate nature is rooted in the learning of general schemes of functions, starting from the initial rudimentary creation of artifacts, then to their combination in more complex artifacts, finally to the application of energy (Leroi-Gourhan, 1943, 1945). The appearance of language greatly improved the ability to transmit knowledge on these schemes (Leroi-Gourhan, 1964). More recent acquisitions point to the emergence of abstract representations of tools as a possible explanation for differential survival chances in early hominids (Schick and Toth, 1993; Gibson and Ingold, 1993). Indeed, the new field of cognitive archaeology is committed to the integration between paleoanthropology, archaeology and neurosciences in order to explain the emergence among hominids of superior cognitive skills, among which technical invention is a crucial one (de Beaune, 2009).

In future works we will review these results more in depth. But the main theme is slowly becoming clear: there is convincing evidence that the ability of humankind to represent functions as separate from objects is distinctive, originated historically in the evolution, has most likely a correlate in brain organization, develops ontogenetically in early childhood, and is responsible for the departure of humans from earlier species. All these elements are so compelling that any theory of technology, in the future, should take them seriously into account.

The discussion so far has led us to postulate that these spaces have different *logical* nature, so they must be represented independently by human beings in their minds. After having stated these foundational points, let us explore in more detail what a theory of functions can deliver to the economics of technology and innovation.

We will develop such a theory in the following steps:

(i)   non-isomorphism
(ii)   abduction
(iii) abstraction
(iv)   representation
(v)   distance
(vi)   exaptation.

5.   TOWARDS A MODEL OF TECHNOLOGY AS SEARCH IN STRUCTURE AND FUNCTION SPACE

5.1   Non-isomorphism

The discussion from philosophy has made clear the need for representing functions and structures separately. It is now useful to investigate how to represent them, and above all how to represent the relation between them. Interestingly, these problems have strong correspondence with the way in which engineering disciplines reflexively represent and model themselves.

There are three main streams of literature within engineering disciplines that are relevant for our purposes. The first is the systematic effort of some authors, mainly in continental European countries, to build a *general theory of design*. In this line of research, experienced academic engineers try to identify common types of problems across all specialized disciplines and to build up a systematic catalogue of procedures used to solve them (Pahl and Beitz, 1984).

The second stream of literature is more pragmatic, since it was originated by an effort to develop *an artificial intelligence approach to design* (Tong and Sriram, 1992; Sriram, 1997). Here the practical problem was how to automate design problems and develop software programs that could substitute for human problem solving. It turned out that many design problems could *not* be automated at all, but the reason for that impossibility was far from clear. This difficulty fuelled research into the abstract nature of design problems. In this direction this pragmatic line of work had important connections with the tradition of analysis of problem solving heuristics and procedures in cognitive science. The failure of artificial intelligence to automatize design has important lessons for theory development.

Finally, there are also a number of *ethnographic* studies, which describe in detail the heuristics and problem solving procedures used by engineers and designers in field tasks (Ferguson, 1992; Bucciarelli, 1994).

In general design theory, the distinction between structural and functional description plays a central role (Pahl and Beitz, 1984; Hubka et al., 1988; Ulrich and Eppinger, 1995; Ullman, 1997). Theories of design as specialized problem solving (Brown and Chandrasekaran, 1989; Coyne et al., 1990; Sridharan and Campbell, 2004) show that the reasoning behind design is based on heuristics about the likelihood that a given structural configuration can implement a desired set of functions, of the form 'generate and test' (Goel and Pirolli, 1992). *There is no logical necessity in this reasoning*, insofar as there are a large number of alternative ways to implement the desired functions. This notion is made even more explicit in the axiomatic theory of design (Suh, 1990).

Let us summarize the main arguments of these contributions by introducing some notions. For the sake of clarity, let us use a naive graphical representation.

Let F be the function space, or the set of all possible functions. This space contains all possible behaviors of objects under any conceivable condition, subject to the constraints that they can be implemented in the physical world. This means that the function 'moving at speed higher than light' is not included in the function space.

Let us remark that functions are *not* needs. The latter are defined in discursive terms by human users of objects. They play a crucial role, which will be discussed below, under the notion of systems of use. Functions are defined in physical terms, as behaviors under specified conditions, which are connected to a general effect. The question how needs are interpreted by firms and are transformed into requirements for functions is a crucial one, and we will address it in the final part of the chapter. In the engineering literature, a certain effort has been put into trying to build up common vocabularies and general catalogues of functions and in developing models for connecting functions to known solutions (see for example Kirschman and and Fadel, 1998; Kitamura et al., 2001; Hirtz et al., 2004; Nagel et al., 2007). As we will show, we have contributed to this literature by developing a very large, highly structured function base, including more than 4000 functional expressions (verb + object), with full analysis of synonyms and antonyms, and also of terms at various degrees of generality (father and son) (Bonaccorsi and Fantoni, 2007; Apreda et al., 2008a, 2008b).

Let S be the structure space, or the set of all possible structures. This includes all natural structures and all conceivable artifacts, the latter subject to the constraints that they do not violate physical laws. This means that the structure 'chocolate bar at 300° C' or the structure 'an engine exhibiting *motum perpetuum*' are not included in the structure space. As Galileo Galilei once noted, a mouse the size of an elephant would not be possible, because the geometry of the mouse skeleton would not support such a large weight. Therefore a very big mouse is not part of the structure space (Griffin, 1962; Bonner, 2006).

At a very general level the main elements of structure are shape, or form, and material (Pahl and Beitz, 1984). Because of their form and material, artifacts have some properties

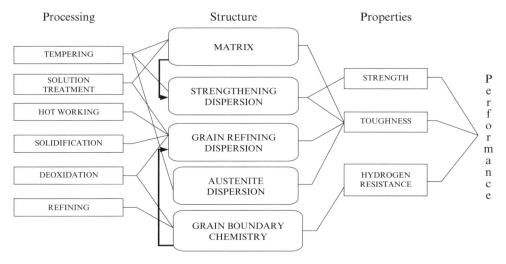

Source: Olson (2002).

Figure 12.1   Flow-block diagrams in materials design (steel)

or behaviors, and due to these exhibit certain performances. More detailed descriptions of structures can be given, depending on specific areas. For example, in mechanical engineering a complex structure like a car is said to have a *macro-function* (for example, to transport people), delivered thanks to an *internal working* (combustion engine) and implemented by drivers through a specific *mode of use* (driving). In delivering the function, cars exhibit *behaviors* that are necessary to implement the function (for example, vibration of the engine) and *effects* that are not necessary (for example, noise emission). In materials technology a rather general representation is a flow-block diagram that links *processing* technologies to physical *structures* (microstructural subsystems such as crystal grain sizes), and these structures to *properties* they control (such as strength and toughness). Finally, properties lead to a desired *performance*, which is needed in order to implement functions when the material is used in an artifact. A representation in the field of steel technology is offered in Figure 12.1.

In the literature on design theory, a distinctive effort has been made by John Gero to articulate the relation between structure and function by introducing an intermediate space, that is, behavior (Gero, 1990; Gero and Kannengiesser, 2002; Dorst and Vermaas, 2005). The idea is that a structure implements a given function because it exhibits some behavior under specific circumstances, namely due to the use of the user. This leads to a more comprehensive model, called Function-Behaviour-Structure (FBS). Our discussion will hold either with a simple structure-function mapping, or with a multi-step mapping model including behavior, as well as a more complex model including values and needs (see below).

In fact, although all these qualifications are important, and are indeed necessary to articulate the design process, we make an abstraction from them. All relevant definitions are summarized in the notion of *structure space*.

Based on the discussion in the sections above, a crucial implication is that human

Function
space

Structure
space

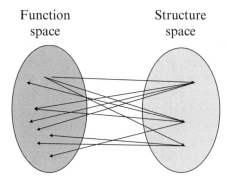

Figure 12.2   Potential many-to-many mapping between function and structure spaces

beings have the distinctive ability to represent functions (perhaps large classes of functions) as *independent* from objects. Their learning takes place not only in the space of structures, resulting from repetition of causal observations, but also in the space of functions, representing them in an abstract way. It is then important to understand what is the relation between functions and structures.

A correspondence between a point or a region in the structure space and a point or region in the function space is called *mapping*.

An important question is as follows: how many mappings are possible for any given point in the two spaces? Following our previous discussion, there are *always* many points in the structure space that can implement any desired function. At the same time, each structure has many possible functions. Consequently, although we observe objects that have a well defined set of functions, there is always a *many-to-many correspondence* between the two spaces (Figure 12.2).

Formally, the two spaces do not enjoy properties of holohedral isomorphism, nor of merohedral isomorphism (Polya, 1945: 46). Holohedral isomorphism, or simply isomorphism, is the property that there is a one–one correspondence between the objects of the two systems S and S' preserving certain relations. It means that if such a relation holds between the objects of one system, the same relation holds between the corresponding objects of the other system. On the other hand, merohedral isomorphism, or homomorphism, implies that there is a one–many correspondence between the objects of the systems S and S' preserving certain relations.

The mapping between S and F, in our case, is a *many–many correspondence*, lacking the inner order and predictability of any type of isomorphism. At the same time, it is clear that this correspondence is definitely *not* a random matching between pairs of points in the structure and function space. The potential mapping is highly structured.

If this is true, why in the real world do we see a close matching between objects and their main functions? Why do objects seem to exhibit a 'natural' propensity[4] to implement just the intended functions, and not others? The answer is an *evolutionary* one: the close matching between structures and functions is only the outcome of a (usually unobserved) selection process. The many-to-many mappings have been filtered through the system of use. This process is only observable in the history of design, which should be an integral part of a functional theory. Alternatively, the selection process may take place entirely in the mind of designers, or in R&D departments, without being subject to *ex post* market selection. In this case only archival research or introspective studies may make visible the selection process.

Let us refine the argument about the precise relation between the two spaces. A structure implementing a function is ultimately subject to a physical description. This description will include a causality relation of the sort: 'the structure of heart produced the pumping of blood'. The flow diagram illustrated for materials science in Figure 12.1 can be read from the left to the right as follows: 'the matrix structure of material K, obtained through a process of tempering and solution treatment, produces certain properties of toughness and hence delivers the performance required'. Would it be possible to go backward from the effect to the cause, that is, from the right to the left? If yes, would it be possible to collect an exhaustive list of all possible structures that produce a desired effect?

In other words, is the mapping reducible to a search within all possible causal explanations? If this were possible, one would build a complete catalogue of all possible causal relations, then would ask what is the desired effect and would generate (almost automatically) all possible mappings.

Unfortunately, this is not logically possible. The mapping can *never* be derived *only* from knowledge of structures. The reason is that causality relations are not of a deductive type, so that it is always possible to conclude whether the set of all possible conditions for a given effect is closed.

Causal relations have to be established inductively. Now, in inductive logic, there is not a process by which it is possible to construct the set of *all* possible causes for an effect (Copi and Burgess-Jackson, 1996; Gustason, 1994). Causal relations must be collected one by one and checked separately. So the catalogue is never guaranteed to be complete. The mapping can never be automated.

This argument can also be defended along the lines of theory of causality (Glymour and Cooper, 1999; Pearl, 2000). Given a causal structure, is it possible to reason back from an effect to all possible causes? The theory shows that this is possible only under very severe assumptions, which are normally violated in design problems. In most cases what one can obtain is a set of non-causal factors, rather than the complete list of causal factors. This points to a fundamental property of mapping: knowledge about physical structures can enumerate exhaustively only all mappings that are not feasible, but never all those that are.

From a cognitive point of view a mapping is a projection from a space into another. There is no logical necessity for such projection. Knowledge of the structure space has limited the admissible region, leaving however a large number of open possibilities.

This leaves us with a difficult theoretical issue (see for example Lombardi, 2008): how to avoid that the combinatorial explosion of all possible configurations makes the problem simply intractable? If each mapping must be generated and tested, even a moderately complex artifact would imply a huge number of possible configurations. The most common answer in design theory, following the tradition of complex problem solving, has been to invoke the power of heuristics. Although this is entirely appropriate, we suggest there is another powerful mechanism: abstract search in the function space, as represented in an appropriate language.

This idea is logically derived by the normativity of functions. To say that a functional description is normative means that it is possible to state whether a given mapping is appropriate (that is, implements a function) or is a failure (that is, is a non-function). Normativity is a crucial feature of functional representations. In the case of technical and biological functions, normativity is eventually rooted in physical mechanisms (usually at several levels of organizational complexity). While it is not possible to derive from the functional description the complete list of all mappings that are appropriate, it will be possible to identify general classes of constraints, that restrict the search for solutions.

Therefore it is not possible to close the set of all possible mappings: in the words of Kauffman (2000) it is not infinite, it is transfinite, it cannot be computed. Even if we know a finite set of physical laws, describing all possible structures, we are not able to build a computable set of all possible mappings, because they have a different logical nature. This is a fundamental reason for abandoning models of technology, such as NK (also the extended NK model!) or genetic algorithms, in which the set of mappings is large but by definition computable.

This does not mean, however, dismissing an analytical stance. It only requires to shifting the emphasis from finding the right algorithm to building the right representation, on which non computable operations can work.

5.2   Abduction

An important consequence of the non-isomorphism of mapping between functions and structures is that the cognitive process needed is not induction.

It is interesting to remark that an authoritative tradition in evolutionary economics has made extensive use of theories of induction to build up models. Holland (1975, 1995) has been widely used as a reference point, but an influential role has also been played by *Induction*, his highly acclaimed work with Holyoak, Nisbett and Thagard (Holland et al., 1986). In a certain sense, while neoclassical economics has traditionally been happy with a nomological-deductive approach (with some conventionalism about hypotheses), evolutionary economics has married a large family of inductive, rule-based, rule-discovery models to instantiate assumptions of bounded rationality and out of equilibrium dynamics. All this should be preserved, but it would be useful to explore some uncharted waters.

Design problem solving cannot be reduced to inductive thinking. It is on the contrary a form of *abductive thinking*, that does not move from antecedents to consequences, but makes the reverse path, from desired consequences (functions) to possible causal factors (structures). In this perspective, design is not the object of logics, but rather of informal logics.

According to Peirce (1878, 1901, 1903) abduction, in fact, is a weak form of logic thinking. Deductive reasoning starts from a general rule (implication), considers a specific case (antecedent) and derives by necessity a result (consequent). Inductive reasoning reverses the path: it starts from a specific case (antecedent), observes a result (consequent) and from that observation produces an inference to a general proposition, or rule (implication). These are the two forms of reasoning most studied in the history of philosophy, in philosophy of science and in cognitive sciences.

However, there is another possibility: abduction. It starts from a result, that is, a desired result (consequent), and tries to identify the applicable general rule (implication) and then establish a specific case by decision (antecedent). Or, in other words, it assumes the existence of a final state, then explores the possibility to reach that state, finally establishing a necessary action, by decision, needed to reach the state (Bonfantini, 1987). Following abduction one identifies one or more ways to reach the desired result, given the knowledge about the applicable general rules, which in the case of engineering is represented by design knowledge, ultimately rooted in natural sciences.

This kind of logic has been largely studied in the field of semiotics and of investigations, because in these fields a similar logic applies (Eco, 1990; Morand, 2004).

A common theme is that abduction *cannot be reduced to induction*, in the sense that even a complete collection of applicable rules (for example, physical laws), when faced with a specific desired result, does not produce the mapping. Consequently the cognitive activity needed to perform abduction is neither nomological-deductive thinking, nor inferential thinking, but rather a complex back-and-forth recursive iteration between possible physical configurations (structures) and desired states (functions). This cognitive activity makes large use of, but is not reducible to, *heuristics*. These are general pragmatic rules to generate possible solutions. But, as we will see below, in design the meaning of heuristics is somewhat different from its classical use in induction.

This conclusion is consistent with developments in artificial intelligence applied to engineering problems. Only trivial problems of routine design can be completely automated. For advanced tasks, automation is always partial and is reduced to a well known portion of the process. Finally, there is no successful experiment in the automation of concept design (Sriram, 1997).

The literature in cognitive science has examined design activity as a particular form of complex problem solving. Problem solving may refer to well structured problems (for example an algebra problem or chess game) or ill-structured problems (Newell and Simon, 1972; Dorner, 1976; Newell, 1990). Design is an extreme case of ill-structured problem solving, in which the statement whether the system is in the final state and the problem is solved (that is, QED in algebra, or check mate in chess) is not well defined. At the same time, design is also a very information-intensive and computationally demanding activity, because a large number of alternatives must be explored (that is, generated and tested) (Goel and Pirolli, 1992; Gero, 1990). In this type of activity, a general finding is that the performance of experts is largely superior to that of novices. Experts are able to move iteratively back and forth between functions and structures, and up and down the product hierarchy, much more rapidly than novices. In addition, due to the hierarchical nature of the two spaces, the feasibility of any given product innovation requires the exploration of the complete function tree. While the design work on product components is usually done in the detailed design stage, expert designers are usually able to identify the possible bottlenecks very early in the conceptual design stage. Although there is a significant tradition that addresses design as a form of expert problem solving, it is true that this literature has given important contributions to well-structured problems, but has failed to identify regularities in ill-structured problems.

Another way of formulating the same idea is that design is a NP-hard problem. For example, a typical representation of a design problem is in terms of constraint satisfaction. There may be approximately optimal algorithms to solve well defined types of design problems, but a general algorithm which is able to produce optimal design algorithms does not exist at all.

However, even this classical notion in problem solving can be challenged when we look at the nature of design problems more closely. A persuasive argument, for example, is that design is even more complex than ill-structured problem solving, because agents change the desired state during the process. In other words, the final state for abduction is not only ill defined, but it can also be modified in the light of successive information generated during the process.

To address this feature the notion of wicked problem, as originally formulated in social planning (Rittel and Webber, 1984; see also Budgen, 2003; Jackson, 2006), has been introduced. These problems are unique, have no definitive formulation, have no stopping rules, have no immediate and ultimate test of a solution, and do not have an enumerable (or an exhaustively describable) set of potential solutions. A wicked problem is such that a solution to one of its parts simply changes the nature of the problem. In Herbert Simon's terms, these types of problems are non-decomposable. This characterization clearly applies to conceptual design and to design processes oriented at radical innovation.

In this sense, the notion of 'search', as applied to technology, is indeed restrictive, in the sense that the space of search has not the characteristics commonly associated to the theory of search in economics or artificial intelligence.

5.3   Abstraction

As we have seen, it is legitimate (and necessary) to speak of functional explanation in the fields of biology and technology, or the living and the artificial systems. These systems survive, hence self-repair, and reproduce. A function can be seen as the characterization of the properties that systems must exhibit, under specified conditions, in order to survive.

A fundamental property of functions is *abstraction*. This means that it is possible to eliminate, or add, details to the functional description, at various levels, still preserving the core function. In moving up in abstraction, functions are less and less circumstantiated, so that we move towards a very general description.

An implication of abstraction is the *hierarchical structure* of the function space. Functions can be hierarchically decomposed, down to elementary units. A functional hierarchy is an iterative decomposition of a high level or macrofunction into more elementary sub-functions (see for a simple example Figure 12.3). The achievement of lower level functions is a requisite for the achievement of higher level ones. Sub-functions are either intrinsically related to the main function as necessary elements, or are generated by the extension of conditions for behavior. Thus the function 'transmit voice from and to a mobile device' is naturally decomposable into several main sub-functions (transmission, reception, recording and so on), each of which has a tree-like structure down to elementary functions such as 'switch on/off' or the like. It is important to note that the detailed functional tree is a very large one in most cases. A full functional tree of a moderately complex device contains a few or several hundred sub-functions, all of which must be satisfied for the main functions to be implemented.

This tree-like structure may be further refined if one adds new conditions under which the same function must be performed, for example, the device must work without recharging for three days (see conditioning below). This means that functions may be *nested* into other functions, at various levels. The nested nature of functions is very important for technological learning, because it dispenses with representing lower level functions if higher level ones can be activated.

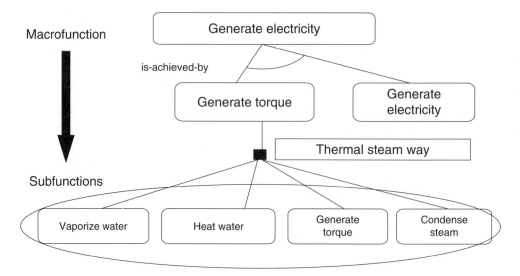

Source: Kitamura et al. (2001).

Figure 12.3   A functional hierarchy of a power plant (portion)

The hierarchical tree does not have a natural vertex. Any node in the tree is a function itself and may be considered the vertex of a new hierarchical tree in the space of functions.

Thus, while any single function may usually be represented by a tree, in general the space of functions cannot be represented by a tree, but rather by a graph. All functions are related to others, following a distance function (more on this below).

The decomposition of functions corresponds to the creation of plans of action, or *planning*. Planning is a hierarchical activity, in which the achievement of a complex goal is subdivided into activities linked by temporal and spatial relations.

An implication of the abstraction of the function space is that searching in it is cognitively highly demanding. Consider the following. Searching in a space of physical structures is greatly helped by the fact that intermediate results can be stored in the memory in the form of examples, pictures, drawings, or the like. Their existence in the external world means that they can be easily accessed during the search activity. In the case of objects they can be manipulated, transferred, moved, combined, juxtaposed in many ways. In the case of functions, they are abstract by nature. The human mind comes to conceive a function by abstracting from examples of physical structures that implement that function. But any possible instantiation of a physical structure that implements the function is just a member of a large and open class of objects.

Consider the problem from another perspective. Inferential reasoning may try to obtain generalizations by applying causality. In causal reasoning it is not necessary for the validity of the claim that we explore *all* possible causes of a phenomenon. It is enough that we establish, with appropriate procedures, that A causes B. It is not the same for abductive reasoning. If I want to get B, it is not enough to know that A may bring me to B: I will have to search for all other ways to obtain B. Unless B is a trivial desired state, this may require extensive search and iteration between the function and the structure space. Due to the non-isomorphism of structure-function mappings, this exploration requires keeping the representation of functions explicit and stable for a certain time. This is extremely demanding for the working memory, which typically contains a few elements (no more than 7 ± 2 units) and forgets the content very rapidly, in around 20 seconds.

A demonstration of this effect is found in the literature on the development of high level skills in infants. In order to think in abstract terms, planning abilities must be in place. Planning requires the ability to create sequences, or hierarchical chains. This ability is common between the acquisition of grammatical abilities and of functional reasoning. The acquisition of grammar is crucial for language and requires the ability to structure sequences of elements in a hierarchical way. Interestingly, in the ontogenetic development, general hierarchical skills are developed early in childhood, but at some point they diverge and specialize. Functional reasoning on artifacts becomes a specialized ability which is then nurtured with education.

Abstraction also leads to generalization as a cognitive process that identifies common elements across several items (Gineste, 1997). Abstraction and generalization are therefore the conditions for *analogy*. It has repeatedly been noted that an important source of invention is given by analogical transfer, that is, the migration of a solution from a known field to a new one. Indeed, the process of analogy is currently considered the more plausible candidate explanation for the invention of stone knapping by *Homo erectus*, which is considered the first example of technological activity of hominids (de Beaune, 2009). The idea is that the deliberate will to produce flakes by knapping a pebble with a hammerstone was originated, in three steps, from the early experience of using pebbles to crack bones, wood or hard fruits.

While the literature on analogy is very large, a common theme is how difficult to draw an inventive analogy is. A large stream of literature (see for a survey Sander, 2000) has documented systematic failures of human agents to identify correct analogies (Gentner, 1983). We suggest that the explanation for such evidence is to be found in the abstraction of the function space. Individuals represent structures much more easily than functions. Functions are abstract sets of properties that are exhibited simultaneously by a (possibly) large number of candidate structures. To make abstraction from any specific instantiation of how a given structure implements a desired function is cognitively demanding. For the same reason, being able to identify analogies means to recognize that, below the surface of structurally dissimilar problems (for example in two different technical or social domains) there are indeed similar clusters of functions. This requires the ability to represent and keep in memory large regions in the function space as separate from examples of structures.

A similar argument applies to other heuristics for problem solving, such as *recombination*. It is often stated that invention comes from the recombination of existing entities in new ways. This is true, but this statement fails to recognize that useful recombination takes place not in the space of structures, but in the space of functions. In order to recognize the potential for recombination, it is necessary to abstract from physical configurations and combine different functions. Again, this is possible only by abstraction, not simply by enumeration of all possible combinations between physical structures. The world of functions is not a Lego world.

5.4   Representation

How are functions represented? This is not a simple question, for several reasons. First, because of the abstract nature of functions, there is a demanding cognitive load in reasoning about functions. Full scale functional representations do not persist in human memory for a long time, but disappear and are difficult to retrieve without external support.

Second, people talk in a language which is mostly related to objects, or technologies, while their mind is working on the underlying functions. This means that functional reasoning is difficult to access by external observers. On the other hand, engineers and designers represent functions in the form of requirements, following specialized technical languages. This type of representation is more accurate, but lacks generality and is typically close to technical (that is, structural) descriptions, rather than to abstract functions.

Third, when people talk deliberately of functions, they use natural language, or common sense language. People intuitively understand what functions mean. But natural language is loose and imprecise as a tool for representation.

Fourth, the language itself is inadequate to represent novelty. New words are needed, but they do not exist yet. Ethnographic studies of engineering design (Ferguson, 1992; Bucciarelli, 1994) consistently report that designers do not always use spoken language, but gesture, mimics, and above all sketches and informal drawings. These practices are indicative of the inadequacy of language.

For these reasons, it is indeed difficult to build complete representations of functions, even for relatively simple objects and technologies. This is a serious reason, of course, for the reluctance of the economics profession to embark on the use of functions. The lack of a standardized dictionary for functions and of a large and friendly repository makes it impractical to use functions outside the highly specialized area of engineering design theories.

But there is good news. Going beyond the limits of existing literature, we have developed a new approach, which may have large potential for economics of innovation, among others. In other technical papers more oriented to the engineering design community, we have developed a full scale theory of functions as represented in physical terms (Apreda et al., 2008a, 2008b). This effort is backed by a long term commitment to produce a large functional dictionary, called Augmented Functional Base, in which lemmas are formed by a functional verb + an object. We have been able to identify, define, and lemmatize more than 4000 functional expressions which cover almost all functions in the mechanical and electromechanical domains – that is, they cover a large part of existing technologies. Table 12.1 offers a small sample of this tool. Each of the entries in the base is indexed in terms of the physical description, the underlying physical principles or laws (if known), the synonyms and the antonyms. Using this base it is possible to represent explicitly the functional map of any artifact, problem, or technology, that has at least some mechanical and control dimensions. Interestingly, the representation can be done in a relatively short time frame (in the order of man/days).

Let us start with the notion that functions exist as a space of possibility constrained by physical laws. Consequently, functions should always be expressed in such a way as to make explicit the physical effect implied. We should always ask 'which state of an observable variable is affected by this function' and 'which is the change in the observable

Table 12.1   A sample of the Augmented Functional Base for a few class functions

Area	Class Functions Equation(s)	Base Functions Parameters of the equations	Detailed Functions Declination of the parameter(s)
Kinematics	Move	Move on closed path	Rotate, Spin, Turn, Flip1
		Move on open path	Advance, Lift1, Translate, Switch, Shift, Pick
		Vibrate	Oscillate1
	Arrest	Arrest	Stop1
	Guide	Transfer	Transport, Deliver, Carry, Convey, Conduct1, Direct, Relocate, Steer
		Position	Locate1, Orient, Align, Place1, Flip2
	Obstacle	Obstacle	Constrain, Restrain1, Resist1, ***Deviate, Scatter, Brake***
Statics	Block DOF	Block DOF	Lock, Hold1, Place2, ***Fasten, Fix1, Secure***
		Capture (=Block DOF + Join)	Inglobate, Contain1, Enclose, Grasp
	Allow DOF	Allow DOF	Open, Unfasten, Unlock, Permit
		Release (=Allow + Separate)	Disclose
	Support	Steady	Hold2, ***Secure, Fasten, Fix1***
		Reinforce	Back, Brace, Line
Dynamics	Interact	Interact	Touch1, Hit, Hammer, ***Bounce***
		Attract	Pull, Lift2
		Repulse	Push, ***Bounce, Deviate, Scatter***
Exchange with External Environment	Import	Import	Input, Absorb1, ***Fill***
		Supply	Provide, Retrieve
	Export	Transmit (useful)	Eject, Emit1, Output, Diffuse2, Conduct2, Transfer2
		Discard (useless) (–E + Remove)	Dispose, Eliminate, Reject
	Store	Store	Accumulate, Reserve, Contain2, Shelf, Register, Record
		Collect	Replenish, Refill
	Add	Add	Addition, Absorb1, Dope, ***Fill, Insulate***
		Create	Generate
	Subtract	Subtract	Empty, Absorb2
		Destroy	Delete, Annihilate
	Detect	Detect (spot)	Sense1, Feel1, Determine, Perceive, Locate2, Measure1
		Monitor (repeatedly)	Track, Time, Control1, Sense2, Measure2, Feel2
	Display	Indicate	Show, Announce, Expose, Emit2
		Label	Denote, Mark

Source: Apreda et al. (2008b).

variable as an effect of the function'? We can represent functions as those measurable aspects of a flow (material, energy, and signal) that evolve (or are prevented from evolving) in time because of an action. Following this definition, a function can *always* be expressed as a pair verb + object, where the verb expresses a flow of material, energy or signal.

It is useful to think of functions as the *dual* of physical properties. The existence of physical forces and effects, at various scales of reality, creates a possibility for functions. In a very precise way, any physical law or effect opens an entire space of possibility for functions: for example, it is because there exists gravity that functions such as picking, gripping, or sustaining may come into existence. Indeed, gravity is involved in almost all mechanical functions!

The more we add physical properties, the more we conceive of complex functions. If we add gravity to the resistance of fluids, and perhaps we include some elements on conditions for survival of a human, we come to conceive a complex function such as 'controlled flight'.

On the other hand, the more we consider fundamental physical laws, the more elementary functions come into existence.

Following the early suggestion of Pahl and Beitz (1984) we therefore stress the physical transformation (or lack thereof) associated to any function and suggest the following definition.[5]

Definition 1 (Function)
A function is any single action or series of concurring actions that interact with one or more physical characteristics (in the broadest meaning of everything that can be sensed objectively) of the system which is the object of the action (namely the flow).

Some notes about the above definition:

1. The concept of interaction means either changing the state of the system or preventing it from spontaneous or unwanted change.
2. The system, object of the action, includes all the flows which are modified by the action. Both the agent and the object of the action modify their statuses (some of their parameters/characteristics) because of their mutual interaction.
3. The definition is not based on (too) generic flows but it recovers the main physical information about the particular aspects of the flows actually modified by the action.
4. The concept of interaction is strictly linked with the time evolution. In turn, time evolution is derived from physics, where the state of a system is uniquely characterized by a certain set of parameters changing with time due to physical interactions.

This definition focuses on those (preferably) measurable aspects of a flow (material, energy, and signal) that evolve or that are prevented from evolving in time because of the action.

Corollary 1.1 (Physical language for functional description)
Any function can be fully described with the same language used to describe the physical constitution of the world.

Of course the above corollary does not state that the description used for functions must be identical to that used for physical laws (such as equations and so on). Actually the emphasis given on the concept of action in the definition of function and the complex nature of products and processes that functional analysis deal with impose that in most cases the two descriptions will be formulated in substantially different ways. The sense of the corollary is that a parallel between the two alternative descriptions (equations versus functions, to name one) must always be possible.

Corollary 1.2 (Physical language for non functional description)
The same physical language may be used for functional and non-functional descriptions.

In a linear feeder the motion of a component along a slope performs the desired function, that is, to feed. The reference equations (a suitable subset of all the equations that could fully describe the phenomenon) are those of kinematics along a tilted plane, those of static mechanics and Coulomb's friction. The same equations govern the motion of a stone that slips along a hill. But in this case we will not say there is a function. This is because there is no agency, hence no action. From Corollary 1 we also derive a Sub-corollary that may be useful as a practical rule for developing an adequate language.

Sub-corollary 1.1.1 (Acceptance criterion for functional description)
Any description that is done in such a way as to make it impossible to identify the relevant physical transformation, is not functional and therefore should be rejected.

Corollary 1.2 makes it explicit that the same physical language can be used in two substantially different ways, one for describing physical structures or laws, the other to describe functions. Polanyi's principle is fully preserved. There will be different syntax and grammar rules, operating however on the same language.

The use of physical language is also a condition to advance functional analysis from the current status of pragmatic discipline to a status of scientific discipline, rooted in scientific understanding of the world, but at the same time preserving the fundamental role of action in the world itself. The former (understanding) defines the boundaries of possible worlds, the latter (action) defines the exploration of particular directions in the space of possibilities. A few other definitions are useful. One introduces a new element in functional analysis, that is, equations. Once we have adopted the physical language to describe functions, there is no logical obstacle to using these highly peculiar representations of relations between physical variables. We limit our definition to the electro-mechanical field, for which the underlying knowledge of physical effects is large and robust. We have developed equation representations for almost all functions in the Augmented Functional Base presented in a vector form in Apreda et al. (2009). In general, equations will not represent functions as such, because they lack the crucial element of action. However, they can legitimately be part of a functional description when coupled with actions. In addition, it will not always be possible to use equations.

Why is this representational choice important? By making explicit the physical transformation involved in any function it is possible to achieve great clarity and completeness. Any technological problem can be fully described in a finite number of steps. Ambiguity with regards to semantic content can be gradually reduced. By using the Functional Base it is possible to draw a *complete map* of all functions of an artifact, or technology, or problem, with a considerable degree of accuracy, up to several dozens or hundreds of elements. All the identified functions are characterized in physical terms, so that the constraints and relations between them are made explicit. If needed, such a functional map can easily be transformed into a directed graph.

Of great importance for economics of innovation, a number of crucial aspects of the dynamics of technology can be fully explained in rigorous terms.

The notion of representation supports the idea that it is useful to conceive *search in the function space* as a crucial explanatory factor for technological progress. In abstract terms, searching the function space means identifying general and abstract conditions for feasible mappings, independently of intentionality. In historical terms, search in the function space is a crucial component of engineering knowledge, as we will see below.

5.5 Distance

What are the topological properties of the space of functions?

This question can be addressed in two different ways. On the one hand, one can assume a given topology, by defining axioms for the space (such as in axiomatic design theory), or creating a purely formal language. In this case we would not know whether the properties of the space are also valid in the real world. On the other hand the approach could be a constructive one: we represent a function space by building a rich dictionary of functional expressions, then we test whether such a space is sufficiently 'knitted' to cover all possible cases. If this is the case, we might conclude that the space has particular topological properties.

This of course would not be a theorem, but a constructive proof. In a work-in-progress paper (Apreda et al., 2009) we have offered evidence that, at least for a portion of the function space, as described using the Augmented Functional Base, a *vector representation* is appropriate. This is a strong characterization. If the function space can be represented as a vector space, it means that any linear combination of two functions in the space is still included in the space. This is not a general characterization of distance in the function space, however. In a work in progress, Apreda and Francaviglia (2009) suggest that non-Euclidean concepts of distance are more appropriate as a general representation. This seems to fit nicely with the suggestion of Stadler et al. (2001) that weaker concepts of space are needed to represent directionality in evolution.

The intuition is clear. Since all functions are ultimately described in physical terms, they must share, at some level of the hierarchy, some physical elements (for example, forces, or effects, or elements). All functions are somewhat linked to other functions, although indirectly.

Following this characterization it is possible to define a notion of *distance* in the function space. Intuitively, two functions are closer if they share some variables in the equations describing the physical effects (irrespective of the specific range of values), that is, share part of the underlying changes in variables brought about by the action that realizes them.

The distance would be a function, on one hand, of the position in a vertical abstraction chain (from more abstract functions, or 'fathers' to more instantiated functions, or 'children') and in a horizontal chain of similarity (synonyms or antonyms), each of which would have an explicit physical description, on the other hand, of the similarity of the ultimate physical description.

Remember that the overall function space is hierarchically related, but is not a tree.

There are multiple fathers, and also it is possible that a given function is the son of different fathers (for example, co-paternity is admitted).

We believe this notion is important for the economic analysis of technology and innovation. Let us assume that the cost of search in the function space is some function of the distance.

With this notion we may build either strategic models in which agents are intentional and explore a function space with some cost function, or evolutionary models in which search takes place due to the properties of a higher order system (living or artificial). The crucial point is that search takes place in the function space, not in the space of structures (or attributes, or technical coefficients, or the like). In this space what matters is the distance between functions and sub-functions, which is a matter of underlying physical effects. Thus it may be possible, for example, to jump from a function to another one, whose technological materialization is completely different, if the underlying functional distance is short. What takes place in the function space is the *hidden* dynamics of the observed technological evolution.

The very simple idea of a cost function defined over a functional distance may give a very precise meaning (and, in the near future, even measurability) to issues such as localized learning, the trade off between exploration and exploitation, the S-shaped curve of technological progress, and many others. Some examples will be given below.

Before that we need to add another element to the theory of dynamics.

5.6   Exaptation and Systems of Use

In a celebrated paper Gould and Lewontin (1979) criticized the adaptationist program in evolutionary biology. They suggested that some biological forms (structures) may owe their existence not to adaptation and fitness, but to the fact they are associated to other forms: they do not have any function at the start, but discover new functions over time. The classical image was that of the 'spandrels' in San Marco mosaic ceilings in Venice: they do not have any function, but were originated by the need to solve the problem created by a circular dome based on a square building foundation. Once created, it was apparent that they could take a role as decorative space. But explaining their existence on the basis of their fitness for decoration is wrong. The discovery of new functions is due to their survival, which is not associated to their own initial function. In a certain sense, they have *latent* functions, not put into exercise, which wait for discovery.

This notion can be generalized. An important stream of research in molecular biology has outlined the notion of *gene sharing*, or the idea that genes and proteins may have different functions according to the context in which they are placed, so that some functions may be latent for a very long time, but still be preserved through the chemical structure, and then be exploited for extremely different purposes. As has been highlighted in a monumental survey of research:

> the gene-sharing concept postulates that protein function is determined not only by the primary amino acid sequence, which remains the same in the multiple functions that are performed by the protein, but also by the micro-environment within the cell and by the expression of its gene. Awareness of gene sharing cautions against assuming that a protein will be used in the same way wherever or whenever it is present, or that it has always done what it is doing at any given moment. (Piatigorsky, 2007: 5)

In other words, gene sharing may be a very general mechanism for exaptation.

An impressive example of the power of gene sharing is given by the evolution of eyes. It is well known that the perfection of the eye has been a problem for evolutionary theory (Darwin himself discussed this issue), because it has very complex aggregate or collective properties, whose emergence from small incremental random mutations seems unlikely (see Parker, 2003 for a reconstruction). Recent research has shown that the proteins responsible for optical functions (transparency and refraction) are indeed multi-functional and can be expressed in tissues where they have non-refractive roles. In evolutionary terms, they initially developed for non-optical functions, survived because of these functions, and then acquired the extremely relevant optical functions when they were placed in a different context.

> The evolutionary scenario of gene sharing emergent from the multifunctional crystallins indicates that independently derived modifications in gene regulation provide a source for functional innovation by placing a protein in another tissue or at a different concentration in the same tissue where it can acquire another molecular role. In short: Changes in gene regulation serve to explore new molecular functions for old proteins. Gene sharing ensues when a differentially expressed protein keeps its original function and takes on one or more new molecular functions. Crystallins exemplify the powerful role of gene regulation for deriving new protein functions. (Piatigorsky, 2007: 95)

This notion is extremely powerful to explain the dynamics of technology, jointly with the idea of a cost function defined over functional distances.

In many relevant cases a new function is ascribed to an artifact, whose reason for survival has nothing to do with it. The artifact survives in use because of its main functions, but then its latent functions are discovered through a social process of discovery. In evolutionary terms, survival from natural selection does not apply to individual entities, but to populations (Lewens, 2004). Now the survival of a population of (roughly) identical artifacts can be predicted only if they exhibit one or more functions for which they are superior to alternatives (either other artifacts or no use at all). No population of artifacts survives if at least some of its functions are not used. The survival of technical artifacts is then subject to the condition of use. If there is not a system of use, whatever its size and location in space and time, artifacts disappear. Thus systems of use are an intrinsic part of technology, not an addendum.

In fact, it is a corollary of the non-isomorphism property that, because all structures have many functions, it is possible that a subset of functions is responsible for its main use, while others stay silent. A classic example of this effect is the origin of SMS, initially conceived as an emergency tool for field telecom technicians, then used for talk between people, creating a huge market. Functions are then *discovered* through use.

This is a powerful idea with long ranging dynamic implications. In fact, it follows from the non-isomorphism property that structures bring with themselves not only those functions for which they are actually selected by the evolutionary mechanism, but also many other hidden functions. These are hidden in those physical features that do not directly contribute to the main function, but are compatible with the overall structure. In this way it is possible to reconcile the deterministic approach of physical explanations with the functional reasoning. The cause for a given feature to be there is simply that its constitution was produced following (relatively invariant) physical laws; the cause for a given feature to be there is also that, at some point in time, it became useful for new functions, which initially were non-existent.

This dynamics seems also at the core of what David Lane has called *generative relationships*. Agents change the meaning of artifacts and their identity through interactions with other agents (*attributional shift*). In turn, these shifts open the potential for further change, in a positive feedback or bootstrap-type of dynamics:

> new configurations in agent/artifact space breed further configurations, mediated by the generation of new attributions: generative relationships among agents give rise to new relations between artifacts (including new artifacts!) which provide new opportunities for generative relationships between agents. (Lane and Maxfield, 1997: 185; Lane and Maxfield, 2006; Villani et al., 2007)

Let us include the idea of exaptation and systems of use into the function-structure framework.

Functions have an abstract nature, corresponding to the space of possibilities, as determined by physical constraints. At the same time, at least in the case of technology, functions are picked up, or activated, from the function space, by systems of use.

In turn, systems of use may be considered themselves complex systems whose main elements are twofold: the *reason* to use, and the *practice* of use.

The reason to use, which we do not analyse here in detail, has to do with needs of users, and ultimately their values (in the most general sense of reason for action). Actors have some (perhaps unobservable) values, which drive their behavior. They also have various needs, partly influenced by values, partly determined by physiological aspects (let us for a moment detach from a more philosophically inclined treatment).

While the mapping between structure and function is mediated by physical possibilities, the relation between needs and function is more complex, because it involves strong symbolic aspects, whose internal laws are perhaps as strong as the physical ones, but are indeed far less understood.[6]

Because there is some reason to use, actors exhibit a practice of use (actual use), to be described in physical terms, and act in a context, or environment. While the description of the context is notoriously a difficult task (for example, in ontological modeling), we may be happy with a pragmatic definition, which is again ultimately linked to the physical effect of the context on the structure-function mapping.

To sum up, we now have a complex system including a system of use (values, needs) and a mapping (function, behavior, structure). This system has an intrinsic internal dynamics.

This is driven by two main elements: the abstract nature of functions, and exaptation. On the first point, functions exist independently of their implementation into structures. If they can be represented, it will be possible to carry out an exploration in the function space, which is independent of the working of specific structures. This means that current mappings may be destabilized. A particularly powerful way of carrying out abstract search in the function space is modern science. While science is not per se aimed at producing solutions for functions, the accumulation of knowledge produces an extensive, sometimes non-directed, search in the function space.

On the second point, the system is put into dynamics by the fact that systems of use, while practicing objects for functions, may discover new functions that were latent in objects themselves, or that can be represented in abstract terms.

In fact, the very nature of a system of use in a human context implies that users of artifacts build up a representation of them. But because of the abstraction of functions, and the separate representation of functions from structures in the human mind, humans start to represent not only variations of existing artifacts, but wholly new entities, whose functions are an extension, or manipulation, or combination, of known functions. By stretching functions, they can build representations of non-existing objects. If however their representation of functions is appropriate (that is, if they are part of the function space, they are possible in physical terms), then what they might end up with is a powerful way to innovate: their imagination may produce the next artifacts. Patrick Flichy (2007) has offered a fascinating and compelling reconstruction of the way in which the technological *imaginaire* may anticipate and guide the birth of new technologies. In a certain sense, the *imaginaire* extends the exaptation mechanism to its limits.

Thus the language of functions is an interesting way to build a dialogue between neo-technological theories, which emphasize autonomy of technology, and the sociology of technology, which on the contrary stresses the role of users, imagination, and interest groups in shaping technology. More recent contributions in this direction (Dourish, 2001; Oudshoorn and Pinch, 2003; McCarthy and Wright, 2004; Suchman, 2007) do not deal with the old question of whether technologies are social constructs or are deterministically produced, but more productively investigate the mechanisms through which systems of use enter into the dynamics. Contrary to old arguments, we believe there is no reason for an opposition between these perspectives.

The theory of functional exaptation can also be extended in other fruitful ways.

For example, one may observe that new functions may be discovered thanks to *complementarity* in use. This is different from the complementarity dictated by technology. The former is a mechanism of inducement of new functions coming from the experience of users of artifacts. For example, it is amusing to observe that the use of mobile phones during walking in urban environments has created new functions for portability of phones (for example, in bags or clothes) or for using only one hand (for example, while steering pushchairs or carrying bags). More seriously, the introduction of the Internet has created a whole new bunch of functions, such as login, encryption, security, and many others, some of which were clearly not anticipated.

These new functions may also be technologically remote from the existing ones, but are elicited through social interactions. In this sense the systems of use, and in modern societies, the sophisticated system of mass consumption, are an integral part of the technological system. They are not simply responsible for *ex post* fitness of technologies and artifacts; they rather come into play at the very early stage, when functions are discovered.

Another intriguing extension of the theory is as follows. We have argued, following Gero, that functions exhibit behaviors that, in turn, implement functions. In the history of technology, a demarcation point is marked between the era of tools, and the era of machines. Tools do not have an autonomous life from the human user. They are an extension of the human body and carry with themselves a functional scheme which is close to the overall experience of human functions. In this period, the conceptualization of distant functions (for example, the human flight) was made possible only by the observation of other natural entities and subsequent extension and imagination (for example, Icarus).

With the advent of machines the situation changes dramatically. Because of the use of energy, machines behave in a way that is, at least relatively and within constraints, autonomous from the human actor. Their behavior is not necessarily an extension of human behavior.

This effect has not been visible until recent years, due to the heavy constraint of energy requirements on mechanical behaviors. But it is now becoming impressive with digital technologies and robotics. Machines may have autonomy. This has important implications: functions can be discovered not only by human actors in systems of use, but by machines themselves. By interacting among them, they exhibit behaviors that are not intended by human actors, or are sometimes non-predictable. This may generate new functions in due time. This effect is a powerful multiplier of the internal dynamics of complex technological systems.

6. THE POTENTIAL OF FUNCTIONAL REPRESENTATIONS FOR THE ECONOMICS OF INNOVATION

A functional theory of technology is able to explain and/or to give richer evidence for several of the effects discussed in the economics of technology and innovation. But in addition, it offers a unified framework to conceptualize these effects, and in a non-distant future, it will allow a rigorous mathematical treatment, and possibly a system for measurement. We offer in this section a short tour of some of the crucial issues in this literature, that might benefit from a functional reconceptualization. In some cases we offer new insights, in others further research is needed, although the general lines for investigation are pretty clear. Also, in some cases we have already made inroads, in others we are only sensing promising research avenues.

6.1 Punctuated Equilibria in Technological Evolution

Evolutionary theories of technological progress have developed in considerable detail the idea that the basic processes of mutation, or variation, selection and retention apply. One crucial issue is how to explain the apparent contradiction between cumulative change, which appears to be gradual and incremental, and the evidence of sudden changes in technology.

Thus for example Basalla (1988) articulates his historical reconstruction in terms of diversity, continuity, novelty and selection, showing with a rich array of examples the specific mechanisms through which discontinuity and continuity are both present. This is consistent with accounts of history of technology that present technological evolution as a collective effort of trial and error even for small and apparently insignificant objects such as paperclips and screwdrivers (Petroski, 1992; Rybczynski, 2000) and point to various cultural mechanisms for transmission of technological knowledge (see Richerson and Boyd, 2005). Ziman (2000) articulates the evolutionary account by taking seriously the suggestion of multi-layered variation and selection.

A classical synthesis is suggested by Sahal (1981), who offers evidence for an S-shaped curve for long term evolution of technology. The idea is that stages of acceleration are followed by stages of saturation and diminishing returns. Similar conceptualizations are at the basis of the management literature on industry life cycles and dominant design (Abernathy and Utterback, 1978; Abernathy and Clark, 1985; Tushman and Anderson, 1986; Anderson and Tushman, 1990) and of analytically based models of industrial dynamics (Klepper, 1996). A natural formulation for this idea is the one of *punctuated equilibria*, initially introduced by Eldredge and Gould (1972).

In all these cases, while the underlying evolutionary ideas are appropriate, most of the discussion takes place in the observed space of technology realizations, or artifacts. The idea that artifacts must be matched with use is clearly articulated, but one rarely finds an explicit recognition of the nature of functions as mediation between use and structure.

A functional theory offers a natural explanation for these evolutionary accounts. Let us make explicit the interesting economic implications of distance in the function space.

First, we need an explanation for discontinuity. Discontinuity takes place because a new mapping is generated from search in the function space. Invariably, these jumps involve some abstraction on functions. We stress that without functional abstraction, discontinuity has no explanation. In fact, in most evolutionary models (for example, industry life cycle models) discontinuity is represented as a random arrival process. In this context, randomness means no explanation. In NK models, the fitness mechanism leads to local maxima, while the jump to global maxima requires an external perturbation.

The functional model offers a powerful explanation: behind any discontinuity there is an abstraction in the function space, for example, a process by which new functions have been discovered and/or existing functions have been mapped in distant structural regions, due to abstract search. What cannot be explained in the structure space, because observed descriptors show large distances, can be explained in the function space.

Once formulated in the function space, the search process which leads to discontinuity may take a variety of specific forms, for example, analogy, or recombination, or others. For example, a large and influential literature has dealt with analogical reasoning (Dreistadt 1969; Holyoak, 1977; Gick and Holyoak, 1980; Holyoak and Thagard, 1989; see for a summary Gineste, 1997; Sander, 2000). One may think of heuristics in terms of operands (in the sense of Stankiewicz and Ziman), but what is crucial here is that they operate in an abstract space, not in the design space, nor in the artifact or attribute space.

Thus, the Wright brothers used a powerful abstract decomposition of the function of manned flight in order to achieve the final solution (Bradshaw and Lienert, 1991; Copp and Zanella, 1993; Johnson-Laird, 2005, 2006). By working at this level they were able to employ fruitful analogies, as shown by Johnson-Laird (2006). More recently, the radical innovation of Stealth aircraft is the result of a purely geometrical abstraction in the space of functions (Rich and Janos, 1994). The invention of computers is the result of several powerful abstractions: the general idea of computation, due to Alan Turing; the notion of a program as executable on a physical machine, due to John von Neumann; and the idea that computations in binary algebra could be implemented by electric circuits, suggested by Claude Shannon, eventually turned into silicon circuits (Wagner, 1998). Similarly, the notion of desktop in PCs has been introduced on the basis of the abstract idea of organization of an office in material terms, to be idealized and reproduced graphically on the screen. Indeed, many radical innovations in the digital world, although historically originated in interactive settings, can be re-interpreted as powerful abstractions in the function space (see Moggridge, 2007).

Second, a natural extension is to argue that there are increasing returns in exploring close regions in the function space, for example, functions at short distance, or sub-functions. Once a new mapping has been generated, the efficiency of searching in close regions greatly increases, leading to a wave of new cumulative refinements. A new mapping is usually associated to a sequence of further improvements that take place in the neighborhood. This idea, commonly found in history of technology (Basalla, 1988), might be precisely measured on functional maps. The shift from radical product innovation, to dominant design and process innovation, suggested by theories of the industrial life cycle, can be explained by extending the functional reasoning from the product to the manufacturing process.

Finally, another interesting line of explanation goes in the direction of the intriguing question posed by Richard Nelson (2003) – why do we see different rates of growth of knowledge in different fields?. Although we have no evidence, we conjecture that an investigation into the underlying function space of lagging technologies might provide a fresh answer.

6.2   Variety

The starting point is a genotype-phenotype representation of technology developed by Saviotti and Metcalfe (1984), according to which 'each product model corresponds to a point in an N-dimensional design space of technical characteristics, and a point in an F-dimensional function space of service characteristics' (Frenken, 2006a: 97). The distinction between technical and service characteristics (Saviotti, 1996: 63ff.) clearly mirrors the distinction between technical attributes (or physical structure) and functions. More precisely, service characteristics refer to benefits to final users, such as, in the case of aircraft, size, range, payload, and speed (Frenken et al., 1999, 2000; see Frenken, 2006a: 108). These are not functions, however, but attributes that keep together both the technical dimension and the benefit/service dimension.

However, this powerful idea is operationalized, in empirical analyses, by merely looking at the attributes of products. Attributes can be described across dimensions (for example, engine type, number of engines, number of blades, number of shafts, number of rotors per shaft in helicopters), in each of which a given range can be identified as discrete alleles, so that entropy measures based on Theil's information theory, or Weitzman's diversity theory, can be fruitfully applied.

While this procedure is extremely useful, what is lost is the critical importance of the relation, or the mapping, between a given technical and a given service characteristic. It is not the addition of a new attribute that has economic value, but the fact that this attribute is a *particular* solution to the problem of adding a new function, or performing existing functions better, so as to deliver more benefits to the user. But when moving from the abstract model to the empirical analysis, the whole discussion collapses into one of measuring the increase in categories of physical attributes, usually at quite a high level of generality.

Clearly the whole field would benefit from a reformulation that makes the distinction between functions and structures, or service characteristics and technical characteristics, fully operational. This would imply specifying, *separately* the space of functions and the space of technical attributes, and then looking at the evolution of the mappings between the two. The possibility open by Augmented Functional Bases, such as the one we have developed, to represent functional maps quite easily will help to enrich this literature.

A reinterpretation of the prediction on increasing variety in functional terms goes as follows: variety increases because new functions are discovered (through exaptation, systems of use, search in the function space). The economic trend towards dominant design is more than compensated by the continuous entry of new functions, which are added to existing ones.

6.3   Science and Technology

A central theme of evolutionary theory of technology is, consistent with history of technology, that technological knowledge is not applied scientific knowledge. Engineering is a peculiar type of knowledge in its own right (Vincenti, 1990). As Basalla puts it, 'technology is not the servant of science. Technology is as old as humankind. It existed long before scientists began gathering the knowledge that could be used in shaping and controlling nature' (Basalla, 1988: 27). And as Rosenberg (1994) has successfully shown, in many relevant cases technology has preceded science.

The relations between engineering and science have been the object of an extremely informative historical literature. While making this distinction problematic, and historically dependent on specific circumstances, still these studies show how engineering progressively became a separate body of knowledge. For example, Gieryn (1983) has examined the sociological demarcation between science and non-science, and Donnelly (1986) looks at the self-representation of chemical engineering in nineteenth-century England, while Sanderson (1978) has shown a remarkable case of an academician working intensely as an industrial consultant for the Sheffield metallurgical industry. Across the Atlantic and considering the nineteenth and twentieth centuries, R. Kline (1995) has reconstructed the interaction between science and engineering as rationalized in public discourse, Seely (1993) has examined the process of institutionalization of curricula in engineering schools, and Kranakis (1989) has offered a fascinating comparison between France and the United States in the relations of academic engineers with industry and society. All these examples point to a process of *separate* institutionalization between science and engineering, which evidently has its roots in different epistemic procedures.

At the same time, another well developed body of literature suggests that, in recent times, science has become more intimately linked to engineering, driving the evolution of technology in many industries, such as IT, biopharma, or materials science (Grupp, 1992; Narin and Olivastro, 1992; Narin et al., 1997; Gittelman and Kogut, 2003; Adams and Clemmons, 2006). How can we reconcile this evidence and the somewhat different views about the relation between science and technology?

During technological progress, functions are discovered in the function space and mappings are projected, sometimes unsuccessfully. An interesting question is: which functions can be discovered *without* the support of a scientific representation of laws of nature? It is clear that a great many functions can be identified randomly, or with the support of practice only. Furthermore, the accumulation of knowledge from practice leads to a partial capability to represent functions in abstract terms.

We predict there will be a limit to the type of functions that can be discovered this way.

This limit can be clearly identified by making explicit the physical laws involved, as we do using the Augmented Functional Base. There are some laws whose scientific explanation is not necessary for handling the functions associated with them: for example, we do not need Kepler, Galileo or Newton in order to exploit gravity by throwing weapons, nor do we need to understand the full chemistry of combustion in order to use fire. But other functions cannot even be conceptualized without a scientific understanding. Feynman could claim that 'there is plenty of room' at the nanoscale, only because he had a magnificent theory of atomic structure; and there is no tissue engineering technology without a full understanding of the cellular and molecular structure of human skin.

Thus it is clear that engineering, as the discipline that cumulates knowledge on realized mappings, and on abstract characterization of functions, is a separate body of knowledge. Its historical relation with science depends on the complexity of the underlying physical effects involved. By complexity here we just mean (quite simplistically) the amount of theoretical and experimental knowledge needed to explain phenomena.

This argument produces a prediction, which will be tested in a work in preparation: there is a clear temporal pattern in the discovery of functions, in which functions whose complexity in the underlying scientific description is limited can be discovered early, while other functions are discovered later in the history of technology.

A related prediction is that the acceleration of scientific knowledge will lead to the discovery of radically new functions, some that cannot even be conceived without science. This is becoming visible, for example, in nanotechnology, where it is the understanding of properties of artifacts based on quantum physics that drives the identification of possible (not yet implemented) functions. Thus science may become an autonomous driver of function discovery, working in the same abstract function space of technology (Bonaccorsi, 2008; Bonaccorsi and Thoma, 2007).

6.4   Diversification and Technological Distance

An intriguing issue in the evolutionary economics of innovation deals with the explanation of growth of firms. One important idea is that growth is driven by the economics of extending the knowledge and skills accumulated in the organization, and stored in routines, to new fields. This extension, however, is heavily constrained by technological cumulativeness and learning: the rate of return of applying existing knowledge to a different field decreases if they are too different. Thus the notion of dynamic capabilities has been proposed to explain the pattern of technological accumulation and of diversification of companies (Teece et al., 1997).

Empirically, however, the notion of technological closeness or distance is operationalized very crudely, for example by computing indexes of proximity between patent classes, as classified by patent offices.

Another more refined methodology uses patent citations to track the flows of knowledge back to original sources. However, these approaches have the serious inconvenience that the content of knowledge is classified using labels that come either from statistical aggregates (that is, industries) or traditional definitions of technologies, indexed through keywords.

A promising way of deepening this literature goes in the direction of making the functional content of the base of knowledge of companies explicit. This can be done by automatically retrieving the functional description of patent texts, using a lemmatizing system based on the Augmented Functional Base. This lemmatization delivers a much more fine-grained representation than the one based on keywords. It also allows the detection of spatial patterns (for example, clustering, branching, migration) directly on functions, not on technologies. The intuition is that companies may move into different fields if they know how to master functions at the appropriate hierarchical level of detail, independently of the industrial label.

In addition, it will be possible to measure the distances in the function space, following for example Apreda and Francaviglia (2009) algorithms. This would open a totally new field of investigation, in which technological proximity is measured at the abstract level, not using statistical descriptors which may be obsolete or obscure the reality.

6.5   Technology Indicators

The issue of measure of technological progress, or of the shift of the technological frontier, is a difficult one.

In many relevant cases there is an obvious measure of technological progress, that is, absolute performance. If something is technically difficult to achieve, its achievement at a given point in history is by itself an advancement of the technological frontier. Thus the absolute speed of an aircraft, or the maximum tonnage of a ship may be considered clear indicators of the shift of the frontier. A large literature on technometrics has therefore rightly collected data on absolute performance of products in order to depict the evolution of the frontier over time.

However, this is not the general case. In many design problems, in fact, the nature of the design trade-offs is such that it is possible to increase the performance if designers add elements to the design. The technology permits better performance to be obtained just by putting more physical constituents in the product. Thus, for example, we can get more thrust from an aircraft engine if we build up larger components and design larger turbines and shafts. This however adds to the weight of the engine, violating a design trade-off, according to which the weight must be kept to a minimum.

Under these conditions, the design problem is not one of getting the maximum performance, but one of getting the best ratio between the physical attributes used and the resulting performance. This problem can be framed in terms of a multidimensional input–output relation, with the physical attributes as vector of inputs, and the performances as vector of outputs. This structure of the problem more closely resembles the structure–function fundamental mapping relation.

In a recent paper we have suggested a new technometrics methodology, one that capitalizes on the distinction between functions and structures (Bonaccorsi et al., 2005). In the paper we used Data Envelopment Analysis, a nonparametric efficiency technique, to estimate the efficiency with which different types of aircraft engines delivered thrust (output) using weight and size. DEA estimators give each observed unit a score, which represents the multidimensional distance from the frontier. By studying these scores for each competitor, we were able to locate radical innovations (that is, a jump in the nonparametric envelope of the frontier) as distinct from the trajectory of increase in thrust, and map very closely technological competition over time.

More generally, once we have a full scale representation of functions, it is possible to measure technological progress by keeping separate the performance over existing functions and the introduction of new functions.

6.6   Patent Scope

A classic problem in the economics of innovation refers to the scope of protection of intellectual property through patents. According to the economic theory of patents, the balance between the social benefits of incentives to innovate and the social losses deriving from monopolization depends, among other things, on the *scope* of protection (Merges and Nelson, 1990). The larger the scope of the patent, in terms of coverage of claims, the stronger the monopoly power granted to the inventor, but also the greater the uncertainty other inventors face in respect of the possibility of infringing the patent in an independent invention. The prevailing view of economists is that it is preferable for patents to have narrow scope (Lévêque and Meniére, 2004).

In a recent paper (Bonaccorsi et al., 2011) we have reviewed the history of legislative changes in two fields, biotechnological inventions and software, in which the applicability of patents had been excluded but was eventually introduced. We have shown that the legal definition of the patent admissibility and scope has evolved over time on the basis of authoritative underlying theories proposed by scientific communities. These theories suggested (in particular, those associated to the so called molecular biology dogma and to automatic computing) that the relation between the object protected (gene sequences, lines of code) and the economically valued functions was indeed narrow, or one-to-one. In other words, they gave the legislator the argument that the protected functions were in reality so narrowly defined that the monopoly granted to inventors did not result in large losses in social welfare. From an economic point of view, these influential arguments distorted the patent system (Cohen and Lemley, 2001).

In fact, subsequent theories (in particular, post-genome and system biology, and theories associated to the Open Source movement) showed how wrong was the argument of a narrow mapping. But when these new arguments established themselves, the legal system had already turned to large scale patentability.

We then suggest that substantive theories about the object of protection and the relation between structure and function should be considered in the economic debate about patent scope. A recent literature applied ontological considerations to patents, with interesting results (Bottani and Davies, 2005). This is another field where a functional theory of technology may be of great help.

7.   CONCLUSIONS

In this chapter we have tried to persuade the economics community working on technology, innovation and complex systems, that a functional representation of technology is possible, useful, manageable, and is able to open several new lines of research.

The argument has been made mainly on a conceptual basis, in order to illustrate the issues at stake. Interested readers are invited to consult the more engineering-inclined papers quoted in the text. We are also actively working on a formal representation of function and structure spaces, as well as of mappings and distances. The paper on vector spaces is a first step in this direction, although much work is still to be done. A large empirical work is also under construction, with several full scale examples of functional representation of technological change. This activity is backed by a powerful lemmatizer, including a large functional base.

We have also tried to show that such a representation may help to address several unsolved issues in the economics of technology, as well as to recapitulate existing knowledge. An extensive agenda for future research is thus identified.

NOTES

1. I have greatly benefited from comments from David Lane, Koen Frenken, Peter Vermaas, Pierre Benoit Joly, Jane Calvert, Patrice Flichy, Gualtiero Fantoni, Riccardo Apreda, Aldo Geuna, Mauro Lombardi and Alessio Moneta. Over the years, criticisms from Rikard Stankiewicz, Ove Granstrand, Ulrich Witt and Philippe Laredo have forced me to sharpen my argument. Carlo Gabbani introduced me to some of the contributions in philosophy of functions. All errors are mine.
2. The first line of directedness ('deterministic consequences of the physical properties of matter' in the words of Gould) is currently actively pursued by biophysicists, exploring the degree to which physical laws constrain the evolution of living materials along directions conducive to higher orders of organization (Fleury, 2003, 2006; Lambert and Rezsöhazy, 2004), as well as by the rapidly expanding field of Evo-Devo, which combines principles of developmental biology on embryo formation with evolutionary considerations, and examines developmental constraints to evolution (Raff and Kauffman, 1983; Carroll, 2005). These developments answer D'Arcy Thompson's famous critique (1961) of Darwinism. The second line develops the idea of exaptation, on which see the discussion below in the text.
3. This is the main reason for our departure from the approach taken by the pioneering work of Rikard Stankiewicz on the economics of design and technology. Stankiewicz (2000, 2002) proposes the notion of design space as a unitary space in which workable solutions evolve in the form of engineering principles realized into *operands*, together with solution embodiments in objects. Operands are demonstrated solutions and allow search to take a cumulative dynamics. While this is an attractive way to give an account of the evolutionary dynamics of technology, we prefer to keep functions and structures separate from a logical point of view. This gives more flexibility in explaining how operands come to the light.
4. This effect is called 'affordance' in the psychological literature: according to Gibson (1977, 1979) individuals do not need to carry out a reasoning process to understand the functions of most everyday objects, but are intuitively right. This idea has been developed extensively by Norman (1988, 1992), Molotch (2003) and Turkle (2008).
5. The following paragraphs (from Definition 1 to Sub-corollary 1.1.1) are reproduced with permission from Bonaccorsi et al. (2009).
6. Needless to say, this is a fascinating field for investigation, linking hard-nosed disciplines to looser treatment in semiotics and marketing science.

REFERENCES

Abernathy, W.J. and Clark, K.B. (1985), 'Innovation: mapping the winds of creative destruction', *Research Policy*, **14**, 3–22.
Abernathy, W.J. and Utterback, J. (1978), 'Patterns of industrial innovation', *Technology Review*, **40**, 41–47.
Adams, J.D. and Clemmons, J.R. (2006), 'Science and industry: tracing the flow of basic research through manufacturing and trade', NBER Working Paper Series 12459, August.
Altenberg, L. (1994), 'Evolving better representations through selective genome growth', in Schaffer, J.D., Schwefel, H.P. and Kitano, H. (eds), *Proceedings of the IEEE World Congress on Computational Intelligence*, pp. 182–87 (quoted in Frenken, 2006a).
Altenberg L. (1995), 'Genome growth and the evolution of the genotype-phenotype map', in Banzhaf, W. and Eeckman, F.H. (eds), *Evolution and Biocomputation: Computational Models of Evolution*, New York: Springer Verlag.
Altenberg, L. (1997), 'Fitness distance correlation analysis: an instructive counterexample', in Baeck, T.

(ed.), *Proceedings of the Seventh International Conference on Genetic Algorithms*, San Mateo, CA: Morgan Kaufmann.

Anderson, P. and Tushman, M.L. (1990), 'Technological discontinuities and dominant designs: a cyclical model of technological change', *Administrative Science Quarterly*, **35**, 604–33.

Antonelli, C. (1995), *The Economics of Localized technological change and industrial dynamics*, Norwell: Kluwer Academic Publishers.

Apreda, R., Bonaccorsi, A. and Fantoni, G. (2008a), 'Rethinking functional analysis', submitted to *Research in Engineering Design*.

Apreda, R., Bonaccorsi, A. and Fantoni, G. (2008b), 'A new architecture for the functional base', submitted to *Research in Engineering Design*.

Apreda, R., Fantoni, R. and Bonaccorsi, A. (2009), 'Functional vector space', Paper presented to the 'International Conference on Engineering Design', ICED '09. 24–27 August, Stanford University.

Apreda, R. and Francaviglia, S. (2009), 'Non-Euclidean distance in the function space', mimeo.

Arrow, K. (1962), 'Economic welfare and the allocation of resources for invention', in NBER, *The Rate and Direction of Inventive Activity: Economic and Social Factors*, Princeton, Princeton University Press.

Arrow, K. (1969), 'Classificatory notes on the production and transmission of technical knowledge', *American Economic Review*, Papers and Proceedings, **59**.

Arrow, K. (1974), *The Limits of Organization*, New York: Norton.

Arrow, K. (1994), 'Methodological individualism and social knowledge', *American Economic Review*, Papers and Proceedings, **84**.

Arrow, K. (1996), 'Technical information and industrial structure', *Industrial and Corporate Change*, **5**.

Arthur, W.B. (2005), 'The logic of invention', *Santa Fe Institute Working Paper*, 19 December.

Arthur, W.B. (2009), *The Nature of Technology: What It Is and How It Evolves*, New York: Free Press.

Arthur, W.B. and Polak, W. (2004), 'The evolution of technology within a simple computer model', Santa Fe Institute Working Paper, 2004-12-042, December.

Balconi, M., Pozzali, A. and Viale, R. (2007), 'The "codification debate" revisited: a conceptual framework to analyze the role of tacit knowledge in economics', *Industrial and Corporate Change*, **16** (5): 823–49.

Basalla, G. (1988), *The Evolution of Technology*, Cambridge: Cambridge University Press.

Bigelow, J. and Pargetter, R. (1987), 'Functions', *Journal of Philosophy*, **84**, 181–96.

Bijker, W.E. (1995), *Of Bicycles, Bakelites, and Bulbs. Toward a Theory of Sociotechnical Change*, Cambridge, MA: MIT Press.

Bijker, W.E., Hughes, T.P. and Pinch, T.J. (eds) (1987), *The Social Construction of Technological Systems: New Directions in the Sociology and History of Technology*, Cambridge, MA: MIT Press.

Birchenhall, C. (1995), 'Modular technical change and genetic algorithms', *Computational Economics*, **8**, 233–53.

Bonaccorsi, A. (2008), 'Search regimes and the industrial dynamics of science', *Minerva*. **46**, 285–315.

Bonaccorsi, A., Apreda, R. and Fantoni, G. (2009), 'A theory of the constituent elements of functions', Paper presented to the International Conference on Engineering Design, ICED '09, 24–27 August, Stanford University.

Bonaccorsi, A., Calvert, J. and Joly, P.B. (2011), 'From protecting texts to protecting objects in biotechnology and software. A tale of changes of ontological assumptions in intellectual property protection', forthcoming, *Economy and Society*.

Bonaccorsi, A. and Fantoni, G. (2007), 'An expanded functional base', paper presented to the ICED Conference, Paris, June.

Bonaccorsi, A., Giuri, P. and Pierotti, F. (2005), 'Technological frontiers and competition in multi-technology sectors. Micro-evidence from the aero-engine industry', *Economics of Innovation and New Technology*, **14**, 23–42.

Bonaccorsi, A. and Thoma, G. (2007), 'Institutional complementarity and inventive performance in nano science and technology', *Research Policy*, **36** (6), 813–31.

Boncinelli, G. (2006), *L'anima della tecnica*, Milan: Rizzoli.

Bonfantini, M. (1987), *Semiosi e abduzione*, Milan: Bompiani.

Bonner, J.T. (2006), *Why Size Matters. From Bacteria to Blue Whales*, Princeton: Princeton University Press.

Boorse, C. (1976), 'Wright on functions', *Philosophical Review*, **85**, 70–86.

Bottani, A. and Davies, R. (eds), (2005), *L'ontologia della proprietà intellettuale*, Milan: Franco Angeli.

Boyd, R. and Richerson, P.J. (1985), *Culture and the Evolutionary Process*, Chicago: University of Chicago Press.

Bradshaw, G. and Lienert, M. (1991), 'The invention of the airplane', in Proceedings of the 13th Annual Conference of the Cognitive Science Society, 7–10 August Chicago.

Brown, D.C. and Chandrasekaran, B. (1989), *Design Problem Solving. Knowledge Structures and Control Strategies*, London: Pitman.

Bucciarelli, L.B. (1994) *Designing Engineers*, Cambridge, MA: MIT Press.

Budgen, D. (2003), *Software Design*, 2nd edn, Harlow: Pearson-Addison Wesley.
Carroll, S.B. (2005), *Endless Forms Most Beautiful. The New Science of Evo-Devo*, New York: Baror International.
Casati, R. and Varzi, A.C. (1999), *Parts and Places*, Cambridge, MA: MIT Press.
Cavalli Sforza, L.L. (2001), *Genes, Peoples and Languages*, London: Penguin Books.
Changeux, J.P. (ed.) (2003), *Gènes et Culture: Envelope Génétique et Variabilité Culturelle*, Paris: Odile Jacob.
Changeux, J.P. (2008), *Du Vrai, Du Beau, Du Bien. Une Nouvelle Approche Neuronale*, Paris: Odile Jacob.
Chisholm, R.M. (1976), *Person and Object*, La Salle, IL: Open Court.
Cohen, J.E. and Lemley, M. (2001), 'Patent scope and innovation in the software industry', *California Law Review*, **89**, 1–57.
Constant II, E.W. (1980), *The Origins of the Turbojet Revolution*, Baltimore: Johns Hopkins University Press.
Cooper, B. (2000), 'Modelling research and development: how do firms solve design problems?', *Journal of Evolutionary Economics*, **10**, 395–414.
Copi, I.M. and Burgess-Jackson, K. (1996), *Informal Logic*, Upper Saddle River: Prentice-Hall.
Copp, N.H. and Zanella, A.W. (1993), 'The flying machine problem: the Wright stuff', in Copp, N.H. and Zanella, A.W (eds), *Discovery, Innovation and Risk*, Cambridge, MA: MIT Press, Chapter 4.
Corballis, M. and Lea, S. (eds) (1999), *The Descent of Mind. Psychological Perspectives on Hominid Evolution*, Oxford: Oxford University Press.
Cowan, R., David, P. and Foray, D. (2000), 'The explicit economics of knowledge codification and tacitness', *Industrial and Corporate Change*, **9** (2), 211–53
Coyne, R.D., Rosenman, M.A., Radford, A.D., Balachandran, M. and Gero, J.S. (1990), *Knowledge-based Design Systems*, Reading, MA: Addison-Wesley.
Cummins, R. (1975), 'Functional analysis', *Journal of Philosophy*, **72**, 741–65.
D'Arcy Thompson, W. (1961), *On Growth and Form*, Cambridge: Cambridge University Press.
de Beaune, S.A. (2009), 'Technical invention in the Palaeolithic: what if the explanation comes from the cognitive and neuropsychological sciences?', in de Beaune, S.A., Colidge, F.L. and Wynn, T. (2009), *Cognitive Archaeology and Human Evolution*, Cambridge: Cambridge University Press.
Dennett, D. (1987), *The Intentional Stance*, Cambridge, MA: MIT Press.
Donnelly, J.F. (1986), 'Representations of applied science: academics and chemical industry in late nineteenth century England', *Social Studies of Science*, **16**, 195–234.
Dorner, D. (1976), *Problemlösen als Informationsverarbeitung*, Stuttgart: W. Kohlhammer (Italian trans. Rome: Città Nuova, 1988).
Dorst, K. and Vermaas, P.E. (2005), 'John Gero's Function-Behaviour-Structure model of designing: a critical analysis', *Research in Engineering Design*, **16**, 17–26.
Dosi, G. and Grazzi, M. (2010), 'On the nature of technologies: knowledge, procedures, artifacts and production inputs', *Cambridge Journal of Economics*, **34** (1), 173–84.
Dourish, P. (2001), *Where The Action Is. The Foundations of Embodied Interaction*, Cambridge, MA: MIT Press.
Dreistadt, R. (1969), 'The use of analogies and incubation in obtaining insights in creative problem solving', *Journal of Psychology*, **71**, 158–75.
Eco, U. (1990), *I limiti dell'interpretazione*, Milano: Bompiani.
Elder, C.L. (2004), *Real Natures and Familiar Objects*, Cambridge, MA: MIT Press.
Eldredge, N. (1995), *Reinventing Darwin. The Great Debate at the High Table of Evolutionary Theory*, New York: John Wiley and Sons.
Eldredge, N. (1999), *The Pattern of Evolution*, New York: W.H. Freeman.
Eldredge, N. and Gould S.J. (1972), 'Punctuated equilibria: an alternative to phyletic gradualism', in Schopf, T.J.M. (ed.), *Models in Paleobiology*, San Francisco: Freeman & Cooper.
Ferguson, E.S. (1992), *Engineering and the Mind's Eye*, Cambridge, MA: MIT Press.
Ferraris, M. (2005), *Dove sei? Ontologia del telefonino*, Milan: Bompiani.
Fleury, V. (2003), *Des pieds et des mains. Genèse des formes de la nature*, Paris: Flammarion.
Fleury, V. (2006), *De l'œuf à l'éternité. Le sens de l'évolution*, Paris: Flammarion.
Flichy, P. (2007), *Understanding Technological Innovation. A Socio-technical Approach*, Cheltenham, UK and Northampton, MA, USA: Edward Elgar (1st edition, Paris, La Découverte, 1995).
Foray, D. (2000), *L'économie de la connaissance*, Paris: La Découverte.
Franssen, M. (2006), 'The normativity of artefacts', *Studies in History and Philosophy of Science*, **37**, 42–57.
Frenken, K. (2000), 'A complexity approach to innovation networks. The case of the aircraft industry (1909–1997)', *Research Policy*, **29**, 257–72.
Frenken, K. (2006a) *Innovation, Evolution and Complexity Theory*, Cheltenham, UK and Northampton, MA, USA: Edward Elgar.
Frenken, K. (2006b), 'Technological innovation and complexity theory', *Economics of Innovation and New Technology*, **15** (2), 137–55.

Frenken, K., Saviotti, P.P. and Trommetter, M. (1999), 'Variety and niche creation in aircraft, helicopters, motorcycles and microcomputers', *Research Policy*, **28**, 469–88.

Frenken, K., Saviotti, P.P. and Trommetter, M. (2000), 'Variety and economic development: conceptual issues and measurement problems', in Cantner, U., Hanusch, H. and Klepper, S. (eds), *Economic Evolution, Learning and Complexity*, Heidelberg: Physica-Verlag, pp. 209–44.

Gentner, D. (1983), 'Structure-mapping. A theoretical framework for analogy', *Cognitive Science*, **7** (2), 155–70.

Gero, J.S. (1990), 'Design prototypes: a knowledge representation schema for design', *AI Magazine*, **11** (4), 26–36.

Gero, J.S. and Kannengiesser, U. (2002), 'The situated Function-Behaviour-Structure framework', *Artificial Intelligence in Design '02*, Kluwer: Dordrecht, pp. 89–104.

Gibson, J.J. (1977), 'The theory of affordances', in Shaw, R.E. and Brandsford, J. (eds), *Perceiving, Acting and Knowing. Toward an Ecological Psychology*, Hillsdale, NJ: Lawrence Erlbaum Associates, pp. 67–82.

Gibson, J.J. (1979), *The Ecological Approach to Visual Perception*, Boston: Houghton Mifflin Co.

Gibson, K.R. and Ingold, T. (1993), *Tools, Language and Cognition in Human Evolution*, Cambridge: Cambridge University Press.

Gick, M.L. and Holyoak, K.J. (1980), 'Analogical problem solving', *Cognitive Psychology*, **12**, 306–55.

Gieryn, T.F. (1983), 'Boundary-work and the demarcation of science from non-science: strains and interests in professional ideologies of scientists', *American Sociological Review*, **48**, 781–95.

Gineste, M.D. (1997), *Analogie et cognition*, Paris: Presses Universitaires de France.

Gittelman, M. and Kogut, B. (2003), 'Does good science lead to valuable knowledge? Biotechnology firms and the evolutionary logic of citation patterns', *Management Science*, **49**, 366–82.

Glymour, C. and Cooper, G.F. (eds) (1999), *Computation, Causation, and Discovery*, Cambridge, MA: MIT Press.

Godfrey-Smith, P. (1994), 'A modern history theory of functions', *Noûs*, **28**, 344–62.

Goel, V. and Pirolli, P. (1992), 'The structure of design problem spaces', *Cognitive Science*, **16**, 395–429.

Goldberg, D. (1989), *Genetic Algorithms in Search, Optimization, and Machine Learning*, Reading, MA: Addison-Wesley.

Gould, S.J. (2002), *The Structure of Evolutionary Theory*, Cambridge, MA: Belknap Press.

Gould, S.J. and Lewontin, R.C. (1979), 'The spandrels of San Marco and the Panglossian paradigm: a critique of the adaptationist programme', *Proceedings of the Royal Society of London*, **B 205**, 581–98.

Gould S.J. and Vrba, E.S. (1982), 'Exaptation – a missing term in the science of form', *Paleobiology*, **8**, 4–15.

Griffin, D.R. (1962), *Animal Structure and Function*, New York: Holt, Rinehart and Winston.

Griffiths, P.E. (1993), 'Functional analysis and proper functions', *British Journal for the Philosophy of Science*, **44**, 409–22.

Grupp, H. (ed.) (1992), *Dynamics of Science Based Innovation*, New York: Springer-Verlag.

Gustason, W. (1994), *Reasoning from Evidence*, New York: MacMillan Publishing.

Hempel, C.G. (1959), 'The concept of function', in Gross, L. (ed.), *Symposium on Sociological Theory*, New York: Harper and Row, pp. 271–307, reprinted in Hempel, C.G. (1965), *Aspects of Scientific Explanation*, New York: Free Press, pp. 297–330.

Hirsch, E. (1982), *The Concept of Identity*, New York: Oxford University Press.

Hirshleifer, J. (1971), 'The private and social value of information and the reward to inventive activity', *American Economic Review*, **61**.

Hirshleifer, J. and Riley, J.G. (1992), 'Research and invention', in *The Analytics of Uncertainty and Information*, Cambridge: Cambridge University Press, Chapter 7.

Hirtz, J., Stone, R.B., McAdams, D.A., Szykman, S. and Wood, K.L. (2004), 'A functional basis for engineering design. Reconciling and evolving previous efforts', *Journal of Research in Engineering Design*, **1**.

Holland, J.H. (1975), *Adaptation in Natural and Artificial Systems*, Ann Arbor: University of Michigan Press (2nd edition, MIT Press, 1992).

Holland, J.H. (1992), *Adaptation in Natural and Artificial Systems*, 2nd edn, Cambridge, MA: MIT Press.

Holland, J.H. (1995), *Hidden Order. How Adaptation Builds Complexity*, Reading, MA: Addison-Wesley.

Holland, J.H. Holyoak, K.J., Nisbett, R.E. and Thagard, P.R. (1986), *Induction: Processes of Inference, Learning, and Discovery*, Cambridge, MA: MIT Press.

Holyoak, K.J. (1977), 'The form of analog size information in memory', *Cognitive Psychology*, **9**, 31–51.

Holyoak, K.J. and Thagard, P. (1989), 'Analogical mapping by constraint satisfaction', *Cognitive Science*, **13**, 295–355.

Hubka, V., Andreasen, M., Eder, W. and Hills, P. (1988), *Practical Studies in Systematic Design*, London: Butterworth.

Iacoboni, M. (2008), *Mirroring People. The New Science of How We Connect With Others*, New York: Farrar, Straus & Giroux.

Jablonka, E. and Lamb, M.J. (2005). *Evolution in Four Dimensions. Genetic, Epigenetic, Behavioural and Symbolic variation in the History of Life*, Cambridge, MA: MIT Press.

Jackson, D. (2006), *Software Abstractions: Logic, Language, and Analysis*, Cambridge, MA: MIT Press.
Johnson-Laird, P. (2005), 'The Wright brothers', *Mind and Society. Cognitive Studies in Economics and Social Science*, **4** (1).
Johnson-Laird, P. (2006), *How We Reason*, Oxford: Oxford University Press.
Kauffman, S.A. (1993), *The Origins of Order. Self-organization and Selection in Evolution*, New York: Oxford University Press.
Kauffman, S.A. (2000), *Investigations*, Oxford: Oxford University Press.
Kelemen, D. (1999), 'The scope of teleological thinking in preschool children', *Cognition*, **70**, 241–72.
Kelemen, D. and Di Yanni, C. (2005), 'Time to get a new mountain? The role of function in children's conception of natural kinds', *Cognition*, **97**, 325–35.
Kirschman, C.F. and Fadel, G.M. (1998), 'Classifying functions for mechanical design', *Journal of Mechanical Design* (ASME), **120**, June.
Kitamura, Y., Kasai, T. and Mizoguchi, R. (2001), 'Ontology-based description of functional design knowledge and its use in a functional way server', Proceedings of the Pacific Asian Conference on Intelligent Systems (PAIS).
Klein, E. and Lachièze-Rey, F. (1999), *The Quest for Unity. The Adventure of Physics*, New York: Oxford University Press.
Klepper, S. (1996), 'Entry, exit, growth and innovation over the product life cycle', *American Economic Review*, **86** (3), 562–83.
Kline, R. (1995), 'Construing "technology" as "applied science": public rhetoric of scientists and engineers in the United States, 1880–1945', *Isis*, **86** (2), 194–221.
Kline, S.J. (1995), *Conceptual Foundations for Multidisciplinary Thinking*, Stanford: Stanford University Press.
Kranakis, E. (1989), 'Social determinants of engineering practice: a comparative view of France and America in the nineteenth century', *Social Studies of Science*, **19** (1), 5–70.
Krohs, U. and Kroes, P. (2009), *Functions in Biological and Artificial Worlds. Comparative Philosophical Perspectives*, Cambridge, MA: MIT Press.
Lambert, D. and Rezsöhazy, D. (2004) *Comment les pattes viennent au serpent. Essai sur l'étonnante plasticité du vivant*, Paris: Flammarion.
Lamberton, D. (ed.) (1971), *Economics of Information and Knowledge*, Harmondsworth: Penguin.
Lane, D. and Maxfield, R. (1997), 'Complexity, foresight and strategy', in Arthur, W.B., Durlauf, S. and Lane, D. (eds), *The Economy as an Evolving Complex System II*, Redwood City, CA: Addison-Wesley.
Lane, D. and Maxfield, R. (2006), 'Ontological uncertainty and innovation', *Journal of Evolutionary Economics*, **15**, 3–50.
Leroi-Gourhan, A. (1943), *Evolution et techniques. Vol. I, L'homme et la matière*, Paris: Editions Albin Michel.
Leroi-Gourhan, A. (1945), *Evolution et techniques. Vol. II, Milieu et technique*, Paris: Editions Albin Michel.
Leroi-Gourhan, A. (1964), *Le geste et la parole. Vol I, Technique et langage, Vol II, La mémoire et les rythmes*, Paris: Editions Albin Michel.
Lévêque, F. and Meniére, Y. (2004), *The Economics of Patents and Copyrights*, Berkeley: Berkeley Electronic Press.
Levinthal, D.A. (1998), 'The slow pace of rapid technological change: gradualism and punctuation in technological change', *Industrial and Corporate Change*, **7**, 217–47.
Lewens, T. (2004), *Organisms and Artifacts: Design in Nature and Elsewhere*, Cambridge, MA: MIT Press.
Lewontin, R. (2000), *The Triple Helix. Gene, Organism and Environment*, Cambridge, MA: Harvard University Press.
Lombardi, M. (2008), 'A morphogenetic approach to the evolution of organisational capabilities', in Leoncini, R. and Montresor, A. (eds), *Dynamic Capabilities Between Firm Organization and Local Systems of Production*, London: Routledge.
Marengo, L. and Dosi, G. (2005), 'Division of labor, organizational coordination and market mechanisms in collective problem-solving', *Journal of Economic Behavior and Organization*, **58**, 303–26.
Marengo, L., Dosi, G., Legrenzi, P. and Pasquali, C. (2000), 'The structure of problem-solving knowledge and the structure of organizations', *Industrial and Corporate Change*, **9**, 757–88.
Margolis E. and Laurence, S. (eds) (2007), *Creations of the Mind: Theories of Artifacts and their Representation*, Oxford: Oxford University Press.
McCarthy, J. and Wright, P. (2004), *Technology as Experience*, Cambridge, MA: MIT Press.
McLaughlin, P. (2001), *What Functions Explain*, Cambridge: Cambridge University Press.
Merges, R.P. and Nelson, R. (1990), 'On the complex economics of patent scope', *Columbia Law Journal*, **90** (4), 839–916.
Merricks, T. (2003), *Objects and Persons*, Oxford: Clarendon Press.
Millikan, R.G. (1984), *Language, Thought and Other Biological Categories: New Foundations for Realism*, Cambridge, MA: MIT Press.
Millikan, R.G. (1993), *White Queen Psychology and Other Essays for Alice*, Cambridge, MA: MIT Press.

Moggridge, B. (2007), *Designing Interactions*, Cambridge, MA: MIT Press.

Molotch, H. (2003), *Where Stuff Comes From. How Toasters, Toilets, Cars, Computers, and Many Other Things Come To Be As They Are*, London: Routledge.

Morand, B. (2004), *Logique de la conception. Figures de sémiotique générale d'après Charles S. Peirce*, Paris: L'Harmattan.

Nagel, E. (1977), 'Teleology revisited', *Journal of Philosophy*, **74**, 261–301.

Nagel, R.L., Vucovich, J.P., Stone, R.B. and McAdams, D.A. (2007), 'Signal Flow Grammar, from the Functional Basis', International Conference on Engineering Design, ICED'07 Paris, France.

Narin, F. and Olivastro, D. (1992), 'Status report: linkage between technology and science', *Research Policy*, **21**, 237–49.

Narin, F.S., Hamilton, K.S. and Olivastro, D. (1997), 'The increasing linkage between US technology and public science', *Research Policy*, **26**, 317–30.

Neander, K. (1991a), 'The teleological notion of "function"', *Australasian Journal of Philosophy*, **69**, 454–68.

Neander, K. (1991b), 'Functions as selected effects: the conceptual analyst defense', *Philosophy of Science*, **58**, 168–84.

Neander, K. (1995), 'Misrepresenting and malfunctioning', *Philosophical Studies*, **79**, 109–41.

Nelson, R. and Winter, S.G. (1982), *An Evolutionary Theory of Economic Change*, Cambridge, MA: Belknap Press.

Nelson, R.R. (2003), 'On the uneven evolution of human know-how', *Research Policy*, **32**, 909–22.

Newell, A. (1990), *Unified Theories of Cognition*, Cambridge, MA: Harvard University Press.

Newell, A. and Simon, H. (1972), *Human Problem Solving*, Englewood Cliffs, NJ: Prentice-Hall.

Noble, D. (2006), *The Music of Life. Biology Beyond the Genome*, Oxford: Oxford University Press.

Nonaka, I. and Takeuchi, H. (1995), *The Knowledge-creating Company*, Oxford: Oxford University Press.

Norman, D.A. (1988), *The Psychology of Everyday Things*, New York: Basic Books.

Norman, D.A. (1992), *Turn Signals are the Facial Expressions of Automobiles*, New York: W.W. Norton and Company.

Olson, G.B. (2002), 'Designing a new material world', in Amato, I. (ed.) *Science. Pathways of Discovery*, New York: John Wiley and Sons.

Olsson, O. (2000), 'Knowledge as a set in idea space: an epistemological view on growth', *Journal of Economic Growth*, **5**, 253–75, September.

Olsson, O. and Frey, B. (2002), 'Entrepreneurship as recombinant growth', *Small Business Economics*, **19**, 69–80.

Oudshoorn, N. and Pinch, T. (2003), *How Users Matter. The Co-construction of Users and Technology*, Cambridge, MA: MIT Press.

Pahl, G. and Beitz, W. (1984), *Engineering Design. A Systematic Approach*, London: Design Council.

Parker, A. (2003), *In the Blink of an Eye*, London: Simon and Schuster.

Pasinetti, L. (1963), *A Multisector Model of Economic Growth*, Cambridge: King's College.

Pasinetti, L. (1974), *Growth and Income Distribution. Essays in Economic Theory*, Cambridge: Cambridge University Press.

Pasinetti, L. (1993), *Structural Economic Dynamics. A Theory of the Economic Consequences of Human Learning*, Cambridge: Cambridge University Press.

Pearl, J. (2000), *Causality: Models, Reasoning, and Inference*, Cambridge: Cambridge University Press.

Peirce, C.S. (1878), 'Deduction, induction, and hypothesis', *Popular Science Monthly*, **13**, 470–82, in *Collected Papers*, Cambridge, MA: Harvard University Press, 1958.

Peirce, C.S. (1901), 'Abduction and induction', in *Philosophical Writings of Peirce*, selected and edited with an introduction by Buchler, J., New York, Dover Publications, 1955.

Peirce, C.S. (1903), 'Pragmatism and abduction', in *Collected Papers*, 5, 180–212 (Italian translation in *Le leggi dell'ipotesi. Antologia dei Collected Papers*, Milan: Bompiani, 1984).

Perlman, M. (2004), 'The modern philosophical resurrection of teleology', *The Monist*, **87**, 3–51.

Perlman, M. (2009), 'Changing the mission of theories of teleology: dos and don'ts for thinking about functions', in Krohs, U. and Kroes, P. (eds), *Functions in Biological and Artificial Worlds. Comparative Philosophical Perspectives*, Cambridge, MA: MIT Press, 17–35.

Petroski, H. (1992), *The Evolution of Useful Things*, New York: Vintage Books.

Piatigorsky, J. (2007), *Gene Sharing and Evolution. The Diversity of Protein Functions*, Cambridge, MA: Harvard University Press.

Pigliucci, M. and Kaplan, J. (2006), *Making Sense of Evolution. The Conceptual Foundations of Evolutionary Biology*, Chicago: University of Chicago Press.

Polanyi, M. (1958), *Personal Knowledge: Towards a Post-critical Philosophy*, New York: Harper Books.

Polanyi, M. (1967), *The Tacit Dimension*, Garden City, NY: Doubleday Anchor.

Polya, G. (1945), *How to Solve It*, Princeton, NJ: Princeton University Press.

Premack, D. and Premack, A. (2003), *Original Intelligence. Unlocking the Mystery of Who We Are*, New York: McGraw Hill.

Raff, R.A. and Kauffman, T.C. (1983), *Embryos, Genes, and Evolution. The Developmental-Genetic Basis of Evolutionary Change*, New York: MacMillan.

Rescher, N. (1996), *Priceless Knowledge?*, Lanham: Rowman and Littlefield Publishers.

Rich, B.R. and Janos, L. (1994), *Skunk Works. A Personal Memoir of My Years at Lockheed*, Boston: Little, Brown and Company.

Richerson, P.J. and Boyd, R. (2005), *Not by Genes Alone: How Culture Transformed Human Evolution*, Chicago: University of Chicago Press.

Riddle, B. and Sinnott, C. (2003), *Letters of the Wright Brothers, Letters of Wilbur, Orville and Katharine Wright in the Royal Aeronautical Society Library*, London: Tempus Publishing.

Rittel, H.J. and Webber, M.M. (1984), 'Planning problems are wicked problems', in N. Cross (ed.), *Developments in Design Methodology*, New York: Wiley, pp. 135–44.

Rizzolatti, G. and Sinigaglia, C. (2006), *So quel che fai. Il cervello che agisce e i neuroni specchio*, Milan: Raffaello Cortina Editore.

Rosenberg, N. (1994), *Exploring the Black Box*, Cambridge: Cambridge University Press.

Rybczynski, W. (2000), *One Good Turn. A Natural History of the Screwdriver and the Screw*, New York: Simon Schuster.

Sahal, D. (1981), *Patterns of Innovation*, Reading, MA: Addison-Wesley.

Sander, E. (2000), *L'analogie, du naïf au créatif. Analogie et catégorisation*, Paris: L'Harmattan.

Sanderson, M. (1978), 'The professor as industrial consultant: Oliver Arnold and the British steel industry, 1900–1914', *Economic History Review*, **31**, 585–600.

Saviotti, P.P. (1988), 'Information, entropy and variety in technoeconomic development', *Research Policy*, **17**, 89–103.

Saviotti, P.P. (1991), 'The role of variety in economic and technological development, in Saviotti, P.P. and Metcalfe, S. (eds), *Evolutionary Theories of Economic and Technological Change. Present State and Future Prospects*, Reading: Harwood Publishers.

Saviotti, P.P. (1996), *Technological Evolution, Variety and the Economy*, Cheltenham, UK and Brookfield, VT, USA: Edward Elgar.

Saviotti, P.P. and Mani, G.S. (1995), 'Competition, variety and technological evolution. A replicator dynamics model', *Journal of Evolutionary Economics*, **5**, 369–92.

Saviotti, P.P. and Metcalfe, J.S. (1984), 'A theoretical approach to the construction of technological output indicators', *Research Policy*, **13**, 141–51.

Saviotti, P.P. and Trickett, A. (1992), 'The evolution of helicopter technology, 1940-1986', *Economics of Innovation and New Technology*, **2**, 111–30.

Schick, K.D. and Toth, N. (1993), *Making Silent Stones Speak. Human Evolution and the Dawn of Technology*, New York: Simon and Schuster.

Seely, B. (1993), 'Research, engineering, and science in American engineering colleges: 1900–1960', *Technology and Culture*, **34** (2), 344–86.

Senker, J. (1995), 'Tacit knowledge and models of innovation', *Industrial and Corporate Change*, **4** (2), 143–51.

Shanahan, T. (2004), *The Evolution of Darwinism. Selection, Adaptation, and Progress in Evolutionary Biology*, Cambridge: Cambridge University Press.

Simon, H.A. (1962), 'The architecture of complexity: hierarchic systems', *Proceedings of the American Philosophical Society*, **106**, December, 467–82.

Simon, H.A. (1969), *The Sciences of the Artificial*, Cambridge, MA: MIT Press.

Sridharan, P. and Campbell, M. (2004), 'A grammar for functional structures', *Design Engineering Technical Conferences* and *Computers and Information in Engineering Conference*, ASME, Salt Lake City, Utah.

Sriram, R.D. (1997), *Intelligent Systems for Engineering*, Berlin: Springer Verlag.

Stadler, B.M., Stadler, P.F., Wagner, G.P. and Fontana, W. (2001), 'The topology of the possible: formal spaces underlying patterns of evolutionary change', *Journal of Theoretical Biology*, **213**, 241–74.

Stankiewicz, R. (2000), 'The concept of "design space"', in Ziman, J. (ed.), *Technological Innovation as an Evolutionary Process*, Cambridge: Cambridge University Press, pp. 234–47.

Stankiewicz, R. (2002), 'The cognitive dynamics of biotechnology and the evolution of its technological systems', in Carlsson, B. (ed.), *Technological Systems in the Bio Industries*, Boston, MA: Kluwer Academic Publishers, pp. 35–52.

Sterelny, K. (2007), *Dawkins vs Gould. Survival of the Fittest*, Cambridge: Icon Books.

Suchman, L. (2007), *Human-Machine Reconfigurations*, Cambridge: Cambridge University Press.

Suh, N.P. (1990), *The Principles of Design*, New York: Oxford University Press.

Teece, D.J. (1986), 'Profiting from technological innovation', *Research Policy*, **15**, 285–305.

Teece, D.J., Pisano, G. and Shuen, A. (1997), 'Dynamic capabilities and strategic management', *Strategic Management Journal*, **18**, 509–33.

Thomasson, A.L. (2007), 'Artifacts and human concepts', in Margolis, E. and Laurence, S. (eds) *Creations of the Mind. Theories of Artifacts and their Representation*, Oxford: Oxford University Press, pp. 52–73.

Tomasello, M. (1999), *The Cultural Origins of Human Cognition*, Cambridge, MA: Harvard University Press.

Tong, C. and Sriram, D. (1992), *Artificial Intelligence in Engineering Design*, Boston: Academic Press.

Turkle, S. (ed.) (2008), *The Inner History of Devices*, Cambridge, MA: MIT Press.

Tushman, M.L. and Anderson, P. (1986), 'Technological discontinuities and organizational environments', *Administrative Science Quarterly*, **31**, 439–65.

Ullman, D. (1997), *The Mechanical Design Process*, New York: McGraw Hill.

Ulrich, K.T. and Eppinger, S. (1995), *Product Design and Development*, New York: McGraw Hill.

van Inwagen, P. (1990), *Material Beings*, Ithaca: Cornell University Press.

Varzi, A.C. (2001), *Parole, oggetti, eventi e altri argomenti di metafisica*, Roma: Carocci.

Varzi, A.C. (2005), *Ontologia*, Bari: Laterza.

Vermaas, P. (2007), 'The functional modelling account of Stone and Wood: some critical remarks', *International Conference on Engineering Design*, ICED 2007, Paris, 28–31 August.

Vermaas, P.E. and Houkes, W. (2003), 'Ascribing functions to technical artefacts: a challenge to etiological accounts of functions', *British Journal for the Philosophy of Science*, **54**, 261–89.

Vermaas, P.E. and Houkes, W. (2006), 'Technical functions: a drawbridge between the intentional and structural natures of technical artifacts', *Studies in History and Philosophy of Science*, **37**, 5–18.

Villani, M., Bonacini, S., Ferrari, D., Serra, R. and Lane, D. (2007), 'An agent-based model of exaptive processes', *European Management Journal*, **4**, 141–51.

Vincenti, W.G. (1990), *What Engineers Know and How They Know It. Analytical Studies from Aeronautical History*, Baltimore: Johns Hopkins University Press.

Vrba, E.S. and Gould, S.J. (1986), 'The hierarchical expansion of sorting and selection: sorting and selection cannot be equated', *Paleobiology*, **12**, 217–28.

Wagner, P. (1998), *La machine en logique*, Paris: Presses Universitaires de France.

Weitzman, M.L. (1998), 'Recombinant growth', *Quarterly Journal of Economics*, **113** (2), 331–60.

Windrum, P. and Birchenhall, C. (1998), 'Is product life cycle theory a special case? Dominant designs and the emergence of market niches through coevolutionary learning', *Structural Change and Economic Dynamics*, **9**, 109–34.

Witt, U. (2004), 'On novelty and heterogeneity', Max Planck Institute Working Paper 0405.

Wright, L. (1973), 'Functions'. *Philosophical Review*, **82**, 139–68.

Ziman, J. (ed.) (2000), *Technological Innovation as an Evolutionary Process*, Cambridge: Cambridge University Press.

PART IV

THE ECONOMIC COMPLEXITY OF STRUCTURAL CHANGE AND DEVELOPMENT

13 Mesoeconomics: a unified approach to systems complexity and evolution
Kurt Dopfer

1. BACKGROUND

The last three decades have seen a rise in interest in evolutionary thinking in economics, paralleled by a large volume of publications in this emergent field. Examining the nature of this research reveals two features that are worthy of note.

First, the growth in the quantity of publications has been matched by an increase in variety, reflecting the fact that the scope of empirical explorations has widened and that the investigations into theoretical issues have become progressively more specialized and differentiated. This development has had far-reaching consequences for the unity and the coherence of the scientific endeavour. While the overall knowledge base has accumulated, the individual pieces of knowledge have tended to become disconnected and unrelated corresponding to the degree that they have undergone theoretical refinement and polishing. This has led to the growing recognition that they should be conceived less as single items and more as component parts of a whole. This recognition is less compelling for the management and related 'micro' sciences (which have furnished important theoretical groundwork and empirical evidence); for the science of economics, though, the macroscopic scope is centre stage, since its very subject matter is the economy as a whole, and any failure to connect the various pieces of theoretical and empirical knowledge may well signal a substantive failure in the theoretical venture. The concern for a valid theoretical architecture is bound to figure prominently on the agenda of evolutionary economics if it is to cope with major problems that relate to the economy as a whole.

A second feature that catches the eye on contemplating the nature of the current research is the fact that a great number of the theoretical and empirical studies stubbornly defy all attempts at classification into the received domains of microeconomics and macroeconomics. There is a broad range of works, dealing with population dynamics, path dependence, industrial sector interactions, industrial clusters, innovation systems, market selection, replicator dynamics, network effects, institutional factors, learning trajectories, and so forth, that cannot be ascribed without a substantial measure of arbitrariness to the domains of micro- or macroeconomics. Against the background of the traditional distinction between micro- and macroeconomics, these studies occupy an intermediate position, and they may be brought together under the conceptual umbrella of 'mesoeconomics'. In this way, mesoeconomics serves as a taxonomic device that allows us to put a great number of theoretical and empirical studies into their proper place in the discipline. This represents no small achievement, and serves as sufficient justification in itself for advancing the idea.

The question arises, however, whether the concept of mesoeconomics must of necessity be confined to the realm of taxonomy or whether it may also play a more substantive role in terms of theory formulation. Is there a deeper reason as to why the various studies do not fit into the established categories? This brings us back to the previous issue, of how to identify and combine the various pieces of theoretical and empirical knowledge into a coherent whole. Is mesoeconomics limited to serving as a conceptual pigeonhole for otherwise unclassifiable studies, or can it also gain an independent and genuine place in the architecture of economics? The core of the research agenda of economics may be captured with two questions: how is the knowledge of an economy coordinated, in terms of structuring economic operations and outcomes, and how do changes in the base of distributed knowledge restructure those operations and outcomes? The validity of any economic theory depends critically on whether or not it provides an explanatory core for tackling these two issues. It has long been acknowledged that neoclassical economics deals well with static allocation problems but fails spectacularly to provide an endogenous core that would allow us to address adequately the questions of generic coordination and evolutionary change. I contend that mesoeconomics provides not only a useful taxonomic format but also, and more importantly, a key theoretical concept that enables us to deal adequately with the questions of structure and change.

Although treating mesoeconomics as a distinct domain is not yet standard practice, it is increasingly recognized that the concept provides the key to a theoretical understanding of structure and change in an economy. Acknowledging that 'between the micro and macro level of economics [there is] the important meso level', Hanusch and Pyka (2007) state succinctly:

> It is the meso level of an economic system in which the decisive structural and qualitative changes take place and can be observed.

The meso domain thus plays a substantive part in constructing the overall theoretical framework of the discipline. It represents not just a taxonomic category but, more significantly, a distinct building block in a new theoretical architecture. The old micro–macro dichotomy is challenged, opening up new vistas for a

micro–meso–macro

architecture.

Having arrived at this point, it is perfectly evident now why the various aforementioned studies were unable to find a home in the received disciplinary schemata. The micro–macro framework of mainstream economics is not designed to tackle problems of knowledge coordination, of the restructuring of economic activities and of self-generating continuous economic change. The studies in question are concerned with precisely these questions, and accordingly they find a home quite naturally in an edifice that is erected on the basis of a micro–meso–macro architecture.

The discussion below starts by highlighting the basic differences in the treatment of economic knowledge and information in mainstream and evolutionary economics. It then proceeds with the construction of a micro–meso–macro architecture on the basis of a unified rule approach demonstrating how 'meso' represents the central explanatory core of a theory dealing with structure and evolutionary change in an economy. The discussion draws on earlier works dealing with various aspects of a rule-based meso approach (Dopfer, 1994, 2001, 2005, 2006; Dopfer et al., 2004; Dopfer and Potts, 2008) with the aims of generalization and integration. As the general theoretic approach adopted covers a great deal of special topics, fields and branches, no attempt will be made to discuss in the text the enormous amount of important literature; instead, a (highly selective) bibliography dealing directly or indirectly with micro–meso–macro subjects in general and meso in particular is provided at the end of the paper.

2.   THE ECONOMY: A GENERALIZED RULE SYSTEM

The complexity of the economy naturally invites differing theoretical views, but the conjecture that it has something to do with many agents who carry knowledge for economic operations should not give rise to serious objections. Despite its simplicity, the statement acknowledges explicitly the theoretical significance of three key categories: agent, knowledge and operations. Viewed from the perspective of agents, they are involved in activities at two levels: the knowledge level and the operational level. Depending on the theoretical intentions, analysis may focus on the level of operations, assuming the knowledge of the agents to be constant, or the level of knowledge, addressing its structural and evolutionary aspects.

Knowledge has an ideational content, or, correspondingly, represents an idea that relates to economic operations. Ideas have an existence of their own, however, meaning that they exist regardless of whether they are actualized in an agent. Ideas constitute a potential for actualization. We therefore call any so-defined ideational potential 'information', and any information actualized by any agent 'knowledge'. Any idea encoded by an agent is said to become 'information', and any information decoded subsequently by one or several agents to become 'knowledge'. There are numerous instances in which the terms 'information' and 'knowledge' can be used interchangeably without giving rise to misunderstanding, and I see no need to labour the linguistic point, but it is worth stating that there are also important cases in which distinguishing an idea in its status of information and of knowledge is essential if conceptual errors or theoretical fallacies are to be avoided – for instance, when coping with the intricacies of the relationship between micro-adoption and meso-diffusion (see Section 5).

The view of the economy as a system composed of many agents carrying knowledge for economic operations is a cornerstone of the theoretical exposition suggested, but the story does not end there. Knowledge is actualized not only in agents but, equally, in all cultural artefacts as they are produced, transacted and consumed by the agents. Both of them – agents and artefacts – can be viewed as representing carriers of knowledge. Given the general term 'carrier', the remaining task is one of defining the particular nature of the various carriers. Building on the above broad distinction of carriers, the question is one of identifying the nature of the agents and of the artefacts.

There are, arguably, various criteria to be employed here, but the one that fits best the theoretical purpose to hand suggests interpreting agents as subjects and artefacts as objects. This characterization allows us, first of all, to deal properly with the particular kinds of knowledge that agents and artefacts carry. The taxonomy of Table 13.1

Table 13.1   Rule taxonomy

Generic rules			
Subject rules		Object rules	
Cognitive rules	Behavioural rules Individual behaviour	Social rules Collective Behaviour	Technical rules
e.g. mental models and schemata	e.g. behavioural heuristics, algorithms and norms	e.g. organization of enterprise or market	e.g. machines, instruments and techniques

acknowledges expressly the relevance of this view. Second, the distinction into subjects and objects allows us to bring into focus the essential theoretical aspects relevant for the explanation of systemic interactions and of the coevolution of knowledge embodied in agents and artefacts. Finally, the categories of subject and object provide a systematic platform for assessing the methodological strands of subjectivism (a subject-related perspective) and objectivism (object-related). The discussion in the subsequent section leads towards an understanding of why these methodological stances are but two sides of the same explanatory coin.

At this juncture it is worth elaborating further on what is being proposed to serve as a conceptual platform for advancing theoretical statements about structure and change. Taking stock, we have the general theoretical terms of 'carrier', 'ideas' and 'operations'. While the term 'carrier' (as specified by subject and object) seems to be quite unambiguous – indeed, this is underlined by its frequent application in theoretical biology – that of 'idea' is surrounded by considerable ambiguity, calling out for a comparably clear-cut definition. It adds to the complication that the term 'idea' often evokes, reflex-like, the reproach of Platonism, which is considered to be generally at odds with the canon of modern science. Considerations of this kind may warrant replacing the term 'idea' by another, but there is a more substantive reason as well for doing so: the notion of 'idea' is not used in a general but, rather, a specific sense. In its present theoretical meaning, an idea is one solely for economic operations; it excludes any other possible application. Looking for better terminology does not relegate the concept of 'idea' from the theoretical plane (in fact, I use the term whenever I feel it may contribute to a better understanding of the matter); it simply acknowledges its particular use.

I propose substituting the term 'generic rule' for 'idea'. A subject or object is said to carry a particular generic rule (or composite of them), allowing it to perform a particular kind of economic operation. We therefore have the following general theoretical terms that, together, define the proposed theoretical exposition: carrier, rule and operations. Before turning to a brief explanation of why this terminology has been adopted, it is necessary to highlight an important point. Economic carriers interact at two levels; and these are considered to constitute two major areas of theoretical investigation.

(1)   Generic level: rules.
(2)   Operant level: operations based on rules.

3.   UNIFIED RULE APPROACH

Employing the term 'rule' leads to two distinct advantages. First, quite a broad range of phenomena relevant for economics are associated with and denoted by the term. The menu of explanatory categories includes social rules, technical rules, organizational rules, cognitive rules, behavioural rules, institutional rules and legal rules – to provide just a few leading examples from a considerably longer list. The term 'rule' functions in this way as a common language upon which a unified approach embracing all the variables relevant for the envisaged theory may be built. Given the distinction in terms of carriers between subjects and objects, the proposed taxonomy introduces as major rule classes subject rules and object rules. In all these particular cases a rule represents an idea for economic operations. A taxonomy differentiating rules into categories on the basis of the distinction between subject and object is given in summary form in Table 13.1.

Second, the term 'rule' (unlike that of 'idea') is variously connected to analytical meanings that are relevant for economics. In its connotation with logic, a rule can be said to represent a deductive format. As processes are a constituent feature of the theoretical approach proposed, the formal apparatus of deduction may be replaced by the idea of an ongoing inferential procedure involving a continuous interplay between induction and deduction. A rule can thus alternatively be said to constitute an abductive format (building on the work of Charles Peirce). The analytical meaning of the term 'rule' facilitates in various ways the translation of theoretical contents into formal or computational renditions, as, for instance, into its more recent vintage simulation models.

The notion of 'generic' is a horse of a different colour. Although the term 'rule' has been informed mainly by practical considerations, the choice of the term 'generic' goes to the heart of the matter, as it addresses the nature of rule. As we shall see next, the term 'generic' concerns the ontological status of rule.

4.   GENERIC MATRIX: COMPLEXITY AND EVOLUTION

Economic entities have been presented as constituting carriers that actualize rules for economic operations. While this brings into focus the general division between generic levels and operant levels, the definitional statement also includes an important distinction that applies more narrowly to the generic level itself. There is, on the one hand, the ideational component stated as rule, and, on the other hand, the process of its physical actualization in time and space. The essential difference between neoclassical and evolutionary economics can be put down to the particular assumptions they make about the nature of rules and their actualizations.

Ever since the seventeenth century the works of the classical sciences have been inspired by a belief in the existence of universal laws. Observed phenomena had to be reduced to their typical characteristics, and the task of science was to make universal statements about them. Universality was based on the twin assumption that real phenomena could indeed be reduced to their homogeneous characteristics and that the laws propounded about their behaviour applied invariantly to all time and space. The assumptions of homogeneity and immutability are at the base of a scientific approach that, in the discourse of methodology, is usually called nomological or nomothetic.

This approach has been challenged by the advent of evolutionary biology in the second half of the nineteenth century. The ontological premise of an immutable universe broke down in the face of the theoretical proposition that the observed variety could not be reduced to any typical average but was itself a consequence of continuous change. The classical assumptions were replaced by those of heterogeneity and mutability, or, in the parlance of evolutionary biology, by extant variety and continual variation. It is indicative of the power of the classical paradigm that there would appear to be no term available in the methodology discourse analogous to that of nomological or nomothetic. Recognizing this deficit, the body of theories based on the above-mentioned non-classical assumptions are denoted as being 'generic'.

In its analytic skeleton, any real phenomenon is an actualization of some rule. Putting generic flesh on it, however, it represents an actualization of a rule of a particular kind at a time and one that changes with the passage of time. For instance, agents operating in a market today may employ quite different decision rules from those they used ten years ago, and the ones they employ today may not be necessarily those they will follow tomorrow. This standpoint is the diametric opposite of the universalistic construct of *Homo oeconomicus*, which assumes that all agents are equally rational and employ the same perfect decision algorithm always and everywhere. The analogous generic characteristics apply to all other rules as they are charted in taxonomic order in Table 13.1.

At this juncture, the question of particular interest is how the generic assumptions bear on the architecture of the theory. What is the nature of the basic theoretical unit designed to serve as a key for explaining structure and change in an economy? This problem has been variously approached by calling for adequate 'micro' foundations, with the result that the discussion often fell at the first hurdle: that of defining what 'micro' actually means.

Employing a generic approach, the key is bimodality: a rule is an idea, and as such it can be physically actualized many times. Put differently, a single carrier of a rule is a member of a population of carriers that have commonly actualized a rule (or a composite of them). By way of an example, there may be a particular technology that is adopted by a population of firms. The technology may represent a blueprint, whereby the physical carrier of the technical rule is a 'paper' medium, or may stand for a technical rule physically actualized in a (technical) object. Similarly, firms may represent a distinct population by way of producing products with the same characteristics; or, returning to the previous example, a decision algorithm of a particular kind may be employed by numerous agents operating in a market. Depending on the kind of rules and carriers employed or specified, it must be expected that models will come in quite different guises with regard to their analytical frames, propositions or hypotheses. Irrespective of this diversity, however, all models belong to the same family with members sharing a common bound: bimodality. There is always one rule, with the potential for multiple actualizations.

Seizing upon this insight, the construction of the architecture of a theory addressing structure and change may be attempted. A structure U is said to be a set of admissible binary relations on U: $R = (R_1, R_2, \ldots)$; a complex structure is a set of elements that are themselves structures: $U = (U_1, U_2 \ldots)$. For instance, the production structure of the economy $U^m a$ is composed of firms that are themselves structures: $U^m ij$, $U^m a = (U^m i_{,1}, U^m i_{,2}, \ldots)$. Following the bimodality assumption, any relation R is composed of an informational part, R_j^I (different rules r), and of a physical part, R_j^C (different actualizations, frequencies F). R_j^I is to be called 'informational relation', R_j^C 'physical connection'. The structure of any existence has therefore a 'deep' invisible informational level $U^I = R^I$ $= (R_1^I, R_2^I, \ldots)$, and an observable physical 'surface' level $U^C = R^C = (R_1^C, R_2^C, \ldots)$. Any structure of an existence is $U^\circ = (U^I, U^C)$, or, respectively, has a 'deep' level of rules and a 'surface' level of physical actualizations.

In this way, for example, a machine can be described as structure. Its elements or component parts form relations that represent functions R^f, and the machine structure may be stated as $U^f = (R_1^f, R_2^f, \ldots)$. In a similar way, a firm may be described as structure composed of relations between tasks or competences. At a higher level, the division of knowledge and labour of the economy may be identified as structure that is composed of industrial, technological elements and a number of associated sectors. Though quite different in their nature, what all structures have in common is that they are composed of relations between rules that are physically actualized.

The machine model may provide inspiration for visualizing the nature of the economy, but can it serve as valid paradigmatic guidance for theory making in economics? Having acknowledged the common features, what then marks the essential difference between the rule structure of a firm or economy, and that of a machine? It is worth noting here that cybernetics, negative feedback and related technical concepts can be and have been successfully applied to the study of the dynamics of economic systems. What is to stop us from following this theoretical course, therefore, with its straightforward mathematics and engineering methodology? The essential difference lies generally not in the rules, or in the relations R^I (as firms, for instance, employ massively technical rules), but in the way they are actualized in time and space. Actualization in the case of a machine means to design a rule and actualize it *uno actu* in a closed process of production. There is no further process of actualization except for its maintenance, given the constraints set by entropy and related physical laws. The structure of the machine does not change over time; it attains law-like (nomological) characteristics: $U = (U_1 = U_2 = \ldots)$.

The actualization process in a firm or economy is quite different, as the structure itself constitutes a major – endogenous – power in the process of actualization determining its meta-stable retention and its continual change over time. The universe of structures is therefore not defined by invariance but, rather, by an order relation with regard to time and space. An essential task in the case of the analysis of economic structures is to make theoretical statements about the logic of the process of actualization. The component parts of any economic structure must be captured theoretically as processes rather than objects or quantities.

Before turning to an account of the actualization dynamic, let us pause for a moment and consider how the major theoretical categories discussed fit into an overall disciplinary scheme. The theoretical key is the bimodal unit that distinguishes between a single rule and its many actualizations. 'Micro' and 'macro' need to be restated in recognition of this theoretical rationale, but at this point the question of immediate interest is how the category itself finds its proper place in the structure of the discipline. Conceptually, the unit features singularity (one rule) and plurality (many actualizations). Drawing on plain natural language, singularity may be associated with 'micro' and plurality with 'macro'. This leads to the identification of 'micro' by reference to the single member of a population, but the conclusion is less straightforward when attempting to nail down 'macro' terminologically. That is to say, there are many members in a population, but there are also many populations in an economy. Both expound plurality, but only one can be labelled 'macro'. By simple inference, the latter, being all-inclusive, is taken to denote 'macro'; the former, being neither 'micro' nor 'macro' but, rather, taking an intermediate position, may be called – not surprisingly – 'meso'. This naturally results in a micro–meso–macro architecture.

It is noteworthy that this conclusion has been reached purely on grounds of theoretical considerations. The earlier discussion suggested introducing it as a practical device for providing a classificatory shelf for a great number of empirical and theoretical studies conducted in evolutionary economics and related topics. Although this endeavour involves basically a terminological matter, the suggested reconstruction of the architecture of the discipline on grounds of theoretical and related conceptual considerations goes far beyond that. It is to be expected that mainstream economists will reject any endeavour involving a micro–meso–macro theme; the explanation of structure and change not being one of their theoretical concerns, meso and its corresponding construal are redundant. The picture is entirely different in the case of evolutionary economists and complexity scientists, as meso here figures prominently in the theoretical agenda. Naturally, the essential point is not the terminology but, rather, the doing of meso in the practice of theory formation. Messieurs Jourdain have spoken prose their whole lives without knowing it.

5.   INTEGRATED VIEW

To address the theoretical questions, the taxonomic building blocks must be given a systematic place in a coherent explanatory scheme. Figure 13.1 attempts to combine micro, meso and macro into a single integrated framework.

In the figure the deep structure is represented by the rules r^a, r^b and r^c. The theoretical analysis of the deep structure embraces a range of issues that relate to the fitting together of the rules. The branch of logic dealing with the nature of the relationships between the parts and the whole is mereology. The questions that arise here are, for instance, in what way technology A is complementary to technology B (object stratum), or what technical behaviour b (subject) is called for with regard to A (object) and is complementary to technical behaviour b called for by B (subject stratum). The central theoretical concern at this level relates to the coordination of the rules on the basis of mereological criteria. The question of rule logic is independent from that of the physical actualization of rules. The problem of adjusting or fitting a rule, say r_a, to rules r_b and r_c arises independently of whether or not the rules are adopted or adopted with a particular frequency. The issue is one of rule coordination as a problem of (mereo-) logic.

Economic agents are bound to operate in this deeply structured environment. They have to adapt to the requirements of particular rule relations prevalent in the sub-domain of the structure of which they are part. The selective criterion is structural adaptation, and the individual behaviour called for may be captured by the term 'efficacious'. Efficacious behaviour needs to be clearly distinguished from efficient behaviour. Rules may be adopted by many agents, leading to competition within a population calling for superior efficiency. For example, a firm producing with lower average costs

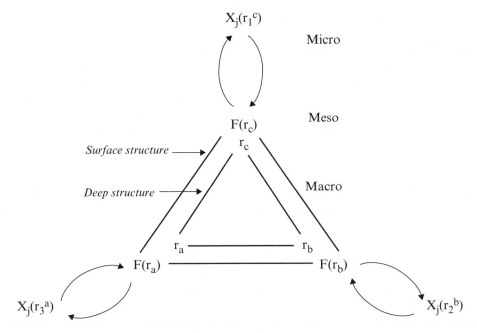

Figure 13.1   Integrated theoretical framework

than those of its competitors will enjoy, *ceteris paribus*, a survival advantage in a market. Unlike efficacy, efficiency is a criterion that works at the level of actualization. It presumes that the behaviour is adapted to the deep rule level, meeting the demands for structural efficacy. Much like competing for deckchairs on board the *Titanic*, a firm may win against its competitors on the basis of superior efficiency but still be destined for disaster if the rule adopted by the population of which it is a member does not fit the macro structure.

Table 13.2   Dual selection contingency

Behaviour	Environment	
Micro	Meso	Macro
Efficiency	Selection by competition	
Efficacy		Selection by adjustment

Selection is effective at the meso level as relative efficiency and at the macro level as the absolute standard of efficacy. There is a double contingency in the selective environment, calling for the combined behavioural efforts of efficacy and efficiency. Historically, it is probably the case that many more firms have disappeared by failing to meet the standards of efficacy than those of efficiency. Let us briefly summarize this finding (Table 13.2).

In Figure 13.1 the complete range of phenomena that relate to the actualization structure are denoted by $F(r_a)$, $F(r_b)$, $F(r_c)$, whereby the letter F signals the significance of (and mostly, but not only, stands for) the relative frequency of the population of adopters.

Note that the component parts of the macro actualization structure are generally not micro but meso units. Micro clearly connects to meso (as the subsequent section shows), and is explicated in the figure by the reciprocal arrows from micro to meso and back; but the power of the macro actualization is seen not as stemming from single micro behaviour but, rather, from the compound behaviour of an entire rule population. The actualization of a rule unfolds along a complex three-phase trajectory embracing, in sequential order, the

(phase 1)   origination;
(phase 2)   selective adoption; and
(phase 3)   retention

of a rule. The actualization at the macro level surfaces as a structure that is composed of many meso processes that unfold along the phase dynamic of a trajectory. The meso units are therefore not only structure components (as rule information bits) but also process components (as physical actualizations in time and space).

The following analysis fleshes out some of the salient features of the meso trajectory as a building block for a theory designed to explain the actualization of macro structure.

6.   MESO TRAJECTORY

Given its bimodality, a meso trajectory falls quite naturally into the categories of the production of an idea and its process of actualization. Both global phases embrace the individual agent but only the phase of actualization includes both the individual agent and a population of agents adopting the same rule. The phase of actualization may itself be viewed in its entirety and theoretically divided into relevant phases highlighting the complete actualization dynamic. A trajectory that comprises the two global phases and breaks these down into distinct phases describing particular characteristics of the meso dynamic may be captured in a single picture. Table 13.3 comprises three distinct process phases, each of which is divided into two sub-phases. (For simplicity, in the following 'sub-phase' is substituted by 'phase' whenever obvious in the text.)

This trajectory dynamic (see Table 13.3) has as its starting point the creative mind of the individual. Any invention has (in this trajectory) its ultimate causal recourse – its uncaused cause – in the cognitive faculties that reside in the human cortex. Methodologically, approaches that emphasize creative cognition as stated in phase I.1 can be associated with the strands of subjectivism of which Austrian economics stands out as a prominent case. Theoretically, the focus on this phase has given rise to interdisciplinary approaches, which, in turn, have led to an extension of the research domains in the already existing field of cognitive economics and the emergence of new ones, such as neuronal (neuro) economics.

Phase I.2 brings into theoretical focus the search and discovery process assuming the context of new ideas as given. Even more than the creative advance of phase I.1, the

Table 13.3   Meso trajectory

I Origination	
Phase 1	Creation of novel idea – i.e. rule invention
Phase 2	Search, discovery and recognition process; internal selection, 'inside the firm'
II Adoption	
Phase 1	First actualization – i.e. rule innovation; rule as 'seed' for macroscopic adoption
Phase 2	External (Darwinian) selection, 'out there' in market; path dependence
III Retention	
Phase 1	Routines selectively retained for ongoing operations; meta-stability of actualization process
Phase 2	Existing regime as breeding ground for novel rule(s); link to phase I

process of recognition in phase I.2 is embedded within the firm in places such as research and development and related departments. In phase I.2, there is an 'internal selection' within the boundaries of the firm as it decides whether or not to continue efforts on a new rule (which may involve decisions to embark on research activities connecting to phase I.1) as well as whether to actualize an available novel rule for the first time. The decision to pursue economically the course of exploiting a novelty is not necessarily conditional upon a firm-internal actualization or its own production (that is, by licensing out), though this course will often be followed in practice.

The macroscopic adoption as stated in phase II starts off with the rule crossing the firm boundaries and entering the domain of 'public' knowledge. Problems arising in phase II.1 touch upon the economically sensitive and often intangible issue of property rights, as related to patents and brands.

Phase II.1 features the Schumpeterian entrepreneur as an innovator, and phase II.2 as a swarm of imitators of a novel rule, such as new production technology. The two sub-phases of trajectory phase II deal with the dynamic of market structures as they evolve from an initial monopoly into an oligopoly, from monopolistic competition to perfect competition, or to the defence of a monopoly.

Phase II includes a quantitative account of the properties of the diffusion path. Its mathematical properties are usually captured by equations that display various forms of the logistic curve or Gompertz curve. A stylized account that combines the quantitative aspects of the numerical pattern of the relative adoption frequency and the qualitative aspects as they underlie the theoretical rationale of the three trajectory phases is provided in Table 13.4.

In an explanatory mould, trajectory phase II embraces the large set of selection models, replicator models and path-dependent models and a range of special models revolving around these master models. Phase II models have been developed into ever greater detail and subtlety, but what is definitely lacking at the current stage of research is the bridging or connecting of the models, both within their class and beyond. Several major lines of theoretical investigation contributing substantially to further scientific advance in this field are currently active; they relate commonly to what may be associated generally with the notion of coevolution.

Table 13.4   Bare numerical bones

Carrier	Origination	Adoption	Retention
C_1	X	X	Y
C_2	Y	Y	Y
...	X	X	Y
C_n	X	Y	Y
Frequency rule Y	$1/n$	Y/n	1
Frequency rule X	$(n-1)/n$	$(n-Y)/n$	0

Note: C_1, C_2, ... and C_n represent agents in the economy.

The field of coevolution encompasses the dynamic interdependence of subject rules and object rules – a most intricate research field, as it brings together not only different theories but also different approaches to theory. The theoretical integration requires coping with theories of cognitive and behavioural economics and related fields, together with theories that deal with the dynamic of technical and social organizational change. Methodologically, the two theoretical approaches build on two different strands, the first one calling for recognition of the subjective (subject-related) aspects and the latter with equal distinction for the objective (object-related) law-like features.

Trajectory phase III deals with theoretical issues that relate to the retention of rules defined as self-maintenance – through a process of recurrent adoption by new generations of agents. While the process of retention is relevant for all kind of rules, it poses particular challenges in the case of cognitive, behavioural and social organizational rules. Subject rules are retained by a single agent as habits and by a population of agents who share a rule as institutions. In the social realm, object rules constitute social (not technical) organizational rules that, when adopted by a population of carriers, form an organized institution. The rule approach proposed here allows us to distinguish clearly between structure and process. An organizational rule is a device for organizing or structuring tasks, an institution a process of recurrent collective behaviour.

Phase III.2 (the terminal phase of the whole trajectory) evokes the aspect of historical contingency. Any economic novelty has an antecedent context as its breeding ground. Phase III.2 is therefore not just a 'closed' historical result of the preceding trajectory dynamic but also the historical departure point for a new trajectory projected into the future. The 'first' cause of phase I.1 represents in this way not only the creative cognition of the individual but also, and necessarily, the particular historical context in which the individual unfolds.

7.   CONCLUSION

The theoretical meso unit is composed of a generic rule, its carrier population and its physical actualization originating from carriers applying the rule. Building on this bimodality, it allows us to describe both the structure and processes of evolutionary change and non-change in an economy. The single information bit is a component part (structure), but one that is actualized in time and space (process). The economy is seen to evolve, as at least one rule has been changing and its structure is broken up, de-coordinating and re-coordinating its meso parts. The rule trajectories (the meso elements of the economy) are embedded in a process structure (the macro) exposing firms (the micro) to a double contingency of the environment. Firms must respond to demands on account of complementarities between rule components with efficacy, and, facing competition within emergent populations, they must meet standards of superior efficiency. Contemporary economics has much to say about efficiency, but leaves efficacy 'under- researched'.

Addressing the complexity of the environment, mesoeconomics provides a most useful analytical platform for theoretical explorations of the management sciences. The latter's success builds on the foundations of economics, signalling the significance of this discipline for the management sciences. There has been much talk about the integration of the two disciplines – which should never have been separated in the first place in the way they are today – yet it seems that, in the final analysis, only a meso approach holds out the promise of a viable synthesis.

ACKNOWLEDGEMENTS

I gratefully acknowledge insightful comments and criticism by Stefania Bandini, Georg D. Blind, Peter Fleissner, Thomas Grebel, Bertram Hofer, David Lane, Sara Manzoni, Stan Metcalfe, Jason Potts, Andreas Pyka, Mike Richardson.

REFERENCES

Dopfer, K. (1994), 'How economic institutions emerge: institutional entrepreneurs and behavioural seeds', in Shionoya, Y. and Perlman, M. (eds), *Innovation in Technology, Industries, and Institutions: Studies in Schumpeterian Perspectives*, Ann Arbor: University of Michigan Press, pp. 299–329.
Dopfer, K. (2001), 'Evolutionary economics: framework for analysis', in Dopfer, K. (ed.), *Evolutionary Economics: Program and Scope*, Boston, Dortrecht and London: Kluwer, pp. 1–44.
Dopfer, K. (2005), 'Evolutionary economics: a theoretical framework', in Dopfer, K. (ed.), *The Evolutionary Foundations of Economics*, Cambridge: Cambridge University Press, pp. 3–57.
Dopfer, K. (2006), *The Origins of Meso Economics: Schumpeter's Legacy*, Paper on Economics and Evolution no. 0610, Jena: Max Planck Institute of Economics.
Dopfer, K., Foster, J. and Potts, J. (2004), 'Micro–meso–macro', *Journal of Evolutionary Economics*, **14** (3), 263–79.
Dopfer, K., and Potts, J. (2008), *The General Theory of Economic Evolution*, London and New York: Routledge.
Hanusch, H. and Pyka, A. (eds) (2007), *Elgar Companion to Neo-Schumpeterian Economics*, Cheltenham, UK and Northampton, MA, USA: Edward Elgar.

SELECTED BIBLIOGRAPHY

Acs, Z.J., Audretsch, D.B., Braunerhjelm, P. and Carlsson B. (2004), 'The missing link: the knowledge filter and entrepreneurship in endogenous growth', Discussion Paper no. 4783, London: Centre for Economic Policy Research.
Aghion, P., David, P.A. and Foray, D. (2009), 'Science, technology and innovation for economic growth: linking policy research and practice in "STIG Systems"', *Research Policy*, **38** (4), 681–93.

Alcouffe, A. and Kuhn, T. (2004), 'Schumpeterian endogenous growth theory and evolutionary economics', *Journal of Evolutionary Economics*, **14** (2), 223–36.

Amendola, M. and Gaffard, J.-L. (2003), 'Persistent unemployment and co-ordination issues: an evolutionary perspective', *Journal of Evolutionary Economics*, **13** (1), 1–27.

Andersen, E.S. (2008), 'Joseph Schumpeter and the essence of evolutionary economics: a centennial appraisal of his first book', Paper presented at International Schumpeter Society conference, Rio de Janeiro, 5 July.

Andersen, E.S. (2009), *Schumpeter's Evolutionary Economics: A Theoretical, Historical and Statistical Analysis of the Engine of Capitalism*, London: Anthem Press.

Antonelli, C. (1997), 'The economics of path dependence in industrial organization', *International Journal of Industrial Organization*, **15** (6), 643–75.

Antonelli, C., Krafft, J. and Quatraro, F. (2010), 'Recombinant knowledge and growth: the case of ICTs', *Structural Change and Economic Dynamics*, **21** (1), 50–69.

Arthur, W.B. (1994), *Increasing Returns and Path Dependence in the Economy*, Ann Arbor, MI: Michigan University Press.

Arthur, W.B., Durlauf, S.N. and Lane, D. (eds) (1997), *The Economy as an Evolving Complex System II*, Redwood City, CA: Addison-Wesley.

Audretsch, D.B. and Feldman, M. (1996), 'Spillovers and the geography of innovation and production', *American Economic Review*, **86** (3), 630–40.

Bandini, S., Manzoni, S. and Vizzari, G. (2004), 'Multi-agent approach to localization problems: the case of multilayered multi agent situated sytems', *Web Intelligence and Agent Systems: An International Journal*, **2** (3), 155–66.

Brette, O. and Mehier, C. (2008), 'Building on the micro–meso–macro evolutionary framework: the stakes for the analysis of clusters of innovation', in Elsner, W., and Hanappi, H. (eds), *Varieties of Capitalism and New Institutional Deals, Regulation, Welfare and the New Economy*, Cheltenham, UK and Northampton, MA, USA: Edward Elgar, Chapter 11.

Brette, O. and Moriset, B. (2009), 'Bringing down territorial inequalities in the digital economy: an evolutionary institutional approach', *Journal of Economic Issues*, **43** (2), 495–502.

Budzinski, O. (2003), 'Cognitive rules, institutions, and competition', *Constitutional Political Economy*, **14** (3), 215–35.

Cantner, U. and Hanusch, H. (2001), 'Heterogeneity and evolutionary dynamics: empirical conception, findings and unresolved issues', in Foster, J., and Metcalfe, J.S. (eds), *Frontiers of Evolutionary Economics: Competition, Self-Organization and Innovation Policy*, Cheltenham, UK and Northampton, MA, USA: Edward Elgar, pp. 228–77.

Cantner U., Krüger, J. and von Rhein, K. (2009), 'Knowledge and creative destruction over the industry life cycle: the case of the German automobile industry', *Economica*, **76**, 132–48.

Castellaci, F. (2009), 'The interactions between national systems and sectoral patterns of innovation', *Journal of Evolutionary Economics*, **19** (3), 321–47.

Cimoli, M. and Porcile, G. (2009), 'Sources of learning paths and technological capabilities: an introductory roadmap of development processes', *Economics of Innovation and New Technology*, **18** (7), 675–94.

Cordes, C. (2005), 'Long-term tendencies in technological creativity: a preference-based approach', *Journal of Evolutionary Economics*, **15** (2), 149–68.

David, P.A. (2000), 'Path dependence and varieties of learning in the evolution of technological practice', in Ziman, J. (ed.), *Technological Innovation as an Evolutionary Process*, Cambridge: Cambridge University Press, Chapter 10.

David, P.A., Foray, D. and Dalle, J.M. (1995), 'Marshallian externalities and the emergence and spatial stability of technological enclaves', *Economics of Innovation and New Technology*, **6** (2–3), 147–82.

Dosi, G., Marengo, L. and Fagiolo, G. (2005), 'Learning in evolutionary environments', in Dopfer, K. (ed.), *The Evolutionary Foundations of Economics*, Cambridge: Cambridge University Press, pp. 255–338.

Dosi, G. and Nelson, R.R. (2009), 'Technical change and industrial dynamics as evolutionary process', Working Paper no. 2009/07, Pisa: Laboratory of Economics and Management, Sant'Anna School of Advanced Studies.

Elsner, W. (2008), 'Why meso? On "aggregation" and "emergence" and why and how the meso level is essential in social economics', *Forum for Social Economics*, **36** (1), 1–16.

Encinar, M.-I. and Muñoz, F.-F. (2006), 'On novelty and economics: Schumpeter's paradox', *Journal of Evolutionary Economics*, **16** (3), 255–77.

Foster, J. (2000), 'Competitive selection, self-organisation and Joseph A. Schumpeter', *Journal of Evolutionary Economics*, **10** (3), 311–28.

Foster, J. (2007), 'A micro–meso–macro perspective on the methodology of evolutionary economics: integrating history, simulation and econometrics', Discussion Paper no. 343, Brisbane: School of Economics, University of Queensland.

Fransman, M. (2007), *The New ICT Ecosystem and the Way Forward for Europe*, Edinburgh: Kokoro.

Frenken, K., van Oort, F.G. and Verburg, T. (2007), 'Related variety, unrelated variety and regional economic growth', *Regional Studies*, **41** (5), 685–97.

Garrouste, P. and Ioannidis, S. (eds) (2001), *Evolution and Path Dependence in Economic Ideas: Past and Present*, Cheltenham, UK and Northampton, MA, USA: Edward Elgar.

Grebel, T. (2009), 'Technological change: a microeconomic approach to the creation of knowledge', *Structural Change and Economic Dynamics*, **20** (4) 301–12.

Hanusch, H. and Pyka, A. (2007), 'Principles of neo-Schumpeterian economics', *Cambridge Journal of Economics*, **31** (2), 275–89.

Hanusch, H. and Pyka, A. (eds) (2007), *The Elgar Companion to Neo-Schumpeterian Economics*, Cheltenham, UK and Northampton, MA, USA: Edward Elgar.

Harabi, N. (1995), 'Appropriability of technical innovations: an empirical analysis', *Research Policy*, **24** (6), 981–92.

Helmstädter, E. (ed.) (2003), *The Economics of Knowledge Sharing: A New Institutional Approach*, Cheltenham, UK and Northampton, MA, USA: Edward Elgar.

Hodgson, G.M. and Knudsen, T. (2006), 'The nature and units of social selection', *Journal of Evolutionary Economics*, **16** (5) 477–89.

Hölzl, W. (2007), 'The evolutionary theory of the firm: routines, complexity and change', in Dietrich, M. (ed.), *The Economics of the Firm: Analysis, Evolution, History*, London and New York: Routledge, pp. 111–26.

Klepper, S. (1997), 'Industry life cycles', *Industrial and Corporate Change*, **6** (1), 145–81.

Knudsen, T. (2002), 'Economic selection theory', *Journal of Evolutionary Economics*, **12** (3), 443–70.

Lane, D. and Maxfield, R. (2004), 'Ontological uncertainty and innovation', *Journal of Evolutionary Economics*, **15** (1), 3–50.

Latham, W.R. and Le Bas, C. (eds) (2006), *The Economics of Persistent Innovation: An Evolutionary View*, Berlin: Springer.

Lazaric, N. and Raybaut, A. (2005), 'Knowledge, hierarchy and the selection of routines: an interpretative model with group interactions', *Journal of Evolutionary Economics*, **15** (4), 393–422.

Llerena, P. and Lorentz, A. (2004), 'Cumulative causation and evolutionary micro-founded technical change: a growth model with integrated economies', Working Papers no. 2004-08, Strasbourg: Bureau d'Economie Théorique et Appliquée, Université de Strasbourg.

Malerba, F. (2006), 'Innovation and the evolution of industries', *Journal of Evolutionary Economics*, **16** (1), 3–23.

Malerba, F., Nelson R.R., Orsinego, L. and Winter, S.G. (1999), 'History-friendly models of industrial evolution: the computer industry', *Journal of Industrial and Corporate Change*, **1** (1), 3–41.

Martin, R. and Sunley, P. (2007), 'Complexity thinking and evolutionary economic geography', *Journal of Economic Geography*, **7** (5), 573–601.

Metcalfe, J.S. (1998), *Evolutionary Economics and Creative Destruction*, London: Routledge.

Metcalfe, J.S. (2005), 'Evolutionary concepts in relation to evolutionary economics', in Dopfer, K. (ed.), *The Evolutionary Foundations of Economics*, Cambridge: Cambridge University Press, pp. 391–430.

Metcalfe, J.S., Foster, J. and Ramlogan, R. (2006), 'Adaptive economic growth', *Cambridge Journal of Economics*, **30** (1), 7–32.

Nelson, R.R. (2005), *Technology, Institutions and Economic Growth*, Cambridge, MA: Harvard University Press.

Nelson, R.R. and Winter, S.G. (1982), *An Evolutionary Theory of Economic Change*, Cambridge, MA: Belknap Press.

Peneder, M. (2003), 'Industrial structure and aggregate growth', *Structural Change and Economic Dynamics*, **14** (4), 427–48.

Potts, J. (2000), *The New Evolutionary Microeconomics: Choice, Complexity and Adaptive Behaviour*, Cheltenham, UK and Northampton, MA, USA: Edward Elgar.

Potts, J. and Morrison, K. (2006), 'Meso comes to markets: comment on "Markets come to bits"', *Journal of Economic Behavior and Organization*, **63** (2), 307–12.

Pyka, A. (2000), 'Informal networking and industrial life cycles', *Technovation*, **20** (1), 25–35.

Rosser, J.B. (ed.) (2004), *Complexity in Economics: Methodology, Interacting Agents and Microeconomic Models*, Cheltenham, UK and Northampton, MA, USA: Edward Elgar.

Saviotti, P.P. (2007), 'On the dynamics of generation and utilisation of knowledge: the local character of knowledge', *Structural Change and Economic Dynamics*, **18** (4), 387–408.

Saviotti, P.P. and Pyka, A. (2004), 'Economic development by the creation of new sectors', *Journal of Evolutionary Economics*, **14** (1), 1–36.

Schnellenbach, J. (2002), 'New political economy, scientism and knowledge: a critique from a Hayekian perspective', *American Journal of Economics and Sociology*, **61**, 193–216.

Silva, S.T. and Teixeira, A.A.C. (2006), 'An evolutionary model of firm's institutional behavior focusing on labor decisions', Working Paper no. 227, Porto: Faculdade de Economia do Porto, Universidade do Porto.

Silva, S.T. and Teixeira, A.A.C. (2009), 'On the divergence of evolutionary research paths in the past 50 years: a comprehensive bibliometric account', *Journal of Evolutionary Economics*, **19** (5), 605–42.

Silverberg, G. and Verspagen, B. (2005), 'A percolation model of innovation in complex technology spaces', *Journal of Economic Dynamics and Control*, **29** (1–2), 225–44.

Simona I. and McCann, P. (2006), '*The structure and evolution of industrial clusters: transactions, technology and knowledge spillovers*', Electronic Working Paper no. 138, Brighton and Hove: Science and Technology Policy Research, University of Sussex.

Uyarra, E. (2010), 'What is evolutionary about "regional systems of innovation"? Implications for regional policy', *Journal of Evolutionary Economics*, **20** (1), 115–37.

Witt, U. (2008), 'What is specific about evolutionary economics?', *Journal of Evolutionary Ecoonomics*, **18** (5), 547–75.

14 Notes on a complexity theory of economic development

Koen Frenken and Ron Boschma

1. INTRODUCTION

For many, the advent of complexity theory at the end of the last century promised an intellectual liberation from the neoclassical straitjacket that dominated the economics discipline for so long. Indeed, quite a few attempts to apply the concept of complexity theory to economic phenomena followed, for example, as collected in the three edited volumes entitled *The Economy as an Evolving Complex System* (Anderson et al., 1988). Taking stock of the progress in the field during the past two decades, one may argue that complexity theory has been successful in providing new explanatory models for a number of isolated phenomena, yet has failed to provide a new research program in economics. This may come as no surprise since complexity theory is best understood as a set of modeling techniques with 'family resemblance', rather than a consistent theory in the proper sense of the word. Thus, to be useful in theorizing, complexity theory needs to be supplemented with an 'ontology' relevant to the question at hand.

The question we raise here is the question of economic development. We understand the process of economic development as a joint process of economic growth and qualitative change (Saviotti, 1996). Furthermore, we also understand the process of economic development as a spatial process, where development is fundamentally uneven across cities, regions and countries (Boschma and Frenken, 2006). Finally, we understand the process of economic development, first and foremost, as a process driven by efforts of firms and cities as the prime loci of the division of labor (Frenken and Boschma, 2007).

We proceed by proposing a minimalist 'complexity theory' of firm growth and urban growth inspired by Gibrat's principle of proportional growth. This framework can be regarded as a 'null-model', in the sense that empirical deviations from the null-model require an explanation that goes beyond the logic of randomness. Following a previous contribution (Frenken and Boschma, 2007), we will take product divisions as the unit of analysis. A growth event concerns the setting up of a new product division within an existing firm or a new firm, and within an existing city or a new city. First, it considers firm growth dynamics and urban growth dynamics as stemming from one single process. Second, it introduces a parental lineage structure between product divisions, which allows one to introduce explicit 'Darwinian' hypotheses regarding the inheritance of relevant knowledge and experience. These hypotheses are further elaborated in the remainder of the chapter.

2.   NULL-MODEL

Conceive of firms and of cities as aggregates of product divisions. Each product division belongs to a particular firm and is located in a particular city. The size of a firm at time t is simply expressed in the number of product divisions it contains at time t. Similarly, the size of a city at time t is simply expressed in the number of product divisions that are located in that city at time t. These definitions imply that a single firm may locate its divisions all in one city or over multiple cities, and, vice versa, a city may host divisions of a single firm or of multiple firms. In short, firms and cities are orthogonal aggregates of product divisions. One can thus derive from a single set of product divisions the firm size distribution by aggregating product divisions into firms and the city size distribution by aggregating product divisions into cities.

In our framework (Frenken and Boschma, 2007), firm growth and urban growth occur simultaneously through the establishment of new product divisions. In terms of Simon's (1955) seminal model, the lumps that drive growth can be considered as product innovations that are exploited by entrepreneurs by establishing a new product division. By reformulating Simon's stochastic model as a growth process fuelled by new product divisions, and by assigning each new product division simultaneously to a firm and a city, the firm size distribution and the city size distribution can be derived from one single growth process.

We further assume that new product divisions are founded by former employees, who become entrepreneurs. One may think of such an employee as someone who comes up with a new product idea, which leads to the founding of a new product division. One can then introduce two *organizational parameters (p and p^*)* and two *locational parameters (q and q^*)*. With probability p the employee will commercialize the innovation in-house leading to a new product division within the parent firm. With probability p^* the employee will commercialize the product innovation in another firm by changing jobs. The remaining probability $(1 - p - p^*)$ is the probability that the employee creates a spin-off firm. And, with probability q the innovation will be commercialized in the city of origin. With probability q^* the innovation will be commercialized in another city where the probability that a particular city attracts the product innovation is proportional to its size. And with the remaining probability $1 - q - q^*$ the innovation will be commercialized in a new city.

This reformulation of Simon's model incorporates nine possible events resulting from a product innovation (see Box 14.1). As such, the framework provides a rich repertoire for formal modeling approaches with only four parameters (p, p^*, q and q^*). Firms and cities being the aggregates of product divisions, the model will produce the Zipf law for both the firm size distribution and the city size distributions in a single model as long as $(1 - p - p^*)$ and $(1 - q - q^*)$ are close to zero and, in case of inter-firm or inter-city mobility, the probability that an employee chooses a firm or city is proportional to its size (otherwise growth ceases to be proportional to size).

3.   GENEALOGY

Mobility patterns of former employees who found their own product division create genealogical trees between product divisions. Such a link is created once an employee

---

BOX 14.1   POSSIBLE EVENTS RESULTING FROM A PRODUCT INNOVATION

$(p)(q)$	Internal firm growth in city of origin
$(p)(q^*)$	Internal firm growth in another city
$(p)(1 - q - q^*)$	Internal firm growth in a new city
$(p^*)(q)$	Firm growth though labor mobility in city of origin
$(p^*)(q^*)$	Firm growth though labor mobility in another city
$(p^*)(1 - q - q^*)$	Firm growth though labor mobility in a new city
$(1 - p - p^*)(q)$	Spin-off in city of origin
$(1 - p - p^*)(q^*)$	Spin-off in another city
$(1 - p - p^*)(1 - q - q^*)$	Spin-off in a new city

Source: Frenken and Boschma (2007).

---

who previously worked for one product division, founds its own product division. Having the arc point from the pre-existing division (parent) to the newly created division (child), the resulting genealogical tree is an a-cyclical, directed graph in which all the nodes have an in-degree equal to one and an out-degree of zero or higher.[1]

In studies of industrial dynamics, genealogy has been used to explain the differential performance of firms (Klepper, 2002). The main idea behind such a genealogical analysis is to explain the performance of a firm from the pre-entry experience of the founder. If the founder has been previously working for a firm active in the same or technologically related economic activity as the newly founded firm, the survival probability of the newly founded firm is higher than if the founder has been previously working for a firm active in an activity that is different from the activity of the newly founded firm. In short, the more related the activity of parent firm and its 'spin-off', the higher the survival probability of the spin-off firm, *ceteris paribus*.

This principle of inheritance can also be introduced in our model where product divisions, rather than firms, are the unit of analysis. We assumed that each new product division comes into existence as a result of a product innovation. This means that the activity of the newly founded division is by definition different from the activity of the parent division. However, the activities of the new division can be more or less technologically related to the activities of the parent division where the founder of the new product division worked before.

Genealogy can be elaborated in our framework in two different ways, which nevertheless both result in the same evolutionary pattern of economic development. One way to incorporate technological relatedness is to assume that entrepreneurs can invent any product with equal probability, which means that the degree of relatedness of the activity of the entrepreneur and the activity of the parent division is a random variable. In that case, those who happen to have invented a product that is technologically related to the product of the parent division will have the highest probability of survival, while those who happened to have invented a product that is technologically unrelated to the product of the parent division, will quickly exit the market. Hence, there will be a correlation between the geodesic distance in the genealogy graph connecting product divisions and the degree of technological relatedness between their products.

Alternatively, one can assume that entrepreneurs have a tendency to develop new products that are technologically related to products of the parent division in order to be able to re-use the knowledge and experience that they have gained as employees, in their newly founded division. This is close to the concept of local or 'myopic' search in evolutionary economics (Nelson and Winter, 1982). Again, there will be a correlation between the geodesic distance in the genealogy graph connecting product divisions and the degree of technological relatedness between their products. Obviously, the two argumentations are not mutually exclusive. Yet, only the latter type of model specification can be fitted in the Simon model, as the former type of specification assumes a differential survival mechanism, which is not part of the logic of the Simon model.

Then, the question that follows is whether the degree of technological relatedness between the product innovation of the entrepreneur and the product of the parent division affects the organizational and locational parameters introduced before.

Concerning the organizational parameters, one can assume that a firm is more willing to accept the creation of a new division by one of its employees, the more the new activities involved are technologically related. A higher technological relatedness will generally result in higher economies of scope, which explains why firms tend to diversify in related products (Teece et al, 1994).[2] In the case the employee's new product is only weakly technologically related to a firm's existing products, the employee may approach other firms that are already active in technologically related activities, because such firms can benefit from economies of scope when they found a new division that produces the new product. In that case, we have again an example of a firm that diversifies in a related product. In the rare instance that an entrepreneur develops a product that is unrelated to the activities of any other firm, the entrepreneur is forced to 'go alone' and found a spin-off firm. Since such a newly founded firm cannot profit from pre-entry experience of the founder, nor from economies of scope associated with the production of multiple products, the chances of observing such firms are rather small. This can explain that – even if technologically unrelated activities are more likely to be organized in a spin-off firm than in an existing firm – most of the spin-off firms that one observes empirically would still be active in technologically related activities. This may also be due to the myopic search behavior of employees, which prevents them from identifying firms in technologically related activities, and which makes them establish their own (spin-off) firms.

Concerning the locational parameters, one can follow the analogous reasoning as for the organizational parameters. An entrepreneur will be prone to stay in the city where (s)he was previously employed, the more the new activity is technologically related to other activities present in the city. By doing so, the entrepreneur will profit from agglomeration advantages associated with the co-location of technologically related products (Frenken et al, 2007, Neffke et al., 2009).[3] In the case the employee's new product is only weakly technologically related to a city's activities, the employee may migrate to another city where technologically related activities are present. Again, the entrepreneur will profit from agglomeration advantages associated with the co-location of technologically related products. In the rare instance that an entrepreneur develops a product that is unrelated to any economic activity, the entrepreneur may found a new city.

The pattern of economic development that follows from our discussion is one where

(i) entrepreneurs tend to move into technologically related activities and, (ii) such technologically related activities tend to be organized as a new product division within the parent firm so as to profit from economies of scope, and within the parent city so as to profit from economies of agglomeration. This implies that the genealogical evolution of products is highly localized within firms and within cities giving rise to related diversification trajectories at firm and city levels (Boschma and Frenken, 2011).

4. ECONOMIC DEVELOPMENT AS A WALK THROUGH PRODUCT SPACE

As entrepreneurs tend to move to technologically related products when setting up a new product division, be it in the same or a different firm and in the same or a different city, the structure of the 'product space' affects the entrepreneurial opportunities for each potential entrepreneur. Following Hidalgo et al. (2007), one can think of the product space as a weighted graph specifying the degree of technological relatedness – or shorter 'technological proximity' – between each two products.

It is most likely the case that such a graph is complex in the sense that it contains dense areas with strong links among products (say, electronics) and sparsely connected areas with weak links (say, natural resources). Attempts to map technological relatedness from the co-specializations in exports (Hidalgo et al., 2007) or the co-occurrences of products in plants (Neffke and Svensson-Henning, 2008) indeed show such patterns.

Depending on a position of a product in product space, entrepreneurial opportunities differ. In case a product is strongly linked to many other products, there are many entrepreneurial opportunities to be exploited. Reversely, in case a product is weakly linked to few products, there are only few entrepreneurial opportunities to be exploited. Indeed, at the country level, Hidalgo et al. (2007) showed that countries tend to move to new export industries that are close to their previous export specializations as mapped in product space. This means that countries that happen to be located in the high-density part of the industry graph grow faster than countries whose industries are located in the low-density parts of the industry graph, as the former countries have many more opportunities to upgrade their export products than the latter countries.

Mutatis mutandis, one expects the same patterns at the level of firms and cities for the reasons just explained. Neffke et al. (2009) have indeed found evidence for that at the regional level in Sweden. They looked at the evolution of the industrial profile of 70 Swedish regions for a period of more than 30 years. Based on more than 2000 events of new sectors entering a region in the period 1969–2002, they found that new sectors have a higher probability of entering a region when these are technologically related to existing sectors in the region. In addition to that, they found that sectors had a higher probability of exiting the region when these are not technologically related to existing sectors in the region. In other words, the Schumpeterian process of creative destruction seems to be strongly conditioned by the degree of technological relatedness between sectors at the regional level.

This can be further illustrated by the evolution of the industry profile of the Linköping region between 1970 and 2000 (for more details, see Neffke et al., 2009). In Figure 14.1, the average industry space of the whole of Sweden for the period 1969–2002 is depicted,

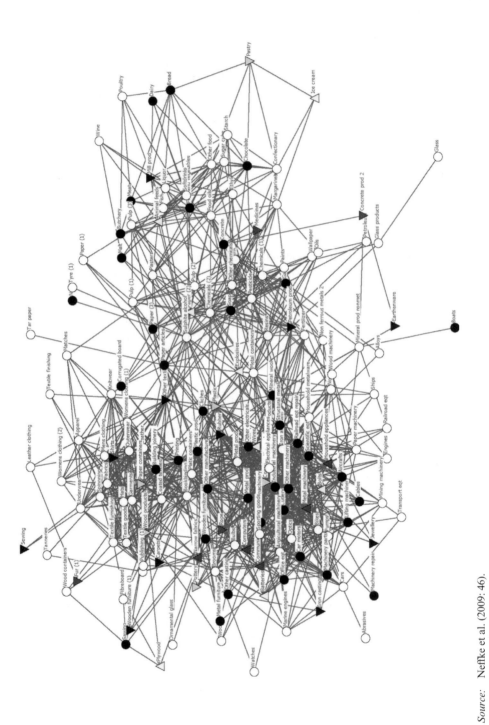

Source: Neffke et al. (2009: 46).

Figure 14.1   Average industry space in Sweden, 1969–2002, with the evolution of the production structure of Linköping

in which each node stands for a manufacturing sector, and each link between two nodes means that these industries are technologically related. The white circles represent industries that were absent in the Linköping region in 1970 and 2000, while the dark circles represent industries that were present both in 1970 and 2000. If we look at the industries that entered this region during this period as indicated by triangles pointing upwards, we can clearly see that most of these were quite centrally located in the more dense parts of the industry space of that region. This is quite opposite to the sectors that exited the region during that period, indicated by triangles pointing downwards, which were in general not supported by a strong technological cluster of related industries in the region. Interestingly, in the upper left corner, we can observe that many industries exited the region from that part of industry space which is associated with textile and wood industries. This cluster was hit hard by the economic crisis of the 1970s, after which other industries in the cluster then became very peripheral to the region's remaining portfolio. This set in motion a domino effect. By the year 2000, the region had lost almost all of its cluster of textiles and wood industries.

To view economic development as solely determined by the position of a country in product space would be overly deterministic. Indeed, it may be possible for firms or cities to make 'long jumps' and to move from low-density parts of the product space to high-density parts of the product space. Following our framework, this can happen when entrepreneurs engage in inventing products that are technologically unrelated to previous activities of the parent firm and parent city, yet decide to organize the product division within the boundaries of the firm and the city, respectively. Such a diversification into unrelated products may require the import of knowledge from different firms and different cities. A second way to make long jumps in product space is when a firm or a city attracts entrepreneurs engaged in technologically unrelated activities. This diversification strategy may require specific policies to attract entrepreneurs to locate their product in firms and cities without related experience. A third way for a firm or a city to cover long distances in product space is to create new products that shorten the distance between the products located in the sparsely connected area and the densely connected area. Such new 'intermediate' products re-combine technology that is already mastered with technology located in the densely connected area. In doing so, the distance towards the high-density areas with many entrepreneurial opportunities has been shortened – by a short-cut as it were – and subsequent efforts to reach this high-density area are made easier. Such Schumpeterian 'Neue Kombinationen' can thus be viewed as products that enable previously unrelated products to become related (cf. Fleming and Sorenson 2001).

5.   CONCLUDING REMARKS

Starting from a 'null-model' based on the Simon model of random growth, we outlined how economic development can be described as an ongoing process of product innovation. With the introduction of a new product, a new product division is created. By assigning this new product division to a firm, existing or new, and a city, existing or new, one can describe the process of economic development in terms of the evolution of firm size and city size distributions. This framework thus considers firm growth dynamics and urban growth dynamics as stemming from one single elementary process, which allows the integration of insights from industrial dynamics and economic geography in one single theory.

Assuming that new product divisions are founded by former employees of already existing product divisions, a parental lineage structure between product divisions is apparent. We argued that it is likely that this parental lineage structure reflects technological relatedness as new products typically emerge out of technologically related products. The degree of relatedness is also expected to affect the organizational and locational dynamics of entrepreneurial events and, hence, the firm size and city size distributions: the more related a new product is to the product from which it emerges, the more likely the new product will be produced in the same firm and the same location as the antecedent product.

The challenge in future research is twofold. First, we need to develop models that capture the evolutionary nature of economic development where new products evolve out of existing products. One possibility is to start from the Simon model and extend this model with explicit representation of technological relatedness along the lines suggested here. Another avenue is to extend the models of economic development developed by Saviotti and Pyka (2004a, 2004b, 2008a, 2008b) in this direction. A second challenge is to construct empirical measures of technological relatedness and to follow the evolution of national and regional economies in terms of entry and exit of new products. This requires high-quality long-term data to construct the evolution of product portfolios of plants. The observed patterns can then inform modifications and the extensions of formal models, which, for now, are admittedly too stylized to capture the rich dynamics in urban and regional performance.

NOTES

1. If one were to take into account all previous employers of the founder, the in-degree would be equal to the number of previous divisions the founder has worked for in the past (cf. Wenting, 2008). We assume here that all employees only work as an employee for a single division, or, equivalently, that only the lineage to the last employer matters.
2. Unless the new product would compete too strongly with related products in the firm, otherwise known as cannibalization.
3. Unless the new product would compete too strongly with related products in the city.

REFERENCES

Anderson, P.W., Arrow, K.J. and Pines, D. (eds) (1988), *The Economy as an Evolving Complex System*, Redwood City, CA: Addison-Wesley.
Boschma, R.A. and Frenken, K. (2006), 'Why is economic geography not an evolutionary science? Towards an evolutionary economic geography', *Journal of Economic Geography*, **6** (3), 273–302.
Boschma, R.A. and Frenken, K. (2011), 'Technological relatedness and regional branching', in Bathelt, H., Feldman, M.P. and Kogler, D.F. (eds), *Beyond Territory: Dynamic Geographies of Knowledge Creation and Innovation*, Routledge, Taylor and Francis, forthcoming.
Fleming, L. and Sorenson, O. (2001), 'Technology as a complex adaptive system: evidence from patent data', *Research Policy*, **30**, 1019–39
Frenken, K. and Boschma, R.A. (2007), 'A theoretical framework for evolutionary economic geography: industrial dynamics and urban growth as a branching process', *Journal of Economic Geography*, **7** (5), 635–49.

Frenken, K., Van Oort, F.G. and Verburg, T. (2007), 'Related variety, unrelated variety and regional economic growth', *Regional Studies*, **41** (5), 685–97.

Hidalgo, C.A., Klinger, B., Barabasi, A.-L. and Hausmann, R. (2007), 'The product space conditions the development of nations', *Science*, **317**, 482–87.

Klepper, S. (2002), 'The capabilities of new firms and the evolution of the US automobile industry', *Industrial and Corporate Change*, **11** (4), 645–66.

Neffke, F., Henning, M. and Boschma, R. (2009), 'How do regions diversify over time? Industry relatedness and the development of new growth paths in regions', Papers in Evolutionary Economic Geography, no. 9.16, Utrecht University, Utrecht.

Neffke, F. and Svensson-Henning, M. (2008), 'Revealed relatedness. Mapping industry space', Papers in Evolutionary Economic Geography, no. 8.19, Utrecht University, Utrecht.

Nelson, R.R. and Winter, S.G. (1982), *An Evolutionary Theory of Economic Change*, Cambridge MA: The Belknap Press.

Saviotti, P.P. (1996), *Technological Evolution, Variety and the Economy*, Cheltenham, UK and Brookfield, VT, USA: Edward Elgar.

Saviotti, P.P. and Pyka, A. (2004a), 'Economic development, variety and employment', *Revue Economique*, **55** (6), 1023–49.

Saviotti, P.P. and Pyka, A. (2004b), 'Economic development by the creation of new sectors', *Journal of Evolutionary Economics*, **14** (1), 1–35.

Saviotti, P.P. and Pyka, A. (2008a), 'Product variety, competition and economic growth', *Journal of Evolutionary Economics*, **18** (3), 323–47.

Saviotti, P.P. and Pyka, A. (2008b), 'Micro and macro dynamics: industry life cycles, inter-sector coordination and aggregate growth', *Journal of Evolutionary Economics*, **18** (2), 167–82.

Simon, H.A. (1955), 'On a class of skew distribution functions', *Biometrika*, **42** (3–4), 425–40.

Teece, D.J., Rumelt, R., Dosi, G. and Winter, S.J. (1994), 'Understanding corporate coherence: theory and evidence', *Journal of Economic Behavior and Organization*, **23**, 1–30.

Wenting, R. (2008), 'Spinoff dynamics and the spatial formation of the fashion design industry, 1858–2005', *Journal of Economic Geography*, **8** (5), 593–614.

15 Innovation networks: formation, performance and dynamics
Uwe Cantner and Holger Graf

1. INTRODUCTION

This chapter refers to work that is concerned with the formation of innovation networks on the one hand and their dynamics and evolution on the other hand. Although the literature on network dynamics is quite rich, considerations of the evolution of innovation networks are still in their beginning. This has to do with the specific concern of innovation networks with information and knowledge exchange among the network participants. The purpose of an innovation network is to exchange knowledge and expertise among cooperating partners. For an understanding of how this works one has to discuss the very nature of knowledge, the incentives of actors to engage in deliberate knowledge exchange, and the dynamic properties of those systems (knowledge dynamics, actor dynamics, and so on) over time.

Networks of innovation are strongly related to the notion of collective invention which has been introduced by Allen (1983). In the historical study of the nineteenth century iron and steel industry he shows that innovative success was the result of the cooperative activities of several different actors. Anecdotal evidence found in Allen's work, in the various studies on Silicon Valley (for example, Saxenian, 1994) or in other success stories of regional innovation (Cooke and Morgan, 1994; Braczyk et al., 1998; Keeble et al., 1999) was enriched by studies on the regional dimension of knowledge flows (Jaffe et al., 1993). Insights into the process of innovation at the firm-level (Kline and Rosenberg, 1986) or the national level (Lundvall, 1992; Nelson, 1993) strengthened the view that the functioning of innovation systems is the basis for innovation-based economic success.

Inspired by the seminal volumes by Lundvall (1992), Nelson (1993), and Braczyk et al. (1998), a large number of investigations build on the systems view in relating innovative activities to measures of economic or innovative success. Since the systemic view of innovation is inherently dynamic and deeply grounded in evolutionary theorizing, empirical studies that take the systems view seriously, should have two ingredients: heterogeneous, interacting actors and the dynamics of these interactions. Unfortunately, many of the empirical studies fail to account for both of these ingredients, which is mostly due to the unavailability of appropriate data. In studies based on aggregate data it is easier to observe the dynamics of the system, as many variables are available as time series. Many studies that account for the interactive structure and the heterogeneity of innovative actors are based on interviews or surveys which are only available at one point in time. This is not to say that system dynamics are not considered important by these authors, but most of the arguments are based on theoretical reasoning rather than on empirical observations.

As a response to this unsatisfying situation, a number of researchers in economics and economic geography started to employ social network analysis to study the interactive structures in the innovation process. The network approach offers a methodology that accounts for heterogeneity and system dynamics. However, its empirical application is subject to rather strong data requirements. Data needs to be more or less complete in terms of actors and relations and in order to conduct dynamic studies it has to be available over long time periods. Information derived from patents or publications has these properties and is therefore increasingly applied in network studies of innovation. For example, networks of co-authorship are used to analyse the development of scientific communities (Barabasi et al., 2002; Moody, 2004), networks of co-invention can help us understand the evolution of local clusters (Fleming et al., 2007; Fleming and Frenken, 2007), investigate university–industry relations (Balconi et al., 2004), or identify channels for knowledge spillovers (Breschi and Lissoni, 2009), and citation networks provide information about the flow of knowledge (Sorenson et al., 2006). The structure and characteristics of clusters and regional networks is explored in a number of recent studies (Cantner and Graf, 2006; ter Wal, 2008; Graf and Henning, 2009; Graf, 2011; Cantner et al., 2010). Apparently, when applied to a local or regional network, there is a trade-off as the information is gained at the cost of other valuable aspects of the regional innovation system. In the case of patent data, the observed relations will only include actors that produce patentable innovations, services are clearly underrepresented and important actors for regional development, such as venture capitalists or local government, are not included.

A different approach in terms of data collection is taken in a variety of studies on clusters and industrial districts (Giuliani and Bell, 2005; Giuliani, 2007; Boschma and ter Wal, 2007). Here, smaller groups of relevant actors are asked about different types of relations to co-located actors, but due to the high efforts related to this research approach, these studies are – with few exceptions (Giuliani and Bell, 2008) – static analyses. Parallel to these developments in economics and economic geography, a lively literature in management and business studies developed that is interested in the organization within firms as in Kogut and Zander (1992) but also in the optimal configuration of alliance networks and the benefits arising from holding specific positions within the network in different environments (Shan et al., 1994).

In the light of this rich conceptual, theoretical, and empirical literature, we attempt to provide a review of what we know about the formation, performance, and dynamics related to networks in the context of innovation. To perform this task, we structure our chapter as follows. In Section 2 we present a small bibliographic exercise on research articles published on the topic of innovation networks to show the relevance and dynamic developments within this field. In Section 3 basic concepts related to innovation and knowledge, to actors and innovative activities, as well as to the motives and conditions for knowledge exchange are presented. Based on these concepts, Section 4 addresses the relationship between an actor's network position and performance. Section 5 investigates the formation of innovation networks and their stability and describes the basic mechanisms of network dynamics, namely preferential attachment, homophily and triad closure. Section 6 concludes.

2.   NETWORKS OF INNOVATION NETWORK RESEARCH

The organization of the innovation process in the form of networks and the consequences of different organizational structures for innovative success is a research field with high relevance for managers and policy makers, and high academic interest. Before we start to review innovation network studies we want to show the increasing interest in this topic, taking a bird's-eye view of the research field. To identify the most important contributions to this field, we perform a bibliographic exercise. From the ISI Web of Science® Social Science Citation Index (SSCI), we downloaded all 2678 publications from 1990 onwards that include the search string 'Network AND Innovat* OR Network AND Invent*' in any field. In the SSCI database one or more subject categories are assigned to every journal. We used this information to refine our data to cover only articles in fields that are related to business and economics (see Box 15.1 for the list).

Further refinement was necessary due to the high number of articles related to network effects or externalities, so we excluded articles with the term 'Network externalit*' or 'Network effect' in title, keywords, or abstract. Other irrelevant articles in the remaining database were on IT infrastructure or production systems and could be identified by the term 'inventory'. The final database consists of 1306 articles. A comparison of the development of the number of articles published in selected subject categories is presented in Figure 15.1. Since journals are assigned to more than one category, we calculated a weighted count, so that every paper is only counted once. As we can tell from Figure 15.1, the field emerged in the early 1990s with almost equal interest in management and economics followed by business, sociology and geography. In the 2000s we observe a sharp increase in publications in management and business journals, a moderate increase in economics and geography but a constantly low number in sociology. As we will show later on, the high importance of sociology for the field is not based on applied network

---

BOX 15.1   SUBJECT CATEGORIES INCLUDED IN THE STUDY

Business
Business, finance
Economics
Geography
Industrial relations & labor
Management
Mathematics, interdisciplinary applications
Operations research & management science
Planning & development
Political science
Social sciences, interdisciplinary
Social sciences, mathematical methods
Sociology
Urban studies

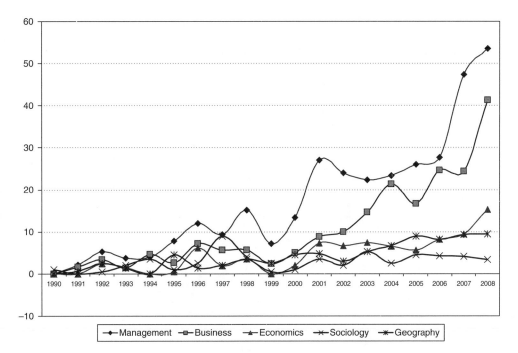

Figure 15.1 Articles on networks and innovation by subject categories

studies on innovation but rather based on sociological theories that are tested in economic and management contexts.

While it is perfectly clear that the topic has received increased attention over the last two decades, we are interested in the theoretical foundations of this literature. To identify the theoretical core of the field, we apply the methodology under investigation to build citation networks from our database. We construct these networks as five-year moving windows starting in the period 1990–94 and ending in 2005–09 where the period refers to the publication date of the citing articles. Visualizations of three of these networks are presented in Figures 15.2–15.4. Figure 15.2 depicts the core network for the starting period 1990–94. Arrows indicate the direction of the citation and node size is proportional to the number of citations a contribution receives (indegree). For clarity, we only include cited papers with an indegree of at least four and the citing papers that connect these most highly cited papers.

The prominence of the sociological literature as a theoretical and methodological input becomes immediately apparent as we find contributions by Everett Rogers on the diffusion of innovation and articles by Mark Granovetter and Ronald Burt on the structure of networks at the center of this network. Other important contributions of this emerging phase are the contributions on innovation in general (Schumpeter, 1934; Mansfield, 1961; Nelson and Winter, 1977) or with a focus on interaction and/or technology management as in Piore and Sabel (1984), Hakansson (1987), von Hippel (1988), Imai and Baba (1989), or Porter (1990).

The citation network for the period surrounding the turn of the century is presented

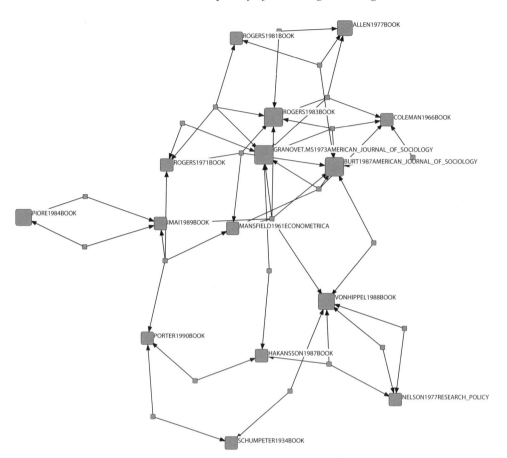

Note: Only publications with an indegree of at least 4 are displayed.

Figure 15.2   Citation network for the period 1990–94

in Figure 15.3. The theoretical basis of articles published between 1998 and 2002 can be aggregated into three groups. In the first group, there are the sociological classics already present in the first period. Mark Granovetter's argument about the strength of weak ties, Ronald Burt's theory of structural holes, and Brian Uzzi's work on overembeddedness show a strong influence on innovation network research. In the second group, we find highly influential research related to the management, organization, and boundaries of firms with the works of Wesley Cohen, Daniel Levinthal, Walter Powell, David Teece, and Oliver Williamson as the most influential representatives. The third group could be labeled innovation systems research. Nelson and Winter (1982) provide the evolutionary theory and von Hippel (1988) identifies interactions between users and producers as valuable sources of innovation. Both are necessary to understand the innovation process as an interactive phenomenon. The books by Nelson (1993) and Lundvall (1992) as well as the article by Freeman (1991) are all on systems of innovation, while Saxenian (1994) and Porter (1990) put more emphasis on geographical aspects. It may be worthwhile to

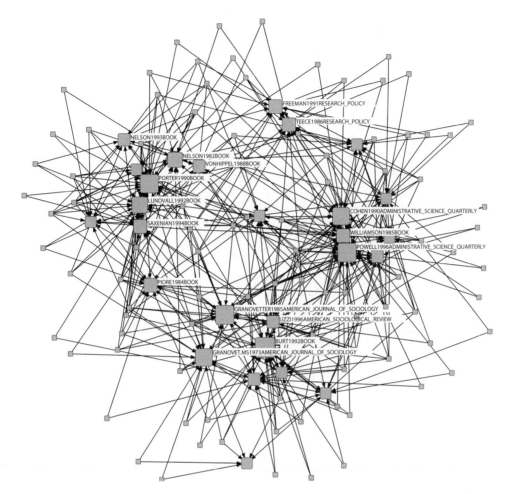

Note: Only publications with an indegree of at least 14 are displayed.

Figure 15.3   Citation network for the period 1998–2002

note that during this period the sharp increase in business and management studies took place.

The consequences of this rise of the management literature to dominate the field today can be observed in Figure 15.4. The sociological classics and publications in the realm of management move closer together and eliminate other disciplines from the top citation spots. A good example for the fruitful combination of sociology and management is the most highly cited work during that period, the empirical study by Walter Powell, Kenneth Koput, and Laurel Smith-Doerr on networks of learning in biotechnology which was published 1996 in *Administrative Science Quarterly*. The paper by Ahuja (2000a) on the influence of firm position within an alliance network on innovation success was published in the same journal and became one of the top cited papers rapidly after publication. From the economic literature only the publications by Nelson and

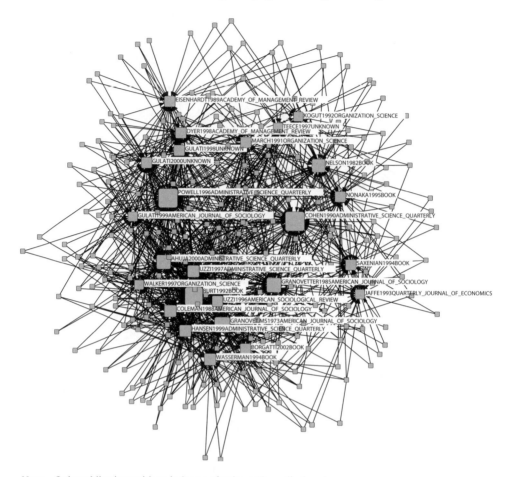

Note: Only publications with an indegree of at least 42 are displayed.

Figure 15.4   Citation network for the period 2005–09

Winter (1982), Jaffe et al. (1993), and Saxenian (1994), who is of course an economic geographer, remain visible. Besides the trend towards management studies, another characteristic development of the most recent years becomes apparent. Frequent citations to the methodological book by Wasserman and Faust (1994) and to software for empirical network studies (Borgatti et al., 2002) indicate an increasing degree of empirical research in the field.

To strengthen this argument, the citation frequency over the last two decades for the top cited references during the period 2005–09 is displayed in Figure 15.5. The classic Granovetter (1973) article is among the top 1 per cent for the whole period and holds the fourth position in the last period. The book by Nelson and Winter (1982) is another classic in terms of citations. The book by Ronald Burt (1992) was the most cited reference for most of the time being replaced by Powell et al. (1996) from the period 2004–08 onwards. The high number of references to Cohen and Levinthal (1990), almost from

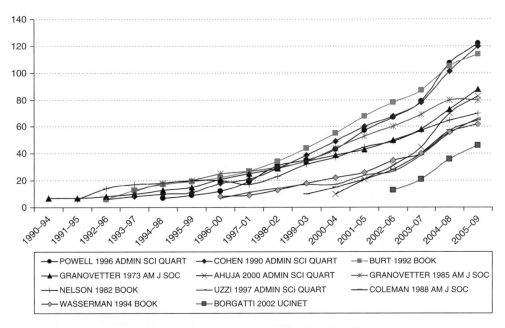

Figure 15.5 *Top ten cited references during the period 2005–09, with Borgatti 2002 added manually*

the beginning, points to the relevance of the concept of absorptive capacity for an understanding of the conditions under which network relations are beneficial in the innovation process.

Overall, the fact that scholars increasingly perform rigorous empirical studies, which is indicated by more frequent citations to methodology and software, surely has to be viewed as a positive development. A development that we, as economists, view more critical is the crowding out of economic fundamentals in this field. While we can gain much insight from the micro perspective of business and management studies we have to keep in mind that the questions asked in these studies are related to the management of single organizations and their positioning within a network. The systemic view of innovation which takes a more macro perspective could benefit from the application of social network analysis but could also provide theories that have to be tested with data on the system level.

3.   INNOVATION, KNOWLEDGE AND COOPERATION

Having discussed the overall importance of the research on innovation networks we now introduce some fundamental concepts required to understand their functioning. The very purpose of an innovation network is to exchange knowledge and expertise among cooperating partners with the ultimate objective of generating new knowledge eventually embodied in new products, services or processes. Hence, in an innovation network already existing, precious knowledge as well as the commonly generated new knowledge is shared among the collaborating actors. For getting appropriate insights into how this exchange and sharing works one has to understand the very nature of the 'commodity' being transferred and commonly used, the character of innovative actors, and their incentives and required conditions for engaging in knowledge exchange.

3.1   Information and Knowledge

To start with, information and knowledge are to be distinguished from commodities and goods. They show an immaterial character on the one hand and they are with a few exceptions not of the type of a purely private good on the other. In the early literature, no distinction was made between information and knowledge; rather they were considered as being the same. In addition both were considered a pure public good meeting the criteria of non-rivalry and of non-excludability. The former maintains that the full amount of services a good under consideration offers can be used by an infinite number of users (there is no rivalry) and that services themselves are not being used up. The later criterion states that no one can be excluded by using that good or, from the side of the producer of the good, there is no way to entirely appropriate the economic returns accruing from that good. Consequently, the incentives to produce information and knowledge fulfilling just these criteria are considerably low if not even nil.

However, classifying information and knowledge in that way requires that they can be encoded into signals required for transmittance between actors and that all potential users have the perfect ability to understand the signals content. Under such circumstances any consideration of the way in which information and knowledge could be transferred and exchanged and what institutional arrangements would be suitable are not required – any network discussion would not make sense. However, the two assumptions put forward can easily be questioned.

A first kind of revision aims at distinguishing between information and knowledge. The former is the representation of some knowledge by signals (words, letters, optical impressions, and so on) which can be transmitted between actors. Knowledge on the other hand is the ability to take up the signals (encoding), to understand their content and to relate it to pre-existing knowledge pieces. For a transfer or exchange of knowledge to be successfully accomplished, its codification, its transfer, its decodification, as well as its basic understanding in the sense of connecting it to the existing knowledge stock, are required.

On the basis of this distinction a second revision refers to giving up the assumption of the perfect ability of actors to understand the content of transmitted signals. Doing so, knowledge is no longer to be taken as a pure public good that by definition was entirely available to everyone at every place and at any time. Due to Nelson (1989), knowledge attached to innovation activities is to be considered a latent public good implying that it enfolds its public good character whenever certain circumstances are met. Among those circumstances most prominent is the ability of the information recipient to understand the signals, to interpret them, and to use them. Cohen and Levinthal (1990) coin the concept of absorptive capacities which comprises characteristics (human capital, smartness, and so on) needed by actors to do so. Transmitting knowledge in that case from one actor to another requires a certain cognitive proximity between them – if the cognitive or technological distance between them becomes too large the communication of knowledge becomes ineffective. Recognizing the interdependence in the process of knowledge exchange, Lane and Lubatkin (1998) suggest the concept of relative absorptive capacity.

The third revision addresses the observation that some encoding of knowledge into signals is not always possible. Drawing back to Polanyi (1967) some part of knowledge has a tacit character. This implies that actors possess knowledge that they use in an appropriate way, but that they are incapable of explaining how it works in detail to others. They are not able to encode it into signals that are transferred to the recipient. Consequently such knowledge cannot be transmitted from one actor to another (Cowan et al., 2000), at least not very easily and by the usual kinds of signals. In that case, knowledge shows the character of a private good – it is embodied within a certain actor who can be hired from the labor market. Thus, this knowledge is not available for the previous employer and can entirely be used by the new one. Hence, the two criteria for a private good, rivalry and excludability, are met. However, beside this market based transfer channel, it seems to be the case that by sheer observation of another even tacit knowledge can be copied. This requires a considerably close interaction between the 'sender' and the recipient, for example face-to-face contact and being at the same place.

3.2 Innovation and Innovative Actors

Understanding innovative activities requires opening up the black box (Rosenberg, 1982) of how actors acquire and apply the knowledge used for creating new combinations. A first step is to briefly address, rather generally, the pattern of the innovation process in modern manufacturing as suggested by Dosi (1988):

(i)   Endogeneity of innovative activities
(ii)   Uncertainty
(iii) Partial dependence on and contacts to science
(iv)   Learning-by-doing, learning-by-using, learning-by-innovating, learning-by-inventing
(v)   Cumulativeness

Features (i) and (ii) point to the fact that economic actors (primarily firms) are engaged in innovation and so they are confronted with strong and therefore non-calculable uncertainty (Knight, 1921; Arrow, 1991). This implies that designing R&D projects in an optimal way is impossible and the search for new ideas is a trial-and-error process. Hence, an understanding of the economic agent different to the *Homo oeconomicus* is required. Drawing on Simon (1955), the concept of bounded rationality is applied, which questions the assumption of ubiquitous information (substantial rationality) available to agents, as well as the assumption of unbounded capabilities (procedural rationality) to use this information. The resulting notion of bounded rationality, although thought of as a conception with rather general importance, seems to be especially relevant for actors engaged in innovative (and also imitative) activities. To create something new, viewed as an experimental activity, implies having imperfect information and imperfect abilities to use it.

The notion of bounded rationality entered the theory of the firm through Cyert and

March (1963) as stable behavioral traits and in Nelson and Winter (1982) an element of adaptive control was added, leading to the concept of a more flexible behavior: routines. Routines are behavioral devices which show certain stability over time as they are often based on idiosyncratic knowledge and competences. They will be changed, however, if their reward does not meet the level aspired to. A further strategic dimension of routines has been developed within the dynamic capability view of the firm (DCV) as introduced by Teece (1988) drawing on the resource based view of the firm (for example, Penrose, 1959; Wernerfelt, 1984; Barney, 1991). A firm's more or less unique knowledge and competencies are just seen as a major resource (characterized as being valuable, rare, imperfectly tradable, and non-substitutable) contributing to its competitiveness. Since these resources are not nature given but are developed and implemented over time, they are labeled dynamic capabilities, implying their role for long term strategic planning. Other firms have to incur non-negligible costs (also to build up respective absorptive capacities (Cohen and Levinthal, 1990)), in order to copy or to imitate knowledge and competences represented by these capabilities, if they are able to.

Features (iii) to (v) indicate how innovative actors act in this trial-and-error process. They gather information and they accumulate knowledge by learning in order to build up dynamic capabilities. The latter in turn enables them to both explore new opportunities and to exploit existing ones (Rosenberg and Nelson, 1994; Zucker et al., 1998; Mowery et al., 2004). To the degree that learning relates to the accumulation of own experience, over time actors become heterogeneous in terms of their technological (as well as economic) knowledge. Taking into account the specific features of knowledge as mainly being a latent public good (and sometimes even being tacit) this heterogeneity is based on an actor specific stickiness of knowledge. In such a context the social dimension of learning assumes a central role and it becomes crucial for the extraction of knowledge from other sources such as science or competitors. An important way to do this is the voluntary exchange of knowledge by cooperating and networking.

3.3   Cooperating in Innovation

For accessing external knowledge a firm has several options. First, required technological knowledge can be bought on appropriate markets (Arora et al., 2001). External R&D expenditures are used to pay someone else to do research and to deliver the results. Licensing fees or buying patents belong to this category. Secondly, a firm can integrate other actors with appropriate technological knowledge into the own firm. Mergers and acquisitions as well as the market for human capital allows for this. A third and for the following relevant mode of accessing external knowledge is research cooperation. Here, different actors agree formally as well as informally to cooperate in inventive and innovative activities. These three cases of accessing external knowledge are related to the concept of organizational proximity introduced by Boschma (2005). In the case of market transaction this proximity is low,[1] the relationships between contracting partners are highly flexible and governed by market prices, and we observe a unidirectional knowledge transfer from the seller to the buyer. Contrariwise, in the hierarchical structure of a firm, proximity is closest, flexibility in the relation between the partners is low and ruled by contract, and we again observe a unidirectional knowledge transfer, here from the subordinate to the chief executive. An intermediate level of proximity applies to any network type of cooperative relationships.[2] This organizational format allows being flexible and switching rather easily from one cooperation partner to another. The transfer of knowledge is bidirectional and based on knowledge exchange. Here the reciprocity of exchanging knowledge is essential but neither necessarily *uno actu* (as in markets) nor contractually agreed upon (as in hierarchies).

Looking more closely on those cooperative relationships one may ask for the conditions that have to be satisfied for actors to become engaged in knowledge exchange. There has to be a common (economic) interest, a certain level of mutual understanding, and a certain degree of controllability and reciprocity in a continuous relation.

With respect to the common interest of actors engaging in knowledge exchange the expected economic benefits are of utmost importance. However, intermediate targets in terms of technological solutions to be achieved commonly, or reciprocal access to specific knowledge can be formulated. In the end, the motives have to be complementary in the sense that all participating actors benefit. A closer look at research cooperation delivers three important motives for firms to get engaged. First, on purely economic grounds research cooperation provides a reduction of risk and a sharing of R&D costs (Deeds and Hill, 1996; Baum et al., 2000). The second motive refers to the combining of complementary assets in order to enhance the propensity of a successful development project (Teece, 1986; Nooteboom, 1999). And third, the internalization of knowledge spillovers (Griliches, 1992), the possibility to exchange knowledge and the resulting interactive learning may lead to higher inventive and innovative success of the participating actors. Obviously, these three motives cannot be seen in isolation but any cooperative arrangement with the aim to further technological development and to invent and innovate will be governed by all of the three motives at the same time – although from case to case by varying degrees.

Having introduced the economic rationales for exchanging knowledge the question arises as to what are the principle conditions to be fulfilled for this interactive process to run effectively. Obviously, actors have to show a mutual understanding combined with enough differences in their knowledge stocks for being creative (creative potential). Boschma (2005) suggested the concept of cognitive proximity as relevant for exchanging knowledge characterized as a latent public good and the concept of geographical proximity for knowledge of the tacit type. Of crucial importance for successful interaction is the cognitive or technological proximity between the interacting agents. The generic potential in cooperative invention and innovation rests on the actors involved being different in their knowledge and competences. However, some overlap in these knowledge bases and thus some degree of proximity in the cognitive or technological dimension is required for a common understanding. This overlap just indicates the (relative) absorptive capacities in the sense that the larger the overlap the higher the absorptive capacities but also the less the generic potential of the relationship. Hence a rather general feature of proximity concepts shows up here, an inverted-U shaped relationship (Wuyts et al., 2005). This means that there is an intermediate level of proximity at which cooperation is highest whereas any deviation from that level (either to lower or increased proximity) leads to a decreased level of cooperative invention and innovation.[3] With respect to the transmittance of tacit knowledge cognitive proximity alone is not sufficient. The face-to-face interaction of the exchanging actors requires spatial or geographical proximity.

Looking at actors' requirement of controlling the knowledge exchange, in markets as well as in hierarchies it may be accomplished by contracts as far as all the contingencies can be taken into account.[4] In network relationships, however, which are often informal, it is not the market or the labor contract but the trust between the cooperating actors which is taken as a controlling device. The mechanism involved is reciprocity of knowledge exchange, not in the sense of *uno actu* but over time. In general, it is social proximity as well as institutional proximity (Boschma, 2005) which governs trust relationships. Trust may be given *ex ante*, before cooperation starts. In that case, the more actors share general habits and attitudes (at the macro level) the closer their institutional proximity and the stronger the trust related to those institutions. Another source of trust (and, of course, distrust) is built up by the very exchange of ideas, concepts and knowledge (*ex post* trust). Here trust is based on social proximity related to repeated interactions along social relationships. This kind of trust is observed on the micro level and is built up by a frequently exchanging knowledge. In this sense it can be labeled as *ex post* trust since it develops after the cooperation has started.

Summarizing, first, at the core of cooperative invention and innovation is a network of actors exchanging ideas. Second, cooperative invention and innovation is based on the combination of different knowledge bases where, however, cognitive or technological proximity should not be too large. Third, with respect to the controllability of network relations, the institution of trust gains importance, itself being determined by institutional and social proximity among the cooperating partners.

4.   NETWORKS AND ECONOMIC PERFORMANCE

This section addresses network structures and prepares for the discussion of network dynamics below. For the network structures we look at we should always keep in mind that they are both the result and the cause of network dynamics. While it will become clear in this section that the network position and its structure have a strong impact on the performance, that performance of the network or of individual agents will also shape the structure of the network. In the following we have a look at whether the basic conditions for networking derived in Section 3, that is economic benefit, mutual understanding and controllability/trust, are related to certain network structures.

Looking at the performance in and of innovation networks, we distinguish several levels of analysis. In a first step, we briefly discuss the mutual benefits and the mutual understanding characterizing innovation networks and their formation. The following two steps are concerned with actor embeddedness and the related performance. Here, we distinguish relational embeddedness, accounting for the frequency and intensity of an actor's bilateral relations, from the integration of an actor in the network, called structural embeddedness. With the latter, an aggregate view of these bilateral relations is taken, allowing us to analyse the structure of such a network and of individual positions therein (Gulati, 1998). At a more aggregated level in the fourth step, we are interested in the influence of the network structure on the performance of the network as a whole. Depending on the definition of the system, applications range from organization studies concerned with knowledge flows within R&D departments to macro oriented studies.

4.1 Network Formation

Network formation has to do with the question of whether there are mutual benefits for individual actors to cooperate in generating new ideas and whether the resulting interaction structures meet the requirements of mutual understanding and reciprocal incentives.

While the relevance of interaction in the production of knowledge is not a new phenomenon, it probably becomes most apparent in the study of Wuchty et al. (2007). They use information from almost 20 million papers and 2 million patents over five decades to study the prevalence and performance of individuals compared to teams. One of their observations is that '[t]eams increasingly dominate solo authors in the production of knowledge' and that '[r]esearch is increasingly done in teams across nearly all fields' (p. 1036). The authors analyse the citation structure to account for the importance of these publications and find that research performed by teams is more and increasingly successful in terms of received citations. Hence there are mutual benefits of cooperating that the team members are not able to achieve as solo authors.

However, to reap those benefits certain requirements concerning the actors involved and their respective knowledge bases have to be satisfied. Looking at the respective interaction structures one may ask to what degree they are governed by mutual understanding and to what degree by actor heterogeneity. Cantner and Graf (2004) analyse regional interaction patterns and show that innovation cooperations are more frequently observed in modestly specialized regions. Their results imply that cooperating firms need related but not too similar technological capabilities. On the basis of patent data Cantner and Meder (2007) look at dyadic relationships in innovation cooperation and find that the knowledge bases of the cooperating firms show a certain degree of overlap. This common knowledge base enhances better understanding and eases the knowledge transfer aspired to. It can be interpreted as a measure for the reciprocal absorptive capacities of the two cooperating partners. The non-overlapping parts of their knowledge bases account for reciprocal incentives prevalent in knowledge exchange. In this respect Cantner and Meder (2007) show that actors are engaged in a knowledge transfer only when each has available a minimal stock of knowledge that is valuable for the partner(s).

Extending this type of analysis from dyadic relations to network structures allows us to find a relationship between absorptive capacity (as a prerequisite for mutual understanding), position in a network and innovative performance. Boschma and ter Wal (2007) find that there is no influence of a firms' absorptive capacity on its network position. They assume the lack of social capital to be a reason for this surprising result. The results of Morrison and Rabellotti (2009) on an Italian wine cluster go in the same direction. They recognize a core-periphery structure of the cluster network where the well-connected actors are barely innovative firms and the periphery consists of highly innovative firms which have no need to integrate in the local knowledge network for external technical advice. Contrary to these results, Giuliani (2007) shows, at least for two of the three wine clusters, that there is a positive correlation between the firms' knowledge bases and their position in the knowledge network.

4.2   Network Position and Individual Performance

In this subsection we look at actors' performance depending on their relational embeddedness. The relational embeddedness of an actor is characterized by the number of ties and other measures of centrality, by the type of collaborative interaction (weak versus strong ties), or the type of collaboration partners.

4.2.1   Number of ties and centrality

As discussed above, the choices of actors to cooperate in innovation should be related to their expected costs and benefits from establishing and maintaining such a relation. Given that, it would be naïve to assume that there is a linear relationship between the number of contacts and performance, at least in contexts where the costs related to establishing and/or maintaining a linkage are non-negligible. The literature is rather clear about the positive effects of network linkages and it is quite hard to find studies that report opposing results to this hypothesis. For the chemical industry a strong positive relationship between the number of alliances (or ties) and innovation is documented in Ahuja (2000a) who performs a longitudinal study of the network of 97 leading chemical firms in Western Europe, Japan, and the United States. Collaboration data for the period 1981–91 is sought to explain patenting activity in the period 1982–92, reflecting a one-year lag between collaboration and patenting. The networks were constructed from information on technical collaborations and joint ventures as documented in business media. By means of panel regression with random effects Ahuja (2000a) finds a significant positive impact of direct ties (degree) on subsequent innovation output. The number of indirect ties also shows a positive influence on subsequent patenting, and, at first sight, these indirect ties seem to be a substitute for direct ties. However, direct and indirect ties serve different functions. Ahuja (2000a) argues that direct ties provide benefits from resource-sharing and information spillover, while indirect ties only serve as a source for spillovers. Equivalent results are reported across a variety of industries such biotechnology (Powell et al., 1996; Walker et al., 1997; Powell et al., 1999; Baum et al., 2000), telecommunications (Godoe, 2000), or semiconductors (Stuart, 1998, 2000).

While there is not much debate about the results regarding direct ties or the number of alliances as most simple measures of network position, other measures of centrality show a less robust impact on performance. A certain advantage of multilateral networks compared to purely bilateral relations is the effect accruing from indirect ties. Here knowledge can flow not just between two actors, but through several nodes of a network, leading to indirect ties (to the partner of a partner). Powell et al. (1996) study the network of dedicated biotechnology firms in the US over a period from 1990 to 1994. The authors obtain rather ambiguous results concerning the influence of a central position in the network on firm growth. In their study, degree centrality (that is, an actor's number of ties divided by the number of possible ties) predicts employment growth, but no significant effects were found for closeness centrality of firms (that is, the reciprocal of the sum of the geodesic distance to each other firm) in the main component. In a subsequent study (Powell et al., 1999) on an expanded dataset for 1988–97, they conclude that (the eigenvector) centrality stimulates growth in size and internally funded R&D and reinforces the use of R&D alliances. Additionally, they find that the returns to networking experience are decreasing. Owen-Smith and Powell (2004) find equivalent results for the Boston biotechnology network.

The generally positive impact of linkages on innovation seems to hold at different levels of aggregation and in differently defined network boundaries. For intra-organizational knowledge networks between business units in two large companies Tsai (2001) shows that the network centrality influences the units' innovative success positively. Looking at regional rather than industry networks, Graf and Krüger (2009) analyse the influence of actor positions on subsequent patenting in four regional networks in Germany. They find a strong positive influence of degree centrality on innovative performance. Being positioned at the interface between the local network and external actors does not seem to be unequivocally positive as the authors find a U-shaped relationship between the intensity of being a gatekeeper (connecting internal and external actors) and subsequent patenting activity. Betweenness centrality – as a measure of how actors serve as a bridge between otherwise unconnected actors in the whole network – seems to have a negative effect on patenting, while the influence of being a member of the main component is not significant.

4.2.2 Weak versus strong ties

Shifting the focus from the number of alliances or ties to their quality leads us to the lively debate related to Granovetter's (1973) argument about the strength of ties. Strong ties are defined as relations to close friends and family, whereas weak ties result from relations to more distant people as well as to suppliers or customers. Granovetter (1973) highlights the importance of weak ties that are supposed to be more important for the acquisition of new and diverse knowledge than strong ties.

To put the argument to an empirical test, Rowley et al. (2000) study two networks constituted by horizontal alliances in the US semiconductor and steel industries. Their main interest lies in the differential influence of strong ties compared to weak ties (as differentiated by the degree of resource commitment to an alliance), and the density of the neighborhood on the return on assets – as a measure of performance. Overall, they find a negative influence of strong ties on performance, but in the exploitation environment of the steel industry they find a positive influence. Weak ties are overall positive, but especially so in the exploration context of the semiconductor industry.

The theoretical arguments concerning the types of relations and their implications for economic success are enriched by Uzzi's (1997) analysis on the basis of an ethnographic fieldwork study at 23 entrepreneurial firms. While his principal findings indicate that strong, embedded ties are favorable for allocative efficiency and complex adaptation, he also points to the problem of overembeddedness. Beyond a certain threshold, embeddedness can '. . . derail economic performance by making firms vulnerable to exogenous shocks or insulating them from information that exists beyond their network' (p. 35). Uzzi (1997) proposes a mix of arm's-length and embedded ties as the optimal network structure, because each type of relation serves different functions: 'Embedded ties enrich the network, while arm's-length ties prevent the complete insulation of the network from market demands and new possibilities' (p. 59). In line with these findings, Cantner et al. (2010) identify an inverted-U shaped relationship between the number of innovation collaborations and the innovative performance of actors in the Jena innovation system – hence at some level of interaction the returns of additional ties become even negative.

Applying an ego-network approach, Ruef (2002) conducted a survey among graduates from a Western US university graduate program who were reported to have tried to start their own business. Innovation is measured by responses regarding patenting and trademark applications during the creation of the start-up and subjective evaluations of their own innovative effort. Innovation is then explained by measures characterizing the entrepreneurs' networks, in particular the sources of inspiration for their business idea. Strong ties are defined as discussions with friends and family, weak ties result from discussions with suppliers or customers, and directed ties are related to discussions in the media or observations of competitors. The diversity of sources was also included to explain innovative outcome. The results imply no significant influence of strong ties on innovation but a positive influence of weak ties, directed ties towards the media, and a diverse set of information sources. A diverse composition of the entrepreneurial team is also advantageous for innovation.

4.2.3 Type of partners

Besides the number and the quality of alliances or ties, the type of partners exchanging knowledge is also supposed to influence performance. Innovation networks consist of different types of partners such as firms, universities and research institutes along the innovation process or different types of firms especially along the vertical value chain. Related to that is a division of labor and a specialization with possibly positive effects on innovative and economic performance. In the context of university-industry relations, Balconi et al. (2004) show that academic inventors are more central and better connected than non-academic ones, implying a vital role of academia for the dissemination of knowledge through interpersonal contacts.

Cantner et al. (2010) investigate determinants of the innovative capacity of firms (as measured by an index based on past innovative success) in the Jena network of innovators. Firms cooperating with public research institutes show a significantly higher innovative capacity. With respect to relations along the value chain, Baum et al. (2000) study alliances of Canadian biotech start-ups in the period 1991 to 1996. They include a number of performance measures such as revenues, employee growth and patents which are to be explained by a variety of measures characterizing the type and partners of their relations. Positive effects are found for alliances with pharmaceutical firms on all performance measures. Alliances with marketing firms are positive except for patenting. R&D expenses and patents are positively influenced by networks characterized by efficiency as measured by the information per alliance, scope (breadth of sectors covered by partners relative to own breadth), and the innovativeness of partner firms.

4.3 Creative Potentials versus Trust Relations

A major issue in networking and interactive innovation is the trade-off relationship between trust and creative potential. Relationships characterized by a high degree of trust tend to be established between actors who are rather similar in their relations (hence rather direct), their knowledge stocks, attitudes and so on. A high degree of creative potential, however, is to be expected between actors who are quite distant in these aspects. Addressing these issues the major problem is to measure trust as well as creative potentials. A possible way out is to look at the structural embeddedness of actors and to infer from that specific structures (as measured by density, structural holes, direct and indirect ties, and so on) that indicate trust relations on the one hand and creative potentials on the other.

A general controversy in this context is – closely related to the discussion of strong versus weak ties – about the structural properties of actors' ego-networks and their influence on performance measures such as innovation. One hypothesis is put forward by Coleman (1988) stressing the importance of a dense local network, that is, actors benefit from a network in which their direct neighbors are tightly connected as well. The argument is that a dense network promotes trust which serves as a prerequisite for knowledge exchange and cooperation among its members. In contrast, Burt (1992) argues that structural holes, that is, structures in which the alters of an ego are unrelated, provide the opportunity to grasp brokerage advantages from the ability to arbitrage non-redundant information exchanges. In this sense structural holes indicate creative potentials. In a more recent article, Burt (2004: 349) states that 'Compensation, positive performance evaluations, promotions, and good ideas are disproportionately in the hands of people whose networks span structural holes.'

Looking at the empirical evidence, the bulk of the literature testing which structure is most conducive to innovation is to be found in business and management journals. One of the most cited references in this field is the work on R&D collaborations in the chemical industry by Ahuja (2000a). In addition to his findings on the relevance of direct and indirect ties, he focuses on the structure of the ego-network of the focal firm. The coefficient of the employed measure for structural holes is negative and significant, indicating more benefits from a dense and closed network than from structural holes in that specific context. Hence, in that network trust seems to be more important for cooperation than creative potentials.

In their study of horizontal alliances in the US semiconductor and steel industries, Rowley et al. (2000) also test the adequacy of the Coleman argument versus Burt's argument of structural holes. They obtain an insignificant influence of the density of the ego-network of firms on the return on assets, which would imply that neither is right. However in separate regressions for each industry they can show that density is important in the exploitation context implying a strong role of trust relations in the steel industry. Weak ties and structural holes are especially important in the exploration context of the semiconductor industry where the creative potentials are acquired through a variety of knowledge sources. Further results imply that strong ties are less positive (or even negative) in a dense network since the benefits of the dense network (trust) can be reaped without the costs of maintaining redundant ties. Building on these findings, Gilsing and Duysters (2008) performed case studies of exploration networks in the Dutch pharmaceutical biotechnology and multimedia industries. Contrasting the results of the literature on exploration, the authors find that a dense network of strong ties can be important as it serves as a selection mechanism.

The issue of trust versus creative potentials is not only studied in an inter-firm context but also within organizations. In a study of a newly created unit within the Italian subsidiary of a multinational computer manufacturer, Gargiulo and Benassi (2000) find a trade-off associated with the safety conferred by cohesive ties (social capital) and the flexibility conferred by ties that connect different parts of a network.

Sorenson et al. (2006: 994) attempt to generalize the discussion and argue that '. . .

the value of social proximity to the knowledge source depends crucially on the nature of the knowledge at hand.' To test their hypothesis, they examine the relationship between patent citation rates and social distance within the inventor collaboration network. In the case of simple knowledge, social proximity is supposed to be irrelevant for diffusion, while complex knowledge hardly diffuses even within close social proximity to its source. Knowledge of moderate complexity, however, allows socially proximate actors to receive and build on knowledge generated elsewhere. Their results support the argument that trust relations among socially proximate actors have the greatest advantage over distant actors for knowledge of moderate complexity.

In a theoretical study, Cowan and Jonard (2007) model knowledge diffusion in a population of agents interacting only over direct ties. Agents are of two different types: traders and givers, where traders demand a quid pro quo for information transfer, while givers do not. With respect to the attitude of the agents, the authors find that giving is superior to trading in terms of efficiency. Clustering is related to Coleman's (1988) argument of the value of social capital. Clustering on the individual level measures the extent to which the alters of a focal firm are connected amongst each other, which is exactly what corresponds to the density of the local (in the perspective of the firm) network. Clustering can then be averaged for the whole network (of the industry for example) to analyse the prevalence of either a cohesive, dense, and clustered structure, or of a sparse network structure characterized by many structural holes. The simulation results imply that when knowledge is scarce, efficiency is higher when there are many structural holes. When knowledge is abundant, networks with high social capital (that is, high clustering) perform better. The scarcity of knowledge is interpreted as an indicator for the maturity of the industry. In their setting, a scarce knowledge environment could represent a young industry while mature industries are characterized by abundant knowledge. As such, the results are in line with the empirical observations by Rowley et al. (2000) who find structural holes to be beneficial in semiconductors (young) but not in the steel industry (old).

4.4   The Influence of Network Structure on System Performance

Having discussed how knowledge transmission affects the performance of individual actors dependent on their relational and structural embeddedness, we now turn to the relationship between the easiness by which knowledge flows and the performance of the network. Of utmost importance in this respect is a network structure called 'small world'. Networks with small-world properties are characterized by high clustering and small average path length and have been identified in various contexts (Watts and Strogatz, 1998).

Cowan and Jonard have a series of papers in which they study how different network structures affect the flow of knowledge by means of formal modeling. In Cowan and Jonard (2003), they analyse the influence of network structure on system performance by means of a formal model. Actors exchange knowledge as a gift (that is, without asking for direct compensation) within the industry as in a process of collective invention described by Allen (1983) and Nuvolari (2004) or to be found in open source communities. One of the results is that the structure of the communication network has a strong influence on system performance. If absorptive capacities are low the small world structure appears to be an efficient architecture, while with high absorptive capacities, short path lengths are especially valuable. In a related model Cowan and Jonard (2004) assume a trading of information instead of giving, which is motivated by the observations by von Hippel (1987) or Schrader (1991) on informal information trading. In that model, the small world structure is always beneficial for the average knowledge level. At the 'optimal' small world structure, variance of knowledge levels is also highest indicating that clustering induces inequality between actors as well. If the coefficient of variation is used to measure heterogeneity, this distributional problem is not evident.

The empirical literature is not so clear about the benefits of a small-world structure for system performance. Uzzi et al. (2007) provide a review of these studies in a variety of contexts and time-spans. Their findings imply that there is no universally true, linear relationship between the small-world structure of a network and its performance, but only a few studies are related to innovation, creativity or the generation of knowledge.

Uzzi and Spiro (2005) build an artist network from information on Broadway musicals to examine the effect of a small world on artists' creativity. Creative performance is measured by profitability and critics' reviews of the shows. The small world property Q is measured as the CC ratio over the PL ratio, where the CC ratio is calculated as the observed clustering coefficient divided by the clustering coefficient of a random network of the same size and similarly for the average path length of the network PL. They argue that a small world affects the performance of a system as well as the performance of the actors within it and suggest a parabolic relationship between a small world and the performance of the actors. The reasoning behind this hypothesis is that for low levels of Q path length is too high for new material to be exchanged between teams and if Q is too high, connectivity and cohesion leads to a homogenization of ideas which undermines creativity. Consistent with this hypothesis, they find that artists were more likely to produce successful shows at a medium level of Q compared to either high or low levels. They also show that seasons with a medium level of Q, produced more successful shows than did seasons with a high or low level of Q.

A study which is closer to our interest in technological innovation is the one by Verspagen and Duysters (2004) who investigate the small-world properties of the network of strategic alliances among firms in the chemical and food and electrical industries. Their data covered 5504 alliances from 1980 to 1996. This alliance network is found to follow a small world pattern with a path length similar to that of a random network and a clustering coefficient exceeding the random one by a factor of 425. While the authors interpret their findings as being a beneficial structure for knowledge transfer, their work does not show a direct connection between the small-world structure and performance. The context dependency of the issue becomes apparent since the authors find remarkable differences in the structure of the networks between the technological fields.

Fleming et al. (2007) compare inventor networks in Silicon Valley and Route 128 in Boston. In their methodology, two inventors are linked if they co-authored a patent. While the networks show small-world properties, they find no relationship between the small-world structure of these networks and regional patenting rates. Short path lengths and the size of the largest component are, however, positively correlated with patenting, suggesting that the level of connectivity within the larger subcomponents of a small world does have an effect on performance. In a comparison of four regional innovator networks, Graf and Henning (2009) provide anecdotal evidence for the influence of network structures on system performance. Successful regions are characterized by a higher and increasing fraction of actors in the main component and public research institutes serve as central actors connecting the network. The same regional networks are analysed in terms of their outward orientation in Graf (2011). It shows that regions that are capable of acquiring external knowledge and communicating it within the network through local network ties are more successful.

Not directly interested in system performance but rather in the individual performance of firms, Schilling and Phelps (2007) study the longitudinal patent performance of 1106 firms in 11 industry-level alliance networks. Their results are consistent with the small-world hypothesis in the sense that the more firms were embedded in networks with small-world properties, the more likely they were to patent at greater rates than firms not in small-world networks. The authors also address the question of when the benefits of networking arise. Models employing a two- and three-year lag show stronger results than those employing a one-year lag, suggesting that innovation benefits of collaboration do not arise immediately.

5.   NETWORK DYNAMICS

Based on the fundamental concepts introduced in Section 3 and the relationship between network structure and performance in Section 4, in this section we discuss the dynamics of innovator networks. The dynamics and evolution of innovation networks appear in the creation of new ties, in the change of the quality and intensity of existing ties, in the entry of new actors and the exit of formerly participating actors. Such dynamics is called a dynamics-of-the-network, which has to be distinguished from a dynamics-on-a-network, where the network structure remains stable but the behavior of the actors is changing over time (Watts, 2003, 54–55). These micro-based phenomena may then lead to characteristic macro or network structures such as the growth or the decline of network, the formation of subcomponents and the dissolution of subcomponents as they fuse into one large component (Fleming and Frenken, 2007), as well as in certain core-periphery structures which show a considerable stability over time.

5.1   Innovation Network Dynamics and the Stability of Network Structures

The dynamics of innovation networks show some specific features related to the (latent) public good feature of information and knowledge. A fundamental point is addressed by comparing the situation of the cooperating partners before and after knowledge exchange. Consider two actors, I and II, who possess several knowledge categories, A to E, and only differ in their competences in B and C, with I being more competent in B and II being more competent in C. In this situation the interests of both to exchange knowledge, the required mutual understanding, as well as the reciprocal benefits are assumed to be given. Consequently, knowledge exchange takes place and – assuming no changes in knowledge categories A, D, and E – may lead to a situation in which I and II show the same, identical expertise in each of the knowledge categories A to E. As soon as this is reached, any further exchange of information and knowledge does not lead to any additional insights for either partner. Consequently, the common interest to exchange information and knowledge has been extinguished. Hence, what we observe and have to take into account in analysing the development and evolution of networks is that the very reasons for undertaking these exchanges, the differences in competencies and knowledge between actors, are vanishing and by this their interest in further collaboration (Cowan et al., 2006).

5.2   Mechanisms of Formation and Evolution

5.2.1   Preferential attachment and path dependency

In the dynamics of networks, preferential attachment is one of the mechanisms that play a major role (Barabasi and Albert, 1999). It describes the dynamics as a process in which the formation of a link from actor I to actor II is dependent on the existing number of links of actor II. The number of links of an actor may serve as an indication of the precious knowledge stock this actor holds or of the cooperative success this actor already has accumulated. Along these lines, Ahuja (2000b) and Stuart (2000) find that firms with more patents are more likely to form further alliances than firms lacking patents.

This suggests that network position and innovation performance constitute a virtuous cycle, implying that the rate of acquisition of information and knowledge from the outside is closely linked to the internally generated expertise and vice versa. Powell et al. (1996) find for the global biotechnology industry that firms which develop experience in managing collaborative R&D relationships garner faster access to centrally positioned organizations. Through accumulating experience in collaboration, firms are able to widen their cooperative network, increase their diversity of partners, and become more visible in the industry (Powell et al., 2005). By a feedback loop a more central position leads to growth in size with a positive influence on the financial situation of the firm accompanied by the ability to coordinate more alliances (Powell et al., 1999).

For the local innovation system of Jena, represented by an innovator network, Cantner and Graf (2006) find that actors entering the system tie themselves rather close to the core of the network made up by actors with a relatively high number of ties and collaboration partners. Compared to that, actors exiting the system are connected mainly to actors in the periphery of the network.

Preferential attachment can also be interpreted on the lines of trustworthiness. Trust within a collaboration might be given right from the beginning (*ex ante* trust) but it may also be developed over time by repeated collaborative projects (*ex post* trust). Lorenzoni and Lipparini (1999) find in a case study on three Italian packaging machine manufacturers that large-scale networks with trustful, repeated and tight relationships to other firms, especially suppliers, increase the innovativeness of a firm. Gulati (1995) shows that partners tend to ally with those close to them in the network and with whom they have previously allied. For the Jena case (Cantner and Graf, 2006), however, the likelihood of an actor to form a new tie in the next period is negatively related to having cooperated in the former period. This raises the question whether the relevant level of trust is related to the dyad relation only or to the system in general. In the latter case, this would imply that a frequent switching between collaboration partners is just taking advantage of specific creative potentials imbedded in a general sphere of broad trust. In the Jena case the connectedness to incumbent collaboration partners increases over time, just sustaining the interpretation of a system wide level of trust.

Network dynamics governed by preferential attachment lead to a sustained core-periphery structure with a few large (in terms of economic, innovative or collaborative success) actors in the core and smaller ones in the periphery (Orsenigo et al., 1998). Clearly, a skewed distribution of the number of ties per actor develops – a case of a scale free network. In a theoretical study, Cowan and Jonard (2007) investigate the implications of a skewed degree distribution on R&D networks. They argue that a skewed network is robust to random failures, but not to specific failures that affect the performance of a star in the network. On the other hand stars can accelerate the diffusion of knowledge through their multitude of relations.

As such, preferential attachment leads to increased clustering; the evolution of an industry then accomplishes a shift from a Burt type of network to a network of the Coleman type. This shift in focus from creative potentials to trustworthy relations can be related to the type of innovative activity pursued. In an exploratory phase creative potentials seem to be of higher importance for generating new technological opportunities. Contrariwise in the phase of exploiting those potentials trust comes into play in order to secure and fairly share the respective rents. Core-periphery structures accompanied by clustering effects just mirror that shift from exploration to exploitation.

The Walker et al. (1997) study hints at a danger in this process as it limits search and therefore reduces variety. This might lead to a technological lock-in as noted by Boschma (2005) in his discussion of proximity concepts. Or as Kogut (2000) puts it 'Since the advantage of the market is the generation of variety, too much structure reduces innovation' (p. 415). However, interpreting or identifying clustered core-periphery structures as constellations characterized by local buzz and global pipelines (Bathelt et al., 2004), the risk of running into a lock-in situation is much reduced.

5.2.2   Homophily

For the establishment of cooperative linkages between actors homophily is considered another major driving force (Skvoretz, 1991). Here, the choice of a cooperation partner is biased towards those actors which are similar. This similarity may be due to close geographical proximity as in the case of clusters or local innovation systems. It may also be based on social proximity in the sense that friends compared to others are preferred cooperation partners. Looking at innovation, however, it is doubtful whether homophily in terms of cognitive proximity really counts. In order to draw on a creative potential, the cooperating actors have to show a considerable difference between their knowledge stocks combined with some overlap indicating the degree of mutual understanding (Nooteboom, 2009). In addition, in terms of trust a rather close social or institutional proximity is required. Hence it is a combination of homophily with respect to trust and mutual understanding on the one hand with some heterogeneity in terms of the respective knowledge stocks and knowledge pieces to be exchanged on the other.

Looking at the empirical evidence, there is some indication that an intermediate level of homophily drives the formation of ties in the future. For cooperation in innovation Mowery et al. (1998) as well as Cantner and Meder (2007) find that the technological overlap (measured on the basis of the IPC classes of their respective patents accumulated until t) between two actors in period t are positively related to the likelihood that they form a cooperation in period $t + 1$. Equivalently, Cantner and Graf (2006) find for cooperation in the case of the Jena network of innovators that the potential to cooperate in period t as identified by some commonality in knowledge and expertise (again measured by IPC classes overlap) determines the likelihood that these actors cooperate in $t - 1$.

With respect to the dynamic relationships between exchanging knowledge, technological overlap and further or continued collaboration three different dynamics can be distinguished. First, by the very nature of frequently exchanging knowledge there is a tendency of the technological proximity between two actors I and II to narrow down. This tendency might be counteracted by a second dynamics related to the potential of any one partner I and/or II to be able to create new knowledge by collaborating with other partners. Hence it is the breadth of ego-network (as measured by the number of different cooperation partners) of each of the partners which governs this potential. Third, by continuously exchanging knowledge with the same partner a higher degree of mutual trust is built up, alleviating and furthering collaboration in the future. Empirical evidence on these relationships is as yet not well developed. However, an indication of effect that by collaboration and exchanging knowhow the degree of overlap between two partners increases is found in Mowery et al. (1998).

5.2.3 Triadic closure

Another force driving network dynamics is triadic closure. It describes the tendency that the collaboration partners of an actor form ties among themselves. For the network dynamics this implies that two actors having one cooperation partner in common are more likely to form a new tie than two actors who are not connected indirectly. Consequently, former indirect ties among actors are turned into direct ones leading to closed triads in a network. Over time this leads to dense cliques of interconnected actors within the network (Skvoretz, 1991).

Dyer and Nobeoka (2000) show how the Toyota production network evolves from a structure characterized by weak ties and numerous structural holes in which mainly codified knowledge is exchanged to a configuration that is based on strong ties and where the structural holes have been closed. This change in structure allowed the network members to increasingly share tacit knowledge. On the other hand Walker et al. (1997) find that brokering positions are persistent, indicating that the exploitation of structural holes is especially profitable.

An explicit test of the mechanisms guiding network evolution is performed by ter Wal (2009) for the inventor network in German biotechnology between 1970 and 1995. He shows that triadic closure gains importance in situations of knowledge exploitation which are characterized by higher levels of knowledge codification and associated risks of unintended knowledge spillovers. This suggests that the transition from exploration to exploitation is accompanied by a process leading to increased clustering through triadic closure and hence from Burt type of networks to a Coleman type.

6. CONCLUSION

In this chapter we reviewed the literature on the basic foundation, the structure-performance relationship and the dynamics of innovation networks. Actors, heterogeneous in the technological knowledge and competences, who seek to cooperate do so for getting access to other actors' knowledge and exchange it against own knowledge.

Connecting such cooperative actors, one ends up at a system or network of innovating firms. Consisting of bilateral knowledge relationships, the network of innovators shows specific structures and dynamics as it may change its size and its structure over time, new relationships come into existence, existing relationships may be cancelled, new actors join the system, and other actors leave it. The principal driving forces behind these structures and dynamics are mutual benefit of cooperating actors, their mutual understanding and creative potential as well as the trust/controllability concerns of the cooperating actors.

Many results on the influence of network position on innovative success seem to be context dependent. Context refers to the type of knowledge to be exchanged, the type of relation under investigation, the task to be performed in collaboration and so on. A robust finding is that relations matter in any context and not only the direct ties but also the broader network of relations. Relations imply access to a variety of knowledge sources but also impose costs of maintaining these relations. While in general, a higher number of relations seem positive for innovation, the problem of overembeddedness shows up whenever there are too many ties. Too much social proximity can then lead to difficulties in adapting to novel situations. Consequently, a network characterized by many structural holes appears to be well suited for exploration tasks, where a variety of external information is beneficial and trust is of minor importance. A dense network of relations is associated with higher trust as it may be needed for exploitation tasks. These ideas could be related to phases of an industry or product cycle where tasks change and the optimal configuration of the network as well. Trusting relations in dense networks show their value whenever complex knowledge is to be exchanged rather than codifiable information.

From our bibliographical exercise but also from our more in-depth review of the literature, we infer that the field of innovation network studies has developed from an interdisciplinary research area that included management, sociology, economics and geography amongst others, into a field dominated by management testing sociological theories on the benefits of individual network positions. While we can gain much insight from the micro perspective of business and management studies we have to keep in mind that the questions asked in these studies are related to the management of single organizations and their positioning within a network. The systemic view of innovation which takes a more macro perspective could benefit from the application of social network analysis but should also provide theories that have to be tested with data on the system level. Future research should go beyond the individualistic and often too static view and move up to analyse system performance. Theories of regional, technological, or sectoral innovation systems should provide a fertile ground for these endeavors.

NOTES

1. In this case of low proximity between actors, flexibility is high and the transfer can take place even anonymously. This mode of exchange or transfer of knowledge might work when knowledge is protected by intellectual property rights and licensing or buying a patent works fine. It might even work in the case of tacit knowledge as one can acquire it by hiring human capital.
2. When appropriate intellectual property rights are absent and the value of a specific piece of knowledge is not known, market transactions usually fail. In those cases a hierarchical relationship among actors may be a solution; here proximity becomes rather close. Paying scientists and researchers just as employees and

pledging them to deliver the knowledge created reflects a high degree of control. Such arrangements for knowledge exchange and transfer are found in large firms running their own R&D laboratory. Of course, flexibility required for creative thinking and exploring and exploiting opportunities is much reduced herein.

3. Discussing technological proximity as a source of new ideas and innovations necessarily leads to discussing the economic relationships among the interacting partners which internalize spillovers or positive technological externalities. From the point of view of economic competition vertical relations along the value chain are rather unproblematic as firms here do not compete on the same markets. On equal terms the exchange of knowledge between firms from different sectors as discussed in Jacobs structures (Jacobs, 1969) is not likely to harm the partners' respective market positions. More problematic in this sense are horizontal relationships (with spillovers of a rather Marshallian type) between the cooperating partners. As far as they compete on the same markets incentive problems may arise and their cooperative venture requires a more formalized and thus controllable design.

4. And here it is questionable whether in the context of innovation activities all the possible outcomes can be really contracted upon, not at least because these outcomes are often uncertain in the Knightian sense.

REFERENCES

Ahuja, G. (2000a), 'Collaboration networks, structural holes, and innovation: a longitudinal study', *Administrative Science Quarterly*, **45** (3), 425–57.

Ahuja, G. (2000b), 'The duality of collaboration: inducements and opportunities in the formation of interfirm linkages', *Strategic Management Journal*, **21**, 317–43.

Allen, R.C. (1983), 'Collective invention', *Journal of Economic Behavior and Organization*, **4**, 1–24.

Arora, A., Fosfuri, A. and Gambardella, A. (2001), 'Markets for technology and their implications for corporate strategy', *Industrial and Corporate Change*, **10** (2), 419–51.

Arrow, K.J. (1991), 'The dynamics of technological change', in OECD (ed.), *Technology and Productivity: The Challenge for Economic Policy*, Paris: OECD, pp. 473–76.

Balconi, M., Breschi, S. and Lissoni, F. (2004), 'Networks of inventors and the role of academia: an exploration of Italian patent data', *Research Policy*, **33**, 127–45.

Barabasi, A. and Albert, R. (1999), 'Emergence of scaling in random networks', *Science*, **286**, 509–12.

Barabasi, A., Jeong, H., Neda, Z., Ravasz, E., Schubert, A. and Vicsek, T. (2002), 'Evolution of the social network of scientific collaborations', *Physica, A*, **311**, 590–614.

Barney, J. (1991), 'Firm resources and sustained competitive advantage', *Journal of Management*, **17** (1), 99–120.

Bathelt, H., Malmberg, A. and Maskell, P. (2004), 'Clusters and knowledge: local buzz, global pipelines and the process of knowledge creation', *Progress in Human Geography*, **28** (1), 31–56.

Baum, J.A.C., Calabrese, T. and Silverman, B.S. (2000), 'Don't go it alone: alliance network composition and startups' performance in Canadian biotechnology', *Strategic Management Journal*, **21** (3), 267–94.

Borgatti, S., Everett, M. and Freeman, L. (2002), *Ucinet for Windows: software for social network analysis*, Lexington, KY: Analytic Technologies.

Boschma, R. (2005), 'Proximity and innovation: a critical assessment', *Regional Studies*, **39**, 61–74.

Boschma, R. and ter Wal, A.L.J. (2007), 'Knowledge networks and innovative performance in an industrial district: the case of a footwear district in the south of Italy', *Industry and Innovation*, **14**, 177–99.

Braczyk, H.-J., Cooke, P. and Heidenreich, M. (1998), *Regional Innovation Systems: The Role of Governances in a Globalized World*, London: UCL Press.

Breschi, S. and Lissoni, F. (2009), 'Mobility of skilled workers and co-invention networks: an anatomy of localized knowledge flows', *Journal of Economic Geography*, **9** (4), 439–68.

Burt, R.S. (1992), *Structural Holes: The Social Structure of Competition*, Cambridge, MA: Harvard University Press.

Burt, R.S. (2004), 'Structural holes and good ideas', *American Journal of Sociology*, **110** (2), 349–99.

Cantner, U., Conti, E. and Meder, A. (2010), 'Networks and innovation: the role of social assets in explaining firms' innovative capacity', *European Planning Studies*, **18** (12), 1937–56.

Cantner, U. and Graf, H. (2004), 'Cooperation and specialization in German technology regions', *Journal of Evolutionary Economics*, **14** (5), 543–62.

Cantner, U. and Graf, H. (2006), 'The network of innovators in Jena: an application of social network analysis', *Research Policy*, **35** (4), 463–80.

Cantner, U. and Meder, A. (2007), 'Technological proximity and the choice of cooperation partner', *Journal of Economic Interaction and Coordination*, **2** (1), 45–65.

Cantner, U., Meder, A. and ter Wal, A.L.J. (2010), 'Innovator networks and regional knowledge base', *Technovation*, **30** (9–10), 496–507.

Cohen, W. and Levinthal, D. (1990), 'Absorptive capacity: a new perspective on learning and innovation', *Administrative Science Quarterly*, **35** (1), 128–52.

Coleman, J.S. (1988), 'Social capital in the creation of human capital', *American Journal of Sociology*, **94**, 95–120.

Cooke, P. and Morgan, K. (1994), 'The regional innovation system in Baden-Wurttemberg', *International Journal of Technology Management*, **9** (3/4), 394–429.

Cowan, R., David, P.A. and Foray, D. (2000), 'The explicit economics of knowledge: codification and tacitness', *Industrial and Corporate Change*, **9**, 211–53.

Cowan, R. and Jonard, N. (2003), 'The dynamics of collective invention', *Journal of Economic Behavior and Organization*, **52** (4), 513–32.

Cowan, R. and Jonard, N. (2004), 'Network structure and the diffusion of knowledge', *Journal of Economic Dynamics and Control*, **28** (8), 1557–75.

Cowan, R. and Jonard, N. (2007), 'Structural holes, innovation and the distribution of ideas', *Journal of Economic Interaction and Coordination*, **2** (2), 93–110.

Cowan, R., Jonard, N. and Zimmermann, J.-B. (2006), 'Evolving networks of inventors', *Journal of Evolutionary Economics*, **16** (1–2), 155–74.

Cyert, R.M. and March, J.C. (1963), *A Behavioural Theory of the Firm*, Englewood Cliffs, NJ: Prentice-Hall.

Deeds, D. and Hill, C. (1996), 'Strategic alliances and the rate of new product development: an empirical study of entrepreneurial biotechnology firms', *Journal of Business Venturing*, **11**, 41–55.

Dosi, G. (1988), 'The nature of the innovative process', in Dosi, G., Freeman, C., Nelson, R.R., Silverberg and G. Soete, L. (eds), *Technical Change and Economic Theory*, London: Pinter Publishers, pp. 221–38.

Dyer, J.H. and Nobeoka, K. (2000), 'Creating and managing a high-performance knowledge-sharing network: the Toyota case', *Strategic Management Journal*, **21** (3), 345–67.

Fleming, L. and Frenken, K. (2007), 'The evolution of inventor networks in the Silicon Valley and Boston regions', *Advances in Complex Systems*, **10** (1), 53–71.

Fleming, L., King, C. and Juda, A.I. (2007), 'Small worlds and regional innovation', *Organization Science*, **18** (6), 938–54.

Freeman, C. (1991), 'Networks of innovators: a synthesis of research issues', *Research Policy*, **20** (5), 499–514.

Gargiulo, M. and Benassi, M. (2000), 'Trapped in your own net? Network cohesion, structural holes, and the adaptation of social capital', *Organization Science*, **11** (2), 183–96.

Gilsing, V.A. and Duysters, G. (2008), 'Understanding novelty creation in exploration networks – structural and relational embeddedness jointly considered', *Technovation*, **28** (10), 693–708.

Giuliani, E. (2007), 'The selective nature of knowledge networks in clusters: evidence from the wine industry', *Journal of Economic Geography*, **7** (2), 139–68.

Giuliani, E. and Bell, M. (2005), 'The micro-determinants of meso-level learning and innovation: evidence from a Chilean wine cluster', *Research Policy*, **34** (1), 47–68.

Giuliani, E. and Bell, M. (2008), 'Industrial clusters and the evolution of their knowledge networks: back again to Chile', Technical report 171, SPRU.

Godoe, H. (2000), 'Innovation regimes, R&D and radical innovations in telecommunications', *Research Policy*, **29**, 1033–46.

Graf, H. (2011), 'Gatekeepers in regional networks of innovators', *Cambridge Journal of Economics*, **35** (1), 173–98.

Graf, H. and Henning, T. (2009), 'Public research in regional networks of innovators: a comparative study of four East German regions', *Regional Studies*, **43** (10), 1349–68.

Graf, H. and Krüger, J. (2009), 'The performance of gatekeepers in innovator networks', Jena Economic Research Papers 2009-058.

Granovetter, M. (1973), 'The strength of weak ties', *American Journal of Sociology*, **78**, 1360–80.

Griliches, Z. (1992), 'The search for R&D spillovers', *Scandinavian Journal of Economics*, **94**, 29–47.

Gulati, R. (1995), 'Social structure and alliance formation pattern: a longitudinal analysis', *Administrative Science Quarterly*, **40** (4), 619–52.

Gulati, R. (1998), 'Alliances and networks', *Strategic Management Journal*, **19** (4), 293–317.

Hakansson, H. (ed.) (1987), *Industrial Technological Development: A Network Approach*, London: Croom Helm.

Imai, K.-I. and Baba, Y. (1989), 'Systemic innovation and cross-border networks', paper presented at the International Seminar on the Contributions of Science and Technology to Economic Growth, OECD, Paris, June.

Jacobs, J. (1969), *The Economy of Cities*, New York: Random House.

Jaffe, A.B., Trajtenberg, M. and Henderson, R. (1993), 'Geographic localization of knowledge spillovers as evidenced by patent citations', *Quarterly Journal of Economics*, **108** (3), 577–98.

Keeble, D., Lawson, C., Moore, B. and Wilkinson, F. (1999), 'Collective learning processes, networking and "institutional thickness" in the Cambridge region', *Regional Studies*, **33** (4), 319–32.

Kline, S. and Rosenberg, N. (1986), 'An overview of innovation', in Landau, R. and Rosenberg, N. (eds), *The Positive Sum Strategy*, Washington: National Academy Press, pp. 275–305.

Knight, F.H. (1921), *Risk, Uncertainty and Profit*, New York: AM Kelly.

Kogut, B. (2000), 'The network as knowledge: generative rules and the emergence of structure', *Strategic Management Journal*, **21**, 405–25.

Kogut, B. and Zander, U. (1992), 'Knowledge of the firm, combinative capabilities, and the replication of technology', *Organization Science*, **3** (3), 383–97.

Lane, L. and Lubatkin, M. (1998), 'Relative absorptive capacity and interorganizational learning', *Strategic Management Journal*, **19**, 461–77.

Lorenzoni, G. and Lipparini, A. (1999), 'The leveraging of interfirm relationships as a distinctive organizational capability: a longitudinal study', *Strategic Management Journal*, **20**, 317–38.

Lundvall, B. (ed.) (1992), *National Systems of Innovation: Towards a Theory of Innovation and Interactive Learning*, London: Pinter Publishers.

Mansfield, E. (1961), 'Technical change and the rate of imitation', *Econometrica*, **29** (4), 741–66.

Moody, J. (2004), 'The structure of a social science collaboration network', *American Sociological Review*, **69**, 213–38.

Morrison, A. and Rabellotti, R. (2009), 'Knowledge and information networks in an Italian wine cluster', *European Planning Studies*, **17** (7), 983–1006.

Mowery, D.C., Nelson, R.R., Sampat, B. and Ziedonis, A. (2004), *Ivory Tower and Industrial Innovation: Technology Transfer before and after Bayh–Dole*, Stanford: Stanford University Press.

Mowery, D.C., Oxley, J.E. and Silverman, B.S. (1998), 'Technology overlap and interfirm cooperation: implications for the resource-based view of the firm', *Research Policy*, **27** (5), 507–23.

Nelson, R.R. (1989), 'What is private and what is public about technology?', *Science, Technology & Human Values*, **14** (3), 229–41.

Nelson, R.R. (ed.) (1993), *National Innovation Systems: A Comparative Analysis*, New York: Oxford University Press.

Nelson, R.R. and Winter, S.G. (1977), 'In search of a useful theory of innovation', *Research Policy*, **6** (1), 36–76.

Nelson, R.R. and Winter, S.G. (1982), *An Evolutionary Theory of Economic Change*, Cambridge, MA: Harvard University Press.

Nooteboom, B. (1999), 'Innovation, learning and industrial organisation', *Cambridge Journal of Economics*, **23** (2), 127–50.

Nooteboom, B. (2009), *A Cognitive Theory of the Firm. Learning, Governance and Dynamic Capabilities*, Cheltenham, UK and Northampton, MA, USA: Edward Elgar.

Nuvolari, A. (2004), 'Collective invention during the British Industrial Revolution: the case of the Cornish pumping engine', *Cambridge Journal of Economics*, **28** (3), 347–63.

Orsenigo, L., Pammolli, F., Riccaboni, M., Bonaccorsi, A. and Turchetti, G. (1998), 'The evolution of knowledge and the dynamics of an industry network', *Journal of Management and Governance*, **1** (2), 147–75.

Owen-Smith, J. and Powell, W.W. (2004), 'Knowledge networks as channels and conduits: the effects of spillovers in the Boston biotechnology community', *Organization Science*, **15** (1), 5–21.

Penrose, E.T. (1959), *The Theory of the Growth of the Firm*, New York: Wiley.

Piore, M.J. and Sabel, C.F. (1984), *The Second Industrial Divide: Possibilities for Prosperity*, New York: Basic Books.

Polanyi, M. (1967), *The Tacit Dimension*, New York: Anchor Books.

Porter, M.E. (1990), *The Competitive Advantages of Nations*, London: Macmillan.

Powell, W.W., Koput, K.W. and Smith-Doerr, L. (1996), 'Interorganizational collaboration and the locus of innovation: networks of learning in biotechnology', *Administrative Science Quarterly*, **41** (1), 116–45.

Powell, W.W., Koput, K.W., Smith-Doerr, L. and Owen-Smith, J. (1999), 'Network position and firm performance', in Andrews, S. and Knoke, D. (eds), *Research in the Sociology of Organizations*, vol. 16, JAI Press, pp. 129–59.

Powell, W.W., White, D.R., Koput, K.W. and Owen-Smith, J. (2005), 'Network dynamics and field evolution: the growth of interorganizational collaboration in the life sciences', *American Journal of Sociology*, **110** (4), 1132–1205.

Rosenberg, N. (1982), *Inside the Black Box: Technology and Economics*, Cambridge, MA: Cambridge University Press.

Rosenberg, N. and Nelson, R.R. (1994), 'American universities and technical advance in industry', *Research Policy*, **23**, 323–48.

Rowley, T.J., Behrens, D. and Krackhardt, D. (2000), 'Redundant governance structures: an analysis of structural and relational embeddedness in the steel and semiconductor industries', *Strategic Management Journal*, **21** (3), 369–86.

Ruef, M. (2002), 'Strong ties, weak ties and islands: structural and cultural predictors of organizational innovation', *Industrial and Corporate Change*, **11** (3), 427–49.
Saxenian, A. (1994), *Regional Advantage*, Cambridge, MA: Harvard University Press.
Schilling, M.A. and Phelps, C.C. (2007), 'Interfirm collaboration networks: the impact of large-scale network structure on firm innovation', *Management Science*, **53** (7), 1113–26.
Schrader, S. (1991), 'Informal technology transfer between firms: cooperation through information trading', *Research Policy*, **20**, 153–70.
Schumpeter, J.A. (1934), *The Theory of Economic Development*, Cambridge, MA: Harvard University Press.
Shan, W., Walker, G. and Kogut, B. (1994), 'Interfirm cooperation and startup innovation in the biotechnology industry', *Strategic Management Journal*, **15** (5), 387–94.
Simon, H.A. (1955), 'A behavioural model of rational choice', *Quarterly Journal of Economics*, **69** (1), 99–118.
Skvoretz, J. (1991), 'Theoretical and methodological models of networks and relations', *Social Networks*, **13** (3), 275–300.
Sorenson, O., Rivkin, J.W. and Fleming, L. (2006), 'Complexity, networks and knowledge flow', *Research Policy*, **35** (7), 994–1017.
Stuart, T.E. (1998), 'Network positions and propensities to collaborate: an investigation of strategic alliance formation in a high-technology industry', *Administrative Science Quarterly*, **43** (3), 668–98.
Stuart, T.E. (2000), 'Interorganizational alliances and the performance of firms: a study of growth and innovation rates in a high-technology industry', *Strategic Management Journal*, **21** (8), 791–811.
Teece, D.J. (1986), 'Profiting from technological innovation: implications for integration, collaboration, licensing and public policy', *Research Policy*, **15**, 285–305.
Teece, D.J. (1988), 'Technological change and the nature of the firm', in Dosi, G., Freeman, C., Nelson, R., Silverberg, G. and Soete, L. (eds), *Technical Change and Economic Theory*, London: Pinter Publishers, pp. 256–81.
ter Wal, A.L.J. (2008), 'Cluster emergence and network evolution: a longitudinal analysis of the inventor network in Sophia-Antipolis', *Papers in Evolutionary Economic Geography*, 08.10.
ter Wal, A.L.J. (2009), 'The dynamics of the inventor network in German biotechnology: geographical proximity versus triadic closure', Druid Summer Conference.
Tsai, W. (2001), 'Knowledge transfer in intraorganizational networks: effects of network position and absorptive capacity on business unit innovation and performance', *Academy of Management Journal*, **44** (5), 996–1004.
Uzzi, B. (1997), 'Social structure and competition in interfirm networks: the paradox of embeddedness', *Administrative Science Quarterly*, **42** (1), 35–67.
Uzzi, B., Amaral, L.A.N. and Reed-Tsochas, F. (2007), 'Small-world networks and management science research: a review', *European Management Review*, **4** (2), 77–91.
Uzzi, B. and Spiro, J. (2005), 'Collaboration and creativity: the small world problem', *American Journal of Sociology*, **111** (2), 447–504.
Verspagen, B. and Duysters, G. (2004), 'The small worlds of strategic technology alliances', *Technovation*, **24**, 563–71.
von Hippel, E. (1987), 'Cooperation between rivals: informal know-how trading', *Research Policy*, **16**, 291–302.
von Hippel, E. (1988), *The Sources of Innovation*, Oxford: Oxford University Press.
Walker, G., Kogut, B. and Shan, W. (1997), 'Social capital, structural holes and the formation of an industry network', *Organization Science*, **8** (2), 109–25.
Wasserman, S. and Faust, K. (1994), *Social Network Analysis: Methods and Applications*, Cambridge: Cambridge University Press.
Watts, D.J. (2003), *Six Degrees: The Science of a Connected Age*, New York: Norton.
Watts, D.J. and Strogatz, S.H. (1998), 'Collective dynamics of "small-world" networks', *Nature*, **393** (4), 440–42.
Wernerfelt, B. (1984), 'A resource-based view of the firm', *Strategic Management Journal*, **5**, 171–80.
Wuchty, S., Jones, B.F. and Uzzi, B. (2007), 'The increasing dominance of teams in production of knowledge', *Science*, **316** (5827), 1036–39.
Wuyts, S., Colombo, M., Dutta, S. and Nooteboom, B. (2005), 'Empirical tests of optimal cognitive distance', *Journal of Economic Behavior and Organization*, **58**, 277–302.
Zucker, L.G., Darby, M.R. and Brewer, M.B. (1998), 'Intellectual human capital and the birth of US biotechnology enterprises', *American Economic Review*, **88**, 290–306.

16 The complex interaction between global production networks, digital information systems and international knowledge transfers

Jarle Hildrum, Dieter Ernst and Jan Fagerberg

1. INTRODUCTION

Innovation has traditionally been a complex undertaking, typically involving multiple actors at different organizational levels who combine diverse resources and ideas through repeated cycles of trial and failure (Van de Ven et al., 1999). This complexity has increased in recent decades as the knowledge necessary for innovation has become more geographically dispersed, and as the modes of interaction between innovators have become more variegated (see Consoli and Patrucco, Chapter 8 in this volume). For instance, in a recent report, the Economist Intelligence Unit (2007) observe a fast growing tendency among large firms to adopt global innovation network models in which R&D is being conducted in multiple globally dispersed sites. In this context, digital information systems (DIS) – meaning electronic systems that integrate software and hardware to enable remote collaborative work (Chandler and Cortada, 2000) – have been attributed a crucial role. Recent generations of DIS are said to be important because they improve people's capacity to collaboratively create, integrate and transfer advanced knowledge across large distances (Foray and Steinmueller, 2003; Ernst, 2003; Foray, 2004; Ernst, 2005c; Gupta et al., 2009).

Focusing on these issues, some authors hold that the interplay between local interactive learning and digitally facilitated knowledge sharing is becoming critical for competitive performance in many industries (Bathelt et al., 2004, Bathelt, 2005; Asheim and Gertler, 2005). For instance, according to Coenen et al. (2004), regions that are successful in harnessing and balancing both localized and remote forms of collaboration are likely to have a more diversified access to knowledge than other regions, and therefore be more innovative and competitive over time. Coenen et al. argue that, while linkages to foreign centres of excellence are important for novel inputs and sustained creativity, well-established local collaborations are often necessary for firms to access global networks and exploit foreign knowledge. This interactive local–global relationship, we propose, is crucial to understanding the complex nature of knowledge in the current economy and for outlining a complexity theory of innovation.

However, while there is by now an extensive body of empirical research on knowledge transfers on the local and regional level, the specific nature of international and digitally mediated knowledge transfers remain much less explored. Only recently has research begun to examine systematically the rising frequency by which firms choose to undertake innovative collaborations within the context of global networks, the increasingly intricate divisions of labor involved and the extensive use of remote interaction in such endeavours (Cantwell, 1995; Borrus et al., 2000; Ernst and Kim, 2002; Ernst, 2005a,

---

BOX 16.1   CONCEPTS AND DEFINITIONS

- **Digital Information Systems (DIS):** DIS are digital systems that integrate software and hardware to enable remote collaborative work (Chandler and Cortada, 2000). Recent generations of DIS uses the Internet as a platform for communication. Important examples are email, videoconferencing, collaborative computer aided design (CoCAD) and remote simulation and training systems.
- **International knowledge transfer:** International knowledge transfer is the process through which the knowledge possessed by one unit in one country (for example, group, department, division or firm) is affected by the accumulated experience and knowledge of a unit in another country (Argote and Ingram, 2000).
- **Information technology (IT) industry:** The global IT industry encompasses all organizations involved in the study, design, development, implementation, service support or management of computer-based information systems. Typical examples, are computer hardware manufacturers like Cisco, software houses like SAP, and IT consultancy firms like Accenture.
- **Global Production Network (GPN):** A GPN is an international multi-firm network centred on the value-chain activities of a network flagship company (Ernst, 2002b).
- **Network Flagship:** A network flagship is a corporation that depends on a global network of affiliates and independent suppliers to develop, produce and market its products. Flagships are typically either original brand name manufacturers (OBMs) or contract manufacturers that produce for the OBMs (Ernst and Kim, 2002). A typical network flagship, such as Cisco or Intel, breaks down their product value chains into a variety of discrete functions and locates them wherever they can be carried out most effectively and where they provide the flagship with necessary competencies(Ernst, 2003).
- **Global Innovation Network (GIN):** A GIN integrates dispersed engineering, product development, and research activities across geographic borders (Ernst, 2009).

2005b, 2009). As Håkansson has put it: '. . . the idea has recently been advanced that through the establishment of "global pipelines" it may be possible to convey . . . knowledge through other means than face-to-face contact. Precisely what sort of mechanisms are at work in such pipelines remains obscure' (Håkansson, 2005: 440).

A promising avenue for exploring this topic further is to focus on the recent expansion of global production networks (GPN), meaning global interfirm networks centered on the value chains of large flagship companies (for definitions of GPN and flagships, see Box 16.1). GPN are relevant in this context because they constitute important arenas for knowledge transfers between internationally dispersed firms, and because they depend heavily on recent generations of DIS to facilitate these transfers. Indeed, as Ernst (1997a, 1997b, 1998, 2002b, 2004) has shown in a sequence of studies from the electronics and information technology industries, GPN flagships outsource an increasing proportion of their value chain activities to globally dispersed independent supplier companies. Whereas outsourcing in GPN has traditionally been confined to lower-end stages of manufacturing, more high-end stages such as knowledge-intensive support services, engineering, product development and applied research are now being dispersed through global outsourcing (Ernst, 2005a, 2009).

For these distributed arrangements to function efficiently the flagships need to transfer knowledge more rapidly and more extensively than before, and to facilitate and coordinate these transfers they are making increasing use of recent generations of digital information systems (Ernst, 2005c). These arguments are supported by studies demonstrating a strong increase in large firms' investments in digital collaboration technologies (Gartner Group, 2007)[1] and by several large-scale surveys showing that large firms increasingly use such technologies to support their knowledge transfer activities (Eppinger and Chitkara, 2006; Boutellier et al., 2008).[2]

Taking the above studies as a starting point, one might hypothesize that the combined expansion of GPN and DIS is making it significantly easier and cheaper to transfer knowledge across distances. There are, however, important reasons to be cautious when assessing the consequences of DIS and corporate networking for the global mobility of knowledge. While there is much research on the individual topics of global production networks, DIS and international knowledge transfer, their mutual interaction is still largely unexplored territory.

The objective of the present chapter is to investigate the different conduits through which knowledge is transferred within GPN, and explore how recent generations of DIS are affecting these knowledge transfers. Through this, we aspire to throw new light on the complexity of internationalized knowledge transfers, and thereby contribute to the present volume's task of delineating a complexity theory of innovation.

We proceed by reviewing past literature about international knowledge transfers and global production networks in the IT industry. Here, we emphasize key operations of current GPN, the geographical expansion of those operations in recent years, and the different types of knowledge that network flagship companies need to transfer globally to efficiently carry them out. Next, we focus on two specific knowledge transfer activities that flagship companies have traditionally relied on in this regard: transfer of technical documentation and expert personnel, and training of employees in best practice locations. At this juncture, we give examples of the ways in which the utilization of two categories of DIS – computer aided design systems and e-learning – are currently affecting those activities. In the concluding section, we briefly discuss the potential implications of these changes for global knowledge transfers and the complexity of innovation processes.

2.   KNOWLEDGE AND INTERNATIONAL KNOWLEDGE TRANSFERS

In any discussion of how DIS affects knowledge transfers, it is important to consider how knowledge differs from information. These concepts are often used with the same meaning and this creates a lot of confusion. As Steinmueller (2002: 144–6) has pointed out, 'It is not knowledge that flows through the circuits of a computer network, but bits of data reaching people as information. . . . What makes knowledge more than "a body of information" is that it involves the ability to extend, extrapolate and infer new information.' This means that the capacity to exchange information is different from the capacity to exchange knowledge (Fransman, 1994: 715).

According to Argote and Ingram (2000) knowledge transfer is the process through which the knowledge possessed by one unit (for example, group, department, division or firm) is affected by the experience and knowledge of another. By international knowledge transfers, we refer to a process in which a department or firm in one country is affected by the knowledge and accumulated experience of another. Knowledge transfers are usually highly valuable for the recipient firm, but it is important to note that this is not always the case: if the knowledge to be transferred is inappropriate for and cannot be adapted to the new context, negative effects on performance can occur (Argote and Ingram, 2000; Greve, 2005). Although knowledge transfer in organizations always involves transfer at the interpersonal level, the topic of knowledge transfer across organizational and national boundaries transcends the interpersonal level to include transfer at higher levels of analysis, such as the group, product line, firm, region and country. In the present chapter, we discuss knowledge transfers that take place both at the inter-personal level in small teams, and knowledge transfers that take place at the inter-firm level in the context of global production networks.

During the past two decades there has been a considerable amount of research on the management of knowledge and knowledge transfers. Early contributions to this literature are characterized by a focus on inherent properties of knowledge such as codification and tacitness, how variations in these properties affect the spatial transferability of knowledge and what firms can do in order to convert knowledge from a non-transferable to a more easily transferable form (Nonaka, 1991; Nonaka and Takeuchi, 1995; Senker, 1995). Prominent in this first wave of knowledge management theories was a focus on technological solutions allowing firms to store and make available information and codified knowledge, such as shared databases and documentation systems. More recently, this research has been complemented by a second wave of knowledge management theories that put less emphasis on inherent characteristics of knowledge, and pay more attention to the specific social, organizational, cultural and technological circumstances in which individuals and firms share knowledge (Brown and Duguid, 1999, 2001). Indeed, the view of knowledge as embedded in social relationships and interactions has led many researchers to focus on the importance of social capital and the notion of evolving communities of practice (CoP), understood as people bound by informal relationships who share common practices (Brown and Duguid, 1999, 2001). In all types of knowledge activities, even where technology is very helpful, people require local communities of some sort in which they develop the skills and motivations necessary to contribute to those activities (Pan and Leidner, 2003: 73). Yet a challenge encountered in knowledge transfer initiatives is to bridge these local CoPs in distributed networks (to enable sharing across distances, not just within, local communities). As a consequence, much research attention has more recently been directed at DIS that facilitate collaboration and social community formation, such as social media and team collaboration software (Fuh and Lee, 2005; Gupta et al., 2009). The purpose of such systems when implemented in a corporate context is to facilitate a knowledge-intensive culture that encourages behaviors such as knowledge sharing and proactively seeking and offering knowledge across functional and geographical boundaries (Alavi and Leidner, 2001: 108). A good way to study this further is to focus on knowledge transfers that take place within global production networks in the IT industry.

3.   GLOBAL PRODUCTION NETWORKS IN INFORMATION TECHNOLOGY INDUSTRIES

To document the growing complexity of global corporate networks of production and innovation, we focus on the information technology (IT) industry, an industry that is unrivaled in its degree of globalization and thus serves as a testing ground for new forms of global corporate networking strategies. What happens here may well signal future transformations in other industries where global production networks have not spread out to an equal extent. Furthermore, emerging economies, especially those in Asia, are playing an increasingly important role as global competitors in this industry.

Competition in the IT industry is driven by rapid changes in technology and markets and by very short product life cycles. A defining characteristic of the industry is 'network externalities' (Katz and Shapiro, 1985). A company succeeds 'when customers expect that the installed base of . . . [the company's] . . . technology [will] become larger than any other,' with the result that the customers 'adopt that technology to the virtual exclusion of others' (Sheremata, 2004: 359). However, network externalities are not sufficient to gain and retain a competitive advantage. Equally important is a capacity to combine cost reduction, speed to market, and product differentiation through significant performance improvements (Ernst 2002b). This requires a broad portfolio of intellectual property (IP) rights and explains why innovation in the IT industry is cumulative rather than discrete (as it is for pharmaceuticals and biotechnology).

A second defining characteristic of innovation in this industry is fragmentation, or 'modularization', and its dispersion across boundaries (of firms, countries, and sectors) through GPNs. Progress in the division of labor in design (through modular design) has created opportunities for vertical specialization in both manufacturing and innovation, enabling firms to disintegrate the value chain as well as to disperse it geographically. Modular design has also provided ample opportunities for vertical specialization in the production of knowledge-intensive services, such as software, information services, engineering, and research and development (R&D). Innovation is being sliced and diced into modular building blocks of specialized tasks for geographically dispersed R&D teams. Innovation in the IT industry thus requires interoperability (or 'compatibility') standards that enable independently designed products and components to work together within a technological system (for example, a laptop, a handset, or a switching system). Increasingly, this process has taken on a global dimension, giving rise to global production networks (Ernst, 2005a).

A GPN encompasses both intra-firm and inter-firm linkages and integrates a diversity of network participants who differ in their access to and in their position within such networks. These arrangements may, or may not involve ownership of equity stakes. A network flagship like IBM or Intel breaks down the value chain into a variety of discrete functions and locates them wherever they can be carried out most effectively, where they improve the firm's access to resources and capabilities and where they are needed to facilitate the penetration of important growth markets. The main purpose of these networks is to provide the flagship with quick and low-cost access to resources, capabilities and knowledge that are complementary to its core competencies.[3] GPNs typically consist of various hierarchical layers that range from network flagships that dominate such networks, down to a variety of usually smaller, local specialized network suppliers.

The flagship is at the heart of a network: it provides strategic and organizational leadership beyond the resources that, from an accounting perspective, lie directly under its management control (Rugman, 1997). The strategy of the flagship company thus directly affects the growth, the strategic direction and network position of lower-end participants, such as specialized suppliers and subcontractors. The latter, in turn, 'have no reciprocal influence over the flagship strategy' (Rugman and D'Cruz, 2000: 84). The flagship derives its strength from its control over critical resources and capabilities that facilitate innovation (for example, Lazonick, 2000), and from its capacity to coordinate transactions and knowledge exchange between the different network nodes. We distinguish between two types of global flagships: (i) 'brand leaders' (BL), like Cisco, GE, IBM, Compaq or Dell; and (ii) 'contract manufacturers' (CM), for instance Solectron or Flextronics, that establish their own GPN to provide integrated global supply chain services to the 'global brand leaders'.

Increasing outsourcing and specialization are the fundamental drivers of this flagship model of industrial organization (Ernst, 2002a). Flagships retain in-house activities in which they have a particular strategic advantage; they outsource those in which they do not.[4] This includes for instance trial production (prototyping and ramping-up), tooling and equipment, benchmarking of productivity, testing, process adaptation, product-customization and supply chain coordination. It may also include design and product development. More specifically, GPNs typically combine global dispersion of value chain activities with spatial concentration of advanced processes in a limited number of specialized clusters. This combination of spatial dispersion and concentration implies two things. First, that some stages of the value chain are internationally dispersed, while others remain concentrated. The degree of dispersion differs across the value chain: it increases, the closer one gets to the final product. And second, the internationally dispersed activities typically congregate in a limited number of overseas clusters.

To exemplify these trends, let us look at computer design and manufacturing (Ernst, 2002b). At one end of the spectrum is final PC assembly, which is widely dispersed to major growth markets in the US, Europe and Asia. Dispersion is still quite extended for standard, commodity-type components, but less so than for final assembly. For instance, flagships can source keyboards, computer mouse devices and power switch supplies from many different sources, in Asia, Mexico and the European periphery, with Taiwanese firms playing a major role as intermediate supply chain coordinators. Concentration increases, however, the more we move toward more complex, capital-intensive precision components. Memory devices and displays are sourced primarily from 'centers of excellence' in Japan, Korea, Taiwan and Singapore, and hard disk drives from a Singapore-centered triangle of locations in Southeast Asia. Finally, dispersion becomes most concentrated for high-precision, design-intensive components that pose the most demanding requirements on the mix of capabilities that a firm and its cluster needs to master. Microprocessors for instance are sourced from a few globally dispersed affiliates of Intel, two secondary American suppliers, and one recent entrant from Taiwan, Via Technologies.

From these latter findings, we might draw several propositions. First, the rapid geographical dispersion of value chain activities suggests that firms within global production networks have become more proficient in transferring knowledge in recent years. The above described outsourcing arrangements would simply not work without being accompanied by extensive international knowledge transfers. On a more specific level, we might propose that the combined expansion of DIS is making it significantly easier and cheaper to transfer knowledge across distances. As we pointed out in the introduction, the expansion of GPNs in the IT industry has taken place in parallel with the widespread diffusion of advanced Internet-based DIS. Moreover, according to several recent surveys, large firms in this industry make extensive use of DIS to facilitate global knowledge transfers (Eppinger and Chitkara, 2006; Economist Intelligence Unit, 2007; Boutellier et al., 2008).

Second, the trend of concentrated dispersion indicates that there are presently clear limits to DIS-mediated knowledge transfers within GPN; the most advanced activities are still carried out by specialized clusters of co-located firms. This suggests that advanced firms depend on frequent co-located interaction with other advanced firms in order to tap into the most knowledge-intensive subsets of GPNs. This resonates with the arguments of Coenen et al. (2004) and Asheim and Gertler (2005) that well-established local collaborations are often necessary for firms to be able to access and exploit international knowledge flows. These authors suggest that, while linkages to foreign centers of excellence are important for novel inputs and sustained creativity, well-established local collaborations are often necessary for firms to be able to absorb and exploit external knowledge. The reason for this is a two-sided one. The first is that few single firms have all the capabilities in-house to supply advanced inputs – such as the production of computer hard drives or memory devices – to global production networks. However, by collaborating closely in specialized local clusters firms may collectively develop the competencies necessary to deliver such inputs. Second, single firms are likely to have difficulty developing the skills necessary to operate advanced international collaborations. But once a local cluster of firms has established a critical mass of linkages with (or pipelines to) global production networks, these firms might draw on each other's international experience and thereby collaboratively develop the skills necessary to efficiently manage those linkages (Coenen et al., 2004).

Judging from the pattern of concentrated dispersion and the above studies, we might preliminarily hypothesize that novel DIS has widened the scope for knowledge transfers within GPN, but that firms still require co-location to collectively develop the capability to participate in (and benefit from) the most advanced network activities. To explore this hypothesis further it is necessary to look more closely at the various activities flagship companies carry out to effectuate knowledge transfers within their GPN, and the ways in which recent generations of DIS have affected these activities. In the remainder of the chapter, we direct attention to the impact of two specific categories of DIS – web-based computer aided design (CAD) and e-learning systems. But first it is important to disentangle the various conduits through which knowledge is transferred within GPN.

4.   KNOWLEDGE TRANSFER ACTIVITIES IN GPN

The extensive geographical dispersion of value chain activities that is currently taking place in IT industries cannot work without substantial international knowledge transfers. These transfers involve a variety of agents, including flagships' subunits and affiliates, independent component suppliers, and contract manufacturers, as well as local technical and business consultancies that market, sell and service the flagship's products (for an elaborate description of these transfer mechanisms, see Ernst and Kim, 2002).[5] There are also many different categories of knowledge involved, such as managerial knowledge, technical knowledge about manufacturing equipment, production and product design, as well as knowledge about sales, distribution, installation and various customer-oriented business services.[6] While all these forms of knowledge transfers play important and interdependent roles in GPN, we focus in the following on knowledge transfers from flagship companies to local independent suppliers of components and services. As we pointed out in the introduction, we do this because we deem these latter linkages to be specifically important for local capability upgrading opportunities in emerging economies.

As we pointed out above flagships need to transfer advanced technical and managerial knowledge to their local suppliers to retain the competitiveness of their GPNs. It is necessary to upgrade the suppliers' capabilities, so that they can meet the technical specifications of the flagships and achieve high quality provision of product and services.[7]

According to Ernst and Kim (2002), there are two dimensions that are specifically important for analysing knowledge transfers within GPN: market mediation and the role of the knowledge supplier (the flagship). Out of these two dimensions, they mark out four distinct categories of knowledge transfer mechanisms (see Figure 16.1).

Quadrant 1 describes a situation where the suppliers are affiliates or formal alliance partners, and the flagship uses formal knowledge-transfer mechanisms such as foreign direct investment (FDI), formal licensing (FL), and independent technical consultancies.[8]

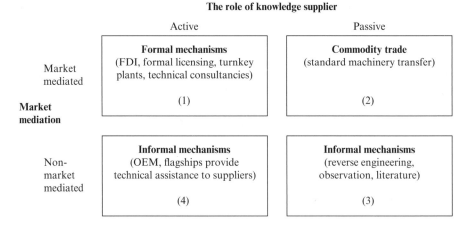

Source: Adapted from Ernst and Kim (2002: 1424).

Figure 16.1   Knowledge transfer mechanisms in GPN

In quadrant 2, independent local suppliers buy standard machinery to improve their productivity in production operations, thereby gaining new knowledge. Flagships are not necessarily the suppliers of this machinery, but they can play an important indirect role by forcing independent local suppliers to purchase more sophisticated equipment to improve their production capabilities.[9] In the third quadrant, independent local suppliers use reverse engineering, observations and the hiring of foreign expert engineers to upgrade their knowledge.[10] As in quadrant 2, flagships exert little direct influence over the way independent local suppliers use such mechanisms, but they may exert considerable indirect influence through increased quality and performance requirements.

Finally, quadrant 4 depicts Original Equipment Manufacturing (OEM) arrangements, an increasingly important way for flagships to transfer knowledge and upgrade capabilities within their global production networks. While these arrangements may appear similar to the ones described in quadrant 1, a major difference is that the suppliers under the latter are formally independent and therefore have greater opportunity to use the knowledge to their own competitive ends. While traditional MNCs relied heavily on activities in quadrant 1 in setting up their plants, flagships transfer knowledge also through mechanisms in quadrant 3. Flagships also tend to transfer more knowledge to their suppliers than do vertically integrated MNC. These transfers are necessary to provide the flagship with competitive products and services, in line with the changing requirements of markets and technology (Ernst and Kim, 2002: 1424) Under these latter arrangements, flagships transfer knowledge to their suppliers through two basic activities.

First, they actively transfer technical equipment, blueprints, technical specifications and technical assistance to ensure that products and services provided by the latter meet the former's technical specifications. But, in most cases, the acquisition of this equipment and documentation alone is not sufficient for the local suppliers to assimilate new knowledge and use it in production. To tackle this challenge, the flagships also send their own engineers to stay at the local suppliers' sites for extended periods during the establishment of new plants or the introduction of new products, processes or services. During these periods, the foreign experts help local technicians debug problems in engineering and manufacturing systems, or in carrying out advanced maintenance and service operations. In addition to immediate learning effects associated with demonstration and instruction, such visits might also serve to build bridges between specialized communities of practice across dispersed sites. More specifically, as flagship engineers stay in different local suppliers' sites, they typically engage with local CoP there, learning about local technical problems and expanding their personal networks. Later, after having returned to their home organizations and their own local CoP these top engineers might maintain regular contact with the supplier companies, giving technical assistance when new technical problems emerge. By virtue of having experiences from several internationally dispersed CoP, they might also take the role of broker, mediating contact between different supplier companies with similar challenges and complementary knowledge. Such extended visits and business travel might over time lead to the interlinking of related communities of practice at different globally dispersed sites, resulting in the build-up of global networks of practice.

Second, to complement the transfer of technical specifications and expert personnel, network flagships typically invite engineers and managers of the local suppliers to their best practice plants and other centers of excellence so that they can receive a systematic training in how actual production systems and products work. Such visits might include instructor-led training, observation of production processes, and actual hands-on operation of technology and equipment. This can help to translate the knowledge gained from the blueprints into actual operations. It also enables engineers from the local suppliers to understand how the flagship's organization and production systems are actually managed, and acquire knowledge from foreign engineers through hands-on training. Finally, these visits enable engineers from the local suppliers to link up with and engage in CoP at the foreign (best practice) plants, thereby establishing contacts and personal relationships that they can capitalize on after they return to their home locations.

Taken together, there are both formal and informal, market and non market knowledge transfer mechanisms. These mechanisms involve exchange of technical equipment and documentation such as blueprints, advanced training in flagships' sites, and most importantly, international mobility of personnel, involving socialization between engineers, on-site practical experience and – over time – the interlinking of local communities of practice and the construction of global networks of practice. However, the question remains of how recent generations of DIS are affecting such knowledge transfer activities. This is the topic to which we turn next.

5.   THE RELATIONSHIP BETWEEN DIS AND KNOWLEDGE TRANSFERS WITHIN GPN

The fast-growing tendency of GPN flagships to use the DIS to facilitate innovation and knowledge transfers is a relatively recent trend that started to expand rapidly around the turn of the millennium (Friedman, 2007; Boutellier et al., 2008). For an example of a global network flagship see Box 16.2. Until the mid 1990s, the primary function of digital information systems was to automate transaction processes and facilitate information sharing, but since then, the focus has shifted to Internet-enabled collaboration infrastructures that can support remote knowledge transfers (Battin et al., 2001; Gupta and Seshasai, 2007; Chu et al., 2008). During the same period, many firms have adopted novel organizational forms and collaboration practices which depend on DIS mediated communication (Gupta et al, 2009). For instance, digital design and prototyping systems are currently the norm in leading product development firms, and high bandwidth networks have enabled these firms to efficiently share their digital product designs on a global scale (Fuh and Li, 2005; Eppinger and Chitkara, 2009; Gupta et al., 2009).

At present, there is no single end-to-end system that is able to cover all knowledge transfer needs in a global production network. Rather, GPN flagships and associated network partners utilize a myriad of DIS which support the organizational processes of knowledge creation, storage, retrieval, transfer and application (Alavi and Leidner 2001: 114). Important examples are email, web conferencing systems, team collaboration systems, collaborative computer aided design, and digital education systems. As we pointed out in the introduction, these technologies have undergone a rapid development in recent years[11] and there is currently a widespread expectation that they will make it cheaper and easier to transfer knowledge within GPN

However, an important limitation in the research literature is that there are no

---

BOX 16.2   CISCO SYSTEMS: A 'WIRED' GLOBAL NETWORK FLAGSHIP

Cisco Systems, the world leading supplier of Internet technologies, offers an interesting example of a network flagship that makes extensive use of DIS to facilitate global knowledge transfers. Cisco's global production network connects the corporation to 32 manufacturing plants worldwide, as well as a myriad lower level suppliers, consultancies and sales & service companies. These suppliers are formally independent, but they go through a lengthy process of certification to ensure that they meet Cisco's technical and financial requirements. The core of Cisco's GPN operation is its website, which encompasses collaboration media and digital training resources associated with all parts of its value chain activities, including design, engineering, production, marketing and sales. Most of the interaction with the suppliers takes place through this website and only major contracts and highly complex projects are handled in person. Cisco has used the Internet and its own information systems to support its strategy in three main ways: (1) to create a business ecology around its technology standards; (2) to coordinate a virtual GPN that allows it to concentrate on product innovation while outsourcing other functions; (3) to showcase its own use of the Internet as a marketing tool. This strategic use of the Internet has allowed the company to dominate key networking standards and sustain high growth rates throughout the 1990s into the 2000s.

Source: Kraemer and Dedrick (2002).

---

studies that systematically examine the use and impact of this complex array of DIS in global production networks. Instead, existing studies typically explore how single DIS affects specific functions and value chain activities within GPN, such as the relationship between online databases and knowledge sharing among technical maintenance personnel (Brown and Duguid, 2001). While these existing studies do not allow us to evaluate the overall impact of DIS on knowledge transfers in GPN, they do allow us to discuss the knowledge transfer potential of these technologies.

In the preceding section, we singled out two kinds of activities that flagship companies have traditionally carried out in order to transfer knowledge to their foreign suppliers: (1) transmission of technical documentation accompanied by technical experts, and (2) on-site training of suppliers' employees in best practice locations. In the following, we review research on two important categories of DIS – computer-aided design and manufacturing (CAD), and e-learning – and discuss whether these technologies have changed the need for, and the impact of, the above knowledge-transfer activities.

5.1   Computer-aided Design Systems and International Knowledge Transfers

An important mode of knowledge transfer between flagships and suppliers is the inter-site transmission of technical equipment, specifications and blueprints, but there have traditionally been important limitations associated with this. As we pointed out above, advanced technical knowledge does not lend itself to be transmitted solely through the diffusion of blueprints and texts (Allen, 1986, for an overview see Olson and Olson, 2003). To compensate for this limitation, flagships have customarily sent expert engineers along with the documentation, helping the local suppliers make sense of this information to build up and improve their manufacturing or service capabilities (Ernst and Kim, 2002). According to several studies, the diffusion of recent generations of computer aided design and manufacturing (CAD) systems – understood as combinations of hardware and graphical software that automates the creation, revision and transfer of technology designs – have reduced the need for personnel transfers in this context (Foray and Steinmueller, 2003; Fuh and Li, 2005).[12]

While CAD systems have been around since the mid 1970s, these technologies have been undergoing a remarkable renaissance during the last few years. This is due to a number of technical improvements such as hardware advances that put 64 bit multi core computers into the mainstream, improvement of 3D graphical designs, new streaming technologies that allow for the efficient Internet transfer of very large CAD files and finally the interlinking of digital visualization techniques with other information management functions such as email and databases (Fuh and Li, 2005). In addition, there is by now widespread acceptance among engineers of the use of CAD systems to represent, integrate and share knowledge.[13] As a consequence, complex digital product models can be easily transmitted over the Internet and even downloaded into computer controlled manufacturing equipment that later converts these into physical products (von Hippel, 2006). This is an important advance over more traditional ways in which engineers exchanged technical knowledge, typically involving extensive face-to-face meetings and the joint drafting and exchange of blueprints and technical specifications.

For instance, analysing evidence from the global semiconductor industry, Macher et al. (2002) shows how CAD and other e-business software have facilitated international knowledge transfers and the development of GPNs in this industry. More specifically, these authors explain, what characterizes the evolution of these GPNs is the so called 'fabless-foundry' model of production: In the first decades of the industry, large integrated producers such as IBM and ATT took care of the design, manufacturing as well as the capital equipment necessary to produce computers. However, from the 1950s onwards, a group of specialized semiconductor manufacturers emerged, and later – during the 1980s and 1990s – hundreds of 'fabless' semiconductor firms that design and market semiconductor components entered the industry. These design firms rely on independent contract manufacturers or 'foundries' for the production of their designs. While the semiconductor design firms are concentrated in the US, Japan and Europe, the foundries are more widely dispersed in manufacturing sites across the globe, particularly South East Asia.

Although shorter product life cycles and requirements for cost cutting, as well as standardization and modularization of semiconductor technology, have facilitated the global dispersion of design and production in the semiconductor industry, new generations of DIS have arguably made this dispersion possible. More specifically, advanced e-business software such as CAD and systems for remote control of manufacturing processes have made it less costly to transmit advanced design and manufacturing knowledge between computer chip design firms and manufacturers, thereby reducing the need for physical co-location of designers and manufacturers.

Seeking to explain the impact of CAD (and other e-business software) on knowledge transfers in the semiconductor industry, Foray and Steinmueller (2003) claim that it is necessary to distinguish between traditional codification and more recent forms of digital 'inscription'. While the former concept refers to the representation of a particular skill by way of recordings and text symbols, the latter refers to creating a script that not only offers an adequate representation of the relevant skill, but also facilitates adequate execution of the skill by the recipient. By using new and powerful inscription tools, such as 3D engineering diagrams and simulation software, organizations are arguably much more capable than previously of creating scripts that facilitate the efficient transfer and re-enactment of tacit skills (Foray and Steinmueller, 2003).

In addition to supporting the transfer of design and manufacturing knowledge, web-based CAD systems are also becoming increasingly widespread as collaboration support in large firms' global product development activities (Fuh and Li, 2005; Li et al., 2005, Chu et al., 2008). This is relevant in the context of global production networks, because flagship firms often collaborate with their suppliers when developing or modifying their products. Collaborative CAD systems (CoCAD hereafter) extend a single-location CAD system to a multi-location CAD application so that two or more geographically dispersed units can work together on a digital product model (Tay and Roy, 2003). In a CoCAD system, designers and engineers can share their work with globally distributed colleagues via the Internet. Furthermore, these collaborative systems allow designers to work closely with suppliers, manufacturing partners and customers to get valuable input into the design chain (Li et al., 2005: 931).

Like the above described transfers of CAD models for manufacturing purposes, these web-based product development collaborations can also carry with them significant knowledge transfers within global production networks (Fuh and Li, 2005). For instance, analysing international product development teams in a global electronics manufacturing corporation, D'Adderio (2001, 2005), demonstrate how virtual prototyping software facilitates the development of online networks of practitioners. More specifically, D'Adderio argues, the digital prototype models – which are developed collectively by internationally dispersed teams of engineers – function as collective knowledge-repositories and as 'intermediaries' between geographically dispersed communities of practice. These communities, which focus on various technical specializations such as design, manufacturing, capital equipment and user-related issues, contribute distinct and complementary knowledge to the digital prototypes. Through repeated interactions around the prototypes, the communities develop direct interpersonal ties, shared work procedures and trust that might form the basis of what Brown and Duguid (1999, 2001) refer to as a global network of practice (NoP).

In spite of these opportunities, however, there are also important limitations associated with CAD and related DIS-based engineering and production tools. According to Söderquist and Nellore (2000) important drawbacks are lack of motivation of people using the systems, low reliability of the information being transferred, and low willingness to render information transparent. Macher et al. (2002) refer to other types of obstacles, such as standards related issues and data-security concerns. Moreover, they argue, basing inter-organizational collaboration and knowledge transfers on digital communication platforms requires far-reaching internal reorganization of business processes, especially by smaller firms. All of these obstacles, these authors point out, suggest that the realization of productivity benefits associated with CAD technologies are likely to occur slowly.

Similarly, in a study of CAD in large construction firms, Salter and Gann (2003) point out that CAD and other engineering software is not a simple substitution for older forms of communication. Instead, their study shows that these technologies are primarily being used to support older forms of communication and problem solving in engineering design (Salter and Gann, 2003). They also argue that engineers frequently suffer from information overload which is intensified by DIS mediated communication, and that personal contact and interaction in local communities is essential for sifting through the information. Drawing on a study of product development teams, D'Adderio offers a similar conclusion. According to her study, the success of collaborative CAD as a tool for knowledge sharing depends on the strength of local technical communities and their capacity to translate and make productive use of the knowledge represented by the CAD models. This latter finding contributes to explaining the pattern of concentrated dispersion of value chain activities in GPN. While web-based CAD systems have made it easier for firms to participate in global knowledge-intensive collaborations, they may require strong local collaborations in order to appropriate and exploit externally developed knowledge.

5.2   E-learning and International Knowledge Transfers

As we pointed out above, an important way in which flagships transfer knowledge to their local suppliers is to bring the suppliers' employees to visit their headquarters or best-practice production plants where they can observe the actual operation of technical equipment, and get systematic on-site training. While such on-site training is an important way of transposing complex and implicit forms of knowledge, it is time consuming and costly as it requires extensive traveling and the withdrawal of key employees from operative work. Several studies have examined whether and how e-learning might reduce the need for or even replace on-site presence and co-located interaction among instructors and students.

Since 2000, e-learning – understood as digital education and training resources delivered or enabled by the Internet (Weller, 2003) – has emerged as an imperative tool to acquire, impart and share knowledge within and across organizations. Recent estimates predict that the world market for e-learning will exceed 52.6 billion dollars by 2010 (Global Industry Analysts, 2007) and research shows that an increasing number of firms – among them technologically leading corporations such as Dow Chemicals and Cisco – presently situate e-learning at the core of their knowledge management strategies (Rosenberg, 2001; Trondsen et al., 2006). While e-learning has traditionally been associated with one-way communication of information mediated through various electronic documents (Rosenberg, 2001),[14] present state-of-the art systems involve extensive contact between students and instructors through interactive communication formats such as blogs and live chats, webcams and wikis, live online courses, simulation systems and interactive 3D computer game environments. For instance, Boston College is presently using interactive computer game technology to organize courses in advanced software programming. Logging in via their PCs, professor and student interact and work together as digital avatars using voice-over Internet to talk or ask questions (Newsweek, 18/25 August 2008).

BOX 16.3   REMOTE LABORATORIES IN CISCO

During the last decade and a half, Cisco has developed a comprehensive e-learning system to improve internal learning processes, and for the purpose of transferring knowledge to its global web of supplier firms (Trondsen et al., 2006). Cisco's e-learning system – which is famed as the state-of-the-art in the industry – consists of a large number of digital training and education resources, including instructional information recorded in various digital formats, online classrooms, electronic chat groups and advanced simulation exercises. A central part of the system is a network of remote laboratories, meaning fully equipped physical laboratories which can be accessed and controlled at a distance through a system of telecommunications, and robotic-controlled technology (Colwell et al., 2002). Technicians can access and operate the remote labs alone, but frequently they get online assistance from an instructor in the relevant field who monitors the lab exercises and who gives advice and step-by-step instructions on how to solve problems (Hildrum, 2009). The students and the instructors, who may be co-located or located in different countries, access the remote lab environment through personal computers with broadband Internet connection, and communicate by way of a video and voice communication link. In 2005, Cisco had 246 remote labs with 350 000 users worldwide, and was in the process of expanding the network of remote labs further.

Hildrum (2009) examines how Cisco's remote laboratories affect knowledge-transfers to the corporation's local sales and system-integrator service firms (see Box 16.3). These system integrator companies – which are dispersed across all major markets of the world – specialize in linking together Cisco's Internet backbone technologies (routers, switches, network software and wireless technologies) and employ a total of 350 000 Cisco-certified network technicians (Waltner, 2006).[15] According to Hildrum, remote laboratory sessions facilitate the exchange of complex and tacit knowledge between technicians who are separated by large distances. Regular online information exchange helps technicians gain a basic understanding of how advanced products work, but the remote lab sessions – where students and instructors jointly solve problems – facilitates the sharing of advanced technical troubleshooting and problem solving skills.[16] This corresponds to previous research on remote laboratories, demonstrating powerful opportunities for remote hands-on learning and training in various fields such as chemical engineering, microelectronics and telecom signal processing (Deniz et al., 2003; Ray, 2006). Nickerson et al. (2005) study remote laboratories and conventional physical laboratories in a mechanical engineering course, concluding that students learned lab content equally well from both types of labs. Similarly, Jara et al. (2008) present a study of robotic-controlled remote laboratories in chemical engineering, concluding that these technologies have a significant potential for improving learning in this area. A number of advanced educational institutions – such as MIT – are using remote lab technology as a means of extending access to laboratory work for science and engineering students who are unable to attend their physical laboratory classes (MIT, 2006; Ray, 2006), and these technologies are also becoming increasingly widespread in the corporate sector (Cisco, 2005).

However, while e-learning systems such as remote laboratories offer new opportunities for long-distance knowledge transfers, there are also important limitations associated with these technologies. Successful e-learning performance depends critically on the degree to which the users are motivated to use the Internet to acquire new knowledge. Indeed, several studies of e-learning state very high drop-out rates, explaining this by a lack of motivation or the inability to uphold motivation over time (Moshinskie, 2001; Bonk, 2002). There are many factors underlying different levels of motivation, such as task relevance, authenticity and the availability of meaningful feedback (Bonk, 2002) but in the perspective of Hodges (2004), the most important motivational factor is past learning performance and the feeling of mastering a task or a discipline. Students who have been successful in e-learning in the past are typically more motivated to engage in e-learning in the future.

According to Hardre (2001), it is possible to activate such virtuous circles of motivation and performance through the formation of local and online communities centered on the e-learning tasks in question. Communities are useful in the sense that they convene together people with similar skills and interests who engage in informal interaction, support one another and give meaningful advice and feedback regarding e-learning tasks and topics of shared interest. In a study of service technicians in Cisco, Hildrum (2009) suggests that motivation can be facilitated through the formation of online networks of practice (NoP) centered on the e-learning activities in question; however, in order to benefit from these networks people require a certain threshold level of technology user-skills and knowledge. This is most easily generated through interpersonal interaction in local communities of practice. Like the above research on CAD systems, Hildrum's (2009) finding supports the argument that firms require good local collaboration in order to benefit from knowledge flows in global production networks.

6.   CONCLUDING DISCUSSION

This chapter has explored various conduits through which advanced knowledge is transferred within global production networks (GPN) in the IT industry, and investigated the ways in which recent generations of digital information systems (DIS) are currently facilitating those transfers. The objective was to throw new light on the complexity of internationalized knowledge transfers, and thereby contribute to the present volume's task of delineating a complexity theory of innovation.

The global IT industry is characterized by a progressive shortening of product life cycles, fragmentation of products into intricate systems of modules and increasing international dispersion of the knowledge that is necessary for developing those modules. This in turn has created a strong demand for corporate networking practices and remote knowledge transfers. An important proposition of our study is that the combined evolution of GPN and DIS has significantly widened the scope for international knowledge transfers in this industry. The fact that GPN flagships outsource an increasing proportion of their high end activities to globally dispersed supplier companies, suggests that knowledge is being transferred more rapidly and more extensively than before. In addition, several studies have shown that flagship companies are increasingly using DIS to facilitate those knowledge transfers. For instance, while flagship companies have traditionally relied on transferring technical personnel to help their suppliers set up new manufacturing operations and services, there is evidence that web-based CAD systems are making it easier for technicians to share knowledge without being co-located. Similarly, new generations of e-learning systems make possible online technical instruction and hands-on training, thereby reducing the need for on-site technical training in best-practice locations.

At the same time, our study suggests that there are clear limits to DIS-mediated knowledge transfers in GPN. The pattern of concentrated dispersion indicates that there are presently clear limits to DIS-mediated knowledge transfers within GPN; the most advanced activities are still carried out by specialized clusters of co-located firms. This suggests that advanced firms depend on frequent co-located interaction with other advanced firms in order to tap into the most knowledge-intensive subsets of GPNs. Coenen et al. (2004) suggest several reasons for this. The first is that few single firms have all the capabilities in-house to supply advanced inputs, but by collaborating closely in specialized local clusters they may collectively develop these. Second, single firms might have difficulty developing the skills necessary to operate advanced international collaborations. However, local clusters of internationalized firms can draw on each other's international experience and management skills and thereby collaboratively develop the competencies necessary to efficiently manage linkages to GPN (Coenen et al., 2004). This interpretation resonates with the above cited studies of CAD systems and e-learning. In order to benefit from these technologies, firms require a certain threshold level of technology user-skills and incentives, as well as the capacity to translate and utilize digitally mediated knowledge inputs. To efficiently develop these skills, incentives and translation capacities, firms arguably require links to strong local communities and collaborations.

The critical proposition that emerges from this literature review is that there is a complementary relationship between local knowledge creation and DIS-based knowledge transfers. Instead of bringing about the demise of localized clusters, the dual expansion of DIS and GPN appear to make such clusters more relevant. These local–global linkages are particularly important in the context of the present volume, because they point to key complexities involved in current innovation processes, namely the practice of inducing and harnessing virtuous circles of local and non-local knowledge transfers. To understand more about these complexities, there is a need for more comprehensive evidence about the degree to which, and how, flagship companies use DIS to facilitate the diffusion of various categories of knowledge within their global production networks. In this chapter, we have merely discussed how two specific categories of DIS facilitate the transfer of certain types of knowledge within specific sub-sections of global production networks. This evidence is quite limited and has mainly been collected on the level of interpersonal communication in small groups. A key problem in the present study is thus to draw inferences from these specific team-level studies to the overall level of the GPN and the industries in which these networks are prevalent. Future studies should cast the net wider and seek to investigate how recent generations of DIS affect the totality of GPNs.

NOTES

1. According to the Gartner Group (2007), a strong demand for information sharing across business functions is driving solid growth for Internet-based collaboration technologies. Through 2011, the report predicts, web conferencing and team collaboration software markets will grow at a rate of 23 per cent and 15.9 per cent respectively.

2. For instance, drawing on a survey of 1000 R&D managers in over 100 large companies in the US, Europe and Asia, Eppinger and Chitkara (2006) document a fast-growing trend to use DIS to support remote knowledge transfers and innovation collaborations. Presenting a comparable study, Boutellier et al. (2008) conclude that new ways of using DIS to support knowledge transfer and innovation have appeared gradually but with a significant impact. Indeed, until the mid 1990s, the primary function of digital information systems was to automate transaction processes and facilitate information sharing. Since the mid 1990s, however, the focus has shifted to the establishment of Internet-enabled, flexible information infrastructures that can support advanced innovative collaboration and transfer of knowledge across organizational and geographical borders (Chu et al., 2008).

3. GPNs do not necessarily give rise to less hierarchical forms of firm organization as predicted for instance in Bartlett and Ghoshal (1989) and in Nohria and Eccles (1993).

4. It is important to emphasize the diversity of such outsourcing patterns (Macher et al., 2002; Ernst, 1997b). Some flagships focus on design, product development and marketing, outsourcing volume manufacturing and related support services. Other flagships outsource as well a variety of high-end, knowledge-intensive support services.

5. It is important to note that there are important differences between these knowledge transfer mechanisms and the areas in which they are employed. For instance, there is a big difference between knowledge flows from network flagships to smaller suppliers and the flagships' sourcing of smaller local knowledge bases (Ernst and Kim, 2002). In any case, recent research suggests that DIS play an increasingly important role in facilitating and coordinating these knowledge flows (Macher et al., 2002; Ernst, 2004; Boutellier et al., 2008).

6. Finally, each of these different kinds of knowledge can be more or less difficult to transfer across locations due to the nature of the knowledge in question (tacitness, systemicness), the strength of social ties between the agents involved, and the absorptive capacity of the receiving organization.

7. Once a network supplier successfully upgrades its capabilities, this creates an incentive for flagships to transfer more sophisticated knowledge, including engineering, and even product and process development. This reflects the increasingly demanding competitive requirements that we referred to earlier. In the electronics industry, product life-cycles have been cut to six months, and sometimes less. Overseas production thus frequently occurs soon after the launching of new products. This is only possible if flagships share key design information more freely with overseas affiliates and suppliers (Ernst, 2009).

8. For instance, when such flagships as Intel, Motorola and Texas Instruments decided to outsource assembly operations of their semiconductor devices, they took the mechanisms of FDI, FL and technical consultancies to establish their subsidiaries in the Philippines, and other countries in South East Asia. They insisted on majority ownership in the subsidiaries and transferred a complete production system.

9. This is also the case with suppliers of local marketing, sales and technical service. For instance, Cisco gives direct financial rewards and better competitive terms to the local sales and service partners that invest more in technical equipment and technical training (Cisco, 2005).

10. In Korea, for instance, the Small Industry Promotion Corporation and industry-related SME associations frequently organize observation tours of foreign firms as a way to acquire new knowledge. Human mobility in quadrant 3 includes not only the repatriation of top-rated engineers trained abroad, but also the active use of experienced foreign engineers who are hired for short periods of time.

11. Focusing on this issue, Ernst (2004) examines two interdependent paths of DIS development that gained rapid momentum from the mid 1990s onwards. First, the development and diffusion of open standard Internet infrastructure – meaning communication protocols (TCP/IP, HTTP), Internet languages (HTML, XML) and web server software (Apache) – allowed for the seamless interconnection of previously detached corporate communication networks, thereby greatly improving opportunities for information exchange. Second, the more recent emergence of e-business software which capitalizes on Internet infrastructure to facilitate knowledge work has improved opportunities for knowledge intensive collaboration across distances. At present, these latter technologies are being adopted by a rapidly increasing number of firms. According to the Gartner Group (2007), a strong demand for information sharing across business functions is currently driving solid growth for Internet-based DIS. For instance, the report predicts that web conferencing and team collaboration software markets will grow at a rate of 23 per cent and 16 per cent through 2011.

12. There are several methods available to create the digital CAD model. For example, the model can be

created interactively in CATIA, a widespread software application, starting from sketches made on the computer by hand, or it can be obtained by scanning hand-made clay models into the computer system. CATIA is the leading CAD application in the worldwide automotive and aerospace CAD markets (D'Adderio, 2001: 1413–14).

13. This is for instance evident from the currently fast-growing market for CAD technology. According to Jon Peddie Research (2008), CAD software vendors gained combined revenues of 5235 million dollars in 2007, which represents a 20 per cent increase compared to 2006.

14. A typical early generation e-learning system included a step-by-step sequence of instructive videos, animations and audio files interspersed with questionnaires that users had to click their way through.

15. The day-to-day work of these individuals consists of configuring, installing, troubleshooting and servicing end-to-end communication networks for public and private organizations.

16. It is important to note here that this study only documents the use of e-learning to support knowledge transfers among sales and service professionals in Cisco's global operations. There is little knowledge about how these technologies might affect knowledge transfer within more advanced operations such as high level manufacturing or R&D.

REFERENCES

Alavi, M. and Leidner, D.M. (2001), 'Review: Knowledge management and knowledge management systems: conceptual foundations and research issues', *MIS Quarterly*, **25** (1), 107–36.

Allen, T.J. (1986), *Managing the Flow of Technology*, Cambridge, MA: MIT Press.

Argote, L. and Ingram, P. (2000), 'Knowledge transfer: a basis for competitive advantage in firms', *Organizational Behavior and Human Decision Processes*, **82** (1), 150–69.

Asheim, B.T. and Gertler, M. (2005), 'The geography of innovation: regional innovation systems', in Fagerberg, J., Mowery, D.C. and Nelson, R.R. (eds), *The Oxford Handbook of Innovation*, New York: Oxford University Press, pp. 291–317.

Bartlett, C.A. and Ghoshal, S. (1989), *Managing Across Borders: The Transnational Solution*, London: Century Business.

Bathelt, H. (2005), 'Cluster relations in the media industry: exploring the "Distanced Neighbour Paradox" in Leipzig', *Regional Studies*, **39**, 105–27.

Bathelt, H., Malmberg, A. and Maskell, P. (2004), 'Clusters and knowledge: local buzz, global pipelines and the process of knowledge creation', *Progress in Human Geography*, **28**, 31–56.

Battin, R.D., Crocker, R., Kreidler. J. and Subramanian, K. (2001), 'Leveraging resources in global software development', *IEEE Software*, **18** (2), 70–77.

Bonk, C.J. (2002), 'Online training in an online world', CourseShare Report (January), Indiana: Indiana University.

Borrus, M., Ernst, D. and Haggard, S. (eds) (2000), *Rivalry or Riches: International Production Networks in Asia*, London: Routledge.

Boutellier, R., Gassman, O. and von Zedtwitz, M. (2008), *Managing Global Innovation. Uncovering the Secrets of Future Competitiveness*, Berlin: Springer.

Brown, J.S and Duguid, P. (1999), *The Social Life of Information*, Boston, MA: Harvard Business School Press.

Brown, J.S. and Duguid, P. (2001), 'Knowledge and organization: a social-practice perspective', *Organization Science*, **12** (2), 198–213.

Cantwell, J. (1995), 'The globalization of technology – what remains of the product life cycle model', *Cambridge Journal of Economics*, **19**, 155–74.

Chandler, A. and Cortada, J. (2000), *A Nation Transformed by Information*, Oxford: Oxford University Press.

Chu, C., Chan, Y. and Wu, P.H. (2008), '3D streaming based on multi-LOD models for networked collaborative design', *Computers in History*, **59** (9), 863–72.

Cisco (2005), 'Cisco formalizes education program, bringing new revenue opportunities to channel partners', Cisco Newsroom, 5 April, accessed at http://newsroom.cisco.com/dlls/partners/news/2005/f_hd_04-05.html.

Coenen, L., Moodysson, J. and Asheim, B.T. (2004), 'Nodes, networks and proximities: on the knowledge dynamics of the Medicon Valley biotech cluster', *European Planning Studies*, **12**, 1003–18.

Colwell, C., Scanlon, E. and Cooper, M. (2002), 'Using remote laboratories to extend access to science and engineering', *Computers & Education*, **38**, 65–7.

D'Adderio, L. (2001), 'Crafting the virtual prototype: how firms integrate knowledge and capabilities across organisational boundaries', *Research Policy*, **30**, 1409–24.

D'Adderio, L. (2005), *Inside the Virtual Product: How Organizations Create Knowledge through Software*, Cheltenham, UK and Northampton, MA, USA: Edward Elgar.

Deniz, D.Z., Bulancak, A. and Ozcan, G. (2003), 'A novel approach to remote laboratories', *Frontiers in Education*, **1** (November), 8–12.

Economist Intelligence Unit (2007), 'Sharing the idea: the emergence of global innovation networks', EIU Survey report for Ireland Inward Investment Agency, retrieved on 2 March at http://www.eiu.com.

Eppinger, S.P. and Chitkara, A.R. (2006), 'The new practice of global product development', *MIT Sloan Management Review*, **47**, 22–30.

Eppinger, S. and Chitkara, A. (2009), 'The practice of global product development', *Business Insight/MIT Sloan Management Review*, 21 November.

Ernst, D. (1997a), 'Partners in the China circle? The Asian production networks of Japanese electronics firms', in Naughton, B. (ed.), *The China Circle*, Washington DC: The Brookings Institution Press.

Ernst, D. (1997b), 'From partial to systemic globalization. International production networks in the electronics industry', The Data Storage Industry Globalization Project Report 97-02, Graduate School of International Relations and Pacific Studies, University of California, San Diego.

Ernst, D. (1998), 'High-tech competition puzzles. How globalization affects firm behavior and market structure in the electronics industry', *Revue d'Economie Industrielle*, **3**, 9–30.

Ernst, D. (2002a), 'The economics of electronics industry: competitive dynamics and industrial organization', in Lazonick, W. (ed.), *The International Encyclopedia of Business and Management (IEBM), Handbook of Economics*, London: International Thomson Business Press.

Ernst, D. (2002b), 'Global production networks and the changing geography of innovation systems. Implications for developing countries', *Economics of Innovation and New Technology*, **11**, 497–523.

Ernst, D. (2003), 'Digital information systems and global flagship networks: how mobile is knowledge in the global network economy?', in Christensen, J.F. and Maskell, P. (eds), *The Industrial Dynamics of the New Digital Economy*, Cheltenham, UK and Northampton, MA, USA: Edward Elgar, Chapter 6.

Ernst, D. (2004), 'Global production networks in east Asia's electronics industry and upgrading perspectives in Malaysia', in Yusuf, S., Altaf, M.A. and Nabeshima, K. (eds), *Global Production Networking and Technological Change in East Asia*, World Bank and Oxford University Press, Chapter 3.

Ernst, D. (2005a), 'Complexity and internationalisation of innovation: why is chip design moving to Asia?', in *International Journal of Innovation Management*, special issue in honour of Keith Pavitt, **9** (1), 47–73.

Ernst, D. (2005b), '"Limits to modularity – reflections on recent developments in chip design', *Industry and Innovation*, **12** (3), 303–35.

Ernst, D. (2005c), 'The new mobility of knowledge: digital information systems and global flagship networks', in Latham, R. and Sassen, S. (eds), *Digital Formations, IT and New Architectures in the Global Realm*, Princeton: Princeton University Press.

Ernst, D. (2009), 'A new geography of knowledge in the electronics industry? Asia's role in global innovation networks', *Policy Studies*, 54, August, East-WestCenter, Honolulu, USA, available at http://www.EastWestCenter.org/pubs/3242<http://www.eastwestcenter.org/pubs/3242.

Ernst, D. and Kim, L. (2002), 'Global production networks, knowledge diffusion, and local capability formation', *Research Policy*, **31**, special issue in honor of Richard Nelson and Sydney Winter, 1417–29.

Foray, D. (2004), *The Economics of Knowledge*, Cambridge MA: MIT Press.

Foray, D. and Steinmueller, W.E. (2003), 'The economics of knowledge reproduction by inscription', *Industrial and Corporate Change*, **12**, 299–319.

Fransman, M. (1994), 'Information, knowledge, vision and theories of the firm', *Industrial and Corporate Change*, **3**, 713–57.

Friedman, T. (2007), *The World Is Flat*, New York: Farrar, Strauss and Giroux.

Fuh, J.Y.H. and Li, W.D. (2005), 'Advances in collaborative CAD: the state-of-the-art', *Computer-aided Design*, **37** (5), 571–81.

Gartner Group (2007), 'Forecast: web conferencing and team collaboration software worldwide 2006–2011', Report G00149624. Retrieved on 6 April at: http://www.gartner.com.

Global Industry Analysts (2007), 'eLearning: a global strategic business report', Report no. 4107 (26 July), San Jose, California: Global Industry Analysts Inc.

Greve, Henrich R. (2005), 'Interorganizational learning and heterogeneous social structure', *Organization Studies*, **26** (7), 1025–47.

Gupta, A., Mattarelli, L., Seshasai, S. and Broschak, J. (2009), 'Use of collaborative technologies and knowledge sharing in co-located and distributed teams: towards the 24-h knowledge factory', *Journal of Strategic Information Systems*, **18** (3), 147–61.

Gupta, A. and Seshasai, S. (2007), '24-hour knowledge factory: using Internet technology to leverage spatial and temporal separations', *ACM Transactions on Internet Technology*, **7** (3), 2–22.

Håkansson, L. (2005), 'Epistemic communities and cluster dynamics: on the role of tacit knowledge in industrial districts', *Industry and Innovation*, **12** (4), 433–63.

Hardre, P. (2001), 'Designing effective learning environments for continuing education', *Performance Improvement Quarterly*, **14** (3), 43–74.

Hildrum, J. (2009) 'Sharing tacit skills on-line – a case study of e-learning in Cisco's Norwegian system-integrator partner network', *Industry and Innovation*, **16** (2), 197–218.

Hippel, E. von (2006), *Democratizing Innovation*, Cambridge, MA: MIT Press.

Hodges, C.B. (2004), 'Designing to motivate: motivational techniques to incorporate in e-learning practices', *Journal of Online Learning*, **2** (3), 1–7.

Jara, C.A., Candelas, F.A. and Torres, F. (2008), 'Virtual and remote laboratory for robotics e-learning', *Computer-aided Chemical Engineering*, **25**, 1193–8.

Jon Peddie Research (2008), 'The 2008 CAD report', Research report, available at: http://www.jonpeddie.com/publications/cad_report/, retrieved 6 April 2010.

Katz, M.L. and Shapiro, C. (1985), 'Network externalities, competition, and compatibility', *American Economic review*, **75** (3), 424–40.

Kraemer, K.L. and Dedrick, J. (2002), 'Strategic use of the Internet and e-commerce: Cisco Systems', *Journal of Strategic Information Systems*, **11** (1), 5–29.

Lazonick, W. (2000), 'Understanding innovative enterprise: toward the integration of economic theory and business history', in Amatori, F. and Jones, G. (eds), *Business History around the World*, New York: Cambridge University Press.

Li, W.D., Lu, W.F., Fuuh, J.Y.H. and Wong, Y.S. (2005), 'Collaborative computer-aided design – research and development status', *Computer-aided Design*, **37** (9), 931–40.

Macher, J.T., Mowery, D.C. and Simcoe, T.S. (2002), 'e-Business and disintegration of the semiconductor industry value chain', *Industry & Innovation*, **9**, 155–81.

MIT (2006), 'The challenge of building internet accessible labs', White Paper, Massachusetts Institute of Technology, available at: http://icampus.mit.edu/iLabs/Architecture/downloads/protectedfiles/ILab Challenge.doc.

Moshinskie, J. (2001), 'How to keep e-learners from e-scaping', *Performance Improvement*, **40** (6), 28–35.

Newsweek (2008), 'Tune in tomorrow: new technology and gas prices are driving a boom in online education across the United States', 18/25 August, p. 63.

Nickerson, J.V., Corter, J.E., Esche, S.K. and Chassapis, C. (2005), 'A model for evaluating the effectiveness of remote engineering laboratories in education', *Computers and Education*, **49** (3), 708–25.

Nohria, N. and Eccles, R.G. (1993), *Networks and Organizations: Structure, Forms and Action*, Boston, MA: Harvard Business School Press.

Nonaka, I. (1991), 'The knowledge creating company', *Harvard Business Review*, **69** (November–December), 96–104.

Nonaka, I. and Takeuchi, H. (1995), *The Knowledge Creating Company*, New York: Oxford University Press.

Olson, G.M. and Olson, J.S. (2003), 'Mitigating the effects of distance on collaborative intellectual work', *Economics of Innovation and New Technologies*, **12**, 27–42.

Pan, Shan L. and Leidner, Dorothy E. (2003), 'Bridging communities of practice with information technology in pursuit of global knowledge sharing', *Journal of Strategic Information Systems*, **12**, 71–88.

Ray, R.H. (2006), 'Learning without barriers: the MIT-Microsoft iCampus connection celebrates innovation', MIT news office, 8 December, available at http://icampus.mit.edu/news/articles/NewsOffice-Symposium. htm.

Rosenberg, M. (2001), *Strategies for Delivering Knowledge in the Digital Age*, New York: McGraw-Hill.

Rugman, A.M. (1997), 'Country case study: Canada', in Dunning, J.H. (ed.), *Governments, Globalization and International Business*, London: Oxford University Press.

Rugman, A.M. and D'Cruz, J.R. (2000), *Multinationals as Flagship Firms. Regional Business Networks*, Oxford: Oxford University Press.

Salter, A. and Gann, D. (2003), 'Sources of ideas for engineering design', *Research Policy*, **32**, 1309–24.

Senker, J. (1995), 'Tacit knowledge and models of innovation', *Industrial and Corporate Change*, **4** (2), 425–47.

Sheremata, W.A. (2004), 'Competing through innovation in network markets: strategies for challengers', *Academy of Management Review*, **29** (3), 359–77.

Söderquist, K. and Nellore, R. (2000), 'Information systems in fast cycle development: identifying user needs in integrated automotive component development', *R&D Management*, **30** (3), 199–212.

Steinmueller, W.E. (2002), 'Knowledge-based economies and information and communication technologies', *International Social Science Journal*, **171**, 141–53.

Tay, F.E.H. and Roy, A. (2003), 'CyberCAD: a collaborative approach in 3D-CAD technology in a multimedia supported environment', *Computers in History*, **52** (2), 127–45.

Trondsen, E., Landon, D., and Edmonds, R. (2006), 'Improving business performance through partner learning', Stanford Research Institute Consulting (SRI) report, August, Stanford, CA.

Van de Ven, A., Polley, D.E., Garud, R. and Venkatraman, S. (1999), *The Innovation Journey*, New York: Oxford University Press.

Waltner, C. (2006), 'Services shine for Cisco channel partners: focus on technical expertise coupled with consultative capabilities during greater revenues and profits', *Cisco Newsroom*, available at: http://news room.cisco.com/dLLs/2006/hd_031506.html, accessed 16 May 2008.

Weller, M. (2003), 'E-Learning', in Jones, D.C. (ed.), *New Economy Handbook*, San Diego, CA: Elsevier.

Wolfe, D.A., and Gertler, M.S. (2004), 'Clusters from the inside and out: local dynamics and global linkages', *Urban Studies*, **41**, 1071–93.

17 The complex dynamics of economic development
Verónica Robert and Gabriel Yoguel[1]

1. INTRODUCTION

In recent decades, the complexity approach has been adopted to explain some characteristics of evolutionary micro-dynamics by different heterodox authors (Silverberg et al., 1988; Dosi, 1991; Dosi and Kaniovski, 1994; Dosi and Nelson, 1994; Foster, 1993, 2005; Witt, 1997; Antonelli, 2007). According to them, taking complex systems as a framework allows an understanding of the morphology and dynamics of innovation systems characterized by (i) micro-heterogeneity in terms of competencies and linkages, (ii) temporal irreversibility, as a result of a dynamic driven by a non-ergodic path dependence, (iii) disequilibrium, non-linear interactions and feedbacks and (iv) the presence of institutional rules.

Nevertheless, some authors of the old development school and post-Keynesian economics have already dealt with some of these features, especially those related to macro-complexity. Kaldor (1972), Myrdal (1957), Prebisch (1959) and Hirschman (1958), among others, had already considered the effects of the economic structure on development, temporal and structural irreversibility, and the existence of divergent dynamics between countries and regions, reinforced by feedback effects between product growth and productivity (Kaldor–Verdoorn law), demonstrating that disequilibrium and non-linear dynamics have a long tradition in the heterodox streams of economic thought.

New emerging literature on development (Ocampo, 2005; Amsden, 2004; Reinert 2007; Cimoli and Porcile, 2009, among others) showed the necessity for the integration of the microeconomic-complexity described by neo-Schumpeterian and evolutionary theories of innovation and the macro-complexity reflected in Latin American structuralism. For example, some of these authors insist on the importance of studying the interaction between the evolution of productivity, aggregate income, and employment levels in the economy, on the one hand, and technical change, learning dynamics, and structural change that could promote or blockade the development path, on the other.

In spite of the macro- and micro-complexity identified by these streams, during the 1990s Latin America experienced the implementation of a model that stands out because of its utter simplicity: the Washington Consensus policies of liberalization and deregulation. The main assumptions of these policies were that trade and financial openness in the region would lead to increased competition and therefore successful performance in local and global markets, under the assumptions of perfect information, the predominance of decreasing returns and technology as a public good. Far from encouraging the development of skills in local firms, this openness brought about the destruction of the capacities built up during industrialization based on import substitution. The openness has also pushed for the internationalization of regional economies based on static advantages such as natural resources, industrial commodities, and low-wage labor-intensive sectors, which has provoked an increase in the structural dualism.

The region's poor growth under the Washington Consensus policies has revived the development debate. The overall objectives of this chapter are to present the major trends in this debate and to contribute to the theoretical integration of the micro-diversity of the evolutionary theory of innovation with the macro-complexity of the old development school under a general framework of complex systems in order to analyse some features of the development problem.

In the introduction to this book, Antonelli points out that 'an innovation economics approach to complexity thinking makes it possible to go beyond the limitations of both general equilibrium economics and evolutionary analysis into a system dynamics approach'. This is the case since for neoclassical theory innovation is not part of the economic process, and for the evolutionary approach innovation is formalized through stochastic processes and then remains exogenous (Nelson and Winter, 1982). The theory of complex systems applied to the evolutionary vision of the economy allows considering innovation as an endogenous property. Hence, innovation is not only the result of the intentional action of each individual agent, but is also an endogenous product of system dynamics. In this sense, innovation constitutes an emergent property of the system because it is not entirely determined on the micro or macro levels, but is – instead – a result of continuous interaction between these two.

Within this analytical framework, we conceive an innovation system as a complex system whose components – organizations, whether firms or institutions – interact and learn to develop their absorption and connectivity capacities, which define the architecture of connections. The interactions between the system's components trigger changes in its capacities. Thus, firms' capacities reinforce themselves through feedback mechanisms, allowing capacities and connections to co-evolve over time. Together, capacities and feedback mechanisms induce firms to undertake different innovation efforts. However, the results of these efforts depend, not exclusively on the firms' behavior, but also on the macro and meso dynamics. We propose that these dynamics can be characterized by the processes of creative destruction, appropriation and structural change, which in turn, will take specific features in developed and developing countries and will define whether the institutional framework is conducive or adverse to innovation (North, 1990; Rivera Ríos et al., 2009). As a consequence of the interaction between these processes and the firms' capacities, innovation endogenously emerges. We assume that the levels of absorption and connectivity capacities, the feedback mechanisms between them, and the characteristics of the meso and macro dynamics could help to differentiate developing and developed countries.

The main questions of this chapter are as follows. Why do different innovation patterns emerge in developed and developing countries? What characterizes the micro interactions (the development of absorption and connectivity capacities and feedback mechanisms between them) in developed and developing countries? What characterizes the processes of destructive creation, appropriation and structural change in developing countries? How do these specificities work in order to explain the way firms react? Finally, in which cases do system dynamics lead to an institutional framework adverse to innovation that limits creative reactions of agents, the generation of positive feedbacks between capacities and knowledge spillovers?

In order to answer all these questions, and following Antonelli (2007), we depart from the idea that the reactions of agents can be both creative and adaptive. Although we assume that agents are able to extend both types of reactions, in developing countries the adaptive reactions stand out. In these countries a productive and commercial specialization profile based on goods intensive in the abundant factors will prevail, which leads to a lock-in in their development path. To escape from this lock-in requires creative responses in the whole system. The creative responses begin with the existence of a critical mass of agents playing against the rules, which help transform the institutional framework. Playing against the rules implies intentional creative reactions of agents that threaten the technological, organizational, and institutional conditions on which quasi-rents are generated and distributed. This means not only promoting the creative destruction process but also the appropriation and structural change processes. The lack of this critical mass blockades the development of positive feedbacks, externalities, increasing returns, and therefore the development of the three mentioned processes. Hence, our characterization of developing countries is that there are indeed agents that play against the rules but there are not enough of them to change the specialization pattern and the main characteristics of meso and macro dynamics. According to North (1990) and Hoff and Stiglitz (2002), endogenous or exogenous shocks are needed to bring about changes in the institutional framework. We assume that the success of these shocks in changing the institutional framework will depend on the existence of a critical mass of agents playing against the rules that enables a phase transition to trigger relevant changes at macro level.

The rest of the chapter is structured as follows. In the second section we briefly introduce some questions related to the development debate in Latin America. The third section introduces the complex systems approach and its specificity to the study of innovation economics and development issues. The fourth section presents an analytical model that explains the dynamics of economic development within a framework that combines Schumpeterian and evolutionary innovation approaches, new development streams, and complex systems theory. In the fifth part, we will apply the analytical framework in order to discuss the specificities of development dynamics. Finally, the closing section deals with the topic of how the complex systems approach obliges development policies to be rethought.

2. THE DEVELOPMENT DEBATE: THE COMPLEXITY OF STRUCTURAL CHANGE

For the well-known development economics school of the 1950s (Rosestein-Rodan, 1943; Singer, 1950; Nurkse, 1952; Myrdal, 1957; Hirschman, 1958; Prebisch, 1959), the fact that the production structure in peripheral economies is a key limiting factor to development is explained by trade and production specialization patterns based on commodities and products intensive in natural resources, deteriorating trade terms, and deficits on the balance of payments.

Some issues related to complexity and feedback effects from a macro perspective can be found in these authors. For example, Myrdal analysed how the divergent paths in developed and developing countries are accumulative, because of cumulative causation between immigration, wages and employment. He stressed that the investment rate depends positively on the previous income level which is reinforced through several mechanisms such as increasing returns, increasing productivity and immigration. According to Myrdal (1957: 162), economy growth increases in receiving areas but decreases in sending areas, bringing about further disparities in wages and employment, leading to additional migration, and ultimately creating a 'circular and cumulative causation of migration'.

In the 1960s, Kaldor (1972) developed his theory of cumulative causation and its effects on dynamic increasing returns, competitiveness, growth, and productivity. The Kaldor–Verdoorn law synthesizes some non-linear dynamics and feedback effects derived from the relationship between productivity and product growth. According to McCombie (1983) the Verdoorn law forms the core of the cumulative causation models.

> The output growth of domestic prices is a function of the growth of wages and the growth of productivity, and the growth of productivity is a function of the growth of output. Hence an increase in output growth will lead to a virtuous circle, with the resulting increase in productivity leading to an improvement in the country's competitive position and hence increasing the growth of output still further. (McCombie, 1983:415)

Other post-Keynesian and structuralist authors (Braun and Joy, 1968; Thirlwall, 1979) followed a similar path and also considered the relevance of economic structure and the specialization pattern in terms of different income elasticity for exports and imports. By this means, all these writers, faithful to the Keynesian tradition, have been attributed a key role in explaining growth rates. However, they did not consider the relationship between micro competition and economic development (Metcalfe et al., 2003). Therefore, their perspective lacks a micro-evolutionary perspective of industrial dynamics and an analysis of the competition process that can take account of micro determinants of productivity evolution. Some attempts have been made by others to provide a micro foundation to the Kaldor model of growth (Boyer and Petit, 1991; Llerena and Lorentz, 2004), nevertheless they were not concerned with development issues.

More recently, several authors belonging to new development economic theory (Amsden, 2004; Ocampo, 2005; Palma, 2005; Ross, 2005; Reinert, 2007; Cimoli et al., 2009; Cimoli and Porcile, 2009) have made important theoretical contributions by combining traditional macro-structure analysis with the new micro-evolutionary foundations of innovation economics. They have criticized the openness and the specialization pattern based on static advantages and decreasing returns. They have shown that the low presence of sectors with high Keynesian and Schumpeterian efficiency in production and trade structure also acts as a constraint to growth. In this case, the problems of specialization are not only related to the macroeconomic effects of international trade but also to the weakness of micro and meso knowledge and technological accumulation derived from feedbacks between international competitiveness and technological capabilities, the lack of exploitation of increasing returns, and the low importance of knowledge complementarities and sectors with steep learning curves in productive structure (Reinert, 1995). In all these cases the micro-macro complementarities and feedbacks are in some sense present in their analysis.

Within a tradition of macro-complexity, the old and new development theories have insisted on the relevance of specialization based on sectors with increasing returns. Nevertheless, in recent years, the development debate seems to have swung back as a consequence of the sharp increase in the prices of food and other industrial commodities.

Since then, some suggestions for rescuing the specialization pattern based on natural resources have returned to the scene. This position is followed by the World Bank and other international institutions and is slightly different from the 1990s Washington Consensus but still remains extremely simple when compared with the old and new development theory mentioned above. For example, according to Lederman and Maloney (2007), 'overall natural resource wealth is good for development and becomes a real development asset when coupled with investment in skill and technological capacities and with good macroeconomic institutions and management'. Within this view, natural resource-based activities are not a resource curse, and from an econometric perspective natural resource exports have a positive effect on economic growth, especially at the recent juncture of high commodity prices.

Some recent heterodox streams are also linked to this approach (Lorentzen, 2008; Andersen, 2009; Pérez, 2010) which has an important background in Ramos's work (1998). Despite the attention that these authors give to the analysis of the characteristics of economic systems such as path dependency, heterogeneity, and learning processes, they remain very close to orthodox analysis, especially with regard to policy implications. According to Pérez (2010), the likelihood of Latin America succeeding in high-tech sectors is rather low. Asian countries that managed to catch up took advantage of a window of opportunity that came with the rise of the ICT-based techno-productive paradigm that has now closed. Therefore, Pérez stresses that by cleverly exploiting existing advantages of high prices, Latin American countries can become suppliers of material inputs, food, and other agricultural goods oriented to developed countries and exploit their expertise to develop skills and add value.

Although economics has complicated their arguments, they remain simplistic. As was noted by Ocampo (2009), the growth boom during the early years of the century was based on a unique combination of four factors that operated positively in the same direction and simultaneously for the first time: high commodity prices, growth in international trade, financial conditions, and exceptionally high levels of remittances. Nevertheless, the emergence of the 2008 crisis showed that these conditions could not be extrapolated into the future. The trade and financial liberalization policies the region experienced in the 1990s fostered an increase in import income elasticity that was not offset by a similar increase in the export income elasticity. This issue inhibits the region from successfully catching up with labor productivity in developed countries. Not even the favorable conditions in international prices have been a powerful enough incentive to produce increasing expenditures aimed at developing technological and organizational capabilities, especially in sectors with increasing returns to scale. Interestingly, despite the strong output growth over those years, the productivity gap between the US and Latin America continued to widen (Cimoli et al., 2009), which reflects the absence of catching-up processes even during exceptional development of economic activity in the region.

In this context, the new development authors have an interesting answer to natural-resources arguments by combining structuralism and micro-evolutionary theory. This stream has not only stressed the presence of several structural problems that should be resolved by changing the specialization pattern, but also the relevance of capacity accumulation at the micro and meso levels. As well as justifying the complexity approach, they point out the need to consider micro and macro interaction in a non-linear way and the impact of both on divergent development paths.

In this regard, the analytical model that we present in the next section explicitly introduces the complexity framework and remains very close to this branch of literature. The overall framework provided by the theory of complex systems can articulate macro- and micro-complexity to give a new meaning to the question of productive specialization and rethink the design of development-oriented policies. The new development theory starts building bridges between the micro specificities described by evolutionary theory and the macro conditions and macro feedback effect stressed by structuralism. Nevertheless, we think that the complex systems theory will help to provide theoretical bases not only for the integration between micro, meso, and macro dimensions but also to explain the evolution of the whole system as a consequence of the feedback between them.

3. COMPLEX SYSTEMS APPROACH TO INNOVATION ECONOMICS

The complex systems approach applied to economics and especially to innovation economics has grown enormously during the last few decades. Although most of these works were applied to developed economies, some of the main questions of development may be tackled from a complex dynamics perspective. In the late 1960s, Simon (1969) introduced, from a static perspective, the notion of the architecture of complexity to economics and modular systems. This stresses the existence of hierarchy and differential relationships between and within modules of an economic system, and especially the idea of simultaneous interactions between micro and macro dimensions. During the 1980s, the idea of self-organization, linked to the study of technological diffusion and competing technologies, was introduced by several authors that emphasized the historical time and the heterogeneity of agents in terms of capacities and strategies (Silverberg et al., 1988; Arthur 1989).

Since then, different authors linked to the Schumpeterian legacy (Dosi, 1991; Foster, 1993, 2005; Dosi and Kaniovski, 1994; Dosi and Nelson, 1994; Witt, 1997; Saviotti, 2001; Antonelli 2007; Metcalfe, 2007) have been using the complex systems approach to explain several aspects of innovation economics within the framework of variation, selection, and retention mechanisms which would account for the relationship between innovation and the processes of creative destruction and structural change. From this perspective, the factor that best explains the evolution of an economic system is the generation of micro-diversity from innovative processes that change agents' routines by interacting in a nonlinear way in conditions of disequilibrium.[2] The idea that brings this group of authors together is that according to them the complex systems approach helps to understand the dynamic nature of economic systems as highlighted by Schumpeter. Therefore, different evolutionary and neo-Schumpeterian economists have introduced complex systems to explain (i) the evolution and dynamics of a capitalist system as an open-ended process of qualitative change led by innovation, as Schumpeter remarked (Fagerberg, 2003); and (ii) the structural changing and self-organizing nature of capitalism, which concerned Marshall. From the latter perspective, Antonelli (2008) and Metcalfe (2007) also explain the differential dynamics of production systems on the assumption that heterogeneous agents have creative reactions. In particular, intentional behavior[3] explains innovation as an emergent property. Nevertheless, other authors use the complexity approach to account for long waves of economy (Silverberg, 2007), economic growth (Metcalfe et al., 2006) and changes in technological paradigms (Lane, Chapter 2 in this volume), following, among other ideas, those of self-organization, far-from-equilibrium dynamics, emergency and self-organized criticality (Prigogine and Stengers, 1985; Kauffman, 1993, and others).

Another group of authors, linked to the economic perspective of the Santa Fe Institute (Arthur et al., 1997, among others), has focused on the study of economics as an out-of-equilibrium evolving complex system. In this case, the emphasis is on the self-reinforcing mechanisms that may even work at an institutional level. Those authors are mainly concerned with (i) non-linearities and positive feedbacks emerging from increasing returns, (ii) the analysis of adaptive complex systems using the biological metaphor (Holland, 2004) and (iii) the history of technology (David, 1985; Lane and Maxfield, 1997). In these cases, they are interested not only in explaining innovation economics and technological change, but also finance topics and macroeconomic dynamics, without abandoning some neoclassical assumptions.[4]

Computational simulations of the Agent Based Modeling type and evolutionary games are frequently used as tools for applying complex systems theory to economics.[5] These models are used to understand innovation economics[6] through a neo-Schumpeterian approach (Silverberg et al., 1988; Dosi 1991; Dosi and Kaniovski, 1994; Dosi and Nelson, 1994) and from the perspective of the Santa Fe Institute (Arthur, 1999; and Tesfatsion, 2003). Other authors linked to the development of a theory of inventions (Fleming, and Sorenson, 2001) use fitness landscape models. Some authors consider that the physical percolation model helps explain the complex dynamics of technology adoption (David and Foray, 1994; Antonelli, 1997; Silverberg and Verspagen, 2005). Finally, authors that focus their analysis on networks and interactions (Cowan, 2004) have been especially interested in methodological tools derived from the study of economic and social networks (Barabási and Albert, 1999; Watts, 2003). Nevertheless, evolution is barely touched upon in this approach.

A common thread among the authors that use the complexity approach to analyse innovation is that they set aside the classical mechanics which have inspired neoclassical economic theory since the Walrasian general equilibrium model. Therefore, all these authors characterize complex systems by taking into account features such as irreversibility, uncertainty, spatial and temporal organization, and heterogeneity of system components. By introducing the idea of complexity to economics, these authors take into account contributions from other disciplines such as physics, chemistry, and biology, which in turn are fed by mathematical modeling (including non-linear dynamics, strange attractors, and agent-based simulations) developed in recent decades. Based on these issues, a complex system is characterized by a set of dimensions that include: (i) adaptive learning and interaction with the environment, (ii) positive feedback, (iii) emerging properties (macrostructure dynamics explained on the basis of local interactions at the micro level), (iv) ontological uncertainty, (v) the creative capacity of the system components, and (vi) the existence of order out of equilibrium (attractors).

In this regard, Metcalfe et al. (2006) emphasize the idea that the complex systems approach can account for some key elements of economic systems, which conventional economic theory has sidelined by resorting to the notion of equilibrium. This approach differs from the arguments supported by traditional economic theory in which equilibrium is considered an optimum state that requires the existence of perfect connections between system components, which implies the assumptions of perfect information (Foster, 2005).[7] Thus, contrary to expectations of conventional economics, the equilibrium of a system is seen, according to complex systems theory, as a situation of disorder and minimal coordination.

Some authors from the Santa Fe Institute also depart from the idea that complex systems can generate order from the interactions of decentralized and dispersed agents. Furthermore, since complex system dynamics are essentially open-ended, the idea of a global optimum is useless by itself. Therefore, the notion of a steady state should change with the concept of evolution. 'Because new niches, new potentials, new possibilities, are continually created, the economy operates far from any optimum or global equilibrium. Improvements are always possible and indeed occur regularly' (Arthur et al., 1997). Therefore, the relevance of complex systems is that this approach can account for some traits of economic systems, such as irreversibility, path dependency, and the presence of increasing returns in which non-linear dynamics and positive feedback mainly occur (Arthur, 1999).

The features of non-ergodic[8] path dependence explain why complex systems are not only sensitive to initial conditions, but also to disturbances occurring along their path, which leads to a diversity of patterns of behavior in the long-term dynamics that affect the overall system (Dosi and Kaniovski, 1994; Antonelli, 2007). In this sense complex systems help to explain why initial differences might increase over time rather than decline, as the neoclassical hypothesis of convergence suggests.

Following Antonelli (2008), we consider the relevance of regarding innovation as an emergent property of a complex system. This property is the result of the intentional creative reactions of agents and their ability to change the architecture of interactions, which are endogenous consequences of the localized action of agents. Creativity is an essential feature of adaptive complex systems (Kauffman, 2003). However, the intentionality of economic agents is the distinctive characteristic of the complex systems in which human beings are involved. Foster (2005) also pointed out the importance of intentionality and agents' creative capacities when he considered interactions not only between agents but also between their mental models.

Absorption and connectivity capacities are key dimensions in understanding both the intentional creativity of agents and their architecture of linkages. The effects of feedback mechanisms between these capacities aid understanding of the non-linear dynamics of learning processes. We propose that a complex system can be conceived as a mechanism for generating order from the reinforcement of absorption and connectivity capacities and between these and the innovation process. The emergent order from micro interaction is one of the most frequently highlighted properties of complex systems. Therefore, innovation emerges from interactions between the absorption and connectivity capacities of creative agents within the framework of specific dynamics in the processes of appropriation, creative destruction and structural change. In this regard, the view of complexity used in the chapter is in agreement with the idea that the complex systems approach applied to innovation economics allows economic evolution to be understood as an ordered macro structure that evolves according to dispersed, decentralized micro interaction which, in turn, is affected by the macro dynamics in which it is involved.

This chapter proposes that a complex system can be conceived as a mechanism for generating order from the absorption and connectivity capacities of its components. Introducing these capabilities into the analysis leads to a ranking of orders of complex systems. This chapter shows a parallel between higher orders of complexity and higher degrees of development of a productive structure. The complex systems of higher orders would require greater absorption and connectivity capacities, which allow access to the skills generated in the multidimensional space in which they operate.

4. COMPLEXITY AND DEVELOPMENT: AN ANALYTICAL MODEL

This section proposes a theoretical model that accounts for the interaction between creative agents and the development of capacities built upon those interactions within a specific institutional framework. Departing from the complex system approach described in the previous section, we argue that innovation can be seen as the result of non-linear dynamics in a learning process driven by mutual reinforcement between absorption and connectivity capacities within the specific dynamics of the processes of creative destruction, appropriation and structural change. The presence of non-linear dynamics involved in learning paths explains why the initial differences in economic development tend to increase.

We assume that the components of the system are firms and other institutions and organizations such as chambers of commerce, consultancies, universities and technological centers, among others. These are endowed with different capacities that lead to creative or adaptive reactions. The firms and institutions are embedded in different systems and networks where they build their architecture of linkages that involves non-exclusive commercial relations but also long-term relationships with other agents. The networks in which firms are embedded constitute the multidimensional space described by Antonelli (2008). Clusters, local systems (Becattini, 1989; Camagni, 1991), sectoral systems of innovation (Malerba and Orsenigo, 1997), production networks (Albornoz and Yoguel, 2004; Bisang et al., 2005; Erbes et al., 2006; Yoguel, 2007), and global value chains (Humphrey and Schmitz, 2002) are historical forms of the spaces where firms build their capacities and interact. Nevertheless, the degree of development of those spaces in terms of the importance achieved by the generation, circulation and appropriation of knowledge (both tacit and codified) involves a gradient of situations ranging from the most virtuous to the weakest. This variety depends on the capacities of firms and institutions, the importance of agents with creative reactions that play against the rules[9] and the development of creative destruction, appropriation and structural change processes. Therefore, this space of interaction will have different characteristics in countries with different levels of development. For example, in developing countries, these multidimensional spaces would be poorly integrated, and the lack of complementarities among agents would limit external economies and negatively impact their learning processes. Meanwhile, in developed countries those spaces work as a quasi-market where firms can find shortage competencies. This multidimensional space is different to the attributes of the firms and institutions that comprise it and therefore lies in a mesoeconomic dimension and cannot be reduced to the sum of its parts. This feature stems from the feedback between the absorption and connectivity capacities of agents, which justifies applying the complexity approach.

Therefore, beginning with the existence of feedback mechanisms between the absorption and connectivity capacities of agents that determine the innovation process, the main hypotheses of this chapter highlight some differential characteristics in developed, developing and newly industrialized countries. These differences are manifested in: (i) the development of absorption and connectivity capacities of agents; (ii) the relevance of feedback effects between them; (iii) the importance of the absorption and connectivity capacities to determine the innovation; and (iv) the relationship between the dynamics of the macro and meso structure and agents' capacities. Therefore, our aim is to understand the learning process as a non-linear one explained by feedback between competencies and linkages in order to identify constraints that may exist in developing countries, which limit the generation of agents' capacities and processes.

The differences in creative and adaptive reactions of heterogeneous agents lead to the emergence of specific patterns of innovation and growth that explain the differences between developed and developing countries. These dynamics tend to consolidate institutional frameworks (macro and meso structures) that could be adverse or beneficial to innovation and that reinforce divergent development paths (Hoff and Stiglitz, 2002; Aghion et al., 2008; Rivera Ríos et al, 2009), which, in turn, would affect the behavior of agents and level of their capacities. As an example, in developing countries adaptive reactions would prevail and therefore the critical mass of agents playing against the rules may not be reached. In this context, there are no forces that provoke institutional change and there would be a consolidation of the institutional framework that is adverse to innovation. Therefore, the institutional framework is the combined result of interactions between heterogeneous agents, in terms of behaviors, skills and connections, and the structural conditions described by appropriation (Teece, 1986; Cohen et al., 2000; Erbes et al., 2006; Pisano, 2006; Antonelli, 2008), destructive creation (Schumpeter, 1934, 1942; Metcalfe, 2002; Metcalfe et al., 2006), and structural change processes (Ocampo, 2005).

The absorption capacity   of the system can be regarded as the ability to recognize new external information, assimilate this and apply it (Cohen and Levinthal, 1989). This capacity is not only related to the possibility of accessing existing knowledge in the multidimensional space, but also implies the ability to identify useful knowledge and generate new knowledge. As a result, absorption is not an ability that can be automatically developed nor is it equally accessible to all systems. Rather, it requires the development of skills within the previous evolutionary path of the system. In this sense, it can be assimilated to the ideas of routines (Nelson and Winter, 1982) and dynamic capabilities (Teece and Pisano, 1994). As long as this capacity is developed, creative reactions will predominate over adaptive ones.

Connectivity capacity   is associated with the system's potential for establishing relationships and generating interaction with other agents whose objective is to increase their knowledge base. Therefore, the different development levels of this capacity provide options for access to knowledge, resources, and opportunities (Richardson, 1972; Freeman, 1991; Teece, 1992; Grandori and Soda, 1995; Mowery et al., 1996; Ahuja, 2000; Coombs and Metcalfe, 2000; Cullen, 2000; Norman, 2002; Laursen and Salter, 2004). Connectivity capacity refers to the agents' ability to establish the architecture of connections and then make changes in the multidimensional space. It requires creative

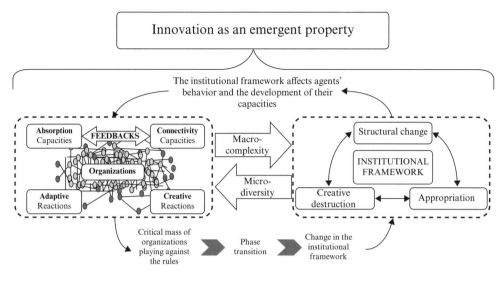

Source: Own elaboration based on Yoguel and Robert (2010).

Figure 17.1   Analytical model

reactions, which in turn are constrained by the dynamics of macro and meso structure. Ultimately, this ability is what defines how open or closed a system is.

The absorption and connectivity capacities are mutually reinforcing (see Figure 17.1). Systems with higher levels of development of their absorption capacity tend to be more open and sustain a higher density in their relationships with other systems. In turn, these are systems that are better able to reap the benefits arising from interactions generated. At the same time, the density of relationships and the degree of openness of the system, defined by the connectivity capacity, help to develop greater absorption capacity when the system is exposed to significant flows of knowledge that it must learn to select and use to obtain quasi-rents (Kleinknecht and Reijnen, 1992; Tether, 2002; Belderbos et al., 2004; Veugelers and Cassiman, 2005; Vega-Jurado et al., 2008; D'Este and Neely, 2008; Eom and Lee, 2008; Tsai and Wang, 2009).

The significance acquired by the absorption and connectivity capacities as well as the existing feedback between them conditions the potential for developing learning processes in firms and hence for generating innovative processes. Meanwhile, in developed countries it is mainly oriented towards R&D, which in turn allow the development of capacities, whereas in developing countries innovation efforts are mainly embodied in capital goods. In the first place, connectivity capacity becomes significant due to the implicit need in the innovative process for relying on knowledge that exceeds that which has been developed internally. This implies that firms should actively seek complementarities which facilitate the development of the innovation process by generating interactions with other agents. Secondly, even when the necessary complementary knowledge exists, firms should rely upon the absorption capacity that allows them to assimilate and exploit external knowledge in order to innovate. In this regard, it is possible to recognize the significance of dimensions such as R&D (Cohen and Levinthal, 1989) and the organizational form (Coriat and Weinstein, 2002) in the differential capacity of firms to obtain a relatively improved economic and innovative performance. Despite the existence of a bi-directional relationship, it can be argued that absorption capacity is a necessary condition for the development of connectivity (Kleinknecht and Reijnen, 1992; Fritsch and Lukas, 2001; Tether, 2002; Miotti and Sachwald, 2003). This result can also be seen from percolation approach (David and Foray, 1994; Antonelli 1997), which states that for knowledge to be absorbed by the system, minimum thresholds in both the absorption and connectivity capacities are required.[10]

Therefore, both capacities jointly define the minimum thresholds that agents need to meet in order to take advantage of local externalities, present in the multidimensional space, positive feedback, and internal learning processes. Thus innovation and the diffusion of it are not randomly governed events, but require specific behavior in individual agents and the particular characteristics of the multidimensional space. Innovation depends on agents' capacities developing sufficiently in order to constitute a critical mass of agents with creative reactions playing against the rules. To reach this critical mass requires what in physics is called 'phase transition'. The idea of phase transition can be useful for understanding the point at which micro interactions trigger qualitative changes in the macro structure. Therefore, the ideas of critical mass and phase transition constitute a first step in understanding the mechanisms that govern emergence within complex systems. When both absorption and connectivity capacities reach significant levels of development, the system can profit from the local conditions of multidimensional space, including opportunities and risks. In these cases, the system can attain an important stage of development in the interconnected processes of creative destruction, appropriation, and structural change (see Figure 17.1).

Creative destruction   From Schumpeter's perspective (1934, 1942), competition between agents is understood as a process of creative destruction that generates variety through innovation but also reduces this variety through selection mechanisms. The generation of novelty by the system depends on the creativity in the agents' reactions and local learning in the multidimensional space. Meanwhile, the selection mechanism remains in the institutional sphere. An institutional framework that enhances innovation will select and reward creative behavior. For this to happen, a critical mass of agents playing against the rules is needed, but it will depend on the extension of markets. In developing countries this extension is lower than in developed ones, which in turn is favored by the low export coefficient in sectors with increasing returns. While the selection mechanisms tend to diminish micro-diversity, the creative component of the creative destruction process helps to increase it. In this sense, they are opposing forces and so interdependent that they should have an impact on both competition and development (Metcalfe, 2010). Within this framework, competition is understood as a space for generating variety and selecting behavior, rather than as an abstractly constructed intersection between the functions of supply and demand.

The appropriation process   (Teece, 1986; Cohen et al., 2000; Pisano, 2006; Antonelli, 2008) refers to a set of mechanisms and skills that allow players to transform knowledge into quasi-rents. This process depends on the way in which technology and knowledge are managed and the dynamics of the creative destruction processes embodied in competition (market share) (Erbes et al., 2006). Agents – by differentiating their routines – attempt to appropriate quasi-rents and extraordinary profits derived from the competition and the demand regime. With regard to this process, it is necessary to consider those aspects that help to explain why the knowledge embedded in products or services and processes produced by agents might constitute a temporary barrier to entry and become a source of quasi-rents. This issue will depend on the absorption and connectivity capacities related to (i) different sources of knowledge, (ii) learning processes, and (iii) the integration of different types of knowledge (Malerba and Orsenigo, 2000). The appropriation regime sets out the rules and institutions that regulate the boundaries of property rights. This means intellectual property rights and other sources of rents, among them tariffs and non tariff barriers to trade, antitrust legislation, and so on. In sum, all are factors that explain the current market structure and the scope of the markets. Nevertheless, these rules can change according to agents' reactions. Regarding appropriation processes, we account for intentional rent-seeking behavior in agents.

The process of structural change   (Ocampo, 2005) describes changes in productive structure that make it more diversified, better integrated, and, thus, more developed. In this sense, the process of structural change involves both a specific direction of change and also, as a consequence, development issues. This process is very close to development theories. It takes into account (i) the reallocation of production factors to higher productivity sectors aimed at reducing structural dualism and collecting the gains from increasing returns, (ii) the development of complementarities between agents, (iii) changes in the specialization pattern, oriented towards differentiated products with a higher income elasticity, and (iv) the development of policies to promote the coordination of investment decisions in a context characterized by technological indivisibilities. Thus, from a strategic point of view, the process of structural change is not spontaneous, but is the result of development policies which imply that players are able to define their behavior in a game in which coordination and information are problems to be solved (Cimoli et al., 2005). This concept incorporates both the contributions made by authors such as Prebisch and Hirshman, among others, in the context of development theories from the 1950s, and those of the new development stream mentioned above.

The three processes help explain the dynamics of meso and macro structure and the evolution of the economic system as a whole. Thus, in more evolved economic systems economic agents perform more complex innovative activities whose benefits are appropriated from different mechanisms, producing a structural change process that modifies the profile of productive specialization. By contrast, in systems with lower levels of complexity, such as those predominating in developing countries, where adaptive reactions prevail, economic development is conditioned by the system's capacity for appropriating knowledge and performing innovative processes.

The degree of development of these processes that jointly explain the main characteristics of the institutional framework is conditioned by the level reached by absorption and connectivity capacities and the feedback mechanisms between them. Therefore, the building of capacities as well as the behavior of agents in terms of adaptive or creative reactions determines the innovation activity of the system and the evolution of the processes of appropriation, creative destruction and structural change. Any system requires not only internally produced knowledge but also knowledge derived from relationships established within the multidimensional space. Therefore, the dynamic of change requires both the existence of linkages with other systems that are functional (connectivity) and skills associated with the identification and implementation of useful knowledge (absorption). Both absorption and connectivity capacities would have strong influences on the agents' creativity.

The relationship between capacities and processes is reciprocal and it is reinforced over time. High levels of absorption and connectivity capacities and the presence of feedback between them lead to the development of innovative processes. Innovation, as an emergent property of a complex system, is located in the center between capacities and processes. Only the creative reaction of agents, through the innovation process, would make changes in the structure of quasi-rents. Nevertheless capacities are also conditioned by the features that the three processes assume. In this way, the specialization pattern would limit the innovative activity due to the lack of technological complementarities present in economic systems characterized by structural dualism. Meanwhile, the processes of appropriation and creative destruction define the basis on which economic agents must compete, develop their capacities and generate innovations. In sum, the three processes describe evolution in the institutional framework and then establish the conditions for the appearance, or the blockading, of creative reactions.

From this perspective, more complex economic systems tend to develop creative capacities that drive changes in the system and in the development path. This dynamic strengthens virtuosity between capacities, innovation, processes and economic development. Also, it shows how capacities determine the development of processes, especially through the accumulation of creative reactions that trigger qualitative changes at an institutional level. At the same time, these feedback dynamics define the possibilities for building up capacities that enable agents' competitiveness to increase.

Nevertheless, this feedback can follow the opposite path: the institutional framework and the features of processes could limit or foster the development of capacities. When agents' absorption capacities remain low, there is little possibility of establishing linkages that allow agents to learn. Therefore, the feedback that leads to learning and capacity development are weak or non-existent. Therefore, there is little possibility of accumulating creative reaction and reaching the critical mass needed to change institutions. In this picture, capacities and processes reinforce themselves but in a vicious manner that inhibits a phase transition that would lead the system to higher development.

5. CAPACITIES AND PROCESSES: THE SPECIFICITIES OF ECONOMIC DEVELOPMENT

In the previous sections we have defined the complexity of an economic system in relation to the level and evolution of capacities and processes and the interactions between them. Following the stream of the new theory of development that combines structuralist and micro-evolutionary approaches, we propose that these relationships operate differently in developed, newly industrialized, and developing countries.[11] Thus, whereas in more complex economic systems, capacities and processes enhance their development path, in the opposite case, different kinds of blockades would limit the feedback between firms' capacities, while the weakness of the processes would constrain the development

BOX 17.1   CAPACITIES AND FEEDBACK IN DEVELOPED
AND DEVELOPING COUNTRIES

The relation between firms' capacities and linkages has been studied by several authors and in most cases statistical relationships between these dimensions were found. For example, in developed countries (mainly European countries), a set of papers have found that absorption capacity is a key determinant in R&D cooperation (Kleinknecht and Reijnen, 1992; Fritsch and Lukas, 2001; Tether, 2002). Other authors assume that the relationship is bidirectional, which means the existence of feedback effects (Veugelers, 1997; Becker and Dietz, 2004; Vega-Jurado et al., 2008; D'Este and Neely, 2008). Others analyse how both absorption and connectivity determine the level of innovativeness in firms (Miotti and Sachwald, 2003; Belderbos et al., 2004; Nieto and Santamaría, 2007; Caloghirou et al., 2004). In the cases of Korea and Taiwan, some papers have found that internal R&D and the acquisition of external knowledge (outsourcing and cooperation) impact innovation (Eom and Lee, 2008; Tsai and Wang, 2009). For Latin American countries, the literature stresses that absorption capacities act as a barrier in the access to connectivity, blockading the feedback mechanisms. Nevertheless, when this happens it has a positive effect on innovation. Therefore, the literature for Latin American countries does not deny the existence of agents that have reached high levels in their absorption and connectivity capacities but these are not enough to achieve the critical threshold required to trigger processes of structural change (Arza and López, 2008; Benavente and Contreras, 2008; Bianchi, et al., 2008; Garrido and Padilla-Pérez, 2008; Kupfer and Avellar, 2008; Erbes et al., 2010). In sum, in developed countries firms' connectivity is oriented mainly to R&D. Besides, in spite of the kind of causality, there is a great difference between these connectivity capacities and those of firms belonging to developing countries.

Source: Own elaboration based on Yoguel and Robert (2010).

of capacities (see Box 17.1). In this sense, in developing countries, the interaction between micro and macro dimensions operates by blockading the feedback mechanisms that foster capacities and provoke reactions against the rules among economics agents. As long as the critical mass of agents playing against the rules cannot be reached, the necessary phase transition does not occur and the institutional framework adverse to innovation continues shaping adaptive reactions. As a consequence, the productive structure in developing countries can be characterized by: (i) an income import elasticity higher than income export elasticity (ii) low complementarities between activities and structural dualism, (iii) scarcity of agents' innovation propensity, (iv) low importance of disembodied innovation efforts, (v) a specialization pattern in low knowledge-intensive products and (vi) a weak position in the global value chains and networks they belong to, limiting the appropriation of externalities and knowledge. Therefore identifying the blockades between the micro and macro interactions becomes the key question for development theory (Cimoli and Porcile, 2009) and for the design of development policies.

Regarding capacities, the different ways in which absorption and connectivity capacities are manifested define different levels of complexity of economic systems. Complexity at the micro level can be accounted for by the diversity and complementarities of agents in terms of capacities, behaviors (creative and adaptive reactions), and the feedback between these. The differences would result in the existence of countries with uneven developmental potential, because the lack of complementarities between capacities would act as a blockade in feedback dynamics and in the number of agents playing against the rules. Therefore, the structural heterogeneity (Ocampo, 2005) would limit the linkages between firms and thus the multidimensional space would be poorly integrated. Firms' possibilities for building capacities would depend entirely on internal efforts that would in turn be diminished by the scarcity of learning opportunities. (See Box 17.1 for references to capacity building in developed and developing countries.)

In turn, the main characteristics of the processes are manifested in the degree of diversification of the specialization pattern, the presence or not of sectors with increasing returns and the extent to which the competition process rewards innovation. As was suggested in the theoretical framework, the relationship described between absorption and connectivity capacities and their feedback effects is reflected in the importance attained by the processes. But also, these processes condition the building of capacities. Therefore, innovation is an endogenous result of feedback between capacities and processes. Its relevance would depend also (i) on the relationships between processes and their influence on capacities, (ii) on the feedback effects between capacities, (iii) on the number of agents playing against the rules that threaten the established position of quasi-rents, and (iv) on the system capacity to counterbalance the possible blockades to develop positive feedbacks that raise agent capacities. In this regard, when these dimensions are relevant the economic system goes through a phase transition that enables institutional changes and development. (See Box 17.2 for some innovation statistics in developed and developing countries.)

In developed and Asian newly industrialized countries, the higher complexity of economic systems is derived from the higher absorption and connectivity capacities and also from the intensity and synergy of the three processes. In such a framework, the minimal threshold of competence that the agents need to reach in order to increase connectivity capacity is lower because of (i) the presence of externalities (public goods, spillovers and infrastructure) and (ii) the existence of networks which enable the appropriation processes of club goods generated within them. In spite of the strong differences between developed and newly industrialized countries, we assume that the dynamic of creative destruction, appropriation, and structural change are similar. What distinguishes these countries from developing countries is that the transition phase has already occurred. In turn, the explanation for this is that the complexity of the multidimensional space reaches the required level of complementary diversity, which allows the interchange of knowledge and learning, thus promoting the development of all three processes (see Box 17.1).

In these countries, the structural change process is favored by the existence of a specialization pattern with complementarities, high intrasectoral homogeneity, and the presence of firms operating in sectors with Schumpeterian and Keynesian efficiency that

---

BOX 17.2   SOME INNOVATION STATISTICS IN DEVELOPED AND DEVELOPING COUNTRIES

Latin American countries show considerable differences from developed and Asian newly industrialized countries. In terms of innovation activities, number of patents per million inhabitants is more than 100 times higher in developed countries than in developing countries (see averages for selected countries in Table 17.1). Regarding R&D expenditure, developed countries show R&D/GDP ratios almost four times higher than developing countries, where this is highly concentrated in the public sector. Other indicators – such as the number of researchers per million inhabitants and the proportion of enrollment in tertiary education in science and technology over the total 24-year-old population – show differences of magnitude that are consistent with the differences in the indicators identified above. Similarly, the low level of innovative activities is consistent with the poor participation of high-tech sectors in the trade specialization pattern.

Latin American countries could not make the transition from acquired capacities to the dynamic technological capacities required for generating appropriation, creative destruction, and structural change processes. The absence of a critical mass of agents playing against the rules constrains the phase transition that newly industrialized countries could make.

---

entail the appropriation of knowledge generated in the form of quasi-rents derived from increasing returns. In a sector with Schumpeterian efficiency, decreasing costs derived from accumulative learning prevail. The existence of externalities and complementarities between agents are key components of systems with highly developed structural change process. However, they are also explained by a strong accumulation of knowledge that, in turn, is derived from agents' absorption and connectivity capacities and feedback between the two. As a consequence, the activities that define the specialization profile in these countries can be labeled as 'Schumpeterian' (Reinert, 2007), since they are characterized by increasing returns to scale, the dynamic existence of imperfect competition, technical progress and relevant disembodied innovation efforts, and strong synergies between sectors that are possible through complex translation mechanisms between agents (Stokes, 1997). The process of creative destruction is aided by the development of market structures arising mainly from a prior accumulation of knowledge, where technology interrelationships are central. In the case of successful economic performance of some East Asian countries Chang (2008) demonstrates that it depends (i) on the change of specialization pattern towards knowledge intensive sectors, (ii) on the support to the infant industry, and (iii) on the key role of industrial and technological policy allowing them to leave a Ricardian or Herscher-Ohlin specialization pattern.

From the perspective of appropriation processes, developed countries stand out because of different appropriation regimes: IPR, secrets, epistemic communities, and high-speed innovation rates. In turn, the resident firms in these countries can reduce the costs of R&D and increase the likelihood of successful innovations by decentralizing

Table 17.1 Innovation in developed and developing countries

	1. Patents granted per million inhabitants	2. R+D expenditure/ GDP	3. % of private R&D over total R&D	4. Researchers per million inhabitants	5. % Tertiary enrollment in science and engineering	6. High tech sector in commercial profile	7. Overall GDP per capita (2004)	8. GDP per capita growth (1960–2004)
France	55	2.12	63.4	3353	8	0.7	26169	204
Germany	119	2.52	70	3386	7	0.69	25610	115*
Italy	25	–	–	–	4	0.39	23174	226
Japan	267	3.4	77	5546	8	1.16	24660	432
United Kingdom	57	1.8	62	3033	10	1.21	26762	158
United States	279	2.61	70	4651	6	1.1	36100	177
Spain	7	–	–	–	6	0.4	20973	322
China	0.5	1.42	71	926	1	1.69	5333	1099
Korea	114	3.23	77	4162	9	1.79	18421	1093
Taiwan	258	–	–	–	8	s/d	20872	1300
Argentina	1	0.49	30.4	895	2	0.08	10945	39
Brazil	0.6	0.82	40.2	461	2	0.21	7204	170
Chile	0.9	0.67	46.1	833	3	0.02	12681	153
Mexico	0.7	0.5	50	464	2	1.22	8168	121

Notes:
1. At the US Patent and Trade Mark Office.
5. As a % over the total 24-year-old population.
6. Reveal comparative advantages. Pharmaceuticals; Electronic data processing and office equipment; Telecommunications equipment; and Integrated circuits and electronic components.
* In West Germany (1960–1997).

Sources: Millennium indicators; United Nations, UNESCO, United States Patent and Trade Mark Office, Penn table; Yoguel and Robert (2010).

activity in many innovative start-ups, which increase diversity and the importance of club goods and commons. One key factor of appropriation processes in developed countries is the whole system's ability to export the institutions that govern the dynamics of this process. Multilateral agreements in the field of property rights (particularly TRIPS, because it is enforced) are an expression of developed economies' capacities to extend the appropriation of technological quasi-rents beyond their own territory.

In addition, in terms of creative destruction and thus the competitive process, high entry barriers – derived mainly from cognitive abilities – prevail. These kinds of barriers are built and torn down by agents playing against the rules, continuously threatening the established market positions. Agents can take advantage of technological interrelationships and knowledge complementarities resulting from the presence of increasing returns to scale, but the better position is subject to constant peril from the competition or is merely temporary. As a consequence, agents compete amongst themselves in concentrated markets through the introduction of innovations. Therefore, the degree of stability of quasi-rents generated by the integration of knowledge is greater than in those systems where agents compete in markets where innovation is not rewarded. Thus, in spite of operating in sectors with strong technical progress and instability, it is possible for them to decode uncertainties.

In Latin American countries, in contrast, the search for new combinations that are oriented towards the generation of innovations aimed at increasing variety and improving selection is less relevant in competition. Learning and technological processes have mainly been embodied and they are poorly fuelled by knowledge derived from basic and applied science (see Box 17.1). This is because of the low levels of complementarities among agents and the absence of a critical mass of agents operating in the most innovative sectors. Although in these countries there are innovative firms that actually compete in global markets or firms integrated in the global value chain, they are not enough to provoke structural change processes. The existence of agents with high absorption capacity does not imply an increase in their likelihood of establishing linkages by themselves. It is critical mass that is needed to generate the complementarities. Therefore, the learning and capacity building processes are developed mainly inside firms because of the weakness of linkages of the multidimensional space where they operate. Linkages with universities and technological centers would be especially helpful in developing capacities.

In explaining the innovation results by means of absorption and connectivity capacities, in Argentina, Erbes et al. (2010) find some evidence that exemplifies firms' behavior in Latin American countries. These authors show that while the level of agents' absorption capacities is central in explaining the results of innovation, the quality of linkages is not significant. The absorption capacity determines the system's potential for accessing the knowledge disseminated in networks and environments to which they belong. Nevertheless, whether or not firms with high capacities exist in the neighborhood also affects the quality of linkages, which is explained by the local search within the multidimensional space. Furthermore, there are other factors at macro level that affect both capacities, such as specialization patterns, firms' positions in the global value chain, and more generally, the weak dynamics of the appropriation, creative destruction, and structural change processes. Both capacities define the minimum thresholds the agents need in order to appropriate the externalities generated in the environment (when these exist) and the results of the processes and learning taking place internally. Thus, dissemination of knowledge does not occur randomly between the components of a system, but a wide variety of capacities are associated with the absorption of knowledge and connections between other agents.

Therefore, as has been illustrated by old and new development theory, in developing countries the structural change process is limited by the low complementarities of absorption and connectivity capacities, and a specialization pattern characterized by the high inter- and intra-sectoral heterogeneity and Malthusian activities prevails (Reinert, 2007). Among the main characteristics of the productive profile should be mentioned (i) the predominance of static comparative advantages, (ii) the prevalence of sectors with technologically low dynamics, with public knowledge, and limited accumulation, and (iii) the major role played by embodied technological progress through the acquisition of capital goods. The latter issue is also evident in the low complexity of networks, although this characteristic does not override the possibility that a few firms in more dynamic industries may exist, grow, and compete globally within the prevalent dynamic specialization profile (Erbes et al., 2006).

Finally, the appropriation process would be characterized by low or null appropriation of quasi-rents because the low absorption and connectivity capacities would inhibit innovation and increase R&D costs, which in turn would affect capacity for catching up (see Box 17.2). Besides, weak absorptive and mainly powerless connectivity capacities in firms would also condition the significance of creative destruction processes. Low capacities would impact on innovation and hence competition would be based mainly on prices and not an increase in variety and the improvement of selection mechanisms. The structural change processes would be constrained by the low feedback effects of absorption and connectivity capacities. A specialization pattern characterized by high income elasticity of imports and low income elasticity of exports blockades the feedback effect between product and productivity and the dynamics implicit in the Kaldor–Verdoorn relation. As was shown before, this specialization pattern would condition the development system component capacities.

This uneven production specialization is reflected in mechanisms for the appropriation of knowledge that are closer to traditional forms of protection and with limited spillover into the productive structure. Reinert (1995) argues that in such countries there are severe constraints affecting the chances of appropriating quasi-rents derived from knowledge and the classical way of spreading the benefits arising from technological progress. As Cimoli et al. (2009) have shown, the non-existence of convergence and the problems linked to a deficit in Schumpeterian and Keynesian efficiency are explained 'mainly because income elasticity of the demand for imports in Latin America has an upward trend which was not matched by a similar increase in exports' and because there is not a convergence of economic structures.

As the three processes mutually reinforce each other, the predominant productive and trade specialization pattern (in goods and services) is defined by limited processes of knowledge appropriation, structural change, and creative destruction. The weakness in specialization patterns is also evident in the low complexity of networks. Developing countries are therefore characterized by the presence of linkages between agents that assign less importance to the endogenous generation of knowledge with learning sources that are basically internal and idiosyncratic. These patterns are associated with diminishing returns, competition based on prices in highly volatile markets, a demand for unskilled labor, the use of low-quality processes, and mainly embodied technical progress. Latin American countries' weakness involves failures in the whole system and not only in firms' behavior. The systemic nature of innovation is less visible in developing countries, resting mainly in individual efforts. Therefore it is easy to find agents performing several functions.[12]

These processes are poorly fueled by knowledge derived from basic and applied science and from firms' linkages with the environment, especially with universities and technological centers. Finally, there is a lack of agents playing against the rules – in the sense mentioned above – and therefore the three processes are very weak. These issues limit the feedback from processes to capacities and act as a blockade to the development path (see Figure 17.1).

Therefore, because of the low complementarities between agents derived from the prevalent specialization pattern, systemic dimensions are weak and firms' individual efforts become more relevant. Low levels of both absorption and connectivity capacities would thus limit emergence of innovations within a framework of weakness in the three processes. Therefore, the improvement of these capacities and the upgrading of feedback effects would be necessary conditions for development. A given economy's specialization profile defines a set of dimensions related to the importance of acquiring knowledge, the kind of returns, the generation of competitive advantages, and market forms which are closely linked to capacities and processes (Reinert, 2007).

This evidence reveals relevant differences between Latin American and Asian countries. In this regard, Cimoli et al. (2008) stress that only the latter have made the transition from production capacities to the technological capacity required for generating technical change.

The presence of these patterns in Latin American countries can then be understood from a complex system approach which stresses that the absence of convergence discussed in the third section is derived not only from the low level and limited feedback between processes but also from the issues associated with a low level of absorption and connectivity capacities and limited or absence of feedback between them. Meanwhile, the blockades to these feedbacks and the absence of a critical mass of agents playing against the rules would explain why the level and composition of innovation as an emergent property of the system is insufficient to overcome the productivity gap with developed countries.

6.   CONCLUSIONS

In the previous sections we have stressed the fact that, in order to generate a development path, developing countries face the challenge of building absorption and connectivity capacities and of increasing the importance of quasi-rents appropriation, creative destruction and structural change processes. For this to happen, positive feedback effects between capacities, and between processes and capacities, should be generated. As a result, innovation would be an emergent property of the system. We have also stressed that when a predominance of decreasing returns is the main characteristics of the specialization pattern, processes and capacities are very weak and hence it is not easy for a group of agents – public or private – playing against the rules to appear and promote institutional change. The possibility of creating a development path and high complexity levels are therefore very low. In consequence, instead of structural change there is structural heterogeneity, a low level of complementarity, and high productivity gaps between sectors. In sum, the weaknesses of the specialization pattern are associated with the low probability of economic development. So, the challenge for developing countries is to increase the complexity of the specialization pattern in sectors where agents are price-formers rather than price-takers, and where the development of absorption and connectivity capacities becomes a key factor in the competition process. As developed countries have absolute advantages in the most technologically dynamic sectors and in most dynamic stages of production networks, the development path needs to catch up. For this to happen, and to reduce the technological gap between developing and developed countries, industrial and technological policies oriented towards generating dynamic market failures in developing countries are key factors. This is because free market conditions will consolidate dominant positions in the world market and a specialization pattern in developing countries intensive in the abundant factors.

The analytical framework based on complex systems theory – and applied to innovation economics – also provides an appropriate framework for the discussion of industrial policies from a systemic perspective. Following Cimoli et al. (2008), industrial policy can be defined as a process of institutional engineering that shapes the behavior of agents and comprises not only support to infant industries, but also trade policies, science and technology, public procurement, and FDI and IPR policies.[13] Under this approach, industrial policies should be able to define the steering of the processes of appropriation, creative destruction, and structural change and foster absorption and connectivity capacities. Those policies ought to promote the emergence of a critical mass of agents playing against the rules, whether they belong to the public sector, are incumbents or new agents.

In this sense, industrial and technological policies should take into account some of the issues discussed in this chapter if they are to meet the objective of increasing the levels of capacities and processes, and hence create potential for development. In particular, assuming that the economic system is a complex system, a set of specific problems needs to be introduced. For example, the outcomes of policy intervention could go beyond policy agency control, and policy makers' decisions could therefore trigger destabilizing positive feedback dynamics if they do not consider the interrelationship that governs the dynamics of capacities, processes, and feedbacks.

Policy makers should also learn from past interventions, because policy should be considered as an experimental and dynamic process (Metcalfe et al., 2004). This experimentation could be carried out in a virtual environment using simulation models in order to learn about qualitative changes in complex dynamics. Nevertheless, these simulations do not provide enough information about the critical determinants in complex systems that involve human behavior (Aghion et al., 2008). The experimental character of policy is therefore crucial.

In order to develop absorption capacities and to spread knowledge and information within and between firms and production networks, incentives must be created for the development of endogenous competencies.[14] One type of policy acting on the improvement of absorption capacities is suggested in Spain by Vega-Jurado et al. (2008). According to them, these policies should strengthen firms' technological competences, which are the main determinants both of innovation and of cooperation with scientific agencies. In this regard, absorption capacities condition the likelihood of generating emulation processes, which also depend on the appropriation regime and the specialization pattern. They also stressed that the accumulation of capacities and knowledge involves improvements in workers' and professionals' skills but also in organization routines. Educational efforts are crucial but from an organizational perspective, policies should be oriented towards resolving persistent inabilities to find opportunities.

The development of connectivity capacities requires linkages between firms and institutions from the perspective of a non-linear model (Stokes, 1997). On the one hand, policies should be oriented towards better positioning local agents in the hierarchy of the global value chain or networks that they belong to. This implies developing a public policy that takes private nucleus–supplier–client relationships into account. In this sense, enhancing the generation, circulation, and appropriation of knowledge in order to create dynamic competitive advantages is necessary. On the other hand, the policy should consider the development of firm–university linkages within a framework that goes beyond individual supply and demand conceptions and human resource training. This requires the prioritization of basic research oriented towards vacancy areas and the development of translation functions between agents in terms of languages and the discovery of new contexts. All of these actions should be complemented with the infrastructure development of free-access ICT.

In term of processes, deep institutional changes are needed to increase their levels of complexity and to overcome the blockades in the feedback dynamics. Policy objectives should then be to create the conditions and rules that promote the actions of new or incumbent agents playing against the rules. The direction of knowledge and capacities accumulation in order to generate catching-up processes is not the same as that which is present in the current institutional framework. Therefore, industrial policy in a broad sense ought to have the political ability to drive development rents towards agents capable of generating structural change, destructive creation, and appropriation processes.

In order to improve the virtuosity of appropriation processes, the extent to which public goods are present becomes a key issue, since these constitute a basic input for the development of club goods. For this purpose, it is necessary to improve the education system – especially at primary and secondary levels – to avoid the increase of perverse selection mechanisms, and to create equal opportunities in access to tertiary education. What is more, from the perspective of the determinants of quasi-rents appropriation, policies should focus on a significant increase in accumulation knowledge embodied into the production of goods and services. This entails not only harnessing the company's external sources by improving the inter-phases between the firms and the scientific system but also improving internal sources by consolidating agents' basic competencies and the circulation of information and knowledge within the companies and networks they belong to. This implies the development of institutions that both allow appropriation as a system of intellectual property rights and reinforce alternative and endogenous forms of protection, such as high innovation rates and high cognitive capabilities, enabling agents to make up epistemic communities in which club goods circulate.

On the other hand, actions oriented towards improving the processes of creative destruction should be related to increasing the weight of knowledge-intensive sectors through the selection of those sectors with potential for development – which increasingly incorporate knowledge – and the promotion of new ones. This requires the application of a vertical policy that would raise the level of knowledge in the present productive structure and modify the specialization profile by taking advantage of the steep learning curves associated with key sectors in the new paradigm. Therefore, the vertical policy must be centered on (i) the promotion of learning processes and competition between agents; (ii) the generation of dynamic market failures and processes of technological accumulation with positive externalities, and (iii) the incentive to innovate and create institutional mechanisms that reduce the failures selection and increase the emergence of agents playing against the rules. In turn, all these policies entail the development of incentives to build complex routines in order to increase knowledge protection and allow greater appropriation of quasi-rents coming from barriers and imperfect competition and from the development of monopolistic rents from emulation patterns (catching-up).

In turn, the promotion of the structural change process would require (i) important efforts to promote infant industry learning and catch-up, especially in the sectors linked to the techno-organizational paradigm, (ii) to induce a complex profile of specialization in goods and services, increasing the weight of sectors with high levels of productivity, and (iii) to develop knowledge and productive complementarities between agents. In both cases the creation and consolidation of organizational structures that connect the market and firms – such as different kinds of networks – are key. These organizational structures have an important role in promoting complementarities between both agents and institutions operating as translators and/or bridging institutions (Casalet, 2005). Moreover, to make these processes more dynamic, the specialization pattern must be discussed, promoting the development of those activities with increasing returns and enabling productivity increases that could spill over into other activities. In turn, these activities favor a more virtuous export specialization pattern in terms of knowledge embodied in products and services.

The ultimate goal of this kind of policy is to move forward on the path of development. Therefore, because of the synergy generated by the processes and capacities associated with complex systems, the policy objectives described above are strongly linked. The improvement of knowledge management by integrating tacit and codified knowledge should have a direct impact not only on the level of agents' absorption capacities but also on their connectivity capacities. In other words, policy tools acting from both the demand and supply perspectives are necessary. However, this also requires significant changes in the organization of firms into more complex structures in order to simultaneously include projects in competition in a context of top-down and bottom-up relationships. Changes in these directions will enable firms to diversify learning sources by complementing the inclusion of embodied technical progress with disembodied progress, such as the development of formal and informal R&D activities, design, knowledge integration from different areas of the organization using specific software, and so on. Therefore, increasing complexity in firms' knowledge management should produce a greater weight of patents, a greater importance of codifiable but un-coded knowledge (displaced code books such as those cited by Cowan et al., 2000), and a greater speed of innovation than that rival firms. Finally, this set of policies associated with each of the processes analysed will also tend to generate a significant increase in agents' absorptive and connectivity capacities.

The design of these policies needs to move along a path in which there is a tension between public and club goods. On the one hand, knowledge is increasingly becoming a restricted access club good derived from the development level of the absorption and connectivity capacities discussed in the previous sections. On the other hand, in the present knowledge-intensive techno-productive paradigm, the chances of development are associated with a wide dissemination of knowledge in the form of public goods as well as club goods because of the growing importance of production networks and linkages between agents. This issue does not imply an inability to capture and generate quasi-rents but does entail more openness in the competitive process (greater variety and better selection) where barriers to entry are generated from agents' different competences on the one hand, and appropriation, creative destruction processes, and structural change, on the other.

Finally, as Reinert (2007) has proposed, from a neo-Schumpeterian approach, it is possible to identify uneven development in developing countries when (a) the appropriation process is weak (classical diffusion), (b) the country specialization is focused on economic activities with low innovation rates and, therefore, (c) the destruction component of the creative destruction process predominates over the creative one. In these cases it is easy to specialize in being poor in the international division of labor. If the specialization pattern is focused on products with exogenous innovation processes, the discussion about appropriation of quasi-rents does not make any sense. As consequence, these types of countries' growth paths will depend strongly on the international prices of the main products in the specialization pattern and not on their absorption and connectivity capacities which, in turn, condition agents' possibilities of innovating and appropriating quasi-rents related to knowledge. As a consequence, policy prescriptions oriented towards a specialization pattern based on static comparative advantages are a luxury that only developed countries can afford (Cimoli et al., 2008).

From this perspective, appropriation, creative destruction, and structural change processes, on the one hand, and absorption and connectivity capacities, on the other, become key points in the development process and structural change path. Developing capacities and processes from a complex systems approach applied to the economy means taking advantage of windows of opportunity by choosing the right technology and knowledge management, and operating in oligopolic markets in order to participate in virtuous global production networks. These windows of opportunity are a moving target (Pérez, 2001; Reinert, 2007), and they depend on the processes, capacities, and properties discussed above.

The complex systems approach presented in this chapter can explain why divergence and heterogeneity are the main trends in the world economy. It is possible to foresee these patterns when there are complementarities and feedbacks in a system but the other mechanisms are absent or very weak. In these cases, the initial differences between developed and developing countries will be amplified and the catching-up process will not be possible.

NOTES

1. A previous version of this chapter was presented at the 17th SJE-KERI-KIF-CEC International Symposium, Seoul, 16 October 2009. We appreciate the comments received by the discussants and by

Keun Lee. We also want to thank Mario Cimoli (Eclac) for his useful comments on a previous draft of this chapter.

2. As part of the Schumpeterian and Penrosean traditions, some authors, like Foster (2005), argue that the biological metaphor is not the most useful one for discussing the specificities of economic systems.
3. Antonelli (2007) stresses that the intentional rent-seeking agents' behavior plays a key role in the analysis of economic dynamics. Within this conception, agents are not automata as they are usually taken into account in computational complexity and in other attempts to apply this approach to economics.
4. Some authors, such as Colander (2009) and Perona (2004), propose that it is likely that complex systems will become a kind of nexus between orthodox and heterodox thinking in economics. We do not agree with this argument because there are differences in ontological assumptions that cannot be reconciled simply by using the same formalizing tool.
5. Among these models, those based on differential equation systems can be differentiated from those that use cell automata.
6. Outside of innovation economics, these models have a multiplicity of applications from financial market analysis and macroeconomics of disequilibrium, to the study of agents' expectations.
7. According to Foster, a dissipative complex system itself organizes exchanges of knowledge with the environment, which reduces losses of entropy through an activity of human creativity.
8. This kind of path dependence occurs when small shocks at any given time affect the trajectory of the long run in a meaningful and irreversible way (Arthur, 1989; Prigogine and Stengers, 1985). It occurs when trajectories emerging from points go away from each other exponentially (nonlinear) over time. Thus, 'minor differences, insignificant fluctuations may, if they occur in appropriate circumstances, invade the whole system, engender a new operating system'.
9. That involve bridge institutions (Casalet, 2005), gatekeepers (Giuliani and Bell, 2005), club goods, diversity and the possibility to establish complementarities, among others.
10. A fundamental property of percolation is that the probability of it occurring is higher in systems with imperfect connectors and high absorption than the opposite. It is necessary to improve absorption capacity so that it is more effective, rather than targeting only increased connectivity.
11. We are referring to Latin American countries from here on.
12. For example, the lack of an appropriate financial system leads to firms self-financing their innovation activities. They may also have to train their employees, substituting educational institutions, among other things. Therefore, attaining a critical mass of agents playing against the rules becomes difficult.
13. As these authors say, institutional engineering implies congruence between capacity development and the institutions that govern the information distribution and the structure of incentives in the economy.
14. The development of these competences should be centered around (i) the systemic training of workers and employees, (ii) the development of continuous improvement and quality assurance processes (Formento et al., 2007), (iii) post-Taylorist forms of work organization and a significant increase in the role of design as a source of quasi-rents.

REFERENCES

Aghion, P., David, P. and Foray, D. (2008), 'Science, technology and innovation for economic growth: linking policy research and practice in STIG Systems', MPRA WP 12096, available at: http://mpra.ub.uni-muenchen.de/12096/1/MPRA_paper_12096.pdf.
Ahuja, Gautam (2000), 'Collaboration networks, structural holes, and innovation: a longitudinal study', *Administrative Science Quarterly*, **45** (3), 425–55.
Albornoz, F. and Yoguel, G. (2004), 'Competitiveness and production networks: the case of the Argentine automotive sector', *Industrial and Corporate Change*, **13**, 619–42.
Amsden, Alice (2004), 'La sustitución de importaciones en las industrias de alta tecnología: Prebisch renace en Asia', *Revista de la CEPAL*, **82**, 75–90.
Andersen, A.D. (2009), 'Institutions, innovation and development – a comment on Erik Reinert's Quality Index', in Andersen, A.D., Johnson, B., Reinert, E., Andersen, E.S. and Lundvall, B.-Å. (eds), *Institutions, Innovation and Development – Collected Contributions from Workshop*, Working Paper Series 5, 6–20.
Antonelli, C. (1997), 'Percolation processes, technological externalities and the evolution of technological clubs', *Empirica*, **24**, 137–56.
Antonelli, C. (2007), 'The system dynamics of collective knowledge: from gradualism and saltationism to punctuated change', *Journal of Economic Behavior & Organization*, **62**, 215–36.
Antonelli, C. (2008), *Localised Technological Change. Towards the Economics of Complexity*, London and New York: Routledge.

Arthur, Brian (1989), 'Competing technologies, increasing returns and lock-in by historical events', *Economic Journal*, **99**, 116–31.

Arthur, B. (1999), 'Complexity and the economy', *Sciences*, **5411**, 107–109.

Arthur, B., Durlauf, S. and Lane, D. (1997), *The Economy as an Evolving Complex System II*, Redwood City, CA: Addison-Wesley.

Arza, V. and López, A. (2008), 'The determinants of firms' distant collaboration. Evidence from Argentina (1998–2001)', 12th Conference of the International Joseph A. Schumpeter Society.

Barabási, A. and Albert, R. (1999), 'Emergence of scaling in random networks', *Science*, **5439**, 509–12.

Becattini, G. (1989), 'Riflessioni sul distretto culturale marshalliano come concetto sosio-economico', *Stato e mercato*, **25**, 111–28.

Becker, W. and Dietz, J. (2004), 'R&D cooperation and innovation activities of firms – evidence for the German manufacturing industry', *Research Policy*, **33**, 209–23.

Belderbos, R., Carree, M. and Lokshin, B. (2004), 'Cooperative R&D and firm performance', *Research Policy*, **33**, 1477–92.

Benavente, J. and Contreras, D. (2008), 'Cooperation partners in manufacture sector, evidence from the Fourth Chilean Innovation Survey', 12th Conference of the International Joseph A. Schumpeter Society.

Bianchi, C., Gras, N. and Sutz, J. (2008), 'Make, buy and cooperate in innovation: evidence from Uruguayan manufacturing surveys and other innovation studies', 12th Conference of the International Joseph A. Schumpeter Society.

Bisang, R., Novick, M., Sztulwark, S. and Yoguel, G. (2005), 'Las redes de producción y el empleo', in Casalet, M., Cimoli, M. and Yoguel, G. (eds), *Redes, jerarquías y dinámicas productivas*, Buenos Aires: Miño y Dávila, OIT-Flacso México.

Boyer, R. and Petit, P. (1991), 'Kaldor growth theory: past, present and prospect', mimeo.

Braun, O. and Joy, L. (1968), 'A model of economic stagnation – a case study of the Argentine economy', *Economic Journal*, **312**, 868–87.

Caloghirou, Y., Kastelli, I. and Tsakanikas, A. (2004), 'Internal capabilities and external knowledge sources: complements or substitutes for innovative performance?', *Technovation*, **24** (1), 29–39.

Camagni, R. (1991), *Innovation Networks: Spatial Perspectives*, London: Belhaven.

Casalet, M. (2005), 'Los cambios en el diseño institucional y la construcción de redes de modernización tecnológica', in Casalet, M., Cimoli, M. and Yoguel, G. (eds), *Redes, jerarquías y dinámicas productivas*, Buenos Aires: Miño y Dávila, OIT-Flacso México.

Chang, H.J. (2008), *Qué fue del buen samaritano. Naciones ricas, políticas pobres.* Universidad Nacional de Quilmes-AEDA, Buenos Aires.

Cimoli, M., Dosi, G. and Stiglitz, J. (2008), 'The future of industrial policies in the new millennium; toward knowledge-centered development agenda', Lem Working Paper series 19, available at: http://www.lem.sssup.it/WPLem/files/2008-19.pdf.

Cimoli, M. and Porcile, G. (2009), 'Sources of learning paths and technological capabilities: an introductory roadmap of development processes', *Economics of Innovation and New Technology*, **18**, 675–94.

Cimoli, M., Porcile, G. and Rovira, S. (2009), 'Structural change and the BOP-constraint: why did Latin America fail to converge?', *Cambridge Journal of Economics*, **34**, 389–411.

Cimoli, M., Porcile, G. and Vergara, S. (2005), 'Cambio estructural, heterogeneidad productiva y tecnología en América Latina', in Cimoli, M. (ed.), *Heterogeneidad estructural, asimetrías tecnológicas y crecimiento en America Latina*, Santiago de Chile: CEPAL-BID.

Cohen, W. and Levinthal, D. (1989), 'Absorptive capacity: a new perspective on learning and innovation', *Administrative Science Quarterly*, **397**, 569–96.

Cohen, W. and Levinthal, D. (1990), 'Innovation and learning: the two faces of R&D', *Economic Journal*, **35**, 128–52.

Cohen, W.M., Nelson, Richard and Walsh, John (2000), 'Protecting their intellectual assets: appropriability conditions and why US manufacturing firms patent (or not)', National Bureau of Economic Research (NBER) Working Paper No. W7552, 1–50.

Colander, D. (2009), 'Complexity and the history of economic thought', Middlebury College Economics Discussion Paper 08-04.

Coombs, R. and Metcalfe, S. (2000), 'Universities, the science base and the innovation performance of the UK', CRIC Briefing Paper 5, available at: http://www.cric.ac.uk/cric/Pdfs/bp5.pdf.

Coriat, B. and Weinstein, O. (2002), 'Organizations, firms and institutions in the generation of innovations', *Research Policy*, **31**, 273–90.

Cowan, R. (2004), 'Network models of innovation and knowledge diffusion', MERIT-Infonomics Research Memorandum series, 16.

Cowan, R., David, P. and Foray, D (2000), 'The explicit economics of knowledge codification and taciteness', *Industrial and Corporate Change*, **9** (2).

Cullen, A. (2000), 'Contracting, co-operative relations and extended enterprises', *Technovation*, **20**, 363–72.

D'Este, P. and Neely, A. (2008), 'What are the factors that drive the engagement of academic researchers in knowledge transfer activities? Some reflections for future research', in Bessant, J. (ed.), *Creating Wealth From Knowledge. Meeting the Innovation Challenge*, Cheltenham, UK and Northampton, MA, USA: Edward Elgar.

David, P. (1985), 'Clio and the economics of QWERTY', *American Economic Review: Papers and Proceedings*, **75**, 332–37.

David, P. and Foray, D. (1994), 'Percolation structures, Markov random fields and the economics of EDI standard diffusion', in Pogorel, G. (ed.), *Global Telecommunications Strategies and Technological Changes*, Amsterdam: North Holland.

Dosi, G. (1991), 'Some thoughts on the promises, challenges and dangers of an "evolutionary perspective"', *Journal of Evolutionary Economics*, **1**, 5–7.

Dosi, G. and Kaniovski, Y. (1994), 'On "badly behaved" dynamics', *Journal of Evolutionary Economics*, **4**, 93–123.

Dosi, G. and Nelson, R. (1994), 'An introduction to evolutionary theories in economics', *Journal of Evolutionary Economics*, **4**, 153–72.

Eom, Boo-Young and Lee, Keun (2008), 'Determinants of industry-academy linkages and their impacts on firm performance: the case of Korea as a late-comer in knowledge industrialization', IDRC workshop on the developmental universities, Mexico, September.

Erbes, A., Robert, V. and Yoguel, G. (2010), 'Capacities, innovation and feedbacks in production networks in Argentina', *Economics of Innovation and New Technologies*, **19** (8), 719–41.

Erbes, A., Robert, V., Yoguel, G., Borello, J. and Lebedinsky, V. (2006), 'Regímenes tecnológico, de conocimiento y competencia en diferentes formas organizacionales: la dinámica entre difusión y apropiación', *Desarrollo Económico. Revista de Ciencias Sociales*, **46**, 33–62.

Fagerberg, J. (2003), 'Schumpeter and the revival of evolutionary economics: an appraisal of the literature', *Journal of Evolutionary Economics*, **13**, 125–59.

Fleming, L. and Sorenson, O. (2001), 'Technology as a complex adaptive system: evidence from patent data', *Research Policy*, **30** 1019–39.

Formento, H., Braidot, N. and Pittaluga, J. (2007), 'El proceso de mejora continua en PyMEs Argentinas: investigaciones y modelos posibles', Colección Publicatión Electrónica Num. 06, UNGS-IDEI, http://www.ungs.edu.ar/publicaciones/pdf/pe06.pdf.

Foster, J. (1993), 'Economics and the self-organisation approach: Alfred Marshall revisited', *Economic Journal*, **103**, 975–91

Foster, J. (2005), 'From simplistic to complex systems in economics', *Cambridge Journal of Economics*, **29**, 873–92.

Freeman, C. (1991), 'Networks of innovators: a synthesis of research issue', *Research Policy*, **20** (5), 499–514.

Frenken, K. (2006), 'Technological innovation and complexity theory', *Economics of Innovation and New Technology*, **15**, 137–55.

Fritsch, M. and Lukas, R (2001), 'Who cooperates on R&D?', *Research Policy*, **30**, 297–312.

Garrido, C. and Padilla-Pérez, R. (2008), 'Cooperation and innovation in the Mexican manufacturing industry', 12th Conference of the International Joseph A. Schumpeter Society.

Giuliani, E. and Bell, M. (2005), 'The micro-determinants of meso-level learning and innovation: evidence from a Chilean wine cluster', *Research Policy*, **24**, 47–68.

Grandori, A. and Soda, G. (1995), 'Inter-firm networks: antecedents, mechanisms and forms', *Organization Studies*, **16**, 183–214.

Hirschman, Albert (1958), *The Strategy of Economic Development*, New Haven: Yale University.

Hoff, C. and Stiglitz, J. (2002), 'La teoría Económica moderna y el desarrollo', in Meier, G.M. and Stiglitz, J. (eds), *Fronteras de la economía del desarrollo. El futuro en perspectiva histórica*, México DF, Banco Mundial-Alfaomega, México.

Holland, J. (2004), *El orden oculto: de cómo la adaptación crea la complejidad*, México DF: Fondo de Cultura Económica.

Humphrey, John and Schmitz, Hubert (2002), 'How does insertion in global value chains affect upgrading in industrial clusters?', *Regional Studies*, **36** (9), 1017–27.

Kaldor, Nicholas (1972), 'The irrelevance of equilibrium economics', *Economic Journal*, **82** (328), 1237–55.

Kauffman, Stuart A. (1993), *The Origins of Order*, Oxford: Oxford University Press.

Kauffman, Stuart A. (2003), 'Investigaciones', Ed. Tusqets, Metatemas. España.

Kleinknecht, A. and Reijnen, J. (1992), 'Why do firms cooperate on R&D? An empirical study', *Research Policy*, **21**, 347–60.

Kupfer, D. and Avellar, A. (2008), 'Appropriability gap and lack of cooperation: evidences from the Brazilian Innovation Survey', 12th Conference of the International Joseph A. Schumpeter Society.

Lane, D. and Maxfield, R. (1997), 'Foresight complexity and strategy', in Arthur, B., Durlauf, S. and Lane, D. (eds), *The Economy as an Evolving Complex System II*, Redwood City, CA: Addison Wesley.

Laursen, K. and Salter, A. (2004), 'Searching high and low: what types of firms use universities as a source of innovation?', *Research Policy*, **33**, 1201–15.

Lederman, D. and Maloney, W. (2007), *Natural Resources, Neither Curse nor Destiny*, Washington, DC and Palo Alto, CA: The World Bank and Stanford University Press.

Llerena, P. and Lorentz, A. (2004), 'Cumulative causation and evolutionary micro-founded technical change. On the determinants of growth rate differences', *Revue économique*, **55** (6), November, 1191–1214.

Lorentzen, J. (2008), *Resource Knowledge Intensity and Development. Insights from Africa and South America*, Cape Town: Human Science Research Council Press.

Lundvall, B., Intarakumnerd, P. and Vang-Lauridsen, J. (2006), *Asia's Innovation Systems in Transition*, Cheltenham, UK and Northampton, MA, USA: Edward Elgar.

Malerba, F. and Orsenigo, L. (1997), 'Technological regimes and sectoral patterns of innovative activities', *Industrial and Corporate Change*, **6**, 83–118.

Malerba, F. and Orsenigo, L. (2000), 'Knowledge innovative activities and industrial evolution', *Industrial and Corporate Change*, **9**, 289–314.

McCombie, John, S.L. (1983), 'Kaldor's law in retrospect', *Journal of Post-Keynesian Economics*, **V** (3), 414–29.

Metcalfe, S. (2002), 'Knowledge of growth and the growth of knowledge', *Journal of Evolutionary Economics*, **12**, 3–15.

Metcalfe, S. (2007), 'Marshall's Mecca: reconciling the theories of value and development', *Economic Record*, **83**, 1–22.

Metcalfe, S. (2010), 'Dancing in the dark: la disputa sobre el concepto de competencia', *Revista Desarrollo Económico*, **50** (197), 59–79.

Metcalfe, S., Foster, J. and Ramlogan, R. (2006), 'Adaptive economic growth', *Cambridge Journal of Economics*, **30**, 7–32.

Metcalfe, S., Ramlogan, R. and Uyarra, E. (2003), 'Competition, innovation and economic development: the instituted connection', *Institution and Economic Development*, **1**, 21–62.

Metcalfe, S., Ramlogan, R. and Uyarra, E. (2004), 'Competition, innovation and development, the instituted connection', in Cook, P., Kirkpatrick, C., Minogue, M. and Parker, D. (eds), *Leading Issues in Competition Regulation and Development*, Cheltenham, UK and Northampton, MA, USA: Edward Elgar.

Miotti, Luis and Sachwald, Frédérique (2003), 'Co-operative R&D: why and with whom? An integrated framework of analysis', *Research Policy*, **32** (8), 1481–99.

Mowery, D., Oxley, J. and Silverman, B. (1996), 'Strategic alliances and interfirm knowledge transfer', *Strategic Management Journal*, Winter, Special Issue **17**, 77–91.

Myrdal, G. (1957), *Economic Theory and Underdeveloped Regions*, London: Gerald Duckworth.

Nelson, R. and Winter, S. (1982), *An Evolutionary Theory of Economic Change*, Cambridge: Harvard University Press.

Nieto, María Jesús and Santamaría, Luis (2007), 'The importance of diverse collaborative networks for the novelty of product innovation', *Technovation*, **27** (6–7), 367–77.

Norman, P. (2002), 'Protecting knowledge in strategic alliances. Resource and relational characteristics', *Journal of High Technology Management Research*, **13**, 177–202.

North, D. (1990), *Institutions, Institutional Change and Economic Performance*, Cambridge: Cambridge University Press.

Nurkse, Ragnar (1952), 'Some international aspects of the problem of economic development', *American Economic Review*, **42** (2).

Ocampo, J. (2005), 'Economic growth and the dynamic of productive structure', in Ocampo, J.A. (ed.), *Beyond Reforms: Structural Dynamics and Macroeconomic Vulnerability*, World Bank-ECLAC.

Ocampo, José Antonio (2009), 'Impactos de la crisis financiera mundial sobre América Latina', *Revista de la Cepal*, **97**.

Palma, G. (2005), 'Four sources of deindustrialization and a new concept of the Dutch disease', in Ocampo, J.A. (ed.), *Beyond Reforms: Structural Dynamics and Macroeconomic Vulnerability*, World Bank-ECLAC.

Pérez, Carlota (2001), 'Technological change and opportunities for development as a moving target', *Cepal Review*, **75**, 109–30.

Pérez, Carlota (2010), 'Una visión para América Latina: dinamismo tecnológico e inclusión social mediante una estrategia basada en los recursos naturales', *Revista de la Cepal*, **100**, 123–45.

Perona, E. (2004), 'The confused state of complexity economics: an ontological explanation', in Salzano, M. and Colander, D. (eds), *Complexity Hints for Economic Policy*, Milan: Springer.

Pisano, G. (2006), 'Profiting from innovation and the intellectual property revolution', *Research Policy*, **35** (8), 1122–30.

Prebisch, R. (1959), 'Commercial policy in the underdeveloped countries', *American Economic Review*, **49**, Papers and Proceedings of the Seventy-first Annual Meeting of the American Economic Association, 251–73.

Prigogine, Ilya and Stengers, Isabel (1985), 'La nueva alianza. La metamorfosis de la ciencia', Ed. Alianza, Ciencias. España.

Ramos, J. (1998), 'Una estrategia de desarrollos productivos a partir de complejos productivos en torno a recursos naturales', *Revista de la CEPAL*, **66**, 105–25.

Reinert, E. (1995), 'Competitiveness and its predecessors – a 500-years cross-national perspective', *Structural Change and Economic Dynamics*, **6**, 23–42.

Reinert, E. (2007), *How Rich countries Got Rich and Why Poor Countries Stay Poor*, London: Constable.

Richardson, G. (1972), 'The organization of industry', *Economic Journal*, **82**, 883–96.

Rivera Ríos, M., Robert,V. and Yoguel, G. (2009), 'Cambio tecnológico, complejidad e instituciones: una aproximación desde la estructura industrial e institucional de Argentina y México', *Revista Problemas del Desarrollo*, **157**, 75–109.

Rosenberg, Nathan (1982), *Inside the Black Box: Technology and Economics*, Cambridge: Cambridge University Press.

Rosestein-Rodan, P.N. (1943), 'Problems of industrialization of Eastern and South-Eastern Europe', *Economic Journal*, **53** (210/211), 202–11.

Ross, J. (2005), 'Divergence and growth collapses: theory and empirical evidence', in Ocampo, J.A. (ed.), *Beyond Reforms: Structural Dynamics and Macroeconomic Vulnerability*, World Bank-ECLAC.

Santoro, M. and Gopalakrishnan, S. (2000), 'The institutionalization of knowledge transfer activities within industry–university collaborative ventures', *Journal of Engineering and Technology Management*, **17**, 299–319.

Saviotti, P. (2001), 'Networks, national innovation systems and self organization', in Fischer, M. and Fröhlich, J. (eds), *Knowledge, Complexity and Innovation Systems*, Berlin: Springer.

Schumpeter, J. (1934), *The Theory of Economic Development*, Cambridge: Harvard University Press, First edition 1912.

Schumpeter, J. (1942), *Capitalism, Socialism, and Democracy*, New York: Harper and Brothers.

Silverberg, G. (2007), 'Long waves: conceptual, empirical and modelling issues', in Hanusch, H., and Pyka, A. (eds), *Applied Evolutionary Economics and the Knowledge Base Economy*, Cheltenham, UK and Northampton, MA, USA: Edward Elgar.

Silverberg, G., Dosi, G. and Orsenigo, L. (1988), 'Innovation, diversity and diffusion: a self-organization model', *Economic Journal*, **98**, 1032–54.

Silverberg, G. and Verspagen, B. (2005), 'A percolation model of innovation in complex technology spaces', *Journal of Economic Dynamics and Control*, **29**, 225–44.

Simon, H.A. (1969), *The Sciences of the Artificial*, Cambridge, MA: MIT Press.

Singer, H.W. (1950), 'The distribution of gains between investing and borrowing countries', *American Economic Review*, **40** (2), Papers and Proceedings of the 62nd Annual Meeting of the American Economic Association, 473–85.

Stokes, Donald (1997), *Pasteur's Quadrant: Basic Science and Technological Innovation*, Brookings Institution Press.

Teece, D. (1986), 'Profiting from technological innovation: implications for integration, collaboration, licensing and public policy', *Research Policy*, **15**, 285–305.

Teece, David (1992), 'Competition, cooperation, and innovation: organizational arrangements for regimes of rapid technological progress', *Journal of Economic Behaviour & Organization*, **18** (1), 1–25.

Teece, D. and Pisano, G. (1994), 'The dynamic capabilities of firms: an introduction', *Industrial and Corporate Change*, **3**, 537–56.

Tesfatsion, L. (2003), 'Agent-based computational economics: modeling economies as complex adaptive systems', *Information Sciences*, **149**, 1–8.

Tether, B. (2002), 'Who co-operates for innovation, and why – an empirical analysis', *Research Policy*, **31**, 947–67.

Thirlwall, A.P. (1979), 'The balance of payments constraint as an explanation of international growth rate differences', *Banca Nazionale del Lavoro Quarterly Review*.

Tsai, K. and Wang, J.C. (2009), 'External technology sourcing and innovation performance LMT sectors: an analysis based on the Taiwanese Technological Innovation Survey', *Research Policy*, **38**, 518–26.

Vega-Jurado, J., Gutierrez-Gracia, A., Fernandez-de-Lucio, I. and Manjarres-Henrıquez, L. (2008), 'The effect of external and internal factors on firms' product innovation', *Research Policy*, **37**, 616–32.

Veugelers, R. (1997), 'Internal R&D expenditures and external technology sourcing', *Research Policy*, **26**, 303–15.

Veugelers, R. and Cassiman, B. (2005), 'R&D cooperation between firms and universities. Some empirical evidence from Belgian manufacturing', *International Journal of Industrial Organization*, **23**, 355–79.

Watts, D. (2003), *Small Worlds: The Dynamics of Networks Between Order and Randomness*, Princeton, NJ, Princeton University Press.

Witt, U. (1997), 'Self-organization and economics – what is new?', *Structural Change and Economic Dynamics*, **8**, 489–507.

Yoguel, G. (2007), 'Tramas productivas y generación de ventajas competitivas: un abordaje metodológico para pasar de la firma individual a la red', in Novick, M. and Palomino, H. (eds), *Estructura productiva y empleo*, Editorial Miño y Dávila and Ministerio de Trabajo, Buenos Aires.

Yoguel, G., Borello, J., Delfini, M., Erbes, A., Kataishi, R., Robert, V. and Roitter, S. (2009), *Redes de conocimiento en tramas productivas argentinas*, Flacso, Mexico and CRDI, Canada.

Yoguel, G. and Robert, V. (2010), 'Capacities, processes, and feedbacks: the complex dynamics of development', *Seoul Journal of Economics*, **23** (2), Summer.

PART V

LESSONS AND IMPLICATIONS FOR ECONOMIC POLICY

18 Coevolution, emergence and economic development: some lessons from the Israeli and Mexican experience

Gabriela Dutrénit and Morris Teubal

1. INTRODUCTION

Whilst everybody agrees that innovation nowadays lies at the heart of economic growth in both advanced and industrializing economies, there is no agreement concerning the processes linking the two. From a simplistic view it can be argued that innovation influences economic growth directly (probably a New Growth Theory's view). Another point of view follows a more structuralist and systems-evolutionary perspective where in order for innovation to affect economic growth it should trigger structural change, which for the purposes of this discussion is identified with new sectors (or widely defined product classes), markets, clusters, large multinational companies, and other forms of what may be termed Higher Level Organizations (HLO). These HLOs can be characterized as multi-agent structures (for example, networks, regional or sectoral innovation systems). In this view, the impact of innovation will be relatively weak if it does not trigger the emergence of these higher-level, multi-agent structures, and will be strong if it does.[1]

Our point of view corresponds to the structuralist/evolutionary perspective to economic growth, which goes back to Schumpeter (1934, 1939) and Kuznets (1971, 1973), and more recently to many authors (for example, Saviotti and Pyka, 2004, among others). A relatively early exponent was Kuznets (1971, 1973), who introduced the concept of modern economic growth, a process which involves, in parallel to the growth of output per capita, a high rate of change in the structure of output and a high rate of accumulation of production relevant knowledge.

The 'early neoclassical' presumption is that structural change does not play an active role in promoting economic growth; but rather the other way around, economic growth 'causes' structural change through supply factors (such as differential rates of growth of capital and labour) and demand factors (such as changes of income and price effects). In contrast, in Kuznets' perspective, radical innovations lead to the emergence of new sectors, which in turn propel economic growth (or structural change).

The structuralist perspective did not consider fully possible coevolutionary processes underpinning the link between structural change and economic growth. Moreover, whilst some analysis of coevolutionary processes of various kinds would gradually become central in research that follows an evolutionary perspective (for example Nelson, 1994, 2007; Saviotti, 1996, 1997; Murmann, 2002, 2003; Breznitz, 2007a, 2007b), the Schumpeterian literature on coevolution still seems to lack a basic analytical framework for incorporating such processes into a broader evolutionary process: still less does it have one linking innovation to economic development (see also Fagerberg et al., 1999; Sotarauta and Srinivas, 2006; Fagerberg and Verspagen, 2007). This chapter makes a contribution in that direction and focuses on coevolutionary and emergence processes in structural change and growth following an industry life cycle perspective (Abernathy and Utterback, 1978; Klepper, 1996; among others).

Previous work (see Avnimelech and Teubal, 2006, 2008a) suggests the importance of characterizing a prior, pre-emergence phase in the contexts of an industry life cycle conceptual framework where the transition to emergence may or may not take place. The pre-emergence phase is characterized by inventions/innovations, which contribute, together with collective and interactive learning, to define both a new product class and a standard product (or platform) configuration. This is the qualitative dimension that lies at the root of new sectors or industries (a necessary but not sufficient condition). But the major impact of innovation on economic growth may depend on a successful transition to the emergence phase, where the quantitative dimension of structural change (or 'scaling up' of the invention/innovation) takes place. Contrary to most industry life cycle theory, this transition is neither assured nor automatic; following a coevolutionary processes approach, there might be a critical mass required to generate an endogenous dynamic. However, our presumption is that there are many socially profitable, invention/innovation-led situations that lead neither to new industries/HLOs nor to the associated quantitative scaling up and high impact. This insight strongly suggests that government policy may have an important role to play to overcome this situation. A related point is the need of updating an analytically satisfying view of what new industries, markets and clusters are, a view that could contribute to differentiate those HLOs with allocative efficiency from those that are characterized by dynamic/technological/Schumpeterian efficiency.[2]

To sum up, the purpose of this chapter is to contribute to the analysis of coevolutionary processes in economic development focusing on their role in the emergence of the above multi-agent structures, and in initiating a self-sustained development process more generally speaking. The coevolutionary processes considered involve the following variables: innovation policy, innovation (including capabilities at firms), innovation finance, and the science, technology and higher education (STE) capabilities and outputs. We will focus on two case studies and then attempt to extract a number of common features about the nature and importance of coevolutionary and emergence processes for growth and development. The two case studies are: (1) Israel, with a focus on the dynamic processes leading to emergence of a venture capital industry and market, and associated entrepreneurial high tech cluster during the 1990s; and (2) Mexico, with a focus on the conditions for successful STE-innovation coevolution.

Section 2 introduces basic ideas from the literature on emergence and coevolution to analyse the coevolution of STE with innovation. Section 3 proposes a conceptual framework to analyse the emergence and coevolutionary processes of these arenas in the context of economic development, and differentiates two cases based on alternative assumptions of decreasing or increasing returns. Sections 4 and 5 illustrate the cases based on evidence from Israel and Mexico, respectively. Section 6 discusses the results and depicts a broad model, and Section 7 contains final reflections.

2. COEVOLUTION AND EMERGENCE IN THE LITERATURE

2.1 Emergence

The concept of complexity is broadly used to approach physical, biological or social phenomena, which are characterized by a set of intricate relationships that arise from the interaction of agents. Based on the idea that these arenas are full of systems, complexity theories draw on relationships, emergence, patterns and iterations. They suggest that, while Darwinian/Lamarckian selection does matter, agents play a role in the evolution of these systems and their adaptation to external changes. Holland (1995) puts forward the most diffused model of complex systems, the complex adaptive system, which is a dynamic network of many agents (the main building block of the system) acting in parallel, and reacting to what the other agents are doing. Agents interact with each other in unpredictable and unplanned ways, but regularities emerge from these interactions and begin to form a pattern, which feeds back into the system.

From a more coevolutive approach it is said that complex adaptive systems adapt to changes but do not learn from the process, whilst a broader concept of complex evolving systems refers to those that learn and evolve from each change enabling them to influence their environment, or more accurately predict probable changes in the future, and prepare for them accordingly (Arthur et al., 1997).

Processes underlying complex systems are dynamic, non-linear and path dependent. Relevant properties are emergence, coevolution and self-organization, others include connectivity, variety and robustness. Emergence, as one of the key concepts in complexity theories, refers to a system's behaviour or structure that arises from the interaction between many individual agents, which happens in random ways rather than being planned or controlled (Kauffman, 1995; Holland, 1998). The outcomes are new properties of the system as a whole which do not exist at the individual agent (or component) level, for example the property of memory not being that of any individual synapses. As asserted by Johnson (2002), from the point of view of the whole it seems as if things simply happen. In some cases the system has to reach a combined threshold of diversity, organization, and connectivity before emergent behaviour appears; in other words, critical masses are needed. Coevolution refers to links between the evolution of the system and its environment, where changes of one induce changes in the other. This property is broadly explored in the next section referring to the populations of STE and innovation. Self-organization refers to the idea that even though complex systems do not have a hierarchy of command, control, planning or management, there is a constant process of re-organization to find the best fit with the environment. The system is continually self-organizing through the process of emergence and feedback. According to Goldstein (1999), the process of self-organization contributes to the arising of novel and coherent structures, patterns and properties. Complex systems are also characterized by being highly sensitive to initial conditions: the butterfly effect illustrates that initial conditions generate specific influences on a non-linear system (Kauffman, 1993).

According to Potts (2000), key components of evolutionary microeconomics are: (i) connections determine the dynamic properties of the system, but diverse sorts of linked structures differ in their dynamic properties; (ii) the dynamics of connections and the emergence of higher-level structures and patterns are the essence of a generalized evolutionary framework in economics; and (iii) system element duality exists, thus once a system emerges as an entity, it can serve as a singular building block for a higher-level system. The definition of an element or a system depends upon the level at which it is viewed. This leads to insights about emergence and hierarchy: twin principles by which systems are constructed into higher-level systems (emergence of Higher Level Organizations, HLO in our terminology) and the resultant structure (hierarchy). A hyper-structure is a system that combines both principles. Also relevant for this chapter are arguments in relation to the emergence of order. Potts (2000) argues that order and coordination emerge in an economic system by the processes of selection and self-organization. Self-organization occurs spontaneously, and much of the order in organisms may not be the result of selection at all but of the spontaneous order of self-organized systems. But, as the whole is greater than the sum of the parts, thus the question of order calls for the emergence and stability of the patterns of connectivity among elements or, more directly, asks how coordination actually comes about. In contrast, Goldstein (2003) makes a case that the emergence of new order is more appropriately constructed rather than self-organized, opening a role for policies.

Emergence opens up fresh insights on the analysis of STE-innovation coevolution and its impact on economic development, which will be referred to in the following sections.

2.2   Coevolution

There is a growing literature that applies coevolutionary concepts to the study of socioeconomic systems, although challenging issues for transferring evolutionary concepts and insights from the biological to the social arenas have been recognized (Norgaard, 1984, 1994; Levinthal and Myatt, 1994; March, 1994; Nelson, 1995; McKelvey et al., 1999; Lewin and Volberda, 1999; van den Bergh and Gowdy, 2003). In relation to science, technology and innovation, Nelson (1994) discusses coevolution between technology, industry and institutions; Murray (2002) between industries and national institutions; Murmann (2003) between Industries and Academic Disciplines; Metcalfe et al. (2005) between clinical knowledge and technological capabilities; Nygaard (2008) between technology, market and institutions; and Breznitz (2007b) between technology policies, industry and the state. Fagerberg et al. (2008) approach the case of the Norwegian National Innovation System (NIS) from a coevolutionary perspective. Sotarauta and Srinivas (2006) relate public policy with economic development in technologically innovative regions, and highlight that self-organization is an emergent feature of development.

The standard evolutionary approach draws on a concatenation of three general causal processes (variation, selection and retention) introduced by Campbell's (1969) model of change. The struggle over scarce resources is seen as a fourth process in the case of the social and economic evolution by some authors (for example, Aldrich, 2001; Sotarauta and Srinivas, 2006), which may lead to new varieties.

Variation, as the introduction of new entities, may be intentional, and so driven by an actively generated alternative and solution to a problem, or blind, and so driven by environmental selection pressures. The selection process happens in a specific environment, which includes both the market and a set of non-market factors (especially institutions). It can be originated in two ways: first, there are forces that lead to differential selection, and, second, it can be a selective elimination of certain types of variations. The evolutionary approach stresses adaptation to the selection environment; and, like most ecological studies, it tends to ignore strategies and intentions of individual actors or collectivities. The retention process involves the mechanisms for preserving, duplicating, or otherwise reproducing selected variations, so that the selected activities are repeated on future occasions or the selected activities appear again in the future. Following Nelson and Winter (1982) and Zollo and Winter (2002), replication is also an important concept in evolutionary models; it refers to the process in which new selected variations are replicated elsewhere, in another organization or in another location. These causal processes may lead to the emergence of an HLO that feeds the coevolutionary process or whose processes involve coevolution among selected variables.

Variation, selection and retention are causal processes that may explain how outcomes are produced from a given set of conditions including resources, incentives and other framework conditions. Very specific features of the environment frequently influence the trajectory of a population. Because environments differ, the same causal process may produce very different outcomes. Usually, if these processes are blind, the environment plays a role in the evolution of populations. However, from a complex systems view, the actions of human agents in the evolving populations not only adapt but to some extent shape their own selection environment.

Coevolution, as the evolution of different populations that are causally linked, was originally confined to two populations. According to this, a coevolutionary explanation requires two conditions: first, two analytically separable populations, each of which experiences variation, selection and retention processes, and second, links between both evolutions; in other words, the evolution of one population influences the evolutionary path of the other. Later on, authors also analysed the coevolution between several populations, various levels within a population, and in terms of populations and their environments.

A coevolutionary process could be either beneficial or risky for the populations involved; this depends on the particular causal relationship that links the parties. Biological ecologists have thought extensively about the relationship between different populations and they have identified six possible kinds of pair-wise interactions or processes: competition, predation, neutralism, mutualism, commensalisms and amensalism (Murmann, 2002).

2.3   Coevolution of STE and Innovation

Most of the developing countries have: a narrow STE and innovation (I) infrastructure; limited science and technology human resources; a business sector in which short-term profits are biased against innovation; weak institutional building; and dramatic social needs. Thus the coevolution of STE and I may be relevant for accelerating a trajectory of development. Most of the catching up processes in the last decades were driven by an extremely acute accumulation of I capabilities, which were fundamentally driven by learning from experience instead of by science or research and development (R&D) activities (Hobday, 1995; Kim, 1997), but it seems that the conditions for catching up and development have changed. There is little dispute about the argument that scientific and technological knowledge is essential for the development process, however the conditions for virtuous cycles of STE-I coevolution are still unclear.

Does the variation, selection and retention model possess an explanatory power on the evolution of STE and I populations? How are new variants introduced into these arenas? How are selection pressures that eliminate some variants generated? Finally, how are the selected variants retained over time to serve as the raw material for a new set of variants?

Following Dutrénit et al. (2008a, 2008b), STE and I are two activities that transform capabilities into outputs, so the populations can be defined in terms of either one or both variables.[3] The population of capabilities for STE is formed by researchers and for I by engineers and technicians, including doctors in science and engineering, involved in innovation activities. Outputs of these populations include human resources (graduates and postgraduates), specific knowledge and new capabilities for STE, and new products, processes and patents for I.

Processes leading to new variants in the population of researchers include those underlying an increase in the number of STE human resources, the creation of positions for new researchers in existent and emergent fields, changes in incentives to stimulate researchers to enter emerging fields, and the creation of new research teams in existing and emerging fields. The selection process results from research proposal requests for grants submitted to competitive research funds, and from publication of papers in peer review journals, among others. Framework conditions, criteria for evaluation and the existing social norms in relation to STE and I determine what is socially accepted. This affects the relationships between the relevant science and technology committees on the one hand and the academic research community on the other, thereby shaping the selection process. The existence of a permanent post with competitive income, availability of resources for research, prestige of the universities or research centres where they work, framework conditions, and the particular social norms affect the retention process.

A parallel process occurs in relation to the population of engineers and technicians involved in business innovation. Note also that salaries and stability, stimulus for developing innovation activities (for example administrative and researchers' careers, and innovation culture of the firms), and the prestige of the organization constitute the retention mechanisms in the population of engineers and technicians, which is also affected by framework conditions and the particular social norms that prevail at the time.

The environment for the variation processes in both populations is formed by the educational system, the domestic and international labour market, the scientific and technological paths, the competitive position of the national industry, and the national postgraduate scholarship policy, among others. The environment for the selection and retention processes is associated with the organization of research, the STE budget, the innovation policy mix, the financial sector, the market structure of the hiring firms, the labour market, the regulatory framework, the existence of innovative firms and their innovation culture. The processes of variation, selection and retention are also influenced by economies of scale and externalities, learning processes and by the macro culture.

Drawing on Murmann (2002), four types of bi-directional causal mechanisms may link the evolutionary trajectory of STE and of I, and may be in the basis of a coevolution of both populations: (i) competition, where each population inhibits the other; (ii) predator/host, where one of the populations exploits the other population; (iii) neutralism, where neither population affects the other (thus it can be evolution of each population but not coevolution of both), and (iv) cooperation, meaning interaction, which is favourable to both populations (named mutualism in the literature). For instance, in the case of cooperation, four significant causal mechanisms may link the evolutionary trajectory of STE and I: mobility of human resources (PhD students, technicians and researchers), training of human resources, exchange of knowledge by formal means (contracts, seminars, stays) and informal networks, and lobbying by each on behalf of the other. These causal mechanisms bring about coevolution as they affect the variation, selection and retention processes that transform STE as well as those that transform I.[4]

The behaviour of the coevolving populations is governed by a set of norms that they have internalized over time, and is also influenced by restrictions associated with these norms. It is worthwhile to differentiate between those norms that shape informal institutions associated with routines, habits, codes and agents' modes of behaviour, and the formal institutions that emanate from constitutions, laws or regulations and set up the rules of the game. Both norms and rules of the game condition the variation, selection and retention processes.

The variation process, in terms of the diversity of behaviours and rationalities, is institutionally conditioned. For instance, if the norm of 'publish or perish' has been introduced in the population of researchers, and at the same time it has been strengthened by incentives derived from specific rules, then the emergence of other behaviours associated with taking risks to explore new ways of knowledge production is difficult. Along the same lines, if the idea that only low cost minor innovations are required to reach high benefits has been introduced in the population of engineers and technicians, it is difficult to generate behaviours associated with evaluating the risks of the emergence of competitors with higher innovation capacities or HLO based on these different behaviours. The selection and retention processes of certain types of agents within the populations are also highly determined by the institutions. They act as filters for the expansion of certain agents in relation to others. For instance, postgraduate scholarships in the case of the researchers' population and public funds for R&D in the engineers and technicians' population are some of the bases for the selection process, which are usually more demanding and have more capacity to distinguish between different competitors than natural selection.

Those institutions located in the interface between universities and firms are the main generators of rules to favour bidirectional mechanisms between both populations. Some of the main characteristics of these intermediary institutions that explain this role are: (i) they are created through agreements between knowledge producers and users, for instance between academic research groups and engineers and technicians groups; (ii) they clearly define the role played by different agents – knowledge producers and users – in their creation, and these agents also fix the operation rules; and (iii) they establish specific rules in relation to the participation that the personnel from the producers and users can play (Puchet, 2008).

This approach to the coevolution of STE and I take into account the initial conditions based on the endowment of capabilities (whether or not they constitute a critical mass to generate dynamics) and the institutional framework. But to transit from a situation without coevolutive processes towards another where those processes are endogenously generated and generalized may require an institutional change. In particular, what is called for is the emergence and consolidation of those institutions that favour variation, selection and retention processes and bidirectional mechanisms. Exogenous factors may also be needed to trigger new coevolutive processes.

Drawing on this approach to coevolutionary processes of STE and I, the next section proposes a model that illustrates such coevolution, and characterizes the endogenous components and exogenous factors. Particular attention is paid to those conditions where both push and pull effects may take place, that is, virtuous STE-I coevolution occurs.

3.   TOWARDS A MODEL OF STE-INNOVATION COEVOLUTION

3.1   The Basic Model

We assume that both STE and I are affected by two distinct relationships or components: a coevolutionary relationship, which we will term endogenous and that could be either 'push' or 'pull', and one or more exogenous components. The coevolutionary components are the variable I, which affects STE directly through a pull effect [f(I. . .)], and the variable STE, which affects I directly through a push effect [g(STE. . .)]. The exogenous component(s) will be any other component directly affecting STE [Xste in (18.1a)] or I [Xi in (18.1b)].

$$STE = f(I. . .) + Xste \qquad (18.1a)$$

f(I. . .) is the 'pull' effect on STE

$$I = g(STE. . .) + Xi \qquad (18.1b)$$

g(STE. . .) is the 'push' effect on I

At this point in the analysis, STE in the above equations represents graduates in the I-relevant disciplines, particularly engineering and sciences, and to some extent from other areas pertaining to the non-technological aspects of I (for example management, finance, and production and marketing of innovative products and processes). Not all the I-relevant graduates will be employed in I by the business sector, since many of the engineering graduates will be employed in the routine operation and maintenance of production equipment and physical infrastructure throughout the economy, and even within the business sector, some of the graduates in the I-relevant disciplines will be employed in routine production and marketing rather than in I. An almost exclusive focus on engineering and other relevant graduates may be particularly important in the early stage of industrialization where imitation and routine types of innovation (rather than more complex innovation) may predominate.[5] Increasingly and particularly in later stages of development, other I-relevant outputs of STE, such as specific knowledge and certain STE capabilities that underpin more complex, multidisciplinary innovations will become increasingly important.[6]

Thus, at this early stage, the left hand side term of (18.1a) (STE) should be regarded as the supply of graduates, both domestic and coming from abroad, which are employable in I in the business sector. This supply is a response to two kinds of demand:

- f(I. . .) is the pull term, which represents an endogenous, short-term demand for STE graduates induced by the aforementioned I;
- Xste could be regarded as 'exogenous' demand by the government or public sector for trained I-related graduates, which are not presently being demanded by the business sector. These are employed by a specific technological infrastructure, Public Technological Institutes (PTI), either for training purposes or for the production of public or semi-public goods (technology and capabilities), which will increase the future business demand for I).[7, 8]

The short-term demand for I-relevant graduates is assumed to be supplied by existing STE facilities and personnel; while the exogenous (and partly long-term) demand is being supplied partly by graduates from the new STE facilities and partly both by students sent abroad to pursue their studies and immigrant STE professionals coming from abroad. They do not need to be presently employed in the business sector either because of lack of demand or due to their post as graduates under training at the PTI.[9] More generally speaking, applied research institutes, usually government-owned or hybrid, or technology centres responding to the future needs of specific industrial branches, could also be the loci of innovative activities involving immigrant returning professionals or returning STE graduates from abroad. The basic idea here is not only to provide provisional employment. Rather it is to employ them in commercially oriented R&D/innovation activities in publicly sponsored institutes even before the business sector is ready to employ them in such activities. An interesting example is Rafael, Israel's Armaments Development Authority, a public research institute, which absorbed both foreign immigrants and returning students, some of whom (including full research groups) were later transferred to the first wave of private companies undertaking R&D in ICT-related areas during the late 1960s (Breznitz, 2007a).[10] This experience is analysed in Section 4.

Similarly the demand for I by the business sector in the left hand side of (18.1b) derives from two sources:

- g(STE. . .) is endogenous, short-term demand resulting from the supply push of I, derived from the availability of employable graduates in business innovation,
- Xi is other, 'exogenous' demand resulting from domestic financial infrastructure, termed here Venture Capital (VC), and by other factors.

A major feature of the push and pull components of STE and I is their reactivity or adaptability and their inducement effect. Thus STE reactivity is the extent to which the level of STE reacts to a particular (or change in the) level of I in equation (18.1a); and STE inducement is the extent by which the above change in STE will induce further changes in I in equation (18.1b). Similarly, we may talk of I-reactivity/adaptability in equation (18.1b), and I-inducement in equation (18.1a). Reactivity and inducement will depend on the structure of STE and of I. Thus, a policy leading to enhanced variation of STE capabilities (see Section 2), may lead to enhancement of the reactivity of STE graduates to I.

In many countries, the exogenous component of STE in equation (18.1a) (Xste) would appear earlier than the pull effect, since – as assumed below – the existence or effectiveness of the pull effect requires a certain level or critical mass of I in the business sector.

Summarizing, Xste in this chapter depends on three factors: (a) creation and operation of new teaching/research universities and other STE facilities, and increase in the number of researchers; (b) sending students abroad to complete engineering and science-related degrees or to enrol in postgraduate studies, both with a proviso requiring them to return at some point in their careers to their country of origin; and (c) promoting immigration of foreign STE professionals and/or the return of professionals working abroad.[11] Moreover all of these must be employed by PTI in order to be ready to be involved in business I.

Government policy will play an important role in kicking off a dynamic process in the system. By assuring a positive and sufficiently large level of Xste, it will facilitate the initiation of I activities, which would also benefit from government subsidies. At some point in the process the levels of STE and I will be sufficiently high for a coevolutionary process to start.

It is worth noting that the coevolutionary processes implied by the relationships of equations (18.1a) and (18.1b) depend on generating a sequence of endogenous and exogenous events, as defined above. However, in this early stage, the time is not yet ripe for significant joint STE-I events that directly affect both I and STE, such as the creation of university–industry centres like those in the US during the 1980s/1990s, the implementation of something similar to Israel's Magnet program in 1992 (after 23 years of supporting regular R&D in firms), or the introduction of vast collaborative mission oriented R&D programs, as in Australia in the last two decades. Whenever joint events (which are directly coevolutionary) are present they should be reflected in an explicit third component to equations (18.1a) and (18.1b).

Equations (18.1a) and (18.1b) require further specification. They are influenced by the capabilities, the creation of systemic components of the system (VC and PTI) and policy variables, but they are also subject to two additional constraints: critical mass conditions and capacity constraints.

Critical mass conditions
A minimum level of STE (STEo) is required for push, and a minimum level of I (Io) is required for pull. Thus:

$$f(I<Io)=0; \ g(STE<STEo)=0 \tag{18.2}$$

The above means that (Io, STEo) represent necessary conditions for a virtuous STE-I coevolutionary process to take place. We will term this the *critical mass condition*. It includes a critical level of I for the pull effect to be effective (Io), and a critical level of STE for the push effect to be effective (STEo).

Capacity constraints
At any moment in time, there exists a maximum level of STE (STE^), termed STE-Capacity and a maximum level of I termed I-Capacity (I^).

$$[STE^\wedge = STE^\wedge (R, K; PTI) > Xste]^{12, \ 13} \tag{18.3a}$$

$$I^\wedge = I^\wedge(N; VC) > Xi^{14} \tag{18.3b}$$

Table 18.1   Summary of main relationships and variables

Dependent variables	Independent components		Capacity constraints
	Endogenous Push and pull	Exogenous (Other and Long term)	
STE	Pull: f[0i I, Sf(ste); Gv]	Xste[R, K; PTI; Sx(ste)]	STE^(R, K; PTI) (<Xste)
I	Push: g[0ste STE; Sg(i)]	Xi[N; VC; Sx(i)]	I^(N; VC) (<Xi)

PTI and VC refer, as mentioned above, to the specific technological and financial infrastructures supporting respectively, STE personnel and business I.

Capacity is also affected by the following variables:

R = number of STE *researchers/teachers* (may be weighted by capabilities)

K = scope of physical facilities comprising the STE infrastructure (buildings, teaching equipment, research facilities, and so on)

N = number of innovative organizations in the business sector (or a relationship between this and skilled personnel in R&D or an index of I-capabilities).

A major distinction is required between capacity and capabilities. For the purposes of this chapter, capabilities refer to the quality (or qualitative aspects) of STE and I, while capacity refers to the quantitative dimension. Thus for a given capacity, some types of capability enhancement may lead to an increase in STE and/or I 'output', when for example 'outputs' are measured in constant quality terms.

There are two types of capability:

- Capabilities which directly affect co-evolution by facilitating enhanced reactivity/adaptability and thereby enhanced 'pull' (0i>1 in Pull equation of Table 18.1) or 'push' (0ste>1 in Push equation of Table 18.1).[15]
- Capabilities which indirectly affect co-evolution through the exogenous term of equations (18.1a) and (18.1b) (see Table 18.1). PTI act directly on the 'quality' (and quantity) of STE outputs through the Xste; and VC acts directly on the 'quality' (and quantity) of I outputs through the Xi term (see Table 18.1).[16]

A set of policy variables influence the various independent variables introduced up to now. There are four types of innovation policy variables that we consider:

- Operational subsidies (S) of which there are two types:
  - Those which enhance pull and push terms f[. . .] and g[. . .] through enhanced reactivity [Sf(ste) and Sg(i)];
  - Those which enhance the exogenous component Sx(ste) and Sx(i).[17]
- Long run public physical and human capital investment or public support of investment oriented to building new universities and research facilities (K) and human capital (R);

- Specific technological and financial infrastructures (PTI and VC);
- Changes in governance at STE organizations (G).[18]

Table 18.1 summarizes the main relationships mentioned above concerning constraints, capabilities and policies; this further specifies the basic model of equations (18.1a) and (18.1b).

Both X_i and $I^\wedge$ depend on the number of innovative organizations (N) and VC. The latter provides the finance and other added value to the former and especially to newly formed innovative SMEs and start up (SU) companies. X_i also depends on operational subsidies $S_x(i)$. VC could be construed as a systemic intermediary in the innovation/knowledge market, and as a locus of innovation capabilities that, by helping innovative SMEs to market their products and access to the right complementary assets and global networks, would contribute to the creation and growth of an innovative SME/SU segment.

The exogenous component of STE (Xste) and STE$^\wedge$ depend on the number of STE researchers/teachers, the STE physical facilities (K), and the network of PTI. PTI could also be considered a systemic intermediary required by the system for the training and creation of those semi-public goods required for effective I.

Note that the exogenous levels of STE and I are strongly related to the capacity levels of these variables, thus policies which increase 'capacity' may generate the critical mass necessary for the pull and push effects of equations (18.1) and, therefore, for the coevolution between these variables. Also the capability coefficients 0_j ($j=i$,ste), which will be enhanced by 'learning' and by changes in 'institutions/governance', may contribute to STE-I coevolution once critical masses are achieved.

3.2 Dynamic Profiles of Coevolution

To identify the dynamic profiles of coevolution, we focus on the $f(I. . .)$ and $g(STE. . .)$ functions of equations (18.1), including the critical masses for push and pull described in (18.2) (STEo and Io), to which we add the exogenous components (Xste and Xi) and STE and I capacities (STE$^\wedge$ and I$^\wedge$). The various cases and sub-cases depend on the initial conditions, which depend on the relationship between the exogenous components and the critical masses, and on the relative slopes of the f and g schedules.

The relevant schedules are drawn on the STE and I phase diagrams in Figures 18.1 and 18.2. There are two main cases. Case 1 is characterized by decreasing returns to push and pull; we assume that 'capacity' variables, capabilities and the exogenous components are constant. Case 2 is characterized by increasing returns followed by decreasing returns as the system approaches capacity levels; we assume non-constant levels of capacity, capabilities and the exogenous components, also during the adjustment process.

3.2.1 Case 1: Decreasing returns to push and pull
Figures 18.1a, 18.1b and 18.1c show three examples of countries' initial conditions under decreasing returns to push and pull; each one of the two variables (STE and I) have low adaptability or reactivity (as embodied in the $f(. . .)$ and $g(. . .)$ functions of equations (18.1)) to increases in the other variable (I and STE, respectively). Moreover, it is assumed that (beyond the relevant critical mass STEo and Io), a given increase in STE

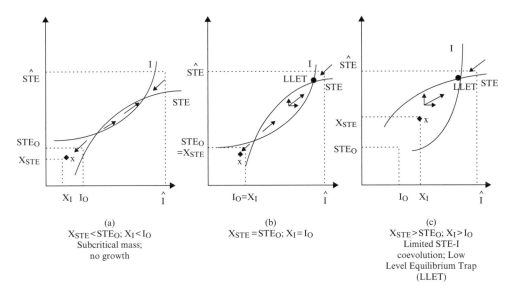

Figure 18.1   Decreasing returns to push and pull

(I) will induce a progressively smaller increase in I (STE), the higher the level of I (STE) already achieved.

The schedules and arrows of the three initial conditions in Figure 18.1 are drawn under the assumption that both the exogenous components of equations (18.1) and the capacity levels of the STE and I systems (STE^ and I^) are constant. Which specific figure is relevant depends on whether the exogenous components of equations (18.1) (Xste and Xi) are correspondingly smaller, equal or larger than the critical mass required for push and pull (STEo and Io).

If the initial conditions are higher than the critical mass required for pull and push effects to take place, the system can coevolve to reach a low-level equilibrium trap (LLET). There would be a coevolutionary process that leads to this point. Once the system reaches this point, it will not move further beyond because it is a stable equilibrium. LLET is a trap because this equilibrium (fixed point) is an attractor.

The existence of decreasing returns in coevolutionary processes is the result of characteristics of both populations and their size. When the size of the STE and I populations is small, for example near point X of Fig 18.1a and even near to LLET of Fig 18.1c, so is the degree of variation between individuals, which diminishes the likelihood of coevolutionary-friendly selection and retention processes. This makes less likely the emergence of links, including virtuous bidirectional links between the populations, a fact that precludes the eventual exploitation of increasing returns. The outcome could be impeding a rapid expansion of the researchers/teachers, students and graduates in academic institutions, and indirectly of engineers and technicians working in firms.

In Figure 18.1a, STEo > Xste and Io > Xi, that is, the exogenous levels of STE and I are lower than the critical masses required for a push and pull effect to take place. Point X (Xste, Xi), the initial conditions, also illustrates all future positions; therefore there are no dynamics. We have a static situation with sub-critical levels of STE and I. In this no-growth context, the only way for the system to start growing is if the exogenous components are increased. In Figure 18.1b, the exogenous components are higher than in the previous situation, reaching exactly the levels of the respective critical masses. In this case the initial position at point X (STEo=Xste, Io=Xi) lies at the outer limit of a space (above the STE curve and below the I curve), where both push and pull may take place. Thus a small increase in the exogenous components may generate a virtuous STE-I coevolution that lead to a LLET, but an extremely low one. In Figure 18.1c, where the exogenous components exceed their respective critical masses, the system will experience a limited STE-I coevolution (up to LLET). Larger exogenous components will lead to a higher LLET and therefore a more extended coevolutionary process (compare Figure 18.1c with 18.1b). But they would not assure that virtuous coevolution would continue in the future beyond the LLET point (which might be quite low from the perspective of national priorities and needs).

Summing up, with decreasing returns to push and pull growth of the STE and I, the system might not be able to take off at all (a critical mass problem), or if it did, the underlying coevolutionary process would be a constrained one. It would eventually reach a LLET point.

3.2.2 Case 2: Increasing returns to push and pull and enhanced capacity
One could say that a longer and more vigorous coevolutionary process is not possible without increases in capacity, which have not been considered explicitly in the analysis of Case 1. This is true, but even then, the decreasing returns to push and to pull will strongly constrain any renewed coevolutionary process, especially at high levels of STE and I. Alternatively it could be stated, 'there will be short-term demand and short-term supply constraints to the full utilization of the system'. This situation will dampen the motivation of policy makers to undertake exogenous increases in capacity even when needed from a broader strategic perspective. In terms of the diagram this failure to act will keep (STE^ and Xste) and (I^ and Xi) at relatively low levels.[19]

The solution to this problem would involve in the first instance a combination of: (i) inducing a shift to increasing returns in push and pull, a result of policies such as improved institutions, capabilities and governance of the STE system, and (ii) increases in capacity, which reflect long term, strategic considerations by policy makers to strengthen STE facilities and I capabilities.[20]

This situation is shown in Figure 18.2 where STE' and I' reflect increasing returns to pull and push, that is, the slopes of the f[. . .] and the g[. . .] functions respectively are increasing. We assume the economy was at the LLET of Figure 18.1c, and that this is either the origin or close to the points of origin of a new set of schedules incorporating, along a defined range of values, increasing returns to push and pull and higher capacity levels (shown by STE^' and I^'). At the DECM point of Fig 18.2, the relative slopes of schedules STE' and I' have switched. DECM stands for dynamically efficient critical mass, since beyond this point, STE-I coevolution could be re-ignited, at least for a certain range of variables up to a HLE (High Level Equilibrium).[21]

The shift from LLET to HLE is not automatic since an explicit policy is required to overcome the HLE-LLET gap. With a constant environment and a set of weakly calibrated and coordinated policies, the system may fail to budge from LLET. Overcoming the HLE-LLET gap may require much more than routine increases in 'capacity'. It may

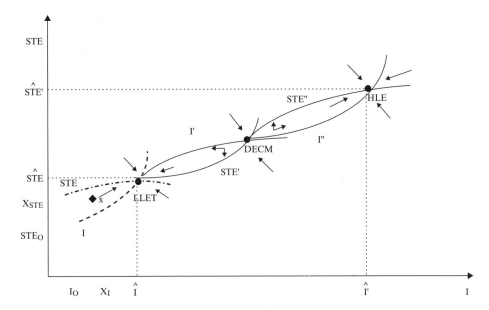

Figure 18.2   Increasing returns to push and pull

require coordinated increases in operational subsidies of I and STE (Sf, Sg) and in the exogenous components of equations (18.1a) and (18.1b) through Sx(ste) and/or Sx(i) and PTI and/or VC.[22]

At some HLE point, beyond DECM, the system must stop again, due to capacity constraints and the likelihood of a shift back to decreasing returns to push and pull as capacity levels are being approached.

Summing up, while a shift to increasing returns (through institutional and governance changes) is important; it may even be critical for the temporary renewal of STE-I coevolution after exhaustion of the first round of the process. Further growth in the system in this second round would require a continuation of the above, namely, further increases in the capacity variables and in policies, which, by increasing the exogenous components of STE and I, may lead to higher critical masses that would trigger a third process of coevolution.

Thus, under this view, the possibility of continued STE-I coevolution would constantly require reinforcements from policy makers and favourable exogenous events.[23] This is not a sufficiently endogenous, and thereby encouraging scenario.

Three events or actions could, in different combinations, make the above coevolutionary process more seamless and automatic. These are: (i) internalization by policy makers of the need to continuously adjust capacity from a long term, strategic perspective (rather than in an ad hoc fashion), one reflecting reasonable expectations and national STE and I objectives; (ii) endogenous capability-enhancing policies, either learning processes enhancing push and pull (increases in 0i and 0ste, see Table 18.1) or systemic enhancements as reflected in PTI and VC; and (iii) introduction of a new set of policies that directly promote coevolution, such as joint STE-I programs (these have not been introduced into the present model).

If the increases in capacity result from a well-founded, continued process of 'strategic innovation policy' broadly conceived, which sets 'area priorities' and a 'vision' while performing higher level coordination as well, then the issue arises as to whether these changes are exogenous or endogenous. In fact we are suggesting an additional endogenous component to the model, which is long-term and part of a policy system where medium and long-term socially desirable supply-demand trajectories are visualized and acted upon by policy makers. Such a policy system would, in part only, compensate for the absence of a capital market (although the existence of such a market does not assure that it would be dynamically efficient), where the current price of a unit of additional capacity would reflect the benefits embedded in the future growth trajectories thereby made possible.

Examples of (iii) are the creation of multidisciplinary research teams at universities with the participation of business; the emerging of new capabilities for undertaking complex, multi-disciplinary projects in the business sector with the participation of researchers from universities; and a capability for undertaking joint projects and for designing and implementing joint university–business sector programs.

Events (i) together with (ii) namely, enhanced learning-based push and pull, would reduce the extent by which policy makers must undertake periodic capacity expansions in an explicit way.

Event (i) would not seem to be enough to move from LLET to DECM in Figure 18.2, and to initiate a new phase of coevolution, an increase in capabilities, as suggested by (ii) above – both that leading to enhanced pull and push 'reactivity' (increases in 0i and 0ste) and that directly affecting the exogenous components of STE and I (as reflected by the PTI and VC variables of Xste and Xi respectively) – may solve at least part of the problem. This can be shown in the figure, where the STE' curve will shift up (a higher STE would result, for each level of I) and the I' curve will shift down, and the effect will be a 'lower' DECM. In this situation, we would add joint STE-I programs as specified above in (iii), then the coevolutionary impact would be even stronger.

Based on this conceptual framework about the STE-I coevolution and the two dynamic profiles of coevolution, the following sections discuss empirical evidence coming from Israel and Mexico, two countries that are at different stages of economic development.

4.   COEVOLUTION AND EMERGENCE OF AN ENTREPRENEURIAL HIGH TECH CLUSTER IN ISRAEL

Israel is an example of a successful dynamic process leading to the emergence of a venture capital industry and market (VC) and associated entrepreneurial high tech cluster (EHTC) during the 1990s. This process started in 1969 when the agency in charge of supporting business innovation (I) was created (Office of the Chief Scientist (OCS), Ministry of Industry and Trade).[24] Three phases were identified during the 1969–2000 period. This section discusses the coevolutionary process underlying this experience; particular attention is given to the initial conditions that are at the base of the potential trajectories available to it.

Our analysis begins with some preliminary background conditions related to STE including the stock and flow of science and engineering graduates. The establishment of Israel's STE infrastructure began long before the state achieved independence in 1948.

Concurrently with the expansion of agricultural and urban settlement, scientific teaching and research institutions were also being established, particularly immediately after World War I. These were frequently staffed by highly accomplished, active scientists who had obtained their knowledge and training abroad. They included a university (the Hebrew University) and an engineering institution of higher learning (Technion – Israel Institute of Technology) both founded in 1925; and later, but before World War II, the Weizmann Institute of Science and the Volcani Center for Agricultural Research. Thus, by the time the state was established, a strong basis for the development of science and technology had been built; as had institutions of higher learning for the training of scientists, engineers and agronomists, as well as some research institutes particularly in agriculture and medicine.

The first years of the state saw a number of attempts to foster applied or directed scientific research. The first central mechanism envisaged was the creation and support by the government of publicly owned and managed, specialized applied research institutions. In 1959 the National Council for Research and Development (NCRD) was established and entrusted with the formulation of a national policy for directed/applied research and the coordination of activities of government ministries, under whose auspices R&D was conducted. Since agricultural research was already flourishing, the emphasis was given to public institutes for industrial research.

Starting in the 1950s, RAFAEL (acronym for Armaments Development Authority) was the first, and for many years, almost the only public research institution in Israel to conduct high-tech industrial R&D, with a focus on computers. Its R&D capabilities were diffused to other defence and civilian companies and organizations (for example, Israel Aircraft Industry in 1962; Elbit, a pioneering private company who later developed the country's first minicomputer; and the Technion's newly created Electronics Lab, two of whose members were instrumental in founding Elscint in 1969, the most prominent civilian high-tech firm of the 1970s). An important factor in expanding the defence R&D sector was the French military embargo, imposed on the eve of the Six Days War (1967). Large amounts of resources were immediately allocated to Defence R&D and other functions in order to ensure rapid growth of Israel's high-technology defence industry. An indirect effect of this was the creation of strong incentives in the labour and education markets to acquire science and engineering skills (Halperin and Berman 1990); consequently during the 1968–74 period Israel had one of the highest growth rates in the world of scientists and engineers employed in the industry: 260 per cent, twice the rate attained by Japan during its miracle decade (Halperin and Berman 1990).

4.1 Three Phases[25]

By the late 1960s a significant STE infrastructure had been established, but R&D in the business sector was practically non-existent. A new institutional setting for innovation policy was established based on the creation of the OCS in 1969. The initial conditions and the continued support both to STE and R&D activity in firms stimulated a 25–30-year evolutionary process eventually leading to the emergence of a VC market and an ICT-oriented EHTC during the second half of the 1990s. From the outset, the policy of the OCS was to enhance social/economic welfare by inducing an innovation-based economic growth process through the diffusion of R&D to the business sector.

The evolutionary process after 1969 and until the year 2000 involved three phases: a background conditions phase (Phase 1, 1969–84), a pre-emergence phase (Phase 2, 1985–92) and the emergence phase (Phase 3, 1993–2000). During the first phase, three new universities and a new set of government owned, applied research institutes were established. These and the already existing institutions in the context of continued support for the STE infrastructure (until the year 2000) led to an increasingly large pool of qualified scientists and engineers. In addition, innovation policy was initiated with the OCS's grants to firms' R&D program followed by the bi-national industrial R&D program (BIRD), which promoted collaborative commercial innovation between Israeli and US firms.[26] Financial incentives were also extended to multinational corporations, a fact that contributed to a strong and relatively early multinational R&D performing presence in Israel. Finally, huge investments in defence R&D (software, communication and instrumentation) were undertaken. The outcome was the establishment and growth of R&D performing companies, particularly in the communications/electronic areas, which has had significant direct and indirect effect on the evolution of Israel's NIS.

The pre-emergence phase (1985–92) included a number of macroeconomic and liberalization policies, such as the successful price stabilization program of 1985 and the liberalization of capital, foreign trade and foreign exchange markets. This phase coincided with global changes, including enhanced capital movements and opportunities for foreign high-tech start-up companies (SUs) to float in NASDAQ, liberalization of communications markets in the US, the UK and Japan, and the internationalization of US investment banks (and their search for investment opportunities in Israel). On the real side of the system, we observe a sharp restructuring of military industry including the very significant cancelling of the Lavi fighter plane project. This contraction caused an increase in the stock of engineers and technicians in civilian industry and a permanent increase in the share of annual flows of engineers and scientists made available for business innovation. It also generated a pool of technological entrepreneurs that could benefit from the OCS's grants to R&D program. A strong learning and experimentation process with respect to entrepreneurship and VC also characterized this phase. It led to identification of the limited partnership form of VC organization, which was subsequently selected by policy makers and embodied in the design of the Yozma Program in 1993.[27]

The outcome was an expansion of informal VC activity; an increased rate of SU formation leading to a critical mass of start-ups (300 in 1992); the appearance of the first VC funds (starting with Athena in 1985); and the creation of companies like Lannet and M-Systems, SUs that successfully floated in NASDAQ. Moreover, individuals (foreign and returning Israelis) and some organizations, such as Advent Private Equity, came to Israel to search for new investment opportunities in high-tech. Underpinning the above was an additional OCS priority: promoting entrepreneurship and SUs, and the establishment of a domestic VC industry to support them. New government programs were implemented: the Inbal Program (1991) that targeted VC and failed, the Magnet Program (1992), and the Technology Incubators Program (1992).

During the early 1990s Israel benefited from a wave of hundreds of thousands of immigrants from the former Soviet Union. Many of them were highly skilled engineers, technicians, and medical doctors, among others, who made a singular contribution to high-tech industry, business innovation and academia. Their impact declined during the course of the emergence phase (1993–2000). This phase was triggered by the implementation of the successful Yozma Program, a policy response to both the weakened impact of the regular grants to industrial R&D program during the second half of the 1980s, and the new opportunities for invention and inventor companies (SUs) opened up by the expansion and globalization of NASDAQ during the 1980s. It targeted a domestic VC market and, indirectly, an EHTC. It triggered a cumulative process with positive feedback based on the entry of new funds and VC organizations, strong VC-SUs coevolution, reputation effects stemming from successful exits in the 1995–97 period, cluster effects in the sense of enhanced scope for the local production of non-tradable intermediate goods and services and the resultant growth promoting effects, and enhanced activity in Israel of large multinationals and foreign investment banks. As a result, the number of SUs increased from 300 to approximately 3000; and VCs and private equity funds from 3 to more than 100. Mergers and acquisitions involving local SUs and foreign multinationals increased and exports of software and hardware products reached 13B$.

Underlying these events were very favourable external/internal conditions of the country. The end of the first Gulf War and initiation of the Oslo Peace Process contributed to reduce Israel's isolation, making it more attractive for business and investments; and the disappearance of the Soviet Union brought in a large number of immigrant scientists and engineers as referred to above. Meanwhile, the grants to industrial R&D program and new-implemented programs continued to expand. The outcome was the emergence of a high impact domestic VC industry and EHTC, with strong links with US product and capital markets. At the bottom of this accelerated process of ICT-oriented growth were the innovation opportunities resulting from the ongoing ICT revolution, from the liberalization of telecom sector, and from the rapid growth of the Internet.

4.2 Coevolutionary Processes

While previous work strongly suggests that the emergence of VC was a central vector of cluster emergence (with VC-SUs coevolution being a central component), the relevant coevolutionary processes started before, with the creation of the OCS in charge of direct support of R&D in firms. Following some leads in a recent paper (Avnimelech and Teubal, 2010), we extend the coevolutionary analysis of the Israeli case to include those processes taking place in Phase 1 (background conditions, 1969–84) and in Phase 2 (pre-emergence, 1985–92).

The coevolutionary framework for analysing the Israeli case links I policy, I, and I finance.[28] The types of coevolutionary links considered in the case of Israel are:[29] (a) I policy-I coevolution, and (b) I-I finance coevolution.

Successful type (a) coevolution implies a two-way, dynamic link between I policy and I. For example, the expansion of capabilities and the enhanced awareness and willingness of entrepreneurs to harness R&D for company growth (resultant from implementation of the grants to industrial R&D program in its early years) created a continued demand for increased OCS budgets as well as for new programs. One example of the latter was the adoption of the Projects of National Importance Program in the second half of the 1970s, which linked industrial R&D with universities in larger and more complex projects (with a higher level of R&D subsidization beyond the standard 50 per cent level). The successful outcome of this type of coevolution during the 1970s is reflected in the enhanced business sector R&D/innovation, and the increase of the innovation capabilities and the numbers of R&D performing firms, particularly in the ICT area (by 1974 there were more than 300 R&D performing firms).

Type (b) coevolution started in the early 1980s when the expansion of actual and desired R&D to be performed in the business sector by far exceeded the increasingly expanded, albeit still limited budgets. It first involved search and adoption of non-OCS mechanisms of financing R&D in firms, such as tax concessions, the so called Elscint Law of the early 1980s (enabling private investors to buy shares in bunches of projects of certain companies), and a precursor VC program oriented exclusively towards foreign investors investing in specific projects (rather than firms), among others. These new mechanisms assured the timely expansion of commercial innovation, innovation capabilities and innovative firms. They also contributed to the creation of a critical mass of 300 SU companies by 1992, a critical pre-emergence condition that signalled the possibility of making a transition to Phase 3.[30]

The upshot is that the operation of both types of coevolutionary processes during Phases 1 and 2 were important for the eventual emergence during 1993–6/7 of Israel's VC industry and a HLO: the EHTC (needless to say, triggering and sustaining such an emergence process also required a new targeted policy, the Yozma VC-directed program). The emergence process that occurred is consistent with Allen's (2004) and Potts' (2000) view about the emergence of structural attractors, which are characterized as complex systems of interdependent behaviour, or higher level structures and patterns.

It should also be mentioned that the emergence process itself in Phase 3 was propelled by a more specific type (b) coevolutionary process – as the SU-VC coevolution – and by other factors (see Avnimelech and Teubal, 2006).[31] Thus towards the end of the 1990s, VC had become the main source of finance of R&D in the business sector, having substituted the government's previous dominant role. Moreover, a large share of the business sector, R&D was being undertaken at the time by SUs.

Following Bar-Yam (1997), the new system involves a new web of connections, which are associated with a new type of organization or agent-VCs, which comprise both a new branch of the business sector (the VC industry) and a new market (for VC services). Their emergence led to a higher-level structure and pattern of the NIS. VCs also coevolve with a pre-existing class of agents (SUs), thereby leading to substantial increases in their numbers. SUs also undergo changes in structure and organization (for example, they take a bi-national form); they lead to the creation of other new types of agents (for example, advisors/consultants, lawyers, accountants, investment banks). This leads to an expansion in the external links/connections of the system (for example, to world global product and capital markets, and to US high-tech industry).

Following Allen (2004), we observe that the agents (mostly of the EHTC), linkages structures and products and services evolved qualitatively during Phases 1 and 2 (1969–92). This is illustrated by the types of financial institutions supporting SUs and R&D that emerged (and the nature of the innovative organization itself). However, following an industry life cycle perspective, we also argue that since the evolutionary process comprising I-I Finance coevolution in Phase 3 (1993–2000) was more specific than that taking place in the previous phases, they involve also a relatively large quantitative component (which could be dominant). The latter can be illustrated by the increase from 3 VCs and 300 SUs in 1992 to more than 100 VC organizations and about 3000 SUs towards the end of the 1990s.[32]

Summing up, the Israeli case is an example of successful transition from background conditions and pre-emergence phases to the phase of emergence of a VC industry/market and an EHTC in the 1990s. This led to strong increases in I, in its share in gross expenditure in R&D (GERD), as well as in the GERD/gross domestic product (GDP) ratio (over 4.5 per cent towards 2007). The success was supported by a strong STE infrastructure (with beginnings in 1925) and sharp increases in the output (and stock of) engineers and scientists during the 1950s, 1960s and beyond. This transition however would not have been possible without an increasingly strong innovative segment of the business sector. I Policy was an important underpinning of I with which it coevolved. Within limits, VC should be considered as a social technology, which could be adapted to serve as the financial structure to a number of ICT and non ICT-based industries, markets or clusters, including clean technologies, biomedicine, and others. Its existence might contribute to rekindle innovation and structural change based economic growth in the present decade (where targeting of new industries/clusters involving tradable goods may be crucial, and where a strategic level of I policy may become an imperative).

This emergence process illustrates the theoretical Case 2, of increasing returns to push and pull and enhanced capacity, described in Section 3.2.2. It involved a number of sub-processes including coevolutionary ones associated with I policy, I and I finance. Coevolution involved largely qualitative changes during Phases 1 and 2 (leading to DECM in Figure 18.2) and quantitative changes (leading to a point like HLE in the figure). They operated in different forms in all phases, in a context where the STE infrastructure continuously adapted itself or expanded to allow for the expansion of innovative activity in firms. I policy-I coevolution was present in Phase 1. It reflected both the creativity and the flexibility of the OCS at the time. Note that I-I finance coevolution in Phase 2 gave the system a new impetus, one based on taking advantage both of the entrepreneurial stage of the ICT revolution and the new opportunities in software and communications, which arose from liberalization of communications, the PC revolution and the Internet.

A major issue to explain in coevolutionary terms is the successful transition from the pre-emergence to the emergence phase. This means overcoming the possibility of left hand truncation, an important issue in industry life cycle theory (see Avnimelech and Teubal, 2006), and a process seemingly capable of explaining the weak VC industries of some European countries during the 1990s (Avnimelech et al., 2010). In the pre-emergence phase and beyond a certain point, the type (b) coevolutionary process was a haphazard, non-regular process with a strong qualitative component involving the mutual adaptation of the strategy and organizational form of VC and SUs. In contrast to this, during the emergence, coevolution is a more systemic and self sustained process, one linked to a broader process of cluster emergence, which involves a strong quantitative component.

5.   STE-INNOVATION COEVOLUTION IN MEXICO

The analysis of the Israeli case ignores an important coevolutionary process, that between STE and I. Our analysis of that country's evolutionary process began when Israel already had a very strong STE infrastructure, a fact which – together with the significant subsequent growth of this infrastructure at least until 2000 – enabled innovation in firms and associated cocvolutionary processes to prosper. In contrast, our analysis of the Mexican case focuses precisely on such a STE-I coevolutionary process. More specifically, it attempts to show how policy may shift a situation characterized by the absence of such coevolution to trigger a virtuous one.

5.1   Two Phases[33]

The building up of STE infrastructure started in 1910 with the re-foundation of the National Autonomous University of Mexico (UNAM). There were two waves of STE infrastructure building, 1935–45 and 1970–82, during which almost all the national institutes, public research centres and universities were created. Both waves were related to economic policy focused on the intervention of the state in the economy and promotion of industrial development. It is worth mentioning the creation of the National Polytechnic Institute (IPN, 1935–38), the Mexican Academy of Sciences (1958), the Centre for Research and Advanced Studies (CINVESTAV, 1961) and the public institutes for scientific research and technological development connected to the main state firms, such as the Mexican Institute of Oil (1965) and the Electric Research Institute (1975).

Before the 1970s, STE strategies were modelled following different approaches and practical actions adopted by the most prestigious research centres and higher education institutions. At the same time, a number of government promotion agencies were created (for example, NAFIN, 1935 and BANCOMEXT, 1937), which had some influence on technological activities. STE and I were stimulated following a linear model based on a top-down approach and a supply-driven, supply-push strategy. With the creation of the National Council for Science and Technology (CONACyT) in 1970, explicit STE policies emerged. From then, several initiatives to foster national development of STE and I capabilities and outputs were designed and implemented, strengthening the supply-driven strategy. However, this trajectory was affected by the 1982 crisis and the economic reforms of 1983. After then, a new approach to development was adopted, where market forces appeared as the only effective way to regulate the economy and provide direction for policy-making decisions.

The idea that innovative capability building was important for competitiveness came to being in the 1990s. STE policies moved to a demand-pull approach, although still in the context of a rather linear model of innovation. The approval of the Science and Technology Laws of 1999 and 2002 brought a set of institutional changes. The Special Program for Science and Technology 2001–06 (PECYT) represents the first formal attempt to design innovation policies based on the double objective of increasing both the share of GERD in GDP and the private-sector contribution to R&D activities. While this program was elaborated with an interactive STE and I perspective, resource allocation evidence reveals the persistence of a linear, science-push approach both by policy makers and the scientific and technological community. The 2000s has been a decade of learning and adaptation to the new institutional set-up, as well as one of confrontation between the winners and losers of these changes. In 2002, creation of a multi-actor structure – the Advisory Forum for Science and Technology – contributed to building the consensus required for the modern institutional set-up.

The analysis of the STE and I evolutionary process since 1970 suggests the existence of two phases: a background conditions phase (Phase 1, 1970–end 1990s) and a Pre-Emergence phase (Phase 2, 2000 on). The first phase started with the creation of

CONACyT, which became the locus to foster the building of domestic capabilities in STE and I. To this end, several policies, programs, and mechanisms were designed and implemented to create and strengthen a set of public academic institutions that were predominantly involved in scientific knowledge production and human resource formation in science and technology, and to the development of scientific communities in certain knowledge fields. During this period two dozen public research centres were created to strengthen scientific research and technological development. On the STE side, a special effort was made to generate a pool of qualified scientists and engineers through the creation in 1971 of a large scholarship program for postgraduate studies, and by implementation of the National System of Researchers program (SNI)[34] in 1984. On the business innovation side, the first programs to promote private sector R&D were implemented (they acted as pilot programs): the Fund for R&D and Technological Modernization (FIDETEC), the Program to Support Technical Modernization (PROMTEC), the Fund for Strengthening Scientific and Technological Capacities (FORCCYTEC), and the Incubator Program for Technology-Based Enterprises (PIEBT). In addition, during the 1990s the Mexican government enacted regulatory changes intended to strengthen innovation and technological transfer, such as updating the Law of Patents and Trademarks to protect intellectual property rights for a more prolonged period, and the updating of quality norms and other metrology standards.

The pre-emergence phase (2000 on) started when the main STE infrastructure was already built and there was already a small pool of qualified scientists and engineers. Although the building of I capabilities had been a major concern of policy makers since the initiation of explicit STE policies in 1970, only at the beginning of the 2000s did they become more consistently oriented toward the promotion of business sector R&D. The approval of the Science and Technology Law in 1999 represented a break in the evolution of STE policies and created the bases for novel forms of governance. This was strengthened by the Science and Technology Law of 2002, the new Organic Law of CONACyT, and the implementation of the PECYT. The latter program contributed to change the previous policy focus on STE to a broader view comprising STE and I. It triggered a pre-emergence process (which is now followed by PECiTI 2007–12), based on a horizontal and non-discriminatory/neutral program (generating variety), oriented to trigger and perhaps sustain the emergence of specific sectors. Other more consistent instruments to promote private R&D were introduced as well, such as the fiscal benefit for R&D, the sectoral fund for innovation and the program for the creation of new businesses from scientific and technological developments (AVANCE, aimed towards the promotion of high-tech SUs). Although CONACyT has been primarily responsible for formulation, implementation, and coordination of the different STE and I policies, changes in the laws contributed to the appearance of new actors and multi-actor structures, such as the Advisory Forum for Science and Technology mentioned above and the National Network of State Councils and Institutions for Science and Technology (REDNACEYT),[35] which made the governance of the system quite a complex process.

Unfortunately, public resource disbursements were insufficient and not consistent with STE and I policy design and objectives. Thus, the share of GERD in GDP was maintained at its historical level of 0.4 per cent. On the other hand, a significant success was achieved raising business sector participation in GERD, from 29.8 per cent to 41.5 per cent, and a three-fold increase in the number of researchers, particularly those working in industry. Also the number of firms that benefited from the fiscal benefit for R&D increased from 679 in 2001 to 1616 in 2006.

5.2 Coevolutionary Processes

The relevant coevolutionary processes started only in this decade, with the changes in the institutional set-up, the introduction of the PECYT, and the consequent growth of innovation in firms. Following some ideas from Dutrénit et al. (2008a, 2008b) this section analyses the processes taking place along the two phases described above with a focus on STE-I coevolution. The basic constraint to STE-I coevolution was the relatively small size and weak growth of these populations, since it meant a narrow process of variation in each one, and a low potential for both selection (or replication) and retention processes, and for mutually adapted bi-directional links. Very specific features of the environment have influenced these processes. One of the main factors is the limited political and social priority that government and society have traditionally assigned to STE and I. This is reflected in the low levels of investment – relative to international standards – in activities such as those mentioned above, and in the failure to reach the planned GERD/GDP share of 1 per cent.

Low size and growth of STE and I
The processes that introduce new variations into the STE population include an increase in the number of academic researchers and the supply of STE graduates and postgraduates, and incentives to stimulate existing researchers to do research and teaching in emerging fields of high potential for the business sector and society as a whole. While overall the researchers' community has grown over time, its size is still relatively small according to international standards and relative to its population and needs. At 44 000 individuals, they represented only 1.1 per thousand employed in the economy in 2005 and 53 per cent of total researchers working in the public research system. This shows the current academic bias of R&D activities in Mexico, a situation comparable maybe to that of Israel up to the late 1960s (prior to the systematic diffusion of R&D in the business sector).

Scholarships were used to increase the supply of STE postgraduates. The program mentioned above started in 1971 and CONACyT sponsored 136 000 scholarships for postgraduate studies in Mexico and abroad. This program was strengthened during the second half of the 1990s. Scholarships have been assigned in different disciplines and approaches, without much prioritization. In 2006 this program represented a third of CONACyT's budget, and together with the National System of Researchers more than half. This illustrates the importance assigned by policy to human resources formation and the generation of a pool both of researchers to work in the STE system and of engineers and technicians to nurture I activities in the business sector. Unfortunately, this financial effort has not been matched with the creation of job positions for the employment and so the retention of graduates/postgraduates in these areas. As a result, the number of researchers and engineers per thousand employees remains low as compared to international standards, a fact which suggests that the pool might still be below requirements. This shortage of the pool of graduates/postgraduates generated by the STE is still far from being overcome. Thus, even though coverage of higher education has increased significantly from 1990 onwards, it only reached 25 per cent of the relevant population in 2006, much lower than countries with similar per capita GDP.

Starting at 2000 with the PECYT, CONACyT introduced, modified or continued implementing several policy instruments and programs to fund research. Seventeen sectoral funds were introduced with partnership from ministries to promote the development and consolidation of STE capabilities according to the strategic needs of each participating sector (for example, basic research, economy/innovation, energy and agriculture, among others). In addition, 30 regional funds were created with partners involving state or municipal governments, which intend to tailor capacities and development projects to local demands. Sectoral and regional funds may largely contribute to increase the size of STE and generate variety across sectors and regions. While new behaviours were promoted, such as teamwork and interactions (for example, the funding provided by the basic science sectoral fund, which is directed to research groups has grown from 16.7 per cent of the total budget in 2000 to 32.4 per cent in 2005), there would seem to be a systematic bias against funding I in CONACyT's budget. In this direction, it is noteworthy that only one of the above sectoral funds is tailored to I activities. Likewise, no regional fund was directly oriented to support I; however, it has to be mentioned that many calls for the funds included requests for proposals directed to its requirements.

Regardless of that, more consistent support for business sector R&D activities was introduced in Phase 2 after the year 2000. The most successful new instrument in terms of resources committed and the number of firms benefited was the fiscal benefits for R&D, coordinated by the Finance Secretary, which has grown from $45 million in 2001 to $413 million in 2007.[36] While firms of all sizes have benefited, 26 domestic and multinational large firms benefited from 54 per cent of the total amount of fiscal benefits assigned. The upshot is that this instrument contributed significantly to the increase of business sector R&D between 1995 and 2005, from 14.1 per cent to 41.5 per cent of the GERD.

A final point concerns the important increase in the number of trained engineers and technicians that are employed in the productive sector in existing and emerging fields, both as percentage of employment in industry (from 0.1 per cent in 1995 to 0.5 per cent in 2005), and as a percentage of total personnel in R&D activities (from 10.3 per cent to 45.3 per cent in the same years). In fact these figures reveal that the number of engineers and technicians in industry has grown more quickly than the number of academic researchers. However, these figures are still very low in comparison to international trends and reveal the possible existence of significant shortages in this resource.

Private sources of finance for R&D continue to be limited. The VC market is very reduced, both in terms of number of funding institutions and in terms of the volume of resources to fund innovation. Thirty investment funds were operating under VC or private equity programs in 2004. Bank credit for funding firms' development, including innovation projects, has been approximately 20 per cent of GDP, lower than Argentina (24 per cent), Brazil (34.2 per cent) and Chile (64.4 per cent). The lack of a VC market is one of the weaknesses of the Mexican NIS.

Bi-directional links

The Mexican case shows that the limited stocks of, and links between, agents that produce and use knowledge do not allow the generation of virtuous cumulative effects. The main source of links would seem to be the flow of graduates/postgraduates from

STE institutions to I in the productive sector, with very little collaboration between STE and I in knowledge creation/use. The National Innovation Survey of 2006 shows that developments by innovative firms are largely based on internal sources and in-house R&D (82 per cent). They tend to cooperate more with other firms (14 per cent) than with universities and research centres (4 per cent). Recent evidence shows that interactions are more associated with hiring graduates, accessing open information (publications, conferences and exhibitions) or training than with joint or contract research (Dutrénit et al., 2010b). The main economic incentives to promote academia–business sector linkages in R&D activities are associated with the fiscal incentives for R&D, the sectoral fund for innovation, a special program (AVANCE) and a pilot experience on public–private partnerships that was underfunded. Additionally, the way selection is carried out, largely influenced by curiosity-driven targets, negatively affects the knowledge production/use-type of bi-directional causal mechanisms. In other words, some relationships are based on cooperation but the most commonly observed causal mechanisms linking the evolutionary trajectories of STE and I are the employment of recent graduates and training. In contrast, the exchange of knowledge by formal means (contracts, seminars, stays) and informal networks, and lobbying by each on behalf of the other are less frequent.

So far the evidence illustrates that the evolutionary path of STE and I has been quite weak, due to the restrictions of each population's variation, selection and retention processes. In addition, there have been difficulties in building bidirectional mechanisms that support coevolutionary processes. The selection environment, the narrow STE and I culture of the society and budget constraints have had a dramatic influence on this aspect of the NIS.

Summing up, our interpretation is that until the year 2000 (Phase 1), Mexico's situation involved subcritical masses of STE and especially of I. Moreover the context was one of decreasing returns to scale in push and pull (see Case 1, Section 3.2.1). This did not permit even a limited coevolutionary process to take place (Figure 18.1a). The situation improved after the year 2000 (Phase 2), especially with respect to I, which increased substantially in both absolute and relative terms. This facilitated a limited STE-I coevolutionary process up to the point of reaching a LLET. Moreover the situation seems to be moving this equilibrium point along the horizontal axis, but as LLET is an attractor, it is impossible to reach DECM in Figure 18.2. A major possible reason for sluggishness in this process could be difficulty in making a transition to increasing returns in push and pull. This means that for a virtuous/endogenous STE-I coevolutionary process oriented to DECM to take place, it is important to improve the conditions for generating variation through significant increases in size and diversity of agents and organizations, as well as assuring effective and mutually adaptable selection and retention processes, which are still in their infancy.[37] This may not be easy due to the still fragile institutional edifice in the STE and I arenas, the evolving multi-actor related governance profile, and the weaknesses of STE and I policy design and implementation.

6. TOWARDS A BROADER POLICY MODEL WHICH INTEGRATES THE ISRAELI AND MEXICAN EXPERIENCE

The model of Section 3 and the Israeli and Mexican experiences suggest a broad conceptual framework on coevolution and emergence in innovation and structural change-based economic development. It takes STE-I coevolution as emphasized in the Mexican case as the central axis of the analysis with the other coevolutionary processes considered in the Israeli case (I-I Policy and I-I Finance coevolution) as influencing this process. The integration of both experiences suggests the existence of three stages:

- *Stage I*   Preconditions: achieving critical mass and limited STE-I co-evolution
- *Stage II*   Strengthening of STE-I coevolution through increasing returns, capability development and specific financial and technical infrastructures
- *Stage III*   continued STE-I coevolution, and widespread emergence.

Table 18.2 links these stages with the phases used to analyse each individual country. Based on the evidence of Israel and Mexico, some key features of each stage are highlighted. Figure 18.3 stylizes the coevolutionary trajectory along the three stages, using a phase diagram.

The evidence reveals that Mexico is situated in Stage I, at an extremely low LLET with a relatively high level of STE relative to I but low absolute levels of both variables. This reflects the focus of that country's innovation policies since the 1970s during Phase 1, with the creation of CONACyT, to build the STE infrastructure with only a limited effort before 2000s devoted to promote I. During the 2000s (Mexico's Phase 2) a greater effort took place to improve the institutional set up along with new programs to foster I. The coevolution that existed during Phases 1 and 2 mostly involved qualitative rather than quantitative changes. Both the weak financial effort and the relative failure at effectively adapting STE and I governance during the last 25 years contribute to explain the current LLET and the limited movement to reach DECM (Figure 18.3).

From 2000 onwards, the stronger pace of STE and I evolution, quicker in the case of the I (beginning of Phase 2), seems to be moving that equilibrium point along the horizontal axis, but not enough to reach DECM. A special effort was made to promote R&D in the business sector, increase the pool of researchers and engineers, promote linkages between the agents and establish conditions for better governance – but these conditions were still insufficient to generate an endogenous coevolutionary dynamic. Also, the time available for introducing changes was insufficient for improved governance to evolve, one that spurred radical changes in agents' behaviour. Moreover, the financial effort by the government was far below minimum magnitudes and standard international levels (and shares of overall effort) to spark or trigger a self-reinforcing coevolutionary process of STE-I, which would involve the economy and society as a whole.

Thus, the main objective may be to set the conditions for re-igniting STE-I coevolution, that is, to sustain a shift to DECM and Stage II (see Figure 18.3), and thereby spur a more endogenous, autocatalytic and coevolutionary path of development. In such conditions, increasing returns and emergence processes of some sectors/clusters may occur.

In Israel, strong support of I after establishment of the OCS in 1969 along with a strong and growing STE infrastructure led to a LLET at the end of that country's Phase 2 in 1984 (Stage I). Moreover, the search and adoption of new non-OCS mechanisms of financing R&D in firms assured the timely expansion of I and contributed to the creation of a critical mass of SU companies by 1992 and attainment of DECM by that year. It is worth mentioning that the transition to such an endogenous process benefited from the

Table 18.2   Stages in the overall evolutionary model (and phases in the evolution of countries)

Israel Period and phases	Mexico Period and phases	GENERAL MODEL
Phase 0: Strong STI system and PTI: before 1969	Phase 1 Background conditions: 1970–end 1990s;	Stage I: Pre-conditions: achieving critical mass and limited STE-I co-evolution
Phase 1 Background conditions: 1969–84	• 1970: creation of National Council for R&D (CONACyT)	• Building up the infrastructure and critical masses of STE and I
• 1969: creation of OCS and grants to R&D program;	• Many programs supporting STE, including those sending students abroad, with a strong bias against programs supporting business innovation	• Qualitative changes in both populations
• Creation of BIRD program;	Phase 2 Pre-emergence: 2000 and beyond	• Horizontal policies to foster variation in STE and I, experimentation of new programs, and learning (including collective learning) about innovation through design and implementation
• Growth in I and beginning of SUs;	• More systematic approach to support innovation	• Institutional set up and building up of effective system governance
• Search for innovation finance mechanisms	• 1999 and 2002: Laws of science and technology	• Creation of some public research institutes to absorb technologies, provide technical services and employ/train immigrant & returning engineers/scientists and students
	• 2001: PECYT	• The above would set the bases for I-I policy coevolution and for limited STE-I coevolution
	• 2002: Fiscal incentives for R&D, enormous increase in business R&D/innovation (a great success)	

Stage II: Strengthening of STE-I coevolution through increasing returns, capability development and emergence of specific financial/technical infrastructures

- Emergence of important innovative small and medium-size enterprises (SME)/SU segment in the business sector
- Quantitative growth in both populations (dynamically efficient critical masses)
- Growing systemic intermediation of support systems: VC and PTI
- Strong STE-I coevolution, supported by push and pull capabilities/governance, and by emergence of VC and PTI
- New qualitative changes and collective learning in new HLO
- Policy: I-I policy coevolution, design and implementation of new programs, more vertical/targeted policies, greater policy mix
- Emergence of new financial segments and markets to finance innovation in SMEs and innovation more generally speaking
- Emergence of new segments of intermediate institutions and markets for training, R&D services and other technical services, especially to the growing segment of innovative firms
- Improving governance, particularly at STE institutions

Phase 2 Pre-emergence: 1985–92

- Ministry of Defence: an important training ground for STE personnel
- Further reinforcement of STE, re-orientation of engineers and scientists from defence to civilian uses
- Strengthening links with the US
- Support of SU becomes a national priority
- Identify qualitative underpinnings of future VC industry (e.g. selection of LP VCs, born global SUs)
- Critical mass of 300 SUs in 1992
- Changes in governance at universities

Phase 3 VC and EHTC emergence: 1993–2000

- Implementation of Yozma Program (a VC-directed policy)
- Emergence of a high impact VC industry/market and successful EHTC
- Thousands of highly skilled immigrants from former Soviet Union, which contributed to build new high-tech cluster

Table 18.2 (continued)

Israel Period and phases	Mexico Period and phases	GENERAL MODEL
Future Phases: 2001 and beyond • Efforts to identify new areas of activity in ICT, biotech, etc; • Initial efforts at creating a strategic level of innovation policy (no impact yet), • Some changes in governance already in operation		Stage III: continued STE-I coevolution and widespread emergence • Implementing a strategic approach to innovation policy to re-ignite STE-I coevolution, set strategic priorities in a supra-ministerial setting, and develop a national vision concerning STE and I (and related issues and areas) • Quantitative and qualitative changes in both populations (new critical masses and enhanced capabilities in emerging areas) • Policy: design and implementation of new programs to foster new sectors (targeting) • Widespread mission-oriented R&D involving institutions in the STE and I arenas • Widespread emergence of new HLOs, e.g. clusters • Collective learning during/after emergence of new HLO and qualitative changes • Improving governance to include new actors

flexibility and creativity of the OCS, which indeed existed at the time. The early activities of this agency, together with the strong STE infrastructure, spurred a strong industrial R&D response that in turn led to expansion of OCS budgets and to some new programs. This is evidence of a strong I-I policy coevolutionary process during the 1980s. We should also mention changes in STE governance and establishment of technology transfer offices at the Hebrew University and Weizmann Institute during that decade. All of these contributed to a relatively fast arrival to DECM, and to the resources to move forward and complete the Stage II during 1993–2000 when a full-fledged VC industry and EHTC were created.

The STE-I coevolutionary process that would initially take off after attaining point DECM would follow a set of relationships, like the push and pull equations described in Section 3. However, new constraints would appear pretty fast both in the area of finance and possibly (maybe more in Mexico than in Israel) of intermediate institutions supporting the increasing amount and variety of firms' technological activities. Referring to intermediate institutions, the broad policy mix introduced in Mexico fostered the emergence of a large number and variety of these institutions, many of which will probably not survive the ongoing selection and retention processes. In the case of Israel, some of these institutions were created prior to 1969, and the OCS in fact reduced its overall disbursements to them during the first half of the 1970s, focusing instead on direct support of R&D projects at firms (see Breznits, 2007a).[38] Concerning the inevitable I finance constraint that would appear during the above Stage II process, some countries should aim at triggering emergence of a domestic I finance and SME-finance segment of agents. This would reinforce I and through this, the overall STE-I coevolutionary process.

By now, Stage III pertains only to the Israeli scene, as Mexico is still in Stage I and it is difficult to close the gap between LLET and HLE in one motion. For Israel, Stage III reflects a rather optimistic future, given the new set of threats and opportunities coming from the global and domestic environments. The major policy challenge would seem to be the creation of a strategic level of I policy, to set up a search and learning intensive path based on a vision of the country and its growth, and a capacity to set strategic priorities in key areas, such as biomedicine, ICT high-tech (with an emphasis on diversification into new applications and fusion of technologies), nanotechnology, water, and so on. Changes are required in both policy process and policy products; in fact the latter is not possible without the former (for a discussion see Sercovich and Teubal, 2009). The central point is that: (i) the global environment and its competition-enhancement effects suggest very strongly that HLO/technology targeting will be more important than in the past to sustain innovation and structural change-based economic growth;[39] and (ii) for this and other reasons as well, the policy process should now increasingly have to include the explicit setting of priorities (and this set of priorities should be coherent with an overall vision). The I-policy institution of the Stage III must be as flexible and creative as OCS was during the 1970s in order to generate, in 'no time', a strong STE-I coevolutionary process, one which would counter the gradual decline in the country's STE capabilities. It should also contribute to link I policy (broadly defined now to include both I and STE directed policies), I (broadly defined to include also capabilities and organizations) and emergence of new HLO (such as new sectors or sub-sectors, markets or submarkets, clusters, regional or sectoral innovation systems, large multinational companies, global

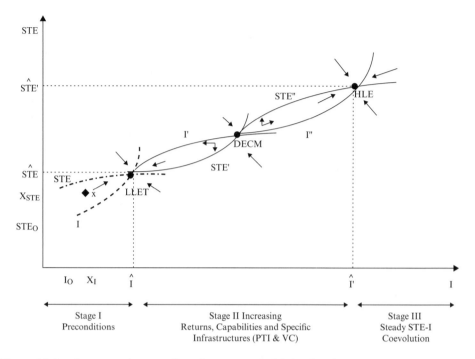

Figure 18.3   Stages in the overall evolutionary model (with a focus on STE-I coevolution)

networks, and so on). Presumably, the targeting of new HLO and specific STE capabilities will figure prominently in that country's new policy portfolio.

Summing up, in some cases, a distinction between two sub-periods of Stage II could be useful. During the first sub-period, IIa, the policy direction would be a STE thrust, while during the second, IIb, it would be an innovation thrust.[40] The capabilities and profile would reflect this distinction. Thus, during IIa, the focus on increasing returns and coevolution would be on 'pull' through an increase in the reactivity capabilities coefficient [0i (>1)], appearing in the f[0i I. . .] function (a weaker or no change would occur to 'push'). Moreover, the specific 'infrastructures' developed would focus on training of STE graduates for incorporation in business innovation.

In contrast, during the subsequent sub-period IIb, the focus on shifting to increasing returns would lie on 'push' through an increase in the reactivity capabilities coefficient [0ste (>1)] in the g[0ste STE. . .] function (thus creating a situation where both schedules of Figures 18.2 and 18.3 would then exhibit increasing returns). Moreover, specific infrastructure development would now focus on the I finance infrastructure – VC, a fact which would then complete the set of infrastructures required.

Both processes will push the economy from LLET to DECM, and would fuel the subsequent coevolutionary process leading to HLE. At this point, the economy will be characterized both by high levels of STE and I and by a set of well developed specific infrastructures, both technological and financial. The latter emerged during the process; and would sustain the growth in STE and I.[41]

7. FINAL REFLECTIONS

This chapter discusses an integrated framework to analyse STE-innovation coevolution into the innovation and structural change-based view of economic growth/development. It argues that STE-innovation coevolution is related to emergence processes (of Higher Level Organizations, like new clusters, markets, sectors, and so on), as emergence requires innovation, and innovation requires STE.

A formal model of STE-push of innovation and innovation-pull of STE (and of overall STE-innovation coevolution) has been presented, in which critical masses, learning and capability building directly affect push and pull, and systemic changes like development of specific financial and technological infrastructures (for example, public technological institutes and venture capital) influence these processes. In this model, graduates/postgraduates from domestic STE or returnees from abroad play an important role in nourishing the pool of qualified scientists and engineers. This could help create critical masses of both populations, hence generating the necessary conditions for the emergence of coevolutionary processes of STE and innovation. The formal model also emphasizes the role of domestic public technological institutes in helping to train graduates, absorb returnees and immigrants and generate other semi-public goods benefiting innovation. The model was used to analyse aspects of the evolutionary history of the Israeli and Mexican NIS in terms of patterns of emergence and coevolution (or lack of them) among key variables associated with innovation and structural change-led economic development. A central coevolutionary process focuses on STE-innovation coevolution (emphasized in the Mexican case); the other ones are innovation policy-innovation coevolution and innovation-innovation finance coevolution (emphasized in the Israeli case).

While the Israeli case study has not considered STE-innovation coevolution explicitly, the historically strong support of the STE infrastructure (reflecting not only economic, but also cultural and defence reasons) continued until the year 2000, thus providing ample space for innovation to flourish. As this situation has changed since the year 2000, any extension of our analysis will require more explicit attention to STE capabilities and to STE-innovation coevolutionary processes and associated policies involving coordination of narrowly defined innovation policies including specific STE policies. Other important coevolutionary processes, such as innovation-innovation policy coevolution (particularly during the 1970s and early 1980s) and innovation-innovation finance coevolution (particularly during the 1980s and 1990s), were also important factors. They contributed to sustain the overall cumulative process of knowledge-based growth (including growth of innovation and STE) during the three decades leading to the year 2000. The Mexican case focuses first on igniting an initial STE-innovation coevolution process in the country. This includes critical mass conditions for the prior existence of a LLET attainable with limited STE-innovation coevolution, and for its transformation into a dynamic increasing returns process that could trigger and sustain a much broader coevolutionary process. A major conclusion of this case is that governments should proactively intervene in a coordinated way, both at the system governance level and in assuring significant increases in resources to both STE and innovation. Piecemeal policies will bring only temporary relief without setting the STE-innovation system into a new, largely endogenous, coevolutionary trajectory.

Drawing on the formal model and the evidence coming from Israel and Mexico, a general evolutionary model based on STE-innovation, and related coevolutionary processes, was also presented. It considers three stages: Stage I refers to the pre-conditions for achieving critical masses, while STE-I coevolution is limited; Stage II considers the strengthening of STE-I coevolution through increasing returns, capability development and emergence of specific financial/technical infrastructures; and Stage III refers to the future growth trajectories that require a re-configured STE-I coevolution and widespread emergence. This framework suggests that a simple policy that would lead to changes in STE and innovation capacity is not sufficient to assure a continued process of STE-Innovation coevolution, and of an innovation and structural change-based process of economic development. It is also important: (a) to adopt a strategic perspective to innovation policy, where increases in capacity become endogenous; (b) to promote enhanced push and pull reactivity through changes in governance and enhanced capabilities (this will generate increasing returns to coevolution); (c) to promote emergence of new segments of public technological institutes, venture capital and other types of financial mechanisms supporting innovative SMEs and high-tech start-ups; and (d) to eventually promote STE-innovation link programs that directly promote bidirectional coevolution. All of these may make the process of STE-innovation coevolution and economic development more seamless and continuous.

The two cases analysed in this chapter and other anecdotal evidence strongly suggests that coevolution and emergence should not be ignored when analysing innovation and its impact on economic development. The possible importance of emergence of new industries/markets/clusters or other Higher Level Organization is consistent both with traditional views of innovation and structural change-led economic development (for example, Kuznets, 1971, among many others) and with modern approaches. What is less standard, although increasingly accepted, is the nature of the process and the possible implications for policy.[42] Concerning this, our work suggests that coevolutionary processes may play important roles both in generating adequate pre-emergence conditions for desirable structural changes and as part of the emergence process itself. Moreover, the new emphasis on qualitative aspects of growth and structural change enhances the importance of an evolutionary targeting perspective (for example, Avnimelech and Teubal, 2008b) and policy targeting in developing countries (see Rodrik, 2004).

The emergence and coevolutionary process relate to positive and normative aspects in an interrelated way. Cumulative emergence, for example, could be initiated in the absence of a proactive innovation policy to overcome system failures, whenever these are present (Avnimelech and Teubal, 2006; Avnimelech et al., 2010). Coevolutionary and cumulative processes may reach a fixed point (like DECM or HLE), in which case the strategic dimension of innovation policy (broadly defined) may have to identify new priorities and possibly new engines of economic development as starting points for a new set of policies and for renewed innovation-innovation policy and STE-innovation coevolutionary processes.

NOTES

1. To exemplify the practical relevance of this perspective, see an analysis of the structural change constraints blocking the renewal of accelerated growth in Chile (World Bank, 2008; Haussman and Klinger, 2007).
2. See Antonelli and Teubal (2011), Avnimelech and Teubal (2010), and Cimoli et al. (2009). Concerning markets for technology see Arora et al. (2006).
3. Moreover, two levels of analysis of populations can be identified: the individual agent level (followed in this chapter), and the organizational level. At the organizational level, the STE population (I population) comprises research centres and universities (innovative firms). As systems mature, monitoring at organizational level becomes relatively more important than at the individual level. But when the institutional structures are still immature, as in the case of developing countries, it is more relevant to focus on individuals.
4. See Murmann (2002) for the case of industries and national institutions, and Murmann (2003) for the case of industries and academic disciplines.
5. Our definition of innovation is a broad one related to newness to the economy rather than to the world, a concept which would include much of imitation in industrializing economies and in general in developing countries (Kim, 1997).
6. These other outputs will be considered more explicitly later on.
7. Xste may result from a strategic perspective to economic growth and to innovation policy, where the creation of a pool of skilled graduates would be part of a strategy of kicking off the demand for I-relevant, highly skilled personnel and the eventual creation of a market for such a critical I input. Thus, Xste could be regarded as the long-term anticipation of demand for trained STE graduates which, for our purposes, means having been employed for a time after graduation by domestic public technological institutes (PTI). Note that the anticipation of demand may relate to expected economic or non-economic needs or national objectives or priorities for STE and associated capabilities. The former could include preparing a pool of STE graduates/postgraduates and 'capabilities' that could serve the future needs of innovation (see Siegel et al., 2003; Geuna and Muscio, 2009; Dutrénit and Arza, 2010). Examples of the latter are related to defence or enhanced national autonomy in STE capabilities in certain critical areas.
8. The level of Xste also relates to students' decisions to pursue I-relevant, higher education studies. These will also be affected by the possibilities of studying abroad and by future employment possibilities.
9. In Korea, this involved employing returnees (presumably in I activities) in a government-owned institute until their eventual absorption by the business sector which largely took place after that country's shift from imitation to innovation (see Lee, 2000 and other articles in Kim and Nelson, 2000). Lee's analysis of Korea's innovation policy during the 'imitation phase' emphasizes the importance of government research institutes in absorbing and assimilating foreign technology for the private sector, attracting Korean scientists and engineers from abroad who otherwise would not have returned, and enhancing the social status and prestige of these scientists and engineers. Many of them played key roles in the development of the heavy and chemical industries and in high tech industry; others also contributed to attract the best students in engineering and science-related departments of universities.
10. The historical experience seems to support our view of the exogenous I-component. This is because in some areas, such as agriculture and other resource intensive sectors, public or hybrid technological centres or institutes played dominant roles in promoting applied research, invention and even innovations (or important components of innovation) for the private sector, which then benefited from their diffusion (see Griliches, 1957; Ruttan, 1961). In a subset of cases, this phase is a prelude to one where the dominant share of innovation is performed in firms (for example, Plastics and Rubber Industry Institute of Israel, an industry-owned organization).
11. Many countries, such as Korea, China and Israel, have extensively used this third mechanism (Kuznetsov, 2006, 2008; Lee and Saxenian, 2009; Yoguel et al., 2009). The Mexican National System of Researchers program has been very successful for the first mechanism and its scholarship program has fostered the second (Dutrénit et al., 2010a).
12. We ignore for the time being that Xste in equation (18.3a) will also depend on numbers of students or student-years in the system.
13. As the Korean government research institutes and Israeli defense organization (RAFAEL) show, publicly financed technology or research institutes stimulate both the return of nationals from abroad and entry of highly skilled immigrants, prior to the existence of a clear demand from the relatively underdeveloped private sector.
14. We should be aware that other exogenous factors may be active as well in equations (18.3a) and (18.3b), for example a wave of global emigration of STE personnel from less advanced to more advanced

economies; or in later stages, enhanced technological knowledge available to the global economy or favourable developments in global markets closely related to the areas of innovation strength of the country.

15. $0j=1$ ($j=$ste,i) will be the unit capability level in the sense that it will prevail initially prior to any process of capability development. We assume this to be the case prior to and up to fulfilling the critical mass conditions (that is, $0j$ could be greater than one and increasing once STEo,Io is achieved). These capability variables appear in multiplicative form in the f and g equations (see Table 18.1).The higher $0i$ beyond 1, the higher f and the higher f' for a given I; and the higher 0ste beyond 1, the higher g and g' for a given STE.

16. Co-evolution will be indirect since an increase in PTI, for instance, will increase STE through Xste (see Table 18.1, first line which corresponds to equation (18.1a)); and this will increase I from equation (18.1b).

17. Sx(ste) includes subsidies to teaching, learning and research in existing facilities (R,K); to support of students abroad and of efforts to locate potential highly skilled immigrants; and to absorb returning students, graduates and immigrants in PTI prior to their employment in the business sector. Sx(i) includes subsidies to firms undertaking innovation. The effectiveness of both depends on capacity and capability variables, including the existing network of PTI (for Sx(ste)) and of VC institutions (for Sx(i)).

18. For simplicity Gv is introduced as a variable in the 'pull' equation of Table 18.1.

19. This situation would also partially justify the assumptions in Figure 18.1 that both the STE and I capacities and exogenous components are constant.

20. Note that increases in STE capacity could be justified if they are accompanied by an explicit policy of kicking off STE demand that is promoting I.

21. DECM should be differentiated from the aforementioned critical mass condition (STEo,Io) which is required to take the system for the first time from a non (STE-I) coevolutionary mode to a coevolutionary mode, albeit a limited one ending in LLET (Figure 18.1c). The justification for attaining critical mass and a first round of STE-I coevolution is to set the stage for generating and exploiting increasing returns to push and pull. As mentioned above, this strongly links with the coevolutionary literature summarized in Section 2, which emphasizes the importance of size and diversity (and the link between the two) of the two populations as preconditions for virtuous coevolution.

22. Note that the exogenous components (Xi,Xste) have automatically increased as part of the same process leading to the enhanced capacity levels of both STE and I (which underlies our mental experiment of the process leading from decreasing to increasing returns).

23. In this case there may be a moving equilibrium that is not shown in Figure 18.2.

24. Much of the material for this early period was obtained from a 1971 document of the National Council for Research and Development (1971).

25. See Pugatch et al. (2010) for a short summary of the pre-1969 STE-related institutional development and policy; and Avnimelech and Teubal (2006) for a broader discussion of Phases 1–3.

26. The grants to industrial R&D program was a horizontal (that is, open to all firms in the business sector) and rather neutral (that is, non discriminatory) subsidies-based program. It became the backbone and dominant I policy program of Israel (its share of total disbursements by the OCS was seldom below 80 per cent).

27. Yozma was a VC-directed, targeted program that was implemented during 1993-6/7. This contrasts with the horizontal/neutral grants to industrial R&D program, which started in 1969.

28. I policy includes not only direct support of innovation or R&D in firms (the main focus) but also other policies, such as VC policies and associated institutional changes; I means not only commercial innovation in firms but also innovation capabilities and creation/growth of R&D performing organizations (such as SUs); while I finance means new private mechanisms of finance of R&D/innovation (for example, VC).

29. We have not explicitly analysed STE-I coevolution in the Israeli case, although we do believe that the STE infrastructure, was until the year 2000 at least, very supportive of commercial innovation in firms (and indirectly, to stimulating the two types of coevolution mentioned above). This also indicates a measure of active coordination between the agency/ministries financing R&D in firms (OCS and the Treasury) and those financing STE (Higher Education Committee of the Ministry of Education, the Treasury and the Ministry of Defence).

30. The two coevolutionary processes may be strongly linked at some point in time, for instance the demands for new mechanisms of finance of an increasingly larger group of R&D performing companies contribute to enable the expansion of I (Type (b) coevolutionary process) and also I policy (Type (a) coevolutionary process), which were eventually expressed, particularly in the 1980s, by new policies including, eventually, the Yozma program of 1993.

31. For instance, the types of organizations involved in the coevolutionary process in Phase 3 were largely fixed (Limited Partnership VC organizations with an early phase, the ICT-oriented investment strategy; and Born Global SU companies oriented not only to product but to technology and capital markets).

These were the result of an interactive selection process which took place in Phase 2, a process we call qualitative coevolution, since it helped to define the type of institutions or organizational forms/strategies that would prevail during the emergence and coevolutionary process of Phase 3. Note that the latter involved significant replication, reproduction and retention), allowing the quantitative expansion of existing organizational forms and strategies of both types of agents.

32. The shifting importance of qualitative and quantitative aspects of interactions among agents and coevolutionary processes leading to emergence is one variant of Allen's (2004) general statement. It could be termed an industry life cycle-type variant, since a central message of such a theory is the eventual appearance of a dominant product design, a qualitative precondition for the subsequent 'growth phase' (Abernathy and Utterback, 1978).

33. See Dutrénit et al. (2008b, 2010a) for a broad discussion of these stages.

34. This is one of the STE instruments with the longest tradition in the country; its main goals include the promotion of the formation, development and consolidation of a critical mass of researchers at the highest level, mostly within the public system of higher education and research. The program grants both pecuniary (a monthly compensation) and non-pecuniary stimulus (status and recognition) to researchers based on the productivity and quality of their research.

35. The Advisory Forum is an independent civil organization for advising the General Council for Scientific Research and Technological Development and CONACyT's Board of Directors (which comprises directors of the main universities, research centres, industrial associations and scientific academies). REDNACECYT is a civil association that embodies a permanent forum for discussing and suggesting initiatives aimed at fostering scientific and technological development throughout the different states of the Mexican Federation.

36. The PECiTI 2007–12, launched in September 2008, replaced this program by a new instrument called Technological Innovation Fund (FIT).

37. This would mean implementing policies acting on the Gv variable appearing in the relationships of Table 18.1.

38. The Ministry of Defence increasingly performed the training and semi-public goods provision function.

39. For the case of Chile see World Bank (2008).

40. This would be linked to but not strictly overlap the two components of Stage II in Figure 18.2 and 18.3: the shift from LLET to DECM, and the transition from DECM to HLE.

41. Throughout both sub-stages we can see a mix between two sources of coevolutionary dynamics: direct effects on STE-I coevolution through capabilities (and governance) changes, which enhance push and/or pull reactivity; and indirect effects that involve the process of emergence of specific infrastructures, which affect the exogenous components of equations (18.1a) and (18.1b).

42. See for instance Breznitz (2007a) for a comparative view of policies–business development coevolution in IT industries of Israel, Ireland and Taiwan; Sotarauta and Srinivas (2006) for an analysis of public policy–economic development in innovative regions in Finland, US and India; and Fagerberg et al. (2008) for a preliminary analysis of the case of Norway.

BIBLIOGRAPHY

Abernathy, J. and Utterback, M. (1978), 'Patterns of Industrial Innovation', *Technology Review*, June–July, 40–47.

Aldrich, H. (2001), *Organizations Evolving*, London: Sage Publications.

Allen, P. (2004), 'The complexity of structure, strategy and decision making', in Metcalfe, J.S. and Foster, J. (eds), *Evolution and Economic Complexity*, Cheltenham, UK and Northampton, MA, USA: Edward Elgar.

Antonelli, C. and Teubal, M. (2011), 'From the corporation to venture capitalism: new surrogate markets for knowledge and innovation-led economic growth', in Dietricht, M. and Krafft J. (eds), *Handbook on the Economics and Theory of the Firm*, Cheltenham, UK and Northampton, MA, USA: Edward Elgar, forthcoming.

Arora, A., Fosfuri, A. and Gambardella, A. (2006), 'Markets for technology: "panda's thumbs", "calypso policies" and other institutional considerations', in Antonelli, C., Foray, D., Hall, B. and Steinmueller, E. (eds), *New Frontiers in Economics of Innovation and New Technology, Essays in Honour of Paul A. David*, Cheltenham, UK and Northampton, MA, USA: Edward Elgar.

Arthur, W.B., Durlauf, S.N. and Lane, D. (eds) (1997), *The Economy as an Evolving Complex System*, SFI Studies in the Sciences of Complexity, Vol. XXVII, Reading: Addison-Wesley.

Avnimelech, G., Rosiello, A. and Teubal, M. (2010), 'Evolutionary interpretation of venture capital policy in Israel, Germany, UK and Scotland', *Science and Public Policy*, **37** (2), 101–12.

Avnimelech, G. and Teubal, M. (2004), 'Venture capital – startup coevolution and the emergence and development of Israel's new high tech cluster', *Economics of Innovation and New Technology*, **13**, 33–60.
Avnimelech, G. and Teubal, M. (2005), 'Evolutionary innovation and high tech policy: what can we learn from Israel's targeting of venture capital?', Technology and The Economy Program Working Paper Series STE-WP-25-2005, Samuel Neaman Institute.
Avnimelech, G. and Teubal, M. (2006), 'Creating VC industries which coevolve with high tech: insights from an extended industry life cycle (ILC) perspective to the Israeli experience', *Research Policy*, **35**, 1477–98.
Avnimelech, G. and Teubal, M. (2008a), 'From direct support of business sector r&d/innovation to targeting venture capital/private equity: a catching-up innovation and technology policy life cycle perspective', *Economics of Innovation and New Technology*, **17**, 153–72.
Avnimelech, G. and Teubal, M. (2008b), 'Evolutionary targeting', *Journal of Evolutionary Economics*, **18** (2), 151–6.
Avnimelech, G. and Teubal, M. (2010), 'The coevolution of ICT, VC and policy in Israel during the 1990s', in Fornahl, D., Henn, S. and Menzel, M.-P. (eds), *Emerging Clusters: Theoretical, Empirical and Political Perspectives on the Initial Stage of Cluster Evolution*, Industrial Dynamics Series, Cheltenham, UK and Northampton, MA, USA: Edward Elgar, forthcoming.
Bar-Yam, Y. (1997), *The Dynamics of Complex Systems*, Reading, MA: Perseus Books (Advanced Book Program).
Breznitz, D. (2007a), *Innovation and the State. Political Choice and Strategies for Growth in Israel, Taiwan and Ireland*, New Haven and London: Yale University Press.
Breznitz, D. (2007b), 'Industrial R&D as a national policy: horizontal technology policies and industry-state coevolution in the growth of the Israeli software industry', *Research Policy*, **36**, 1465–82.
Campbell, D.T. (1969), 'Variation and selective retention in socio-cultural evolution', *General Systems*, **14**, 69–85.
CBS (2008), *Central Bureau of Statistics*, Israel, available at: http://www.cbs.gov.il.
Cimoli, M., Dosi, G. and Stiglitz, J. (2009), *Industrial Policy and Development*, New York: Oxford University Press.
Commission on Growth and Development (2008), 'Chilean growth through Asian eyes', typescript, February.
Dutrénit, G. and Arza, V. (2010), 'Interactions between public research organisations and industry in Latin America: a study from the perspective of firms and researchers', *Science and Public Policy*, **37** (7), 541–53.
Dutrénit, G., Capdevielle, M., Corona Alcantar, J.M., Puchet Anyul, M., Santiago, F. and Vera-Cruz, A.O. (2010a), *El sistema nacional de innovación mexicano: estructuras, políticas, desempeño y desafíos*, Mexico: UAM/Textual SA.
Dutrénit, G., De Fuentes, C. and Torres, A. (2010b), 'Channels of interaction academy–industry and benefits from firms and researchers' perspective: evidence from Mexico', *Science and Public Policy*, **37** (7), 513–26.
Dutrénit, G., Puchet Anyul, M., Sanz-Menendez, L., Teubal, M. and Vera-Cruz, A.O. (2008a), 'Coevolution of science and technology and innovation: a three stage model of policies based on the Mexican case', in Cozzens, S.E. and Berger Harari, E. (eds), *2007 Atlanta Conference on Science, Technology, and Innovation Policy*, Piscataway, NJ: IEEE.
Dutrénit, G., Puchet Anyul, M., Sanz-Menendez, L., Teubal, M. and Vera-Cruz, A.O. (2008b), 'A policy model to foster coevolutionary processes of science, technology and innovation: the Mexican case', Globelics Working Paper Series, No. 08-03.
Dutrénit, G., Santiago, F. and Vera-Cruz, A.O. (2006), 'Influencia de la política de ciencia, tecnología e innovación, sobre los incentivos y comportamiento de los agentes: lecciones del caso mexicano', *Economía, Teoría y Práctica*, **24**, 93–118.
Fagerberg, J., Guerrieri, P. and Verspagen, B. (1999), *The Economic Challenge to Europe: Adapting to Innovation Based Economic Growth*, Cheltenham, UK and Northampton, MA, USA: Edward Elgar.
Fagerberg, J., Mowery, D. and Verspagen, B. (2008), 'Innovation-systems, path-dependency and policy: the coevolution of science, technology and innovation policy and industrial structure in a small, resource-based economy', Working Papers on Innovation Studies, Centre for Technology, Innovation and Culture, University of Oslo.
Fagerberg, J. and Verspagen, B. (2007), 'Innovation, growth and economic development: have the conditions for catch up changed?', *International Journal of Technological Learning, Innovation and Development*, **1**, 13–33.
Foster, J. and Metcalfe, J.S. (2001), *Frontiers of Evolutionary Economics: Competition, Self-Organization and Innovation Policy*, Cheltenham, UK and Northampton, MA, USA: Edward Elgar.
Geuna, A. and Muscio, A. (2009), 'The governance of university knowledge transfer: a critical review of the literature', *Minerva*, **47**, 93–114.
Goldstein, J. (1999), 'Emergence as a construct: history and issues', *Journal of Complexity Issues in Organizations and Management*, **1**, 49–72.

Goldstein, J. (2003), 'The construction of emergence order, or how to resist the temptation of hylozoism', *Nonlinear Dynamics, Psychology, and Life Sciences*, **7**, 295–314.

Gompers, P. and Lerner, J. (1999), *The Venture Capital Cycle*, Cambridge, MA and London: MIT Press.

Gompers, P. and Lerner, J. (2001), 'The venture capital revolution', *Journal of Economic Perspectives*, **15**, 145–68.

Griliches, Z. (1957), 'Hybrid corn: an exploration in the economics of technological change', *Econometrica*, **25**, 501–22.

Halperin, A. and Berman, E. (1990), 'Skilled labor, security and growth', in Brodet, D., Justman, M. and Teubal, M. (eds), *Industrial–Technological Policy for Israel*, Jerusalem: Jerusalem Institute for Israel Studies (in Hebrew).

Haussman, R. and Klinger, R. (2007), 'Structural transformation in Chile', typescript, June.

Hobday, M. (1995), *Innovation in East Asia. The Challenge to Japan*, Aldershot, UK and Brookfield, VT, USA: Edward Elgar.

Holland, J. (1995), *Hidden Order: How Adaptation Builds Complexity*, Reading, MA: Addison Wesley.

Holland, J. (1998), *Emergence: From Chaos to Order*, Reading, MA: Addison Wesley.

IAEI (2008), *Israel Association of Electronics and Information Industries* (www.iaei.org.il), Israel.

IVC (2008), *Israel Venture Capital Research Center Database* (www.ivc-online.co.il).

Johnson, S. (2002), *Emergence: The Connected Lives of Ants, Brains, Cities, and Software*, New York: Touchstone.

Justman, M. and Zuscovitch, E. (2002), 'The economic impact of subsidized industrial R&D in Israel', *R&D Management*, **32**, 191–200.

Kauffman, S. (1993), *Origins of Order: Self-Organization and Selection in Evolution*, Oxford: Oxford University Press.

Kauffman, S.A. (1995), *At Home in the Universe*, New York: Oxford University Press.

Kim, L. (1997), *From Imitation to Innovation: The Dynamics of Korea's Technological Learning*, Boston: Harvard Business School Press.

Kim, L. and Nelson, R. (eds) (2000), *Technology, Learning and Innovation: Experience of Newly Industrializing Economies*, Cambridge: Cambridge University Press.

Klepper, S. (1996), 'Entry, exit, growth, and innovation over the product life cycle', *American Economic Review*, **86** (3), 562–83.

Klepper, S. (2001), 'Employee startups in high-tech industries', *Industrial Corporate Change*, **10**, 639–74.

Klepper, S. (2006), 'The evolution of geographic structure in new industries', *Revue OFCE*, June.

Kuznets, S. (1971), *Economic Growth of Nations: Total Output and Production Structure*, Cambridge, MA: Harvard University Press.

Kuznets, S. (1973), 'Modern economic growth: findings and reflections', *American Economic Review*, **63**, 247–58.

Kuznetsov, Y. (ed.) (2006), *Diaspora Networks and the International Migration of Skills: How Countries Can Draw on their Talent Abroad*, WBI Development Studies: Washington DC.

Kuznetsov, Y. (2008), 'Mobilizing intellectual capital of diasporas: from first movers to a virtuous cycle', *Journal of Intellectual Capital*, **9**, 264–82.

Lane, D., Pumain, D., van der Leeuw, S. and West, G. (eds) (2009), *Complexity Perspectives on Innovation and Social Change*, Berlin: Springer-Verlag.

Lee, J.H. and Saxenian, A. (2009), 'Do we need a double-edged sword? Triggering the contributions of Silicon Valley's Korean diaspora to domestic institutional transformation', Working Paper, Science & Technology Policy Institute, Korea.

Lee, W.Y. (2000), 'The role of science and technology policy in Korea's industrial development', in Kim, L. and Nelson, R. (eds), *Technology, Learning and Innovation: Experience of Newly Industrializing Economies*, Cambridge: Cambridge University Press.

Levinthal, D. and Myatt, J. (1994), 'Coevolution of capabilities and industry: the evolution of mutual fund processing', *Strategic Management Journal*, **15**, 11–28.

Lewin, A.Y. and Volberda, H.W. (1999), 'Prolegomena on coevolution: a framework for research on strategy and new organizational forms', *Organization Science*, **10**, 519–34.

March, J.G. (1994), *A Primer on Decision Making. How Decisions Happen*, New York: Free Press.

Marshall, A. (1890), *Principles of Economics*, 8th edn (1948), New York: Macmillan.

Maskell, P. (2001), 'Toward a knowledge-based theory of the geographical cluster', *Industrial and Corporate Change*, **10**, 921–43.

McKelvey, B., Baum, J.A.C. and Donald, T. (1999), 'Campbell's evolving influence on organization science', in Baum, J.A. and McKelvey, C.B. (eds), *Variations in Organization Science: In Honor of Donald T. Cambpell*, New Delhi: Sage Publications, pp. 1–15.

Metcalfe, J.S. and Foster, J. (eds) (2004), *Evolution and Economic Complexity*, Cheltenham, UK and Northampton, MA, USA: Edward Elgar.

Metcalfe, J.S., James, A. and Mina, A. (2005), 'Emergent innovation systems and the delivery of clinical services: the case of intra-ocular lenses', *Research Policy*, **34**, 1283–304.

Murmann, J.P. (2002), 'The coevolution of industries and national institutions: theory and evidence', working paper, FSIV02.14, Social Science Research Center Berlin.

Murmann, J.P. (2003), 'The coevolution of industries and academic disciplines', working paper, WP03-1, Kellogg School of Management, North-western University.

Murray, F. (2002), 'Innovation as coevolution of scientific and technological networks: exploring tissue engineering', *Research Policy*, **31**, 1389–403.

National Council for Research and Development (1971), *Scientific Research in Israel*, Center for Scientific and Technological Information.

Nelson, R. (1994), 'The co-evolution of technology, industrial structure and supporting institutions', *Industrial and Corporate Change*, **3**, 47–63.

Nelson, R. (1995), 'Recent evolutionary theorizing about economic change', *Journal of Economic Literature*, **33**, 48–90.

Nelson, R. (2001), 'The coevolution of technology and institutions as the driver of economic growth', in Foster, J. and Metcalfe, J.S. (eds), *Frontiers of Evolutionary Economics: Competition, Self-organization and Innovation Policy*, Cheltenham, UK and Northampton, MA, USA: Edward Elgar.

Nelson, R. (2007), 'What makes an economy productive and progressive? What are the needed institutions?', Staff Papers 13728, University of Minnesota, Department of Applied Economics.

Nelson, R. and Winter, S.G. (1982), *An Evolutionary Theory of Economic Change*, Cambridge, MA: Belknap Press of Harvard University Press.

Norgaard, R. (1984), 'Coevolutionary development potential', *Land Economics*, **60**, 160–73.

Norgaard, R. (1994), *Development Betrayed: The End of Progress and a Coevolutionary Revisioning of the Future*, London: Routledge.

Nygaard, S. (2008), 'Coevolution of technology, markets and institutions – the case of fuel cells and hydrogen technology in Europe', PhD thesis, Centre for Innovation, Research and Competence in the Learning Economy (CIRCLE), Sweden.

OCS (2008), *Office of Chief Science*, Ministry of Industry, Trade and Labor (www.moit.gov.il), Israel.

OECD (2004), 'Venture capital: trends and policy recommendations', DSTI/DOC, STI Working Papers, Paris.

Porter, M. (1998), 'Clusters and the new economics of competition', *Harvard Business Review*, Nov.–Dec., 77–92.

Potts, J. (2000), *The New Evolutionary Microeconomics: Complexity, Competence and Adaptive Behavior*, Cheltenham, UK and Northampton, MA, USA: Edward Elgar.

Puchet Anyul, M. (2008), 'Incentivos, mecanismos e instituciones económicas presupuestas en el ordenamiento legal mexicano vigente de la ciencia y la tecnología', in Valenti, G. (ed.), *Prioridades para la definición de la agenda en ciencia, tecnología e innovación*, Mexico: IBERGOP Y FLACSO.

Pugatch, M., Teubal, M. and Zlotnick, O. (2010), 'Israel's high tech catch up process: the role of IPR and other policies', in Odagiri, H., Goto, A., Sunami, A. and Nelson, R. (eds), *Intellectual Property Rights, Development and Catch-Up*, Oxford: Oxford University Press.

Rodrik, D. (2004), 'Industrial policy for the twenty-first century', Working Paper Series rwp04-047, Harvard University, John F. Kennedy School of Government.

Roelandt, J., Gilsing, V. and Sinderen, J. (2000), 'Cluster-based innovation policy: international experience', Erasmus University Rotterdam, Research Memorandum 0012.

Ruttan, V. (1961), 'Usher and Schumpeter on invention, innovation, and technological change', *Quarterly Journal of Economics*, **LXXV**, 596–606.

Saviotti, P. (1996), *Technological Evolution, Variety and the Economy*, Cheltenham, UK and Brookfield, VT, USA: Edward Elgar.

Saviotti, P. (1997), 'Innovation systems and evolutionary theories', in Edquist, C. (ed.), *Systems of Innovation: Technologies, Institutions and Organizations*, London: Pinter Publishing.

Saviotti, P. and Pyka, A. (2004), 'Economic development by the creation of new sectors', *Journal of Evolutionary Economics*, **14**, 1–35.

Saxenian, A. (1994), *Regional Development: Silicon Valley and Route 128*, Cambridge, MA: Harvard University Press.

Schumpeter, J. (1934), *The Theory of Economic Development* (1st German edition: 1911), Cambridge, MA: Harvard University Press.

Schumpeter, J. (1939), *Business Cycles: A Theoretical, Historical and Statistical Analysis of the Capitalist Process*, New York: McGraw Hill.

Sercovich, F. and Teubal, M. (2009), 'Strategic innovation policy: a systems evolutionary perspective', paper presented to the Georgia Tech 'Science and Technology Policy' meeting, October.

Siegel, D.S., Waldman, D.A., Atwater, L.E. and Link, A.N. (2003), 'Commercial knowledge transfers from universities to firms: improving the effectiveness of university–industry collaboration', *Journal of High Technology Management Research*, **14**, 111–33.

Sotarauta, M. and Srinivas, S. (2006), 'Co-evolutionary policy processes: understanding innovative economies and future resilience', *Futures*, **38**, 312–36.

Syrquin, M. (2009), 'Kuznets and Pasinnetti on the study of structural transformation: never the twain shall meet', typescript.

Teubal, M. (1997), 'A catalytic and evolutionary approach to horizontal technological policies', *Research Policy*, **25**, 1161–88.

van den Bergh, J.C.J.M. and Gowdy, J.M. (2003), 'The microfoundations of macroeconomics: an evolutionary perspective', *Cambridge Journal of Economics*, **27**, 65–84.

Volberda, H.W. and Lewin, A.Y. (2003), 'Co-evolutionary dynamics within and between firms: from evolution to coevolution', *Journal of Management Studies*, **8**, 2111–36.

World Bank (2008), *Commission on Growth and Development*, Washington DC: World Bank.

Yoguel, G., Tacsir, E. and García, M. (2009), 'Aprovechando el conocimiento argentino en el exterior', Working Paper, Washington DC: World Bank.

Zollo, M. and Winter, S.G. (2002), 'Deliberate learning and the evolution of dynamic capabilities', *Organization Science*, **13**, 339–51.

19 Network models of innovation process and policy implications*
Paul Ormerod, Bridget Rosewell and Greg Wiltshire

1. INTRODUCTION

Understanding the innovation process is key to understanding how capitalism has created levels of productivity which were previously undreamed of. However, the standard models of the firm or of macroeconomic growth do not address this very effectively. This is largely because innovation is fundamentally a disequilibrium phenomenon – it is about the constant adjustment towards a new equilibrium that is never reached because further innovation is always occurring. Innovation is a disturber and a re-adjuster, to both the firm and the economy. Since innovation is a dynamic process, analysis using comparative statics fails to capture the nature of the process. Schumpeter pointed out long ago that 'innovation . . . does not lend itself to description in terms of a theory of equilibrium' (Schumpeter, 1928), and more recently Antonelli notes that 'innovation is the distinctive element of a dynamic process which cannot be analysed with the equilibrium approach' (Antonelli, 2008).

This chapter addresses the dynamics of innovation by considering the process by which a particular innovation might be made effective. To do this, we look at the networks by which organizations might discover and adopt innovations. Glückler notes that growth and innovation largely result from network dynamics, and this is the starting point this study takes (Glückler, 2007).

Innovation is the deliverable realization of an invention. It is important not to treat technological improvement or invention as identical to innovation (Metcalfe, 2007). Metcalfe notes that even were technological advancement to end today, there would still remain a considerable amount of potential for innovation within an economy. Innovation is more than just invention; it can also involve the use of a better production process, a new service, or the changing of the network structure itself (Antonelli, 2008). Metcalfe tells us 'innovation requires access to and command of many more kinds of knowledge and capability than are summed up by the phrase "science and technology"'. Innovation is the economic realization of an invention and requires an understanding of consumer and user needs as well as knowledge of the market and organization if it is to occur. Primarily it is the application of new combinations of resources to the economic process.

The most relevant indicators of innovative outcomes should reflect the efficiency and effectiveness in producing, diffusing and exploiting economically useful knowledge (Lundvall, 1992). One measure of the success of an innovation is the proportion of the total possible market the innovation has penetrated (Mansfield, 1961). We model the spread of an innovation through the market and, through seeing how far the innovation has penetrated, gain a metric that measures innovation.

We go on to look at the impact that different structures have on the speed and effectiveness of the spread of innovation and how public policy might affect this.

A network model of the innovation process needs to capture those features that are relevant to the spread of innovation between firms. We estimate the number of links firms have with others, their own ability to generate innovations, and their abilities to both disseminate and absorb knowledge and innovation from the wider network of firms in which they are embedded.

The ability of an industry to have a high degree of innovation will be a function of various features of the network and the firms within it. The number of links within a network may have a positive or negative bearing on its amount of innovation (Ormerod and Rosewell, 2009) depending on the decision rule used by agents in deciding whether or not to adopt the innovation. The propensity individual firms have to innovate, disseminate innovation and absorb innovation will all be important determinants of an industry's innovation. The model approach described here can be applied to a variety of cases and the methodology is relevant to any problem where the process of change needs to be examined.

We use here data from a study of Manchester in the UK to provide an example of the calibration of a model of this innovation process.

2. THE NETWORK MODEL

2.1 Methodology

Figure 19.1 outlines the approach used to model the adoption of a single innovation across a network while Table 19.1 describes the parameter values and ranges used in this study.

The model takes an initial innovation to be exogenous and it is taken up by one agent/organization at the outset. The characteristics of the agents are governed by their willingness to innovate, their desire to keep innovation to themselves, and their willingness to communicate with others. The innovating agent will be connected to other agents via the network structure, and at the next step of the model the innovation will be passed on according to the extent agents discover the innovation and their own willingness to take it up. At further steps of the model further agents may be able to discover and take up the innovation, until eventually no further take up occurs.

2.2 Innovation Behaviour of Organizations

We define two different methods by which innovation may be passed on via the network linkages. The first is a direct relationship between two partners, while the second is a group relationship.

First, an organization with an innovation will provide it to another firm only if its level of secrecy, or the propensity of a firm to try to retain the benefits of its innovations, is less than the absorptive capacity, or the degree to which a firm actively engages in activities which enable it to identify and adopt new innovations, of the firms it is linked with. This method of adopting an innovation represents a mutual relationship

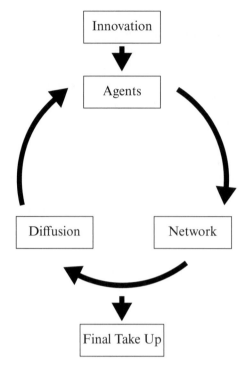

Figure 19.1   Model overview

or exchange between firms and implies a degree of trust or collaboration. It is probable that this relationship is more likely to exist with customers, suppliers or third parties than with competitors.

The second method for spreading an innovation we describe as a *copying* behaviour. Here if a firm looks at the spectrum of organizations to which it is linked and finds that the proportion that have adopted an innovation is higher than their own personal threshold, they will mimic their behaviour and adopt the innovation. In some circumstances this threshold may be very high and only when all or nearly all of the firms an organization has relationships with have taken up an innovation will they be persuaded to do the same. For other organizations relatively few businesses may have to have the same innovation before they adopt it. This mechanism represents a copying behaviour. This may occur even when a firm may not fully understand the reasons and benefits of an innovation but relies on observing that other businesses have adopted it. This behaviour is more likely to be a response to competitor behaviour.

There is a growing body of literature that indicates that a range of macro consumer behaviour, such as the take up of bank accounts by unemployed people (Volterra Consulting Ltd, 2006) and the binge drinking behaviour of young adults in the UK (Ormerod and Wiltshile, 2009), can be explained by such decision making mechanisms.

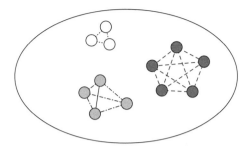

Figure 19.2   The initial stage of generating a network structure for a given industry using
           k-*cliques*

2.3   Network Behaviour

The network behaviour is not set a priori. One of the important aspects of this chapter is
that we are able to calibrate the network across which any innovation percolates to the
actual networks that we observe in our survey. To enable us to use these distributions in
the model a variable is introduced called the network scaling factor (S_0). This is essentially the maximum number of links, or degree, a firm can have in the model (while the
minimum is $\alpha\, S_0$). Once this is set the number of links of all firms can be determined. As
S_0 is increased the number and therefore the density of links is increased.

The *k*-clique algorithm

As discussed the model starts by taking the value for S_0 and calculating the implied
degree distribution of links. It then builds the network to match this distribution as
closely as possible by generating a series of what are called *k*-cliques. For example, there
may be three firms who should have two links, four firms that should have three and five
firms that should have four links. In this case the firms that require the same number of
links are connected into a fully connected sub-graph or *k*-clique as shown in Figure 19.2
Links formed using this method are reciprocated, which means that an innovation can
be spread in both directions.

At this stage the network is therefore highly clustered and each cluster is isolated.
In order to move towards a more realistic network structure half of the links in the
model are re-wired to randomly selected firms while the degree of each firm is retained,
as shown in Figure 19.3. What is achieved is a hybrid network structure where quasi-
clusters of firms exist as part of a larger region wide network. However, it is not always
possible to guarantee that the program will find a way to rewire 50 per cent of the
links within the computational constraints. Table 19.3 presents the average percentage that the algorithm achieved across the 1000 networks generated for each industry
parameterization.

2.4   The Parameters

The model parameters are set out formally in Table 19.1, alongside the ranges used in the
model, which reflect the data used and are more fully described in Section 3.

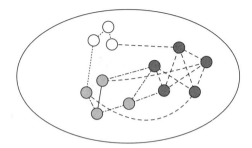

Figure 19.3 *The second stage of generating a network structure for a given industry where the* k-*cliques are rewired but the degree distribution is retained*

Table 19.1 *Parameters used in the generation of the network model for each industry*

Parameter	Description	Value/Range
n	Number of agents or firms in network	1000
α	The lower limit to the distribution for the threshold of agents to adopt an innovation based on an evaluation of agents connected to them by their business network. – copying	0–1.1
ε	The upper limit to the distribution for the threshold of agents to adopt an innovation based on an evaluation of agents connected to them by their business network. – copying	1–1.1
S_0	Network scaling factor, equals the highest number of business links a firm can have in the model. – size of network	8–64
β_a	Absorptive Capacity Scalar: this is the scaling factor applied to each firm's absorptive index when drawn from the industry distribution	0–10.05
β_s	Secrecy Scalar: this is the scaling factor applied to each firm's secrecy index when drawn from the industry distribution	1
periods	The number of time steps from the point that the first innovation is generated, that the model runs for	50
Repeats	The number of iterations that each parameterization is repeated in order to find by the average and range of possible outcomes	1000

The steps that the model takes in disseminating an individual innovation are described in detail in the flow charts in Figure 19.4. The model enables us to determine the final take-up of an innovation, given the parameters of the model. It also allows us to consider the effectiveness of different behaviours, agent characteristics and network structures on the likelihood of an innovation being adopted by all firms – a global cascade.

2.5 Choice of Model Parameter Ranges

Number of agents – n
The number of agents is chosen as a balance between providing a population of firms that enable the various distributions to be well reflected in a single repeat of the model

and the computational demands of running 315 model parameterizations, for each of four industries, all of which are averaged 1000 times. Even at a second per repeat this equates to 15 days of pure computation, a time that does not include the time needed to build the 20 000 network structures.

Boundaries to copying – α and ε

α and ε are used to define the maximum and minimum boundaries of the uniform distribution used to allocate firms their personal threshold used in their copying behaviour. The maximum is held at one throughout this study while the minimum varies. The impact of this is shown in Figure 19.5, as α is increased, on average, firms require a higher proportion of their connections to possess an innovation before they will adopt it. The values of α in Table 19.1 studied here relate to the entire range of possibilities between 0 and 1. The special case of a and e equal to 1.1 corresponds to the copying behaviour being turned off.

No data is available from our survey to enable us to calibrate this kind of behaviour.

Maximum number of links – S_0

S_0 is the maximum number of links of any firm in a given network structure that is then used to define the degree distribution for all other firms. The distribution used is based on the survey data discussed in Section 3.1, where the smallest non zero bin is 0.125. In order to avoid biasing the model by rounding the number of links a firm has it is therefore necessary that S_0 is an integer multiple of eight. It follows that eight itself is the lowest possible value as this will produce firms with only a single link in the network ($8 \times 0.125 = 1$). The upper range of S_0 is open ended: for the purposes of this study connectivity an order of magnitude higher than that implied by the minimum was studied.

The survey can only tell us the distribution of links and not the total number, so this is an essential assumption. Results are later shown for different configurations of S_0.

Scaling factors on absorption and secrecy – β_a and β_s

The parameters β_a and β_s are used to vary the values, but not the distribution of, the absorptive and secrecy indices of the firms. When these are initially drawn the values generated are the upper limits of the bins used in the survey (0, 0.1, 0.2 . . .1.0), these are then multiplied by the values of β_a and β_s. Figure 19.6(a) shows this for the generalized case, for example when β_a equals β_s a firm with an absorption index of $0.5\beta_a$ (the dark grey area) will be able to adopt all of the innovations of firms with an secrecy index of up and including $0.4\beta_s$ (the light grey area). Figure 19.6(b) and (c) show two examples where the two scaling factors are unequal. When $\beta_a = 0.25$ and $\beta_s = 1$ the same firm will only absorb the innovations of firms with secrecy indexes of 0.1 and zero whereas when $\beta_a = 2.05$ and $\beta_s = 1$ the same firm will be able to absorb the innovations of all firms.

These examples demonstrate three characteristics of the engineering of this mechanism and the parameter ranges presented in Table 19.1. First, that this research does not have to explore a parameter space for β_a and β_s independently. This is because increasing β_a is equivalent to reducing β_s, therefore we hold $\beta_s = 1$ throughout this study and only modify the characteristics of the exchange behaviour by changing the value of β_a. Second, it explains why the model requires firms to have a *higher* absorptive index than the secrecy

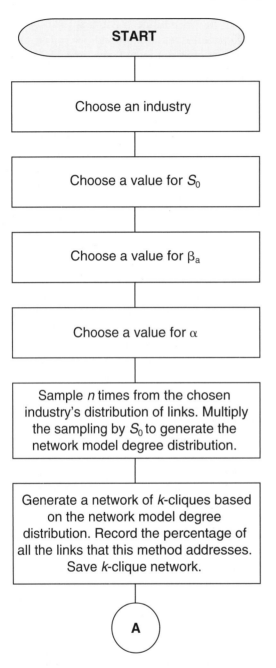

Figure 19.4   The network model

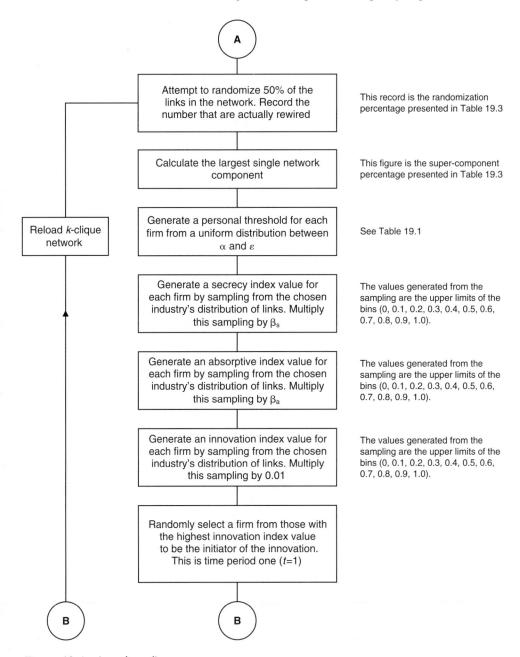

Figure 19.4 (continued)

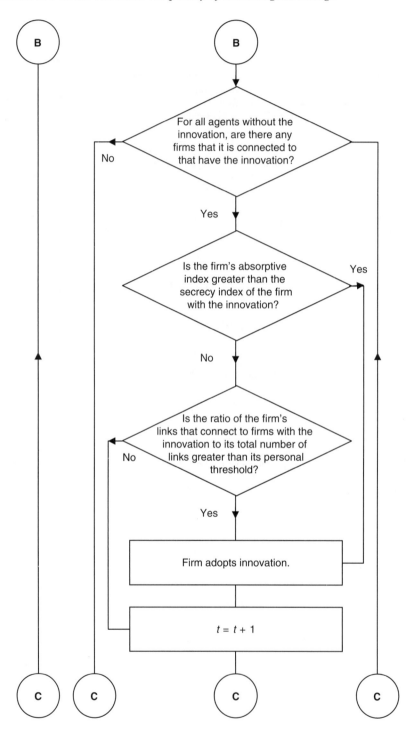

Figure 19.4 (continued)

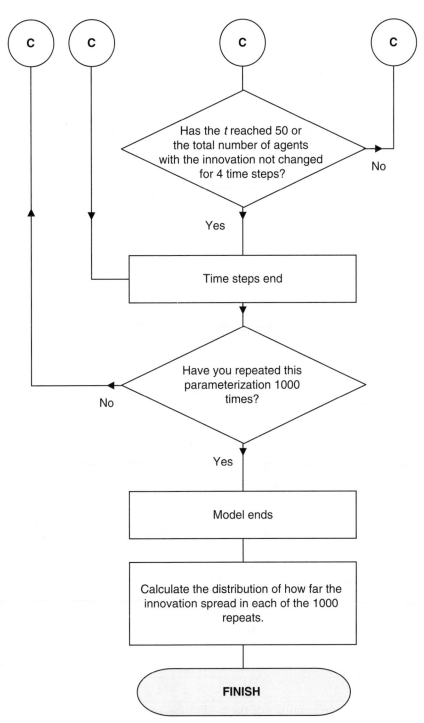

Figure 19.4 (continued)

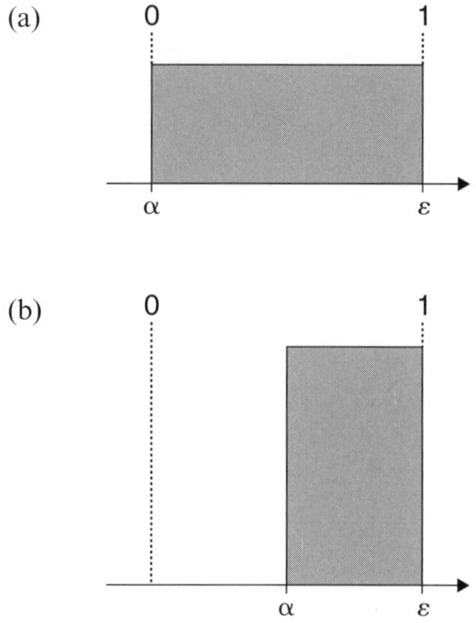

(a)

(b)

Figure 19.5   *Specification of α and ε for determining the distribution used for the personal threshold of agents used in their mimicking behaviour for (a) α=0 and ε=1 and (b) α=0.5 and ε=1*

index of a firm that has an innovation and that it is connected to, rather than *higher or equal to*. We do this to avoid the case that a firm with an absorptive index of zero could adopt the innovation of a firm with a secrecy index of zero, which would be counter intuitive, especially when $\beta_a = 0$. The consequence of this is that when $\beta_s = 1$ and $\beta_a = 0$ the exchange method of innovation adoption is turned off and that when $\beta_a > 10$ all the firms, except those with an absorption index of zero, adopt any innovation they are connected to because any non-zero absorption index will be larger than any secrecy index.

Periods
The number of periods over which to run the model was chosen so that each repeat of the model was given ample time to reach the maximum contagion determined by the parameterization. The program was set up so that warning flags would be recorded if the model did not reach equilibrium by the end of the steps.

Repeats
This was based on establishing standard deviation of cascades.

3.   THE DATA

This section gives some examples of the calibration of this model to data drawn from a study in Manchester, UK. Both statistical and survey evidence are necessary to this calibration.

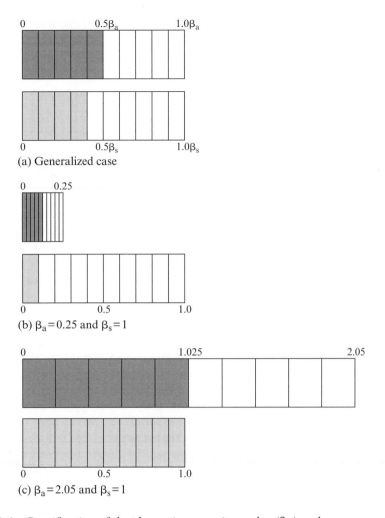

Figure 19.6   Specification of the absorptive capacity scalar (β_a) and secrecy capacity scalar (β_s) to change the amount of adoption of innovation, due to the exchange mechanism, available in a model for three cases

We examine evidence from four separate industries: financial and professional services; health sciences; creative/digital/new media/IT/communications; and engineering and textiles, in the Manchester City Region (MCR). These industries span quite different types of industrial activity and so provide a broad evidence base. In addition, using data from different industries enables us to examine contrasts between industries in the drivers of innovation. The primary research was conducted as part of a broader study to examine the prospects and policies of the Manchester City Region.[1] This information was used to calibrate the agent based model described in Section 2 for firms in each of the industries.

The firms are connected by a network, and direct flows of innovation can only take place between firms which are connected. The particular structure of the network is based on the evidence of the business relationships between firms.

Drawing on the primary research, we obtain the distributions across firms of the networks and the three key parameters of the innovation model. These are:

- The propensity of a firm to innovate
- The secrecy index, which is the degree to which firms seek to protect their innovation
- The absorptive index, which reflects the willingness of firms to discover and participate in innovation.

Given the distributions across firms of these three key parameters and the structure of the networks across which firms are connected, we are able to analyse the propensity of innovation to spread across the firms of an industry, and to identify the parameters to which the spread is most sensitive.

3.1   The Network Structure

The network structures used in the model for each industry are derived from the relations between firms in the MCR identified from the surveys. Organizations were asked what proportion of their purchases and their sales are made within the Manchester City Region. The responses for both questions had similar distributions so they were combined into a single entity.

The resulting distribution for each industry gives us the proportion of firms that perform a specific percentage of their business within the MCR, both upstream and downstream in their supply chain, but not what absolute level this represents.

These distributions are used to calibrate the relative degree of connectivity or links between firms in the network model for each industry. Note that this implies that organizational size does not affect the degree of connection with other organization. Evidence suggests that larger firms focus their supply chains so that fewer firms are involved, while developing stronger relationships with those that remain, which would be consistent with this (Rhodes et al., 2006).

Supply chain relationships are important to the spread of innovation between firms. Dyer and Singh (1998) argue that 'a firm's alliance partners are, in many cases, the most important source of new ideas and information that result in performance-enhancing technology and innovation'.

Table 19.2 shows the mean percentage of business performed within the MCR for each of the four industries while Figures 19.7–19.10 show the overall distributions.

Figures 19.7–19.10 demonstrate that a surprisingly high proportion of firms identified themselves as performing no proportion of their business within the MCR. In the network model this is equivalent to an organization having no links. Since the aim of the network study is to understand the drivers that enable the innovation of one firm to spread to others, these isolated firms are unable to spread or receive an innovation and are therefore redundant.

These distributions do not allow us to know how many links a given firm within the

Table 19.2   Mean percentage of links within the MCR for organizations within each industry

Industry	Mean % of business links within the MCR	
	Including those that do not have any MCR links	Excluding those that do not have any MCR links
Creative/digital/new media/IT/ communications	28	43
Financial & professional services	38	52
Health sciences	53	70
Engineering & textiles	22	34

MCR actually has; it simply tells us the relative connectivity of the population of firms. For example, in the case of the health sciences industry we know that there are three times as many firms with all of their business relationships contained within the MCR as there are firms who have 26–50 per cent of their links within the region. We do not know how many links this corresponds to.

Note also that the firms' networks do not distinguish here between the kinds of linkages – they are the linkages of firms from a particular kind of business but with all kinds of organizations.

Comparison between questionnaire derived and model degree distributions
In practice the distributions derived from the questionnaire are not perfectly replicated using the k-clique algorithm discussed earlier. Residuals may exist in the distribution that cannot form a perfect k-clique. Table 19.3 shows typical values for the percentage of links that this method successfully incorporated into the network as a proportion of the total in the questionnaire derived distribution; this is called the degree of reciprocation.

Table 19.3 indicates that the algorithm is capable of assigning over 90 per cent of the links in all but the densest networks (where S_0 is 64); even then it is above 85 per cent. As S_0 decreases and the network structure becomes less dense the algorithm improves in efficiency.

There are two options at this point regarding how to deal with the residual differences between the questionnaire derived and model degree distributions. First, since the degree of distribution is adequately high across all parameterizations the differences could be ignored, second, the difference could be removed by including un-reciprocated links (links where an innovation can only be adopted in one direction).

The second method was chosen so that the degree distribution in the model exactly matched that of the questionnaire but as a result a residual proportion of these were unreciprocated.

Network super-component size
One consideration with the method developed to generate the network structures is that there is a probability that not all of the 1000 firms in the model end up connected into a single component. This increases in likelihood as S_0 is reduced. It is important to

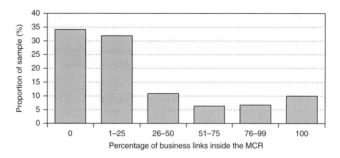

Figure 19.7   Distribution of links in creative/digital/new media/IT/communications

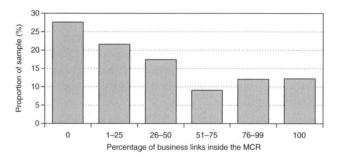

Figure 19.8   Distribution of links in financial and professional services

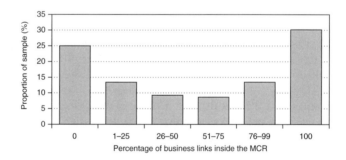

Figure 19.9   Distribution of links in health sciences

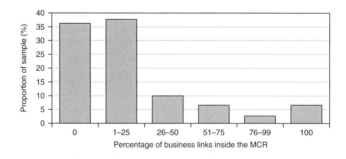

Figure 19.10   Distribution of links in engineering and textiles

Table 19.3   Analysis of the performance of the network generating algorithm for each industry distribution and value of S_0

Industry	S_0	Typical degree of reciprocation (target of 100%) %	Average randomization (target of 50%) %	Average super-component size %
Creative/digital/new media/ IT/communications	8	99.2	49.96	82.2
	16	98.5	49.97	100
	24	97.7	–	100
	32	95.6	49.97	100
	64	91.7	–	100
Financial & professional Services	8	98.5	49.93	94.5
	16	98.2	49.97	100
	24	97.9	–	100
	32	97.5	49.97	100
	64	88.6	49.96	100
Health sciences	8	99.8	49.96	97.5
	16	98.3	49.96	100
	24	97.5	–	100
	32	96.1	–	100
	64	97.0	–	100
Engineering & textiles	8	97.9	49.94	67.8
	16	96.1	49.98	100
	24	96.0	–	100
	32	96.9	49.97	100
	64	86.4	–	100

understand what the average maximum component size is for each parameterization of the network.

For example if on average when S_0 is 8 the largest connected component, or super-component, is 80 per cent of all of the agents in the model, then this acts as a ceiling to the maximum percolation that a single innovation can achieve.

The average super-component size was calculated for each of the five network parameterizations used for each industry. The results of this analysis (Table 19.3) show that the super-component size only needs to be considered when the industry networks are at their lowest density or when S_0 is 8. The relative size of the industry super-components under this parameterization is simply a restatement of the average number of links presented in Table 19.2.

3.2   Agent Characteristics

The secrecy index or innovation protection

The secrecy index in the model measures the strengths of the barriers to the spread of innovation. The market pressures that lead firms to innovate will also mean they attempt

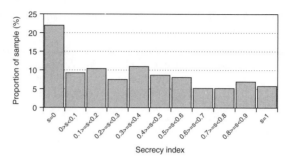

Figure 19.11   Distribution of secrecy index in creative/digital/new media/IT/communications

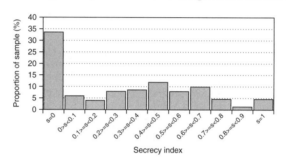

Figure 19.12   Distribution of secrecy index in financial and professional services

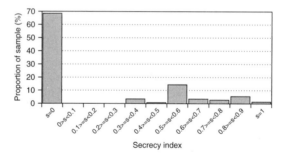

Figure 19.13   Distribution of secrecy index in health sciences

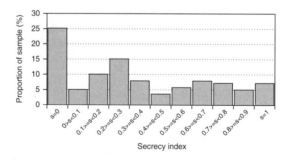

Figure 19.14   Distribution of secrecy index in engineering and textiles

Table 19.4   *P-values of Kolmogorov–Smirnov tests to evaluate whether any two secrecy index distributions are statistically equivalent*

	(1)	(2)	(3)	(4)
Creative/digital/new media/IT/communications (1)	–	0.37	<**0.01**	0.74
Financial & professional Services (2)	0.37	–	**0.01**	0.74
Health sciences (3)	<**0.01**	**0.01**	–	<**0.01**
Engineering & textiles (4)	0.74	0.74	<**0.01**	–

Note: Cells in bold indicate distributions that are statistically dissimilar at the level shown, non bold cells are statistically similar at the level shown.

to prevent the spread of the innovation to competitors. The literature shows the importance of the structures of knowledge governance to the spread of innovation (Antonelli, 2008). If firms protect innovations, the ability of a network structure to spread innovation is reduced.

In order to construct the distribution for the secrecy index of organizations in the model the survey asked firms about the importance they placed on various methods for protecting innovations. These protective measures were:

- Registration of design
- Trademarks
- Patents
- Confidentiality agreements
- Copyright
- Secrecy
- Complexity of design
- Lead time advantage on competitors.

From these answers we can build a picture of how active firms in an industry are in protecting their innovations, and thus part of the picture of how easy it is for innovations to spread. The exact methodology is presented in Appendix 19A.1. Figures 19.11–19.14 present the resulting distributions of the secrecy indices for each industry.

Table 19.4 presents the results of Kolmogorov–Smirnov tests which evaluate the statistical probability that the derived distributions are samples from the same underlying distribution. The health sciences industry is clearly distinct from the others, but there is a 73 per cent chance that the creative/digital/new media/IT/communications and financial and professional services' distributions are in fact the same.

Table 19.5 gives an average secrecy index of each industry. A high secrecy score indicates an industry in which there are higher barriers to the sharing of innovations, and a lower score means there are lower barriers to sharing.

Absorptive index or pursuing innovation
Spreading an innovation using the exchange process is a two way relationship – the firm with the innovation must be willing to share it, and the firm without the innovation must

Table 19.5   Mean secrecy index of each industry

Industry	Mean secrecy index
Creative/digital/new media/IT/communications	0.34
Financial & professional services	0.31
Health sciences	0.20
Engineering & textiles	0.34

be actively pursuing and able to adopt it. The ability to absorb an innovation depends on a number of factors:

- The knowledge parity between the firms with and without the innovation
- The importance that the firm without the innovation places on absorbing innovations
- The involvement of a firm in wider networks – knowledge transfer partnerships, business networks, links with higher education institutions, trade organizations, cluster organizations, and so on.

The survey asked firms about their involvement in the final factor, as this is the most relevant from a network perspective, and from this we are able to construct an absorptive index for each firm. The literature showed that the ability to absorb innovation was intimately tied to firms' involvement in the network of firms around them (for example, Cowan and Jonard, 2004). The absorptive methods asked about were:

- Publicly funded joint research programmes
- Other research associations
- Joint R&D agreements
- Licensing and second sourcing agreements
- Knowledge transfer partnerships and hosting research studentships
- Other links with higher education
- Member of/attends: trade associations, cluster organizations, business networks
- Member of other general business organizations.

The exact methodology for calculating the index for an individual firm is detailed in Appendix 19A.2. Figures 19.15–19.18 present the resulting distributions of the index for each industry.

Table 19.6 again presents the results of Kolmogorov–Smirnov tests which evaluate the statistical probability that the derived distributions are samples from the same underlying distribution. There is a 73 per cent chance that the health science industry's distribution and both the financial and professional services and the creative/digital/new media/IT/communications' distributions are in fact the same.

As for the secrecy index, we can give a mean absorptive index for each industry to give an initial description of the ability of firms within that industry to absorb innovations. This is shown in Table 19.7.

An absorptive capacity of one indicates a firm that undertakes every method of

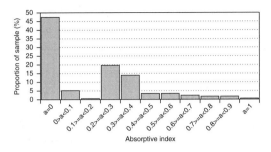

Figure 19.15   Distribution of absorptive index in creative/digital/new media/IT/ communications

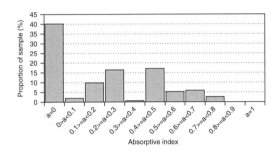

Figure 19.16   Distribution of absorptive index in financial and professional services

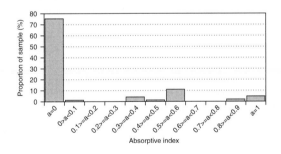

Figure 19.17   Distribution of absorptive index in health sciences

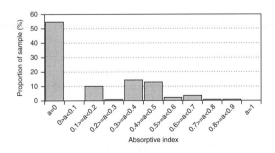

Figure 19.18   Distribution of absorptive index in engineering and textiles

Table 19.6   P-values of Kolmogorov–Smirnov tests to evaluate whether any two absorptive index distributions are statistically equivalent

	(1)	(2)	(3)	(4)
Creative/digital/new media/IT/communications (1)	–	0.74	0.37	0.74
Financial & professional services (2)	0.74	–	0.37	0.99
Health sciences (3)	0.37	0.37	–	0.99
Engineering & textiles (4)	0.74	0.99	0.99	–

Note: Distributions are statistically similar at the level shown.

Table 19.7   Mean absorptive index of each industry

Industry	Absorptive index
Creative/digital/new media/IT/communications	0.18
Financial & professional services	0.22
Health sciences	0.14
Engineering & textiles	0.17

absorbing innovations that the survey identified. Such a firm has a very high ability is absorb innovations from other firms it is connected with. An absorptive capacity of zero indicates a firm that undertakes none of the methods of absorbing innovations. Such a firm is unable to extract innovations from the wider network of firms in which it is embedded.

Propensity to innovate
The final distribution derived from the survey was the propensity of organizations to innovate in each industry. Firms were asked whether or not they had engaged in a range of activities conducive to creating an innovation, over the three year period 2005–07. Specifically, they were asked whether they had performed the following:

- In-house R&D
- Acquisition of external R&D
- Acquisition of machinery, equipment and software
- Acquisition of external knowledge
- Training to support new products, services, or business and process improvement
- Design expenditure
- Marketing and advertising specifically related to new and improved services or products
- Major changes in business structure, practices or processes.

From the responses a propensity to innovate was constructed for each firm. The method of calculation is detailed in Appendix 19A.3.

Table 19.8   P-values of Kolmogorov–Smirnov tests to evaluate whether any two
innovation index distributions are statistically equivalent

	(1)	(2)	(3)	(4)
Creative/digital/new media/IT/communications (1)	–	0.99	**0.05**	0.74
Financial & professional services (2)	0.99	–	**0.05**	0.74
Health sciences (3)	**0.05**	**0.05**	–	0.15
Engineering & textiles (4)	0.74	0.74	0.15	–

Note: Cells in bold indicate distributions that are statistically dissimilar at the level shown, non-bold cells are statistically similar at the level shown.

Table 19.9   Mean innovation index of each industry

Industry	Innovation index
Creative/digital/new media/IT/communications	0.50
Financial & professional services	0.48
Health sciences	0.29
Engineering & textiles	0.51

Table 19.8 presents the results of Kolmogorov–Smirnov tests which evaluate the statistical probability that the derived distributions are samples from the same underlying distribution. The health sciences industry is clearly distinct from the creative/digital/ new media/IT/communications and financial and professional services' distributions but there is an 85 per cent probability that it is the same as the engineering and textiles distribution.

An innovation index close to one indicates a firm that engages in a high number of innovation-generating activities. An index close to zero indicates a firm that undertakes very few innovation related activities. Table 19.9 shows the mean innovation index of each industry.

Figures 19.19–19.22 show the distribution of innovation index of each firm within an industry. This is only relevant in the second of the two network models when more than one innovation can be generated and spread amongst firms.

4.   RESULTS

4.1   Cascades

The output of a single execution of the model is a time series of the percentage of firms that adopted the original innovation. Figure 19.23 shows two examples for the creative/ digital/newmedia/IT/communications industry using the same parameterization. It shows two contrasting examples: first, the lower line where over 50 time steps the innovation spread to 3.5 per cent of the firms in the network and second, the upper line where

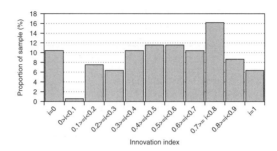

*Figure 19.19   Distribution of innovation index in creative/digital/new media/IT/
communications*

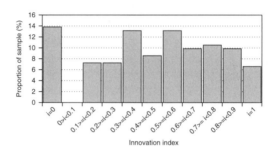

Figure 19.20   Distribution of innovation index in financial and professional services

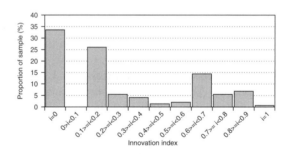

Figure 19.21   Distribution of innovation index in health sciences

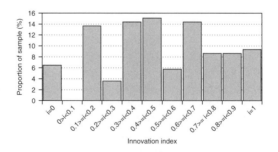

Figure 19.22   Distribution of innovation index in engineering and textiles

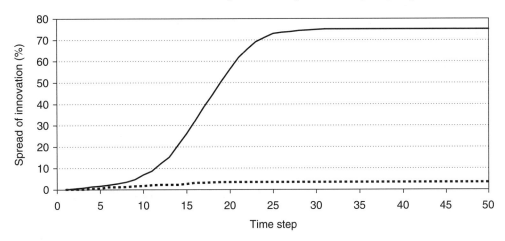

Note: ($\alpha=0$, $\varepsilon=1$, $S_0=16$, $\beta_a=0.25$, $\beta_s=1$).

Figure 19.23   *Example results for single runs of the model for the creative/digital/new media/IT/communications industry*

a much larger contagion occurred and 75 per cent of the agents adopted the innovation over the same number of steps.

Figure 19.23 demonstrates that even for the same parameterization the results of individual runs of the model can be very different. This variation is a result of differences in the arrangement of the network such as the degree of connection of the firm that generates the innovation as well as the randomly assigned personal thresholds, absorptive and secrecy indices. It is unrealistic to expect to be able to map the real world network and assign each firm its actual behavioural characteristics so this process of randomization is necessary to explore the possible impacts of the myriad arrangements. It is for this reason that the model is repeated 1000 times for each parameterization, for each industry. The final spread of the innovation (3.5 and 75 per cent in the examples shown in Figure 19.23) across these 1000 repeats is plotted as a histogram for each industry parameterization, as shown in Figure 19.24.

Figure 19.24 shows that the cascades that occur form two distinct distributions. It is the upper symmetric distribution that is of interest for this study. We will call it the global cascade (as opposed to the lower skewed distribution which we call the local cascade). As discussed, the aim of this analysis is to understand the drivers that create this wider spread contagion, the assumption being that the Manchester City Region will benefit if the innovations of one firm are enabled to spread to others in the regional economy.

In order to evaluate these drivers, the characteristics of the upper symmetric distribution need to be captured. These characteristics include its mean, standard deviation and proportion of the 1000 repeats it includes. This analysis focuses on the first of these. In order to evaluate the mean of the distribution the lower skewed distribution needs to be removed from the data.

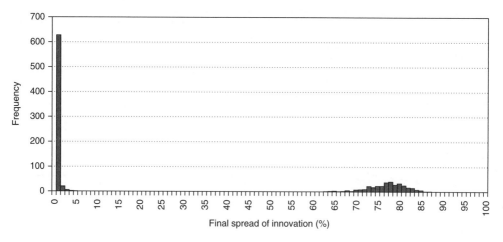

Note: ($\alpha=0$, $\epsilon=1$, $S_0=16$, $\beta_a=0.25$, $\beta_s=1$).

Figure 19.24   *Histogram of the final spread of innovation from 1000 runs of the model for the creative/digital/new media/IT/communications industry*

4.2   Significance of Global Cascade Mean

Before moving on to the more substantive results it is important to evaluate the statistical robustness of the mean of the global cascade. For example the mean value would vary significantly when comparing runs of the model that only used ten repeats in the averaging. If we repeat the model 1000 times how different could we expect the results of this to be compared to a second run of 1000 repeats?

Figure 19.25 shows an analysis of the standard deviation of the mean of the global cascade across ten runs of the model, for different number of repeats. This standard deviation is expressed as a percentage of the mean. It shows that the standard deviation decays as a power law. When using 1000 repeats, 68 per cent of the time the mean can be expected to vary by less than 0.1 per cent.[2] Of course this only applies to this parameterization but even if the variation were an order of magnitude higher, this level of accuracy would be acceptable.

Table 19.10 illustrates the mean global cascade and timeframe characteristics of the model across the sectors for this particular set of parameters. It highlights that the different industry survey distributions have a significant impact on the characteristics of innovation contagion. It is probably most helpful to think of the sectors as capturing variation of performance of firms of different types as much as different industries.

4.3   Network Descriptions

Betweenness and average shortest path length

There is an extensive range of characteristics associated with the structure of a network; two relevant ones for the innovation model are shortest path length and betweenness. The first is a network parameter called the average geodesic distance which measures

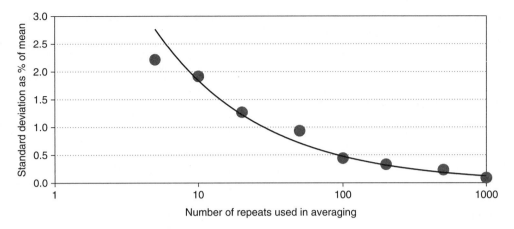

Note: ($\alpha=0$, $\varepsilon=1$, $S_0=16$, $\beta_a=0.25$, $\beta_s=1$).

Figure 19.25   *Standard deviation of the mean of ten runs of the model using different numbers of repeats for the creative/digital/new media/IT/communications industry*

Table 19.10   *Comparison of the mean global cascade, its standard deviation and the proportions of runs of the model that result in global cascades for the four industries using a single parameterization*

Industry	Mean global cascade (%)	Standard deviation (%)	Proportion of runs that are global cascades (%)
Creative/digital/new media/IT/ communications	76.7	4.2	34.3
Financial & professional services	92.8	1.8	55.2
Health sciences	81.3	4.5	71.4
Engineering & textiles	57.0	8.0	22.6

Note: ($\alpha=0$, $\varepsilon=1$, $S_0=16$, $\beta_a=0.25$, $\beta_s=1$).

the shortest path between each pair of firms, in terms of number of links, and finds the average. Second is betweenness, a parameter associated with each agent that measures the frequency of involvement of that firm in the shortest path between all other pairs of firms. This is therefore a measure of the presence of key actors in a network. A higher maximum betweenness indicates the presence of a key actor that dominates the shortest paths between firms.

Summary results for these characteristics are shown in Table 19.11, which shows that as the density of links increases in a network, both the maximum betweenness and the average shortest path length decrease. The health sciences industry is identified as the network structure that has both the shortest average path length and lowest maximum in betweenness. On this measure then this industry appears to have a network structure conducive to spreading an innovation.

Table 19.11   *Analysis of the maximum betweenness and average shortest path length for each industry distribution and value of* S_0

Industry	S_0	Maximum firm betweenness	Average shortest path length
Creative/digital/new media/IT/communications	8	25247	5.7
	24	12610	3.5
	64	7290	2.6
Financial & professional services	8	15423	5.3
	24	7273	3.2
	64	5072	2.4
Health sciences	8	11615	4.5
	24	4827	2.9
	64	3100	2.2
Engineering & textiles	8	45608	7.2
	24	17923	3.8
	64	11653	2.7

4.4   Results for the Exchange Mechanism

Figure 19.26 shows how the mean of the global cascade varies for each industry when the only method by which an innovation can be adopted is through the exchange mechanism.

- The model captures the impact that differences in both structure and behaviour between the industries on the mean size of a global cascade.
- Increasing the density of links (S_0) increases the spread of an innovation. The strength of this increase varies between industries, with health sciences and financial and professional services seeing less sensitivity to the density of the network than the others.
- The most significant driver of producing larger global cascades is the absorptive capacity scalar. As this increases the cascades become larger, although the effect is minimal in the health sciences industry. This effect is strongest in the creative/digital/new media/IT/communications and engineering and textiles industries.
- The health sciences industry is the least responsive to changes in the absorptive capacity scalar. This is for a range of reasons:
  - The industry has the highest proportion of organizations with absorptive capacities of zero (around 75 per cent). These firms are unaffected by increases in β_a.
  - In comparison, the industry network has a disproportionate number of organizations in the category with the highest number of links. This is what drives the low average shortest path and betweenness. In this respect the network can be viewed as more cohesive where even at the lowest scaling factor there are already multiple routes between organizations for the innovation to spread.

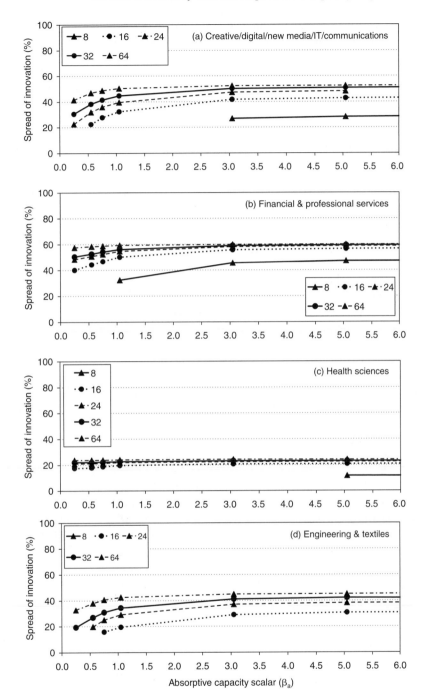

Figure 19.26 *Spread of a single innovation for different network scaling factors (S_0) for each industry as a function of the absorptive capacity scalar (β_a) when no mimicking behaviour is allowed ($\alpha=1.1$, $\varepsilon=1.1$)*

Table 19.12   Analysis of the percentage of links in an industry's network available for transmitting innovations using the exchange method

Industry	Proportion of links in the network where the exchange of an innovation is possible for a given value of absorptive capacity scalar (%)		
	$\beta_a = 0.25$	$\beta_a = 0.55$	$\beta_a = 0.75$
Creative/digital/new media/IT/ communications	13.0	20.0	24.8
Financial & professional services	21.9	26.1	30.3
Health sciences	16.9	17.2	18.7
Engineering & textiles	12.5	18.4	23.3

Increasing this scaling then has a proportionately smaller impact compared to the other industries.

- Although the health sciences industry is characterized by a significant lack of absorptive capacity, sufficiently dense network links exists that the remaining 25 per cent of firms share multiple paths through which innovations can reliably spread. This reliability is demonstrated by Table 19.10 which shows that the industry has the highest proportion of runs of the model that result in global cascades.
- The system is the most sensitive to changes in the absorptive capacity scalar when it is between 0 and 1. If we ignore the health sciences industry, which as we have said is less affected by changes in the scalar, the strength of the response for the other three can be understood in terms of the proportion of links in a network that can be used to spread an innovation (that is, where the absorptive capacity at one end is greater than the secrecy index at the other).

  Table 19.12 shows that the financial and professional services industry has 22 per cent of its links that meet this criteria when $\beta_a = 0.25$; this rises to 30 per cent when $\beta_a = 0.75$. This increase is less than the doubling shown by both the engineering and textiles and the creative/digital/new media/IT/communications (Table 19.12) and explains why their global cascades shown in Figure 19.26 respond much more strongly to changes in the absorptive capacity scalar between 0 and 1.

A simple indicator of the response of an industry to changes in the absorptive capacity scalar in this range is the difference between the mean absorptive and secrecy index of an industry.

- Figure 19.26 shows that when the absorptive scalar is greater than 1 the network scaling factor becomes more influential in driving how far global cascades can reach. Each system appears to have a maximum limit; if we again exclude the health services industry which we have covered already, this limit can be readily understood.
- If we take the financial and professional services industry this shows the best average ability to spread innovation for a given parameterization. However it also

shows the second highest proportion of firms with an absorptive capacity of zero. This is mitigated by its higher levels of connectivity. This argument is exactly the same as the one outlined for the health services sector above. What we see is an antagonism between the influence of the behavioural distributions and the structural ones. These can mitigate each other in the middle ground but when one side wins we get a system like the health services sector and when the other does we get results like the financial services sector.

4.5   Spread of Innovation Through Copying Behaviour

Figure 19.27 shows an analogous set of results to Figure 19.26 but where innovation can only be adopted through the mimicking mechanism. Note that lower α corresponds to greater ease of innovation.

- The copying behaviour appears incapable of creating the high cascades seen for the exchange behaviour.
- For all values of the minimum threshold the spread of an innovation is low and decays rapidly as it is increased.
- The conclusion is that copying behaviour is a poor method of spreading an innovation. In fact the relative strengths of the two ways in which innovation can spread were of the 100–100 000 to 1.[3]
- The reason that copying behaviour is less successful is not because the parameterizations chosen in some way force this to be the case. When α is 0 one fifth of all firms in the model will only require less than a fifth of their links to possess an innovation in order for them to mimic their behaviour and adopt it themselves. This is comparable to the case when $\beta_a = 0.55$ in Table 19.12. However, for the exchange relationship this leads to mean global cascades 10–30 times larger than for the copying behaviour. Again this demonstrates the relative effectiveness of the two mechanisms.

Spread of innovation through both behaviours: a case study
Figures 19.28 and 19.29 show the mean global cascade values when both the copying and exchange methods of adoption are allowed for different strengths of each. In Figure 19.28 the parameterization of the copying behaviour is held constant while the relative strength of the exchange behaviour is varied, while the opposite is true for Figure 19.29. Only the creative/digital/new media/IT/communications industry is included in the interests of brevity although the conclusions are valid across all of the four industries.

- The exchange behaviour must be present for global cascades to occur.
- The exchange mechanism is not a replacement for the mimicking behaviour, together they achieve cascades that neither can achieve on its own. In some cases the addition of copying behaviour doubles the size of the cascade.
- Extremely large cascades can be achieved with even relatively low absorptive capacities, so long as there is strong copying behaviour. However, unless there is some absorptive capacity, copying will be insufficient.

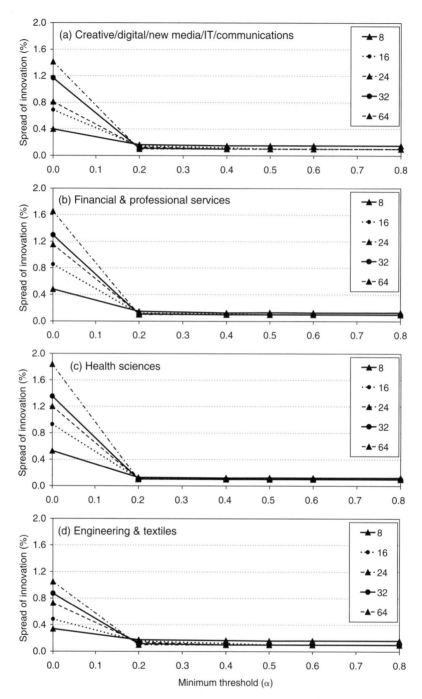

Figure 19.27   Spread of a single innovation for different network scaling factors (S_0) for each industry as a function of the minimum threshold (α) when no exchange behaviour is allowed ($\beta_a = 0$)

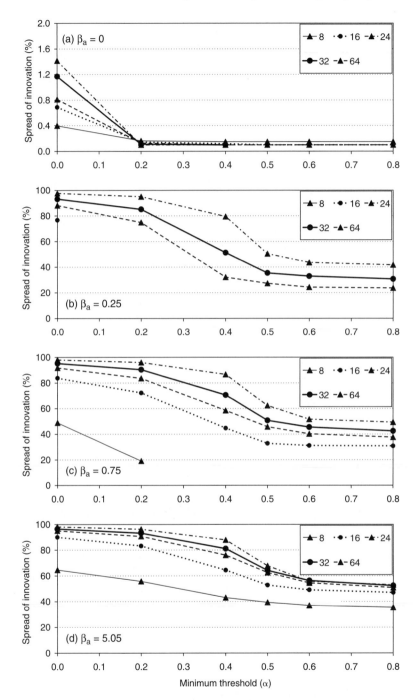

Figure 19.28   *Spread of a single innovation for different network scaling factors (S_0) for the creative/digital/new media/IT/communications industry as a function of the minimum threshold (α) for various values of the absorptive scalar*

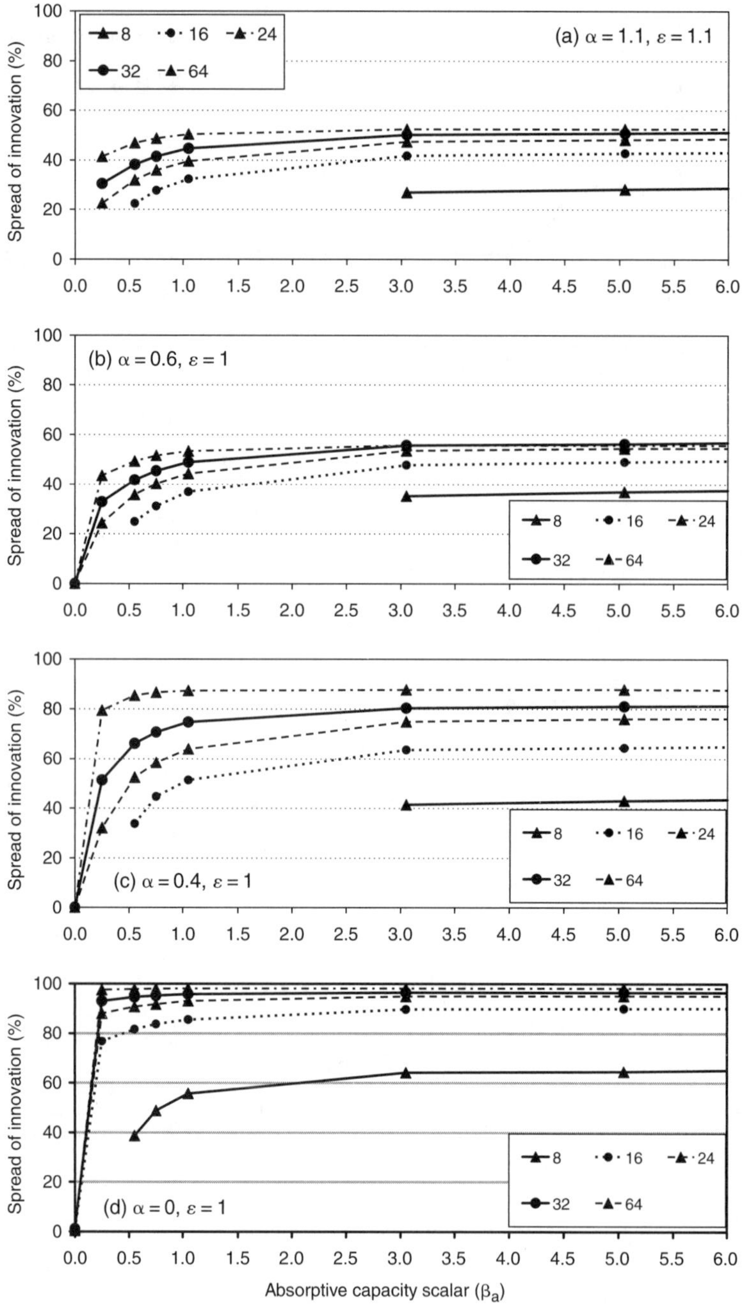

Figure 19.29   Spread of a single innovation for different network scaling factors (S_0) for the creative/digital/new media/IT/communications industry as a function of the absorptive capacity scalar (β_a) for various values of the minimum threshold (α)

• The real difference is that the addition of the copying behaviour removes some of the limits that we have discussed in Section 4.4. If an industry has a high proportion of firms with an absorptive capacity of zero then the copying behaviour allows for these organizations to still adopt an innovation *and* to subsequently pass it on. If an industry is relatively unconnected then the copying behaviour allows for multiple methods by which the innovation can spread amongst the existing links.

The net effect of adding the copying behaviour to the exchange based one is to increase the maximum possible sizes of the global cascades and reduce the sensitivity of the system to the absorptive capacity. This sensitivity was discussed in Section 4.4.

4.6 Length of Time to Spread Innovation

So far we have examined how the spread of innovation is determined by the parameters of agent behaviour and its distribution. In this section we look at the number of steps taken to achieve this spread. Figure 19.30(a) shows the histogram of the spread of innovation for a particular case. For both the global (upper component) and local (lower component) cascades a histogram of the number of time steps it took to reach the maximum percolations is shown in Figures 19.30(b) and 19.30(c) respectively.

Naturally global cascades require more time steps than the local ones but the initial pattern of both is within the same range. It is only when innovation continues to spread after four to ten steps that we can be sure that there will be a cascade of some size. The model does not directly identify the size of a time step but a natural interpretation would be around three months. This is a reasonable time for an organization to identify and implement an innovation. So it takes at least a year and maybe more than two years before we can be sure that an innovation will not be generally successful. Moreover, it will take between four and seven years for an innovation to reach its maximum extent on this basis.

Figures 19.31 and 19.32 show the upper and lower boundaries for local and global cascades from 1000 runs of the model. They show that there is a wide range of potential behaviour, with spreads of innovation to between 10 and 70 per cent of organizations within 15 time steps in global cascades. For local cascades, it is clear that some innovations peter out after three steps, while others take longer.

Finally, we look at the relationship between the parameters of the model and the time steps to a cascade. We concentrate on the results for the financial and professional services industry since this demonstrated the most pronounced variations in behaviour.

Figure 19.33(a) shows the average percolation of the industry's global cascade for various parameterizations. As copying becomes less effective, the total spread of innovation falls, and this is also true when the density of the links in the network are reduced (S_0 decreases). It also decreases as the absorptive capacity, β_a, is reduced.

Figure 19.33(b) shows the corresponding average number of time steps taken for the innovation to reach its maximum (similar distributions for the local cascade are also available but the averages are less meaningful because the distributions are asymmetric). It indicates that as copying becomes more difficult or absorptive capacity falls, or the network is less dense, it takes more time to reach the maximum spread of innovation.

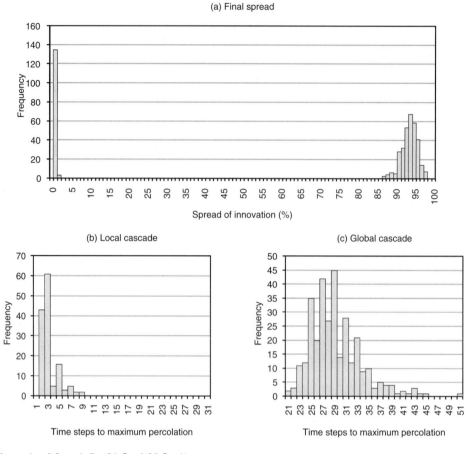

Note: ($\alpha=0.2$, $\varepsilon=1$, $S_0=24$, $\beta_a=0.25$, $\beta_s=1$).

Figure 19.30   (a) Histogram of the final spread of innovation from 1000 runs of the model for the financial and professional services industry and time steps to maximum percolation for (b) local and (c) global cascades

However, once there are further restrictions on the ability to percolate, both the extent of the spread and the number of steps are both reduced – there is simply less effective innovation.

This transition occurs because, as it is made easier for an innovation to spread, this initially opens up portions of the network that were previously inaccessible. When these bottlenecks are removed the additional organizations that the innovation spreads to are further away from its origin and so the time taken to reach these groups adds a few additional time steps to the model before the model reaches its maximum.

Figure 19.33(c) shows the ratio of (b) and (a), or in other words the time steps per effective innovation. It shows that this rate appears to be more strongly influenced by the density of the links rather than the behavioural rules of the agents themselves.

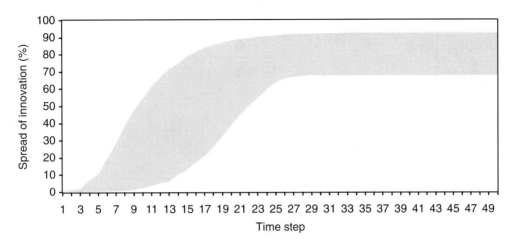

Note: ($\alpha=0.4$, $\varepsilon=1$, $S_0=24$, $\beta_a=0.25$, $\beta_s=1$).

Figure 19.31   Upper and lower boundaries for the percolations across 310 of the 1000 runs which were global cascades

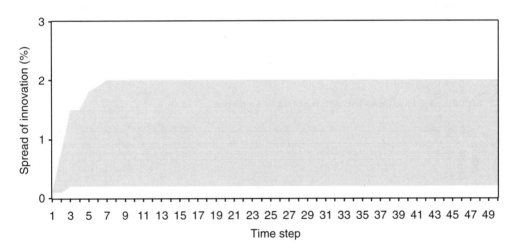

Note: ($\alpha=0.4$, $\varepsilon=1$, $S_0=24$, $\beta_a=0.25$, $\beta_s=1$).

Figure 19.32   Upper and lower boundaries for the percolations across 71 of the 1000 runs which were local cascades

5.   CONCLUSION AND IMPLICATIONS FOR POLICY

This model offers a way of thinking about innovation based on dissemination across a network where the behavioural rules of innovating organizations also have a bearing on the outcome. This seems an entirely plausible way to approach this problem, though

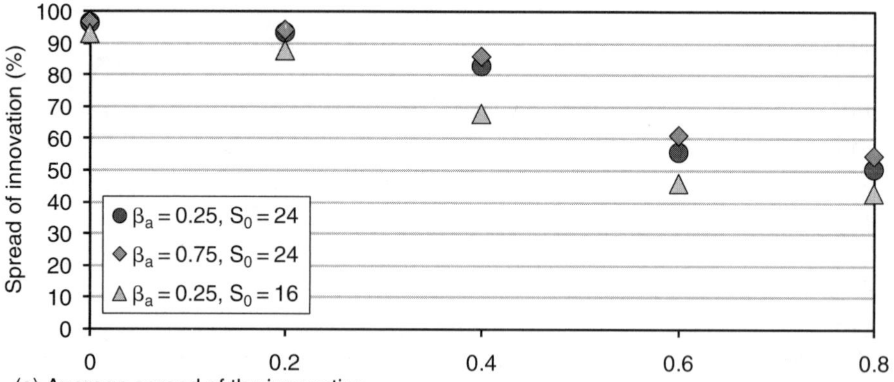

(a) Average spread of the innovation

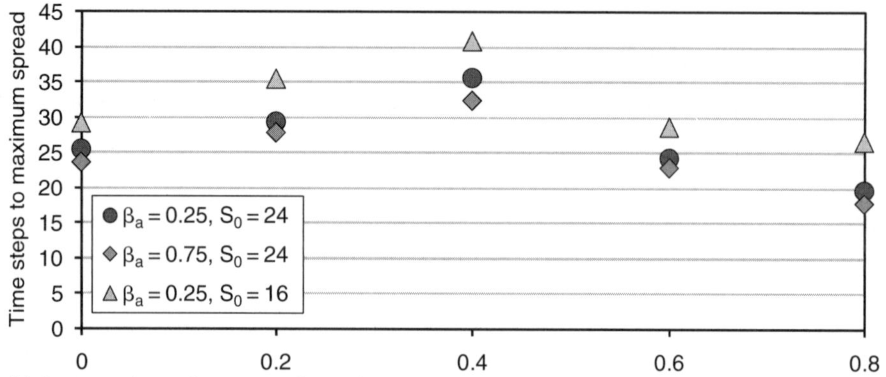

(b) Average time taken to reach maximum percolation

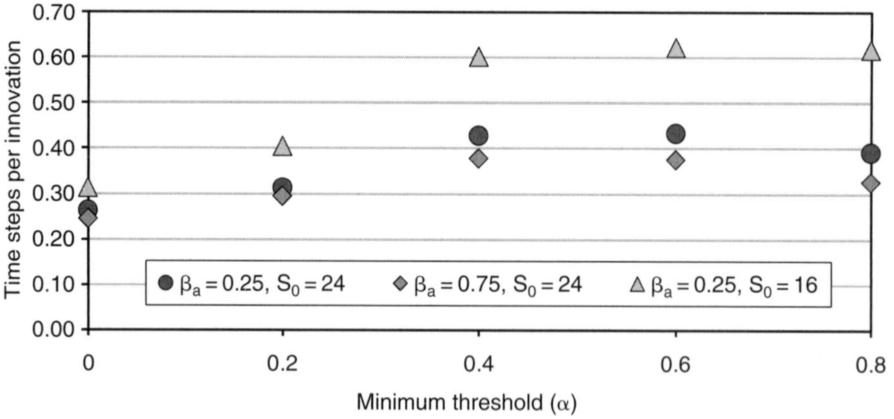

Minimum threshold (α)

(c) Average number of organizations that adopt the innovation per time step

Figure 19.33 *Analysis of the average properties of global cascades arising from the 1000 runs of the model for the financial and professional services industry ($(\varepsilon=1, S_0=24, \beta_s=1)$ for $\beta_a=0.25$ and $\beta_a=0.75$ and ($\varepsilon=1, S_0=16, \beta_s=1$) for $\beta_a=0.25$)*

even so there are many simplifications around the type of innovation under consideration, let alone the way the innovation comes into being in the first place.

In spite of the considerable simplifications of this model, there still emerge many interacting parameters. Network structure, copying behaviour, and the willingness to exchange interact in different ways according to how they are varied.

Moreover, we are also able to show that the distribution of these parameters across groups of agents also matters. The ability to calibrate these distributions to survey results in a region of the UK enables us to investigate the importance of the distributions as well as the average values of the parameters.

The survey results for the various industries examined do not show very large differences in average behaviour for most of the industries – health sciences appears to be an exception. However, when these differences interact across the various parameters, it changes the outcomes very significantly.

In addition, our results also show that the ability to distinguish a successful, global, cascade of innovation at the outset is very limited. Whether a cascade emerges or not is not predictable at the outset.

These two results, taken together, mean that it is impossible to design policy levers with any certainty as to how they will be effective. We can see that industry surveys with similar results for innovation behaviour and attitudes can nonetheless produce very variable outcomes. Moreover, initial success cannot predict the final outcome.

Classically, policy has concentrated on identifying innovation that ought to be supported, and on creating sector support groups. In the UK, the latest policy initiative has been the establishment of NESTA (National Endowment for Science, Technology and the Arts). A recent pronouncement suggested setting up new sector groups, to look at different ways innovation takes place in 'non-traditional' sectors. How this is likely to help change the parameters of the kinds of behaviour which generate innovation take-up is not at all clear.

However, the models do suggest that there are ways to help maximize the likelihood of innovation spreading. The model shows that:

- The willingness to exchange innovation is a major driver
- Well-connected but not too dense networks help
- A willingness to copy others helps

Policy can help create networks by events and the support of the widest possible networks. Note that these need to be more broadly focused that on just one sector. Policy to support the willingness to absorb innovation is much more difficult. The policy instinct is to provide grants or tax breaks. However, there is no guarantee these would support the sort of innovation that organizations can readily use, which may be hard to identify in policy terms.

The conclusion can only be that a continual policy of supporting test and try which does not worry too much about an *ex ante* analysis of the potential for success is the only option.

The modelling approach presented here provides a way of thinking about the process of innovation which captures the key potential parameters of take-up and which is capable of calibration using fairly limited survey data. It enables the user to think about innovation without requiring analytical and equilibrium solutions and to illustrate the limitations and capacities of a location.

NOTES

*   We are grateful for the support of the Manchester Independent Economic Review in undertaking much of this research.
1.   The Manchester Independent Economic Review is a group of several projects looking at various aspects of the city's economy. The models described here have been developed in one of these projects.
2.   And only 0.2 per cent 95 per cent of the time, assuming that the mean of the global cascade distribution follows a normal distribution.
3.   In the case when either method could have spread the innovation in a given time step then this was counted in both the numerator and denominator in this calculation.

REFERENCES

Antonelli, C. (2008), *Localised Technological Change: Towards the Economics of Complexity*, London: Routledge.
Cowan, R. and Jonard, N. (2004), 'Network structure and the diffusion of knowledge', *Journal of Economic Dynamics and Control Volume*, **28** (8), June, 1557–75.
Dyer, J.H. and Singh, H. (1998), 'The relational view: cooperative strategy and sources of inter-organizational competitive advantage', *Academy of Management Review*, **23** (4), October, 660–79.
Glückler, J. (2007), 'Economic geography and the evolution of networks', *Journal of Economic Geography*, **7** (5), 619–34.
Lundvall, B.-Å. (1992), 'Explaining inter-firm cooperation and innovation – limits of the transaction cost approach', in Grabher, G (ed.), *The Embedded Firm: On the Socioeconomics of Industrial Networks*, London: Routledge.
Mansfield, E. (1961), 'Technical change and the rate of imitation', *Econometrica*, **29**, 741–66.
Metcalfe, J.S. (2007), lecture delivered at University of Jena.
Ormerod, P. and Rosewell, B. (2009), 'Innovation, diffusion and agglomeration', *Economics of Innovation and New Technology*, **18** (7), 695–706.
Ormerod, P. and Wiltshire, G. (2009). '"Binge" drinking in the UK: a social network phenomenon', *Mind and Society*, **8**,135–52.
Rhodes, E., Warren, J. and Carter, R. (2006), *Supply Chains and Total Product Systems: A Reader*, Oxford: Blackwell Publishing.
Schumpeter, J.A. (1928) 'The instability of capitalism', *Economic Journal*, **38** (151), September, 361–86.
Volterra Consulting Ltd (2006), 'The spread and containment of behaviour across social networks', prepared for the Financial Services Authority, UK.

APPENDIX 19A.1

Calculating the Secrecy Index

Calculating a secrecy index for each firm was done by the following formula:

$$\sum_{k} A_k \times \left(\sum_i A_k \times \sum i \right) \div \sum_k \left(3 \times \sum_i A_{kk} \times \sum i \right)$$

where i is a firm within a particular industry,
k is an action to protect an innovation,
A_k is a dummy variable that can take values between zero and 3. Zero means the firm
    did not undertake an action while 3 means the firm attaches high importance to the
    action,
A_{kk} is a dummy variable that is zero when a firm's value for A_k is between 0 and 2, and
    takes the value 1 when a firm's value for A_k is 3.

Each method of protecting an innovation is weighted by its revealed importance to the
sector, where revealed importance is the percentage of firms saying the method was very
important to them. A firm is then given an innovation index, which is the sum of the
weights of the methods of protection it did undertake multiplied by the importance the
firm put on each method (between 1 and 3). This is then divided by the sum of all
the weights multiplied by three. The result is a firm can be given an index between zero
and 1. A score of 1 indicates a firm that uses every method of protecting innovation that
the survey asked about. A score of zero indicates a firm that used none of the methods of
protecting innovation that we asked about.

APPENDIX 19A.2

Calculating the Absorptive Index

Calculating an absorptive index for each firm was done by the following formula:

$$\sum_{m} A_m \times \left(\sum_i A_m \times \sum i \right) \div \sum_m \left(\sum_i A_m \times \sum i \right)$$

where i is a firm within a particular industry,
m is an activity conducive to absorbing an innovation,
A_m is a dummy variable equal to 1 when a firm performed activity m and zero when it
    did not.

Each method of absorbing innovation is weighted by its revealed importance to a sector.
This weight is effectively the percentage of firms in that industry who undertook that
method of absorption. A firm is then given an absorptive index which is the sum of the
weights of those actions it did undertake, divided by the sum of all the actions' weights. A

firm can therefore be given an absorptive index between zero and 1. Zero indicates a firm that undertook none of the methods of absorbing innovations that the survey identified. A score of 1 indicates a firm that engaged in every method of absorbing innovation that the survey asked about.

APPENDIX 19A.3

Calculating the Innovation Index

Calculating an innovation index for each firm was done by the following formula:

$$\sum_j A_j \times \left(\sum_i A_j \times \sum i \right) \div \sum_j \left(\sum_i A_j \times \sum i \right)$$

where i is a firm within a particular industry,
j is a type of activity conducive to innovation,
A_j is a dummy variable equal to 1 when a firm performed activity j and zero when it did not.

Each innovation is weighted by its revealed importance to a sector. This weight is effectively the percentage of firms in that industry who undertook that innovation. A firm is then given an innovation index which is the sum of the weights of those innovations it did undertake, divided by the sum of all the innovation weights. A firm can therefore be given an innovation index between 0 and 1 with a lower value indicating a lower propensity to innovate.

20 Government as entrepreneur: examples from US technology policy[1]

Albert N. Link and Jamie R. Link

1. INTRODUCTION

Throughout intellectual history as we know it, the entrepreneur has worn many faces and played many roles. The entrepreneur is the person who assumes the risk associated with uncertainty, the entrepreneur is the person who supplies financial capital, the entrepreneur is an innovator, the entrepreneur is a decision maker, the entrepreneur is an industrial leader, the entrepreneur is a manager or superintendent, the entrepreneur is an organizer and coordinator of economic resources, the entrepreneur is the owner of an enterprise, the entrepreneur is an employer of factors of production, the entrepreneur is a contractor, the entrepreneur is an arbitrageur, and the entrepreneur is an allocator of resources among alternative uses.[2]

These themes are not mutually exclusive descriptions of his or her roles or actions, but they all are themes that have been offered by scholars as identifiable entrepreneurial activities that occur within a market setting. But government actions, which are the theme of this chapter, are not necessarily market-based.[3] Markets operate through the laws of supply and demand, and economic actors within markets respond to explicit and implicit prices.[4] A similar analogy does not always hold for public sector actors or activities.[5]

What do we mean by the phrase *government as entrepreneur*?[6] Based on the economic principle of market failure, government involvement in market activity – the provision of technology infrastructure, in particular, to remove the innovation barriers that bring about the market failure, technology market failure in particular – is warranted. The marginal social benefit of involvement is greater than the marginal social costs, assuming of course that government involvement is efficient.[7]

Not all such government involvement is entrepreneurial. We argue, based on the historical perspective of who the entrepreneur is and what he does, from a technology-based perspective, that: *Government acts as entrepreneur in the provision of technology infrastructure when its involvement is both innovative and characterized by entrepreneurial risk.*

The programmatic mechanism or organizational structure for this involvement, at least as we use this concept herein, is the public/private partnership.[8]

Thinking of government as entrepreneur is a unique lens through which we characterize a specific subset of government policy actions.[9] As such, our viewpoint underscores the purposeful intent of government, its ability to act in new and innovative ways, and its willingness to undertake policy actions that have uncertain outcomes.

Of course, we do not believe that all government policy actions are entrepreneurial. Certainly, aspects of monetary and fiscal policy are theoretically based and have predictable outcomes. Such policy actions are not necessarily innovative, and aside from timing issues are generally not, in our view, characterized by entrepreneurial risk.[10]

We do not take the position, much less advocate, that government should be more or less entrepreneurial. Rather, we argue that a new aspect of a taxonomy of government policy actions should be considered, and we are sanguine about its usefulness. Viewing particular policy actions through an entrepreneurial lens could be useful in at least two broad dimensions. First, viewing particular government policy actions as entrepreneurial underscores the forward looking nature of policy makers as well as the need to evaluate the social outputs and outcomes of their behavior in terms of broad spillover impacts. Second, government acting as entrepreneur parallels in concept similar activities that occur in the private sector. Baumol et al. (2007: 2) suggested that: 'if the United States wishes to continue enjoying rapid growth, it must find a way both to launch and promote the growth of innovative entrepreneurial enterprises. . . .' Viewing government as entrepreneur, albeit in selected areas and for selected policies, places a realistic (and positive, we believe) spin on such activities because it equates entrepreneurial government policy actions with the spirit of the private sector that has led to economic growth and prosperity in all industrial nations.

Viewing particular innovative policy actions through an entrepreneurial lens does not necessarily imply that all such policy actions are productive. Baumol (1990: 3) argued, within the context of a market, that '. . . at times the entrepreneur may even lead a parasitical existence that is actually damaging to the economy.'

The remainder of the chapter is outlined as follows. In Section 2, we define more completely the concept of government as entrepreneur.

In Section 3, we overview selected theories of innovation and technological development to illustrate the absence of the concept of government as entrepreneur.

In Section 4, we illustrate our concept of government as entrepreneur through six US public/private partnerships. The partnerships discussed are both retrospective and prospective. The retrospective examples are intended to ground our concept of government as entrepreneur; the prospective example is intended to underscore the importance of viewing government policy actions through an entrepreneurial lens. These six partnership examples illustrate government affecting a reallocation of entrepreneurial resources that lessens barriers to innovation. We believe that these examples are indeed examples of government as entrepreneur.

Finally, in Section 5, we conclude the chapter with summary remarks.

2.   DEFINING GOVERNMENT AS ENTREPRENEUR

As we suggested in the introduction, government acts as entrepreneur in the provision of technology infrastructure when its involvement is both innovative and characterized by entrepreneurial risk (that is, uncertainty).[11] Our conceptualization of government as entrepreneur draws directly from the intellectual thought of Cantillon (1931), and those scholars who built upon his idea that the entrepreneur is one who assumes the risk associated with uncertainty – entrepreneurial risk;[12] and on the intellectual thought of Baudeau (1910) and Schumpeter (1928) who fostered the idea that the entrepreneur is one who innovates and applies new techniques. Cantillon's entrepreneur was not an innovator, but the entrepreneur of Baudeau and Schumpeter was, as he assumed entrepreneurial risk and undertook uncertainties.

We draw specifically on Schumpeter's (1928: 380) characterization of entrepreneurial leadership: 'some are able to undertake uncertainties incident to what has not been done before; [indeed] . . . to overcome these difficulties incident to change of practice is the function of the entrepreneur.'

Many of the earlier writers about the entrepreneur envisioned his actions within a market setting, and his actions led to or maintained market equilibrium. Schumpeter, writing about the entrepreneur in the context of a theory of economic development, envisioned economic growth occurring through the innovative actions of the entrepreneur who, through creative destruction, moved an economy away from its current static equilibrium toward a new one in which there was greater efficiency. With respect to government policy actions, following Schumpeter, the public sector embraces new combinations of policy tools to move a segment of the market from inefficiency (for example, market failure) toward efficiency.

The government, by providing technology infrastructure, acts in a Schumpeterian manner as entrepreneur. In a dynamic fashion, government exhibits leadership by perceiving opportunity and acting on that perception.[13] The opportunity at hand with respect to technology policy is the provision of a public or quasi-public good – the technology infrastructure itself – that leverages the ability of firms and other actors in a national innovation system to participate efficiently in the innovation process and thereby to contribute to technology-based economic growth.

Technology infrastructure, or a technology-based institution, has many dimensions. It supports the design, deployment, and use of individual technology-based components that comprise a knowledge-based economy. Technology infrastructure can be classified legitimately by the set of physical and virtual tools, methods, and data that enable all stages of technology-based economic activity: the conduct of R&D, the control of production processes to achieve target quality and yield, and the consummation of market transactions at minimum time and cost. The government, primarily at the national level, provides technology infrastructure through public and quasi-public institutions, as well as through public and quasi-public goods and services that leverage the innovation process. Through public/private partnership mechanisms, government supports institutions and platforms that lessen innovation barriers that bring about market failure as related to investments in all stages of technology-based economic activity; government supports the design, deployment, and use of both individual technology-based component goods and the systems of such component goods that enhance a knowledge-based economy; and government is involved in the provision of services that leverage innovation by making private-sector R&D more effective. By perceiving opportunity and acting on that perception to provide such technology infrastructure – institutions, goods, and services – and assuming the entrepreneurial risk associated with it, government acts as entrepreneur.

While government as entrepreneur is a concept that transcends national innovation and technology policies, the examples in the following sections have a distinct, and somewhat exclusive, US policy focus.

3.   THEORIES OF INNOVATION AND TECHNOLOGY DEVELOPMENT

In this section we briefly overview various theories or conceptualizations of innovation and technology development for the purpose of emphasizing the absence of government as entrepreneur in this body of thought.

Within the evolution of US technology policy, most scholars and policy makers point to Vannevar Bush for first using the term *basic research*. In his 1945 report to US President Roosevelt, *Science – the Endless Frontier*, Bush used that term and defined it to mean research conducted without thought of practical ends. Since that time, policy makers have been concerned about definitions that appropriately characterize the various aspects of scientific inquiry that broadly fall under the label of R&D and relate to the linear model that Bush proffered, as discussed below. From this document many have gleaned what has come to be called the linear model:[14]

- *Basic Research → Applied Research → Development*

Bush's linear model is often referred to more broadly as a linear model of the innovation process, and in that context we represent it in four alternative ways:

- *R&D → Innovation → Economic Growth*
- *R&D → Knowledge → Innovation → Technological Advancement → Economic Growth*
- *Basic Research → Applied Research → Development → Innovation → Economic Growth*
- *Basic Research → Applied Research → Development → Innovation → Production → Diffusion → Economic Growth*

Regardless of the representation, the source of innovation is investment in new knowledge represented by investments in R&D, in total or by character of use. And, regardless of the representation, the concept (or reality) of government as entrepreneur is absent.

4.   EXAMPLES OF GOVERNMENT AS ENTREPRENEUR

Six examples of US public/private partnerships through which government acts as entrepreneur are described in this section. All are summarized in Table 20.1.

4.1   Research Joint Ventures

Both public and private organizations participate in RJVs, and public resources are indirectly used to encourage the partnership formation.[15] The National Cooperative Research Act of 1984 lessened the prevailing antitrust laws and created a legal environment conducive for cooperative research. It is this legal environment that is the technology infrastructure. The so-called legitimization of RJVs (that is, the relaxation of antitrust laws to stimulate private-sector R&D) was the innovative policy action. It

Table 20.1   Examples of government as entrepreneur

Public/private partnership	Technology infrastructure	Innovative policy action	Entrepreneurial risk
RJV structure	Legal environment conducive for collaborative research	National Cooperative Research Act of 1984: use of antitrust laws to stimulate private-sector R&D	If the benefits to firms from participating in an RJV outweigh the costs
Advanced Technology Program	Cost-sharing environment conducive for cooperative research	Omnibus Trade and Competitiveness Act of 1988: use of public resources to leverage private-sector R&D, that would otherwise not have been undertaken, through cooperative research	If the jointly funded research will be successful and if so, whether it will accelerate the development of generic technology
National Institute of Standards and Technology	Voluntary industrial standards	Organic Act of 1901: use of public resources to promulgate voluntary standards to reduce the technical and market risk of private-sector R&D	If the promulgated voluntary standard will be accepted by industry, and if accepted in a timely manner, whether it will enhance competitiveness
Biomass Research and Development Initiative	Cost-sharing environment conducive for making domestic biofuels cost competitive with gasoline	Biomass Research and Development Act of 2000: use of public resources to accelerate the development of biofuels	If the publicly supported research will be successful in generating advanced biofuels to meet the most recent renewable fuel standard
University research park	Environment conducive for industry/ university research collaboration and academic entrepreneurship	The Building a Stronger America Act: use of public resources to establish and/or expand existing parks	If the new or expanded park will attract tenants, and if so, whether they will actively participate in the two-way flow of knowledge between the university and the park
Small Business Innovation Research program	Funded environment conducive for commercializable research	Small Business Innovation Development Act of 1982: use of public resources to target and support research in small firms	If the funded research will result in a commercializable product, process, or service

removed the innovation barriers that were suspected of causing an underinvestment in private-sector R&D. The entrepreneurial risk is if the benefits to firms from participating in an RJV outweigh the costs.

Through RJV activity, firms potentially benefit from the opportunity to capture knowledge spillovers from other members of the venture, reduce innovation costs due to a lessening of duplicative research, realize faster commercialization because the fundamental research stage is shortened; and realize the opportunity to develop an industry-wide competitive vision.[16] These listed potential benefits are based on the theoretical literature, anecdotal evidence from the successful Japanese experience with research collaborations in the mid to late 1970s and early 1980s, and a few limited empirical studies.

The realization of these potential benefits is subject to entrepreneurial risk because, in fact, they might not be realized, and if they are realized, the benefits will not likely be appropriable without a cost. This cost includes appropriability loss because research results are shared among participants in the venture, and it includes the inevitable managerial tension among venture participants as each learns to trust the others and work in concert. Anticipation of such categories of cost could deter initial participation in the venture.

4.2   Advanced Technology Program

The Advanced Technology Program (ATP) was established within the National Institute of Standards and Technology (NIST) through the Omnibus Trade and Competitiveness Act of 1988, and modified by the American Technology Preeminence Act of 1991.[17] The goals of ATP, as stated in its enabling legislation, are to assist US businesses in creating and applying the generic technology and research results necessary to commercialize significant new scientific discoveries and technologies rapidly, and refine manufacturing technologies. ATP's public financial resources leverage private-sector R&D.[18] The use of public resources, authorized by the Omnibus Trade and Competitiveness Act of 1988, to leverage private-sector R&D that would not otherwise have been undertaken lessens barriers to innovation and creates a cost-sharing environment conducive for cooperative research. It is this cost-sharing environment conducive for cooperative research that is the technology infrastructure. The entrepreneurial risk associated with the activities of ATP is if the jointly funded research will be successful and if so, whether it will accelerate the development of generic technology.

4.3   National Institute of Standards and Technology

NIST leverages public-sector and private-sector R&D through the direct provision of infrastructural and research resources that reduce the technical and market risk of developing infrastructure technologies – infratechnologies – that become the technical basis for standards, voluntary standards in particular.[19] This public support is necessary because infratechnologies and hence standards are quasi-public goods and they suffer from underinvestment by the private sector (Tassey, 2007). The Organic Act of 1901 is the innovative policy action that authorizes using public resources to support development of voluntary industrial standards (the technology infrastructure). Promulgating voluntary standards lessens barriers to innovation by reducing both technical risk (for example, through public-sector research that diffuses through the private sector) and market risk (for example, through the reduction of transaction costs). The entrepreneurial risk associated with the activities of NIST is if the promulgated voluntary standard will be accepted by industry, and if accepted in a timely manner, whether it will enhance competitiveness.[20]

4.4   Biomass Research and Development Initiative

The Biomass Research and Development Initiative (BRDI) uses public financial resources to leverage both public- and private-sector R&D. The use of public resources to support public- and private-sector R&D lessens barriers to innovation and creates a cost-sharing environment conducive for accelerating the development of advanced biofuels and other biobased products.[21] It is this cost-sharing environment, authorized by the Biomass Research and Development Act of 2000 and amended by the Food, Conservation, and Energy Act of 2008, which is the technology infrastructure.[22] The innovative policy action, set forth in the form of a new renewable fuel standard (RFS) by the Energy Independence and Security Act (EISA) of 2007, established a schedule for the adoption of advanced biofuels, including some that are not yet commercially viable. Much of the federal funding dedicated to developing advanced biofuels is awarded through the BRDI. The entrepreneurial risk associated with the activities of the BRDI is if the publicly supported research will be successful in leveraging the development of advanced biofuels to meet the RFS set forth by the EISA of 2007.

4.5   University Research Parks

The university research park (URP) organizational structure is another public/private partnership through which government acts as entrepreneur.[23] Government, state government specifically, has traditionally allocated funds to support URPs. The allocation of these funds is direct, in terms of state resources earmarked for the creation of a park, as well as indirect in the sense that a state university allocated its operating funds for the creation and ongoing activities of the park.[24] Among the many objectives of the park, an important one is that the park serves as an environment conducive for industry/university research collaboration and academic entrepreneurship. Thus, the environment created by the park is a technology infrastructure that facilitates leveraging both public (for example, the university or public-sector tenants in the park)[25] and private R&D. The Building a Stronger America Act, which has been introduced in the US Senate but not passed into law, aims to expand the size and scope of existing URPs and to help create new URPs through a federal loan guarantee program. This enabling legislation authorizes the innovation policy action of using public resources to establish and/or expand existing parks and lessens barriers to innovation by reducing technical risk (for example, through expanded R&D activities). The entrepreneurial risk associated with the Building a Stronger America Act is if the new or expanded parks will attract tenants, and whether they will actively participate in the two-way flow of knowledge between the university and the park.

4.6   Small Business Innovation Research Program

The Small Business Innovation Research (SBIR) program leverages, through the direct provision of financial resources, private-sector R&D in small firms. The use of public resources to target and support private-sector R&D in small firms lessens barriers to innovation (much like ATP) and creates a funded environment conducive for commercializable research (unlike ATP) that would not otherwise have occurred.[26] It is this funded environment conducive for commercializable research, enabled initially by the Small Business Innovation Development Act of 1982, which is the technology infrastructure.[27] The entrepreneurial risk associated with the activities of the SBIR is if the funded research will be successful, meaning that it will result in a product, process, or service to commercialize.

5.   SUMMARY REMARKS

Our theme is that government acts as entrepreneur in the provision of technology infrastructure when its involvement is both innovative and characterized by entrepreneurial risk. Thinking of government as entrepreneur is, we have argued, a unique lens through which to view particular government policy actions.

As summarized in Table 20.1, we have, as a means of illustrating our premise, overviewed six US innovative policy actions: the National Cooperative Research Act of 1984, the Omnibus Trade and Competitiveness Act of 1988, the Organic Act of 1901, the Biomass Research and Development Act of 2000, the Building a Stronger America Act (pending), and the Small Business Innovation Development Act of 1982.

Each of these six policy actions resulted in a public/private partnership that had the economic objective of leveraging public-sector R&D, private-sector R&D, or both.

While the examples and data presented and discussed in this chapter were selectively chosen, based primarily on our previous research experiences and current research interests, they do illustrate the entrepreneurial dimensions of government's provision of technology infrastructure. While these examples and data are specific to the United States' policy experience, the concept of government as entrepreneur is, we believe, universal and is an applicable lens through which to characterize a subset of governmental policy actions.

All too often policy initiatives that involve entrepreneurial risk are criticized a priori because they lack precedent and/or predictable outputs and outcomes. When precedent and/or predictable outputs are not available, the temptation is to stick to the status quo of tried and true policy instruments. Our challenge to policy makers is to leapfrog the status quo and thereby to embrace innovative policy actions through their entrepreneurial behavior.

Hopefully, this chapter will serve as a vehicle for policy makers and scholars to think about entrepreneurship, or more specifically the entrepreneurial actors in an economy, in a new way. Through example we have discussed realistic situations – albeit specific to the United States and to US innovation policy – that demonstrate our theme. As such, viewing government as entrepreneur broadens the scope of thinking about tools and frameworks available for providing technology infrastructure. If innovation policy to provide technology infrastructure is to be used effectively as a national competitiveness strategy, imitating what has been done in the past or what other nations are doing may well be a second-best approach. Perception of new infrastructure opportunities may require actions that are characterized by what we have called entrepreneurial risk.

NOTES

1. This chapter is based on Link and Link (2009), and the references therein.
2. For an academic trace of the intellectual history of the entrepreneur, see Hébert and Link (1988, 2006, 2009).
3. According to Holcombe (2002: 155), '[p]olitical entrepreneurs, like those in the market, discover and act on unexploited profit opportunities. In many ways, there are parallels between political exchange and market exchange, and the political marketplace is, indeed, a market.'
4. Of course, firms within markets must contend with a wide-ranging and often complex set of standards, legal issues, and regulatory bodies, all of which they not only live with but also are entrepreneurially active in shaping.
5. We are aware of the public choice argument that governmental officials do respond to price-like incentives.
6. We first used the term *government as entrepreneur* narrowly in Link and Siegel (2007).
7. Inefficient government involvement in market activities, both in terms of timing and level, is often referred to as government failure.
8. US policy actions are our primary focus because of our previous policy experiences. Certainly, our entrepreneurial view of government is conceptually applicable across nations.
9. Fligstein (1991) and others have argued within the institutional entrepreneurship literature that many non-market actors serve the role of government as entrepreneur.
10. One could argue that supply management policies are both innovative and characterized by entrepreneurial risk. We agree that some innovative supply management policies could be representative of government as entrepreneur, especially if they involve new and innovative means of providing technology infrastructure. But, a supply management policy that affects innovation is not necessarily an innovative policy. The 1981 research and experimental (R&E) tax credit is one such example. For a firm that qualifies for the tax credit, the marginal cost of innovation decreases, and if its innovation is successful and diffuses as a technology, aggregate supply will increase. The R&E tax credit was not innovative, in fact a number of other countries had implemented such a credit long before the United States did (Leyden and Link 1993).
11. Lane and Maxfield (2006) discuss the concept of ontological uncertainty. One interpretation is that the consequences of public-sector agents are not predictable, that is, they are uncertain. Our view of government as entrepreneur is narrower, focusing only on the innovative actions of government.
12. Recall that Cantillon (1931) argued that uncertainty is a pervasive fact of everyday life, and likely, we suggest, a pervasive fact of many public policies.
13. Perception and action characterize much of the Austrian School's thought about the entrepreneur. Both are required.
14. According to Godin (2006: 640), 'One would be hard-pressed, however, to find anything but a rudiment of this [linear] model in Bush's [1945] manifesto. Bush talked about causal links between science (namely basic research) and socioeconomic progress, but nowhere did he develop a full-length argument based on a sequential process broken down into its elements or that suggests a mechanism whereby science translates in socioeconomic benefits.'
15. The development and evolution of the material in this chapter is discussed in Link (1999, 2006).
16. These benefits are elaborated upon in Hagedoorn et al. (2000) and Combs and Link (2003). See also Belderbos et al. (2004).
17. This section draws, in part, on Link (2006).
18. The development and evolution of the material in this chapter is discussed in Link (1999, 2006) and Link and Scott (2005).
19. The development and evolution of the material in this chapter is discussed in Link (1999, 2006). Market risk is associated with infrastructure technologies because of the cost and time associated with their development. A standard imposes additional market risk because resources are required to promulgate it.
20. A standard is a prescribed set of rules, conditions, or requirements concerning the following: definitions of terms; classification of components; specification of materials, their performance, and their operations;

and delineation of procedures, and measurement of quantity and quality in describing materials, products, systems, services, or practices.

21. Note that government agencies have long been funding research on biofuels. BRDI created an interagency initiative on the topic and mandated that investments in biofuels be accelerated.
22. The purpose of the BRDI, as stated in the 2000 Act, is: '. . . to stimulate collaborative activities by a diverse range of experts in all aspects of biomass processing for the purpose of conducting fundamental and innovation-targeted research and technology development; to enhance creative and imaginative approaches toward biomass processing that will serve to develop the next generation of advanced technologies making possible low cost and sustainable biobased industrial products; to strengthen the intellectual resources of the United States through the training and education of future scientists, engineers, managers, and business leaders in the field of biomass processing; and to promote integrated research partnerships among colleges, universities, national laboratories, Federal and State research agencies, and the private sector as the best means of overcoming technical challenges that span multiple research and engineering disciplines and of gaining better leverage from limited Federal research funds.'
23. A URP is a cluster of technology-based organizations that locate on or near a university campus in order to benefit from the university's knowledge base and ongoing research; the university not only transfers knowledge but expects to develop knowledge more effectively given the association with the tenants in the research park (Link and Scott, 2005).
24. Link (2008) reported, based on data from the Association of University Research Parks (AURP) that over 80 per cent of URPs rely in one way or another on public funds.
25. Although many private universities have research parks, those universities still have a degree of publicness in the sense that much of their internal research agenda is publicly funded.
26. ATP was concerned with accelerating the development of generic technology while the SBIR program funds accelerated the development of proprietary technology and commercialization.
27. The 1982 Act stated that the objectives of the program are: (1) to stimulate technological innovation, (2) to use small business to meet Federal research and development needs, (3) to foster and encourage participation by minority and disadvantaged persons in technological innovation, and (4) to increase private sector commercialization of innovations derived from Federal research and development.

REFERENCES

Baudeau, Nicolas (1910), *Premiere Introduction a la Philosophie Economique*, edited by Dubois, A., Paris: P. Geuthner.

Baumol, W.J. (1990), 'Entrepreneurship: productive, unproductive, and destructive', *Journal of Business Venturing*, **11**, 3–22.

Baumol, W.J., Litan, R.E. and Schramm, C.J. (2007), 'Sustaining entrepreneurial capitalism', *Capitalism and Society*, **2**, 1–36.

Belderbos, R., Carree, M. and Lokshin, B. (2004), 'Cooperative R&D and firm performance', *Research Policy*, **33**, 1477–492.

Cantillon, R. (1931), *Essai sur la nature du commerce en general*, edited by Higgs, H., London: Macmillan.

Combs, K.L. and Link, A.N. (2003), 'Innovation policy in search of an economic foundation: the case of research partnerships in the United States', *Technology Analysis & Strategic Management*, **15**, 177–87.

Fligstein, N.D. (1991), 'The structural transformation of American industry: an institutional account of the causes of diversification in the largest firms', in Powell, W. and DiMaggio, P. (eds), *The New Institutionalism*, Chicago: University of Chicago Press.

Godin, B. (2006), 'The linear model of innovation: the historical construction of an analytical framework', *Science, Technology, & Human Values*, **31**, 639–67.

Hagedoorn, J., Link, A.N. and Vonortas, N.S. (2000), 'Research partnerships', *Research Policy*, **29**, 567–86.

Hébert, R.F. and Link, A.N. (1988), *The Entrepreneur: Mainstream Views and Radical Critiques*, New York: Praeger.

Hébert, R.F. and Link, A.N. (2006), 'The entrepreneur as innovator', *Journal of Technology Transfer*, **31**, 589–97.

Hébert, R.F. and Link, A.N. (2009), *A History of Entrepreneurship*, London: Routledge.

Holcombe, R.G. (2002), 'Political entrepreneurship and the democratic allocation of economic resources', *Review of Austrian Economics*, **15**, 143–59.

Lane, D. and Maxfield, R. (2006), 'Ontological uncertainty and innovation', *Journal of Evolutionary Economics*, **15**, 3–50.

Leyden, D.P. and Link, A.N. (1993), 'Tax policies affecting R&D: an international comparison', *Technovation*, **13**, 17–25.

Link, A.N. (1999), 'Public/private partnerships in the United States', *Industry and Innovation*, **6**, 191–217.

Link, A.N. (2006), *Public/Private Partnerships: Innovation Strategies and Policy Alternatives*, New York: Springer.

Link, A.N. (2008), 'The evaluation challenge', presented at the National Academy of Sciences Workshop on Understanding Research and Technology Parks, Washington, DC.

Link, A.N. and Link, J.R. (2009), *Government as Entrepreneur*, New York: Oxford University Press.

Link, A.N. and Scott, J.T. (2005), *Evaluating Public Research Institutions: The US Advanced Technology Program's Intramural Research Initiative*, London: Routledge.

Link, A.N. and Siegel, D.S. (2007), *Innovation, Entrepreneurship, and Technological Change*, Oxford: Oxford University Press.

Schumpeter, J.A. (1928), 'The instability of capitalism', *Economic Journal*, **38**, 361–86.

Tassey, G. (2007), *The Technology Imperative*, Cheltenham, UK and Northampton, MA, USA: Edward Elgar.

Index